"Connecting theology to a variety of disciplines and intellect companion provides an exciting sample of the current work of postmodern theologians. Many of the essays are ground-breaking, as the fields of theology and religious thought move forward into the next century. This is a valuable sequel to Ward's *The Postmodern God!*"

Robert Gibbs, University of Toronto

"If you think you know what postmodern theology is, or think you don't know, either way these remarkable essays will change your mind: written by Jews, Christians and atheists; indebted to Plato, the Bible and Augustine; haunted by Heidegger, Levinas, Foucault and Derrida; dealing with jazz, the Shoah, the ecological crisis, the American prison system and many other topics; some long and patient, others short and cryptic, all asking to be read more than once; ... You may still not know at the end but you will certainly have seen the variety and vitality of what theologians are doing, in these postmodern times, and the zest with which they do it."

Fergus Kerr O.P., Regent of Blackfriars, Oxford

"Among the delights of this collection are the essays that dare to reconsider some of the 'bad guys' in the official postmodern story: thus Catherine Pickstock endeavours of rescue Plato from his Nietzschean decriers by rereading the *Republic* through the *Laws* to offer an account of Plato's politics as liturgical rather than totalitarian; while Jean-Luc Marion even seeks to learn from the much-despised Descartes."

Literature & Theology

"[A] useful and exciting volume, bringing together the work of religious scholars and theologians across a wide spectrum, creating space for their current work independently from a given theme, showing them sometimes in agreement, sometimes in heated argument with each other."

Anglican Theological Review

Blackwell Companions to Religion

The Blackwell Companions to Religion series presents a collection of the most recent scholarship and knowledge about world religions. Each volume draws together newly-commissioned essays by distinguished authors in the field, and is presented in a style which is accessible to undergraduate students, as well as scholars and the interested general reader. These volumes approach the subject in a creative and forward-thinking style, providing a forum in which leading scholars in the field can make their views and research available to a wider audience.

Published

The Blackwell Companion to Judaism
Edited by Jacob Neusner and Alan J. Avery-Peck

The Blackwell Companion to Sociology of Religion
Edited by Richard K. Fenn

The Blackwell Companion to the Hebrew Bible
Edited by Leo G. Perdue

The Blackwell Companion to Postmodern Theology
Edited by Graham Ward

The Blackwell Companion to Hinduism
Edited by Gavin Flood

The Blackwell Companion to Political Theology
Edited by Peter Scott and William T. Cavanaugh

The Blackwell Companion to Protestantism
Edited by Alister E. McGrath and Darren C. Marks

The Blackwell Companion to Modern Theology
Edited by Gareth Jones

The Blackwell Companion to Christian Ethics
Edited by Stanley Hauerwas and Samuel Wells

The Blackwell Companion to Religious Ethics
Edited by William Schweiker

Forthcoming

The Blackwell Companion to the Study of Religion
Edited by Robert A. Segal

The Blackwell Companion to Eastern Christianity
Edited by Ken Parry

The Blackwell Companion to Christian Spirituality
Edited by Arthur Holder

The Blackwell Companion to the Bible and Culture
Edited by John Sawyer and Paul Fletcher

The Blackwell Companion to the New Testament
Edited by David Aune

The Blackwell Companion to Comtemporary Islamic Thought
Edited by Ibrahim Abu-Rabi

The Blackwell Companion to Postmodern Theology

Edited by
Graham Ward

University of Manchester

© 2001, 2005 by Blackwell Publishing Ltd
Editorial matter and arrangement © 2001, 2005 by Graham Ward
"Musee des Beaux Arts", © 1940 and renewed 1968 by W. H. Auden, from *W. H. Auden: Collected Poems* by W. H. Auden. Used by permission of Random House, Inc.

BLACKWELL PUBLISHING
350 Main Street, Malden, MA 02148-5020, USA
9600 Garsington Road, Oxford OX4 2DQ, UK
550 Swanston Street, Carlton, Victoria 3053, Australia

The right of Graham Ward to be identified as the Author of the Editorial Material in this Work has been asserted in accordance with the UK Copyright, Designs, and Patents Act 1988.

All rights reserved. No part of this publication may be reproduced, stored in a retrieval system, or transmitted, in any form or by any means, electronic, mechanical, photocopying, recording or otherwise, except as permitted by the UK Copyright, Designs, and Patents Act 1988, without the prior permission of the publisher.

First published 2001
First published in paperback 2005 by Blackwell Publishing Ltd

2   2006

Library of Congress Cataloging-in-Publication Data

The Blackwell companion to postmodern theology / edited by Graham Ward.
    p. cm.— (Blackwell companions to religion)
    Includes bibliographical references and index.
    ISBN 0-631-21217-5 (alk. paper) — ISBN 1-4051-2719-8 (pbk : alk.paper)
    1. Postmodernsim theology.   I. Ward, Graham.   II. Series.

BT83.597 .B53   2001
230'.046—dc21

                                                              2001037469

ISBN-13: 978-0-631-21217-1 (alk. paper) — ISBN-13: 978-1-4051-2719-6 (pbk : alk.paper)

A catalogue record for this title is available from the British Library.

Set in 101/2 on 121/2 pt Photina
by Best-set Typesetter Ltd, Hong Kong
Printed and bound in the United Kingdom
by TJ International, Padstow, Cornwall

The publisher's policy is to use permanent paper from mills that operate a sustainable forestry policy, and which has been manufactured from pulp processed using acid-free and elementary chlorine-free practices. Furthermore, the publisher ensures that the text paper and cover board used have met acceptable environmental accreditation standards.

For further information on
Blackwell Publishing, visit our website:
www.blackwellpublishing.com

To

Martha, Grace and Nicola

ὑμεῖς γάρ ἐστε ἡ δόξα ἡμῶν καὶ ἡ Χαρά
(1 Thess. 2.20)

Contents

List of Contributors   x
Introduction: "Where We Stand"   xii
Graham Ward

Part I   Aesthetics   1

1   Postmodern Theology as Cultural Analysis   3
    Mieke Bal

2   The Man Who Fell to Earth   24
    Gerard Loughlin

3   Communion and Conversation   48
    Regina M. Schwartz

4   The Ends of Man and the Future of God   68
    Janet Martin Soskice

5   "Lush Life": Foucault's Analytics of Power and a Jazz
    Aesthetic   79
    Sharon D. Welch

Part II   Ethics   105

6   The Midwinter Sacrifice   107
    John Milbank

7	Postmodernity and Religious Plurality: Is a Common Global Ethic Possible or Desirable? *Gavin D'Costa*	131
8	The Christian Difference, or Surviving Postmodernism *Stanley Hauerwas*	144
9	Justice and Prudence: Principles of Order in the Platonic City *Catherine Pickstock*	162
10	Visiting Prisoners *William C. Placher*	177
11	Suffering and Incarnation *Graham Ward*	192
12	Earth God: Cultivating the Spirit in an Ecocidal Culture *Mark I. Wallace*	209

Part III Gender   229

13	An Ethics of Memory: Promising, Forgiving, Yearning *Pamela Sue Anderson*	231
14	Is Macrina a Woman? Gregory of Nyssa's *Dialogue on the Soul and Resurrection* *Virginia Burrus*	249
15	"They Will Know We are Christians by Our Regulated Improvisation": Ecclesial Hybridity and the Unity of the Church *Mary McClintock Fulkerson*	265
16	On Changing the Imaginary *Grace M. Jantzen*	280
17	Companionable Wisdoms: What Insights Might Feminist Theorists Gather from Feminist Theologians? *Serene Jones*	294

Part IV Hermeneutics   309

18	Shattering the Logos: Hermeneutics Between a Hammer and a Hard Place *Daniel Boyarin*	311
19	The Renewal of Jewish Theology Today: Under the Sign of Three	324

Peter Ochs

20 Intending Transcendence: Desiring God   349
    Edith Wyschogrod

Part V Phenomenology   367

21 Transfiguring God   369
    Richard Kearney

22 Presence and Parousia   394
    Jean-Yves Lacoste

23 The Formal Reason for the Infinite   399
    Jean-Luc Marion

24 Religions as Conventions   413
    Joseph S. O'Leary

Part VI Heideggerians   425

25 The Self-Saving of God   427
    Thomas J. J. Altizer

26 The Subject of Prayer: Unwilling Words in the
    Postmodern Access to God   444
    Laurence Paul Hemming

27 The Christian Message and the Dissolution of Metaphysics   458
    Gianni Vattimo

Part VII Derrideans   467

28 The Poetics of the Impossible and the Kingdom of God   469
    John D. Caputo

29 Anti-Discrimination   482
    Don Cupitt

30 Is There a Postmodern Gospel?   490
    Walter Lowe

31 Indian Territory: Postmodernism Under the Sign of the Body   505
    Carl Raschke

Index   517

List of Contributors

Thomas J. J. Altizer is Professor Emeritus of Religious Studies at the State University of New York.

Pamela Sue Anderson is Fellow in Philosophy and Christian Ethics, Regent's Park College, Oxford.

Mieke Bal is Professor of the Theory of Literature, University of Amsterdam, and A. D. White Professor-at-Large, Cornell University.

Daniel Boyarin is Professor of Talmudic Culture at the University of California, Berkeley.

Virginia Burrus is Associate Professor of Early Church History at Drew University.

John D. Caputo is David R. Cook Professor of Philosophy at Villanova University.

Gavin D'Costa is Reader in Christian Theology at the University of Bristol.

Don Cupitt is a Fellow of Emmanuel College, Cambridge.

Mary McClintock Fulkerson is Associate Professor of Theology at Duke University, Divinity School.

Stanley Hauerwas is the Gilbert T. Rowe Professor of Theological Ethics at Duke University, Divinity School.

Laurence Paul Hemming is a lecturer in Systematic Theology at Heythrop College, University of London.

Gavin Hyman is Lecturer in Religious Studies at the University of Lancaster.

Grace M. Jantzen is Research Professor of Religion, Culture, and Gender at the University of Manchester.

Serene Jones is Associate Professor of Theology at Yale Divinity School.

LIST OF CONTRIBUTORS xi

Richard Kearney is Professor of Philosophy at University College, Dublin and Visiting Professor of Philosophy at Boston College.

Jean-Yves Lacoste is a Life Fellow of Clare Hall, Cambridge.

Gerard Loughlin is Senior Lecturer in Christian Theology, Ethics, and Philosophy of Religion at the University of Newcastle upon Tyne.

Walter Lowe is Professor of Systematic Theology at the Candler School of Theology, Emory University.

Jean-Luc Marion is Professor of Philosophy at the University of Paris, Sorbonne and Visiting Professor at the University of Chicago.

John Milbank is the Frances Myers Ball Professor of Philosophical Theology at the University of Virginia.

Peter Ochs is the Edgar Bronfman Professor of Modern Judaic Studies at the University of Virginia.

Joseph S. O'Leary teaches Philosophy of Religion at Sophia University, Japan.

Catherine Pickstock is a Lecturer in Philosophy of Religion at the University of Cambridge and a Fellow of Emmanuel College, Cambridge.

William C. Placher is Charles D. and Elizabeth S. LaFollette Professor in the Humanities at Wabash College, Indiana.

Carl Raschke is Professor of Religious Studies at the University of Denver.

Regina M. Schwartz is Professor of English at Northwestern University and Director of the Institute of Religion, Ethics, and Violence.

Janet Martin Soskice is Lecturer in Christian Theology at the University of Cambridge and Fellow of Jesus College, Cambridge.

Gianni Vattimo is Professor of Philosophy at the University of Turin.

Mark I. Wallace is Associate Professor in the Department of Religion, Swarthmore College.

Graham Ward is Professor of Contextual Theology in the Department for Religions and Theology at the University of Manchester.

Sharon D. Welch is Professor of Religious Studies and Women's Studies at the University of Missouri.

Edith Wyschogrod is J. Newton Rayzor Professor of Philosophy and Religious Thought at Rice University.

Introduction: "Where We Stand"

Graham Ward

In the spring of 1829 Thomas Carlyle composed his eloquent, yet biting essay *Signs of the Times*. Much later, in 1848, Matthew Arnold would publish his own condemnation of soulless materialism and utilitarian functionalism in *Culture and Anarchy*, and Ruskin would follow, in 1861, with his essays in *Unto This Last*. But it is with Carlyle's essay that we begin because he recognized early, before Marx, what later became known as the sociology of knowledge. He knew the importance of asking about where we stand.

> We were wise indeed, could we discern truly the signs of our own time; and by that knowledge of its wants and advantages, wisely adjust our own position to it. Let us, instead of gazing idly into the obscure distance, look calmly around us, for a little, on the perplexed scene where we stand. Perhaps, on a more serious inspection, something of its perplexity will disappear, some of its distinctive characters and deeper tendencies more clearly reveal themselves; whereby our own relations to it, our own true aims and endeavours in it, may also become clearer.[1]

Postmodernity promises neither clarification nor the disappearance of perplexity. It is debatable whether theology promises these things either. Nevertheless, Carlyle's call to take stock of where we stand is pertinent, for the whole conception of there being a distinctive "postmodern theology" rests upon the notion that our thinking and our cultural/historical context are profoundly related. And part of what I wish to investigate in this Introduction is the profundity of that relationship – the ways in which theological speaking and doing are implicated in contemporary culture, both as its products and its producers.

Where We Are Now

In 1998 Nicholas Boyle produced a stimulating collection of essays entitled *Who Are We Now? Christian Humanism and the Global Market from Hegel to Heaney*.[2] My question is different (the existence of the unity of any subject that can be so strictly identified with the interrogative pronoun "Who" is doubtful), but my theological enquiry into our contemporary situation is similar. My question is: "Where are we now?" And before I begin to answer that question with respect to what is variously termed "the end of modernity," "late-capitalism," "post-Fordism," "postmodernism," and "globalism," I wish to distinguish between two forms of cultural transformation.

The first form is a transformation within the logics of a certain movement. This transformation might radicalize elements already apparent within an historical epoch. For example, the postmodern thinking on the aesthetics of the sublime by Jean-François Lyotard (one of the earliest to write theoretically about the phenomenon of postmodernity)[3] extends Kant's own analysis of the sublime in his *Critique of Judgement*. This form of transformation may develop what is already there in the tradition.

The second form of transformation is a radical break with the cultural logic of the past or present. The postmodern thinking of Michel de Certeau wishes to examine the Christ event as "an inaugurating rupture," and several poststructural thinkers employ words like "rupture," "diachrony," and "event" to mark an encounter with a wholly Other whose difference cannot be calibrated within the continuities of narrative. The Other fractures the symbolic systems that constitute any given cultural milieu. Some cultural analysts suggest postmodernity performs such a radical break with respect to the thinking and practices of modernity. I, along with others, would question that. Nevertheless, the times always change and when we come to recognize that change then consciousness marks a present situation from a past one.

I believe this distinction between two forms of cultural transformation is important when assessing where we are now, or, to put it more theologically, when we read the signs of the times. For whatever label we place on the present cultural scene – and a very Westernized, Americanized scene it is – the context issues from complex forms of transformation. Put briefly, the cultural situation we find ourselves in both develops certain themes evident in modernity (like the social arena as composed of barely repressed struggles and competitions regulated through contract), but also breaks with categories that maintained the hegemony of modernity (its naturalisms, positivisms, essentialisms, dualisms, and humanisms, for example). I am going to label where we are now "postmodernity." I do this because some of the other labels (post-Fordism, late-capitalism, even globalism) are too tied to economic discourse and I want to demonstrate that where we are now is not simply a place economists can define. To understand economics is fundamental for understanding history (Marx has taught us that), but the postmodern condition as Frederic Jameson and David

Harvey (both left-wing thinkers) now see is not simply the effect of free-market capitalism.[4] Things are more complicated. Neither does the current fashion for describing where we are as at "the end" of something – the end of history (for Fukuyama), the end of metaphysics (for Derrida), the end of modernity (for Vattimo), the end of art (for Danto) – actually tell us anything. It simply spatializes time and maps us at the end of a promontory. Such labels can inform us about the current cultural scene in terms of the first form of transformation, but not the second. So, like Jameson, I can say

> I occasionally get just as tired of the slogan of "postmodernism" as anyone else, but when I am tempted to regret my complicity with it, to deplore its misuses and its notoriety, and to conclude with some reluctance that it raises more problems than it solves, I find myself pausing to wonder whether any other concept can dramatize the issue in quite so effective and economical a fashion.[5]

Unlike Jameson, I do want to continue to maintain a distinction between postmodernism and postmodernity.[6] It is not a watertight distinction, but it is functional and, as I will demonstrate, helpful. I follow Lyotard in seeing postmodernism as the other side that haunts the modern – Lyotard even suggests it comes *before* modernism, making it possible. It is characterized, according to Lyotard, by its acceptance of the plural and the rejection of grand narratives of progress and explanation. It is also characterized by a nonfoundationalism, a hybridity, an appeal to a certain excess, the employment of masks, irony, anti-realism, and self-conscious forms of representation. As such postmodernism is both an aesthetic and a critical moment within the ideology of the modern. It is, on the one hand, a matter of style – Pop Art and John Portman buildings – and, on the other, a genre of theoretical para-Marxist writing. The Baroque and Weimar culture of the 1920s has been viewed by historians like Stephen Toulmin as protopostmodern.[7] Writers like Rabelais, Kierkegaard, Mallarmé and, of course, Nietzsche are then viewed as protopostmodern. What postmodernism suggests is that a certain social sea-change is occurring; new emphases and sensibilities are making themselves felt and older ways of looking at and explaining the significance of the world are becoming otiose or no longer credible. If I were asked what was the substance of those emphases and sensibilities, then, very broadly, I would say (and this returns us to the theological) that the death of God had brought about the prospect of the reification and commodification (theologically termed idolatry), not only of all objects, but of all values (moral, aesthetic, and spiritual). We have produced a culture of fetishes or virtual objects. For now everything is not only measurable and priced, it has an image. It is the image which now governs what is both measured and priced. And so the age of the Promethean will to power – in which human beings rationally measure, calculate, predict, and control – turns into the age of Dionysian diffusion, in which desire is governed by the endless production and dissemination of floating signifiers.[8] Furthermore, this cultural sea-change was paralleled by the closing down of a certain political space for credible challenge. That is, it paralleled the weakening of socialism – the one discourse that, in a galloping secularism, had been able to arrest the social conscience for more than a hundred years.

We can see these two cultural changes taking place – the production of what Guy Debord, nearly thirty years before the development of virtual reality, termed "society's real unreality,"[9] and a realization of the ineffectiveness of any cultural critique – in an astonishing essay written by Michel de Certeau in August 1968, following the riots in Paris. The essay is called, significantly, "A Symbolic Revolution." It argues that the May riots had left in their wake the sense of a cultural trauma and the explicit feeling of powerlessness:

> Something that had been tacit began to stir; something that invalidates the mental hardware built for stability. Its instruments were also part of what shifted, went awry. They referred to something *unthinkable*, which late May, was unveiled while being contested: values taken to be self-evident; social exchanges, the progress of which was enough to define their success; commodities, the possession of which represented happiness.[10]

The principles of established order have become questionable and what remains is a "hole, opened by a society that calls itself into question." It is a hole that cannot be covered over; nor can it be avoided. No quick-fix solutions like a better division of goods or the call for true community are credible. And yet de Certeau ends his essay on a rhetorical high, speaking of "revolution," "revision," and "challenge." He dispatches the sense of failure and loss by making speech itself a transformative event, replacing the political revolution with a symbolic one. A real transformation has become a virtual one. And de Certeau is too astute not to allow the uncertainties of that victory to be registered: "taking speech is neither effective occupation nor the seizure of power,"[11] he opines. He recognizes that this rhetorical gesture only turns political and ethical values into aesthetic ones; nevertheless, this is the only way forward that he can see. Out of failure and a lack of resources a virtual triumph is fashioned which, for the moment, curtains the void, the hole. It is fashioned out of words.

I call this "hole" the implosion of secularism and it is the many consequences of that implosion that postmodernism explores and postmodernity expresses. The implosion of the secular has also facilitated a new return to the theological and a new emphasis upon reenchantment: a return not signaled by theologians but by filmmakers, novelists, poets, philosophers, political theorists, and cultural analysts. Let me define more closely what it is I mean by the implosion of secularism, because it will be fundamental for understanding the nature of the change and its consequences.

The Implosion of Secularism

First, we have to conceive of the secular according to a world of immanent values which has disassociated itself from, and in its various important discourses – the natural and human sciences – even discredited, the transcendent. It is a world grounded, resourced, and evolving according to its own internally conceived laws: physical laws like Newton's laws of motion and Maxwell's laws of thermodynamics; psychical laws like Freud's Oedipal triangle; the laws Descartes believed observable by "natural light." In order to compose and possess knowledge in such a world, there must be what Descartes describes as "the search for first causes and true principles which enable us to deduce the reasons for everything we are capable of knowing."[12] The world must constitute an integrated system. The secular, therefore, is conceived as a world-system, constituted by forces it is increasingly coming to understand and which integrate various aspects of its systematicity. This world began to emerge in the late fifteenth and early sixteenth centuries.

Second, we have to understand how it is that any system implodes. A thing is exploded when an external force is required to detonate and facilitate the explosion; an external force or principle which can tear the system apart and render it incoherent. But the radical immanence of secularism (which rejects an exteriority) cannot be exploded. Theologically, certain figures in Weimar Germany who propounded dialectical theology (founded upon a certain revelatory positivism) were trying to explode the secular, and religion as implicated within secularity. With the rallying calls of Crisis and Judgment, they challenged the secular world-system itself. One commentator on the second edition of Karl Barth's *Der Romerbrief* suggested that the book was the pitching of a hand-grenade into a playground full of diehard liberals. The implosion of a system, on the other hand, comes about through internal processes, forces, or principles which no longer regulate the immanent order but overshoot it.

A worldview becomes acceptable by being internalized. Its internalization brings about its naturalization. But various forms of critical thinking – from the so-called Masters of Suspicion (Marx, Nietzsche, Freud) to the work of the Frankfurt School and the poststructural critical strategies of Foucault, Derrida, and Irigaray, among others – have challenged aspects of this naturalization. Each, in their own way, reminded the secular that it was produced, that it was self-constituted, and that such a constitution was governed by a certain cultural politics with particular ideological investments and presuppositions. Hence, the secular value-system was always unstable and fragile. The work of Bruno Latour and Alain Touraine has done much to develop our notions of the instability of modernity or the secular worldview. Their historical analyses help us to understand the cultural background of postmodernity and something of its future. Touraine, in particular, believes the crisis and collapse of modernity is due to the advancing critiques of rationalism which took a rabid turn when left-wing intellectuals in the late 1960s, disillusioned with modernity's hopes and freedoms, turned against it. "[A] purely critical vision of modernity became a total rejection of the very idea of modernity and then self-destructed when it became postmodernism."[13] I accept this, but on Touraine's model of modernity's collapse we are left with a choice: either to continue the nihilistic drift which will lead to the fascisms and fundamentalisms of neo-tribal diversity, or to return, a little wiser now, to modernity's project. "If we do not succeed in defining a different conception of modernity – one which is less haughty than that of the Enlightenment but which can still resist the absolute diversity of cultures and individuals – the storms that lie ahead will be still more violent than the storms that accompanied the fall of the *anciens régimes* and industrialization."[14] Touraine, albeit in a different way, joins forces with that neoliberal thinker Jürgen Habermas.[15] But the implosion of modernity I am arguing for leaves us with no opening to resurrect its project (though that does not deny the benefits modernity has bequeathed to us). We live in the trajectory of what is coming to us from the future; we never return to the same place twice to rethink the choices abandoned. Furthermore, all these critiques and rejections of modernity, in already accepting secular immanence, can offer nothing to overturn the system. As rational extrapolations from the secular world, they can only attempt to ground the secular more securely (fostering a divorce between literary form and intellectual content – in Hume and Schopenhauer, for example – that Nietzsche sutured). The system turns increasingly into a hideous chimera that adapts itself to absorb the challenges posed and takes delight in its own destructive powers, rather like those proliferating aliens of contemporary science-fiction films whose strength and intelligence lie in their ability to adapt, virus-like, to new conditions and to turn attacks against themselves into a mechanism for further self-development. Let me give some examples here.

In Kant the noumenal renders fragile an appreciation of the phenomenal because it makes evident its constructedness and contingency. Nevertheless, the analysis on the basis of intuitions, synthetic *a priori*, and the teleology of transcendental reasoning reinforces the universal power of rationality itself. The Kantian critique then provides (as Kant himself intended it would in the face of Hume's skepticism) the metaphysics, the architectonics, for the instrumental reasoning required by ethics, aesthetics, and science. The liberating postmodern nihilisms of Baudrillard, Lyotard, and Deleuze are based upon returning to and employing this Kantian distinction and emphasizing the delights of the fragile appreciation of the phenomenal. The system adapts to serve another purpose.

Let me give a second example with respect to the critiques of commodity fetishism by Marx and various members of the Frankfurt School, for the postmodern shift from value to image fetishism is culturally pervasive. These early critiques of fetishism – in which the authentic is betrayed by the mass-produced, by the reification and alienation of the worker's labor from the value of the object-product – did not and do not lead to the end of mass production, nor the collapse of the bourgeoisie. In fact, attention to commodity fetishism, to the processes of reification, could be absorbed and harnessed by market economics. Thus, on the one hand, the "authentic," the "handmade," and the "customized" could become that which is most marketable; while, on the other, the first step towards the mass reproduction of Van Gogh's *Sunflowers* is the production of Van Gogh's work as an aesthetic object with a certain magic appeal, the aura of the authentic. An observation by the contemporary Slovenian philosopher Slavoj Žižek with respect to *The Communist Manifesto* and Marxian communism develops this point:

> This notion of a society of pure unleashed productivity *outside* the frame of Capital, was a fantasy inherent to capitalism itself, the *capitalist* inherent transgression at its purest, a strictly *ideological* fantasy of maintaining the thrust towards productivity generated by capitalism, while getting rid of the "obstacles" and antagonisms that were . . . *the only possible framework of the actual material existence of a society of permanent self-enhancing productivity*. . . . Capitalism and Communism are not two different historical realizations, two species, of "instrumental reason" – instrumental reason *as such* is capitalist, grounded in capitalist relations; and "actually existing Socialism" failed because it was ultimately a subspecies of capitalism, an ideological attempt to "have one's cake and eat it," to break out of capitalism while retaining its key ingredient.[16]

The demise of socialism as a critique of capitalism is itself evidence of the way the secular system (which renders all values internally exchangeable and transferable) absorbs internal critiques.

The secular, modernity, is founded upon the strength of its integrating mechanisms. Critiques and even rejections are themselves only turns within a certain secular logic that remains itself uninjured. The most that can be achieved from such critique is the ontologizing of politics – which returns us to Hobbes or, more recently, the work of Thomas Keenan and William Connolly.[17] One cannot rebuild an imploding system, nor reject it from within – just as one cannot turn a black hole back into a red dwarf, nor counter the gravitational pull from within the black hole itself. According to Touraine's analysis, then, the alternative is a drift towards cultural nihilism, the replacement of value by image. But that alternative, too, is based on a view from within the system. Another possibility, which installs the theological project, can radically challenge the system from elsewhere, from an exteriority, or what Ernesto Laclau calls a "constitutive outside."[18] Challenged from outside, a transformation of the cultural in the second mode outlined above becomes possible.

How then does the implosion take place if critique is already inherent to, or a subspecies of, the system? I suggest it does so when the system comes to recognize itself *as* a system, rather than *as* a natural order; when it recognizes what it produces *as* production, rather than discovery of what is out there. How does this recognition take place? Well, modernity maintained a hierarchical order among secular values, an order predicated on a series of dualisms: public–private, mind–body, reason–passion, universal–particular, nature–culture, object–subject, in which, generally, the former was valued more highly than the latter. These dualisms and separatisms structured a space for public action: they founded the liberal state. In postmodernity's development of the logic of modernity, these dualisms and the hierarchical system of values associated with them have collapsed. How this collapse took place is complex to narrate, but it has something to do with modernity's need, in the face of establishing this system of dualities, for finding ways of mediating between them.[19] For it is not the case that "subject" and "object," "natural" and "cultural," "public" and "private" are on some kind of spectrum in modernity's thinking. They are rendered essentially distinct from each other in order better to facilitate a program of public accountability (transparency). Diversity of opinion, democracy itself, is only made possible by such institutional quarantining. Nevertheless, to establish a principle of difference and contradiction *as such*, at the heart of what *is*, can lead to skepticism of the Cartesian kind: that is, how can I as a subject know with certainty that the objective world I see is really there at all? Or, read politically, why – if I can indulge my private pleasures without interruption – should I be at all concerned for the public welfare? For Descartes, God is the only guarantee of the world beyond the "I." In the wake of the death of God, however, there is no transcendental mediation. The tools, the mechanisms for mediation between the dualisms, have to be found in-house. Methodologically, dialogue, dialectic, debate, reconciliation, synthesis, and the establishment of common self-interest offer themselves as means of mediation. So, for example, political representation of various kinds mediates between the private and the public; institutions such as the law and education mediate between nature and society; and nature itself is examined through certain constructions (like the vacuum pump) and the results published in various acknowledged journals. The implosion occurs when the processes of mediation – dialogue, dialectic, and debate – can no longer be held to operate; when certain incommensurable perspectives become apparent; when the subject increasingly loses the distinctiveness of its position and likewise the object; when the natural is seen as already cultivated; when the private is increasingly subject to social policy and internalizes a public surveillance; when the universal is recognized as representing a certain power/knowledge interest which necessarily marginalizes other interests. And so the hierarchy of values implodes, with no appeal possible to an authority outside the system itself – no principle, no shared ontology, no grounding epistemology, no transcendental mediation. And so we move beyond the death of God which modernity announced, to a final forgetting of the transcendental altogether, to a state of godlessness so profound that nothing can be conceived behind the exchange of signs and the creation of symbolic structures.

The godlessness which was inherent but not fully apparent in the secular world-system is now realized and spawns a variety of responses (including public enquiries into theological questions). In *A Contribution to the Critique of Political Economy* Marx discusses the social implosion in terms of the logic of capitalism. I find this significant because of the associations between capitalism, modernity, and postmodernity. "At a certain stage of their development, the material forces of production come in conflict with the existing relations of production.

... From forms of development of the forces of production these relations turn into their fetters."[20] More recently, Ernesto Laclau and Chantal Mouffe have written about "a new logic of the social" which has begun "to insinuate itself, one that will only manage to think itself by questioning the very literality of the term it articulates."[21] From these two observations we could say that the forces of secular production forged an understanding of the world whose very constructedness came increasingly to haunt and obsess it, so that the relations produced, instead of continuing to work on behalf of the system, came increasingly to shackle and finally dismantle it. Secularity then gets locked into the virtual realities it has produced; locked into the paranoias of David Cronenberg's *eXistenZ* and the Wachowski brothers' *The Matrix*. The godlessness which was inherent but not fully apparent in the secular world-system is now realized. The system has exhausted its own self-conceived, self-promoted symbols. The symbolic itself collapses (as Baudrillard observes, plaintively) because it is not standing in for or symbolic of anything. Liberal tolerance become post-symbolic indifference in the face of the endlessly plural and contingent relays of connections, disconnections, and erasures. In the implosion of the secular the weightless flow of signs which constructed the secular as a symbolic system views itself as such and, now, without alternative. The real is the simulated[22] that installs an omnipresent commodification, a trading on emptiness, a pervasive cultural fetishism. Postmodernity is then characterized by simulation, the play and creation of virtual realities, the surface suggestions of depth – like the Opryland Hotel in Nashville where acres of woodland and rocky gorges, with a river, gladed pools, and waterfalls, lie beneath a great canopy of glass. The rooms of the hotel, each with their balconies, look inwards over the country idyll with its bandstands and cascades, clock-towered clapboard buildings and cobbled streets. Space collapses in carefully crafted perspectives and temporal distance dissolves; one is both resident and tourist, set adrift in a highly organized culture of nostalgia for a premodern world.[23]

This implosion of the secular produces a vacuum without values, a *horror Vacui*. What de Certeau calls the hole, Heidegger called the *Zeug*, and Derrida and Irigaray have called the *Khora*. Fascination with it can transform it, too, into a commodity fetish. We need to examine this fetishism more closely, for it characterizes contemporary culture, as I have suggested, and it focuses the effects of the implosion of secularism.

Fetishism

Contemporary accounts of fetishism weave Marx's observations on the magical nature commodities take on in the process of reification (*Capital*, vol. 1) into Freud's and Lacan's analyses of the nature of desire. For Freud and Lacan, desire does not seek its fulfilment, for that would terminate the pleasure of desiring. Desire promotes the allure and attraction of an object that stands in for what it lacks, but its enjoyment lies in not having what it wants. The commodified object then becomes the cause of desire rather than the object of desire itself. In fact, pleasures issue from not having what you want – which produces what I have called elsewhere the cultural prevalence of sado-masochistic desire.[24] It is significant that the structure of commodity fetishism involves both a recognition that the fetish is a substitute, not the object desired itself, and, simultaneously, a disavowal of its substitutional character. It has the grammatical structure of "I know, but even so. . . ." As Jacques Lacan pointed out, this intrinsic disavowal renders desire itself unstable. The desire can then continually displace itself onto new objects.[25] The pleasure of not getting what you want drives consumerism. Consumerism becomes an endless experience of fetishism – as Marx was inchoately aware.

The point I am making is that the effect of the implosion of the secular is a hole that is at once longed for and disavowed. Contemporary culture both wishes to embrace the nihilism of the abyss and screen it through substitutionary images. Another way this might be put, which draws upon the work of several feminist thinkers (from Hannah Arendt and Adriana Cavarero to Grace Jantzen and Catherine Pickstock) and a statement by John Paul II in *Evangelium Vitae*, is that a profound necrophilia emerges: 'a culture of death', a longing and a *frisson* for oblivion. Postmodernity embraces this fantasy and is sustained by it in the same way that certain people are able to cope with the ongoing struggle with life only by repeatedly fantasizing about suicide, fatal accidents, and terminal illnesses. "Beam me up, Scottie" expresses a more pervasive desire for vaporization, a total immersion in forgetfulness.

A certain paradoxical cultural logic, the logic of fetishism, is evident in postmodernity: David Harvey (from the New Left perspective) can lament the political vacuum, while Ernesto Laclau (from the post-Marxist perspective) can find hope in the radical politicization of everything. Now you see it; now you don't. The same fetishist logic pertains to the theological in contemporary culture. I have argued that the deepening sense of godlessness is the apotheosis both of the secular worldview and, simultaneously, the generator of theological questions, motifs, images, and mythemes articulated by a variety of secular sources in contemporary culture. What is this announcing but a certain pathological enjoyment of a postmodern sensibility; an enjoyment of the absence of God by the commercialization of God's presence – through angels and miracles, through stigmatas and sacramentalisms, through philosophies of charity and appeals to the "social divine?"[26] In Michel Serres's book *Angels: A Modern Myth*, the angels announce a pantheistic world of immanent fluxes, a world in which the Word is to be made flesh. But beyond the angelic hosts is the Most High or the All High God to whom all glory is due. Nevertheless, Serres concludes: "if our will becomes sufficiently good for us to make an agreement between us to accord the glory only to a transcendent absent being, then we will be able to live in peace."[27] The logic of the fetishist desire is that pleasure is found in the failure to attain what one desires; pleasure is taken in absence itself. And so the profound alienation that the hole evokes is veiled and curtained. We will have to return to this when we examine what postmodern theology is doing.

Where does this leave us? Where do we stand? Michel de Certeau was in no doubt about the questioning which circled the hole at the heart of the social. "Our society has become a recited society, in three senses; it is defined by *stories* (*recits*, the fables constituted by our advertising and informational media), by *citations* of stories, and by the interminable *recitation* of stories."[28] In a recited society people believe what they see and what they see is produced for them – hence, simulacra-created belief which installs the logic of fetishism: "The spectator-observer *knows* that they are merely 'semblances' . . . *but all the same* he assumes that these simulations are real."[29] This "objectless credibility" is based upon citing the authority of others. Thus the production of a simulacrum involves making people believe that others believe in it, but without providing any believable object. There is what de Certeau calls the "multiplication of pseudo-believers"[30] promoted by a culture of deferral, credit, and accreditation.

By the 1980s the culture of deferral and credit, the culture of the virtually real, had not yet taken on the pervasiveness which is registered our current globalism. Nevertheless, postmodernity now becomes an epochal term describing a culture in which postmodernism is seen as the dominating worldview.

Postmodernity and Postmodernism

It is exactly here that I want to argue for the helpfulness of a distinction between postmodernity and postmodernism. It is a distinction that enables us to see why so many of the postmodern theological voices in this volume have turned to various forms of postmodern critical theory to help them analyze the contemporary cultural phenomena that most concern them. Postmodernism enables us to distinguish certain elements in our contemporary world which are other than postmodern and yet, all too often, can be lumped together as characteristics of postmodernity. For example, it enables us to distinguish between globalism and postmodernity. Put briefly, advocates of globalism such as Francis Fukuyama and historians of the world-system such as Immanuel Wallerstein quite explicitly discuss their ideas in terms of the grand narratives of Hegel (Fukuyama) and Marx (Wallerstein). In fact, along with the various forms of neo-Darwinism – right-wing political and social thought and its biological equivalent in the work of someone like Richard Dawkins – and neoliberal economic progressivism, grand narratives are making something of a cultural comeback. Certain postmodern "values" or "emphases" – on simulacra, pastiche, irony, the kitsch – and certain postmodern understandings of space and time are developed considerably by what David Harvey terms "accumulative capitalism." Nevertheless, it is important not to view these developments as antinomies of postmodernism but, rather, ways in which, within postmodernity, cultures become complex weaves of ideologies, values, symbols, activities, and powers. The danger of tying postmodernism to developments in capitalism and conflating postmodernism with postmodernity, postmodernism with globalism – as Jameson, Eagleton, Harvey, and Soja do – is that we can lose sight of postmodernism's critical edge. Its critical edge is important for the way it can sharpen theology's own analytical tools, enabling theology not only to read the signs of the times but to radicalize the postmodern critique by providing it with an exteriority, a position outside the secular value-system. That exteriority is founded upon the God who is revealed within, while being distinctively beyond, the world-system. Without that exteriority academics in cultural studies are faced with a dilemma: how is it that critical theory, which has been one of the driving forces behind postmodernism and which, in many ways, appeared as a mutation in the history of Marxist thinking, leads to and advances global consumerism? Academics in cultural studies face the challenge Nicholas Boyle speaks of when he states that "Post-Modernism is the pessimism of an obsolescent class – the salaried official intelligentsia – whose fate is closely bound up with that of the declining nation-state.... The Post-Modernist endlessly repeats what he believes to be his parricidal act of shattering the bourgeois identity."[31] In other words, without the radicality that a theological perspective can offer the postmodern critique, the postmodernist is doomed also to inscribe the ideology he or she seeks to overthrow. The radical critique is not radical enough. Hence the important contribution that theological discourse can make in postmodernity when "the historical *modus vivendi* called secularism is coming apart at the seams."[32]

When, in the early 1970s, Jean Baudrillard first introduced his thinking on simulation and simulacra; when, in the late 1960s, Roland Barthes first turned our attention to the empire of signs, and the erotic pleasures of surfaces without depth or shadows; when Thomas Pynchon was composing *The Crying of Lot 49* and Guy Debord began instructing audiences on the society of the spectacle, the Cold War was still being played out, American money was still related to the gold standard, Keynesian economics and the GATT trading agreement still held, Mandel had not yet written his *Late Capitalism*, cable TV and video were unheard of, and the linking of two or more computers so that they might "talk" to each other was still a science-fiction fantasy. There was postmodernism before there was postmodernity. The erection of John Portman's Peachtree Plaza did not catapult Atlanta into postmodernity. Neither do the ethical concerns for alterity and difference in the writings of Emmanuel Levinas, Jacques Derrida, Luce Irigaray, and Julia Kristeva inevitably supplement the cultural logic of late-capitalism. On the one hand, what is happening today is the vast commodification of postmodern sentiments. On the other, the inevitable incommensurabilities of pluralism are coming to the fore – where the insistence upon difference vies with narratives of historical progress towards global democratization, the bureaucratic call to transparency and the fulfilment of Bentham's Panopticon dreams, the erasure of the other as nonconsumer, and the flattening of differences in a world market.[33] It is this very process of turning objects into idols, fetishism itself – which is more than just a matter of analysing economic processes – that theological discourse challenges. That *is* the theological difference, the theological critique. This theological difference has the potential for transforming culture in the second mode of cultural transformation I alluded to: that is, radically. That is why postmodern theology is not simply a product of the new reenchantment of the world, but an important mode of critical analysis in such a world.

The essays in this volume testify to the variety of theological responses to the critical and aesthetic contributions of postmodernism and the complex cultural logics of postmodernity. They testify also to the implosion of secularism while, simultaneously, they attempt to think creatively beyond it. Theologians are never above and beyond the cultural situation in which they work. Theological discourse not only employs the language of its times, but also inhabits many of its dreams and aspirations. Hence the question must arise as to the commodifications and fetishisms of its own projects. There is no room for a dogmatism that is not strategic, for polemic which is not self-consciously rhetorical, for categorical assertion which does not foreground its *poeisis*. Theology, too, is mediated and mediates, encultures and is encultured. It is a discourse which, as I have argued, has public relevance and can offer certain cultural critiques and insights. But it is a *discourse*. It traffics in signs and seeks to make its own beliefs believable. It must, on the one hand, make judgments while, on the other, rendering itself vulnerable to interruption, critical reflection, contestation, and engagement. There is no moral high ground.

For a long time I wrestled with the attempt to situate the essays in this volume with respect to various categories elaborated in an earlier essay on postmodern theology[34] – liberal and conservative postmodern theology, postliberal and radical orthodox theology. But the categories did not hold. There are too many shades of liberal to conservative theological thinking, too many people working creatively between the positions, say, of Thomas Altizer and Don Cupitt on the one hand, and Jean-Luc Marion on the other. The development of the postliberal position, the emergence of a constructive theological project in the United States (associated with Kathryn Tanner, Serene Jones, and Mary McClintock Fulkerson, among others), has close concerns with those of radical orthodoxy. Hence, the categories collapsed because they proved unhelpful, too reductive, and too restrictive.

I had decided to present the theological voices in alphabetical order when Robert Gibbs alerted me to how the failure to provide an architecture signaled a failure to do justice to the contending differences evident in the material.[35] It was he who suggested the present architecture of this collection of essays. The groupings, rather than categories, that emerged – aesthetics, ethics, gender, hermeneutics, phenomenology, Heideggerians, and Derrideans – point to important foci not only for postmodern theology but in postmodernism more generally. As I argued in my introduction to *The Postmodern God*, along with structuralism, Heidegger and the French phenomenologists are important genealogical roots for postmodern thinking. The turn towards encountering the Other raises ethical and political questions. And deconstruction's attention to semiotics rather than semantics opens up issues fundamental to aesthetics and hermeneutics. It is then no accident that these foci for critical attention in postmodern theology are prominent thematics in postmodernism itself. Nevertheless, the groupings for the essays in this volume are fluid. The theological essays of a phenomenological nature are all highly indebted to Heidegger, for example, and the concern of those in the hermeneutics group with the interpretation of founding theological texts is not intended to diminish the ethical questions with which they are also preoccupied. If the boundaries of the groups are drawn on water, then the essays within them are also transgressive and some could have been placed in another grouping entirely. The architecture of the volume reflects the postmodern emphasis upon a space of flows.[36] But setting out the material in this way allows the differences of approach, emphasis, argument, and conclusion between thinkers to take on the prominence which makes postmodern theology diverse, creative, and not without its frictions. Robert Gibbs was right: it is important to portray some of those frictions. Putting contributions in alphabetical order would have dissipated the frictions in a very modernist fashion. Now I can see this collection as a gathering of friends and colleagues to a supper – not a formal supper where the discussion is ordered, but more a buffet supper in a British pub, where food, drink, and uninhibited conversation can circulate between a long oak bar top and a spitting log-fire. People are not ensconced in seats; rather, they stand, are flexible, and are ready to move on. Laughter and the clashing of opinions strongly held can be heard throughout, for it is distinctiveness that matters, not typology.

Accordingly, each thinker is introduced and their work to date outlined in order to provide a context for the essay they have contributed. All of the essays are from work currently undertaken by these writers, but my introductions explicitly mention their other work in order to facilitate further reading. The judgments made in these introductions are my own and are therefore inevitably partial; another editor would have written other things, sketched other portraits. Several of these thinkers have been very productive indeed over many years; where this is so, I have made a selection from the long list of their available titles. But if conversations are to begin then – lacking a venue and the ability to coordinate 31 different diaries – it is the reader who will conduct them, introducing each to each, catching the reflection of one in the eyes of another, the clink of glasses raised together, and the flush of cheeks inflamed with argument. For this is a *Festschrift* of its kind, for friends.

This introduction began with the words of Thomas Carlyle, so it is fitting that he should conclude it. Having outlined the darknesses and fetters of his own age and offered his analyses and critiques, *Signs of the Times* ends on a note of qualified optimism:

> On the whole, as this wondrous planet, Earth, is journeying with its fellows through infinite Space, so are the wondrous destinies embarked on its journeying through infinite Time, under a higher guidance than ours. . . . Go where it will, the deep HEAVEN will be around it. Therein let us have hope.[37]

Notes

1 *Thomas Carlyle: Selected Writings*, ed. Alan Shelston (Harmondsworth: Penguin Books, 1971), pp. 63–4.
2 Nicholas Boyle, *Who Are We Now? Christian Humanism and the Global Market from Hegel to Heaney* (Edinburgh: T. & T. Clark, 1998). See the essay by Stanley Hauerwas in this volume which treats this book in more depth.
3 See his *The Postmodern Condition: A Report on Knowledge*, trans. Geoffrey Bennington and Brian Massumi (Manchester: Manchester University Press, 1988). For his work on aesthetics see *The Inhuman*, trans. Geoffrey Bennington and Rachel Bowlby (Cambridge: Polity Press, 1991) and *Lessons on the Analytic of the Sublime*, trans. Elizabeth Rottenberg (Stanford, CA: Stanford University Press, 1994). Lyotard's work on aesthetics forms an important philosophical backdrop to those essays treating works of art in part one of this volume.
4 For Jameson, compare his early book *Postmodernism, or, The Cultural Logic of Late Capitalism* (London: Verso, 1991) with his collection of essays *The Cultural Turn* (London: Verso, 1998). For David Harvey, compare his early book *The Condition of Postmodernity* (Oxford: Blackwell Publishers, 1989) with his volume *Justice, Nature and the Geography of Difference* (Oxford: Blackwell Publishers, 1996).
5 Jameson, *The Cultural Turn*, p. 49.
6 I made this distinction in the essay "Theology in Cyberspace" which introduces my edited collection *The Postmodern God* (Oxford: Blackwell Publishers, 1998). This *Companion to Postmodern Theology* is conceived as an extension of that project, so I will not rehearse in this introductory essay the *historical* move towards postmodernism. I concern myself here with what Foucault would term an archeological (rather than a genealogical) analysis of postmodernism and theological discourse's relationship to it.
7 See Stephen Toulmin, *Cosmopolis: The Hidden Agenda of Modernity* (Chicago, IL: Chicago University Press, 1990).
8 See Michel Maffesoli, *The Contemplation of the World: Figures of Community Style* (Minneapolis: University of Minnesota Press, 1996), pp. 61, 72.
9 Guy Debord, *The Society of Spectacle* (Detroit, MI: Black and Red, 1977), axiom 6.
10 Michel de Certeau, *The Capture of Speech and Other Political Writings*, trans. Tom Conley (Minneapolis: University of Minnesota Press, 1997), p. 4.
11 Ibid, p. 10.
12 *The Collected Philosophical Works of Descartes*, vol. 1, trans. John Cottingham et al. (Cambridge: Cambridge University Press, 1985), p. 181.
13 Alaine Touraine, *Critique of Modernity*, trans. David Macey (Oxford: Blackwell Publishers, 1995), p. 172.
14 Ibid, p. 198.
15 See ibid, pp. 336–43 for an account of how Touraine differs from Habermas with respect to rethinking democracy.
16 Slavoj Žižek, *The Fragile Absolute: Why the Christian Legacy is Worth Defending* (London: Verso), pp. 18–19.
17 For Keenan see *Fables of Responsibility* (Stanford, CA: Stanford University Press); for Connolly see *Why I am Not a Secularist* (Minneapolis: University of Minnesota Press, 1999). In *Ecce Homo* Nietzsche proclaims quite clearly that only after him does grand politics become possible.

18 See Ernesto Laclau, *New Reflections on the Revolution of our Time* (London: Verso, 1990), pp. 16–18. In their different ways both Levinas and Laclau are searching for that orientating exteriority. See section 3 of Levinas's *Totality and Infinity*, trans. Alphonso Lingis (Pittsburgh: Duquesne University Press, 1969).

19 See Bruno Latour, *We Have Never Been Modern*, trans. Catherine Porter (Cambridge, MA: Harvard University Press, 1993).

20 Karl Marx, *A Contribution to the Critique of Political Economy* (New York, 1970), p. 20.

21 Ernesto Laclau and Chantal Mouffe, *Hegemony and Social Strategy* (London: Verso, 1985), p. 8.

22 See Susan Stewart, *On Longing: Narratives of the Miniature, the Gigantic, the Souvenir, the Collection* (Baltimore, MD: Johns Hopkins University Press, 1984), p. 23.

23 See John Frow, *Time and Commodity Culture: Essays in Cultural Theory and Postmodernity* (Oxford: Oxford University Press, 1997), p. 86.

24 See my essay "Suffering and Incarnation" in chapter 11 of this volume.

25 For a clear account of this logic see Henry Kipps, *Fetish: An Erotics of Culture* (London: Free Association Books, 1999), p. 24.

26 See the work of the contemporary French social anthropologist Michel Maffesoli.

27 Michel Serres, *Angels: A Modern Myth*, trans. Francis Cowper (Paris: Flammarion, 1993), p. 288.

28 Michel de Certeau, *The Practice of Everyday Life*, trans. Steven Rendall (Berkeley: University of California Press, 1984), p. 186.

29 Ibid, pp. 187–8.

30 Michel de Certeau, *On Signs*, ed. Marshall Blonsky (Oxford: Blackwell Publishers, 1987), p. 202.

31 Nicholas Boyle, p. 318.

32 William Connolly, p. 19.

33 The return of scientific, social, and economic Darwinism would not count against a postmodern reading of contemporary culture. What it introduces is an incommensurability between determinisms and pragmatists – Fukuyama on the one hand, Rorty on the other. The incommensurability itself would be enough to demonstrate that while determinism requires the *acceptance* of a grand narrative, it does not demonstrate the *existence* of a grand narrative. This is Lyotard's more subtle point in *The Postmodern Condition*: it is not that construals of development, progress, and explanation have disappeared, but that with the conflict of interpretations fostered by radical pluralism – that is, where perspectives are incommensurable – they are viewed as just one way of making sense of the world. And because they are now only *one* way they are *petits récits* and not *grands récits*.

34 See David Ford (ed.), *Modern Theologians* (Oxford: Blackwell Publishers, 1997).

35 Gibbs was invited to contribute to the volume himself but because of other commitments was unable to do so in the time available. His eleventh-hour suggestions were nevertheless welcome and it is very satisfying to me that he made the volume after all.

36 The term is adopted from Manuel Castell's discussion of postmodern architecture in *Rise of the Network Society* (Oxford: Blackwell Publishers, 1996).

37 *Thomas Carlyle*, pp. 84–5.

PART I
Aesthetics

1	Postmodern Theology as Cultural Analysis	3
2	The Man Who Fell to Earth	24
3	Communion and Conversation	48
4	The Ends of Man and the Future of God	68
5	"Lush Life": Foucault's Analytics of Power and a Jazz Aesthetic	79

CHAPTER 1

Postmodern Theology as Cultural Analysis

Mieke Bal

Mieke Bal is probably one of the best-known academics in the Netherlands today, recognized not only for her contributions to many disciplines (biblical studies, hermeneutics, literary studies, aesthetics, feminist theory) but also her frequent appearances on Dutch television. Her intellectual range is awe-inspiring. Her work is characterized by its interdisciplinary breadth. In the mid to late 1980s, having published in English her book first produced in Holland in 1980, *Narratology: Introduction to the Theory of Narrative* (Toronto, 1985), she began working on a series of studies of narratives from the Hebrew Bible which employed literary analytical skills. Her familiarity with structuralist and poststructuralist forms of criticism, linguistic and genre analysis, and her commitment to feminist theory came together in three autonomous but interrelated publications six years later. The first of these, which explicitly developed from her interests in narratology, was *Lethal Love: Feminist Literary Readings of Biblical Love Stories* (Bloomington, IN, 1987). Here she took narratives concerning women – Delilah, Tamar, Ruth, and Eve – and refigured them for feminists in a way more sophisticated, but nevertheless complementary, to the work done in the United States by Phyllis Trible. In the second book, *Murder and Difference: Gender, Genre, and Scholarship on Sisera's Death* (Bloomington, IN, 1989), she employed Umberto Eco's semiotic theory – where signs are considered to constitute a series of overlapping cultural codes in which reality is represented – to argue for the possibility of a distinctively feminine authorship for the song of Deborah. Here, possibly, one could find a woman's song in a man's epic. This suppressed feminine voice she investigated further in what is her most mature study, *Death and Dissymmetry: The Politics of Coherence in the Book of Judges* (Chicago, IL, 1986). In examining (even deconstructing) the obsession evident in the Book of Judges with military and political chronology, Bal paid attention to the accounts of *lady* killers and lady *killers* (as she puts it in the following essay). In doing so she exposed the repressed other side of the chronological obsession: the theme of gender-bound violence. Her series of books came to something of a conclusion with her edited volume *Anti-Covenant: Counter-Reading Women's Lives in the Hebrew Bible* (Sheffield, 1989).

In the 1990s Bal developed her interests in terms of much broader concerns with cultural production itself. Her explicit methodological employment of theory led to an appreciation of the theoretical as a cultural practice of interpretation, a cultural engagement attempting not simply to offer analysis but also critique. This account of the value of the theoretical informed a collection of essays (coedited with Inge E. Boer) entitled *The Point of Theory: Practices of Cultural Analysis* (Amsterdam, 1994). Bal's interest in narrative, particularly biblical narrative, never waned, but simply took another turn. For her Northrop Frye Lectures in Literary Theory she chose to look at the production of biblical scenes (featuring Susanna, Hagar, Samson, and Delilah) in the paintings of Rembrandt. These lectures were published in the beautiful volume *Reading "Rembrandt": Beyond the Word–Image Opposition* (Cambridge, 1991). Until this point Bal's attention had focused on the literary, but now she became increasingly interested in the visual and the nature of the relationship between the visual and the verbal. This raised theoretical questions about what it is to read. If her Rembrandt explorations led to an account of how to read visually, then her later book on Proust provides an account of how to look discursively. In *The Mottled Screen: Reading Proust Visually* (Stanford, CA, 1997) she examined Proust's fascination with the optical – figured in references to paintings, telescopes, magnifying glasses, magic lanterns, and photography – and the way this affected his highly visual writing. Throughout this new development in Bal's work a continuity remains, based upon her commitment to gender studies. Even in her Proust volume she draws attention to how the poetics organizing Proust's *A la recherche du temps perdu* issue from the appearances and disappearances of Gilberte/Albertine.

Bal's exposure to art museums following her research for her book on Rembrandt became the basis for a series of reflections on collective memory and the framing of the past. These were published in two books: *Double Exposures: The Subject of Cultural Analysis* (New York, 1996) and *Acts of Memory: Cultural Recall in the Present* (Dartmouth, MA, 1999). We see the further development of these reflections in the essay that follows.

Points of Departure

Western culture as we know and live it today was built on several interlocking structures, one of which was theological, specifically, Christian. Present-day culture in the West, therefore, cannot be understood without theology. *Postmodern theology is the study of this presence of the past within the present.*

For all our postmodern protestations in the form of either post-Enlightenment atheism, postcolonial religious pluralism, or even, as is deplorably fashionable today, sentimental returns to a God generated by millennial anxiety, the cultural present is unthinkable, indeed, unimaginable, without an understanding and acceptance of three premises. First, Christianity is there; that is, here (in Europe and the Americas, at least). Second, Christianity is a cultural structure that informs the cultural imaginary, whether one identifies with it in terms of belief and practice or not. Third, Christianity is just that; hence, it is neither the only cultural structure nor the only religious structure around. While these premises define the cultural present, it is my assumption in this essay that they also underlie any possible postmodern theology. In other words, theology in our time must be a cultural discipline, and the study of religion must be a branch of cultural analysis, whose boundaries with other cultural disciplines are porous and provisional. In such a conception, no privilege can be granted to any particular religious tradition or any cultural structure – such as religion – over any other – such as politics, education, or "culture" in the narrow sense, as the practices and products of the imaginary.

This position is grounded in a number of further premises. The first of these premises concerns history as the study of the past. The importance of history lies not in attempts to reconstruct the past but in understanding the present. Understanding culture serves the purpose of making the world we live in understandable and thereby a place with more freedom, with all kinds of choices. Knowledge of the past derives its relevance from this ongoing presence of the past within the present, not as its precursor or source but as an ineradicable, integral part of the present. The pervasive presence of religion in the past is therefore a presence in the present as well, a presence that no one can escape, that informs politics and education, moral behavior and juridical decisions alike.[1]

A second further premise concerns the cultural disciplines. If "culture" is the object of study in the disciplines of art history, literary studies, classics, and such social disciplines as anthropology, then the endeavor, again, must be an understanding of the present as integrative and dynamic. This conviction entails a need for interdisciplinary work as an indispensable framework for any study within separate disciplines. Moreover, no field within this large arena can afford to limit itself to its traditional self-identity. The fundamental permeability of fields of study concerns both the "medium" – literature cannot be isolated from visual art, for example – and the social area – "high" and "popular" art cannot be isolated from each other. Visual and verbal culture interpenetrate, as do everyday culture and the more contemplative, imaginary cultures of leisure. Religion is part and parcel of the cluster constituting this fundamentally mixed culture.

While this position precludes any practice of theology in separate endeavors, it also makes the study and understanding of the religious legacies whose offshoots pervade Western culture an indispensable element of the analysis of culture. It is a flaw in current academic practices such as cultural studies that they underestimate the importance of the integration of what used to be "theology" or "religious studies" in any attempt to grasp how we live the past inside the present.

I have argued and explored these premises in earlier work, which I can only refer the reader to here. In a recent study, I made an argument for the consequences of this position for historical work in the domain of visual art (*Quoting Caravaggio: Contemporary Art, Preposterous History*, Chicago: University of Chicago Press, 1999). Earlier, I was involved in exploring ways in which biblical literature could be interpreted as both strange – "old" and "foreign" – and relevant to today's post-Enlightenment culture (this work is probably why I have ended up in this volume). Elsewhere, I explored the interrelations of verbal and visual culture (1991 around Rembrandt; 1997 around Proust), and the negotiations carried out in the present to deal with that mixture, specifically in the practice of exhibiting. For the purposes of this volume, I would like to present one spin-off from that earlier work and touch upon one later development of it, in order to argue for the importance of the integration of the traditional topics of study in a radically different analytical setting which – why not? – might go by the name of "postmodern theology."

Theology, then, is the name for a specialization within the domain of cultural analysis that focuses, from the point of view of the integrative premises outlined above, on those areas of present-day culture where the religious elements from the past survive and hence "live." Consequently, a postmodern theology must account for those aspects of that special domain that are "other" to the past. If the field of study is the Bible, then postmodern theology must account for the social meanings, including the "literary," political, and artistic ones, of biblical literature in today's world – within the context of the heritages of other religions, other cultures. Sometimes the field of study is what is traditionally called "art history," namely those portions of visual culture that represent or evoke, or otherwise engage, religious traditions, or, to put it differently, those elements of religion that function in the visual domain. This field includes medieval stained-glass windows as well as films such as Robert Duvall's *The Apostle* (1997). But the visual can no more be distinguished from expressions in other media than fictional or aesthetic objects can be from objects of everyday life. Postmodern theology is liable to study gospel traditions and convent life, denominational schools and the ideological makeup of charitable foundations, and the presence of religious discourse in lay politics and religious tenets in the practice and theory of law. But to make this field less large and muddled, without falling back onto the traditional text-based sources, let me confine the discussion here to postmodern "visual theology."

It is obvious that the cultural heritage of Western art is to a large extent bound up with past religious purposes and events. In such cases the work to be done by a postmodern theology with such imagery is to account for it, that is, to examine and analyse it in order to understand the effective and affective result of encounters in the present with such "works of art." For the sake of integrating the premises indicated above, I will select the cases for my demonstration from the latter domain, not traditionally considered directly theological.

In the limited space of this contribution I will outline two case studies that I have conducted recently within which these premises have proved productive. The first concerns an attempt to articulate an approach to some of Caravaggio's paintings of religious subjects. This is a spin-off of my book on the painter as revised by contemporary art. The paintings attract flocks of tourists, many of whom profoundly enjoy the images without necessarily sympathizing with the religious content, or even recognizing, let alone understanding, it. Far from deploring this "loss of tradition" as conventional art history would tend to do, or explaining the meanings of the original work, the attempt, then, is to offer an explanation for – and to argue on behalf of – the continued relevance of elements of our visual culture that are not understood today in the terms of the past (nor need they be). The second case study concerns an inverse itinerary: to present an image that, far from suffering a loss of tradition, suffers from an excess of it. Here, I was dealing with an image that is already overgrown with the weeds of later ideological reception. The goal was to bring to this image a fresh understanding, in a culture which is not only post-Enlightenment in its overt atheism, but which is also – or should be – post-misogynistic in its confused reception of the narratives that came to us from older religious traditions.

Caravaggio Today

There's a dogma in the discipline of art history which says that images from the past must be understood in terms of the artists' and patrons' intentions. In the many cases where the documentation is insufficient and intention diffuse, such as where the Italian master Michelangelo Merisi da Caravaggio is concerned, this dogma is particularly problematic. We know that many of his images represent biblical scenes or religious moments: conversions, callings, or devotional scenes. It is relatively easy to track down the precise meanings of the details in such images; for example, in terms of the patron's wishes to make a stand in favor of a theological fine point that matters to the religious order that commissioned the painting. Such research, standard in the history of art, pertains to what I would call a modernist theology, one based on historical reconstruction and the purity of theological meaning as directly derived from theological documents.

At the same time, however, today the most striking aspect of Caravaggio's work is seen to be the profound sensuality of his representations of the human body, especially the male body. It is a well-known fact that, although the painter depicted scenes figuring, for example, the Virgin and Mary Magdalene, no female nude by his hand is known. His male figures, on the other hand, saints or not, are often sensuously depicted nude or semi-nude bodies. The status of this aspect of such paintings cannot be accounted for in the terms that are offered by modernist theology or art history. This sensuality cannot be attributed to the artist's overt intention, especially not in cases of commissions by religious authorities, but neither can it be construed as unintentional. We simply don't know and perhaps shouldn't care; instead, we ought to accept that the mind is unreadable and does not dictate meaning and effect. Instead, it seems more important to recognize that the tension between the paintings' sensuality and their religious content is the product of the present and its dogmas. For it is our time, not Caravaggio's, that appears to find a tension between these two areas of human experience. As if to disavow the aspect of Caravaggio's paintings that troubles scholars most today, art-historical work labors to make the case for either the artist's deep religiosity or his faithful execution of his patrons' wishes.[2] What I referred to above as modernist theology is not "pure" theology, but an active, polemical repression of bodily and sensuous aspects of life from theology. This repression has its counterpart in art history's reluctance to acknowledge the importance of studying the tradition of the female nude and its many variations and ramifications.[3]

My interest is not in contesting the artist's religiosity, of which we know nothing apart from his paintings, or the influence of his patrons on their iconography. What I find relevant for the articulation of a postmodern theology would be, rather, the acknowledgment of the scholars' deep commitment to "save" the art from itself. This commitment has nothing to do with any theological "truth" – God – Christian or other. The compulsion to explore Caravaggist iconography in the most subtle theological detail in order to "reconstruct" its historical meanings is in fact profoundly anachronistic, either as art history or as theology. For it is based on a division between body and spirit which is, I contend, *not* historical, but rather an anachronistic projection from a more recent past, often indicated by the term "Victorian," which is still rampant in present-day morality.[4] To be sure, such studies can be relevant and useful for their precision and the underlying acknowledgment of a mixed-media culture in the past. But instead of, or in addition to, such studies, I see the sensuality in Caravaggio's images as being utterly compatible with, indeed, an integrated part of a baroque religious sensibility that was, so to speak, the everyday life of the Counter-Reformation. More importantly, it accounts for the images' appeal to viewers in the present. And, according to my premises, its theological relevance, if any, must be anchored in that appeal. Far from leading to anachronistic interpretation as my work has often been accused of doing, I contend it is only from this "presentist" perspective that a historical account can be meaningfully attempted.[5]

Perhaps trying to satisfy his clients' wishes or, at other times, only paying lip-service, this artist was, for all we know, primarily a painter invested in probing the possibilities of his art from the perspective of his lived reality. This reality included – we must surmise from what we see – the presence of sensually rich, enticing bodies in his representations. Caravaggio's images are profoundly and decisively erotic. It can only be on and in such bodies that the religious content took hold. If theological interpretation is to be meaningful, its task is to account for this bodily aspect of religious experience, not to dismiss it as idiosyncratic or to privilege one domain over the other.

The sensuality and religiosity must be taken together, not only to account for Caravaggio's specificity as a painter, but more importantly, to learn from these images something about religion as lived experience instead of dead, authoritarian letter. This lesson concerns what has been called "relationality."[6] And if religion, etymologically if not essentially, concerns relationality, then chances are that the very sensuality of Caravaggio's paintings *is* their theological content, for which the references to the dogmatic position he was commissioned to depict is no more than a frame.[7]

As it happens, contemporary – postmodern – conceptions of art are also more invested in art's relational potential, its performativity, than in its iconography. Thus the bond between a theological interpretation of images based on traditional religious content and an account of art's powers has more than an incidental common ground in relationality. We can learn something from painting, not as a transparent medium of representation but as alternative semiotic production. Painting offers something we don't know, or have forgotten: something books don't teach us but images can; something, ultimately, that, in more senses than one, *matters*.

By exploring sensuality and representation together, Caravaggio was the first to make utter illusionism into a statement on the body. Two of his works on religious subjects give a sense of what this entails. *The Crucifixion of Saint Peter* and *The Conversion of Saint Paul*, both from 1601–2 and both large canvases (230 × 175 cm), were commissioned as a set. They were painted to be companion pieces in the Cerasi Chapel of the Church of Santa Maria del Popolo in Rome, where they are still found today. The site, the hanging, and the duration of their time in this chapel constitute a frame in the double sense. In the first place, these paintings in their past and present site also suggest what Caravaggio's bodily illusionism does *not* entail. Here, there is no narrative "in the third person," no telling stories of others that concern us only for the lesson drawn from them by church authorities. There is no referential illusion that the temporality of the image is safely ensconced within the historical past of the dramatic events. The painstaking theological–iconographic analysis carried out in a spirit of modernist historiography, correct and therefore valuable as it otherwise is, utterly fails to account for this defining aspect of the works.[8] Yet, here they are, in this church, where thousands come to see them. In order to benefit from these paintings-in-situ, we must endorse the obvious fact that tourism, not religion, the lust for art not for God, sensuous visual appeal not spirituality, brings most viewers into this church, and to these paintings. So what experience do they solicit and enhance that might have cultural, even specifically theological, relevance today?

First, there is the site itself, the conditions of viewing that allows or forbids. To see the paintings fully, one needs to stand between them, something the casual visitor, under pressure of time because of the 100-lire piece inserted into the automatic lighting machine, is not allowed to do. As far as temporality is concerned, this pressure ironically makes up for the limited access, for on this utterly mundane level one is made acutely aware of bodily frustration and the effect of duration. Instead of standing between them, one cranes one's neck and feels the pressure of seeing quickly, amidst so many others, and obliquely. A lack of access is inherent to this viewing experience; a sense of the partial and the transient, the impossibility of possessing these images, to stare at them at leisure, to own and objectify them.

The second relevant aspect of the experience concerns the kind of representations the images offer. These are figurative paintings, proposing not just a fictional happening but a specific bias towards that happening as well.[9] To summarize the result of a long analysis of their painterly mode as it clashes with their *mise-en-scène*, these two paintings are totally *illusionistic* in their texture yet totally *artificial* in their figurativity. This disjunction between illusion and realism sharpens the qualification of illusionism as a tool for attracting the embodied look which the figuration further elaborates. Both scenes are utterly theatrical. This theatricality solicits a look that is both engaged and devoid of mimetic illusion. This is powerfully visible, for example, in the figure of Peter. He is lifting his head and shoulder to look away in boredom at having to pose in an uncomfortable position for too long. Similarly, Paul is displaying his muscles, tense from holding up his arms for the length of time it takes to paint him so painstakingly. Thus, the figures don't come to us as saints from biblical stories but as people, actors playing these saints, in a play staged for us.

Why is that important? The tension between illusionistic painting and artificial, anti-narrative figuration has been brought to awareness most effectively not by art-historical commentary but by Derek Jarman's 1986 film *Caravaggio*, another visual work of art, made in and for our time. The transformation of the acting friends and assistants who set up the tableaux vivants for Michele as he paints, into the actual paintings that result, is a precious tool for art history classes, for it drives home a sense of the performativity that mediates between illusion and theatricality. And while this film seems to be indifferent to theological knowledge, it seems less in tension with the paintings-in-situ than with the art-historical iconographic readings that ignore their frame and their actual effect. For it turns the sensuality of the studio, the intimacy of lived reality in which the paintings were made, into a plausible way of being with the stories of the apostles.

The clash – or harmony – between illusionism and theatricality impels the viewer to look differently at the details of the scene and the painter's work. Peter's fingernails are dirty but his hand does not bleed, is not pierced by the nail. And, in case you are mistaken, the arbitrary spatial direction of the nail, doubly oblique, confronts you with the impossibility of reconciling but also of ignoring the two modes of representation at stake. For the nail is bent away from the wood and towards the picture plane. Thus it drives home the point that it does not connect to the wood to which it is supposed to fix the hand. Instead, the posing man is holding it, but, due to the duration of the session, loosens his grip, forgets to keep it straight. This is a real man, not a legendary saint or a historically remote narrative figure. It is a man who does odd jobs, who, just one or two years ago, saw a turn-of-the-century celebration, who perhaps witnessed the burning of Giordano Bruno at the stake a few streets from the studio, and who is now posing for Michele. Illusionism serves not realism but its opposite. What can we do with such a scene of crucifixion? We are accustomed to associate crucifixion with the utter sacrifice – of life for faith – that Christianity proposes as a model for religion. What if it is presented to us as a play and, if not as playful, as an act rather poorly performed, and thereby perversely comical, conveying the contagious fun of an afternoon among friends?

The point, I submit, of Caravaggio-according-to-Jarman is to do with community, with intimacy, as a value of intensity; a relationality which does not require compliance with the exclusivist morality of heterosexual monogamy. The narrative *on* religion – as distant, in the past, and regarding others who can only be models – is overwhelmed by a narrative *of* religion. At least, if we conceive of religion in the lay sense of binding and bonding outside of the discourse of possession and permanence that continues to characterize thought on relationships that involve the body.

This relationalist activism of the paintings is more specific than this. *The Crucifixion of Saint Peter* manifests this activism against narrative third-person distanciation and the temporal closure it entails most famously in the figure of the man holding the shovel. This figure is helping out the other actors for whom lifting the cross with a live man on it is not the easiest way to spend an afternoon. He has the dirty feet of a street worker, the rough, reddish elbows of a manual laborer, and an incredibly live, fleshy pair of buttocks that press through his pants so as to make you look twice both at them and at the shapely, manly shoulder. This man's body is totally real; its back is turned obliquely towards the viewer, seducing you to come in, or at least, to stay captivated. You keep throwing in 100-lire pieces. Looking, even at religious imagery, clearly, is not a disembodied flight into piety but an act mediated through the body.

This look, then, engaged in an intense travel across the picture plane, stops at the sight of the dirty soles of feet, the fingernails, the irritated facial expression, and the fleshy, tactile buttocks. Thus, the viewer, body and soul, is drawn *inside* the event, this world of sensuality and bodily engagement with a collaborative existence of pleasure and work, of enjoyment and helping out, of something whose intensity makes it so special without enforcing a specific interpretation of what one sees.

Once the viewer is caught by the painting's way in, the painting at the right-hand side of the chapel continues the spatial captivation in a time-consuming process. It also seems to comment on a feature of the *Crucifixion*: the fact that this painting resists eye contact.[10] The figures hauling up St Peter's cross are too busy to look at us. The helper who most directly pulls us in does so by turning his buttocks to us. And Peter, whose face is more or less directed towards the viewer, only seems to face us because he is looking away from the others, clearly aggravated, as if thinking, or saying to the audience in a theatrical aside: What's all the fuss about?

Standing in the crowd, craning our neck to see, it may occur to us that the fuss is, among other things, about space, or the lack of it. Caravaggio has been accused of a lack of spatial skills; his spaces seem over-crowded, sometimes arbitrarily cropped and unharmonious. But continuing our adventure in Rome, we come to realize that this is all for the good. *The Conversion of Saint Paul* clearly demonstrates that Caravaggio knew exactly what he was doing with his famous confined spatiality. This painting is an extreme case of the claustrophobic representation of space. Yet the center of the picture is a deep black hole. As one critic phrased it, "the clarity has a bare-bones drive; the man's stretched arms and the corresponding horse's legs set up the center of the drama as a deep hole."[11] The low point-of-view makes you almost afraid of the horse's bulk and menacing lifted foot. And whereas the figures in the *Crucifixion* look in different directions, here they are blind.

This is most emphatic, of course, in Paul himself, whose shell-covered eyes – cleverly taken up by Jarman, who covers the eyes with coins – are close to us, symmetrical to the man's buttocks in the other picture. But the clearest structural device used to bind the two pictures together from left to right, despite the chronological oddity – the *Paul* represents the beginning, the *Peter* the end of apostleship – is *light*. In the *Peter* the light comes from somewhere at the left, in front of the picture plane. Once attracted, you follow it to step inside. In the *Paul* the light comes from somewhere to the right, behind the picture plane. It leaves the back of Paul's head in the dark, emphasizing the skin of his chest and the inside of his arms, as well as the large flank of the horse and the balding forehead of the older man holding the horse. This man is also afflicted by blindness.

Paul is lying with his legs spread open, his arms and hands stretched out to receive whatever it is the light brings. Grace, revelation, the third-person story of modernist theology would say; and, thanks to the predominance of iconography, the painter could make sure that this third-person story passed muster.[12] But this second-person story invited ordinary people with live bodies into the scene, just as the helper in the *Peter* did with his buttocks. The space has grown more confined, the body more passive, receptive. Taken together, the erotic quality becomes poignantly concrete, so much so that the blindness comes to signify the substitution of touch for sight, a radicalization of the thought of visual tactility.

This reading is not a homosexual interpretation in any simple, anecdotal sense. In a postmodern theology it is pointless to either attribute or deny homosexuality to the artist. But writing homosexuality out of the present "work" of Caravaggio's saints would be another gesture of modernist purification. Instead, before embarking on an analysis of this body of images, we must declare and endorse the presence of this centering of sensuous appeal on male bodies. In a sense that is not confined to identity politics, this art is both theological and homosexual. Contemporary American painter David Reed adopts the theoretical thought implied in Caravaggio's pair of paintings but radically changes it. For no body can be seen in his painting. Yet the utter physicality, the sense-based involvement of the body, is just as keen. The body, in his work, is made drastically present, but not as an actor on the stage. The body that cannot escape, does not wish to escape, the *touch* of this painting, is that of the viewer. It makes the

POSTMODERN THEOLOGY AS CULTURAL ANALYSIS   13

erotic quality equally intense but infinitely malleable. The viewer becomes the sole actor and the painting the sole seducer, a "trisexual" figure whose primary characteristic is to be universally available, for whom it may concern.[13]

What temporality is at stake here? As a result of the visual erotics, the mobilized body, conjured into participation *qua* body, is the same body whose eyes are doing the looking. Hence, these paintings militate against the disembodied gaze we have learned to cast on images. That gaze is atemporal and does not even know that it has a body, let alone a body involved in looking.[14] Instead, the Caravaggio works propose a mode of looking which is not only a desirable one for these paintings but also the only possible one, the only one that leads to *seeing*. They solicit a participatory look, one beyond that of "participatory observation" based on coevalness, the long-standing ideal of anthropology.[15] This intellectual posture, this embodied look, is not only epistemologically indispensable, as was participatory observation for modernist, self-conscious anthropological knowledge; it is ontological. Taking into account the deceptiveness and other drawbacks of this epistemological mode, the notion of *performance* would seem more appropriate for characterizing it.

Performance, in anthropology, is the construction of knowledge about a culture *with* the people and through collective research and discovery, as Fabian argued in a study which, loyal to its thesis, is an account of just such an endeavor. Performance is an act; it is doing. Most often the word is used to indicate ontological dynamism, as in J. W. Austin's famous linguistic theory of performativity. In theater, performance is when a play becomes a play; without performance, it remains a text. In reception-oriented theories of reading the same notion of performance is used to define a specific ontological status of textuality. Without reading, the book remains a dead object, existing only as a thing in space.[16] Text and image belong rigorously in the same ontological domain here, for neither one exists as "pure."

Caravaggio's two religious paintings draw their viewers through a double play on the concept of performance. Their emphatic theatricality opens the audience up to the idea that one can play various parts, provisionally participate in – experience from within – an event that took place in the past but that is also being enacted in the present; an event perhaps not otherwise available to each of us. We are offered this participation in a light, voluntary tone, with a wink, so to speak. This is a liberal seductiveness, easy to accept. But then things get more serious. The sensuous appeal of the two paintings together, in their neck-craning site, perform, also, *qua* painting. They operate in this respect through their visual modality as distinct from, but cooperating with, their theatricality. This performance in the second sense thickens the first one. This mode is no longer so voluntary; its appeal is more powerful, punitive, the penalty of refusal being the impossibility of seeing and enjoying the paintings beyond superficial and quick glancing.

On the one hand, then, each viewer is given the opportunity of playing a part in an erotic relationality clearly homosexual in kind: the men-only, the attraction from behind, the dark cavity, all encourage male homosexual fantasies; a relationality based on unexpected encounters and brief, provisional role-playing. But it would be a mistake to reduce the images' work to a specific, limiting kind of sexuality. The second performativity enables the once-seduced viewer to relate to the bodies in the images in any way he or she wishes. The point of the general "trisexual" sexiness available is not to enforce an experience that is alien for some, too common for others. The point is to offer a different experience of bodiliness and relationality through the encounter with vision. Far from the appropriating eroticism of the pornographic visuality, these images propose an alternative visual seduction, no less erotic, but unabusive, unexploitative; a decolonized erotics of vision.

Whether or not one recognizes theological relevance in this relationality does not preoccupy me greatly. But even if one limits the field of theology to the more classical sense of the remnant of past fantasies and imagery, of stories and myths that we call biblical literature as they remain present today, the use of sacred stories for the deployment of the double performativity of Caravaggio's paintings of religious subjects must be recognized as relevant. Personally, I would be more interested in a conception of theology as the exploration of alternative possibilities for relationality which traditional morality, religion and, indeed, art history do not enhance, so that it can be brought into connection with the bodily experience of otherness available in the church of Santa Maria del Popolo. It is precisely because of, not despite, its location in a church that the sexuality embodied here entails an experience that is by definition different, and more profound than whatever a particular viewer's sexual practice might be.

Reframing Judith

Two factors obstruct this expansion of religious subject matter. First, some subjects are already so tenaciously overdetermined, overwritten by ideological interpretation, that they are not open to the kind of experience the Cerasi Chapel offers. Second, churches are not the only locations of art that might have theological relevance in a postmodern perspective. Museums, the worldly version of churches, are more likely places for it, with their equally ritual function and ideologically imposing power. In the second case study, I would like to focus more on framing, which is the companion to performativity in a postmodern cultural analysis, with or without theological specialization.

To do justice to the differences between the members of the public and the aspects of the art works that museums display, I have proposed, in my book *Double Exposures*, to work with the concept of framing – in its double meaning as mentioned above. That book was based on the idea that the concept of framing enables museum workers to display art while also showing what they do, how they do it, and why. Easier said than done, is an obvious objection, and until the summer of 1998 I had no answer that would satisfy those who mustered that appeal to the alleged rift between theory and practice. At that moment I received a request from the Museum Boijmans Van Beuningen in Rotterdam to help present a newly acquired, early seventeenth-century non-canonical painting to the public. This provided me with the precious opportunity to test if, and how, such revisionist presentations are possible in practice.

My experimental exhibition was primarily an attempt to work with the notion of framing as a way of freeing exhibition practice from the constraints of traditional monography and narrative itinerary. Underlying this experiment was Derrida's rich text on the frame as parergon, as a kind of supplement to the work of which it is also a part; to simplify: the notion that the frame is the link between work and world, not the cut between them, however hard it tries to be just that cut. As it happens, the object I was to work with had a place in the theological canon. The painting in question was *Judith Shows Holophernes' Head to the People of Bethulia*, by Gerrit Pieterszoon Sweelinck, from 1605. Given the expectation – frame as set-up – that I would reiterate the misogynistic castration theme so often projected on this subject, I did not wish to do a thematic presentation. Thematics so often seems to be the sole alternative to monographic shows, and so easily becomes totally ahistorical, that I was reluctant to endorse it, even though there was some pressure from others in the museum to do so. I have reported on the experiment elsewhere;[17] here, I would simply like to point out how, *in practice* – a practice not of viewing, as in the Cerasi Chapel, but of exhibiting – a kind of cultural–analytical perspective can again gain relevance for a postmodern theology. With Caravaggio I attempted to place the engagement with the sensate body and the erotics of relationality within the religious subject rather than to see it as its repressed other. In the museum, in contrast, the possible theological potential is paradoxically situated in the movement away from theology.

Beneath an introductory text at the entrance to the exhibition space, at a distance of 1 meter from the wall, I put a display case with seven household utensils on which Judith and other biblical heroines were depicted. An information leaflet outlined the concept of the show. It began with the title of the show, followed by the title of the painting, and then continued with a presentation of the painting as part of the collection. The paintings mentioned there were displayed, in the traditional manner, side by side, on the long left wall, with enough space between them to allow looking at each of them in isolation. This modernist mode of hanging fitted the content of this section – or frame – which was based on a traditional preoccupation of art museums. Only the painting on a related subject, *Jael Showing the Body of Sisera to Barak*, by Speckaert, had an individual caption. This painting most obviously invited comparison with the Sweelinck and was hung closest to the new work but on the opposite wall; it also served as a shifter to the following section. Its caption read: "With her sensual mouth, looser hair and bare leg, Jael is much more sensually depicted than Sweelinck's Judith. There is more narrative movement in this painting; the story isn't finished yet." My hope was that the comparison might invite viewers to consider the two paintings, not in terms of relative aesthetic merit or of reiterations of a theme, but as two different modes of visually dealing with a narrative subject.

The second section, described subsequently in the information leaflet, was central to the entire presentation. Paradoxically perhaps, I titled this section of the leaflet "*Judith* as masterpiece," adding the somewhat different meaning of the phrase, due to a quote from Sweelinck's contemporary critic Karel Van Mander, to the effect that Sweelinck had mentioned to him that he'd rather be a "good painter . . . than a great monarch." This quote brought in a topic of great resonance today: ambition.

The use of the problematic term "masterpiece" was meant to trigger reflection on it, since the category is not at all self-evident for this painting. What followed then reflected my intuitions about the ambitious quality of the painting. This was both the most complex and the most paradoxical frame: the painting itself was the frame, spilling over into the surrounding works that had been brought together on a variety of grounds; it was, after all, about the internal variety of the painting. A screen with two wings was placed just before the two short walls that led to a transitional cabinet. Hence, the works on these sections of walls were half-hidden – by the wings of the screen – from the visitor as he entered.

The right-hand corner was crowded, with six portraits of women, all from the first half of the seventeenth century, some oval, and, stylistically as well as canon-wise, totally unrelated. Only one caption accompanied this ensemble. Whereas the women's portraits served, literally, as a backdrop, I put four other works closer to the Sweelinck on the wings of a screen, to foreground the genres represented within the painting. Here, I had to contend with "historical evidence." Van Mander reports Sweelinck's own words about his ambition, albeit in indirect discourse. These words were put on the screen in large print above the painting: ". . . a good painter rather than a great monarch." The point was not to ignore this evidence, or to give it more status *as evidence* than such indirect, gossipy reporting warrants; this is why I avoided historicizing lettering, choosing a modern typeface instead. Nor did I want to infuse the centrality of the painting with more canonizing intentionalism.

But the historical "effect of the real" that such quotes produce did have a historicist purpose. The notion of ambition – a word used in the information leaflet but not on the wall – has a contemporary resonance today. By drawing attention to the ambition of the artist, who, by all accounts, would be considered mediocre by traditional art historians and art critics, the viewers were enabled to frame the work with empathy. Thus, by mentioning Sweelinck's ambition instead of glorifying great art or putting the painting at a historical distance from today, the viewers were helped to identify with the artist, across time, enabling those who wished for it to have what one historian would call a "historical experience" – which is emphatically not based on a conflation between past and present. On the contrary, as Didier Maleuvre argued about the historicity of things in his 1999 book *Museum Memories*: "To be historical, an object must have seceded from time: it cannot be one with its temporal becoming. The historical object is therefore one that belongs neither to its original setting – from which it has been singled out – nor to the present – in which it resists assimilation."[18] And the historical experience consists of living through the caesura that inheres in the historical: "The historical is the stuff of the past which, by being remembered in the present, desists from being in the present: it is what cannot be reconstituted in the present." The frame, precisely, separates, acknowledges the separation, and thus *links* present to past, and this experience infuses subjects in the present with the temporal density that "history" provides.

Moreover, the ambition of the painting seemed not simply to be its desire to excel. Instead, the ambition took a specific turn, embodied in the attempt to excel *in many genres*. This aspect provided a frame through which to "read" the painting on its own terms, while keying it into an historical experience based on empathy. This specific ambition was visually indicated by surrounding the work with paintings from the collection exemplary of each of these genres; paintings, again, not selected for their canonical status or their aesthetic quality but because they could serve to explain Sweelinck's work, just as that work honors these genres; glosses or visual footnotes, rather than stylistic commentaries. This multiple-genre frame seemed all the more attractive because it allowed the viewers to realize for themselves not only *that* genres in painting differ, but also *which* genres they individually find most interesting. The four "footnotes" were: a still life underscoring the lower left corner; a domestic scene with a curtain, referring to the upper left; a landscape on the upper right; and a portrait on the lower right.

How does this presentation – of which I have had to simplify the account here – bear on the question of a postmodern theology? The foregrounding of framing and the deconstructive dispersal of the canonical interpretation of the Judith story are a strategy for achieving a relevance for theology as cultural analysis. The strategy of dispersal and the foregrounding of framing itself by means of pluralized frames were attempts to account for the painting in terms that were not thematic, that did not immediately focus on the Judith subject. But, clearly, to present a *Judith* without paying attention to the most obvious frame, the thematic one, would be disingenuous and beside the point. Visitors would expect it, and might quickly lose interest if the theme were artificially avoided. But three traps lurk here: the predictably misogynistic interpretation of the theme, the ahistorical reification of any theme, and the visual tedium of repetition.

My endeavor was to exploit the thematic frame by blowing it up from the inside, so to speak. This was done in several ways concurrently. The thematic part of the show was divided into two sections: the prints and drawings, and some paintings. Wishing at all costs to avoid the kind of thematics that surround castration anxiety or more general misogynistic fantasy, I divided the prints and drawings according to two sub-themes, and, forced by the limitations of the collection – but then, wholeheartedly – I presented the paintings in terms of ambiguity, not concentrating on powerful women, the famous lady killers, but on a variety of power relations between women and men. *Lady* killers confronting lady *killers*.

However, the ambiguities could easily get lost on viewers keen on connecting this frame with the subject of the painting. To recall that subject while undercutting its centrality, I made two interventions. First, Speckaert's *Jael*, which appeared in the section devoted to the Boijmans collecting policy, was moved from that wall to be closer to the thematic section. Second, I added, in the small section to the left of the entrance, a number of color photographs of other *Judith* paintings and one drawing, all related to Sweelinck's representation of the theme in specific ways, thus countering thematic conflation.

The two most famous *Judith Beheading Holophernes* paintings – the one by Artemisia Gentileschi and the other by Caravaggio – were perhaps most likely to confront the viewers with aspects such as horror and admiration for a job well done (the Gentileschi) and the contradictory feelings evoked when the face of the decapitated figure turns out to be a self-portrait (the Caravaggio), aspects which enhance the Sweelinck in unexpected ways. These irreverent photographic copies were also meant to shock viewers into realizing the difference between imagery as such and the material work of painting; to reflect on what matters to them, the work as image or the work as thing.

The point of this working around the Judith theme was twofold: narrative and representational. First, like the Samson story, the story of Judith is often depicted in art. It has great dramatic potential. The combination of beauty and virtue presents a challenge to the subtle painter. Moreover, it juxtaposes two loyalties: Judith saves her people but is a threatening figure to men. As usual, the older woman, Judith's maid, is important for introducing nuances. In many representations she is depicted as a "madame," something which is given sexual expression in the form of the younger woman. This is why such a female figure is often placed next to Delilah, although the Bible gives no cause for this. In more subtle works, by being contrasted with the older woman, the heroine is depicted as beautiful, attractive and hence, indirectly, sexual.

But Gerrit Pieterszoon is subtler still. He has the women resemble each other, which suggests cooperation, without an emphasis on sexual "weapons." His Judith virtuously looks away. The older woman represents her to the viewer; she looks us straight in the eye and thus assumes responsibility for our response to the event. The tension between virtue and the use of sexuality as a weapon is thus dramatically presented to the viewer. At this juncture it seemed useful to broaden the biblical frame by comparing the case of Judith with that of Jael, represented in the nearby Speckaert.

The story of Judith is similar to the subject of Speckaert's *Jael and Sisera*, a canonical Old Testament theme (Judges 4 and 5).[19] Here, too, a beautiful heroine takes action, saving her people through ruse and sex appeal. In Jael's story, unlike in Judith's, no mention is made of her virtue. Accordingly, she is rather voluptuous in Speckaert's rendering. The moment is presented when Jael is proudly about to show her prey to Barak, who was unable to achieve the same victory. A double triumph, therefore, of one woman over two men. And, in a certain sense, a theatrical performance *within* the story.

The foundation was now laid for a more integrated comparison that relates the stories to their cultural life, their popularity to the tensions between men and women, and the various traditions of depiction to the paintings and objects on display. Why is the story of the beautiful – or deadly – heroine so popular that it is so often depicted, and even tangibly present, on household utensils, whereby housewives and maids are confronted with it on a daily basis? If such artifacts have any theological relevance then, in our postmodern perspective, this popularity of the story, its cultural presence, must be accounted for. Along with stories about Samson and Jael, the story of Judith is one of the popular mythical stories in which the power struggle between men and women ends in favor of "the weak(er) sex." These stand next to, or opposite, other stories, which have also been frequently depicted, in which women are the victims of (sexual) violence, like when Lucretia was raped and, to save her honor – or her husband's – committed suicide. Susannah (in the Book of Daniel) barely escapes the same fate: she resists the threats of her two attackers and is saved from death from stoning by the young Daniel, who isolates the two Elders and is thus able to catch them out on contradictions. The domain of such stories and their ongoing popularity is mythological.

Myth, whether we like it or not, is part and parcel of religion. For a postmodern theology that neither denies the persistence of myth in the present nor endorses the naturalization of myths, this intersection between myth and religion is an important area of contestation. The most important aspect of the thematic frame thus became the *variety* of such tensions, not the uniform focus on dangerous women. For me, this was the key to making this show *work*: not repeating what one already knows (or thinks one knows) but drawing upon other knowledge, to increase insight into more varied relations. It is a mistake to explain such stories simply as those of victims, of women's wickedness, or of a carnivalesque upside-down world in which women get the upper hand. Instead, they belong, together with more ambiguous and ambivalent stories, to a series of stories about women, men, and power.

Moreover, a one-sided reading often deprives one of what the depiction, visually, reveals. Many depictions, in which the story on which they are based points in one direction, visually suggest the other side of the same story. Thanks to the depiction we see that the other side was embodied in the story from the beginning. The languid nymph about to be raped by the powerful faun emerges as a raging Fury; the lethal Delilah, the murderous Jael and Judith sometimes seem more like the caring mother worrying about her child. If we look back at the text, which seems to have been so inappropriately interpreted, we see instead that the depiction reveals a new – and until then unseen – side. This confrontation offers an implied argument for the adoption of visual imagery in the domain of – mostly text-based – theological study.

The feelings and loyalties dealt with in such stories are ambivalent indeed. The vulnerability of the drunken or sleeping man can be seen as a rendering of the more common insight that men do not have all the power; that women cannot be totally subjugated; that uncertainty and vulnerability always also influence relationships.

The makeshift print cabinet had to be isolated from the room where the paintings were displayed because of light restrictions. In line with suggestions made by Julia Kristeva in her exhibition at the Louvre but not fully elaborated there, I wanted to draw attention to the intimate connection between beheading and portraiture.[20] I now wanted to theorize the fine portrait of Holophernes in this Sweelinck – already foregrounded by the juxtaposition of the *Judith* with the portrait of his famous brother – in more general terms. But to make that point an even more general aspect of the depiction of the human body needed to be explored. On the one hand, bodies in interaction pose the problem of delimitation. What comprises an individual body, as opposed to the mass of lines and planes that suggest bodies embracing or bodies killing each other? The sleeping body displays a vulnerability that seems to visually raise the question of whether sleep doesn't invite the kind of killing actions that biblical heroines represent. The question of individual wholeness is also raised by decapitation as such. For is a body without a head still a human being?

The two walls with the prints and drawings were linked by my favorite quote from the original biblical story. On the left, above the works, were the words: "Look! there lies Holophernes..." and on the right: "...and his head is missing!" A head apart: from dissection to composition. Such stories about women's victory and such experiments in depicting individual limbs, vulnerable sleeping figures, and heads without bodies recur in numerous prints and drawings in the Boijmans collection. A beautiful series by Lucas van Leyden depicts no less than three of the popular "lady killers" from the Bible: Jael, Delilah, and Salome. In Ferdinand Bol's drawing of Tamar and Amnon he reveals the other side of the story: a man rapes a woman, who has been lured with a trick.

Unlike the impersonal, separate body part or the headless body, the decapitated head stands for the essence and limits of the individual. At this point I wanted to invite the viewers to retrace their steps and take a second look at Sweelinck's painting, and perhaps at the entire room. A suggestion to do so was given in a daring, perhaps dubious, connection, presented as open to reflection and decision. On the back of the screen – in the middle of it and surrounded by a few particularly remarkable prints and drawings – I placed one of the two drawings by Sweelinck, a depiction of Saint Luke at the easel. This striking sketch shows the same jaw, cheekbone, and eyebrows that made the two women in the painting resemble each other so closely.

Looked at with this in mind, Sweelinck's *Judith* became even more surprising. Could it be a coincidence that the unusual shape of the face of both Judith and the older woman who resembles her – the prominent cheekbones and the distinct jaw – was also found in the face in this sketch? Seen in this light, it was striking that Holophernes' head again resonated in Gerrit Pieterszoon's most beautiful portrait: that of his brother, who achieved greater fame.

This last sentence, which leads back to the painting and its two primary features – ambition and portraiture – risks reintroducing relative canonicity and aesthetic judgment. As it happens, these are two major elements of the ideological power of religion framed as authoritative structure, and hence both were in need of analysis and critique. But I also wished to connect with preoccupations I could be sure would be entertained by visitors. It made no sense to expect people to come into the room with blank, empty minds. Framed as they invariably are by the traditional discourse on art, it seemed more meaningful to include such considerations – but putting them in a pluralist perspective – than to ignore their important influence.

Visually, this connection between the less successful brother, here in charge and at the center, and the more famous one who ends up decapitated – but then, also, beautifully portrayed – was based solely on the visual imprint, in the memory of the visitor, of the striking, strong features of the two murderous women, now projected over the light, barely readable sketch. Bathing in the blood-red color of the ground, the sketch and painting may or may not have anything to do with each other.

With this experimental presentation of Sweelinck's *Judith* I tried to make the most of that obnoxious notion, the "work of art." I was attempting to confront the various visitors who might wander into Room 4 of the museum with a different kind of confrontation with art, one that *concerns* the people who inhabit today's society, that *shocks* them into looking at old masters not as venerated yet antiquated remnants of the past, but as something that belongs to a present that entertains a lively relationship with its past.

My point was/is that there are different ways of working in museums that can increase both enjoyment and visual literacy: ways that do not reproduce, in vulgarized form, the historical scholarship conducted by museum professionals; that connect art to social and cultural life, without moralizing; that bring objects to life and life to bear on the objects otherwise so easily severed from what preoccupies the culture around them. What is usually called "a work of art" is ultimately an object, a thing that works, which occupies, in our culture, just such a position – that of a *key* between itself and the world, and vice versa.

As long as religious themes and narratives permeate a culture, they partake of the ideological makeup of that culture. Clothed in the joint authority of moralism and aesthetics, the forms they take – be they framed as "high art" or as "popular culture" – belong to that domain of contemporary culture where theology has its part to play in the general critique, or deconstruction, of what makes that culture constrictive and limiting. A postmodern theology, then, need not decide whether God exists or not, and which one God has privileges over which other Gods in a multiple society. Instead, staying rigorously on the side of the human subjects who make up and are shaped by that culture, such an atheological theology can break open the confining limitations imposed by authoritarian religion and open up possibilities of different forms of relationality that are insensitive to old, ill-conceived taboos. If I have it my way, then this is theology's postmodern mission – if such a thing is thinkable, which, perhaps, it isn't.

Notes

1 For this historical position see a number of contributions in Bal, *The Practice of Cultural Analysis: Exposing Interdisciplinary Interpretation* (Stanford, CA: Stanford University Press, 1999), esp. Ankersmit.
2 Two examples of close analyses that nevertheless escape the work itself in favor of theological finery are Bert Treffers, *Caravaggio: Genie in Opdracht* (Nijmegen: SUN, 1991) and Pamela Askew, *Caravaggio's Death of the Virgin* (Princeton, NJ: Princeton University Press, 1990).
3 For an excellent account see Lynda Nead, *The Female Nude: Art, Obscenity and Sexuality* (London: Routledge, 1992).
4 In fact, to call this morality Victorian is an anachronistic repression of the same structure as the attribution to Caravaggio of a non-bodily religiosity.
5 For such a rejection of my work on Rembrandt, see Michael Podro, "Reading 'Rembrandt': Beyond the Word–Image Opposition," *Burlington Magazine* October 1993, pp. 699–700. In contrast, Griselda Pollock, "On Reading 'Rembrandt,'" *Art Bulletin*, LXXV (3. 1993), pp. 529–35. Pollock's own art-historical work, although theoretically grounded in a different social history than the one underlying my work, ends up in a similar practice. See, for example, her recent study of the canon, *Differencing the Canon: Feminist Desire and the Writing of Art's Histories* (London: Routledge, 1999).
6 See Leo Bersani and Ulysse Dutoit, "Beauty's Light," *October* 82 (Fall 1997), pp. 17–30.
7 A frame in the double sense of the material frame of the church in which the works were to be displayed and the ideological frame of the theological context they were called on to enhance. For this meaning of framing, see Derrida's famous essay on "parergon"; also Didier Maleuvre, *Museum Memories: History, Technology, Art* (Stanford, CA: Stanford University Press, 1999) and Paul Duro (ed.), *The Rhetoric of the Frame: Essay on the Boundaries of Artwork* (Cambridge: Cambridge University Press, 1996).
8 See, for example, Treffers, *Caravaggio*, but many other examples can also be alleged.
9 I am alluding to the narrative structure of any representation of happenings, where a narration – here, in paint – is inevitably colored by a represented vision, either the narrator's or a represented character's. For the narrative theory underlying these remarks, see my *The Mottled Screen: Reading Proust Visually* (Stanford, CA: Stanford University Press, 1997).
10 If one accepts this resistance as inhering in the painting, one must also reject Michael Fried's obsessive application of the pair absorption–theatricality to Caravaggio in "Thoughts on Caravaggio," *Critical Inquiry* 24 (1997), pp. 13–56. Note, in this context, the idiosyncratic use of the latter term in Fried's work, which is not to be conflated with the more common meaning I am using here, of theatricality as referring to, evoking, or imitating the stage.
11 Creighton E. Gilbert, *Caravaggio and His Two Cardinals* (University Park, Pennsylvania State University Press, 1995).
12 He did this so well that even today this story gets all the attention. But such iconographic analyses do not account for the *painting*, only for what is "behind" it, outside of it. In other words, the most established of art-historical methods treats the painting as a text.

13 The term "trisexual," not its content, has been borrowed from Christopher Bollas, *The Shadow of the Other: Psycho-analysis of the Unknown Thought* (New York: Columbia University Press, 1987), pp. 82–96.
14 See Norman Bryson, *Vision and Painting: The Logic of the Gaze* (London: Macmillan, 1983) for an early version of this distinction.
15 On coevalness as the failed potential of anthropology, see Johannes Fabian, *Time and the Other: How Anthropology Makes its Object* (New Haven, CT: Yale University Press, 1983).
16 The concept of reading as performance is current and most characteristic of postmodern literary analysis. Its best-known early proponent was Wolfgang Iser, *The Act of Reading: A Theory of Aesthetic Response* (Baltimore, MD: Johns Hopkins University Press, 1978); for an inquiry into the feminist and postcolonial implications of Iser's approach, Mary Louise Pratt *Imperial Eyes: Travel Writing and Transculturation* (London: Routledge, 1992) and Jane P. Tompkins *West of Everything: The Inner Life of Westerns* (Oxford: Oxford University Press, 1992).
17 Mieke Bal, *Travelling Concepts in the Humanities: A Rough Guide* (Toronto: University of Toronto Press).
18 Maleuvre, *Museum Memories*, pp. 48–9.
19 I devoted a study to this story and the ways biblical scholarship has dealt with it in *Murder and Difference: Gender, Genre and Scholarship on Sisera's Death*. trans. Matthew Gumpert (Bloomington, Indiana University Press, 1988).
20 See Julia Kristeva, *Vision Capitales* (Parti Pris. Paris: Museé du Louvre, 1998).

CHAPTER 2
The Man Who Fell to Earth

Gerard Loughlin

Gerard Loughlin is a theologian with style and imagination. Having completed his doctoral work on a highly critical evaluation of John Hick's approach to theology, he was drawn to examine a subject that has preoccupied him since: narrative. In his first book, *Telling God's Story* (Cambridge, 1996), Loughlin sets a distinctly Roman Catholic mark on what has been, since Hans Frei and the development of postliberal theology, a Protestant project: narrative theology. Not only does the book emphasize a far more sacramental perspective; not only does it draw upon the premodern theological tradition in a manner not really pursued by postliberal theologians like Lindbeck and Hauerwas. The book also learns from and employs the structural and poststructural analyses of narratology. In this way postmodern thinking plays a therapeutic role in an explicit theological exploration.

Loughlin has since produced several essays, in journals and edited collections, which have taken his interests in critical theory, postmodernity, and narrativity much further. His essay in *Radical Orthodoxy: A New Theology* demonstrates the place erotics and the body have come to play in his thinking. His work as review editor for the journal *Theology and Sexuality* promoted the new direction of his theological investigations. Deftly weaving theological insights on the trinity and Marian doctrine with visions of erotic excess in Bataille's work and Dante's *divina commedia*, Loughlin produces a richly suggestive, even provocative theological argument about God's sex. This splicing of different narrative clips is characteristic of the creativity and imagination of Loughlin's work. Holding to and working from within a committed Catholic faith, his writing is composed of the dialogue partners he introduces to each other. Often with a dash of indecency, and always with a certain insouciant, Rabelaisian wit, Loughlin's method brings major theological voices – Aquinas, Barth, Balthasar, Rahner – into unexpected company and

> gets them talking. The effect on the reader is one of surprise, curiosity, and illumination. His texts are comprised of what film critics would call "jump-cuts": creative leaps from one *mise-en-scéne* to another; from one discursive practice to another: from theology to philosophy or queer theory or a novel or a passage from the Bible. Increasingly, Loughlin has been drawn to film as a vehicle for his theological explorations and the essay included here is a fine example of his sensitivity to and absorption in that aesthetic medium. The essay comes from his forthcoming book *Alien Sex*, which takes its title from the film series featuring Sigourney Weaver. Loughlin's theological voice is utterly original, profoundly intra- and intertextual and, to that extent, intensely incarnational. With Christ central as mediator, Loughlin reflects upon mediation and media, figuring for us, in the words of John Milbank, the Word made strange.

From the beginning, heavenly visitors have walked the earth, such as the "sons of God," who seeing the fairness of men's daughters took them as wives.[1] Indeed, once upon a time, even the Lord God would walk the earth "at the time of the evening breeze."[2] And though God and his "sons" ceased to visit, the world having grown more historical, other divine beings still came to earth, angelic ambassadors such as the three men who appeared to Abraham "by the oaks of Mamre," as he sat at the door of his tent in the "heat of the day";[3] or the two "angels" who came to Lot as he was "sitting in the gateway of Sodom."[4]

Heavenly visitations have not ceased in the long history of human story-telling, though the names of the visitors have changed, as also the places whence they come. In modern times their homes are more closely mapped among the stars, the trajectory of their flight more carefully calculated, but their arrival on earth is still uncanny. They still appear in the time it takes to raise your eyes or turn your head, coming along the road toward you, where before no one was to be seen, as when a caped gentleman suddenly strides toward two pilgrims on their way to Santiago de Compostela, at the beginning of Luis Buñuel's *La Voie Lactée* (*The Milky Way*, 1969). He comes along the road toward the two pilgrims, as once angels strode out of the day's heat, or walked up to the city gate, but now he appears in the blink of a shutter, out of the unseen darkness between two frames of a film. And such a visitor still fascinates and frightens, seduces and repulses, occasioning the embrace of blows.

Coming to Town

Thomas Jerome Newton, the visitor in William Tevis's 1963 novel *The Man Who Fell to Earth*, arrives in the morning, when it is still cool, having walked for 2 miles, from where we are not told, but arriving in the small town of Haneyville, population 1,400. In Nicolas Roeg's masterful 1976 film of Tevis's book, which tells the story as a tragicomedy, the visitor is first seen in silhouette, on the ridge of a shale escarpment, taking exaggerated, awkward steps, as small stones and shards of rock roll from beneath his feet on the steep incline. He is descending toward a disused mine, the rusting remnants of a redundant industry, including the incongruous hulk of a steam engine.[5] He wears a short, dark greenish-brown duffle coat, and even with its hood up we can tell that he is a gaunt, spindly figure. This visitor arrives alone, without companions, a stranger come among strangers.

Nicolas Roeg (b. 1928) is a reticent storyteller, interested in visual rather than verbal narrative, and narrative under strain. His films require active rather than passive viewing. They are examples of what Roland Barthes called writerly (*scriptible*) texts, as opposed to readerly (*lisible*) ones. The latter are texts – novels or films – that we already know, or think we know, how to read. They gratify instantly because they repeat forms we have already learned and that have become conventional. They exemplify familiar genres. Writerly texts, on the other hand, are produced ahead of the conventions that will allow us to comprehend their meaning. As such, they may cause dyspepsia, for they have to be well chewed. The reader has to write the text; the viewer has to script the film.[6]

> The writerly text is a perpetual present, upon which no *consequent* language (which would inevitably make it past) can be superimposed; the writerly text is *ourselves writing*, before the infinite play of the world (the world as function) is traversed, intersected, stopped, plasticized by some singular system (Ideology, Genus, Criticism) which reduces the plurality of entrances, the opening of networks, the infinity of languages.[7]

For Barthes the writerly is an ideal that exists, if it exists at all, before or in the writing, but not afterward, when at least in part the text will become readable, interpretable. The ideal writerly text is a "galaxy of signifiers, not a structure of signifieds; it has no beginning; it is reversible; we gain access to it by several entrances, none of which can be authoritatively declared to be the main one; the codes it mobilizes extend *as far as the eye can reach*, they are indeterminable."[8] Roeg's films do not attain to this pitch of indeterminacy, which is hardly realizable, but are what Barthes calls "incompletely plural texts, texts whose plural is more or less parsimonious."[9] The films are neither univocal nor equivocal, but in Barthes' terminology, polysemous, connotative. They are suggestive of multiple allusions, which attend a story that while it can be told, can never be fully determined, that escapes total comprehension, differing each time it is recollected. Roeg's films do not so much unfold stories as baroquely complicate them, folding them upon themselves, intricately.

Roeg refuses a straightforward narrative structure, a zero degree of dissonance between the story and its telling.[10] The narrative is often elliptical, and uses analepses that may be either recollections or premonitions, or even pure fantasies, scenes from another story, another film. The viewer is forced to construct and reconstruct his or her own account of the story being told. In this, Roeg's cinema relocates a biblical narrativity that already refuses the simply sequential and consistent. Abraham, sitting at the door of his tent, sees three men, but addresses them as one Lord. Sarah makes three cakes and having eaten them, they ask after her, but he – the one Lord – promises her a son, and asks why she laughs, and then rises to go on his/their way.[11] The text is undecided and undecidable as to there being one man or three.[12] It is as if two similar but slightly different scenes had been intercut, producing an unsettling effect; a tremor of uncertainty in the narrative. Yet even if we suppose that the text in Genesis is the result of confusing two or more sources,[13] the final form of the narrative is entirely fitting for its purpose, the disclosure of the divine in the mundane. As Karl Barth remarked of this and other visitations, the "contradiction in the statements is the appropriate form for indicating at least what has to be said. The apparent obscurity of these presentations is the real clarity with which the matter has to be presented."[14] The presentation of Roeg's story is similarly appropriate, producing a sense of the uncanny in the everyday, of something out of joint.

Matters are more straightforward in Tevis's novel, in which we learn from the first that Newton is an alien visitor, who only seems to be human.

> He was not a man; yet he was very much like a man. He was six and a half feet tall, and some men are even taller than that; his hair was as white as that of an albino, yet his face was a light tan color; and his eyes a pale blue. His frame was improbably slight, his features delicate, his fingers long, thin, and the skin almost translucent, hairless. There was an elfin quality to his face, a fine boyish look to the wide, intelligent eyes.... There were other differences, too: his fingernails, for example, were artificial, for he had none by nature. There were only four toes on each of his feet; he had no vermiform appendix and no wisdom teeth.... Yet he did have eyelashes, eyebrows, opposed thumbs, binocular vision, and a thousand of the physiological features of a normal human. He was incapable of warts; but stomach ulcers, measles and dental cavities could affect him. He was human; but not, properly, a *man*. Also, man-like, he was susceptible to love, to fear, to intense physical pain and to self-pity.[15]

Newton is not properly a man, but nor is he a divine being. He is already too human to be anything other than a fallen creature, fallen into our world and away from a biblical ideal of the heavenly visitor. Though in some sense a warning angel, who has come to earth to save humanity from destroying itself and thereby securing a new home for his own species, the Antheans,[16] he succumbs to the terrors and beauties of our world. He is defeated by the loss of home and family, and by fear and desire of our alien environment. "This world is doomed as certainly as Sodom," he tells Nathan Bryce, "and I can do nothing whatever about it."[17] He is an angel who stays in the city, while "brimstone and fire" rain down upon it.[18]

Looking Beneath the Skin

Roeg's film is not really interested in why Newton has come to earth, but it is interested in the earth to which he has come, the advanced capitalist society of North America in which he seeks salvation. It is also interested in the fears and desires that Newton's seeking provokes in others. In the film, Newton has come from a desert planet, dying for lack of water. "Where I come from," Newton tells Bryce, "there's a terrible drought. We saw pictures of your planet on television. In fact our word for your planet means 'planet of water'." The fortune that Newton amasses through the exploitation of his alien technologies is to fund the building of a space ship that will allow him to return home, but in the film it is never explained how this might help his family. Will the ship somehow transport water to his planet,[19] or bring his people back to earth, as explained in the novel?[20] Roeg and his script writer, Paul Mayersberg, are not really interested in the mechanics of the story, but in the alien visitor's experience of our dissociated world, a world that has already become alien to itself.[21]

We see a society in which images proliferate, but none of which pictures the society as it is, except in and through their proliferation. It is a society that looks but does not see. "Television!" Newton exclaims to Bryce. "Strange thing about television is that it doesn't tell you everything. It shows you everything about life on earth, but the true mysteries remain. Perhaps it is in the nature of television. Just waves in space." The same might be said of Roeg's films, which seem to show us more than we need to know about the simple stories they narrate, but at the same time do not tell us enough, since we are never quite sure what we have seen, can never quite determine the lineaments of the story we have watched. For Roeg, simplicity is unobtainable, identity forever uncertain.

> Perhaps it's naiveté on my part, but I don't think a story of any kind can be simple. If you were to ask me to summarize my own life, I'd never be sure if I described it accurately. The past changes all the time for me. Finally, I come to the conclusion of never talking about it. Even if I described it exactly, I'd finally have to say it was not exactly that way.[22]

The irony, of course, is that photography in general, and film in particular, is taken to be a guarantor of identity. As if the photograph, still and moving, were a reproduction rather than a representation of the things and people it images. This is why we have photographs in our passports. When we look like our photographs we can traverse boundaries without loss of identity.

The most prominent of all Newton's products, by which he makes his fortune, is a photographic system, camera and self-developing film, that in Roeg's movie also seems to have the ability of taking pictures from a point of view at some distance from the camera. Newton's invention thus produces a seemingly objective image that is freed from the partial eye of the photographer. Bryce, the scientist who comes to work for Newton and later betrays him, first becomes aware of

Newton's company when he notices one of his cameras, used by the student with whom Bryce is having sex to take pictures of their cavorting in bed. But for Bryce these photographs do not proffer an excitement or truth of the body, but a mystery to be solved.

Prior to his arrival on earth, Newton has learned about our world through the study of television transmissions. He knows us by our own constructed self-images, and when he comes to earth he surrounds himself with television sets, which grow in number as the film proceeds. It is as if these simulations of earthly life are more comforting than the lives of those around him. He also seeks to communicate with his family on Anthea by appearing on television commercials for his products, in the hope that the pictures may reach his wife and children. But even if they reach his family they will communicate only the distance between them, the distance that is opening within Newton himself, as his alien and human identities diverge.

The commercial starts with a recurring Roeg conceit: Newton standing with his back to the camera, unable to see his observer. When he turns around he is holding one of his cameras, that might actually have taken the picture from behind him, creating a loop between camera and image, observer and observed: photographic mediation is lodged within the sight of oneself. The commercial which both shows Newton while refusing his identity (through denying us sight of his face) is watched by Bryce and Newton together. Bryce wants to know Newton's identity, but cannot see it in his face. He has arranged secretly to take an X-ray photograph of Newton that will reveal his alien form. It is only by photography that he can see the alien in the human. But the photograph will constitute only another loop, displaying only another photographic skin, and not what is beneath the skin. By the end of *The Man Who Fell to Earth* the attempt to remove Newton's skin, in order to see the alien beneath, will have been literalized, as surgeons attempt to detach his nipples. But flesh is all they find, for identity is only skin deep.

As already indicated, Newton is a heavenly messenger who succumbs to that which he foretells, the doom of Sodom. Like the angels who come to Lot, he is at first welcomed and entertained by people who are happy to profit from the commercial exploitation of his science. But after he has revealed the reason for his visit, which is in part, or so he says, to save humankind from self-destruction, the "men of the city," the shadowy overseers of American society, seek him out in order to "know" and destroy him.[23] In the novel Newton is arrested by FBI agents for being an "unregistered alien"[24] and interrogated by them and by members of the CIA. In the film their provenance is more vague, an undefined alliance of state and corporate interest. The chief agent is Mr Peters (Bernie Casey), who is reminded by his superior that he is not working for the Mafia, but for people determining the nation's "social ecology." The unprecedented success of Newton's corporation – World Enterprises – is "technologically overstimulating," destabilizing the nation's economy, and Peters must take "flexible," "elastic" measures to put things right. "This is modern America and we're going to keep it that way."

Unlike Lot's visitors, Newton does not escape through smiting his enemies with blindness.[25] Instead, he loses his own sight. Newton is then more like one of the servants sent to the vineyard, who are variously beaten, stoned, and killed by the wicked "husbandmen."[26] Newton's loss of sight is actual in the novel, but metaphorical in the film. In the novel he is blinded when some FBI agents, seemingly ignorant of his alien physiology, insist on taking an X-ray picture of his eyes. "Haven't you been informed about me? Haven't you been told about my eyes? Certainly they know about my eyes. . . . They are sensitive to X-rays."[27] But Newton's alien eyes are unseen behind his contact lenses, and when he offers to remove them he finds that he cannot, and the doctors cannot see them. So, like Alex in Stanley Kubrick's *A Clockwork Orange* (1971), Newton is restrained, his head held in place, and he is made to look into the binocular lenses of the X-ray camera that will permanently change the way he sees the world. As the camera is fired, Newton screams: "Don't you know I'm not human? I'm not a human being! . . . I'm not a human being at all."[28]

In the novel Newton's blinding seems to confirm his claimed identity. In the film, however, the X-ray camera does not blind Newton but fuses the contact lenses onto his eyes, or so he claims, so that he can no longer establish his alien identity, even to himself. Thus neither he, nor any of the other characters in the film, nor we the viewers of his story, can be sure of his identity. Perhaps his recollections of his home world are fantasies, delusions. *The Man Who Fell to Earth* is replete with shots of people looking in mirrors and at reflections, and through windows and lenses, whether worn as eye-glasses or used in laboratories. Sight is always mediated; knowledge always imagined. Everything is as it *appears*.

Indifferent Suffering

Roeg is not only uninterested in the mechanics of his science-fiction story, he also seems less concerned than Tevis with its religious resonance, and more concerned with its sexual aspects. But in fact it is rather that the religious is subsumed in the sexual, as will be discussed below. Furthermore, the film does explicitly, if fleetingly, connect alien visitations with religious concerns. When Newton, alone in the desert with Bryce, admits his alien identity, he also insists that the earth has always been visited. "On my own planet we found evidence of 'visitors'. You must have seen them here. . . . I've seen them. I've seen their footsteps and their places." Bryce denies such knowledge, arguing that the supposed traces of visitors are speculations, not facts, to which Newton gnomically responds: "I know all things begin and end in eternity."

In Tevis's novel Newton is explicitly associated with Christ. In the country home of Newton's lawyer, Oliver Farnsworth, there is a "large painting of a religious figure" whom Newton recognizes as "Jesus, nailed to a wooden cross." He is startled by the face of the crucified man because its "thinness and large piercing eyes" remind him of his own face, "the face of an Anthean."[29] During a drunken conversation between Bryce and Newton, Bryce suggests that the "big war" will begin in five years, and that only Christ's Second Coming might stop humankind from destroying itself. Newton, who needs ten years to complete his space ferry and bring the rest of the Antheans to earth, laughs, "soft and pleasantly."

> "Maybe it will be the Second Coming indeed. Maybe it will be Jesus Christ himself. In ten years."
> "If he comes," Bryce said, "he'd better watch his step."
> "I imagine he'll remember what happened to him the last time," Newton said.[30]

These words stay with Bryce, who increasingly entertains the idea that Newton is an extraterrestrial, possibly a Martian, but a drunken Martian? "But why not a drunken Martian? Christ himself drank wine, and he came down from heaven – a wine-bibber, the Pharisees said. A wine-bibber from outer space."[31]

If the novel's religious references seem lacking in the film, it is only because they are not verbally expressed, and the film visually develops the novel's other figure of alien descent, the fall of Icarus. The first and last of the novel's three unequal parts are respectively entitled "1985: Icarus Descending" and "1990: Icarus Drowning."[32] *The Fall of Icarus*, attributed to Pieter Brueghel (ca. 1525–69),[33] pictures the end of the story of Daedalus and Icarus as told in Ovid's *Metamorphoses*. It shows Icarus in the bottom right-hand corner, having fallen headlong into the sea, his legs thrashing above the waves, while in the foreground a plowman concentrates on cutting his furrow, while in the middle-distance a shepherd rests on his staff, looking up into an empty sky, with his back to the disaster at sea. The painting not only combines in one image the various elements that are set forth sequentially in Ovid's text, but it turns the rural laborers from amazed witnesses of human flight, as they are in Ovid, into indifferent bystanders of the disaster. Ovid's story was newly translated into English by Brueghel's contemporary, Arthur Golding (1536–1606).

> He fastened to his shoulders twaine a paire of uncoth wings.
> And as he was in doing it and warning him of things,
> His aged cheekes were wet, his handes did quake, in fine he gave
> His sonne a kisse the last that he alive should ever have.
> And then he mounting up aloft before him tooke his way
> Right fearfull for his followers sake: as is the Bird the day
> That first she tolleth from her nest among the braunches hie
> Hir tender yong ones in the Aire to teach them for to flie.
> So heartens he his little sonne to follow teaching him
> A hurtfull Art. His owne two wings he waveth verie trim,
> And looketh backward still upon his sonnes. The fishermen
> Then standing angling by the Sea, and shepherdes leaning then
> On sheepehookes, and the Ploughmen on the handles of their Plough,
> Beholding them, amazed were: and thought that they that through
> The Aire could flie were Gods. And now did on their left side stand

> The Iles of *Paros* and of *Dele*, and *Samos*, *Junos* land:
> And on the right, *Lebinthos*, and the faire *Calydna* fraught
> With store of honie: when the Boy a frolicke courage caught
> To flie at randon. Whereupon forsaking quight his guide,
> Of fond desire to flie to Heaven, above his boundes he stide.
> And there the nerenesse of the Sunne which more hote aloft,
> Did make the Wax (with which his wings were glewed) lithe and soft.
> Assoone as that the Wax was molt, his naked armes he shakes,
> And wanting wherewithall to wave, no helpe of Aire he takes.
> But calling on his father loud he drowned on the wave:
> And by this chaunce of his, those Seas his name for ever have.
> His wretched Father (but as then no Father) cride on feare
> O *Icarus* O *Icarus* where art thou? tell me where
> That I may find thee *Icarus*. He saw the feathers swim
> Upon the waves, and curst his Art that so had spighted him.[34]

Brueghel's strange, dream-like vision of Ovid's tale, combining mythic drama with bucolic serenity, is differently rendered in what is arguably the first proper scene of Roeg's film, showing the impact made by Newton's space craft as it crashes into the still waters of a Kentucky/New Mexico lake,[35] sending huge sprays of foamed white water into the air. This shot comes immediately after a sequence constructed from stock footage of rockets and spacecraft, which is perhaps meant to indicate the arrival of Newton's spaceship, or humankind's first steps into space at the same time as a starman steps onto earth. As in the painting, which shows Icarus just after he has entered the water, so the film cuts to the crash of Newton's ship just after it has entered the lake. We see the effect of its arrival but not the arrival itself, a spume of water without apparent cause, seemingly inexplicable, its violence contained by the indifferent silence of the forested hills surrounding the lake.

In the novel a print of Brueghel's painting hangs in Bryce's university office; in the film it appears in a book published by Newton's corporation – *Masterpieces in Paint and Poetry* – that Bryce receives from his daughter. The picture is printed facing the last verse of W. H. Auden's 1938 poem, "Musée des Beaux Arts," on which the camera lingers, for the audience to read, and which Bryce partly quotes in the novel, "in a soft, ritualistic voice, without any particular expression or feeling."

> In Brueghel's *Icarus*, for instance: how everything turns away
> Quite leisurely from the disaster; the ploughman may
> Have heard the splash, the forsaken cry,
> But for him it was not an important failure; the sun shone
> As it had to on the white legs disappearing into the green
> Water; and the expensive delicate ship that must have seen
> Something amazing, a boy falling out of the sky,
> Had somewhere to get to and sailed calmly on.[36]

The painting, which Bryce takes with him when he goes to work for Newton, provides him with a clue to Newton's alien identity, and he reflects that "Icarus had failed, had burned and drowned, while Daedalus, who had not gone so high, had escaped from his lonely island."[37] Later, when Newton proposes to Bryce that they fly to Chicago, Bryce quips, "Like Icarus?" and Newton replies, "More like Daedalus, I hope. I wouldn't relish drowning."[38] Newton sees the picture in Bryce's house and remarks how its landscape, the "mountains, snow, and the water," resembles that of Kentucky.[39] He draws Bryce's attention to the fact that the sun is setting in the picture, but that it was noon when Icarus fell.[40] "He must have fallen a long way. In the picture, the sun was half-way below the horizon, and Icarus, leg and knee flailing above the water – the water in which he was about to drown, unnoticed, for his foolhardiness – was shown at the moment after impact. He must have been falling since noon."[41] Newton has been falling for a long time, and falling fast, and soon he will be drowning. It is during the same conversation in which they discuss the picture that Bryce secretly takes the X-ray photograph of Newton that will confirm his alien identity.

The figure of Icarus, who pervades both book and film, is also a clue to Newton's Christic identity, since the concern of Auden's poem is not so much the "foolhardiness" of Icarus as the indifference of the world to "the disaster," to the miracle and the martyr, to the "important failure"; in short, to human suffering, and in particular the suffering of Christ. We eat while torturers practice their trade.

> About suffering they were never wrong,
> The Old Masters: how well they understood
> Its human position; how it takes place
> While someone else is eating or opening a window or just walking dully along;
> How, when the aged are reverently, passionately waiting
> For the miraculous birth, there always must be
> Children who did not specially want it to happen, skating
> On a pond at the edge of the wood:
> They never forgot
> That even the dreadful martyrdom must run its course
> Anyhow in a corner, some untidy spot
> Where the dogs go on with their doggy life and the torturer's horse
> Scratches its innocent behind on a tree.

Auden's poem may also be read as alluding to Brueghel's *The Census at Bethlehem* (1566) and *The Adoration of the Kings in the Snow* (1567), in both of which their putative subjects – the arrival of Mary and Joseph in Bethlehem and the visitation of the magi – are almost lost amidst the Netherlandish townsfolk, going about their business, unaware of the birth that is imminent in one picture and celebrated in the other. In both, children play upon the ice, though skating on "a pond at the edge of the wood" is more accurate of some of Brueghel's other paintings. The poem also alludes to Brueghel's *The Massacre of the Innocents*

(1566), in which "dogs go on with their doggy life," while soldiers, horsed and on foot, snatch children from their mothers and slay them in the snow, while others look on – though no horse "scratches its innocent behind on a tree." Dogs also pursue their own interests in *The Procession to Calvary* (1564), in which the figure of Christ drags his cross almost unnoted by the crowds of people who are making their way to the site of execution, far distant in the top right-hand corner of the painting. Like the dogs, few of the people are concerned with what is happening to Christ, most attending to their own business, while some are walking out of the picture. Even the figures of John and the three Marys, foregrounded in the bottom right of the painting, have their backs to the scene, consumed by grief.

Brueghel's paintings display a profoundly incarnational theology. His divine subjects are not signaled with golden halos or other penumbra, but are simply men and women amongst other men and women. Only our looking will show a difference. *The Man Who Fell to Earth* displays a similar sense of the extraordinary in the ordinary, of epiphany in the mundane. Taken up with the daily round, most people fail to notice what is passing before their eyes, and those who notice something, think it less trouble to turn and look the other way. Just as the ship sails on, having "somewhere to get to," after seeing "a boy falling out of the sky," so in Roeg's film the powers of this world refuse to be turned from their course by the arrival of an alien being, as once they refused to be stirred by the advent of God's Messiah. The potentially disturbing is ignored or dispatched.

From the first, Newton's arrival has been noted by government agents. In the opening scenes of the film, as Newton makes his way down the stony hillside, the camera zooms out to reveal the figure of a watcher, standing on a higher promontory. He will turn out to be an agent of the state, just as Newton's hired driver and body-guard – named Brinnarde in the book – will prove to be an FBI agent.[42] Newton's arrival has not gone unnoticed, but nor has it astounded. It is merely another fact to be scrutinized, catalogued, and controlled. Newton disturbs not because he is an alien, but because his hugely successful business threatens to destabilize the world market. As with Christ, what matters about Newton is not his offer of a new world order, but his threat to the existing one. Consequently he has to be neutralized.

The latter part of Roeg's film plays out a passion narrative. Newton is the forlorn Messiah, Nathan Bryce and Mary Lou his erstwhile disciples. More than the novel, the film portrays Bryce as Judas. In the novel his betrayal of Newton is inadvertent, taking the X-ray photograph for his own interest, and unwittingly conversing with Newton in rooms that are bugged by the CIA. But in the film Bryce is complicit in Newton's downfall. Newton, having twice before asked for Bryce's trust, declares his own trust in Bryce, having spent the day with him, alone in the desert, explaining who he is and why he has come to earth. Bryce cannot look him in the face, but traces a pattern in the sand with a stick. Later, after Newton's arrest, we see Bryce in Peters's company, reassuring him that he can persuade Newton to see things their way. "I'll talk to him. I know he'll be all right." Bryce becomes a watcher, like the man on the hill at the beginning of the film, the camera pulling back to reveal him in the operating theater, when surgeons unsuccessfully try to remove Newton's skin in order to reveal the alien beneath. As they cut into him, Newton sees Bryce and cries out for help, but Bryce runs away.

The scene in which Bryce dissembles his betrayal to Mary Lou, denying that he has seen Newton, is counterpoised with the confession of another cinematic traitor: Holly Martins (Joseph Cotton) in Carol Reed's *The Third Man* (1949). Martins is himself a kind of alien, an American in postwar Vienna, who betrays his old friend, Harry Lime (Orson Welles). The scene of Bryce and Mary Lou dining in a restaurant is cross-cut with that of Newton in his hotel prison, undergoing a further medical examination while watching Reed's film on a large projected television screen. "Well, they asked me to help take him, and I'm helping," Martins tells Anna Schmidt (Alida Valli), referring to her lover Harry Lime, but through Roeg's cross-cut it is also what Bryce doesn't say to Mary Lou about her lover. The effect is typical of Roeg's metonymic cinema, his cutting between two discrete scenes producing a third, a coagulation in the viewer's imagination as the different scenes from the two films bleed into one another. Like the illusion of cinematic motion itself, produced between the still frames of the film in the mind of the viewer, so Roeg produces significance from the intercut, in the space between scenes. Moreover, Bryce's betrayal of Newton gains its biblical resonance from the intercut of film and scripture. The same is true of Mary Lou, whose name, changed from that of Betty Jo in the novel, suggests her figuration of Mary of Nazareth, Christ's mother, and Mary Magdalene, Christ's disciple and, in some Gnostic stories, Christ's lover.[43]

When Mary Lou first encounters Newton she is working as a chambermaid in the hotel where he is staying. She operates the elevator, but it moves too fast for Newton, who hemorrhages and collapses on the floor. Mary Lou picks him up and, cradling him in her arms, carries him, *pietà*-like, to his room, where she continues to look after him. It is in his vulnerability that Newton is perhaps most Christ-like. Apart from the later scenes where he becomes frustrated with Mary Lou, because frustrated with himself, he is remarkably passive throughout the film. He offers little resistance when he is finally arrested and imprisoned. Like Christ, his actions provoke violence in others, but he does not instigate or return it. Roeg admits to admiring people who are "fragile and receptive."[44]

Queer Bodies

Where Roeg's film most departs from Tevis's book is with regard to Newton's body and its sexuality. Tevis's alien is albino, but Roeg's alien has flame-red hair, revealed near the beginning of the film, when having almost walked into an oncoming car, Newton removes the hood from his head and walks away from the camera. It is the second of three little shocks, the third being a large inflated plastic clown, partly unmoored and buffeted by the wind, seemingly jeering at Newton as he enters Haneyville. The red hair is worn by David Bowie, in whom Roeg had found the perfect actor to play his alien.

David Bowie (b. David Jones 1947) was already a hugely successful pop-star, who had, with other singers like Marc Bolan (T. Rex) and Bryan Ferry (Roxy Music), reinvented British rock'n'roll music at the start of the 1970s, producing a fusion of rock and pop idioms that became known as "glam" or "glitter rock." He did so, moreover, through the creation of his most famous persona, Ziggy Stardust, a parody of pop-star pretensions, in whose habitation Bowie had become an influential and successful performer, twice removed from the originary David Jones. Ziggy and his band – the Spiders – first appeared on stage in January 1972, and on vinyl in the same year, to be followed in 1973 with a third character, Aladdin Sane.[45] "Bowie was attaining rock-mythological status by becoming one huge aggregation of real and imagined personalities. As if releasing an alien virus, Bowie had set in train the *idea* of David Bowie – a one-man collective of media personae – changing form and content rapidly, shedding personalities like unwanted shards of skin and inhabiting different terrains of pop music and culture in the process."[46]

By the time Bowie came to film *The Man Who Fell to Earth* in 1975 he had already left Ziggy and Aladdin behind, metamorphosing into what his biographer, David Buckley, calls the "gouster" – a "streetwise, sharp-talking, coolly dressed all-American dude"[47] – and then into the character of the Thin White Duke, who first appears in Roeg's film. According to Buckley, Newton's sartorial appearance in the film – "crimson and blond centre-parted hair, jacket and fedora" – was devised by Bowie,[48] and Newton's famished, insomnious look was the result of Bowie's "astronomic" consumption of cocaine.[49] All rock stars are supposed to live the emotions they perform, their music a heart-felt expression of their inner state, and so – even for Buckley – Bowie is the alien, having "spent his first forty years on the planet acting like a man from the Andromeda galaxy."[50] Certainly, he had performed the alien from the earliest days of his career, when, against the background of the American moon landing (July 20, 1969) and Stanley Kubrick's *2001: A Space Odyssey* (1968), he released what was to become his first major hit, "Space Oddity" (1969). As Ziggy Stardust, the "space invader" ("Moonage Daydream"), Bowie sang of the "starman waiting in the sky" who would "like to come and meet us" but "thinks he'd blow our minds" ("Starman"); and the reason for that was not his celestial origin or music, but his body; his sexuality and gender.[51]

In January 1970 the British gay magazine *Jeremy* published an interview with David Bowie, and in January 1972 he came out as gay in an interview with Michael Watts for *Melody Maker*.[52] Already in 1971 he had appeared on the cover of his third album, *The Man Who Sold the World*, with long hair and wearing a silk dress and reclining on a *chaise-longue*. As Ziggy Stardust and Aladdin Sane his hair would be cropped but dyed red, and he would wear lipstick and mascara, in a provocative refusal of normative gender behavior for British men. Same-sex relations between men (aged 21 and over) had only become legal in 1967, in the long wake of the Wolfenden Committee on Homosexual Offences and Prostitution.[53] Bowie's "coming out" was commercially risky, but gained attention and proved to be astute publicity.

As a self-declared gay man Bowie nevertheless slept with women. At the time of the interview he was still married to Angie Barnett, whom he had married in 1970, and who had given birth to their son in the following year, and from whom he would not divorce until 1980.[54] Yet even if Bowie was a heterosexual posing as a homosexual,[55] as John Gill insists, the adoption of a queer persona not only enhanced the allure of Bowie's androgyny for would-be rebellious teenagers, but it helped to create a space in popular culture where even heterosexual men could, for a time, be relieved from the burden of normative heterosexuality. In Bowie's performance of himself as alien it became possible to see that what was supposed natural for the body might at the same time be alien to it.

It may have been because Bowie's body was already marked as queer, the site of an ambiguous, ambidextrous sexuality, that Mayersberg and Roeg dropped the suggestions in Tevis's novel of a homosexual sheen to Newton's character. When, in the novel, Newton remains unmoved by Betty Jo's (Mary Lou's) attempt to seduce him, she momentarily wonders if he is "queer" – "anybody who sat around reading all the time and looked like he did" – but then reflects that "he didn't talk like a queer."[56] But then again, and though married, "maybe he was queer – being married didn't prove anything that way."[57] Almost the first thing that Nathan Bryce notices about Newton is the way that he walks.

> He walked slowly, his tall body erect, but with a light gracefulness to the movement. There was an indefinable strangeness about his way of walking, a quality that reminded Bryce of the first homosexual he had ever seen, back when he had been too young to know what a homosexual was. Newton did not walk like that; but then he walked like no one else: light and heavy at the same time.[58]

How do queers walk? Like Ziggy Stardust? Like an alien, unused to earth's gravity? Like an angel, "light and heavy at the same time?" How do they talk? Like Tommy Newton? Like an Englishman in a world of Americans? Not quite, for while there are no homosexual characters in the novel, there are in the film. Mayersberg and Roeg not only make Newton's lawyer, Oliver Farnsworth (Buck Henry), gay, but they provide him with a lover, Trevor (Rick Riccardo).[59] We see Oliver and Trevor eating breakfast together, we see them getting ready for bed, Oliver undoing his bow tie, while Trevor, still in his dinner jacket, is laying out his tarot cards; and, briefly, we see Oliver embracing Trevor. The bedroom scene is ominous, for though Trevor claims to see nothing in the cards, he might have espied that he and Oliver will be the only two characters to die in the film. The short scene of their embrace comes after that of their deaths.[60]

When the "men of the city" decide to rein in Newton's World Enterprises, kidnapping him while he is making his way to his now completed space ship, they also decide to eliminate his lawyer, the man who oversees the running of World

Enterprises. Farnsworth is thrown through the window of his high-rise apartment. The window doesn't break on the first throw. Farnsworth apologizes to his assailants and they tell him not to worry, and with a second swing he smashes through the glass and falls to his death, the camera following his descent, with his breathing and quickened heartbeat amplified on the sound track. He is shortly followed by Trevor, and Trevor by his dumb-bells.

Oliver and Trevor's weights fall in silhouette against a dark blue sky, and are followed almost immediately by another silhouetted figure, falling through the air against the glare of the sun, and which at first we take to be a continuation of the previous scene, which has been briefly interrupted by the short scene of Oliver and Trevor embracing. But in fact the silhouetted figure is the instigator of their murder, Mr Peters, who is not falling but diving into his swimming pool. The camera, in one of the film's most arresting shots, smoothly follows Peters' lithe and naked body as he enters the water, swims beneath its surface to where his wife, also naked, is standing in the water. As the shot continues in slow motion, he lifts her out of the water and places her on the pool side, where he joins her. They embrace, in bright sunlight and with precise focus, as drops of water glisten on their skin, and the diamonds on her rings catch the light. The immediately following scene shows Peters and his wife putting their children to bed, and he muses if they always say and do the right thing. "To the children?" his wife asks. "No, everything," he replies. This entire sequence is open to a number of readings. Is it an affirmation of familial heterosexuality, the city having been cleansed of deviations? Is it but a brief interlude, an aside, showing how white corporate America – symbolized in pool, diamonds, and wife – has come to embrace the once disenfranchised black man? At another level, Peters' dive into the pool and his emergence from it into the arms of his wife is a counterpart to Newton's own fall into the lake at the start of the film, from which he too emerges into the arms of Mary Lou. Perhaps Peters is another Icarus, and his marriage and family another way of drowning.

The scenes of murder and familial domesticity, linked by those of bodies in air and water and sexual embrace, are original to Mayersberg and Roeg, having no basis in Tevis's novel, and would seem gratuitous. But they can be seen as part of the film's complex consideration of alien sex, the intercut of bodies. *The Man Who Fell to Earth* suggests that it is above all in sexual congress, in the relationship that promises loving union, that we are both most alone and at the same time most liable to lose or find our identity. Just as Roeg's scenes bleed into one another, as if they simultaneously occupied the same space, so also the bodies of his characters are seeking but rarely achieving a single occupancy of space, an interpenetration of flesh.

The film presents a series of couplings, all of which are fraught with social anxiety. Professor Bryce has sex with his female students, to whom he stands *in loco parentis*, as each compares her father's penis with his; Farnsworth has sex with another man, and Peters, who arranges Farnsworth's death, is a black man who has sex with his white wife. Finally, Newton, the alien Anthean, has sex with the human, Mary Lou. Each relationship crosses a divide, whether of age, gender, race, or species. Each can be named as a perversion: incest, homosexuality, miscegenation, bestiality. They comprise an almost levitical list of abominations; variations on the theme of crossing the border between the same and the other.

Sleeping with Angels

In Genesis God's sons are lured to earth by the beauty of women; they come to have sex with the daughters of men. (If some were also lured by the beauty of men's sons, we are not told, nor of their attraction for the women they took.) This archaic coupling of divine and human is exemplary of all relationships that seek to cross frontiers, and its results are monstrous, issuing in the Nephilim or giants.[61] Thus St Paul warned the Christian women of Corinth to veil their heads, lest their beauty attract the angels.[62] Mary Lou, who attends church, might have known of this injunction, but if so is unheeding, and wantonly seeks to seduce her angel.[63] In the novel Newton disdains Betty Jo's advances, but in Roeg's film the sexual relationship between alien and earth woman is central.

The first scene of Newton and Mary Lou's sexual intercourse is tender and romantic; a mutual caressing of bodies by candle light. It contrasts with the earlier scenes of Bryce frolicking with his students, shots of him with different girls alternating in quick succession so as to suggest his interest in them as young flesh rather than as individuals. Moreover the first of these scenes is intercut with one of Newton eating in a Japanese restaurant, where a kabuki-style sword-play is being performed.[64] The ritualized thrusts of the sword fighters enact the mounting excitement of Bryce and his partner, whose ecstatic moans are heard but not seen. Disturbed, Newton leaves the restaurant as the off-screen lovers climax. Newton's own lovemaking with Mary Lou has no such violent connotations. They gently explore one another's bodies, each having licensed the other's hands to venture upon a "new found land."[65] The scene is intercut with shots of Mary Lou exploring other new worlds: amoebal life on a microscope slide, and, through a telescope and impossibly, the sun, which in its excitement appears to be giving off coronal spermatozoa.[66] It is almost as if Roeg had replaced scopic metaphors (cosmic and microcosmic) for John Donne's geographic metaphor of America as the body of his mistress; and for Donne, union with his mistress was union with an angel.[67] In the film Newton is the angel and Mary Lou his lover, whose new found land is not America, but England. Yet at the same time she is a bodily synecdoche of his new found land, America.[68] Each is the other's alien, a strange body in which they may either find or lose themselves.

The scene of Newton and Mary Lou's lovemaking ends with them curled in one another's arms, asleep, almost indistinguishable from one another. Moreover, immediately prior to these concluding shots we are shown two iconic portrait images, framed by burn-outs to white. In the first Newton and Mary Lou are in profile, facing one another, their faces filling the cinemascope screen. In the second they are still side by side, but now facing the camera, looking directly at the audience. Both shots are bleached white, so as to flatten the image and enhance the similarity of their faces. The second in particular recalls Ingmar Bergman's *Persona* (1966), and the striking composite image of Liv Ullmann and Bibi Andersson, their faces fused in order to suggest their psychological merger. Roeg's faces do not merge, but they are rendered almost identical: the same face, but different.[69] It is at one and the same time a picture of the proximity and distance between Newton and Mary Lou, and of the distance within themselves. Framed by white light, this double portrait is the still central image of the film, to which the first half moves and from which the second departs. It is the image of a possible union that the film will find to be impossible, a conjunction attempted but failing. And because of the angelic and Christic identity of Newton as alien, this impossible possibility resonates with the attempted union of divine and human that is the possible impossibility ventured in religious, and, more specifically, Christian faith.

The growing distance within Newton leads to a distance growing between himself and Mary Lou, which she doesn't understand and cannot accept. Finally, he attempts to show her how far they are from one another, while at the same time still attempting to traverse the distance between them. After their most acrimonious exchange, when Mary Lou in her desperation has both entreated and jeered at Newton, he locks himself in the bathroom and stands naked in front of two mirrors. The scene is shot from behind, accentuating Newton's vulnerability, and the viewer's sense of watching something private. Moreover, the viewer is now like Newton, unable to see his face, only its reflection in the mirrors, one of which magnifies and distorts. Newton feels his false nipples, and then, just out of shot, below the level of the picture frame, his false penis. In a close-up, but again shot from behind, we see him raise a pair of tweezers to his eyes in order to remove his human contact lenses. He then unlocks the bathroom door, and with staring yellow snake eyes, shows himself to Mary Lou: hairless and without nails, nippleless and unsexed, castrated. Touching her on the neck, he passes by her on his way to the bedroom, and she stands immobile with terror and urinates on the floor.[70] Newton lies on the bed, on his back, his naked body clearly ungenitalled. This contrasts with the earlier scenes in the film, where Nathan Bryce's penis is inspected by the college girls, as he too lies on his back. Mary Lou fights her fear and approaches Newton, and after first removing her pants and skimpy chemise, climbs on to the bed beside him and with a terrified touch begins to caress his now visibly alien flesh.

While Mary Lou can see only Newton's transfigured body, he recollects or phantasizes making love to his wife on Anthea, shots of which are interposed with those of him and Mary Lou. Anthean sex appears to be like an aerial ballet, a gymnastic engagement of almost weightless bodies in midair. More startlingly, both of them are entirely covered in a viscous white liquid, which appears to emanate from their skin, and occasionally splashes across the entire screen: a non-specific all-over ejaculate.[71]

In response to Mary Lou's caresses Newton places a hand on her body, and as he takes it away, leaves behind his bodily secretion. This proves too uncanny for Mary Lou, and with a scream she flees the bedroom. The sequence ends with a shot of her crouched and whimpering in the kitchen, still naked, as if seen through Newton's alien eyes, the image horizontally distorted. Then he is again standing in front of the mirror in the bathroom, one human contact lens already in place, while he inserts the other with a pair of tweezers.[72]

Though Newton returns to his human form, and in the final part of the film briefly resumes his sexual relationship with Mary Lou, they never regain their former intimacy, and eventually they admit that they no longer love one another. Their final sexual encounter is very different from their first, shots from which are intercut with the later scene, as also of alien sex between Newton and his Anthean wife. In their last meeting Newton and Mary Lou are clearly having sex, as opposed to making love. He postures aggressively, threatening her with a gun, which turns out to fire blanks, an obvious symbol of his now all too human impotence. Newton and Mary Lou have become like Bryce and his students, making bodily contact but no emotional connection.

The Man Who Fell to Earth offers two paradigms of sexual union, the one phallic and violent, the other asexual and pacific. The sexual antics of Bryce and his students, and later of Newton and Mary Lou, exemplify the first, encounters that are truly deadly, emotionally and spiritually sterile. The other kind of sexual union is only ever partly realized, and presented as a past or future possibility, as a dream or phantasy. A joyful, tender reciprocation of bodies is presented as alien sex; as something almost beyond corporeal possibility. It is also presented as sex outside the law of the phallus.

In his alien form Newton ceases to be identifiably male. One might read this unmanning of his body as its feminization, revealing the woman beneath the skin, so that his encounter with Mary Lou becomes a scene of lesbian, same-sex intercourse. However, this would be to overdetermine the scene, and would require thinking woman's sex as lack, as the absence of the phallus, as in the traditional Freudian gesture; so that what terrifies Mary Lou about Newton's alien form is seeing in it the truth of her own emasculated body. Instead, however, we can see Newton's alien body as beyond the sexual polarity of male and female, as a third androgynous sex.

Newton's unmanning destabilizes the web of gender relations in which he is placed, most notably with regard to his "wife" on Anthea. For if Newton is not humanly male, the designation of "husband" and "wife" are clearly borrowed terms, translating a relationship we can only imagine. Perhaps he is the "woman" to her "man"; or perhaps, like the Gethenians on the planet Winter, in Ursula Le Guin's novel *The Left Hand of Darkness*, they are asexual except when in a state of "kemmer" or sexual potency, when they develop masculine or feminine features for the period of their kemmering, their particular sexualization being temporary and unknown beforehand.[73] These speculations go beyond anything presented in the film, which merely offers the union of alien and human as an impossible ideal, suggesting, perhaps, that it is the impossible ideal of all human relationships.

I earlier suggested that in Roeg's film the religious is not so much displaced in favor of the sexual, as that the latter subsumes the former. This is most evident in the scene where Mary Lou makes love to Newton as alien, when he has shed his human skin. Their intimacy bespeaks the intimacy of human and divine lovers, the latter folded upon the former. To love God and be loved by God is, on the face of it, the love of aliens; a love that is most to be desired and feared. *The Man Who Fell to Earth* invests the attempted lovemaking of Anthean and human with religious dread and yearning, and, at the same time, nostalgic regret at its failure.

When Mary Lou screams at the sight of Newton in his alien form it is the scream of any terrified girl in countless horror films; the scream of the girl who has desired to see, or to see too much.[74] But it is also the terror of one who has seen the face of God, since no one can see God's face and live. Moses once survived God's presence because God, as he passed by, covered Moses with his hand, so that Moses saw only God's back, not his face.[75] Mary Lou, however, sees the face of her divinity, who is more fully incarnate, figured as a lonely, melancholic Christ. The scene of her terror is also a scene of his desolation, of his loss and yearning. As Newton lies prostrate and naked on the bed, in a room suddenly grown dark, he has become the deposed Christ, lying in the tomb, awaiting his anointing for burial. As Mary Lou climbs on to the bed with him, raising and kissing his hand, we are reminded of Christ cradled in the arms of mourning women, and of Newton, similarly cradled by Mary Lou at the beginning of the film, when she picked him up from the hotel floor and carried him to his room. "I lifted you up once," she reminds him as she kisses him, and he replies: "You must believe Mary Lou."

While Roeg's Christ cannot save, cannot overcome the distance within and between bodies, because already too distant from himself, the Christ of whom the church tells has journeyed to earth in order to traverse the distance, the difference, figured by Roeg's alien. Christ has come so that we might learn to love the alien, within and between ourselves; might learn that the distance we are from ourselves, and between ourselves, is the distance we are from Christ, and that it is only by joining and journeying with Christ that we too can traverse the distance between one another. But for this to be possible we have to recognize the alien in Christ, that there is a difference between ourselves and him that has to be, and can be, traversed. If Christ becomes too familiar we cannot see the distance between ourselves and him; we think the journey already completed. But if Christ is too alien, too strange, we fail to see the point of the journey; we become oblivious of the distance that yet remains. We must meet with Christ when he is both familiar *and* strange, human *and* alien. The place of that meeting is the garden, where nature is both extravagantly itself and yet companionable, wild and tamed. But that must be the subject of another essay.[76]

Notes

1. Genesis 6.2.
2. Genesis 3.8. See also Genesis 7.16, 8.21, and 11.7.
3. Genesis 18.1.
4. Genesis 19.1.
5. Trains recur throughout the film, symbols of promise and possibility. The rusting engine we see at the film's beginning, however, is an ominous sign of how the visitor's journey will end.
6. As Roeg has said, the "film belongs as much to the spectator as the director . . . if not more so." Roeg quoted in Gordon Gow, "Identity: An Interview with Nicolas Roeg," *Film and Filming* (January 1972), pp. 18–25.
7. Roland Barthes, *S/Z*, trans. Richard Miller (London: Jonathan Cape [1970] 1975), p. 5.
8. Ibid, pp. 5–6.
9. Ibid, p. 6.
10. For the nature and importance of the distinction between *narrative* and *story* see Gerard Loughlin, *Telling God's Story: Bible, Church and Narrative Theology* (Cambridge: Cambridge University Press [1996] 1999), pp. 52–63.
11. Genesis 18.1–16.
12. One man in verses 3, 10, 13–15; three men in verses 2, 4, 5, 8, 9, and 16. Like Abraham's visitor(s), Buñuel's stranger (Alain Cuny) in *La Voie Lactée* is both one and three: a magician who, as he walks away from the two pilgrims, is suddenly accompanied by a dwarf who throws a dove over his shoulder, becoming a vaudeville trinity.
13. See Claus Westermann, *Genesis 12–36: A Commentary*, trans. John J. Scullion SJ (Minneapolis, MN: Augsburg Publishing House/London: SPCK [1981] 1985), pp. 272–82. Westermann supposes that Abraham addresses the leader of the three men, but recognizes that this does not explain the textual vacillation between them and the one who speaks and is addressed, which he ascribes to the combination of two variant stories (p. 278).
14. Karl Barth, *Church Dogmatics*, vol. 3, pt 3, trans. G. W. Bromiley and R. J. Ehrlich (Edinburgh: T. & T. Clark, 1960), p. 491.
15. Walter Tevis, *The Man Who Fell to Earth* (London: Bloomsbury [1963] 1999), pp. 6–7. Two other Tevis novels were made into major films: *The Hustler* (filmed by Robert Rossen, 1961) and *The Color of Money* (filmed by Martin Scorsese, 1986), both starring Paul Newman as Fast Eddie Felson.
16. Tevis, *The Man Who Fell to Earth*, pp. 127–8.
17. Ibid, p. 182.
18. Genesis 19.24. Richard Dyer sees a similar affinity between the angel – "an archetypal 'sad young man', beautiful but melancholy" – and the people whose destruction he has come to announce, in the film *Lot in Sodom*, made in 1930 by Melville Webber and James Sibley Watson. See Richard Dyer, *Now You See It: Studies on Lesbian and Gay Film* (London: Routledge, 1990), p. 110.
19. This is supposed in John Izod, *The Films of Nicolas Roeg: Myth and Mind* (London: Macmillan, 1992), p. 88.

20 When the film was released in America audiences were provided with explanatory notes. Neil Sinyard, *The Films of Nicolas Roeg*, Letts Film Makers (London: Charles Letts, 1991), p. 58.
21 For Mayersberg's account of working on the screenplay with Roeg see Paul Mayersberg, "The Story So Far . . . *The Man Who Fell to Earth*," *Sight and Sound* (Autumn 1975), pp. 225–31. The sense of a "dissociated" society is partly the result of Mayersberg and Roeg's attempt to make a film in the form of a "circus." "It has dozens of scenes that go together, not just in terms of plot, but also like circus acts following one another; the funny, the violent, the frightening, the sad, the horrific, the spectacular, the romantic and so on" (p. 231).
22 Roeg quoted in Joseph Lanza, *Fragile Geometry: The Films, Philosophy, and Misadventures of Nicolas Roeg* (New York: PAJ Publications, 1989), p. 16. Lanza's book is by far the best of those on Roeg's cinema, being lively, appreciative, and imaginative.
23 Genesis 19.4–5.
24 Tevis, *The Man Who Fell to Earth*, p. 138.
25 Genesis 19.11.
26 Matthew 21.33–41; Mark 12.1–12; Luke 20.9–19.
27 Tevis, *The Man Who Fell to Earth*, p. 165.
28 Ibid, p. 168.
29 Ibid, p. 15.
30 Ibid, p. 85.
31 Ibid, p. 88.
32 The second part of the novel is entitled "1988: Rumplestiltskin."
33 The attribution of the painting is questioned. See, for example, John White, *Pieter Brueghel and the Fall of the Art Historian*, Charlton Memorial Lecture (Newcastle upon Tyne: University of Newcastle upon Tyne, 1980).
34 Ovid, *Metamorphoses*, trans. Arthur Golding (1567); reprinted as *Shakespeare's Ovid*, ed. W. H. D. Rouse (London: Centaur Press [1904] 1961), bk 8, ll. 282–311 (pp. 165–6). See also Ovid, *Metamorphoses*, trans. Mary M. Innes (Harmondsworth: Penguin Books, 1955), bk 8, ll. 183–235 (pp. 184–5).
35 The film relocates the novel's Kentucky scenes to New Mexico.
36 W. H. Auden, *Collected Poems*, ed. Edward Mendelson (London: Faber and Faber, 1967), pp. 146–7. Only the last three lines are quoted in Tevis's novel (p. 21).
37 Tevis, *The Man Who Fell to Earth*, pp. 87–8.
38 Ibid, p. 111.
39 Ibid, p. 108.
40 This identifies the painting as the one which hangs in the Musées Royaux des Beaux Arts in Brussels. A second version of the painting belongs to the D. M. van Buuren Collection (Brussels). It shows the sun at its proper place in the sky, consistent with its reflection in the sea, and the shepherd looks up at Daedalus, as he successfully flies away from the sun. But the former painting is the more uncanny of the two. "Nothing is real in this reality. All is a dream. There is no straining at the harness for this horse; no jerking at the reins or heaving at a juddering handle for this tiptoeing ploughman as the blunt board of his wooden plough turns easy furrows, neat as ribboned felt. There is no wind to catch the ploughman's coat. There is no whisper in the air to stir a single leaf, and still the ship sweeps on, its great sail billowing, its rigging creaking, in a ghostly, silent gale of its own making." White, *Pieter Brueghel*, p. 27.

41 Tevis, *The Man Who Fell to Earth*, p. 109.
42 While the "watcher" has a function in the plot, he also represents the viewer of the film, seeking to understand the characters and their story. For Roeg, the "watcher" also serves as a reminder that we are always observed by others, including ourselves. "We *are* being watched, if not by other people, then by ourselves, which can be even worse.... No matter what you do, you are always accountable to another person. Someone is formulating your life from an angle you may know little about." Roeg quoted in Lanza, *Fragile Geometry*, p. 113. The "angels" who consort with men's daughters in Genesis (6.4) are also known as "watchers" in later renditions of the story, in the Genesis Apocryphon and the Testament of Reuben (5.4–6).
43 The blurring of boundaries between characters is common to both Roeg's cinema and Christian reading of scripture. For example, St Ephrem (306–73) and other Syrian writers confused or elided Christ's mother with Mary Magdalene in her meeting with the risen Christ in the garden. See Robert Murray, *Symbols of Church and Kingdom: A Study in Early Syriac Tradition* (Cambridge: Cambridge University Press, 1975), pp. 146–8.
44 Lanza, *Fragile Geometry*, p. 23.
45 *The Rise and Fall of Ziggy Stardust and the Spiders from Mars* (RCA 1972); *Aladdin Sane* (RCA 1973).
46 David Buckley, *Strange Fascination: David Bowie: The Definitive Story* (London: Virgin Books, 1999), pp. 143–4.
47 Buckley, *Strange Fascination*, p. 212. Bowie performs as the "gouster" on his tenth album, *Young Americans* (RCA 1975).
48 Ibid, p. 232.
49 Ibid, p. 229.
50 Ibid, p. 14.
51 Another allusion to Bowie's character and song would appear in John Carpenter's 1984 film, *Starman*, in which Jeff Bridges plays an alien, returning the calling card dispatched to the galaxy on Voyager II (1977). The conceit of an alien response to human missives (to the gods) had been used earlier by Robert Wise in *Star Trek: The Motion Picture* (1979).
52 Michael Watts, "Oh You Pretty Thing," *Melody Maker*, January 22, 1971, pp. 19, 42.
53 See Jeffrey Weeks, *Sex, Politics and Society: The Regulation of Sexuality Since 1800*, 2nd. edn. (London: Longman [1981] 1989), pp. 239–44; Richard Davenport-Hines, *Sex, Death and Punishment: Attitudes to Sex and Sexuality in Britain since the Renaissance* (London: Collins, 1990), pp. 314–29.
54 Bowie married Iman Adulmajid in 1992.
55 John Gill, *Queer Noises: Male and Female Homosexuality in Twentieth-Century Music* (London: Cassell, 1995), pp. 106–13.
56 Tevis, *The Man Who Fell to Earth*, p. 57.
57 Ibid, p. 58. The alien visitor in Carpenter's *Starman* (1984) also walks oddly, being unused to the human body he has appropriated. He is also taken for queer, when, ignorant of the etiquette of human urination, he stands smiling at a urinating man in a gas station rest room: "Every God damn place you go."
58 Tevis, *The Man Who Fell to Earth*, p. 79.
59 Scott Salwolke espies a third gay character in Newton's servant–jailer: *Nicolas Roeg Film by Film* (Jefferson, NC: McFarland, 1993), p. 68.

46   GERARD LOUGHLIN

60   Vito Russo identifies *The Man Who Fell to Earth* as one of the few American films to present homosexuality as incidental rather than constitutive of its gay characters: Vito Russo, *The Celluloid Closet: Homosexuality in the Movies* (New York: Harper & Row, 1981), p. 187. Nevertheless, Oliver and Trevor's relationship is not thematically incidental, since, along with all the other relationships in the film, it counts as "alien" (queer) to normative heterosexual (white) marriage.

61   Genesis 6.4; Numbers 13.33. The primeval story of the coupling of angels with humans and their offspring also features in the Book of Enoch (1 Enoch or Ethiopic Enoch) which, written before the third century BC, was influential in the early church, though later rejected and lost. See Margaret Barker, *The Lost Prophet: The Book of Enoch and Its Influence on Christianity* (London: SPCK, 1988). See also the Book of Jubilees (second century BC).

62   "For this reason a woman ought to have [a symbol of] authority [*exousia*] on her head, because of the angels" (1 Corinthians 11.10). In Greco-Roman culture the veil that a woman placed upon her head symbolized her authority to avert a shaming male gaze (human or angelic), and yet also her subordination to the gazer(s) thus denied. Tertullian understood Paul's curious remark about the angels as referring to such as the lustful angels in Genesis 6 ("On the Veiling of Virgins," 1.7), as did other ancient authorities (Clement of Alexandria, Paulinus of Nola), and as also several modern scholars. See, for example, Gail Patterson Corrington, "The 'Headless Woman': Paul and the Language of the Body in 1 Corinthians 11.2–16," *Perspectives in Religious Studies*, 18 (1991), pp. 223–31; Dale B. Martin, *The Corinthian Body* (New Haven, CT: Yale University Press, 1995), pp. 244–7.

63   Mary Lou takes Newton to church, where, in his honor as a visiting Englishman, the congregation sing an old English hymn, William Blake's "Jerusalem" (from the preface to "Milton," 1804–8): "And did those feet in ancient time / Walk upon England's mountains green? And was the holy Lamb of God / On England's pleasant pastures seen?" Candy Clark (Mary Lou) has good reason to grin throughout the scene, for not only do the lines have multiple significance within the film, but it is the only scene in which Bowie sings, or tries to sing.

64   The stylized violence of Japanese theater is associated with Bryce, while the serenity of other aspects of Japanese culture attract Newton, who adorns his house with Japanese artifacts. See Mayersberg quoted in Lanza, *Fragile Geometry*, p. 89.

65   The allusion is of course to John Donne's 19th Elegy, "To his Mistress Going to Bed": "Licence my roving hands, and let them go / Before, behind, between, above, below. / O my America, my new found land" (ll. 25–7).

66   One has to suppose that the telescope is one of Newton's strange inventions.

67   "Now off with those shoes, and then safely tread / In this love's hallowed temple, this soft bed. / In such white robes heaven's angels used to be / Received by men; thou angel bring'st with thee / A heaven like Mahomet's paradise; and though / Ill spirits walk in white, we easily know / By this these angels from an evil sprite, / Those set our hairs, but these our flesh upright" ("To his Mistress Going to Bed," ll. 17–24).

68   In the film David Bowie not only plays an Englishman in America, but is an Englishman surrounded by American actors. *The Man Who Fell to Earth* was heralded as the first entirely British-financed film to be shot in America. It was made by British Lion.

69 Roeg had explored the merging of faces and characters in his first film, made with Donald Cammell, *Performance* (completed 1968; released 1970), in which Chas Devlin (James Fox) fuses with the ex-rock star Turner (Mick Jagger).

70 This shot, along with several others, adding up to some twenty minutes, was cut from the film for its initial release in America. A complete version was eventually released in 1980. See Lanza, *Fragile Geometry*, pp. 53–4.

71 Roeg's visualization of Newton's wet dream clearly proved too much for Neil Feineman, who nevertheless missed the point or was being coy when he described it as "a process that can best be described as the mutual splashing of mud on each other's bodies." See Neil Feineman, *Nicolas Roeg* (Boston: Twayne Publishers, 1978), p. 115. The scene is so rarely remarked in commentary on the film that it would seem to have embarrassed most critics.

72 The framing of the alien sex sequence between shots of Newton in the bathroom, looking at himself in the mirror, allows for the possibility that it has only taken place in his imagination. The dialogue between him and Mary Lou after their aborted encounter could as well refer to what they said before it, as during it.

73 Ursula Le Guin, *The Left Hand of Darkness* (London: Virago [1969] 1997). The Gethenians consider people of a fixed, determinate sex, male or female, as "perverts." I am grateful to Rowan Williams for bringing this novel to my attention.

74 Lanza (*Fragile Geometry*, p. 145) suggests that Mary Lou's "Grade B scream" on seeing "David Bowie's Grade B alien suit" is a tribute to directors like Herschell Gordon Lewis, who was notorious for such gory "meat-movies" as *Blood Feast* (1963) and *Color Me Blood Red* (1964). Roeg, at an earlier stage in his career, had worked with the master of horror B movies, Roger Corman, as lighting cameraman on *The Masque of the Red Death* (1964). Its famous tracking shot of Jane Asher walking through a series of coloured rooms, is reprised in *The Man Who Fell to Earth*, when a waiter pushes a trolley through a series of garishly decorated rooms on his way to the bedroom where Newton is imprisoned.

75 Exodus 33.20–3. Moses, while denied sight of God's face, was also, of course, privileged to see God's face and live. This contradiction in the narratives renders the story indeterminate, so that we can have little idea of what it would be to "see" the "face" of God.

76 See further Gerard Loughlin, *Alien Sex: Desire and the Body in Cinema and Theology* (Oxford: Blackwell Publishers, forthcoming).

CHAPTER 3
Communion and Conversation

Regina M. Schwartz

The work of Regina Schwartz relates to several of the authors in this collection, although with her dual interest in literary theory and the Old Testament she is closest perhaps to Mieke Bal. Along with Stephen Moore, she has served as a general editor for *The Book and the Text: The Bible and Literary Theory*, a series which opened with a collection of essays by that title edited by Schwartz (Oxford, 1990). The books in this series are intended to reread biblical literature through various theoretical frames – philosophical, social, and psychological among others. Schwartz has also been involved in *The Postmodern Bible* project.

All of Schwartz's work focuses upon creation and justice as redemption. To pursue these interests she has developed a highly interdisciplinary reading of literature, philosophy, and theology. Before moving to Northwestern University, she taught at Duke University along with Stanley Fish, Fredric Jameson, and Ken Surin. With Fish she shared a passion for Renaissance literature, and her first book was a scholarly study of Milton's hermeneutic of charity in his Divorce Tracts. *Remembering and Repeating: On Milton's Theology and Poetics* (Cambridge, 1988) took up the problem of distinguishing compulsive repetition from ritual repetition, and it locates the center of Milton's theology of redemption (which is simultaneously a poetics of redemption) in creation. This book won a Milton Society of America Prize for the best book of the year.

Continuing her interest in the field of religion and literature, Regina Schwartz explored the cultural reception of biblical literature in *The Curse of Cain: The Violent Legacy of Monotheism* (Chicago, 1997). Explicitly advocating religious toleration, this book is a critique of embracing religious identity at the expense of religious ethics (very much in the tradition of Jeremiah inveighing against the Temple worshipers, or Erasmus complaining that monks worry more about the color of their habits than about charity). It

> demonstrates the complex ways in which biblical narratives have been used to underwrite religious intolerance when they could instead be read as offering eloquent protests against it. It contrasts a law of scarcity with a vision of plenitude. This vision of plenitude repeats a theme found earlier in her book on Milton: the hermeneutic of charity and a theological interpretation of creation (literary and cosmic). It is as a further development of this theme that, more recently, Schwartz has been examining the ways in which conversation, praise, and lament can offer a way out of the instrumental use of language noted in *The Curse of Cain*, and we can see something of her thinking here in the essay that follows. Schwartz is currently writing a book on communion and conversation, one that takes a long look at the debates about the eucharist in the theology and poetry of the English reformation. During this period concepts of the one and the many, the relation of matter to spirit, linguistic signification, cosmology, authority, community, and ideas of justice were all at stake. The poets of the period experimented with imaginative possibilities unthinkable to those caught up within explicitly theological debates; furthermore, they engaged in a process of expanding the sphere of the sacred from ritual to verse. The essay here is an introduction to this new engagement in what might be termed a theological poetics.

From different angles, both Jacques Derrida and Jean-Luc Marion have critiqued ontotheology: Derrida for its metaphysics of presence, Marion for its metaphysical concept of God as a causal Being. But as Marion notes, Heidegger himself saw the problems of a conception of God as equivalent to *causa sui*, writing: "Man can neither pray nor sacrifice to this God. . . . The god-less thinking which must abandon the God of philosophy, God as *causa sui*, is thus perhaps closer to the divine God."[1] I would add that it may be that the "god-less thinking which must abandon the God of narrative" is perhaps closer to the divine God. Like the God of metaphysics, narrative tries to offer up a God of determinate meaning. And like the God of metaphysics, narrative tries to offer up a God of causes. To ask, as I do, how can the divine God break through narrative is similar to asking how the divine God can survive metaphysics. Both are human stories, preoccupied with Being and beings, cause and effect, motive and meaning. If we were to search for the more divine god, we would need, as Marion puts it, "to think God without pretending to inscribe him or to describe him."[2] We would turn to a different understanding of language, not one that presumes to convey meaning, but one that performs otherwise.

Let us distinguish between two views of language. First, *descriptions* that claim to inscribe, describe, explain, or capture, that purport to answer questions – "who, what, where, when, and why" – leave the reader with either a false sense of epistemological satisfaction or frustration that all his questions have not been answered; here, language functions as a tool to convey meaning. This instrumental, idolatrous use of language differs little, it seems to me, from turning to a golden calf to ensure prosperity. As such an instrument, language is destined to miss its mark, to misfire (the violence of these metaphors, not mine, is apt). As Derrida showed in his persuasive critique of Austin's speech-act theory, whatever the illocutionary intent, the perlocutionary effect is not the same: the conditions of an utterance are inevitably infelicitous for such success.[3] Hence, if I use language as a tool, it is an unruly one, for it does not do what I mean for it to do. Misfires multiply: using language as a tool to convey meaning is one idolatry, but added to the misunderstanding are intentional misuses of language. Using language as a tool can look more like using language as a weapon. Whatever the biblical story of the so-called curse of Ham intended to convey (the narrative describes the curse of Canaan), it certainly misfired. And the bullets have ricocheted throughout history. Genesis 9:25–6 reads: "Accursed be Canaan. The lowest of slaves will he be to his brothers. Blessed be the Lord, the God of Shem. May Canaan be the slave of Shem." Either set of questions – "What meaning is this narrative trying to convey?" "Why is Canaan cursed? What is the explanation?" or with a different ideological lens, "Why should Canaan be victim to this terrible curse?" – presumes that the narrative is a tool conveying a meaning, and that presumption of instrumentality is the condition for its legacy of violent uses. The curse falls where it will, far beyond the ancient Canaanites. The narrative was used as a weapon to justify slavery in the antebellum American South: Josiah Priest was among the ministers who used a version of the story to preach that a whole race of humankind was cursed by Noah to be subjugated to another race and that this was the will of God. "Accursed be Ham [changing the curse to Ham to suggest that the curse of the Hamites was of Africans]. He shall be his brother's meanest slave; blessed be Yhwh God of Shem, let Ham be his slave. May God extend Japheth, may he live in the tents of Shem and may Ham be his slave." This kind of reading has recently been revived by white supremacists. One writes in a manifesto alarmingly titled, "A Scriptural Justification of Racism,"

> The curse was in his descendants in the form of spiritual and moral deformity, and Canaan's descendants were a cursed people [he is presuming Canaan's descendants were African-Americans]. These were the sinful people living in the Promised Land when the Israelites entered it. In Deuteronomy 7, God's people were told to destroy them and not intermarry with them, but Israel disobeyed and consequently these people were always in trouble in the land, acting as pricks and thorns.

The violence of such overt instrumentality is apparent. Elsewhere, I have called it not the curse of Canaan but of Cain, to recall the violence between the first brothers, a violence we are apparently heirs to, for we continue to murder our brothers.

Is there a way to approach language without such instrumentality? Is there a way to overcome the curse of Cain? There *is* a very different way to view language: not as instrumental, purporting to describe, explain, or capture, even a way to understand language concerned explicitly with divinity without attempting to capture it. This language simply praises or laments, rather than describes.

To hear such language we would not attend to referential or predicational functions, but to rhythm, to the alternation of silence and utterance. Rhythm marks not only the performance of poetry, drama, and ritual, but also conversation. Conversation, in turn, unfolds into many nuances: con*verse*, going to and fro, versing to and fro, but also it has suggested dwelling among, living, and then, *converse*, the opposite, the negation of verse, and *conversio*, a transformation, and *conversio realis, the conversio realis*.

What happens when we hear the creation narrative in Genesis 1 as a conversation, or as an expression of gratitude, a hymn of praise, instead of an idolatrous description of divine activity? Is it possible to read an account of the beginning without satisfying (or frustrating) our craving for an explanation of the beginning? Can it perform instead of describe performance – albeit that magnificent first performance of creation? The prose is marked by a strong rhythm – each day is punctuated by the repetitive *Qui tov*, "and it was good," a praise that exceeds the instrumentality of description – and when it turns to the creation of man, it even breaks into verse:

> God created man in the image of himself,
> in the image of God he created him,
> male and female he created them. (Gen. 1.27)

This narrative intones the creation – "God created man . . . God created him . . . he created them" – with no interest in delimiting either the subject or object. Among other reasons, this ritual, liturgical quality has even prompted biblical scholars to call this biblical source the "priestly writer." This example demonstrates that we would be mistaken to ask questions about the performative nature of the *narrative*, when we should be asking about its *reception*. Whether we hear Genesis 1 as an idolatrous narrative of description – telling us what really happened at the creation – or a liturgical poetry of praise are questions of perception; this narrative can have different effects on different hearers at different times in differing contexts. For some readers Genesis 1 will always describe the creation of the world; for others, including those who understand its rehearsal as keeping chaos at bay another year, it creates the world. That means that if one way of apprehending the biblical narratives sees God described and inscribed as a Being who constitutes a people, protects them, secures their borders, guarantees the destruction of their enemies, and authorizes their collective violence, those very stories *can* be experienced differently, as praise and lament, as a poetry that does.

Here, I must confess that I am guilty of idolatry. I have used the narratives of the Bible, but mind you, with the best of intentions: to inspire toleration, even respect, for the Other, to deplore violence against our brothers, especially the perverse notion that God could sanction genocide. And idolator that I am, this intention has often misfired. When I turned my attention to Cain and Abel, pained that we continue to murder our brothers, I wondered if the story offered an explanation for man's inhumanity to man. Looking to be satisfied by some explanation or description, I found, sure enough, explanations and descriptions: the pain of a rejected gift, the humiliation of injured merit, failed efforts to please, competition for favor, sibling rivalry, jealous rage, murderous envy, the pain of punishment, the pain of exile – any or all of these familiar mental landscapes were described in the story that said so little about divinity, but too much about hamanity. And I was preoccupied with a problem: if the narrative wanted to depict human competition and violence that way, fine, but why did it seem to implicate God in that scenario? Why didn't it describe God valuing the sower and the shepherd equally so that then there would be cooperation, rather than violent competition between the first brothers?

> Abel kept flocks and Cain worked the soil. In the course of time Cain brought some of the fruits of the soil as an offering to the Lord. But Abel brought fat portions from some of the firstborn of his flock. The Lord looked with favor upon Abel and his offering, but on Cain and his offering he did not look with favor. So Cain was very angry and his face was downcast. (Gen. 4.2–5)

My suspicion that God is implicitly described as playing favorites was confirmed by later narratives of sibling rivalry, narratives describing one brother prospering at the expense of the other, and that described this condition as the will of God.

In the story of Jacob and Esau, after Jacob steals his elder brother's blessing, the unsuspecting Esau approaches his father to ask for his blessing – only to learn that because his younger brother has already been blessed, there is no blessing left for him.

> When Esau heard his father's words, he burst out with a loud and bitter cry and said to his father, "bless me – me too, my father!" But he said, "Your brother came deceitfully and took your blessing." . . . Haven't you reserved any blessing for me?" Isaac answered Esau, "I have made him lord over you and have made all his relatives his servants and I have sustained him with grain and new wine. So what can I possibly do for you, my son?"

And then Esau asks a profound question, one that reverberates from the ancient Israelites and Edomites through subsequent history of religious strife between peoples: "Have you only one blessing, my father? Bless me – me too, my father." And he weeps: "he burst out with a loud and bitter cry."

These narratives of neglected, rejected, or exiled brothers have been used instrumentally, and the use to which they were most often put involved justifying some hatred or other, hurting, even killing the Other in the name of God. Examples are rife: not only slavery in the US but the expulsion, persecution, and genocide of Jews, of indigenous peoples in the New World, and ethnic cleansing in Bosnia. For me, these stories of scarce blessings and pain were proleptic of historical tragedy. But if I turned to the story of Jacob and Esau, attending not to description but to performance, what would I hear? Not the divine sanctioning of injury and the terrible purposes to which that has been put, but the weeping of Esau. And what would I hear from the story of Cain and Abel? The blood of Abel crying from the ground. Cries from the injured. Cries for justice.

I want now to follow the fate of grain. In this instance, unlike in that of Cain's offering, it is not offered to God, but by God. In the story of manna, God is not described as being short on blessings, but as infinitely charitable, infinitely giving, with blessings for all. This narrative describes a God who rains bread from the heavens, enough for everyone. Greed, the notion that some would take more than they need and hoard it, is addressed in a didactic narrative that schools the Israelites in an equitable distribution of their resource.

> "That," said Moses to them, "is the bread God gives you to eat. This is God's command: Everyone must gather enough of it for his needs." . . . When they measured in an omer of what they had gathered, the man who had gathered more had not too much, the man who had gathered less had not too little. Each found he had gathered what he needed. (Ex. 16.15–18)

But the Israelites fail to accept this divinely ordained distribution of resources – each according to his needs. Moses said to them, "no one must keep any of it for tomorrow." But some would not listen and kept part of it for the following day, and it bred maggots and smelt foul; and Moses was angry with them (Ex. 16.19–20). Used as a tool, what message does this narrative seem to convey? That despite all evidence of dearth, despite their starving in the wilderness, the Israelites are asked to trust in a God who will provide for them and they are asked to base their actions on that belief in divine generosity so that they will not hoard their resources. This "message" of divine bounty recurs in the New Testament where it describes Jesus miraculously multiplying the loaves and fishes so he can feed everyone. Needless to say, the heavens do not rain bread when the needy cry for it. When people are dying of starvation, loaves and fishes do not multiply for them. Children are hungry. Even using such narratives, not descriptively but for ethical norms, to inspire generosity, can collapse under the weight of a different instrumentality: in an op ed in an Italian newspaper about the Albanian refugees fleeing to Italy, a spokesperson for the Right wrote, "We can offer them a plate of pasta but not open the cafeterias. Even Jesus who multiplied bread and fishes did not open trattorias. He transformed water into wine, but, it seems to me, only once, and even then, for a wedding. Albania, like Bosnia, is not our problem, but the problem of Europe." A story that I thought describes miraculous generosity is used to justify just the opposite. But because the manna and the loaves and fishes miracles fail on the level of verisimilitude, does that mean that they succeed in other terms? Has something of divinity shone through? An endless divine giving? The glory of the Lord? From an apophatic perspective, neither a realistic nor utopian (nor perverse) *description* can capture divinity, because no descriptions, not even beautiful ones, capture the divine. The hazards of narrative idolatry seem to outweigh the benefits.

There is another way to understand grain: not describing the curse of Cain or the blessing of manna. Not descriptions of withholding deities or bountiful ones, not descriptions at all; but effects, transformations. The cries of Abel, the tears of Esau, and curse of Canaan can do. Indeed, these narratives are performed and transformed every time there is a mass; the murder of our brother, the breaking of his body, is performed, transformed as a sacrifice. "Then he took some bread, and when he had given thanks, broke it and gave it to them, saying, 'This is my body which is given for you; do this in remembrance of me.'" The violence of that sacrifice does not destroy another; it is transformed into a gift by that other. Abel's blood crying from the ground of an unjust murder has been transformed from robbing to giving life. "He did the same with the cup after supper, and said, 'This cup is the new covenant in my blood which is poured out for you.'" The bread rained from heaven in the wilderness no longer describes a superabundant generosity that feeds the starving; it is transformed into a bread that nourishes beyond material feeding: take, eat, this is my body which is broken for you. But is this cheating, for I have invoked the performance of a religious ritual, rather than a way of reading a story? I will make the case that language does not only act in religious ritual, but in all its forms: in verse, in meter, rhythm, the spaces in between words, the spaces that make poetry, and that make conversation.

Communion

Given the rhythm of verse, the deliberateness of its stops, it is no accident that Pseudo-Dionysius's *Mystical Theology* begins with a poem. That poem depicts an alternative revelation to the one at Sinai – not thunder and lightning, but silence and darkness; not words graven on stone tablets soon dashed to pieces, but a mystic scripture whose words need not be cut or broken, for they "lie simple" in the brilliant darkness of a hidden silence. To approach them we, too, must be silent and blind; the revelation only occurs when our senses and our understanding are left behind, so that our sightless minds can be filled with treasures beyond – beyond being, goodness, and all beauty.

> Trinity!! Higher than any being, any divinity, any goodness!
> Guide of Christians in the wisdom of heaven!
> Lead us up beyond unknowing and light,
>   up to the farthest, highest peak of mystic scripture
> where the mysteries of God's Word
>   lie simple, absolute and unchangeable
>   in the brilliant darkness of a hidden silence.
> Amid the deepest shadow
>   they pour overwhelming light
>   on what is most manifest.
> Amid the wholly unsensed and unseen
>   they completely fill our sightless minds
>   with treasures beyond all beauty.

Everything in the poem points beyond itself: from the invocation of the first line, "Higher than any being," to the revelation conferred in the last of "treasures beyond all beauty." In no case does the verse try to describe or contain what it points to. Instead, the eloquence of this silence "beyond" challenges us to think silence without a determinate meaning. And this silence betrays neither a discernible origin – which is the first silence? – nor a seamless continuity, for it disrupts, erupts into speech. This pointing beyond, this grasping and yearning and desiring more, more than the language can say, more than the hymn can express, characterizes not only sacramental poetry, but arguably, all poetry. Among other changes wrought by the Reformation, its insistence on a symbolic commemoration rather than a ritual reenactment of Christ's sacrifice in the mass ushered in an overtly sacramental poetry. If the bread was not transformed into the body of Christ through the priest's words of institution, it was still transformed in that most democratic of forms, as Derrida once called it, literature.[4] The work of the seventeenth-century Anglican pastor, George Herbert, illustrates this movement from liturgy to poetry, in effect broadening the liturgical functions to poetry. His compendium of lyrics, *The Temple*, was then and is now widely regarded as the greatest compendium of religious lyrics written in the seventeenth century, England's great age of religious poetry, but the lyrics were also perceived as not only a source of religious inspiration but a model for practical devotion. In *The Poetry of Meditation* Louis Martz says of *The Temple* that it is "hardly too much" to call it "a book of seventeenth-century psalmody."[5] In his lyric "Providence" Herbert eloquently expresses the apophatic "Unnameable of all Names," the yearning for more than finite words can say:

>Each thing that is, although in use and name
>It go for one, hath many wayes in store
>To honour thee; and so each hymne thy fame
>Extolleth many ways, yet this one more.

A sign cannot point to only one thing, but to more, and that excess is impelled by desire. For Herbert, that desire erupts into praise; and all things are impelled to praise. The ancient Israelites understood death as the state when we can no longer praise: "for Sheol does not sing thy praise, Death does not celebrate thee" (Isaiah 38). "The dead, they do not praise Yahweh, nor any who sink to the silent land. But we, we will bless Yahweh from this time forth and for evermore" (Psalm 115.17). To live *is* to praise; this is the very purpose of life. Mystical theology asks us to think of praise as a gift that has been made to us, as an offering we return, and as such, a ceaseless activity. Within the language of praise, God is always praised "*as* . . ." and the *as* constitutes an "index of inadequation" for Marion. So praise does not designate a subject or predicate; it does not claim to describe, to inscribe; rather, it admits with its every utterance that "what" we praise is not a "what"; indeterminate and inaccessible, it is the pure expression of desire.[6]

"Higher than any being, any divinity, any goodness! Lead us up!" says the prayer/poem, simultaneously praising and desiring. But how can gratitude be expressed when the request is not yet granted? Lead us up, says Pseudo-Dionysius, amidst his praise, but we are not yet led up, so why be grateful? Grateful for what? For desire, for what is given *is* this desire: hence, to feel desire is to be grateful, and when we express gratitude we also express desire: this is the heart of the paradox that governs liturgical language. "God is not governed by our desire," writes Henri de Lubac, the relation is precisely the other way around – it is the giver who awakens desire. "It remains true that once such a desire exists in the creature it becomes the sign, not merely of a possible gift from God, but of a certain gift. It is the evidence of a promise, inscribed and recognized in the being's very self." This is precisely the logic of Herbert's "The Altar," where each part of the poet's heart, cut by God, desires only to praise, and so the poem is visibly shaped, not only like an altar, but to form the shape of the pronoun I – the speaker is the offering made at the altar. De Lubac writes that the desire we have for God, the longing for the beyond that informs mystical theology, is no accident; rather, it belongs to the humanity that is called, it is our response to the call.

Praise also encompasses, in a seeming paradox, lament, for in the very act of lamenting we are already celebrating what we have: a listener, someone to hear us; in complaint, something beyond us gives us the sense that something is lacking, and to even know that is a gift. Long before a request is heard or honored, there is a prior response to it: the presupposition of responsiveness. The biblical psalms are the classic expression of this dynamic. Even as the speaker laments he demonstrates his confidence that God will not fail him. Conversely, in the very act of celebrating God the speaker expresses his longing for him. While the scholar whose exhaustive study of the psalms, Sigmund Mowinckel, has separated psalms of lamentation from psalms of praise as heuristic structures, he acknowledges that, liturgically, the distinction does not hold. Mowinckel discerns that the vow in the psalms of lamentation indicates that they were offered in a cultic setting when some distress had been overcome, as a song of thanksgiving. The *todha*, or thanksgiving psalm, had two functions: to offer testimony to the saving work of God, and to thank God for that salvation. Such psalms begin with praise: "I will extol thee, Yahweh, for thou hast lifted me up" (Psalm 30) and proceed to an account of affliction, and then to an account of salvation. "On the very day I cried unto thee Thou answeredst me at once" (Psalm 138). The verb *hvdh*, generally translated as "to praise," properly means "to confess" or "to accept," so that praising includes a confession of unworthiness and acceptance of the judgment for that unworthiness. Gerhard von Rad points to the "avowal" component of praise: "in accepting a justly imposed judgment, the man confesses his transgression, and he clothes what he says in the mantle of an avowal, giving God the glory." This is praise from the depths, the praise of Jonah from the belly of the whale, the praise of the afflicted Job. "God gives these songs in the night" (Job 35.10).

Herbert's brief lyric, "Bitter-sweet," compresses both understandings of praise so resonant in the psalms: lament and gratitude, lack and fullness, desire and love. That compression begins with the hyphenated title, one word that combines the bitterness of affliction with the sweetness of praise:

Bitter-sweet

Ah my deare angrie Lord
Since thou dost love, yet strike:
Cast down, yet help afford;
Sure I will do the like.

I will complain, yet praise;
I will bewail, approve;
And all my sour-sweet days
I will lament, and love.

They that sow in tears shall reap in joy (Psalm 126.6). Here again, praise and lament are not "subjects" of discourse: they are modes of speaking or of silence, and they are part of a conversation.

Herbert writes in his lyric "Deniall" that if we are unable to be heard, then we are unable to speak. There is no cry when there is no anticipation of a response.

When my devotions could not pierce
Thy silent ears;
Then was my heart broken, as was my verse:
My breast was full of fears
And disorder: (ll. 1–5)

But if we are heard, we can speak: we can verse – we can *only* verse – when we converse.

O cheer and tune my heartless breast,
Defer no time;
That so thy favours granting my request,
They and my mind may chime,
And mend my rime. (ll. 26–30)

In "A True Hymn" Herbert approaches the problem of verse and converse again:

the fineness which a hymn or psalm affords
Is, when the soul unto the lines accords.

What is this congruence between the soul and a line of poetry? Elaborating, Herbert points out that a poet who wants to offer everything in his poem – all mind, soul, strength, and time – has every right to be disappointed if instead he only produces rhyme. To make the point, he offers just such an impoverished stanza.

He who craves all the minde,
And all the soul, and strength, and time,

> If the words only ryme,
> Justly complains, that somewhat is behinde
> To make his verse, or write a hymne in kinde.

While Deuteronomy says, "Thou shalt love the Lord thy God, with all thy heart, with all thy soul and with all thy might" (6.5), Luke changes it to "all thy heart, soul, strength, and mind" (10.27). Neither speak of time. But Herbert's poem speaks of mind, soul, strength, and time – and in the process he substitutes time, poetic meter, for heart. But if the heart is missing in that stanza, it appears twice in the final one.

> Whereas if th' heart be moved,
> Although the verse be somewhat scant,
> God doth supply the want.
> As when th' heart says (sighing to be approved)
> *O, could I love!* And stops: God writeth *Loved.*

Here, the poet fears he offers a verse too short, but God supplies the rest of the line. The heart sighs, lamenting, and then stops. The heart stops, the verse stops, time stops, life stops, but this is not an end, only a pause. For then God writes more. The poet speaks; God responds. The obvious answer to the cry, "O could I Love" would be "You *can* love," but the response that is offered is different: "Loved." This is God's word, from scripture: "We love him because he first loved us" (1 John 4.19). The true hymn, then, is a yearning heart that is answered, a sigh and response. No description of God is offered, no predication, no denomination, just *loved*.

Pseudo-Dionysius writes of the Unnameable with all Names, "they especially call it *loving* toward humanity, because in one of its persons it accepted a true share of what it is we are, and thereby issued a call to man's lowly state to rise up to it."[7] The Incarnation itself is described as part of a dialogue, a call to man which is framed so that man can respond. But even as he speaks of the Incarnation he sounds like he is speaking of language, of poetry:

> Since the unknowing of what is beyond being is something above and beyond speech, mind, or being itself, one should ascribe to it an understanding beyond being . . . in our reverent awe, let us be drawn together toward the divine splendor. For . . . the things of God are revealed to each mind in proportion to its capacities; and the divine goodness is such that, out of concern for our salvation, it deals out the immeasurable and infinite in limited measures.[8]

These limited measures can be understood as the measures of poetry, that is, the immeasurable is made proportionate to man not only in the Incarnation, but also in poetry, another kind of incarnation, the Word made words. Hence, what follows in *Mystical Theology* could be an apt description of the metaphors in Herbert's poetry: "the Transcendent [comes to us] clothed in the terms of being, with shape and form on things which have neither, and numerous symbols are employed to convey the varied attributes of what is an imageless and supranatural simplicity." "We now grasp these things in the best way we can, and as they come to us, wrapped in the sacred veils of that love toward humanity with which scripture and traditions cover the truths of the mind with things derived from the realm of the senses. But if God offers a revelation proportionate to man's capacities, how could man respond? What could be our answer? The eucharist, thanksgiving, the hymn of praise awakened by the desire that invites us beyond ourselves. This is a conversation, not a thunderous clap from the beyond that flattens the listener into shock; a conversation – not a devastation. Not the kind of overwhelming ravishing that crushes, like Donne depicts in "Batter-my-Heart," where the speaker says to God, "nor ever chaste unless you ravish me." A conversation, not a human call that echoes in a cavern, a lonely call that is unanswered, only deferred endlessly until it fades away. The mystery of this conversation "according to our proportion" is the mystery of the eucharist. And this mystery is called Love by both Pseudo-Dionysius and George Herbert. Pseudo-Dionysius: "The sacred writers lift up a hymn of praise to this Good. They call it beautiful, beauty, love, and beloved. They give it the names which would convey that it is the source of loveliness and the flowering of grace." It is called beauty, he goes on to say, not because it possesses beauty, but because it bestows it, confers love . . . And there it is ahead of us as Goal, as the Beloved."[9]

"Love (III)," Herbert's final poem in *The Temple*, a collection that begins with "The Altar" written by his heart, an altar that he asks to be sanctified so that he may receive the sacrifice that he subsequently offers, concludes by understanding that sacrifice as conversation. To be more precise, it is a conversation that is framed as an invitation to dinner, and the guest feels unworthy of the host. In the course of the conversation the host lifts the guest up to her level, qualifying the guest to dine.

>Love (III)
>Love bade me welcome: Yet my soul drew back,
>   Guilty of dust and sin.
>But quick-eyed Love, observing me grow slack
>   From my first entrance in,
>Drew nearer to me, sweetly questioning,
>   If I lack'd any thing.
>
>A guest, I answer'd, worthy to be here:
>   Love said, You shall be he.
>I the unkinde, ungratefull? Ah my deare,
>   I cannot look on thee.
>Love took my hand, and smiling did reply,
>   Who made the eyes but I?
>
>Truth Lord, but I have marr'd them: let my shame
>   go where it doth deserve.

> And know you not, sayes Love, who bore the blame?
> My deare, then I will serve.
> You must sit down, sayes Love, and taste my meat:
> So I did sit and eat.

Like all of Herbert's poetry, "Love (III)" is dense with biblical allusion, here, to the passages describing God inviting man to a feast: Song of Songs 2.4, "he brought me to the banquetting house, and his banner over me was love"; psalm 23, where God is a gracious Host; Matthew 26.29, "I tell you I shall not drink again of this fruit of the vine until that day when I drink it new with you in my Father's kingdom": Luke 12.37, where the master comes and serves his servants; Rev. 3.20 – the promised messianic banquet: "Behold I stand at the door and knock; if any one hears my voice and opens the door, I will come in to him and eat with him, and he with me"; Matt. 22.1–10, Luke 14.7–24, the parables of the great supper – Luke 14.7 is especially apt:

> Now he told a parable to those who were invited, when he marked how they chose the places of honor, saying to them, "When you are invited by any one to a marriage feast, do not sit down in a place of honor, lest a more eminent man than you be invited by him; and he who invited you both will come and say to you, "Give place to this man" and then you will begin with shame to take the lowest place."

And the drama of the poem follows:

> But when you are invited, go and sit in the lowest place, so that when your host comes, he may say to you, "Friend, go up higher" then you will be honored in the presence of all who sit at table with you. For every one who exalts himself will be humbled and he who humbles himself will be exalted.

A guest worthy to be here. "Worthy" is the term used in Matthew's version of the parable, "the king said to his servants, The wedding is ready, but those invited were not worthy" (Matt. 22.8) But Herbert's use is different. Luke's version says:

> A man once gave a great banquet, and invited many; and at the time for the banquet he sent his servant to say to those who had been invited, "Come; for all is now ready." But they all alike began to make excuses. The first said to him, "I have bought a field, and I must go out and see it; I pray you, have me excused." And another said, "I have bought five yoke of oxen, and I go to examine them; I pray you, have me excused." And another said, "I have married a wife, and therefore I cannot come." So the servant came and reported this to his master. Then the householder in anger said to his servant, "Go out quickly to the streets and lanes of the city, and bring in the poor and maimed and blind and lame." And the servant said, "Sir, what you commanded has been done, and still there is room." And the master said to the servant, "Go out to the highways and hedges, and compel people to come in, that my house may be filled. For I tell you, none of those men who were invited shall taste of my banquet." (Luke 14.16–24)

Herbert changes the plot. In his version Love does not simply invite a guest who says I am not coming and then is pronounced unworthy and someone else is invited; nor are they claiming to be unworthy and so the host gives up on them. Love does not give up with the invitation. Love will not be refused. She invites him, not only to her meal, but into a conversation, sweetly questioning if he lacks anything. In the course of this conversation the guest not only disclaims that he is not a worthy guest and is told that another has borne the blame and so has imputed worthiness to him, this is not only a discussion about worthiness; rather, in the course of the conversation, the guest becomes worthy – first by acknowledging his lack of worth, then by listening when he is told that his unworthiness has been acknowledged and accounted for, then because he then understands he is a servant and wants to serve, and all of these change him, qualify him, for the communion. We cannot ask who is speaking and who is spoken to as though they are prior to the conversation, because being addressed and responding constitute the addresser and addressee, as such.[10] Subjectivity is not constituted apart from the conversation; rather, it is forged actively, in the course of the conversation, in dialogue. Who issues this invitation? A subject? Beyond the subject? God? Love, but what is love? Love is welcoming, observing, questioning, offering, explaining, and inviting.

In "Love (III)" the feast of love to which God has invited man is both the earthy communion (with the implied pun on host) and the heavenly marriage banquet it anticipates.[11] "Behold I stand at the door and knock; if any one hears my voice and opens the door, I will come in to him and eat with him, and he with me" (Rev. 3.20). The Book of Common Prayer makes that very association, invoking the parables of the marriage feast and the wedding garment in the communion service. The Prayer Book exhorts those who are "negligent to come to the holy Communion," using the parable of the great supper as Herbert does:

> Yea know how grievous and unkind a thing it is, when a man that prepared a rich feast, decked his table with all kind of provision, so that there lacketh nothing but the guests to sit downe, and yet they which be called (without any cause) most unthankfully refuse to come . . . If any man say, I am a grievous sinner, and therefore am afraide to come: wherefore then doe you not repent and amend? When God invite you, be you not ashamed to say yee will not come?[12]

In the parable the guests are condemned, but in the Song of Songs love is not angered by her rejection: "I opened to my beloved, but my beloved had withdrawn himself, and was gone." There, love is not angered, but determined to win him back.

The mystery of language, then, is the way that praise and lamentation can be joined, as silence is to speech, as God is joined to man; the mystery of a cry and a response, of conversation. The English Reformed poets inaugurated modernity, not by turning away from this mystery, but by making sure that poetry was its chief vehicle with their sacramental signification. In this understanding of language what we say is immaterial, and its relation to reality, let alone its ability to confer that reality to another, is inconsequential. For in such a conversation some *thing* is not passed from one to another; rather, it is circulation itself. Love is understood as an invitation that is accepted, and the drama of the poem focuses with exquisite intensity on the invitation and the question of its acceptance. An invitation accepted, a call answered, a prayer heard – none of these suggest the content of the conversation. Herbert shows no interest in the content of the gift, in the meal served (although the status of the wafer and wine, as symbolic or transubstantiated into the body and blood of Christ, was the heated controversy of his time), only in the invitation and acceptance, the calling and answering. Over and over, the scripture avoids interest in the content of the conversation to focus instead on the call and answer: "Abraham," "My Lord," "Moses, Moses," "My Lord," "Jeremiah," the call that Jonah tries so desperately to evade, the one that Isaiah is made qualified to hear, the death of Christ understood as an invitation accepted, a call heard, a prayer offered in praise and in pain. This then is the mystery: that an utterance could be heard, that a call could be answered, that someone – unnameable, unknowable, incomprehensible, is at the receiving end of language. If the performative seems to lurk around this discourse it is because it permeates it: my emphasis is on speaking, hearing, listening, and answering as performed, as liturgy is performed, rather than on ontic categories.

Silence

To speak, to cry, to write, is not only a performance, but an act of faith: to believe someone will understand, someone will answer. I cried out to the Lord, says the psalmist, and he answered me. Our first breath is a cry that signals our entry into conversation, into response and responsibility. The rhythm of conversation is marked by silence. It is in this silence – unspoken and unwritten – that response is located. This silence is waiting, an anticipatory, full of expectation of an answer. It is also the silence of attention, of hearing, that precedes and occasions a response. Sometimes it can be the briefest of silences, barely noticeable for the overlapping of voices; sometimes an agonizingly long, even interminable silence. But sometimes the expectation of an answer becomes exhausted, waiting gives up, and belief gives way to hopelessness. Silence signals that there is no reason to cry, for there will be no response. There is, then, another, less sanguine kind of silence – neither of expectation nor of hearing, but of indifference and exhaustion. That silence is not a mystical achievement, a caesura in a verse, or a pause in the conversation, but the stunning silence that signals no answer. Where is the answer to the cry during earthquakes, massacres, death-camps? And that question leads inexorably to another: how can we know when the conversation is still going on, when there is still hope for a response, and when it is over?

It is possible to read biblical narratives as obsessed with this question, offering, as they do, so many eloquent versions of the human cry. One of its answers is the complete satisfaction of justice: God hears the cry, responds to the pain, delivers from distress: "And now the cry of the sons of Israel has come to me, and I have witnessed the way in which the Egyptians oppress them, so come, I send you to Pharaoh to bring the sons of Israel, my people, out of Egypt" (Ex. 3.9–10).

Another answer, Christ's last words from the cross, seems to lament the failure to be heard: "My God my God, why have you forsaken me?" But Jesus is quoting psalm 22, a psalm that begins with the poignant cry that God does not hear, that the speaker's appeals are fruitless, only to, indeed, be heard:

> Why art thou so far from helping me,
> from the words of my groaning?
> my God, I cry by day, but thou dost not answer;
> and by night, but find no rest.

The speaker recalls that cries were once answered. That is his very genealogy: the one whose father's cries were heard.

> Yet thou art holy,
> enthroned on the praises of Israel.
> In thee our fathers trusted;
> they trusted, and thou didst
> deliver them.
> To thee they cried, and were saved;
> in thee they trusted, and were not disappointed.

And then, toward its close, the psalm bursts into praise, expressing complete confidence that the cries of the afflicted are heard:

> I will tell of thy name to my brethren; in the midst of the congregation I will praise thee: You who fear the Lord, praise him! . . . For he has not despised or abhorred the affliction of the afflicted; and he has not hid his face from him, but has heard, when he cried to him.

In conversation, the very dynamic of cry and answer, speech and silence, holds forth the promise of justice itself. It can be no accident that one of the earliest allusions to justice in the Bible occurs, then, in the midst of a heated conversation. Abraham is bartering with God, trying to drive down the price of sin. This speaker at the beginning of the psalm is not the same as the speaker at the end. One of the earliest allusions in the Bible to divine justice takes place in the midst of a heated conversation. Just such conversation holds forth the promise of justice: Abraham is bartering, driving down the price of sin.

> Abraham remained standing before Yahweh. Approaching him he said, "Are you really going to destroy the just man with the sinner? Perhaps there are fifty just men in the town. Will you really overwhelm them, will you not spare the place for

the fifty just men in it? Do not think of doing such a thing: To kill the just man with the sinner, treating just and sinner alike! Do not think of it! Will the judge of the whole earth not administer justice?" Yahweh replied, "If at Sodom I find fifty just men in the town, I will spare the whole place because of them." Abraham replied, "I am bold indeed to speak like this to my Lord, I who am dust and ashes. But perhaps the fifty just men lack five: will you destroy the whole city for five?" "No," he replied. "I will not destroy it if I find forty-five just men there . . ." (Gen. 18.22–9)

Abraham suggests that God's terms, fifty just men, are too high, that justice requires lowering the number: ten should be enough to stave off destruction. As Abraham questions the divine dispensation of justice, he sets new stipulations, testing and subverting the old ones with each of his challenges. And with each new divine promise new laws are forged. Justice is redefined in the course of their conversation. Justice is depicted, extraordinarily enough (given how frequently God is depicted as absolute, whose will is law), as a negotiation. Fifty righteous men would have been necessary to save Sodom; now it will be saved if there are only ten. But that fails: "Rising early in the morning Abraham went to the place where he had stood before Yahweh . . . he saw smoke rising from the land, like smoke from a furnace" (Gen. 19.27–8).

Silence, then, runs the spectrum from complete communication – nothing need be said, so complete is understanding – through a pause in a conversation when one is listening and endeavoring to understand and respond, to indifference: no response, no hearing. While the first sense, the silence of complete communication, has been the purview of mysticism, constituting the achievement of mystical experience, the last, the refusal to respond, has been the purview of legal and political discourses of injustice, attaining its ultimate expression in the criminal silencing of murder and the political crime of genocide. While mystical silence ultimately abandons the will, leaving its conscious efforts behind, on the political side of the spectrum it is difficult to think of silence without the context of the will. Indeed, the verb forms reflect this attachment to agency: "to silence" is to will that someone be silent. "To be silenced" is to have one's will to speak out be denied by another's will, to be oppressed. "To fall silent" is to will retreat from the context of speaking. Only the willed nature of silence and silencing makes sense of the Vatican's apology for its silence during the Nazi genocide. Not simply an omission, a failure of the will, the implication is that this silence was willed, and as such, must be atoned for.

Historians tell us that the Vatican's response to Galileo concentrated on silence: his punishment for the Copernican hypothesis was not only house arrest, but the final provision was that "he was never to speak on these matters again." That sentence of 1633 responded to the provision of 1617 that he would neither "hold, teach, or defend" the Copernican hypothesis. The copy of that provision in the papal archives, however, differed significantly from Galileo's own: it reads that Galileo must not "hold, teach, defend, or discuss" the hypothesis. The omission of "discuss" has led historians to believe that he felt free to discuss his theory so long as he did not advocate it. They conclude that he was framed: he was now explicitly silenced for the unspecified crime of not being silent. The fate of the papal records of the trial of Galileo embroils them still deeper in the issue of silence. When the troops of Napoleon invaded Italy in 1797 and sacked Rome, they seized the papal archive, hauled it to Paris, and in their anti-papal propaganda they published the part of the trial of Galileo that seemed most damaging. After the fall of Napoleon the archive was returned to Rome, but the Galileo case was missing. Galileo was silenced again. When the case resurfaced (in the 1840s) the Vatican published the official documents of Galileo's trial, but a historian, Pietro Redondi, accidentally discovered a letter recently that was in no published record. Written close to the time of the 1617 agreement the letter indicates that Galileo will be prosecuted for heliocentrism while his real threat is another; his atomism threatened the doctrine of the eucharist. From the beginning, according to Redondi, the trial that silenced Galileo was intended to completely silence the real danger he posed, not even deliberating over the real force of his critique and contribution. Is this the silencing of oppression or indifference? Which does Job suffer? Can we tell the difference?

Recent discussions of sacrifice have returned to the question of the gift: we are told that the gift must be given with no expectation of return for it to be a gift, that it must not be reciprocal, for to give with an expectation of return is not to give a gift, but to enter into a kind of contract, or economic exchange. I would like to leave this framing by economy to frame the question in a different context, not economic, but linguistic; specifically, the context of conversation. For if we shift the trope from gift to language, to conversation, something else happens: not an exchange of goods, but a response that evokes a further response.

When Derrida sought to change the paradigm for how we think about signification, with his essay "Différance" suggesting that what the sign points to is not here and not now, that what is signified is both different and differed, he opened a way to understand his project as not simply in the Heideggerean tradition, but also the heir of mystical theology with its explicit abandonment of the project of naming, signifying. When invited to put his work in that context of mystical theology – an invitation first made by Kevin Hart and later provoked into dialogue by Jean-Luc Marion – his response was to clarify (to the extent that he clarifies) that no, Derridian difference is not de-negation, for the mystical way names even as it refuses to name, holds forth a hyper-essentiality, a Being beyond beings, so that in the end he indicts the mystical tradition for being guilty of the dreaded "presence" – however indirect its approach. I am not going to argue (as some have) that his own *différance*, with the sign's deferral and difference from the referent, places him in a mystical tradition that he disavows. Rather, I want to suggest that mystical theology can offer us a new theory of language, and all irony about its newness is intended. In the wake of deconstruction the central literary project has been expanding the canon of texts to those written by women, blacks, and in postcolonial settings – all of whom had been marginalized when the center was white, male, European. If this is one debt to Derrida, a political one, the other, the project of how language means, has been largely at a standstill.

I want to take it up again, asserting that mystical theology offers a fruitful key to the understanding of signification as conversation: a call that evokes a response, an offering of words that were already given, an expression of gratitude or praise that precedes, indeed, is the condition of the reception of what we are grateful for, speaking and being heard. The miracle of language is the very recognition and reception of the gift. In conversation, the concern is not to designate or nominate, to describe or inscribe the speakers, but to attend to the conversation. To converse, to verse across, to and fro, to speak and to elicit a response, con-verse, versing against, not-versing: we should attend to all of these meanings. Utterances go back and forth and in between them is the silence where the gift of hearing is given and received of listening. This silence is where the conversation really takes place, if it does, for this is the silence of responsiveness, responsibility, and response. Without this silence each utterance could in fact be a monologue; what makes it a dialogue is what occurs in the silence: a gift of attention, a gift of a hearing. To converse is to exchange responses – and, as Derrida writes in "Faith and Knowledge," response is at the very heart of religion. "Is it not there, perhaps, that we must seek the beginning of a response? Assuming, that is, that one knows what responding means, and also responsibility. Assuming, that is, that one knows it – and believes in it. No response, indeed, without a principle of responsibility: one must respond to the other, before the other, and for oneself."[13] These last remarks allude to the rich contribution of Levinas to our understanding of responsibility, for response is inseparable from the ethical. The burden (or privilege) of this response is not from God, but is for humanity.

In his theophany to Moses in Exodus 3, God is famously unwilling to name his name, and Pseudo-Dionysius makes much of this: the divine is both all names and no name. But before there is even any discussion of naming, before Moses asks who shall I say sent me, God tells Moses that he is the one who *hears* and knows of the Israelites' affliction – indeed, this is why he appears to Moses, to say *he has heard and seen and means to save*: "I have seen the affliction of my people who are in Egypt, and have heard their cry because of their taskmasters; I know their sufferings, and I have come down to deliver them out of the hand of the Egyptians, and to bring them up out of that land to a good and broad land" (Ex. 3). The parallelism suggests that hearing, seeing, and saving are versions of the same act: response. Ex. 6.5 reiterates this claim that God has heard: "Moreover I have heard the groaning of the people of Israel whom the Egyptians hold in bondage and I have remembered my covenant." I've remembered my promise to hear. And these scenes contrast the Lord hearing the people with the people's deafness to the divine message when Moses delivers it: "Moses spoke to the people of Israel; they did not listen to Moses." But ultimately the word of the Lord does not come back empty, according to the prophet. The words that God has given man are heard and a response is made. As Hans Urs von Balthassar has written about dialogue,

Looking back over two thousand years of Christian theology, it is astonishing how little attention it has received.... After all, at the very center of the biblical events lies the Covenant between God and man, in which God gives man, whom he has created and endowed with freedom, an area of independent being, an area where he can freely hear and answer and ultimately cooperate responsibly with God.... There is also the area... of taking up a position, of possible refusal.... His astounding masterpiece is to elicit the Yes of his free partner from the latter's innermost freedom.[14]

What comes after the subject and the death of the author is conversation, not between not-beings, whether authors or readers, but between those who are only constituted in dialogue as calling and responding, praying and hearing, yearning and loving.

Notes

1 Jean-Luc Marion, *God Without Being*, trans. Thomas Carlson (Chicago: University of Chicago Press, 1991), originally *Dieu sans l'etre: Hors-Texte* (Paris, 1982), p. 35.
2 Ibid, p. 45.
3 Jacques Derrida, "Signature, Event, Context," *Glyph* 1 (1977), pp. 172–97; the response by John Searle, "Reiterating the Differences: A Reply to Derrida," *Glyph* 1 (1977), pp. 198–208, and Derrida, "Limited Inc.," *Glyph* 2 (1977), pp. 162–254.
4 Derrida, "This Strange Institution Called Literature: An Interview," *Acts of Literature*, ed. Derek Attridge (New York: Routledge, 1992), pp. 33–75.
5 Louis Martz, *The Poetry of Meditation: A Study in English Religious Literature of the Seventeenth-Century* (New Haven, CT: Yale University Press, 1962), p. 280.
6 Here I depart from Derrida who accords this inaccessibility to prayer rather than to praise. I understand prayer as containing the possibility for instrumentality.
7 Pseudo-Dionysius, "The Divine Names," *The Complete Works*, trans. Colm Luibheid (New York: Paulist Press, 1987), p. 52.
8 Ibid, p. 49.
9 Ibid, p. 76.
10 See Marion's rich discussion of the addressee and addresser in *Etant Donné* (Paris: Presse Universitaires de France, 1997).
11 See Chana Block, *Spelling the Word* (Pittsburgh, PA: University of Pittsburgh Press, 1980), p. 100.
12 Book of Common Prayer, 1604.
13 "Faith and Knowledge," trans. Samuel Weber, in *Religion*, ed. Jacques Derrida and Gianni Vattimo (Stanford, CA: Stanford University Press, 1998), originally *La Religion: seminaire de Capri* by Editions de Seuil and Editions Laterza, p. 26.
14 Hans Urs von Balthassar, *Theo-Drama: Theological Dramatic Theory*, vol. 1, trans. Graham Harrison (San Francisco: Ignatius Press, 1988), p. 34, originally *Theodramatik: Erster Band: Prolegomena* (1983).

CHAPTER 4
The Ends of Man and the Future of God

Janet Martin Soskice

Canadian by birth, Janet Soskice crossed the Atlantic to read for a doctorate in the philosophy of religion at Oxford, working with Basil Mitchell and Rom Harré. The imprint of the Oxford analytical approach to philosophy, which I have commented on with respect to several authors in this volume (Grace Jantzen and Pamela Sue Anderson particularly), is most evident in her early work, *Metaphor and Religious Language* (Oxford, 1985), but already in that volume there were the hints of a distinctive line of thinking to follow. The book's main purpose was to metaphor its fully cognitive and creative role after its side-lining in the "merely ornamental" by the empiricist tradition; metaphors can be fully referential and "reality depicting." In this way metaphor provided grounds for both a theological realism and a scientific realism that was not simply positivist and espousing positivist theories of language. Soskice's subsequent work in numerous published essays has taken up and considerably developed the emphases within that first book. First, her interest in metaphor led, rather as it did in the work of Paul Ricoeur, to an interest also in narrative, hermeneutics, and the theory and practice of reading. In turn this fed into theological engagements with both Augustine and Schleiermacher and, as she became interested in feminism, in the operations of gendered metaphors in Christian texts and tradition. Second, the argument for theological realism developed into the adoption of a more explicit theological methodology in her writing. The move Soskice made might well be characterized as a shift from philosophy of religion to philosophical theology. As is evident from her contribution to this volume, her thinking begins from faith, from within the tradition-based reasoning of Christianity (with a particularly Roman Catholic orientation). Third, drawing upon the theological tradition, Soskice continues her interest in cultural context. This essay brings together her concerns with science and scientific culture, religious language, and aesthetics.

Hope is one of the three theological virtues, but hope seems to us different from faith and charity. You can dispose yourself to faith and charity – try to be more kind or more devout. With hope you either have it or you do not. In contemporary culture hope is represented, often even by the churches, as a psychological mood: lack of faith and charity can be treated by prayer but lack of hope is treated with anti-depressants. But surely this points to what is flawed in this commonplace understanding of hope, at least for theological purposes. Christian hope is neither a psychological mood nor an emotional commodity, but a gift and a grace. The same is true of faith and love. We don't "possess" these or a certain quantity of them as commodities, any more than we will possess God as a commodity when we see God face to face. Rather, we are constituted in these theological virtues by God. This is what is meant, in part, by saying that hope, like faith and love, *abides*. Hope in God will not dissolve once it possesses its "object" as do profane hopes, because this hope is not directed towards some *object* or end but towards God.

Many theologians have pointed to the difference between this hope in God and profane hopes. J.-B. Metz has said that the difference from secular utopian vision is this: secular utopias envision a time which will be marvelous for those lucky enough to be alive then, but offer little solace to those whose lives have been a means to this glorious end. A study of some of the "brave new worlds" of the past hundred years will tell us all we need to know about utopianism gone wrong. Hope in God does not have in hand some well-delineated sketch of the future but looks forward to God's time, the kingdom, when all will be well and when every tear will be dried – when all the suffering of the world through its ragged and jagged history will be made whole. Such hope could only be hope in God.

However, religious hope is not only hope for the future but hope for the present and past. This hope is quite different from a saccharine optimism that "blue skies are just around the corner." This hope is quite different from a saccharine optimism that all is right in the world when clearly all is not. Christians have learned from Jews out of the horror of the Shoah that hope in God can abide even in the midst of profound evil, and without ignoring that profound evil.

Just as hope in God is not simple optimism, the opposite of hope in God is not pessimism or even despair, but nihilism.[1] Whereas despair is a transient mood, nihilism, like hope, is a fundamental orientation to the world. You can have a happy, even jolly, nihilist. There are many of these people around: garrulous dinner-party nihilists who are optimistic about pay rises or their summer holiday but skeptical as to questions of meaning, truth, values, goodness, or integrity.[2]

Depending on who one listens to in the intellectual cacophony, nihilism is in the ascendant in the postmodern West and hope is on the way out. From the religious point of view the period of European modernity has been one of sustained and continuing loss of beliefs; loss of belief in the authority of scripture, church, tradition, and even common sense. God, in dying – so this story goes – has dragged other cherished fancies to the grave. Most recently we have seen loss in belief in those "idols" which tried to take the place of the absent God – loss of belief in progress, in beauty, in Marxism, in the Enlightenment, in psychoanalysis, all the secular narratives of salvation – a true twilight of the idols.

There is a certain consensus that science has played a large part in the stripping away traditional certainties, in "disenchanting" the universe. On this view the growth of scientific knowledge with its convincing accounts of order in the world is directly responsible for the decline in religious belief and the values of traditional culture. The phrase "disenchanted universe" is Max Weber's, but it has an update in Jean-François Lyotard's book *The Postmodern Condition*, where the writer argues that this postmodern condition is undoubtedly the product of the progress of science.

What interests me about this putatively "empirical" account of modernity and the decline of faith is that it has so little empirical warrant. There is no direct correlation between advance in scientific knowledge and decline of religious allegiance. Where we see dramatic declines in church attendance, say in modern Greece between the 1950s and the 1980s, it was not new scientific knowledge that paved the way, although secularism may have something to do with advancing technology and technocratic culture. The causes of religious decline are undoubtedly complex, and nor should Western Europe be our template. It is not the case that everywhere modernity has meant the loss of religion. It may even be quite distinctive to the modern West. Three billion of the world's people are still religious and these are not all "unmodern" people. Indeed, secularization has proceeded at quite different rates in Western countries where acquaintance with the scientific culture was roughly the same.

What, in any case, are we meant to have learnt from science that was so shocking to the religious mind? Is science meant to have shown that there is a totalizing and atheistic explanation of the universe? No scientific explanation has achieved as much.[3] Are Christians meant to be shocked by the revelation that the Bible is not useful when read as a book of astrophysics? Are they meant to be shocked by the possibility that the universe was not really made in six days? Sometimes we are given the impression that all Christians were biblical literalists until Darwin.

We do a disservice to our great-grandparents to imagine their faith uniformly so simple that the trauma of the nineteenth century in matters of science and religion was simply one of fundamentalists encountering Darwinists. Paradoxically it is not because a great gulf had emerged during the Enlightenment between science and religion that the nineteenth century saw a crisis. In Britain we might say that the reverse was true – *because* the theological apologetics of the eighteenth century had been so closely wedded to the science of their time, with its support for the arguments from design, that the controversies over evolutionary theory in the nineteenth century came as such a blow. Religion's dearest ally had turned on it. Science, which had been proving the truths of religion only a hundred years before, now proposed naturalistic explanations for the perfections and order of the natural world. The divine clock-maker was redundant.

But what is the nature of this fall? What was destroyed? What was it about scientific advance that so devastated the Victorians? I have already indicated that we do them a disservice to imagine that they all were biblical literalists, stunned into sudden atheism by the suggestion that the world was not made in six days.

Consider the case of two of the most distinguished minds of Victorian England, the art critic John Ruskin and the poet Alfred, Lord Tennyson.

Ruskin's aesthetic theory in the early parts of *Modern Painters* brimmed with praise for the ingenuity and beauty of creation. The fluting and veining of a leaf, the way in which the clouds were formed, the way in which water divides over a cascade, all received his devout attentions. And all of this was connected with his belief in a divine providence ordering all that is and all that we see. When scientists produced explanations to rival – indeed, to better – that of the grand designer, it was not simply that Ruskin feared he would lose his faith in God. He feared to lose his *faith in beauty*. How can we say the leaf is beautiful if it just happens to be that way for adaptive reasons – for reasons that can be determined completely scientifically? A gap seems to yawn between the world as described by science (the "real world" of quantification and measurement) and the world as seen by unassisted human eyes. If the leaf and the clouds are not designed, why do we call them beautiful? Are they not just there? Are they not just natural phenomena which we happen to call beautiful? Is our judgment of beauty then nothing to do with the world as it really is in itself but merely subjective effusion? Even more worrying than this loss of foundation for aesthetics, must we not say that all human values, whether aesthetic or moral, are merely subjective?

The same fears haunt one of the finest nineteenth-century works on the tensions of science and religion, Tennyson's "In Memoriam." Ostensibly, this poem mourns the loss of Arthur Hallam, a young college friend, but at another level what is lost and what is mourned in the poem is a world where God's providence and man's preeminence are unquestioned assumptions. Tennyson was a keen reader of scientific writings and his poem is punctuated throughout with references to then-contemporary scientific ideas. Particularly influential, in these pre-Darwinian days, were the finds of the geologists. Tennyson was deeply affected by the demonstration, from fossil records, that whole species such as the "giant reptiles" (that is, dinosaurs) should have flourished and now are no more. On such a cosmic scale, where whole species have gone into extinction, what matters the life and work of a single man like Hallam or, for that matter, like Tennyson?

> Are God and Nature then at strife,
> That Nature lends such evil dreams?
> So careful of the type she seems,
> So careless of the single life . . . (LV)
>
> 'So careful of the type?' but no.
> From scarpèd cliffs and quarried stone
> She cries, 'A thousand types are gone:
> I care for nothing, all shall go.' (LVI)

All forms of life, man amongst them, are destined for extinction.

In another place Tennyson describes a visit to the street where Hallam had lived.

> Dark house, by which once more I stand
> Here in this long unlovely street

The word "unlovely" is carefully chosen. The street once was lovely, but is now unlovely. It is not a merely neutral street, it is positively ugly. His friend has gone; it is empty. The natural world, too, once lovely because suffused with God's purpose and providence, is now empty. Tennyson writing again of Hallam, but also of God, says

> He is not here; but far away
> The noise of life begins again,
> And ghastly through the drizzling rain
> On the bald street breaks the blank day. (VII)

Tennyson's choice of phrase bitterly echoes the angel's words in Luke to the women disciples at the empty tomb – "He is not here, but is risen" – but in Tennyson's vision there is no resurrection and no life, only bald streets and blank day. A clearer statement of the anxiety of modernity you will find nowhere. It is a world empty of God and empty of hope – a vision of cosmic futility.

If I may draw together the themes that I have been tracing under three points they are these: (1) In the modern period "man"[4] seems to have been swiftly demoted from being the crown of God's good creation to being just one more creature in a line of creatures destined for extinction, one more ultimately meaningless episode in the history of nature. (2) A gap seems to have emerged between the world as it is in itself and the world as we just happen to see it – sometimes described as the world of facts and the world of values. (3) The single individual – the individual man or woman, or the individual ivy leaf or drop of water – seems of no importance compared to the law-like generalizations which govern the whole.

These philosophical anxieties, or ones close to them, predate the nineteenth century. Already in the eighteenth century some feared the hegemony of science. Yet Romantic soul-searching was not simply nostalgia, or hostility to progress, but motivated by fear that, despite the benefits that science brought, science was suggesting that its description of the world was the only one and that the real world was a world of brute facts to which values, whether aesthetic or ethical or religious, were merely inessential decoration. It was, they feared, being suggested by the ideology of science, if not by science itself, that the real accounts of the world were those subsumable under laws and generalities and the real truths about the world were quantifiable and susceptible to formal analysis. In this the particular, the singular, and the individual were lost. As I have said, not just religion but ethics and aesthetics – all merely human values – on this account look sham.

The Nobel laureate Ilya Prigogine and his coauthor Isabelle Stengers make a related observation, saying that it appeared during this period that classical science "revealed to men a dead, passive nature, a nature that behaves as an automaton which, once programmed, continues to follow the rules inscribed in the program."[5] We might say that the real fear of Tennyson when faced with the demotion of man to just one more episode, and the fear of many now when faced with more extreme kinds of scientific reductionism, is not that science has proved that God is dead, but rather that science has proved that man is dead, that all we really are is perceptual apparatus of a particular sort, destined for extinction like all other life. As one of my friends put it, "From data you have come and to data you shall return."[6]

Mention of the death of man may recall for us Nietzsche, or perhaps Lyotard or Lacan, for we have arrived at an influential thesis of "postmodernism." Nietzsche's version of "the death of man," the ancestor of many postmodernist variants, is not so different from that we have discerned in Tennyson, and it goes something like this: the death of God does not mean merely the end of theism but is, in a sense, the death of any claim to absolute value, the death of any transcendental grounding of values, and the death of man as a privileged knower whose knowledge is underwritten by God. Postmodernist successors suggest that the Enlightenment "project" itself, with its pretensions to objectivity and universal truth, now stands in ruins. "Man," as a privileged knower, is dead.

It is very much man as a privileged knower that Lyotard indicates is in crisis in *The Postmodern Condition*, a book tellingly subtitled "A report on knowledge." As mentioned, this crisis is the product of the progress of science. "Science," Lyotard states baldly, "has always been in conflict with narratives," most of which, by the yardstick of science, are but fables. Yet science itself, if it attempts to move beyond the stating of regularities and seek "truth," must produce its own narrative of legitimation and this it cannot do, or at least not without being vulnerable to the criticisms of other legitimating narratives.[7] According to Lyotard, Nietzsche was correct in seeing European nihilism as the result of the truth requirement of science being turned back on itself. Following the failure of positivism adequately to demarcate the bounds of science we can only, on Lyotard's view, acknowledge that science itself is but one more "little narrative," bounded by its own conventions. "Science," says Lyotard, "plays its own game; it is incapable of legitimating the other language-games."[8] Yet a remarkable feature of Lyotard's book is that for all its putative postmodernity it employs very old-fashioned conceptions of science. The natural sciences in particular emerge as rankly positivistic, incapable of bending at all in the direction of the narratives and traditions that characterize the human life-world. On this construal, perhaps, all we can have is what Lyotard proposes: competing language-games, rhetorical strategies for success, little and local narratives locked in combat.

This agonistic scenario does not seem particularly new or postmodern. In fact it looks remarkably like an epistemological variant of Hobbes's war of all against all. Is it really so that our crisis is epistemological? The purpose of my excursus from Tennyson on the "death of man" through Lyotard on "the crisis of knowledge" is to raise this question. Many voices suggest that science has been complicit with epistemological crisis. With the collapse of master narratives, the demise of ideological systems (or systems perceived as ideological), and even the implosion of scientific certainty itself, we *do not know what to believe any more*, not just on matters religious but about anything; hence Lyotard's subtitle. I wish to suggest, especially but not only from the point of view of religious faith, that the crisis conflict of our modern period is not over knowledge; that our crisis, if it is such, is not epistemological so much as anthropological and, as such, a crisis of hope. Our problem is not so much that advance in scientific knowledge leads to loss of religious conviction, but with the suggestion, more scientistic than scientific, that the human race is epiphenomenal and human values superfluous. It is this that leads to anomie and sometimes to despair.

This essay's title speaks of "the ends of man," a phrase chosen to be neatly ambiguous between two meanings, "the aspirations of humanity" on the one hand, and the "end," that is, the demise of "man" as conceived by Western modernity, on the other. This last is what I am calling the anthropological crisis. Lyotard's "report on human knowledge" stands within the recognizably modern tradition of Western philosophy which, as Charles Taylor has pointed out, takes it as evident that a theory of knowledge will be philosophy's main contribution to scientific culture. Epistemology will make clear which knowledge claims are valid – which scientific claims are valid and, we might well add, which religious claims are valid. To a considerable extent religious apologetics has bought into this presentation of the case.

But look at the implicit anthropology this sets up: we, as knowers, address objects of knowledge which are "out there," whether these be objects of science or of theology. We are plunged immediately and almost inevitably into a definition of knowledge as "correct representation of an independent reality."[9] With this is introduced the split between the world "out there" and the knowing self "in here," the world of facts and the world of values.

The "representational epistemology" outlined above implies an anthropology wherein the knowing agent is somehow set apart from, maybe outside of, the world that is known.[10] Essential to this enterprise is the disengagement of the subject.[11] The subject is rational and objective only to the extent that it is disengaged from natural and social worlds and even from its own body, which can then be seen as both an object of study and a source of deception.

The disengaged or "punctual self," in Charles Taylor's phrase – rational and free, but languageless, cultureless, historyless – is an anthropological notion apparent in many of the texts of the modern period. In the twentieth century this concept of the self faced sustained attack: Iris Murdoch, Michel Foucault, Alison Jaggar, Luce Irigaray, and Ludwig Wittgenstein are just some of its critics. Indeed, there would seem to be a remarkable consensus across theorists from a variety of philosophical traditions that only an untenable construal of knowledge can be based on this idea of the punctual, disengaged self. Notably, interest in language and in the philosophy of language in our century has convinced many of the inadequacy of any account of human knowing which does not take account of our participation in natural languages.

Now one might at first think, since science is so important a factor in the modern period, that "science" itself is naturally aligned to this anthropology of a disengaged or "punctual self." Some early modern thinkers would have thought so. But over and against this we should note that the challenge to this anthropology has come in recent years as much from science as from anywhere else. In science and philosophy of science there is increasingly the conviction that the ideal agent of knowledge is not a disembodied mind, but one located in culture and history, not detached from the world but deeply attentive to it. Mary Hesse states the obvious but often overlooked fact when she points out that we must use "some natural language or other when we talk about the real world."[12]

This point, that science is bound up with and can only be understood in terms of human culture in general, is made with insistence by Prigogine and Stengers. It is an adjunct to their thesis that classical science (from the sixteenth century to fairly recently) – a science in which disengaged observers studied a world which was seen as essentially simple, static and law-determined – is a thing of the past. This conception of the scientific task was killed, not by philosophers, but by the progress of science itself. Nor was it only the scientists who, in previous centuries, were charmed by the notion of the model of the "punctual self" in the mechanical universe. Theologians as much as scientists favored the mechanical model of the universe in the seventeenth century. Man was, for many of them, "emphatically not part of the nature he objectively described" but, rather, dominated from the outside.[13] With God as guarantor of his interrogations of a mute and passive nature (notoriously rendered by Baconian science in female imagery) man could, as it were, see things from "a God's-eye view." By means of his "objectivity" he could separate fact from value, control the products of nature and also of "less fully rational" peoples – notably women, slaves or "primitives," peoples of "lesser" cultures.[14] It was a most useful anthropology for the early modern West. "The debasement of nature is parallel to the glorification of all that eludes it, God and man."[15]

The interest of these remarks by scientists lies in the suggestion, first, that what is defective here is the anthropology (although a defective epistemology flows from it) and, second, that the defect is *au fond* theological – "man" lays claim to a "God's-eye view." If we know anything of the "God's-eye view" it must be that only God can have it.

Like most heresies this one is a good theological tenet gone out of control – in this case the idea that to be in *imago dei* (construed as participating in divine rationality) means in some sense, epistemologically, to be God. It is curious that Christianity, whose central doctrine is the Incarnation, could be used to underwrite an epistemological program in which man attempts to distance himself from the human condition. In aspiring to be totally "in control" while fearing we are "out of control" (to take only two examples, think of reproductive technology and genetic engineering), we stand at what is arguably a hope-less period of Western intellectual history – one in which we recognize that confidence in progress and control has sometimes masked arrogance and mismanagement, yet see no clear way forward.

"Man" is, in a certain sense, dead, yet we should not be too concerned with his passing, for this is not the death of "man" *per se* but the death of a particularly intoxicating and alluring fiction – that of man as completely rational, completely wise, and completely in control. This essentially Promethean vision has never been the Christian one. Yet to say that we cannot see things from a "God's-eye view" is not to say that we cannot see truly at all. Rather it is to admit to the human condition, as good theologians and scientists always have done. We know as men and women and not as angels. Lyotard's mistake seems to be in saying "if we can't say we know with absolute certainty, we can't claim to know at all"; or otherwise put, "If I can't be God then I don't want to play." Nihilism is the reverse negative of presumption.

Hope, says Karl Rahner, is a matter of "letting one's self go." It is death to presumption. "Hope alone is the *locus* of God as he who cannot be controlled or manipulated, and so of God as such. . . . Presumption *and* despair both entail the same basic refusal to commit oneself and so to abandon oneself to the incalculable and uncontrollable."[16] If you prefer your sources to be French and philosophical rather than German and theological, Paul Ricoeur in his recent writings makes similar points about the deep religious and human value of being able to "let go." In its openness to the future of God, hope is far from being a deadening opiate, rendering us passive and immobile in the face of our present challenges. On the contrary, hope is angry for a better world, and it is that which both commands and enables us to move forward.

Hope, in this life, has a temporal quality, and not merely in its sense of the future and its sorrow for the past. Hope, like faith and love, is a state of readiness which is displayed in action. A mother or a father, out of love for the children, washes their clothes or buys the toy that is a sudden playground necessity. While doing this the parents may be thinking of what to get for dinner, or something that needs doing at work. They do not always think of the children as they wash their clothes or plan their meals, and yet the love for the children flows into these actions, for they would not be doing them at all without it.

Hope in God is a little like this. It is not a transient and optimistic *emotion*. It is a readiness to act, a directedness, a commitment, a passionate practicality. Hope is attentive and it changes your life.

It is perhaps fitting to end with the reflections of a scientist – another Nobel laureate – and with a return to what might unite the poet and the scientist and point to a way forward for the rest of us. "Good research," Barbara McClintock has said, "requires a disposition to hear what the material has to say to you." This is not simply a device to fathom the reasons governing the world. "It is," as her biographer notes, "a longing to embrace the world in its very being, through reason and beyond," a capacity for union with that which is known.[17] It is not too much to describe this, in the life of a research scientist, as a religious longing. It is a desire to move beyond "mere certainty" to a reverence for the given, "a disposition to hear what the material has to say to you."

Samuel Taylor Coleridge's great poem, *The Rime of the Ancient Mariner*, tells the story of a sailor cursed for his gratuitous slaughter of an albatross. He is condemned to wear this dead bird around his neck as, one by one, his shipmates die around him and his ghostly ship is trapped on windless seas. The spell is broken when he sees some sea snakes and, taken out of himself for a moment by their beauty, the mariner blesses them unawares. Yet surely, as Coleridge knows, the grace had already come, for only God can bless and enable us to bless. The albatross falls from the sailor's neck, the fresh water falls from the sky, the winds pick up, and he is saved. He has glimpsed the glory. Note something about the sea snakes: the poem does not lead us to believe that the sighting of sea snakes was an extraordinary thing and the mariner fortunate to note them at their rare moment of appearance. The sea about the stricken boat may, for all we know, have been full of these creatures throughout the time of deathly stillness, but the mariner, turned in upon himself, could not see them and still less see that they were beautiful. The scientist, like the artist or the person of faith, believes that we may on occasion glimpse a greater glory – a beauty that surrounds us but which we are too blind to see. To move towards this "given" in hope and attentiveness, in reverence and with awe, is a shared project of science and of faith. It is also the ground for an anthropology based not in epistemology but in eschatology. In this we would seek not our limited ends but the future of God, which is after all our true end, and in doing so we might discover what it is to be truly, fully human beings.

Notes

This essay first appeared in Michel Welker and John Polkinghorne (eds.), *The Ends of the World and the Ends of God* (Trinity Press International, 2000).

1   This is a somewhat overworked term and I do not, for the purposes of this essay, intend to give an extensive account of the varieties of European nihilism, whether philosophical or other. Let it rest, for our purposes here, in the contrast with despair. Nihilism in this sense is not an emotional state.
2   For a diagnosis of this nihilism and its attendant moral confusions see the papal encyclical *Fides et Ratio* (1998).
3   And were someone to produce so totalizing an account it is interesting to ask whether we would call it "science" rather than ideology.
4   The English collective term "man" is used here deliberately to indicate a particular Enlightenment construction of the human condition.
5   Ilya Prigogine and Isabelle Stengers, *Order Out of Chaos: Man's New Dialogue With Nature* (New York: Bantam Books, 1984), p. 6.
6   I owe this quip to my colleague Timothy Jenkins.

7   Jean-François Lyotard, *The Postmodern Condition: A Report on Knowledge* (Manchester: Manchester University Press, 1991), p. xxiii.
8   Ibid, p. 40.
9   Charles Taylor, "Overcoming Epistemology," in Kenneth Baynes, James Bohman, and Thomas McCarthy (eds.), *After Philosophy: End or Transformation?* (Cambridge, MA: MIT Press, 1987), p. 466.
10 This representational epistemology was, as Charles Taylor has argued, most useful to the new, mechanistic science of the seventeenth century. For Aristotle, knowledge was, in a sense, participational: in knowing, the mind becomes one with the object of thought. Descartes is more interested in science as certainty and certainty is achieved procedurally. For Descartes, but not only for Descartes, rationality becomes a property of private thought, rather than a vision of reality. It is achieved by a method or procedure, albeit one guaranteed in Descartes' system by a trustworthy God.
11 Charles Taylor argues this in his big work on the concepts of "self" and agency in Western philosophy, *Sources of the Self: The Making of Modern Identity* (Cambridge: Cambridge University Press, 1989), and in a series of articles.
12 "Science Beyond Realism and Relativism," in D. Raven, L. van Vucht, et al. (eds.), *Cognitive Relativism and Social Science* (Utrecht: University of Utrecht, 1988).
13 Prigogine and Stengers, *Order Out of Chaos*, p. 50.
14 For an interesting account of the extent to which the deists' *imago dei* influenced seventeenth- and eighteenth-century philosophy see Edward Craig's *The Mind of God and the Works of Man* (Oxford: Clarendon Press, 1987).
15 Ibid, p. 51.
16 "On the Theology of Hope," *Theological Investigations*, vol. 10 (London: Darton, Longman and Todd, 1973), pp. 245–59.
17 Evelyn Fox Keller, *A Feeling for the Organism: The Life and Work of Barbara McClintock* (San Francisco: W. H. Freeman, 1983), p. 199.

CHAPTER 5

"Lush Life": Foucault's Analytics of Power and a Jazz Aesthetic

Sharon D. Welch

One of the most important contributions feminist theology has made to academic Christian thinking is in the realm of social ethics. Christian social ethics, from F. D. Maurice and William Temple, to Ulrich Duchrow and Michael Novak, has been dominated by economic issues. The measure of social justice has been correlated to the soundness of economic policy, some arguing that there was justice in welfare-led, redistribution-orientated policies and others that free-market capitalism promoted not only democracy, autonomy, and increased participation in government, but also the kingdom of God. In the United States there had been more ethical discussion beyond the confines of economics, as the work of Edward Farley (one of Welch's teachers) and Stanley Hauerwas demonstrates. Nevertheless, Welch begins her first two books with important sections on the turpitude, even bankruptcy, of Christian ethics.

It is fair to say that new forms of critical thinking about gender and new analyses of the various forms and operations of power developed new styles of ethical enquiry among Christian thinkers which, while not ignoring economic issues, refused to reduce sites of cultural contestation to issues concerning property, scarcity, and capital. Into the complex matrices of daily life, theologians like Welch (and Mary McClintock Fulkerson) inserted gender, racial, and ethnic considerations. This is evident in Welch's first book, which emerged from her doctoral thesis, *Communities of Resistance and Solidarity: A Feminist Theology of Liberation* (Maryknoll, NY, 1985). In a sense, what is methodologically exciting about this book is that Welch has listened to the work of various liberation theologians (James Cone, Dorothy Soelle, Rosemary Radford Ruether, Johann B. Metz, Jon Sobrino, and Gustavo Gutierrez are all mentioned) and introduced their conversations to the work of Michel Foucault. As we see from the following essay, Foucault has remained an important influence.

> The influence of Foucault is not only methodological, it is political. Welch practices in her own work something of the analytics of power which Foucault increasingly came to see as fundamental to his writing of history as both archeology and genealogy. But Welch also takes up something of Foucault's pragmatism with respect to ethics and the political pursuit of cultural transformation. Her essay quotes Foucault's commitment to "pessimistic activism." This is a commitment to accepting that there is no "final or universal resolution to injustice." There is no room in Welch's thinking for Christian triumphalism or even apocalyptic. Justice is an ongoing work and Christians make a contribution to it: they cannot hegemonically command its operations. Through participation in communities of resistance and protest (always self-critical), a political actionism is nurtured which can "manifest accountability and creativity." Attention to the creativity of such resistance and protest has always been an important part of Welch's analysis, from her citation of Wallace Stevens in her first book, to her use of Toni Morrison's fiction in *A Feminist Ethic of Risk* (Minneapolis, 1990), to her reflections on jazz in the essay below. Limited as this may be in terms of the global plans for salvation produced by various utopias, nevertheless there is voiced in this "activism" (and in the sheer conviction that Welch's work conveys) a refusal to allow, after Auschwitz, Vietnam, and El Salvador, disillusionment to have the final word. Welch's own term for what might be called her tragic politics is "risk." Risk and, concomitantly, vulnerability, becomes a major defining characteristic of a new Christian ethics.

> I can't help but dream about a kind of criticism that would try not to judge but to bring an oeuvre, a book, a sentence, an idea to life; it would light fires, watch the grass grow, listen to the wind, and catch the sea foam in the breeze and scatter it. It would multiply not judgments but signs of existence; it would summon them, drag them from their sleep. Perhaps it would invent them sometimes – all the better. All the better. Criticism that hands down sentences sends me to sleep; I'd like a criticism of scintillating leaps of the imagination. It would not be sovereign or dressed in red. It would bear the lightning of possible storms.[1]

The Necessity and the Danger of Critique

What keeps us from realizing Foucault's dream? Why is it that much of our critical work has precisely the opposite effect, not multiplying signs of existence but amplifying our sense of isolation, cynicism, and despair?

We find ourselves at an interesting juncture culturally and politically. Unlike periods of seeming complacency and confidence in the social order, our era is one of widespread recognition of a host of crises and social injustices, and an equally widespread awareness of the fallibility of political leaders and economic and governmental institutions. It is no longer shocking to learn of political malfeasance, no longer unusual to distrust the wisdom and efficacy of institutions of finance, education, transportation, and healthcare.

While critique is widespread, the solutions offered are often simplistic and uninspiring. Instead of heedless globalization, we are offered simple calls for democracy, economic justice, and human rights. While these humanistic goals are certainly laudatory, the actual implementation of these goals is far from within reach.

Foucault claims that while there is a need for continuous critique, it is no longer satisfactory to stay merely with critical analysis. In a dialogue published in 1977 Foucault addresses specific policy recommendations that can redress the problems he and others have raised in regard to the use of psychiatry as a means of policing public health.

> People may ask why I've allowed myself to get involved in this – why I've agreed to ask these questions. . . . But, in the end, I've become rather irritated by an attitude, which for a long time was mine, too, and which I no longer subscribe to, which consists in saying: our problem is to denounce and to criticize; let them get on with their legislation and their reforms. This doesn't seem to me the right attitude.[2]

Instead of remaining in the stance of critique, Foucault points to other tasks of critical reflection:

> The work of an intellectual is not to shape others' political will; it is, through the analysis that he carries out in his field, to question over and over again what is postulated as self-evident, to disturb people's mental habits, the way they do and think things, to dissipate what is familiar and accepted, to reexamine rules and institutions and on the basis of this reproblematization . . . to participate in the formation of a political will (in which he has his role as a citizen to play).[3]

What does it mean to operate as a citizen, as a political activist, thoroughly grounded in Foucault's unsettling reproblematization of specific discourses? How do we avoid the paralysis of ineffective critique without succumbing to the heedless exercise of an uncritical political will? While he does say critique must continue, Foucault does not advocate every sort of critique. Like any other exercise of power, our critical work is also "dangerous." Foucault, for example, rejects polemics and claims that "we shouldn't confuse useful criticism of things with repetitive jeremiads against people."[4]

In an interview conducted by Paul Rabinow in 1984 Foucault answered a simple question, "Why don't you engage in polemics?" by emphasizing that "a whole morality is at stake, the morality that concerns the search for truth and the relation to the other." Not only are polemics unproductive ("Has anyone ever seen a new idea come out of a polemic?"), but polemics function as "an obstacle in the search for truth."[5]

> Very schematically, it seems to me that today we can recognize the presence in polemics of three models: the religious model, the judiciary model, and the politi-

cal model. As in heresiology, polemics sets itself the task of determining the intangible point of dogma, the fundamental and necessary principle that the adversary has neglected, ignored, or transgressed; and it denounces this negligence as a moral failing; at the root of the error, it finds passion, desire, interest, a whole series of weaknesses and inadmissible attachments that establish it as culpable. As in judiciary practice, polemics allows for no possibility of an equal discussion: it is processing a suspect; it collects the proofs of his guilt, designates the infraction he has committed, and pronounces the verdict and sentences him.... But it is the political model that is the most powerful today. Polemics defines alliances ... it establishes the other as an enemy, an upholder of opposed interests against which one must fight until the moment this enemy is defeated and either surrenders or disappears.[6]

Foucault challenges us to forgo the ready satisfactions of polemics while yet being attentive to the continuing presence of error and domination. How is it possible, though, to see error and domination and yet avoid polemical and repetitive jeremiads against people and against global structures of imperialism and domination?

While repetitive jeremiads are isolating and paralyzing, action without self-critique is foolhardy and dangerous. Foucault warned of the folly of "technocratic humanism":

It must surely be possible to engage in a left-wing politics which does not exploit all these confused humanist myths.... The technocrats, now, are humanist.... They in fact consider that they are the only ones in possession of the card game which would allow a definition of what the "happiness of man" is and its realization.[7]

We can see such *naïveté* and denial of fallibility in many of the social visions offered in public debate in the United States. In an article in *The Atlantic Monthly* Steven Weinberg criticizes five widely held utopian visions. The first is "The Free-Market Utopia."

Government barriers to free enterprise disappear. Governments lose most of their functions, serving only to punish crimes, enforce contracts, and provide national defense. Freed of artificial restraints, the world becomes industrialized and prosperous.[8]

Leaving aside the question of the ecological impact of a fully industrialized world, Weinberg warns of the tyranny of industry, unacknowledged and unredressed in this social vision:

For many Americans the danger of tyranny lies not in government but in employers of insurance companies or health-maintenance organizations, from which we need government to protect us. To say that any worker is free to escape an oppressive employer by getting a different job is about as realistic as to say that any citizen is free to escape an oppressive government by emigrating.[9]

The second social vision is "The Best and Brightest Utopia" in which "public affairs are put in the hands of an intelligent and well-educated class of leaders."[10] Weinberg's critique of this vision is succinct: is there any group that can be trusted with such power?

> There never has been a governing elite in any age that did not eventually come to give priority to its own interests.... There is no reason to imagine that a ruling elite drawn from business leaders would do any better. H. G. Wells and other utopians have imagined putting public affairs in the hands of scientists, but I know my fellow scientists too well to be enthusiastic about this proposal.... Power is not safe in the hands of any elite, but it is not safe in the hands of the people, either. To abandon all constraints on direct democracy is to submit minorities to the tyranny of the majority.[11]

The other three utopias are marked by similar denials of fallibility and the history of political corruption. "The Religious Utopia" envisions "a religious revival [that] sweeps the earth, reversing the secularization of society that began with the Enlightenment. Many countries follow the example of Iran, and accept religious leaders as their rulers.... Scientific research and teaching are permitted only where they do not corrode religious belief."[12] Those who advocate a "Green Utopia" hope for a time when "the world turns away from industrialism and returns to a simpler style of life. Small communities grow their own food, build houses and furniture with their own hands, and use electricity only to the extent that they can generate it from sun, wind, or water."[13] Weinberg argues that those who advocate this view fall prey to the "common" tendency "for those who don't have to work hard to romanticize hard labor."[14] The fifth vision, "The Technological Utopia," does not address the negative ramifications of the loss of cultural diversity, or the environmental costs of a technology-saturated world. It extols, rather, "the development of information processing, robotics, synthetic materials, and biotechnology [that] increases productive capacity so much that questions about the distribution of wealth become irrelevant. National borders also become irrelevant, as the whole world is connected by a web of fiber-optic cables."[15]

All of these utopian visions avoid the ubiquity of error, corruption, and unintended consequences. The mode of strategic political engagement proposed by Foucault is far from the moral certitude that accompanies any utopian vision. Foucault does not offer a clarion call for the purity and forcefulness of revolution, but rather, calls us to "hyper and pessimistic activism" in the face of ongoing social and political dangers.

> You see, what I want to do is not the history of solutions – and that's the reason why I don't accept the word *alternative*. I would like to do the genealogy of problems, of *problematiques*. My point is not that everything is bad, but that everything is dangerous.... If everything is dangerous, then we always have something to do. So my position leads not to apathy but to a hyper- and pessimistic activism.

I think that the ethico-political choice we have to make every day is to determine which is the main danger. Take as an example Robert Castel's analysis of the history of the antipsychiatry movement.... I agree completely with what Castel says, but that does not mean, as some people suppose, that the mental hospitals were better than antipsychiatry; that does not mean that we were not right to criticize those mental hospitals. I think it was good to do that, because *they* were the danger. And now it's quite clear that the danger has changed. For instance, in Italy they have closed all the mental hospitals, and there are more free clinics, and so on – and they have new problems.[16]

Why do we continually confront danger, and why do these forms of danger change? The cause of any danger and of new forms of danger is quite simple – we humans are the species marked, not primarily or solely by reason, or by freedom, but also by error. James Faubion argues that this attention to error makes Foucault's work not a pragmatic philosophy but a "philosophy of fallibility" in which the history of thought is interpreted as "a history of trials, an open-ended history of multiple visions and revisions, some more enduring than others."[17] As Foucault writes:

The opposition of the true and the false, the values that are attributed to the one and the other, the power effects that different societies and different institutions link to that division – all this may be nothing but the most belated response to that possibility of error inherent in life. If the history of the sciences is discontinuous – that is, if it can be analyzed only as a series of "corrections," as a new distribution that never sets free, finally and forever, the terminal moment of truth – the reason again is that "error" constitutes not a neglect or a delay of the promised fulfillment but the dimension peculiar to the life of human beings and indispensable to the duration [*temps*] of the species.[18]

The sources of error are many: some are benign, such as partiality and specificity; others are more disquieting, such as ignorance, carelessness, jealousy, arrogance, malice, greed, and cruelty. Rather than seeing these elements of human behavior as distortions to be denounced or eradicated, Foucault challenges us to recognize them as factors in ourselves, not just in others. It is this attention to fallibility that leads him to both criticize domination and yet to disavow the possibility of utopian power relations.

The idea that there could exist a state of communication that would allow games of truth to circulate freely, without any constraints or coercive effects, seems utopian to me. This is precisely a failure to see that power relations are not something that is bad in itself, that we have to break free of. I do not think that a society can exist without power relations, if by that one means the strategies by which individuals try to direct and control the conduct of others. The problem, then, is not to dissolve them in the utopia of completely transparent communication but to acquire the rules of law, the management techniques, and also the morality, the *ethos*, the practice of the self, that will allow us to play these games of power with as little domination as possible.[19]

I would argue that this is true even of feminist goals of power-with or power-from-within. Our attempts to avoid control and to interact openly with others are also fraught with danger. Our efforts to "play games of power with as little domination as possible" often falter in the presence of difference and serious disagreements over theory and specific strategies.[20]

Although it is easy to spend one's life and academic career caught up in the analysis of patterns of domination and exclusion, Foucault argues that resistance to unjust power relations is not enough.

> Those who resist or rebel against a form of power cannot merely be content to denounce violence or criticize an institution. . . . What has to be questioned is the form of rationality at stake. The criticism of power wielded over the mentally sick or mad cannot be restricted to psychiatric institutions; nor can those questioning the power to punish be content with denouncing prisons as total institutions. The question is: how are such relations of power rationalized? Asking it is the only way to avoid other institutions, with the same objectives and the same effects, from taking their place.[21]

How do we act after our analyses of the rationalization of various forms of power? As if these challenges were not sufficiently daunting, Foucault raises a further challenge for self-critical political engagement. How do we act without romanticizing the challenges facing us as a fundamentally new or ultimately decisive break in human history?

> Here, I think, we are touching on one of the forms – perhaps we should call them "habits" – one of the most harmful habits in contemporary thought, in modern thought even; at any rate, in post-Hegelian thought: the analysis of the present as being precisely, in history, a present of rupture, or of high point, or of completion or of a returning dawn, and so on. The solemnity with which everyone who engages in philosophical discourse reflects on his own time strikes me as a flaw. I can say so all the more firmly, since it is something I have done myself. . . . I think we should have the modesty to say to ourselves that, on the one hand, the time we live in is not *the* unique or fundamental or irruptive point in history where everything is completed and begun again. We must also have the modesty to say, on the other hand, that – even without this solemnity – the time we live in is very interesting; it needs to be analyzed and broken down. . . . It is a time like any other, or rather, a time that is never quite like any other.[22]

How do we act and think *after* our recognition of the challenges of our time, after our analyses of the rationalization of various forms of power?

This is not a task completed by Foucault. He points to the need for such work not only in his dream of a criticism that "would light fires" but in his assessment of the "turning period" in "European thought."

> This turning point, on an historical scale, is nothing other than the end of imperialism. The crisis of Western thought is identical to the end of imperialism. This crisis has produced no supreme philosopher who excels in signifying that

crisis.... There is no philosopher who marks out this period. For it is the end of the era of Western philosophy. Thus, if philosophy of the future exists, it must be born outside of Europe or equally born in consequence of meetings and impact between Europe and non-Europe.[23]

We find here a concise description of Foucault's own work. It can be readily argued that he is a philosopher who signifies this crisis, and who provides intimations of a philosophy of the future, based on the impact of meetings between the "Others" of Europe, prisoners, homosexuals, the cultures, symbols, and knowledges of madness and illness. The latter work, the meeting and impact between Europe and non-Europe, has been the task of many activists and scholars in religious studies for the past thirty years. Witness the vast work in theologies of liberation, the works in ethics, theology, and the comparative study of religion based on the voices of "others" – the liberation theologies from Africa, Latin America, and Asia, and the voices of the "others" within Western societies – African-Americans, Latinos/Latinas, Asian Americans, Native Americans, women, the disabled, the poor and working class, people who are gay, lesbian, bisexual, and transgender.

What is the analytics of power that can serve these voices, that can embody the philosophy of the future? Critique of injustice is essential. We must hear the voices of rage, pain, and suffering. But what do we do after we have heard these critiques? What do we do, those of us who have relative power and access to institutional and cultural power? What do we do as citizens? What shape can a political will take that occurs within this engagement with difference, conflict, and injustice? How do we act after we accept Foucault's challenge and realize that there are no foolproof formulas, that all of our actions are dangerous, subject to error and challenge?

The challenge that Foucault poses for the philosophy of the future is intriguing and daunting. In this essay I describe such a form of critique, an "analytics of power," drawing on the suggestions made by Foucault but amplifying them in light of the directions for thought and action that emerge from learning from jazz, and from the critical works of social theory by many of those designated as "Other" within a dominant culture – women, gay men, African-Americans, and Native Americans.

"Write *The Word?* No. But tie the knot with life again, yes."[24]

In this essay I explore the ramifications of one particular "meeting" between dominant and marginalized cultures. How do we acknowledge the costs of domination, our fallibility, and yet hold a vision that can direct a creative and accountable political will? We can find a clear expression of such an ethos of vision and self-critical accountability in the artistry, critical social theory, and political activism of some African-Americans. I will explore the artistry of jazz, the critical social theory of Patricia Hill Collins, and the political work of Ronald Dellums.

It is now clear to many social critics why we listen to "Others" and why we who are the "Other" speak; but why, specifically, should we learn from jazz? To think about jazz and to learn from it is to enter a compelling engagement with a complex, changing, intricate form of art. What can be learned from the beauty, complexity, and depth of insight that is art? Art has, of course, its own logic, its coherence, its evocative power. It is meaningful and valuable in its own terms. And yet, if we immerse ourselves in this complex play of insight and form, what can we discover?

I will explore the power of a jazz aesthetic, following the brief yet evocative discussion by Foucault of the import of another form of music, that of Boulez. What Foucault found in Boulez, many of us find in jazz. Foucault claimed that

> to encounter Boulez and his music was to see the twentieth century from an unfamiliar angle – that of the long battle around the "formal." It was to recognize how in Russia, in Germany, in Austria, in Central Europe, through music, painting, architecture, or philosophy, linguistics and mythology, the work of the formal had challenged the old problems and overturned the ways of thinking.[25]

Foucault provides provocative insight into the significance of the work of Boulez:

> One is apt to think that a culture is more attached to its values than to its forms, that these can easily be modified, abandoned, taken up again; that only meaning is deeply rooted. This is to overlook how much hatred forms have given rise to when they have come apart or come into existence. It is to ignore the fact that people cling to ways of seeing, saying, doing, and thinking, more than to what is seen, to what is thought, said, or done.[26]

The power of a jazz aesthetic is that it provides a different form, different ways of seeing, saying, thinking, and doing. We can learn from jazz how to act knowing that our actions are dangerous, open to error and mistakes, that they are experiments without solid grounding in ahistorical foundations or universally recognized rationality. As Foucault states, our challenge now is to work and think within a framework in which we acknowledge limits and risk.

> The critical ontology of ourselves must be considered not, certainly, as a theory, a doctrine, nor even as a permanent body of knowledge that is accumulating: it must be conceived as an attitude, an ethos, a philosophical life in which the critique of what we are is at one and the same time the historical analysis of the limits imposed on us and an experiment with the possibility of going beyond them [*de leur franchissement possible*].[27]

There is in jazz, and in the blues, an aesthetic form to this work on limits.

Before we explore the implications of the form of jazz, a caveat is in order. Not only is it a tenuous task for any intellectual to work with the insights of any form of art, continuously running the risk of reductive or instrumental interpretations, it is doubly dangerous for those of us who are white to speak about jazz. In speaking of what we have learned from this art form, we must acknowledge the racism that is part of the history and continued struggles of jazz artists. Jazz is the creation of African-Americans, a form of beauty that emerges from the intense struggle to live deeply and well, even in the face of a racist society. Stanley Crouch, for example, writing on the legacy of Louis Armstrong emphasizes both Armstrong's awareness of suffering and the ways in which his artistry "in the service of happiness" embodied "spiritual exaltation."[28]

Jazz artists have historically seen their work misinterpreted and misappropriated. Krin Gabbard reminds us of the twin errors that befall white interpretations of jazz: disparaging it as sensual, ecstatic, and emotional, or romanticizing it for the same "primitive" traits: "But whether the music was demonized or romanticized, the result was the same: jazz was the safe contained world of the Other where whites knew they could find experiences unavailable to them at home."[29]

The damage of these distortions is twofold: the damage to the lives of men and women who are not given recognition and respect, and the loss to white culture of a deep appreciation of an art, a style that, to use Ralph Ellison's words, "reduces the chaos of living to form."[30] The effects of jazz performance are often profound: Mary Lou Williams, noted jazz pianist, would often implore inattentive audiences to "Listen, this will heal you."[31]

What is the healing power of jazz? Jazz is a different form of seeing, saying, doing, and thinking. What is seen through a jazz aesthetic is what is seen now by many: conflict, difference, failure, mistakes, suffering, meaning, beauty, commitment to justice, grief, outrage at suffering and injustice. The form of jazz can provide a modality of critique, of social engagement that enables the actualization of Foucault's dream, his dream of a criticism that "would try not to judge but to bring an idea to life.... It would multiply not judgments, but signs of existence."

We can learn much about creativity and freedom, social critique and political activism, from the life and work of artists such as Billy Strayhorn. While known by a few as a creative genius during his lifetime, in the public eye Strayhorn was known only as a collaborator with Duke Ellington. David Hajdu's biography brings us a fuller picture, an evocative portrait of a compelling person.

> I found that Strayhorn led an extraordinarily active and influential life despite his near anonymity. In time, it became evident that Strayhorn composed far more music than the listening public knows.... Urbane and a bon vivant, he lived well and hard. Strayhorn was a homosexual, and he never seemed to care who knew. He lived in Harlem and loved Paris, where he collaborated on a musical drama with Orson Welles. His dearest friend was Lena Horne.... He worked for the civil rights movement, often closely with the Reverend Dr. Martin Luther King, Jr. Strayhorn suffered demons, and he smoked and drank until the effects killed him.[32]

Strayhorn's compositions, like his life, escape easy characterization. One of his most famous compositions, "Lush Life," is described as a "cynical moan" and a musically sophisticated "prayer" that "exquisitely weds words and music."[33] Listening to such compositions is intellectually challenging and aesthetically satisfying. It can also be profoundly healing.

What are some of the elements of a jazz aesthetic? What form does it embody? In this essay I will emphasize five.

Sorrow and joy

One element of a jazz aesthetic is a creative expression of sorrow and joy. One hears in "Lush Life" and in many other works an evocation of loss and suffering, but without despair or self-pity. Crouch recognizes this multidimensionality in the work of Louis Armstrong: "He almost single-handedly begat a new spirit of freewheeling but perfectly controlled improvisation, tinged with playfulness, sorrow and sardonic irony."[34] James Baldwin states that he hears in "some gospel songs, for example, and in jazz . . . and especially in the blues . . . something tart and ironic, authoritative and double-edged. [By contrast] white Americans seem to feel that happy songs are happy and sad songs are sad."[35] Eric Lott also sees this complex vision as central to the artistry of Charlie Parker: "Jazz was a struggle which pitted mind against the perversity of circumstance, and . . . in this struggle blinding virtuosity was the best weapon."[36]

The individual and the larger community

Another key element of jazz is the interaction between the individual and a larger collective. Take, for example, the multiple ingredients in successful improvisation. In improvisation the individual artist expresses technical skill and the achievement of a supple musical imagination. Improvisation also requires a thorough understanding of the harmonics, rhythm, and stylistic possibilities of the musical work that serves as the framework and basis of improvisation. Further, to paraphrase James Colliers, to improvise well one has to listen.[37] One has to know not only the contours of a specific piece, and the possibilities of one's own instrument and level of skill, but one builds on an understanding of what the other musicians are doing in their improvisations and in their accompaniment of each other. Jazz improvisation is a mixture of individual creativity and astute participation in a multi-layered dialogue – a dialogue with other players, with the particular musical work, and with the history of jazz performance.

Improvisation emerges from a fluid interaction between individual skill and group synergy. It embodies a sense of the strongly individuated yet deeply connected social self described by Karen and Garth Kasimu Baker-Fletcher. They write of the power of generations in the constitution of the self and the community, and cite the cosmological community principle "muntu" of the Bantu peoples of Southeastern Africa: "I am because we are; and we are because I am."[38] They also remind us that "generations must not be romanticized": "when we idealize the elders we learn far less of what life has taught them or can teach us than if we learn from their strengths and their weaknesses."[39]

Risk

This complex interaction between self and others, between the past and the present, is, not surprisingly, fraught with risk. Central to the jazz aesthetic is pushing to the limits, taking the risk of mistakes, and learning from those mistakes. Ann Douglas describes the interaction between the freedom to make mistakes "intelligently" and the power of jazz.

> Even the musicians' strike of 1942, which banned recording, had its advantages. Errors were taboo in a big band or a recording studio, where mainstream taste set the standard. But Monk urged musicians: "Make a mistake. Play what you want and let the public pick up" on it.
>
> The purpose of bop's irregular phrasings, side-sliding harmonies and whirl-wind pace, was, in Kenny Clarke's words, to "raise the standard of musicianship," to tell people, "whatever you go into, go into it intelligently."
>
> Together these men [Charlie Parker, Thelonious Monk, Dizzie Gillespie, Earl (Bud) Powell] created a new musical language. . . . In a 70s interview, Gillespie said that be-bop was "a love music." Bop is mind-dancing: it's about seduction, about hearing notes that are intimated rather than played, ghostly air-sketching in dialogue with intense bravado, an impossible mix of intellect and rapture.[40]

Within the jazz ethos of "dialogue and bravado" we acknowledge that we are all capable of error: there are no infallible institutions, systems, or groups of people. We can be wrong as can every person, force, institution, and system we trust. Yet, even with error, our work can be fitting, beautiful and evocative, "an impossible mix of intellect and rapture."

Ceremonies of gratitude

This form of creativity emerges from participation in, and celebration of, the potentials of the present. This is not the stance of prophetic denunciation, standing outside a system and decrying its flaws and proclaiming a pure vision of beauty and justice. The creativity of jazz emerges from seeing, valuing, and enhancing the potentials within the present, within a song, a musician, an ensemble. Both Duke Ellington and Billy Strayhorn were noted for this aspect of their work, their ability to compose original works and orchestrations that built on the strengths of certain artists. David Hajdu recounts one such instance, the experience that the trumpeter Clark Terry had working with Strayhorn in a recording session with the Ellington Orchestra:

> "I didn't know what to expect picking up a part for one more version of 'Sophisticated Lady,'" said Terry. "Then I played it, and I told Strayhorn . . . 'That chart we just played . . . is really the most fantastic chart I have heard in a long time.' And he said to me, 'Did you enjoy your part?' I'll never forget that. . . . That man was always thinking about *you*." (Strayhorn told a magazine interviewer, "I have a general rule. Rimsky-Korsakov is the one who said it: All parts should lie easily under the fingers. That's my first rule, to write something a guy can play. Otherwise, it will never be as natural, or as wonderful, as something that does lie easily under the fingers.")[41]

As we live out of an affirmation of the present and the everyday, seeking political actions that "lie easily under the fingers," we can avoid the "soul murder" described by Jonathan Rieder:

> For some time now, the cultural left has been going around in a funk, deconstructing everything in sight, wavering between scolding a culture that seems hostile to liberation and conducting a promiscuous search for signs of resistance to that culture's dominating symbols. But in all this rage for representation, the left has often committed soul murder too, projecting disappointment onto the objects of its gaze, representing itself rather than the complex reality of a vibrantly imperfect culture.[42]

Success: ephemeral, yet real

Finally, in jazz, success is both ephemeral and real, an evocation of beauty that is fitting for now, embedded in the creativity of the past, and evocative of further creativity in the future. The past is honored not by repetition or imitation, but by participation – learning from other musicians and emulating not their specific music styles but their degree of virtuosity and responsiveness to other musicians. There is no progress in jazz, but there is connection, a legacy of learning from the past and from other musicians in the present. A jazz artist cannot know in advance what the response will be to a particular improvisation – will the other musicians hear it? If so, what will they do in response? Outside of a particular performance, one cannot know what future generations will make of one's legacy. How will they be inspired to find their own style, their own mode of creative response?

Our goal now, again to use Foucault's words, is an experimentation with technologies of the self that enable us to use power creatively and self-critically.[43] If we seek to use power truthfully, our goal is not a final or universal resolution to injustice but, rather, actions that manifest accountability and creativity. This focus is an extension of Foucault's understanding of the challenging task now being not that of "authenticity" but "creativity."

> Q But if one is to create oneself without recourse to knowledge or universal rules, how does your view differ from Sartrean existentialism?
> MF I think that from the theoretical point of view, Sartre avoids the idea of the self as something that is given to us, but through the moral notion of authenticity, he turns back to the idea that we have to be ourselves – to be truly our true self. I think that the only acceptable practical consequence of what Sartre has said is to link his theoretical insight to the practice of creativity – and not that of authenticity. From the idea that the self is not given to us, I think that there is only one practical consequence: we have to create ourselves as a work of art.[44]

If we seek creativity, but not authenticity, we find ourselves immersed in a kind of "truth game"[45] in which our primary concern is not denouncing or stopping the immoral acts of others, but, rather, the intensification of desire and pleasure in the interest of transforming institutions and structures, and the intensification of desire and pleasure in the interest of living as justly as possible in any given moment. The goal of our technology of the self is the evocation of actions that are creative, accountable, and aware of the contingent circumstances that fuel their emergence. Foucault claimed that

> one of the great problems of Western culture has been to find the possibility of founding the hermeneutics of the self not, as was the case in early Christianity, on the sacrifice of the self but, on the contrary, on a positive, on the theoretical and practical, emergence of the self . . . that was the aim of political and philosophical theory – to constitute the ground of the subjectivity as the root of a positive self. . . . Maybe the problem of the self is not to discover what it is in its positivity. . . . Maybe our problem is now to discover that the self is nothing else than the historical correlation of the technology built in our history. Maybe the problem is to change those technologies. And in this case, one of the main political problems would be nowadays, in the strict sense of the word, the politics of ourselves.[46]

A jazz aesthetic can serve as a model for another hermeneutics of the self, one shaped by an awareness of domination, of limits, and equally shaped by virtuosity, audacity, and joy. Our work in multicultural education, our work in all sorts of political, cultural, and managerial tasks, can be such a differential practice of the self.

If we follow a jazz aesthetic we depart from Foucault, however, at a key juncture. Foucault was critical of humanism and defined it at the "political level" "as any kind of attitude that considers that it is possible to define what the 'happiness of man' is and [the means of] its realization."[47]

A founding principle of a jazz aesthetic is not just the *possibility* of happiness, but the *lived reality* of happiness, virtuosity, and beauty in the face of suffering and limits. Like Foucault, however, jazz does not rest with any particular production of beauty and happiness, any particular expression of virtuosity. The technocratic claim of being able to define in advance the nature of happiness or beauty, and the rules of its emergence, are as foreign to the production of jazz as they are to Foucault's technology of the self.

In order to understand more fully the import of a jazz aesthetic, we can examine other works by African-Americans that explore similar combinations of radical openness to error and critique with innovation and a vital commitment to justice. What is key in all of these works is that critique does not mean denunciation. To point out errors is not to denounce a project, an individual, or a system. It is, rather, participation in the ongoing work of social justice. A punitive or judgmental form of critique assumes that it is not only odd, but somehow shameful, to be embedded in given systems of power and knowledge. The energy of critique in a jazz aesthetic is quite different: our critique emerges from within a social system, and from our affirmation of the possibilities for justice within the present.

In *Fighting Words* sociologist Patricia Hill Collins writes of the imperative of "moving beyond critique" and is critical of the illusions of utopian, linear "grand narratives": "Even as they move people to action, linear visions ironically disempower their followers when the utopic end of the line fails to materialize. Why work for something that one knows can never happen?"[48] While utopian visions may be dangerous, Collins claims that it is equally devastating when people lack any sort of "visionary thinking."

> Social engineering projects that tinker with poverty, homelessness, institutionalized racism, illiteracy, domestic violence, and other social problems through incremental reforms represent technical Band-Aids slapped on historically entrenched, systemic social problems. In the United States, American citizens clamor for recipes, rules, and quick-fix solutions that give the illusion, if not actual evidence, that things are getting better. When short-term solutions fail, apathy and cynicism flourish.
>
> Postmodernism as practiced within some academic disciplines provides a compelling case of a discourse that counsels local, pragmatic action as a stimulus for change but whose actual politics undermines its own critical edge.... Without some larger vision, continual deconstruction that looks at the specific, the concrete, the everyday can foster a nihilism as crippling as that accompanying the death of utopic visions.[49]

Collins argues that it is possible to find an alternative to utopian thinking or cynicism and despair. She analyzes her own childhood experiences and interprets them as the expression of "visionary pragmatism."

> As a child growing up in an African-American, working-class Philadelphia neighborhood, I wondered how my mother and all of the other women on our block kept going. Early each workday, they rode long distances on public transportation to jobs that left them unfulfilled, overworked, and underpaid. Periodically they complained, but more often they counseled practicality and persistence, stressing

the importance of a good education as the route to a better life.... Their solution: we, their daughters, were to become self-reliant and independent.... Despite their practicality, these same Black women also held out hope that things would be better for us.... They always encouraged us to dream.[50]

Collins states that "visionary pragmatism" cannot be reduced to a "predetermined destination," but signifies participation in a larger, ongoing collective struggle.[51]

Thus, although Black women's visionary pragmatism points to a vision, it doesn't prescribe a fixed end point of a universal truth. One never arrives but constantly strives. At the same time, by stressing the pragmatic, it reveals how current actions are part of some larger, more meaningful struggle. Domination succeeds by cutting people off from one another. Actions bring people in touch with the humanity of other struggles by demonstrating that truthful and ethical visions for community cannot be separated from pragmatic struggles on their behalf.[52]

Although she extols the power of this vision, Collins argues that it no longer shapes black civil society.

Sadly, both my childhood neighborhood and the version of visionary pragmatism expressed by its African-American female residents no longer exist.... Since 1970, the quality of life in Black working-class communities like the one I grew up in has changed dramatically in the United States.... Who could have anticipated how deeply the combination of racial desegregation and drugs, violence, and hopelessness in poor African-American neighborhoods would tear the very fabric of Black civil society?... Now that Black women's community work seems increasingly ineffective, what will replace it?[53]

Despite these political changes her goal is to live and work out of this vision: "the fundamental question raised by the Black women on my block remains: how can scholars and/or activists construct critical social theories that prepare future generations for lives that we ourselves have not lived?"[54]

How can our critical social theories inform creative political action? Collins argues that "remain[ing] in a stance of critique leaves one perpetually responding to the terms of someone else's agenda.... The next step lies in moving beyond critique and crafting something new."[55] Like Foucault, and like those who practice a jazz aesthetic, Collins urges us to participate in the ongoing work of action and critique.

What keeps this continuing critique, however, from becoming enervating and nihilistic? The difference lies not in the content of our critiques, but in the form and tone of those critiques. Within a utopian or cynical worldview such critiques function as judgments and denunciations. Within jazz, within Foucault's analytics of power, errors are accepted, not judged; they are seen, noted, and serve as a spur for further acts of virtuosity and creativity.

If we live out of this ethos of visionary pragmatism Collins claims that our theories do not function as "a dogma or a closed system," but "as a story or narrative."[56] Collins adds here a telling element of these narratives:

> Certainly their [the black women on her block] visionary pragmatism was shaped by a commitment to truth, a belief in freedom, a concern for justice, and other ethical ideals. They clearly had an arsenal of pragmatic skills that helped them deal with difficult situations. However, I think that their ability to persist was rooted in a deep love for us. . . . I talk of the power of intense connectedness and of the way that caring deeply for someone can foster a revolutionary politics.[57]

What does visionary pragmatism look like in practice? We can see such an exercise of political power grounded in deep connection in the work of Ronald Dellums. In *Lying Down with the Lions* Dellums recounts the history of his work in politics and the commitments and strategies that have shaped his work. His career is marked by the connections described by Patricia Hill Collins: he was continually open to listening to the voices of those who were marginalized and exploited, open to hearing their stories of injustice and hope.

> While many with whom I shared governance on the Berkeley City Council and then later in Congress would decry the protests, demonstrations, and other expressions of outrage as a discordant noise – incoherent and strident – I heard a chorus. I heard harmony in the claims for equality by African Americans, by Native Americans . . . and by Latinos and Asian Americans. I heard the counterpoint added by the assertions of women, lesbians and gay men, and the disabled, all of whom were being denied full participation in the economic, social, and political life of the community. I heard syncopation from the environmentalists and from peace movement activists, who were seeking to defend the life of the planet from ecocide and its people from self-destruction. I found inspiration in this music of protest and I believed that its powerful voices deserved representation in a body that all too often seemed to refuse to listen or to respond. In her essay "Where is the Rage?" June Jordan, an African American and an extraordinary activist, poet, and professor, captures the legacy of that era: "unabashed moral certitude and the purity – the incredible outgoing energy – of righteous rage."[58]

Although affirming the "moral certitude" and "righteous rage" of those who are oppressed, Dellums's own political engagement led him away from self-righteous denunciations of other people and social structures. In responding to those voices of suffering and rage, Dellums recounts that he had early on to make a choice: was he going to be a "rhetorical activist" or "an effective legislator committed to securing social change through the process of governance?"[59] Dellums chose the latter path and describes for us the elements of being an effective legislator committed to social justice. The first is simple in principle yet daunting in practice. He learned from his mother "that you have to start by dealing with people as they are and seek to change their views from where they start, not from where you want them to be. It was a lesson that would be invaluable in both my professional and political careers."[60] This insight was reinforced by his professional training as a social worker. "Another professional tenet I'd learned forbade either condemning or condoning behavior: by forbidding passing judgment on a person, this principle allowed the social worker to focus on understanding behavior and its roots, and better understanding enhances the prospect of problem solving."[61]

Dellums learned the importance of these principles early in his political career. In a speech in Milwaukee in 1971 he referred to colleagues in the House of Representatives as "mediocre prima donnas," "with no real understanding of the pain and human misery being visited upon our people."[62] Back on the floor of the house, Representative Wayne Hayes verified that the statement was accurate, and then asked Dellums, "I just wonder if you then want a bunch of mediocre prima donnas to pay more serious attention to your amendment?"[63]

The lessons here were clear:

> I realized I could not afford to let myself become cynical – which was the implication of my statement in Milwaukee. I had not come to Congress to attack and alienate my colleagues; I had come to challenge their ideas. I needed to step back from the personal. . . . I had to return to the educative role that Dr. King had laid out in his challenge to leadership. I needed to become better informed, to understand my opponents and be able to best them in open debate. I had to bring them along with me, not demand that they reject themselves. . . . I could not be content with a role as the radical outsider if I wanted people to pay heed to our radical ideas. I needed to develop arguments that my fellow legislators could take home to *their* constituents and imagine articulating at *their* constituents' day meetings.[64]

Dellums writes of the challenge this poses for political work, and repeats Martin Luther King's understanding of transformative social critique.

> His exhortation to all to translate the "jangling discourse of stridency and discontent," to deliver the message in terms that did not disturb the ear and therefore could be heard, related to my experiences in the antipoverty campaign and on the city council. I was beginning to learn that if you proffer the message and people are turned off by how you say it, then you are talking to yourself. You need to conceptualize and articulate issues in terms that allow you to be heard, terms that invite people to come to your side. That was King's strategy – take the stridency of the antiwar movement and replace it with the tones of the civil rights movement so that people of all political persuasions could hear the beauty and truth of the argument.[65]

The form of Dellums's work was educational and transformative. There was confrontation, of course, but not in the form of polemics, but, rather, in a form that invited debate, dialogue, and further discussion.

Another key aspect of Dellums's work was "moving beyond critique" to provide alternatives to what he and others saw as destructive political policies.

As he introduced his first budget to the Congress, President Reagan issued a challenge to potential opponents: "If you don't like or cannot support this budget, pose an alternative." Reagan perhaps understood that it is easier to oppose something than to make the effort to develop and successfully promote a comprehensive alternative. Especially for those used to being outside the system, it is significantly easier to concur in opposition than to unite with others to do the hard work of developing a program, building a constituency, and defending it against criticism. The CBC [Congressional Black Caucus] was not afraid. . . . Under Walter Fauntroy's leadership, the CBC agreed to develop, draft, and propose an entire budget alternative.[66]

While his political goal was coalition, Dellums also argued against "compromising too soon." Genuine coalition is built on "educating others and [being] educated oneself," it takes time, and it is a process without "guarantees of success or definitive and lasting progress."[67] Dellums is forthright about the continual possibility of failure and defeat. This shapes his views of "the role of the progressive":

> Whether in victory or defeat, the challenge is not so much to prevail at the moment as it is to remain faithful to the ideas and to the struggle, and to refuse to yield to the powerful temptation of cynicism. People often ask themselves, "Will this succeed?" "Will this be effective?" . . . Whether I have been successful or effective I leave to other people to assess. Others ask, "Why bother? You can't change anything." At the end of the day, I never felt that I could guarantee the effectiveness of an action, or control an outcome. What I did have control over, however, was my own faithfulness to the ideas and principles of our movement, and a willingness to do my work diligently in pursuit of the legislative goals that could achieve them. Simply put, showing up and being prepared for the fight is the first step. And sometimes that alone has powerful unanticipated consequences.[68]

Dellums's acknowledgment of "unanticipated consequences" is crucial. His is a philosophy of fallibility, of accountability, of unanticipated and unpredictable consequences.

Like Collins, he argues that our successes do not solve all problems for all times. Rather, there will be challenges in the future to what we accomplished, as well as challenges that we are not able to foresee.

> The generation that came of age in the 1960s believed we could change the world – and in many ways we did. We ended a war, prevented the deployment of the MX and Pershing missiles. We forced the Reagan administration back to the arms negotiation table. We secured passage of important environmental laws. We ended legal discrimination against racial minorities and helped to break down some of the barriers that limit the choices of women, gays and lesbians, persons with disabilities, and others who have historically been oppressed or exploited.

> Everything we have struggled for remains under attack – and in some measure it always will. Some will always reject equality as a first principle and will do no more than pay lip service to the idea that the common good means including everybody.

... Some will always believe that war is the inevitable solution to international affairs. ... Some will always seek to consume rather than preserve the environment. ... And so it will go.[69]

Dellums's work is a manifestation of the pleasure of fluid, educational, political engagement. It is an engagement that maintained his connection with those who are oppressed and also created connection with opponents who became allies in the work for justice. He recounts the joy of finding common ground with people who had earlier rejected his political analyses, and the joy of maintaining connection with others also committed to justice.

> After over thirty years I have learned that one doesn't make a difference by oneself. ... We did it, when millions of people took the time to coalesce into a mighty force that could bend the political process to its will. ... Linking hands with them [his constituency] and with countless other activists across the nation and around the world in the service of their legislative agenda has been the highest privilege imaginable.[70]

In the words of Michel Foucault, Dellums's work can be seen as critical engagement with "transformable singularities."[71] What, then, does all of this mean for social justice? Contrast the jazz-inflected ethos of visionary pragmatism with the apocalyptic fervor of polemics. If we examine any exercise of political will it is, by definition, limited in range and scope. Take, for example, one political challenge: developing forms of multicultural education that address the systemic, communal, cultural, and individual effects of centuries of oppression. We may develop an effective program in a school or school district, and questions still arise. Will this be implemented everywhere? How do we know that change will effectively occur on all pertinent levels – individual attitudes and behaviors, systemic changes in social values, and in which groups have access to cultural, economic, and political power, institutional change – the creation of institutions that systematically and self-critically embody these values? These limits, held in a jazz form, do not create cynicism or despair. One face of cynicism is the argument that any action is limited and inadequate. None of our policies or interventions simultaneously sweep away the old corrupt social system and instantaneously implement a glorious new world of justice and freedom. Our response to the criticism that we have not ushered in a new age, that we do not know the scope or depth of our actions, is simple: the critics are right. We are not the members of the revolutionary vanguard; we are not the harbingers of the long-awaited apocalypse. We are, rather, grateful daughters and sons, mothers and fathers, friends and colleagues, artists "tying the knot with life."

Living within the ethos of jazz, living within the framework of visionary pragmatism, is profoundly freeing. In an interview in 1980 conducted by Christian Delacampagne, Michel Foucault points to the contrast between a politics founded on "lament" and one founded on self-critical affirmation.

> CD Let's risk a few concrete propositions. If everything is going badly, where do we make a start?
>
> MF But everything *isn't* going badly. In any case, I believe we shouldn't confuse useful criticism of things with repetitive jeremiads against people. As for concrete propositions, they can't just make an appearance like gadgets, unless certain general principles are accepted first. And the first of such general principles should be that the right to knowledge [*droit au savoir*] must not be reserved to a particular age group or to certain categories of people, but that one must be able to exercise it constantly and in many different ways.[72]

Foucault understands the impulse to remain critical, but argues that there is another form of engagement possible.

> It is understandable that some people should weep over the present void and hanker instead, in the world of ideas, after a little monarchy. But those who, for once in their lives, have found a new tone, a new way of looking, a new way of doing, those people, I believe, will never feel the need to lament that the world is in error, that history is filled with people of no consequence.[73]

If we begin our political and intellectual work with the jazz form of continually expanding dialogue, with an expanding range of dialogue partners, our energy can more easily be expended in action, and not in cynical or nihilistic critique.

We can "tie the knot with life" because of our participation in particular communities, particular narratives of connection, of love, respect, self-critique, and virtuosity. The meaning of this form of social engagement can be seen not only in jazz, but in the approach to social justice taken by some Native Americans. The "Beauty Way," as described by Carol Lee Sanchez, for example, is an "analytics of power" that "multiplies signs of existence." Sanchez argues that "focusing on destructive forces all the time causes feelings of despair and, too often, a sense of powerlessness to do anything to change these dreadful circumstances."[74] She offers instead the "Beauty Way," a technology of the self grounded in practices of respect, self-critique, and gratitude.

> Center yourself in the region where you make your home and introduce yourself to the spirits of your place. Greet the plant, creature, mineral, wind, water, earth, and sky spirits.... If ... you will attune yourself to your homeplace, and if you make it a point to acknowledge your nonhuman surroundings on a daily basis (several times a day, preferably), your environment will begin to respond to you. ... Welcome all your relatives into your immediate family. Approach each day in a sacred manner and with a healthy sense of humor. Our relatives will help us if we ask them to help. Our relatives will forgive us if we ask for their forgiveness and make a serious commitment not to repeat our previous mistakes.... If we all open our hearts and minds to this rich legacy, we may discover many creative solutions to our ecological dilemmas.[75]

To work for a fitting response, but not a final or definitive response, is to respond with beauty and evocative creativity to the ambiguity and domination of life. This work is not cynical, nihilistic or utopian. It is not triumphalistic, but evocative, for it embodies an intelligent, vital engagement with the complexity of life.

Notes

"Lush Life" is the title of a composition by Billy Strayhorn. Copyright 1949 (renewed) by Tempo Music Inc./Music Sales Corporation (ASCAP). It is also the title of the biography of Strayhorn: *Lush Life: A Biography of Billy Strayhorn* by David Hajdu (New York: North Pint Press, 1996).

1 Michel Foucault, "The Masked Philosopher," interview conducted on April 6–7, 1980 by Christian Delacampagne, reprinted in *Michel Foucault, Ethics Subjectivity and Truth, Essential Works of Foucault 1954–1984, Volume I*, ed. Paul Rabinow (New York: New Press, 1997).

2 Michel Foucault, "Confinement, Psychiatry, Prison," in *Politics, Philosophy, Culture: Interviews and Other Writings, 1977–1984*, ed. L. D. Kritzman (New York: Routledge, 1988), p. 209.

3 Michel Foucault, "The Concern for Truth," in *Politics, Philosophy, Culture: Interviews and Other Writings 1977–1984*, ed. L. D. Kritzman (New York: Routledge, 1988), p. 265.

4 Foucault, "The Masked Philosopher," p. 326.

5 Michel Foucault, "Polemics, Politics, and Problematizations: An Interview with Michel Foucault," conducted by Paul Rabinow in May 1984; in Rabinow, *Michel Foucault, Ethics*, pp. 111–12.

6 Ibid, p. 113. An example of the distortions caused by polemics can be seen in my erroneous interpretation of Foucault in *Sweet Dreams in America: Making Ethics and Spirituality Work* (New York: Routledge, 1999), pp. 9–15. In that book I contrasted a Foucault who denied the possibility of happiness, who valued transgression and suffering, with a jazz aesthetic founded in the affirmation of finitude. This interpretation distorted Foucault's own very clear definition of transgression as that which "affirms limited being." In the same essay Foucault also makes it clear that transgression has nothing to do with the scandalous or subversive: "A Preface to Transgression," in *Language, Counter-memory, Practice: Selected Essays and Interviews by Michel Foucault*, ed. Donald F. Bouchard (Ithaca, NY: Cornell University Press, 1977), p. 35. Even in his discussion of sado-masochism, the Iranian revolution of 1978/9, and the demonstrations in Paris in May 1968, Foucault's focus is not violence or cruelty, but the vital expansion of possibilities. For me to cite James Miller's paraphrase of Foucault's ethos as "be cruel" led to an inaccurate presentation of Foucault's work. In his discussion of sado-masochism Foucault addresses not suffering, but "relationships of differentiation, of creation, of innovation." He states quite clearly that "the S & M ghetto in San Francisco is a good example of a community that has experimented with, and formed an identity, around pleasure": see "Sex, Power and the Politics of Identity," in Rabinow, *Michel Foucault, Ethics*, pp. 166–7. In a similar vein, what was thought-provoking to Foucault in the Iranian revolution

was not violence, but a "political spirituality" ("Iran: The Spirit of a World Without Spirit," in Kritzman, *Politics, Philosophy, Culture*, pp. 211–24). Furthermore, while some of the participants in the revolts in Paris in May 1968 may not have known what they were about, and were merely caught up in the joy of destruction, what is significant for Foucault is not the violence *per se* but the opening of new possibilities and questions. ("Polemics, Politics, and Problematizations," p. 115.)

7   Michel Foucault, "Who Are You, Professor Foucault? (1967)," reprinted in *Religion and Culture: Michel Foucault*, ed. Jeremy R. Carrette (New York: Routledge, 1999), pp. 100–1.
8   Steven Weinberg, "Five and a Half Utopias," *The Atlantic Monthly*, vol. 285, no. 1 (January 2000), p. 108.
9   Ibid, p. 109.
10 Ibid.
11 Ibid, p. 110.
12 Ibid.
13 Ibid, p. 112.
14 Ibid.
15 Ibid, p. 113.
16 Michel Foucault, "On the Genealogy of Ethics: An Overview of Work in Progress," interview conducted by Paul Rabinow and Hubert Dreyfus in April 1983, in Rabinow, *Michel Foucault, Ethics*, p. 256.
17 James D. Faubion, "Introduction," *Michel Foucault: Aesthetics, Method and Epistemology, Essential Works of Foucault, Volume Two*, ed. James D. Faubion (New York: New Press, 1998), p. xxxii.
18 Michel Foucault, "Life: Experience and Science," in Faubion, *Michel Foucault: Aesthetics*, p. 476.
19 Michel Foucault, "The Ethics of the Concern of the Self as a Practice of Freedom," in Rabinow, *Michel Foucault, Ethics*, p. 298.
20 See, for example, the discussion of conflicts among women in *Making Face, Making Soul*, ed. Gloria Anzaldua (San Francisco: Spinsters, 1990) and *Conflicts in Feminism*, ed. Marianne Hirsch and Evelyn Fox Keller (New York: Routledge, 1990).
21 Michel Foucault, "Pastoral Power and Political Reason (1979)," in Carrette, *Religion and Culture*, p. 152.
22 Michel Foucault, "Structuralism and Post-structuralism," in Faubion, *Michel Foucault: Aesthetics*, p. 44.
23 "Michel Foucault and Zen: A Stay in a Zen Temple (1978)," trans. Richard Townsend, in Carrette, *Religion and Culture*, p. 113.
24 Patrick Chamoiseau, *Texaco*, trans. Rose-Myriam Rejois and Val Vinokurov (New York: Pantheon Books, 1997), p. 294.
25 Michel Foucault, "Pierre Boulez, Passing Through the Screen," in Faubion, *Michel Foucault: Aesthetics*, p. 242.
26 Ibid.
27 Michel Foucault, "What is Enlightenment?" in Rabinow, *Michel Foucault, Ethics*, p. 319.
28 Stanley Crouch, "Wherever He Went, Joy was Sure to Follow," *New York Times*, March 12, 2000, p. 16.
29 Krin Gabbard, "Introduction: Writing the Other History," in *Representing Jazz*, ed. Krin Gabbard (Durham, NC: Duke University Press, 1995), p. 2.

30 Ralph Ellison, *Shadow and Act* (London: Secker and Warburg, 1964), p. 190.
31 Mary Lou Williams, as quoted by Neil Leonard, *Jazz: Myth and Religion* (New York: Oxford University Press, 1987), p. 58.
32 Hajdu, *Lush Life*, p. xii.
33 Ibid, pp. 250, 36.
34 Crouch, *New York Times*, p. 1.
35 James Baldwin, as cited by Theophus Smith, *Conjuring Culture: Biblical Formations of Black America* (New York: Oxford University Press, 1994), p. 123.
36 Eric Lott, "Double V, Double-Time: Bebop's Politics of Style," in *Jazz Among the Discourses*, ed. Krin Gabbard (Durham, NC: Duke University Press, 1995), p. 243.
37 James Collier, *Jazz: The American Theme Song* (New York: Oxford University Press, 1993), p. 52.
38 Karen Baker-Fletcher and Garth Kasimu Baker-Fletcher, *My Sister, My Brother: Womanist and Xodus God-Talk* (Maryknoll, NY: Orbis, 1997), p. 204.
39 Ibid, p. 184.
40 Ann Douglas, "Feel the City's Pulse? Be-bop, Man!" *New York Times*, August 28, 1998, B26.
41 Hajdu, *Lush Life*, p. 148.
42 Jonathan Rieder, *New York Times Book Review*, December 26, 1998, p. 15.
43 Michel Foucault, "Technologies of the Self," from a seminar given at the University of Vermont in October 1982, in Rabinow, *Michel Foucault, Ethics*, pp. 224–5.
44 Michel Foucault, "On the Genealogy of Ethics: An Overview of Work in Progress," in Rabinow, *Michel Foucault, Ethics*, p. 262.
45 Michel Foucault, "Technologies of the Self," p. 224.
46 Michel Foucault, "About the Beginnings of the Hermeneutics of the Self (1980)," in Carrette, *Religion and Culture*, pp. 180–1.
47 Michel Foucault, "Who Are you, Professor Foucault?" p. 101.
48 Patricia Hill Collins, *Fighting Words: Black Women and the Search for Justice* (Minneapolis: University of Minnesota Press, 1998), pp. 187–9.
49 Ibid, p. 189.
50 Ibid, pp. 187–8.
51 Ibid, pp. 189–90.
52 Ibid.
53 Ibid, pp. 190–1.
54 Ibid, p. 191.
55 Ibid, pp. 194–5.
56 Ibid, p. 200.
57 Ibid.
58 Ronald V. Dellums and H. Lee Halterman, *Lying Down with the Lions: Public Life from the Streets of Oakland to the Halls of Power* (Boston, MA: Beacon Press, 2000), pp. 2–3.
59 Ibid, p. 76.
60 Ibid, p. 17.
61 Ibid, p. 30.
62 Ibid, p. 74.
63 Ibid, p. 75.
64 Ibid, p. 76.
65 Ibid, p. 49.
66 Ibid, p. 107.

67　Ibid, p. 70.
68　Ibid, pp. 144–5.
69　Ibid, pp. 200–1.
70　Ibid, p. 201.
71　Foucault, preface to the *History of Sexuality*, vol. 2 in *Ethics*, p. 201.
72　Foucault, "The Masked Philosopher," p. 326.
73　Ibid, p. 327.
74　Carol Lee Sanchez, "Animal, Vegetable, Mineral: The Sacred Connection," in *Ecofeminism and the Sacred*, ed. Carol J. Adams (New York: Continuum, 1993), p. 226.
75　Ibid, pp. 226–7.

PART II
Ethics

6	The Midwinter Sacrifice	107
7	Postmodernity and Religious Plurality: Is a Common Global Ethic Possible or Desirable?	131
8	The Christian Difference, or Surviving Postmodernism	144
9	Justice and Prudence: Principles of Order in the Platonic City	162
10	Visiting Prisoners	177
11	Suffering and Incarnation	192
12	Earth God: Cultivating the Spirit in an Ecocidal Culture	209

CHAPTER 6
The Midwinter Sacrifice

John Milbank

For some time now John Milbank has been writing essays on the themes of sacrifice and the gift. He is not the first to see that there is a relationship between these things – both Mauss and Derrida in their different ways have been exercised by the mutual workings of their logics – but Milbank weaves these anthropological and philosophical construals (and Marion's theological analyses) into a meditation upon the nature and operation of Christian ethics itself. "The Midwinter Sacrifice" is one of these periodic essays, which leaves me to surmise that Milbank's next major project is to do for ethical theory what he has already done in his first major book for social theory.

The repercussions of that first work, *Theology and Social Theory: Beyond Secular Reason* (Oxford, 1990), are still being registered in postgraduate theses and academic publications. The implications of the rhetorical method, the theological vision, the incisive critique of fields as diverse as sociology, political theory, and ethics, and thinkers as distinctive as Durkheim and Deleuze, are still being mulled over. There is no doubt in my mind that the book will establish itself as a landmark in twentieth-century British theology. And as the academic machinery turns slowly and reflectively over its pages, Milbank adds to the *oeuvre*. In 1996 a collection of erstwhile essays was melded into a further thesis entitled *The Word Made Strange* (Oxford, 1996). This is a key work, I suggest, for appreciating the theological vision informing much of Milbank's passion, his criticism, and his concern with recovering the Christian tradition. Here, in brief, is a *summa* (Milbank is nothing if not ambitious in his thinking), drawing together views of the world and the *polis*, language and representation, into a Christian account of Christ as Logos, and the Trinity as the mediation (and articulation) of difference.

Where Milbank's postmodernism expresses itself is in the strangeness of the Word that can now receive expression. Although he is critical of postmodern thinking, his project issues from the critiques of modernity with its master

> narratives and liberal humanism. He moves beyond but remains indebted to Deleuze, for example, and it is Derrida (with whom he disagrees) who enables him to articulate his distinctively Christian position. Finding the right debating partner is important; many of Milbank's are postmodern thinkers.
>
> In 1998, along with Catherine Pickstock and myself, he edited *Radical Orthodoxy: A New Theology*, a book which launched both a series of titles and a new Christian sensibility. He published in the series a joint book with his former postgraduate student Catherine Pickstock, *Truth in Aquinas* (London, 2000). It is another important book. Throughout his work Aquinas and Augustine have been the Christian theologians most appealed to. He once called his project a postmodern theology in an Augustinian vein. In recovering the tradition, in voicing again the premodern in the postmodern (not *as* and *for the sake of* being premodern, but as an indication of the Christian worldview *per se*), Milbank's project is both genealogical and constructive. His very act of writing is a Christian *poeisis* and an act of continuing the Christian tradition, of bearing a past towards the possibilities of a *new* future and a final, *eschatological* future.

Usually, Christianity is seen as suppressing "moral luck," or the idea that, to a degree at least, we require good fortune if we are to be good. However, in this essay, I want to argue, to the contrary, that Christianity embraces moral luck to such an extreme degree that it transforms all received ideas of the ethical.

In the course of this argument, I shall try to show that these received ideas of the ethical, which may or may not permit some play to "moral luck," all ascribe to a "sacrificial economy." And that they do so in two different variants: either in terms of the giving up of the lesser for the greater, or else of a more radical notion of absolute sacrifice of self for the other, without any "return" for, or of the self, in any guise whatsoever. The second variant, which would usually see itself as *escaping* the sacrificial economy of *do ut des*, but which I will argue is but this same economy taken to its logical extreme, has been recently espoused in different but profoundly analogous ways by Jan Patocka, Emmanuel Levinas, and Jacques Derrida.[1] Against this view, which now enjoys a wide consensus, I shall argue that a self-sacrificial view of morality is first, immoral, second, impossible, and third, a deformation, not the fulfilment, as Patocka echoed by Derrida claims, of the Christian gospel.

The article has two parts: first, a consideration of "moral luck" accompanied by an intermittent analysis of Shakespeare's late play *The Winter's Tale*. Second, a more systematic spelling out of the implications of this analysis for a consideration of "morality, gift and sacrifice."

I

Let me first rehearse, briefly, the usual arguments concerning "moral luck."[2] Morality, for the Greeks, concerned the attainment of the truly happy life. True happiness was regarded as secure, abiding happiness, impregnable to assault. Hence it came to be associated with self-possession and "autarchy" or *self-government*, whether of the city or of the self, and increasingly of the immaterial soul, deemed to be free of need. However, there was a tension implicit in this notion of a secure happiness. Happiness usually concerns reception of gifts from without, and a total immunity would lock a person within a tower where neither sorrow *nor* joy would be able to gain entrance. Hence Aristotle, for at least part of his output, articulates a compromise: the ethical life is to be found in the *relative* security of the *polis*, and within the *polis* in the *relative* security of the well-born, good-looking man, owning sufficient store of goods to permit him to exercise a virtuous generosity, and *through this* to sustain his relative power and independence. This example indicates that while the Greeks fundamentally defined the ethical in opposition to fortune or luck they were sometimes prepared to admit, to a degree, fortune or luck as a necessary precondition for the ethical: a circumstance which Martha Nussbaum terms "the fragility of goodness," although she repeatedly loses sight of the fact that a security of self-possessed good *remains* Aristotle's fundamental determining notion. It is nonetheless true that, for Aristotle, just as we need good fortune to begin to be good, so we must continue to enjoy it if we are to remain good. If we fall, for example, under the rule of a tyrant who commands us either to betray the city or else to allow a member of our own family to die, we have, by bad stroke of fortune, been tragically removed from the context in which we can continue to be unambiguously virtuous people.[3]

The Greeks therefore, *first of all* in defining the ethical goal as secure happiness, deemed the good and fortune to be opposites, but in the *second* place did tend to admit an element of moral luck. And after all, their very deliberations involved a presupposition of the supreme moral luck of being born Greek and not barbarian. However, in later times of greater political anxiety, thinkers sought a more absolute total security of the inner citadel of the soul. Since such security precludes joy as well as sorrow, the goal of happiness tended to be redefined as a passionless *tranquillity*: this roughly speaking is the stoic position.[4] Now how, in this late antique period and later, has it stood by contrast with Christianity? It will usually be noted that Christianity permitted no such stoic security: the Christian was not offered any inner refuge against what time may bring, nor was an utterly passionless (in the sense of emotionless) life regarded as desirable. It may, however, also be noted that, for a Christian, "to be good" was dependent on "fortune" in the new guise of the grace of God. Such grace does involve external circumstance since it is in part externally mediated, and furthermore it renders *even the inner citadel of the soul* subject to an arrival from without. This observation already introduces a note of considerable uncertainty into construals of the Christian stance *vis-à-vis* moral luck. However, it is also usually concluded that Christianity radically extirpates this thematic, since it holds that every person, whatever their birth and whatever their degree of learning (so one does not have to live the minority life of a philosopher) can always, in every situation, respond in a moral fashion – even in an unambiguously moral fashion. This is partly because virtue itself has now been redefined:

the more apparently "passive" modes of humility, patience, forgiveness, suffering unto death, even the non-despairing endurance of tragic dilemma, are modes universally available in every situation. These virtues can be perfectly performed by us "alone"; they can be offered to the world as gifts all the more secure in their gratuity by the possibility of their derelict abandonment through the refusals of others.[5] One might, perhaps, qualify this in the direction of saying that one needs the initial fortune to belong to the *community* of such a novel form of practice: that to be able to give and forgive one must first have the sense that one is oneself given and forgiven; that one owes in gratitude a certain return and a certain repetition. In other words, it is true that we never entirely originate our own virtuous acts – they are responses, even mere continuations in the face of the gift that we have always first received. However, this point is after all but a small qualification, since God, for the Bible, has never been without witnesses, and the church through typology and prolepsis is a universal reality. No one anywhere, by virtue of mere human birth alone, would appear to be entirely outside the logic of donation, which seems to permit a certain immunity to moral luck.

Now I do not, without qualification, accept the above account as true. However, supposing, for the moment, that it is, there is one all-important point to take note of. This is that Christian ethics, *so construed*, retains the antique requirement of security, and, indeed *maximizes* it, yet wrenches it away from its original logical foundation in the pursuit of happiness which even the stoics still followed – albeit to the point of logical collapse. Christianity apparently still thinks of the ethical life as the deepest identity, *as that of which we cannot be dispossessed*, and therefore as that which we have *no excuse* to lack, and yet this inner possession may not make us happy, at least in any recognizable worldly sense, and according to later mystical writers celebrating "indifference," whose legacy passes to Kant, not necessarily happy in any sense at all.[6] Christian ethics, on this latter construal, has ceased to pursue "happiness" and instead has become "other-regarding."[7] The orientation to the other, by intentional gesture, is that which we alone can own. There is a latent paradox here, because the priority given to the other at the limit demands the laying down of our own life. Hence what we "own," the ethical, is nothing other than radical self-dispossession. However – and this will become relevant for my wider argument – this paradox does *not* necessarily overthrow the logic of ownership: to the contrary it dialectically preserves it at the limits of contradiction. The idea of a non-eudaemonistic other-regarding ethic is finally that, to be ethical, is to offer your life as a gift without hope of return in time (since your offering outreaches your death). Such a stance remains always possible, for what we absolutely cannot be robbed of is indeed (as Heidegger realized) our own death.[8] Hence also we cannot be robbed of the will to offer ourselves, if necessary, in death.

This account of Christian ethics as "other-regarding" appears then, at first glance, to be logically coherent. It regards the ethical attitude as essentially one of altruism, which is only *guaranteed* by the gesture of self-sacrifice, the willingness to give oneself even unto death. It is *this* gesture, or the latent will to this gesture, of which we cannot be deprived, which appears absolutely immune to "moral luck."

However, at this point we need already to note something else. If this *is* the Christian stance *par excellence*, then it can be readily secularized, as Patocka argued, because omission of the hope for resurrection and eternal life will tend to *purify* the strictly other-regarding motive still further. Thus Patocka, and Derrida ambiguously in his wake, urge on us a "heretical" Christianity which is nonetheless really a demythologized one, more Christian than Christianity so far. In this new, perfected Christianity, the injunction of St Luke not to invite to feasts those who can invite you back (Luke 14.26), thereby guaranteeing the austerity of your giving as "unilateral" and self-sacrificial – is no longer to be contaminated at the eschatological level by the Lucan promise that such conduct will receive a reward from our heavenly father.[9]

Hence, if the construal of Christian ethics as most essentially "other-regarding," and in consequence sacrificial, is valid, then it might well be the case that Christianity's true destiny is to be demythologized and secularized.

However, this construal may be called into question. *Should* one read Christian ethics as abandoning the antique concern with happiness, and yet sustaining its requirement for secure self-possession (even if this is now reduced to the will to the gesture of absolute non self-possession)? Or *can* one construe things precisely the other way round? That is to say, that Christianity, unlike stoicism, was able to stick with and even augment the goal of happiness or beatitude through a novel *abandonment* of the goal of self-possession, *even* in its mode of ethical reduction? And along with the notion of self-possession, to abandon also the cognate themes of self-achievement, self-control, and above all self-government, which rule nearly all our inherited ideas of what is ethical? This is what I eventually wish to argue.

Let us, however, for the moment strategically remain with our two inherited notions of the ethical (as identified by Robert Spaemann) which are *both* linked to the supremacy of self-possession and self-government. On the one hand, classical eudaemonism, on the other hand, post-Enlightenment (perhaps post-Renaissance) other-regarding ethics whether Kantian or utilitarian (the latter at least in its altruistic versions (Sidgewick)). I now want to show (drawing freely on Spaemann, Derrida, and Bernard Williams) how both notions are subject to inner dialectical collapse (or deconstruction) in a fashion concerning precisely their attempts to manage and control "fortune."

First of all, eudaemonism. Can one secure happiness? No, it seems that it is never present as secure, and so never present as genuine happiness that need not turn its face away from reality to seek refuge in illusion. At most we have only "virtual happiness." Why? First, because to open ourselves to the most and most genuine happiness (for example, one including friendship, as Aristotle stipulated) risks also the greatest ultimate sorrow, and therefore for self-protection we must remain to a degree self-enclosed and will never be free from the anxious calculus of precisely to what degree this should be the case; exactly what balance of adventure and security we should espouse. Second, because happiness is not punctual;

as Aristotle realized, it is rather the course of a whole life. Yet we never get to the end of our lives, nor their upshots; we are bound to "die before our time," and only others will read our lives as a whole, rather than as still open to further development. It is for them to say "happy" or "unhappy," yet they *cannot* say this, since, as Spaemann argues, happiness retains something of a secret unpredictability and inviolability relating to *my* specific physical body, whose movements are not entirely subject to cultural control.[10] Third, happiness is comparative. To take Spaemann's example: for the Portuguese poet Fernando Pessoa in one of his poems, the shepherd in Arcadia is happy *over there*, for *me*, the non-Arcadian.[11] But no more than the shepherd will experience his own death, does he (even in Arcadia) know, reflectively and consciously, his own pastoral joy. Again, it seems that one's own happiness is known only by the other and yet it is still not *his* happiness. Happiness is nowhere replete and therefore never itself: nowhere in life and nowhere in space. Likewise in the fourth place, it is nowhere in time. For happiness must be present to us now, yet now is never, but always over or yet to come. Perhaps, indeed, happiness might be just this stretched-out anxiety, this "joy over time." But not, at least, in our time, since for now the past is always contaminated by loss and mourning, and the future by fear and anxiety. Happiness must be present, without these negations, yet *cannot* be so. And in these four ways, not just *ordinary joys* remain illusive, but *also* our tranquil enjoyment and realization of a consistent ethical excellence (or even of an unperturbed entry into impersonal communion with abiding Platonic forms).

Antiquity, therefore, early and late, still underrated the contamination of morality by luck or fortune. How stands it, by contrast, with modern, "other-regarding morality" from Kant and Bentham to Levinas and Parfitt? Its plight is equally dire. First of all, there is Hegel's critique of Kant, in its broad thrust: as soon as we act, with patience, humility, forgiveness, suffering unto death and so forth, we run the risk that this act will be mistaken, misinterpreted, and abused (perhaps because we have badly *expressed* it, since aesthetics can always contaminate and ruin the ethical imperative) in a fashion that is both not our fault, and yet somewhat our fault, because of our tactlessness, and often both in a disentanglable fashion. What use then, are these derelict, abandoned acts: are they, as Jean-Luc Marion would have it,[12] still perfect gifts, since he takes the content of a gift to be a mere "sign" of the real ethereal gift of intention or more fundamentally the unobjectifiable passage of the "self-giving" gift itself? Surely, one should argue, they are not, for intentions (or rather passages) are only ever instantiated in signs and gestures and are therefore always somewhat particular, somewhat content-specific. The abandoned, useless gift is to the contrary reduced to the most *general* and therefore impotent, unintending invitation to be patient, humble, suffer unto death and so on. Abandoned, inert, without upshot, it is reversely corroded even in its most original intention – it is, in short, *objectified*. A duty, therefore, which fails to make the other happy surely ceases to be a moral act (and perhaps not just Hegel, but even Kant himself remained haunted by this thought). Other-regarding ethics *cannot* ignore happiness, yet happiness is often the child of whim and circumstance.

Therefore "other-regarding ethics" is also undermined, as we have seen, by the self-implosion of the notion of pure duty. But hard on the heels of this "loss of duty" comes also "loss of self." Can we possess ourselves as ethical through a sacrificial self-offering in death? If this alone proves the good, then we *need* the misfortunes of others to demonstrate our worth – and therefore this seemingly ethical self is utterly lost in its secret longing for the sorrows of others as the occasions of its own heroism. Moreover, *till* we are martyrs, we can never be sure that we possess ourselves as ethical, since martyrdom is the paradigmatic test – passing it, at the end beyond ourselves, we also lose ourselves and *never* come to possess a good will, ever. For always, in the next gasp before expiry we *may* despair, we may recant, we may come to curse the very one we think we propose to save. And if even the *dying* self is not immune to luck (the "weakness of the flesh" in dying) then *a fortiori* we have lost the living self who enjoys his life but is subject to still greater uncertainties and contingencies.

These contingencies are, supremely, the *needs of others*. In the case of the moral subject of consequentialist ethics this subject is liable to limitless persecution by the needs of others, who are regarded contradictorally as *not* subject to this persecution, but as somehow already in the endlessly, postponed telos of "enjoyment."[13] And just the same "bad infinite" haunts the seemingly greater refinement of Kantian and Levinasian ethics. Both exhibit the same obliteration of the living self in the form of the circular pointlessness of a subjectivity constituted through its respect for the (free or suffering) subjectivity of the other which is only subjective in returning that respect. Modern ethics, just because it enthrones altruism, is pathological in its degree of obliteration of the possibility of *consummation*, or of the beginning of beatitude in a time simply to be enjoyed, and a conviviality to be celebrated by the living self.

However, if, as we have seen, the living and dying self of self-sacrificial ethics is not after all secure – save in a bizarre kind of hope for a gesture of martyrdom which can never arrive, which is just how Derrida construes it[14] – nor, in the third place, is the self of the other whom we are supposed to "regard" secure in its turn. Insofar as the other is alive, I will tend to take her for granted, and her visibility (here I am strategically somewhat agreeing with Levinas), will tend to make her "part" of me, like a kind of extension of my body. She cannot, by appearing, fully appear as other. Her otherness will rather emerge in her absence, especially her death, which partially defines her uniqueness and non-dispossessibility. When she is gone, I mourn, and first come to value her as irreplaceable, in a way that I could *not* have done while she lived. But now she can no longer speak to me and so she has emerged as irreplaceable in that very moment in which she has lost that *other* crucial aspect of otherness, namely free spontaneity. Indeed, a mourning which neglects this second aspect of otherness can degenerate into the most ferocious mode of possession of the other. And moreover, mourning, although *it alone* tends to *reveal* to us the subject as subject of our ethical concern (as irreplaceable), is also a domain in which we can sing an orphic song but do no ethical deed towards the other, just as she can no longer respond to us. For this reason there is *no* virtue in mourning, and yet if we cease to mourn, the other is lost and we forget the only occasion for the realization of the possibility of virtue and thereby become supremely evil. For what is more evil than to burn a human body like an animal without a funeral? But if mourning is a vision, it is not a work, for the work of mourning or of coming to terms with loss is immoral and unchristian since it would always mean we *forget* the subject as irreplaceable. And yet to act again towards the living we *must* recover, must betray the good, must become evil.

This situation is acutely dramatized when it is uncertain whether someone is dead or alive, for they have merely *disappeared*. In Michelangelo Antonioni's film *L'Avventura* (1959) a woman, Anna, disappears, and her fiancé immediately starts to court her best friend, Claudia. If she is dead, this relationship may retrieve something from her decease, yet if she is alive it is contaminated by guilt. But given her mere disappearance, a state of irresolvable uncertainty pertains: life simply cannot go forwards. Likewise in the film *Le Colonel Chabert* (based on a short story by Balzac), a soldier returns "from the dead" to find his wife remarried. Should she resume her previous life, or abandon a later life undertaken in good faith? Both the earlier and the later lives have now become unresumable as ethical imperatives. So, on one level, these stories show how we need *definite death* to sustain morality; to pass to a new good, an earlier claim on our attention must be "over." And that in itself is enough to cast suspicion on "morality" as such: why does it require absolute death for its repeated exercise? Yet at a deeper level still, these stories indicate how death itself functions *only* as "disappearance." For we can only register the dead one as "missing," not in a state of death, since death is *not* a state. Hence in any case, even if Anna is really dead, Claudia will be faced with the choice between guilt and a certain callousness, and the only answer to her dilemma, as to that posed by *Le Colonel Chabert*, is Christ's answer to the Pharisees that in heaven "there will be neither giving nor taking in marriage."

In the case of Shakespeare's late play, *The Winter's Tale*, we have the case of a death and a presumed death which turns out to be only a double disappearance. But the one who mourns, Leontes King of Sicily, treats the death from the outset like a "disappearance" which cripples the very possibility of moral action. Hence Leontes' courtiers beseech him to forget his dead wife and son and lost daughter and resume his rule again, for politics requires self-control, although morality seems after all to disallow it (Act V, Scene 1). Here mourning is complicated by guilt (but it usually is). Leontes' false accusation of his wife as adulteress has led to her death, the death of his heir, and loss of his daughter, Perdita. His courtiers urge that he has now *atoned* through mourning, thereby claiming that mourning is a moral work that may be completed. But Leontes, echoing Lear's repeated "Never" after the loss of Cordelia, absolutely denies this. *Nothing* could compensate for the monstrousness of his deed, since he has betrayed what for him are the unique, irreplaceable ones; only reconciliation with them could cancel out the deed, and that is impossible since they are dead and lost. Time, with its irreversibility, Leontes perceives, is stern: it permits justice and the punishment that sin automatically incurs. But it does not permit forgiveness and reconciliation, because that would be to trivialize a past that in the mode of the death of responding persons can be irretrievably lost.

Leontes, via his loss, has finally come to love. He loves because he is wounded, and so at last sees what is missing. He enjoys, one might say, this one advantage, that unlike those chronically wounded *by others* he is not rendered incapable of love, and yet this advantage is cancelled in that his mainly self-inflicted wounds permit him only the futile *gesture* of love. Like the initially complacent in general, he sees what is lost with absolute clarity only too late, and therefore tragically. Hence in our world half the potential moral subjects – the wounded – see too late, and only through loss of the other, which is either their fault, or has been inflicted upon them from the first. By contrast, the other potentially moral subjects – the *apparently innocent* – who have abundantly received love from the living, and therefore are able to pass this gift on, are always infected by complacency, the non-realization of the fragility of the gift in its passage through time. They have always been too sheltered in their development from the knowledge of wounds inflicted elsewhere. Not having lost, they do not sufficiently attend to the voice of the present loved one. And since *all* are either wounded and complacent, or rather all are relative mixtures of both, since this is an exhaustive human typology, there exist *no* potential moral subjects at all. Rather we are all embroiled in the *aporia* of the present versus the absent other, where neither can adequately fulfil the role of the other; neither the living beloved, nor the dead.

"Other-regarding ethics," whose paradigm is self-sacrifice, has now therefore lost its duty, its self and its other to regard. It is ruinously subject to the vagaries of fortune in the first case, and in the second two cases to the universal bad fortune of temporal loss and death combined with the subjection of even the best human wills to a kind of routinization in respect of the other, which sometimes, as in Leontes' case, spills over into suspicion.

However, things are worse than this. As Spaemann details, there are no criteria by which to *prioritize* either the pursuit of self-fulfilling happiness or the regard of the other. To pursue *entirely* the latter path of self-sacrifice would pathologically erode the self which is alone able to offer itself. But then, when to live and when to give? A further anxiety enters the picture, and as Bernard Williams once suggested, a further dimension of moral luck.[15] Was the painter Gauguin right to leave wife and children to go to Tahiti? (Against Williams one can conceive the pursuit of aesthetic self-fulfilment as *also* a moral choice, but this merely renders more acute the dilemma he invoked.) Williams suggested that only the success of Gauguin's wager on being a good painter can retrospectively justify this decision. He comes to enjoy the moral luck of finding he has talent (a "gift"), or that his talent was able to come to fruition. But it might have been otherwise. Williams's analysis assumes that this instance is an anomaly, and that *normally* an intention to do something is not at all like Gauguin's intention to be a painter. Hence one can usually know that one can realize one's intention, and exactly what that intention is (whereas Gauguin does not really know what *kind* of painter he will turn out to be). However I think, to the contrary, that all of us are always in the situation of Gauguin. This is for two reasons: first of all, as Derrida suggests,[16] the giving of ourselves to one person or purpose frequently involves sacrificing other goods or people, and often without reason. Our sense of responsibility *must*, in order to fulfil itself, be always exceptional and particular because attentive to a specific unique demand, yet to be responsible it must also by definition be answerable to a public forum. But how can these two demands ever be reconciled? And what explanation could ever be given to the neglected ones? There are *never*, it seems, any *adequate*, that is to say, publicly stateable reasons for lavishing devotion on one person rather than another – to the public gaze this will always appear excessively aesthetic or erotic. Yet to the private impulse it may appear to fulfil the logic of the ethical itself. Second, an intention is never precise until we begin to formulate it in words, which already amounts to a kind of actual performance. We *never* know in advance, strictly speaking, what we are going to do or say. Intentions "come to us," as it were, from the Muses, and we are not in command of them. (Intention is therefore merely the way an intention turns out to be.) Heterogenesis of ends (beyond Hegel) has *always already begun*. Even to formulate a good intention, it seems, we need moral luck.

But here, at last, at the most extreme point of ruination of even the ethical intention, everything can run into reverse. Christianity is, perhaps (sporadically), the history of this running into reverse. Suppose it is the case that to be ethical is not to possess something, not even to possess one's own deed. Suppose it is, from the outset, to receive the gift of the other as something that diverts one's life, and to offer one's life in such a way that you do not know in advance what it is you will give but must reclaim it retrospectively. A total exposure to fortune, or rather to grace. Were it *simply* the former, then one would have run resignedly into nihilism – all the *aporias* of the ethical already sketched would still stand, but one would simply embrace the impossibility of the ethical and yet the necessity of temporary ethical conventions. Perhaps, in addition, one would qualify this, like Derrida (and Levinas?), with a mysticism of infinitely postponed hope for the arrival of the good. Life would either be construed as utterly arbitrary after Lear or Schopenhauer, or else as a comedy beyond the ethical, in "postmodern" mode. However, the Christian construal of the total sway of moral luck is to understand fortune, as always, however disguisedly, the personal gift of grace: to believe therefore that only *utter exposure* constitutes the ethical. It follows from this that no secularization of Christian ethics along the lines proposed by Patocka is possible: we have already seen how the mere attitudes of patience, humility, and so forth, regarded as things we can of ourselves perform, can turn out to be not ethical at all. To the contrary, they only assume an ethical complexion as a waiting on God – in other words, as a kind of meta-ethical trust that it *will* (beyond perpetual postponement) be given to us to be ethical, given to us again to receive and again to give in such a way that a certain "asymmetrical reciprocity" or genuine community, will ceaselessly arrive (for now in part and eschatologically without interruption). It ceases, on this perspective, to be the case that the Christian is the person who knows that he can be good in any merely *given* situation. On the contrary, the Christian can rather be seen as the person who recognizes that there is no *apparent* good to be found or performed in any given situation. Original sin and death (the results of the fall) are perceived as locked in a complicity which prevents the ethical from coming to pass. By naturally and culturally inherited contamination of our wills, we are all either wounded or complacent or both, capable only of valuing what is lost, obliged therefore to take measures to prevent future loss, congratulating ourselves on these measures (law) and so secretly celebrating loss as the occasion for our greatness, and instead of festively enjoying present loved ones, subject to boredom with them tending always to suspicion. Death, the experience of loss, contaminates our wills: this leads in turn to more barriers, more wars, more loss. Loss is ineradicable, and so we tend to assume that ethics is a sort of maximum possible minimization of loss. Yet I have shown that so long as there is loss, there *cannot* be any ethical, not even in any degree. Hence hope, hope that it may be given to me in the next moment to act well, is inseparable from hope that there may be universal acting well, and at last a non-futile mourning; to be ethical therefore is to believe in the resurrection, and somehow to participate in it. And *outside* this belief and participation there is, quite simply, no "ethical" whatsoever.

From these considerations I would argue that there are three aspects to ethics. First, the mundane, everyday hope that community is possible, that people and objects can analogically blend beyond identity or difference, though we can never prove such a possibility *a priori* or *a posteriori*. We can only receive instances that we judge to constitute such blending and seek, in hope, to perpetuate them: here hope is conjoined to receptive charity. Both the living out and the search for such a life in common is neither simply eudaemonistic nor "other-regarding," but as Spaemann puts it, "ecstatic." However, this is neither a self-sacrificial nor a sado-masochistically erotic ecstasy (and are not these two things secretly natural counterparts?) since both these courses are unto death and thereby subject to the aporia I have already outlined (we cannot live to enjoy it). Rather, this ecstasy passes *through* death, or in trusting it *will* be given to us to offer in death, and not just *to* death (which would be ethical/masochistic) but through death because in hope of our own return along with the return of others. Thus to look for our collective participation in divine fullness of being is to transcend in an "objective" and self-less manner either egotistic *or* self-sacrificial concerns. For Spaemann this ecstasy is epitomized by the *feast* in which mere bodily need is transfigured in collective celebration: here we eat only because and when others eat, and yet we do not renounce ourselves, for we eat also.[17]

Hence the everyday ethical hope naturally leads to hope for resurrection. However, by contrast, the second two aspects of ethics are not mundane, but mythical, miraculous, magical, indeed in a sense child-like (and therefore Christian). After Shakespeare had written *Lear*, there was no possibility of him remaining with the unsurpassability of the tragic, because this would actually be to *underestimate* the end of *Lear*. Since this play discloses a universal tragic sway (we cannot redeem our losses and misdeeds, there is no forgiveness), one cannot either mitigate this circumstance nor come to terms with it; that is to say *accept* it, even though it is true. It is so bad, it *should* be turned away from, and yet it cannot be. It *must* be turned away from because it leaves *no possibility for the ethical* (and this is where "a piety of the tragic" such as that of Donald Mackinnon, simply will not do, partly because it *still*, after all, *evades* the tragic). Hence the late Shakespeare has to imagine "another place," or a mythical post-tragic sphere. Herein lie the second two aspects. First of all, Christianity *refuses*, having recognized a universal tragic condition, to ontologize this, but makes the extraordinary move of seeing the universal itself as but a contingent narrative upshot. Hence the story of the fall, and to ontologize this story in the manner of Hegel, is to miss what here profoundly disturbs the entire project of "ontology" itself. For without the fall, or with the substitution of the notion of a necessary fall, one starts with an irreducible scarcity and egotism, and the ethical becomes that which reacts to a bad situation which it is secretly in love with, and needs ceaselessly to reinstate, despite the fact that this compromises the very character of the ethical. Therefore one *needs* the myth of the fall in order to think a genuine good, which to be non-reactive can only be an original plenitude. However, the danger here is to imagine that the fall originated in the *doing* of something bad. How can this be, if originally and by divine intention, to give or receive the gift in ignorance is always to give or receive an unknown good action? If, that is to say, the *entire* field of action is by definition "good" in a manner that cannot be qualified by the character of an intention. In this case original sin must instead mean *refusal* of the field of action itself, defined as giving with joyful uncertainty in faith, a refusal which commences in the suspicion that one does not, after all, receive a good gift from the other. This is articulated better by Shakespeare than by Genesis: in *The Winter's Tale*, Leontes and Polixenes, Kings of Sicily and Bohemia respectively, passed their boyhoods in seeming innocence, as if outside of time. Early in the play, Polixenes interprets their meeting with women, their future wives, or the arrival of "the other" in the course of time, as the moment of fall. But Hermione (Leontes' wife) to the contrary ascribes marriage still to the reign of innocence, and indeed views the arrival of the women as the event of grace itself (an association that is maintained throughout the play) (Act I, Scene 2). This is an ironic passage, for in the context of the play the fall is still to come, and involves not a first *misdeed* by Leontes, but rather a first *suspicion* that Hermione has committed the sin of adultery. Here the fall is not an act, but rather a first mistrusting of the joyfully confident "risk" and uncertainty constitutive of the field of action (or, one might say, it is a first diminishing of act). Leontes misreads the *signs* of Hermione's affection for Polixenes, and thereby offends against necessary trust in the secrecy of the other. Hence "original sin," on this rendering, is the imagination of sin, the reading of the unknown as source of threat or poison rather than potential or gift. (In Locke's *Essay Concerning Human Understanding* the philosopher notes that the Hebrew words for adultery (*niouph*), and jealousy (*kinneah*), would have been invented by Adam[18] before the *actuality* of adultery on the grounds of suspicion alone.)

This reading of original sin therefore understands original blessedness by implication, not as deliberately "doing good," but as a state of good moral luck or reception of grace. And original sin is here seen as nothing but the imagination that there could be a perversion of the field of action, malice from the other, such that the bad dream gives birth to a bad reality. The third aspect of ethics we have already indicated as hope for resurrection. Again *The Winter's Tale* is instructive. Were this play more "realist" in the mode of Shakespeare's earlier plays, it could not be post-tragic. Were Leontes to relent from mourning, resume control over his kingdom and ask pardon from Polixenes whom he has accused of adultery with Hermione, it would not, after all, for reasons we have seen, reinstate the ethical, although equivalents to such actions are our only usual recourse. The ethical, to the contrary, only returns fabulously with the return of Perdita and the seeming "resurrection" of Hermione (Act V, Scene 3). The reappearance of the latter as, at first, apparently a statue, who only gradually moves, is of crucial significance. For it dramatizes our fracture between a world of life which is real, in which the other can speak to us for a time and yet is doomed to be lost in a manner which renders life irredeemable, unforgivable and therefore *meaningless*, with a world of meaning or 'art' (one could say language and culture) which is permanent, deathless and yet sterile: the statue cannot speak (and indeed only speaks again once, to acknowledge Perdita, the lost daughter). This fracture between meaningless life and lifeless meaning is another way of expressing our fallenness and incapacity to be good. Hence when Hermione returns, she is not just resuscitated, but returns as *both* life and art, returns indeed like a kind of *perfected human intention*, where it is shown that the only good deed that could be given to us would be the capacity to raise another from the dead (after the fashion of the one good man who walked on earth). And, in addition, Hermione's continuing to be a statue means that her loss as living person is not simply *cancelled* – the spectators *continue* we are told in the play, to sorrow, and are not sure whether their surprised ecstasy is one of mourning or of joy. In the resurrection of the dead, the dead one is given back to the living as in a sense still dead, still wounded, and yet uniquely innocent, so that he or she appears in the space of living exchange as surprising gift, beyond our life now in time, which is always the mere pursuit of security. In other words, Shakespeare does not articulate magic on this earth, but magic in another, transfigured earth which is the earth given back as manifest gift, rather like the walking crippled boy and the once again blooming garden of the forever mourned dead wife of the Lord of the Manor in Frances Hodgson Burnett's *The Secret Garden*.[19]

The transfiguration at the end of *The Winter's Tale* culminates in a double marriage: first of all of Perdita to Florizel, and so of Sicily to Bohemia (Act V, Scene 3). Thereby in a final mutual giving of all future time, fallen anxiety is mended: for this had begun with the separation of bounded political kingdoms that were traditionally close allies. Again this separation had commenced with suspicion, not deed. Leontes considered that he had become too friendly with Sicily (in the person of Hermione) – conversely, Polixenes wondered whether he had already stayed too long as a guest; in other words, received too much from Leontes, thereby incurring an unreturnable debt (since he comes from poorer, less exotic, northern Bohemia) The lack of permanent bonding, the lack of marriage and the ceaseless need for guarantees, with the consequent problematic of interpretation of signs, means that there is an anxiety about duty and extent of duty between the two kingdoms, and anxiety about *when* to live, enjoy and consummate, and when to sacrifice and give to the other. This, as we have seen, renders ethics undecidable and impossible. Anxiety is only surmounted when enjoying and giving coincide in a communal ecstatic feast which is perpetual and so secure, no longer in need of any contractual reestablishment (which is not to preclude the need for constant mutual readjustments within the security of faith). Marriage is clearly a figure for this, as is confirmed by the second marriage in the play, of Camillo (Polixenes' servant) to Paulina (Hermione's maidservant) as the *final* deed of the play. Camillo had been in service to Leontes, but deserted to Polixenes, because he refused to go along with Leontes' suspicions. He nonetheless longed to return to Sicily, but Polixenes says to him that as he has come to *rely* on Camillo's sacrificial gifts of service, if Camillo *ceases* to give them, he will in effect *take back* all that he has so far given. (George Herbert was soon to confront God with the same *aporia* in his poem *Gratefulnesse*.) Here an *aporia* of gift follows from a situation of forced obligation and alienated exile. But once again marriage restores free but mutual giving in asymmetrical reciprocity, since in marriage there is no interval of *debt* between gift and return (which would reduce gift to a contractual economy) but rather absolute eternal coincidence of gift and exchange in the same moment which is ceaselessly perpetuated. Once Camillo is returned to his home, once political *order is restored in the light of resurrection*, the *aporias* of gift and the ethical are both suspended and resolved.

Nonetheless, we must at this point bear the examples of *L'Avventura* and *Le Colonel Chabert* in mind; Leontes might have remarried, and yet still resurrection could betoken a healing of the inevitable guilt involved. If the angelic state (as Christ says) does not inaugurate new marriages, then this implies a compatibility in the resurrected order of all erotic unions entered into on earth, since somehow they will all be taken up into the more general eschatological marriage of the church as bride with the crucified lamb of God.

The opposite to the condition of married reconciliation in *The Winter's Tale* is the condition of utter abandonment. When Perdita was lost she was left in the capitalist north (Bohemia) with a cache of money (Act IV). As *only* alive, estranged from the inheritance of honor down the generations (which is all her mother Hermione declares she lives for: Act III, Scene 2, 92–115), she is reduced to a thing, a commodity. For that which is abandoned, outside donation, reception, and mutuality, is after all such a mere *object* and *not* as Marion would have it, a gift. Hence Derrida, Marion, Levinas, and Blanchot have all utterly failed to see that the private, supposedly "free" gift of market society is identical precisely *as* abandoned, with the commodity of the capitalist mode of exchange.[20] Thus in Bohemia the abandoned Perdita has fallen into the world of calculating exchanges for money presided over by Autolycus, son of the mediating god Mercury. This is already the world in which we live, a modern world in which, unlike the past, nothing shields *anyone* from tragedy or the doom of endless "choice" which results in the sacrifice of some for others and unresolvable dilemmas and unhealed regret: a poisoning of the heterogenesis of ends which issues in ceaseless perversion of our intentions. Am I saying that our mercantile reality then reveals the raw truth of life in fallen time? Yes, but I am not, like Derrida, ontologizing this truth. For I insist instead on the possibility of imagining the counter-reality of resurrection, and the possibility that this world already mysteriously participates in that reality. Embracing this possibility leads us to hope, even now, after the fall and before the end, for the gracious arrival of something better and to act within this hope. Such hope will note that the resolution of *The Winter's Tale* is political as well as religious – that Camillo, at home in the restored *polis* and *oikos*, can at last give freely. Hence should *our* polity be restored by grace, would not anxiety about our necessary preference for some not others, and our apparent sacrifice of some for others, be eased in the knowledge that we are to love our *neighbors*, because we know that others are loving theirs? In other words we would rediscover that even the condition of *agape* can only be fulfilled within a polis where each of us exercises a particular – albeit unique and non-identically repeated – role. Equally, should hopeful ventures be encouraged and not thwarted, we would tend to rejoice at the course taken and laugh at the courses thereby not taken, in the confident knowledge that everything is in any case excess, and there is an infinity on which all roads may be taken in the end. And, thirdly, if we lived in an economy of gift we would not be indifferent to the consequences of our acts, now treated like sellable products, but we would "go" with our gifts, and others in receiving them creatively would continue to care for us in this employment. Joyfully estranged from ourselves, we should sometimes find in this loss our gain, and always know that it would finally be so.

II

Through the above reflections, incorporating a partial rereading of one of Shakespeare's late plays, I have sought to suggest first, that the ethical is only genuinely imaginable as a mutual and unending gift-exchange, construed as an absolute surrender to moral luck or absolute faith in the arrival of the divine gift, which is grace. Secondly, that the sustaining of such an exchange requires a notion of resurrection and faith in the reality of participation in resurrection. The first element, gift-exchange, is paradigmatically figured either as feast or as marriage, and therefore is appropriately combined with the second element, resurrection, in terms of images of the heavenly banquet or the eschatological marriage of God and humanity, heaven and earth. Outside an overcoming of the present economy of death *as well as* sin, I have argued, and a practice which seeks to anticipate the resurrection Sabbath, there can be no notion of the good that does not fall prey to irresolvable *aporias*. Hence, in theological terms, I am arguing that resurrection is an inseparable moment of atonement, or that sacrifice is only ethical when it is also resurrection.

This complex of ideas, or characterization of the ethical as gift-exchange, feast, marriage, and resurrection, I am seeking to set in deliberate opposition to a recent consensus which would try to understand the ethical as *primarily* self-sacrifice for the other, without any necessary "return" issuing from the other back to oneself. This consensus itself involves an alternative complex of ideas: first of all, one has the notion that only an entirely sacrificial giving without any expectation of a counter-gift distinguishes the gift from a form of self-interested *contract*. Second, one has the notion that *death*, far from being complicit with evil (as I would understand it to be), is the *necessary condition for the event of the ethical as such*.[21] This is supposedly for two reasons: first only our *vulnerability*, the possibility that we might die, allows us to make an appeal as needy people to our neighbor; only this circumstance provides the condition for an ethical demand. Second, only the capacity of the ethical subject to respond to the needy person if necessary with his own death, guarantees his deed as truly ethical, as truly disinterested gift. Thirdly, one has the notion that "God" must be reduced to a shadowy hypostasized other lurking just behind the human other, because any God who interfered to "reward" the disinterested giver would undo the purity of this disinterest and the purity of the ethical realm. And so, in the fourth place, one arrives at the paradoxical affirmation that the true nobility and purity of religious self-sacrifice is only realized in a *secular* sphere, that here alone a dying for the other achieves genuine sacred value. These positions are common to Patocka, Derrida, and probably Levinas, while the first point is espoused by Marion (although logically it should lead to the other three).

Let me now, in this second part of the essay, summarize and make more explicit the grounds for my rejection of ethics as unilateral gift and sacrifice in favor of ethics as gift-exchange and openness to divine grace, dealing with each of these four notions in turn. First, the idea of a fundamentally sacrificial, or unilateral gift, makes absolute one's inalienable self-possession of a will to sacrifice and so *preserves* the Hellenic notion of the ethical as the overcoming of moral luck or the arrival of that which imperturbably belongs to one, even if, or *especially* if, as for Derrida, this belonging or identity is only secured when one is no longer, when one is dead, and even if, or *especially* if, this identity is construed as with Marion as the debt to a giver which inaugurates subjectivity as such (for this subjectivity supposedly outside all agency and judgment is thereby all the more inviolable). There is no true respect for the other involved here, since the gesture which allows the other to persist outside of his communication with you is seen as more definitive of the good than the living communication which you enjoy with the other: hence Levinas sees the other as only genuinely present in "trace," not in present image. But if we truly value the other we must value meeting him in his specificity and therefore *my* presence before the other is ineradicable from a situation which is paradigmatic for the ethical. Of course, one's celebration of such an encounter may *require* one in certain circumstances to sacrifice oneself, even unto death, and one can go further to say that in a fallen world the only path to the recovery of mutual giving will *always* pass through an element of apparently "unredeemed" sacrifice and apparently unilateral gift. But the point is that this gesture is not *in itself* the good, and indeed, I have argued, is *not* good at all outside the hope for a redemptive return of the self: albeit that this is an eschatological hope which never permits us to expect a return at any particular place or specific moment of time, or to elicit any specific *mode* of return. To speak of such a return is not at all, however, to surrender to the lure of contract, because it is not the case that actual, self-present life is a mode of self-possession which we then *surrender* in the sacrificial gesture unto death. Quite to the contrary, it is when we are giving, letting ourselves go, sometimes with unavoidable sacrificial pain, that we are always receiving back as ever different a true, abundant life (this is the gospel). Therefore the resurrection hope preserves this logic at the limit: we do not hope (as Patocka and Derrida allege) for an extrinsic super-added reward for our giving up of an illusory self-possessed life; rather, we take it that a final surrender of an isolated life, a life indifferent to the pain of others issues of itself – dare one say *automatically* – in a better more abundant life (and this 'automatic' self-raising dimension of Jesus's resurrection, clearly articulated in the New Testament, is shamefully glossed over by the pseudo-piety and mythologizing bent of exegetes who wish to speak only of a "mighty act of the Father": John 11.25; 12.24).

The fuller more abundant life is a return of life always afresh, always differently. Hence, as I have argued elsewhere, what distinguishes gift from contract is not the absolute freedom and non-binding character of the gift (this is our Western counterpart to the *reduction* of exchange to contract which remains entirely uncriticized by Derrida and Marion, who are unable to assimilate the more truly critical lesson of Mauss), but rather the surprisingness and unpredictability of gift and counter-gift, or their character in space as *asymmetrical reciprocity*, and their character in time as *non-identical repetition*.[22] It should also be noted here that Derrida regards the event of a gift construed as a free, unilateral gift as an *impossibility*, since, short of death, one always does cancel one's giving in receiving something back, be it only the consciousness that one is a giver.[23] Only the dead person, on this account, only the subject who has passed beyond subjectivity, can be a true giver, just as the only disinterested gift is to an absolutely anonymous other – paradigmatically the enemy, says Marion – and cannot possess any identifiable content beyond the gesture of giving, because there is nothing about an object on *this* construal that makes it in itself a gift – although I would argue that the content of a gift alone determines whether it is an *appropriate* gift and therefore a gift at all.[24] For Derrida, therefore, a gift is only ever a promise of a gift, perpetual postponement. And Marion's attempt to show that this impossible gift is really a phenomenologically *reduced* gift, having its special mode of being present outside the "presence" of Being and the mutual coincidence of giver and receiver, will not work. For this reduced gift which is no identifiable object, and derives from no known source, and passes to no known willing recipient, can only be "recognized" in a fashion that can make no conceivable difference to actual ethical life. Such recognition acknowledges only the idol of an abstract God, whose gift is as effectively abyssal and absent as that of Marion's atheistic interlocutors. And where there is no intimation *whatsoever* of the donating source, a gift is simply an impersonal intrusion, whose lack of objectifiable content further renders it *arbitrary* on our part to interpret it *as* gift, rather than as violent rupture. Equally, where there is no knowledge of a recipient, and one assumes even that he is hostile, there cannot truly be a gift, because a true gift must be considered and *appropriate* to its donee; hence one must *already* have entered into an exchange with her. Before a gift *can* be given, it must already have started to be received. For gift-giving is a mode of social being, and in ignoring this, both Derrida and Marion remain trapped within Cartesian myths of prior subjectivity after all. However, Derrida is right, against Marion, to deconstruct his unnecessary Cartesian starting point, and one can agree with him that a unilateral, purely sacrificial gift can *never* occur. If there is a gift that can truly be, then this must be the event of reciprocal, but asymmetrical and non-identically repeated exchange.

The second element in the complex of notions which construes the ethical as sacrificial is the idea of death as the ground of morality. I have already indicated how this manifestly celebrates something negative as the precondition of something positive, in a way that is self-contradictory, and I have already shown also how a self-surrender without hope of self-return *gives up on* the hope for ecstatic communication, for "feasting" and for "marriage," which is the only viable paradigm for the good itself. Although I take this paradigm to be fully articulated only by Christianity, it is notably anticipated by Plato in the *Phaedo*, when he insists that warriors who die for the city out of fear of loss of honor are trading lesser fear for greater and lesser pain for greater pleasure of anticipation of undying fame (*Phaedo* 68d–69e). Socrates, in this dialogue, refuses this idea that virtue is a kind of coinage, and therefore refuses an ethical market economy which is also a *sacrificial* economy – something is given up, abandoned, in order to gain more. By contrast, the *philosopher* is in his essence a person who begins with absolute confidence, with the vision of the Forms as that which cannot possibly be endangered, and therefore acts with genuine positivity, without fear and not with a merely apparent fearlessness that is in thrall to an even greater fear. For this reason the philosopher is good as first merely knowing, or *receiving* the vision of the Forms and *not* as acting or as sacrificing in the sense of giving up something. (And indeed the Pythagorean tradition which precedes Plato already refrained from bloody, sacrificial rituals.)[25] Only in a secondary moment, out of the plenitude of vision, does he offer himself entirely, giving his whole body over to death, if the occasion arises (as it has, for Socrates). This is not, as modern philosophy tends to claim, *itself* an aspect of a sacrificial economy, in the sense of a "giving up" of the body and the passions for the gain of knowledge, since formed materiality and the passions are for Plato simply weak participations in a fuller ontological and erotic reality. Nothing real is lost here: there is only in *this* exercise of virtue, a passage from lesser to greater. And later, in the

Christian era, the records of the deaths of martyrs record a similar acceptance of suffering out of an already commenced plenitude of paradisal vision.[26] (One should also note that the above implies a qualification of Nussbaum's verdicts on Plato and Aristotle: it is *Aristotle*, seeking a relatively secure inner citadel in time who limits "moral luck," whereas for Plato one entirely abandons oneself to the Forms which arrive through the erotic lure of the other.)

This leads me to a discussion of the fourth notion in the complex of ideas which define the ethical as sacrificial: this is the idea that the sacred is fully realized in an atheistic or demythologized mode. What this notion seeks ideologically to occlude from our view, is the ever-present role of the city or the state intervening in order to maintain civic order[27] within our relationship to the other person or to God. This mediation is fundamentally inscribed in the very historical "transport" of sacrifice from practice to metaphor. One can mention two moments here in particular. First, the way in which, as Marcel Detienne has recounted, in Greek sacrifice the same scents and spices were involved in erotic play as in religious sacrifice, and it was in consequence thought important to divert an excess of sensation from the horizontal to the vertical plane. Unlike the Platonic instance, the bodily erotic is here not regarded as participatory, but as a real thing to be limited, kept in its place and to a degree "given up." The burning spices should most appropriately spiral upwards to the divine realm. Here then is a kind of "giving up" or offering of material passion in favor of its sublimation, and so a limitation and confinement of its scope of operations.

In this context one should note that the specific language of "sacrifice of passions" does not, as far as I can see, occur in Greek philosophy. This is because, after Pythagoras, the more immaterialist tendency tended to advocate a non-bloody, non-civic, sacrifice in which the passage upwards of smoke indicated not so much the *offering* of passion as the transmutation of passion within the philosopher into higher passion.[28] Hence amongst the Neoplatonists, sacrifice is specifically construed as *initiatory passage*, rather than as gift or offering.[29] It is only, perhaps, with Paul in *Romans* that one gets the language of "sacrifice of passions" and so an "internalization" of sacrifice – but the import here is entirely different from the vertical deviation of horizontal scents and spices. Rather, Paul is talking about an offering of self (soul and body) to a personal God which implicitly involves a trust in a return of self as a more abundant living soul and body.

The second moment concerns, as Martin Hengel has described, the way in which the death of the hero for the city was construed by the Greeks (and later still more the Romans) as equivalent to sacrifice, and indeed as rendering the hero himself a fit recipient of sacrifice in turn.[30] In both these instances – that of the sacrifice of passion and of the sacrifice of the hero – one has the idea of the subsumption of something ontologically real and irreducible into a greater whole: in the one case the city, in the other the cosmic order. There is a notion here of loss without return, save for the posthumous praise of celebration of one's austerity or bravery. A return of the *living self* is not involved, save in rather shadowy intimations of an after-life. But the point here to grasp is that modern secularity gets rid of even such intimations, and so *perfects* pagan logic, a logic of sacrificial obliteration of self either for an ideal, or for the city, or for both. Such a logic elevates *an abstract space*,[31] the notion of the perpetually abiding city which outlasts the lives of its citizens and is elevated in value above the lives of individual humans, even where this is disguised in the form of the notion of "sacrifice for future generations." For since *every* generation should logically be subject to the same imperative, consummation is forever postponed, and indeed morality itself is *defined* as perpetual postponement or else as self-sacrifice (this *aporia* applies both to consequentialism focused upon the capital of pleasure, and to Kantianism focused upon the capital of "freedom"). Hence, already (as I have recounted elsewhere),[32] nineteenth-century positivism proclaimed that the secular, science-based community understands the true sacrality of sacrifice as "altruism" or surrender of the self for the future, for science, and for the state. And when our contemporary "postmodern" or else Levinasian thinkers discover the good, or the moral act, or self-giving sacrifice to be perpetual postponement, they are simply perfecting this cruel and annihilating logic under whose tyranny we all now live. The *opposite* to this tyranny was remarkably articulated by John Buchan in his novel *Midwinter*, in which (in a highly Kierkegaardian fashion) the Jacobite hero of the story puts the salvation of a young girl in whom he is erotically interested before the well-being of his political cause, and indeed, according to the plot of the novel, destroys that cause altogether. The extremity of his situation is not downplayed: "He saw his clan, which might have become great again, reduced to famished vagrants," and yet, encouraged by a fictionalized "Dr Johnson," and the mysterious "Midwinter," who represents in the story the mysteries of Diana, he is reconciled to his option as a truly Christian one: "Love had come to him, and he had passed it by, but not without making sacrifice, for to the goddess [Diana] he had offered his most cherished loyalties. Now it was all behind him – but by God, he did not, he would not regret it. . . . He had sacrificed one loyalty to a more urgent, and with the thought bitterness went out of his soul. Would Lochiel, would the Prince, blame him? Assuredly no."[33] Reduced to a Lear-like "nakedness," he is yet consoled by the thought that instead of sacrificing the singular to the all, he has sacrificed an (after all idolatrous and finally merely nominal) "all" to the singular, and so affirmed the resurrection hope for the return of each and every one, beyond the *aporia* of sacrificial options.

My claim, therefore, is that the idea of self-sacrifice unto death without return for the sake of "the whole," even if that be the rule of moral duty to an unspecified other, is *not at all* the true moral kernel of the Jewish and Christian legacy, but much more a transcription of secular modernity which reads time not as a gift-of-self in the hope of an eternal return, but rather as a giving-up-of-self in time for a future absolutized space which will never truly be set in place. One may note, for example, that parents who entirely sacrifice themselves for their children, thereby betray them, since they fail to present them with any *telos* and example of a lived, enjoyed (and sexual) adult life. This claim can be substantiated from the evidence of the Bible. Biblical criticism shows that a typically near-

Eastern idea that "doing good" is a one-way operation proceeding downwards from the king towards those in need – "the widows and orphans" – was heavily qualified in the intertestamental period by the influence of Greek notions that good can be done by anyone – even a slave – and is more reciprocal or "exchangist in character."[34] (And it would also be premature to conclude that the earlier Jewish perspective is wholly "unilateral" – this would ignore in particular the notion of "covenant.")[35] A tension between the two perspectives appears to be registered in the New Testament itself, where in Luke's gospels "benefactors" or those who wield power by giving are regarded with suspicion, where one is adjoined to love one's enemies and also, as already noted, *not* to invite to feasts those who can invite you back (Luke 6.32–5)[36] (though one may contrast this with the way Jesus's death is preceded in this gospel by a *symposium* amongst friends). This is Derrida's favoured locus for the Christian essence, and yet it is surely to be contrasted with St John's gospel where there is no mention of loving enemies, where love seems to ceaselessly circulate amongst friends – I in you, and you in me – where there are erotic gestures, and where the disciples are described as the Father's "gift" to the son, just as the Son is his gift to the disciples. Also one finds here an integration of Hellenistic notions (deriving from the Socratic paradigm) of a dying for friends rather than the city, which is also a dying for the truly *ethical*.

Now it may very well be argued that Christianity has combined both perspectives on giving, but if it has done so it is surely more fundamentally under the *aegis* of reciprocity, even though the eschatological character of this goal requires a "quasi-unilateral" moment for the gift in our fallen present time. The final gift from the divine height (to "widows and orphans") is received only as a gift also returned from below, in the incarnation of the *logos*, as the return of humanity to the Father. Likewise, God ceases to be a gesture of lonely superabundant giving, but instead his gift which is the Holy Spirit only *results* from, and is the manifestation of, the perfect mutuality of Father and Son. And, finally, the Son offers himself *not at all* for the earthly city, and not at all as the giving up of something for the sake of an even greater something else, not even himself for the sake of the cosmos or the other. For the manner in which "he dies for his friends" is indeed not that they should live their self-possessed lives while he has lost his – as if he had saved them from drowning, or defended them in war – but rather in defence of the truth he has taught them, which is the absolute creative power of the Father, a truth only maintained and indeed fully taught in his resurrected return. It is this return that is commemorated when in the eucharistic gesture there is offered up to God *without division* bread and wine, and yet the people immediately consume this all themselves in its return to them as God's very flesh and blood.

In the eucharistic liturgy, humanity enters in advance into the divine Sabbath, the eschatological banquet and the cosmic nuptial, into the realm where once again we can entirely trust our *every* act as good precisely because we know that it will not merely follow our intention but be transformed and given back to us in a different and surprising mode.

Here, therefore, in the eucharist, we see the only possible paradigm for gift and therefore for ethics, not as one-way sacrifice but as total surrender for rereception. Within this paradigm we can realize that to the degree that we are involved in some sense at certain times in both "feast" and "marriage" we are transported by the divine *logos*, which gives, only to those reclined at the *symposium*, already above the time of death, such that we participate already in the time of resurrection. At this *symposium* and within this *connubium*, we give up everything, but not for the terrestrial city, and not even primarily for others: here we give up "absurdly" to God in order to confess our inherent nothingness and to receive life in the only possible genuine mode of life, as created anew. Here we hold on to nothing, here we possess nothing securely, in contrast with exclusively ethical models which are also sacrificial. Here instead we render ourselves entirely prey to the mere good fortune that it might turn out that we have been ethical. But the name of this fortune is secretly grace, the gift or the Good; those names which convey all our Western longing.

Notes

Originally published as "The Midwinter Sacrifice" in *Christian Ethics*, vol. 10, no. 2, 1997.

1 Jan Patocka, *Essais hérétiques sur la philosophie de l'histoire*, trans. E. Abrams (Paris: Verdier, 1981); Jacques Derrida, 'Donner la Mort' in *L'Éthique du Don*, ed. J.-M. Rabaté and Michael Wetzel (Paris: Metailié-Transition, 1992); Emmanuel Levinas, "Time and the Other" (extract) in *The Levinas Reader*, ed. Séan Hand (Oxford: Blackwell Publishers, 1989), *Autrement qu'être ou au-delà de l'essence* (Paris: Kluwer, 1990).
2 Bernard Williams, "Moral Luck" in *Moral Luck Philosophical Papers 1973–80* (Cambridge: Cambridge University Press, 1981), 20–39; Martha Nussbaum, *The Fragility of Goodness: Luck and Ethics in Greek Tragedy and Philosophy* (Cambridge: Cambridge University Press, 1986).
3 Aristotle, *Nicomachean Ethics*, 1109630–111068.
4 See Robert Spaemann, *Glück und Wohlwollen: Versuch über Ethik* (Stuttgart: Klett-Cotta, 1989), pp. 85–95: "Die Antinomien des Glücks."
5 As seems to be affirmed by Jean-Luc Marion. See "Esquisse d'un Concept Phénoménologique du Don" in *Archivio di Filosofia* LXII, 1994 N.1–3, 75–94.
6 See Hans Urs von Balthasar, *The Glory of the Lord, Vol. V. The Realm of Metaphysics in the Modern Age*, trans. Oliver Davies et al., (Edinburgh: T. & T. Clark, 1995), pp. 451–597.
7 See Spaemann, *Glück und Wohlwollen*, for this characterization especially. "Vorwort," pp. 9–11.
8 Martin Heidegger, *Being and Time*, trans. John Macquarrie and Edward Robinson (Oxford: Blackwell Publishers, 1978), pp. 279–312.
9 Derrida, "Donner la Mort," pp. 64–5.
10 Spaemann, pp. 85–95: "Die Antinomien des Glücks,' pp. 110–22: "Vernunft und Leben," pp. 123–40: "Wohlwollen."
11 Spaemann, p. 89.
12 Marion, "Esquisse d'un Concept Phénoménologique du Don."

13 For the arid pursuit of such conundra to their bitter end without *aufhebung*, see Derek Parfit, *Reasons and Persons* (Oxford: Oxford University Press, 1984).
14 Jacques Derrida, *Given Time: I Counterfeit Money*, trans. Peggy Kamuf (Chicago: University of Chicago Press, 1991).
15 Bernard Williams, "Moral Luck."
16 Jacques Derrida, "Donner la Mort," pp. 54, 64.
17 Spaemann, pp. 110–22: "Vernunft und Leben," especially pp. 114–15.
18 John Locke, *An Essay Concerning Human Understanding* (Oxford: Oxford University Press, 1975), III, VI, 44–7 and V, 1–8.
19 Frances Hodgson Burnett, *The Secret Garden* (Oxford: Oxford University Press, 1993). These magical aspects are very well brought out in Agnieszka Holland's film of this novel (1994).
20 Marion, "Esquisse."
21 See, especially, Derrida "Donner la Mort." And for a critique of this, Catherine Pickstock, *After Writing: The Liturgical Consummation of Philosophy* (Oxford: Blackwell Publishers, 1998), ch. 3, "Signs of death."
22 John Milbank "Can a Gift be Given?" in *Rethinking Metaphysics*, ed. L. G. Jones and S. E. Fowl (Oxford: Blackwell Publishers, 1995), pp. 119–61.
23 Derrida, *Given Time*. However, it might be contended here that there is no real contradiction between being truly disinterested and a virtuous satisfaction at a meta-level of awareness that we *are* disinterested. The unilateral gift is not so much impossible as objectionable as a final *telos*, even if in a fallen world it is normally an inescapable *imperative*. Marion's attempt to regard gratitude as an awareness which does not cancel the gratuity of the gift by returning it in terms of his universal conception of the gift will *not*, however, work, because there is an imperative to *display* generosity and to do this in a delightful manner: gratitude *is* a counter-gift.
24 See Milbank, "Can a Gift be Given?"
25 Diogenes Laertius, *Lives* VII, 13, 22 and see Marcel Detienne, *The Gardens of Adonis* (New York: Hassocks, 1975).
26 I am indebted to Villiers Breytenbach for this point.
27 Detienne, *The Gardens of Adonis*.
28 I am grateful for discussions with Hildegard Caneik-Lindemaier on this point.
29 See Robert Alun Jones, 'Robertson Smith, Durkheim and Sacrifice,' *Journal of the History of the Behavioural Sciences*, XVIII (April 1981), pp. 184–205.
30 Martin Hengel, *The Atonement*, trans. John Bowden (London: SCM, 1981), pp. 1–32. I am indebted to Wolfgang Stegemann for the point that Antique texts often use *sphagein* (whole-offering) rather than *plusia* in this context. It should be said, however, that Hildegard Caneik-Lindemaier thinks Hengel and Stegemann exaggerate lightly metaphorical usages.
31 See Pickstock, *After Writing*, ch. 2.
32 John Milbank, "Stones of Sacrifice" in *Modern Theology*, vol. 12, no. 1, January 1996, pp. 27–56.
33 John Buchan, *Midwinter: Certain Travellers in Old England* (Edinburgh: B & W Publishing, 1993), pp. 229–30. The "Sacrifice to Diana" which Buchan has of course derived from reading J. G. Frazer and Margaret Murray is here deployed typologically (a) as a figure for genuine Christian sacrifice (a trope used also in the equally remarkable *Witchwood*) and (b) to suggest that since the foretype is still included, there can be an integration of a Platonic erotic and romantic moment in Christianity. (Again *Witchwood* conveys the same message and suggests that a "Catholic"

and "Platonic" Christianity holds the balance between a bleak uncharitable puritanism and a demonic neopaganism; in the latter novel it is Calvinist "justified sinners" who are also devil worshipers, implying that a fatalistic construal of grace, where our "return" of love is irrelevant and the divine decree is impersonal and arbitrary is *dialectically identical* with an equally "returnless" love for the powers of darkness and destruction.)

34 See Hendrik Bolkestein, *Wohltätigkeit und Armenpflege in Vorchristlichen Alterturn* (Utrecht: A. Oosthoek, 1939) and Willem Cornelis van Unnick, "Eine Merkwürdige Liturgische Aussage bei Josephus (Jos. Ant 111–113)" in *Josephus-Studien*, ed. O. Betz et al. (Göttingen: Vandenhoeck & Ruprecht, 1974), pp. 362–9.
35 See Milbank, "Can a Gift be Given?"
36 See Willem Cornelis van Unnick, "Die Motivierung der Feindesliebe in Lukas VI, 32–35" in *Novum Testamentum*, vol. VII, 1996, pp. 284–300.

CHAPTER 7

Postmodernity and Religious Plurality: Is a Common Global Ethic Possible or Desirable?

Gavin D'Costa

From his first volume, *Theology and Religious Pluralism* (Oxford, 1986), to *The Trinity and the Meeting of Religions* (New York, 2000), Gavin D'Costa has been concerned with the practices of other faiths. Although D'Costa continues to use the word "religion" he is more than aware that the concept has a genealogy. Modernity constructed a discourse on religions, then turned to the study of religions and, more recently, the comparison of religions. D'Costa's work challenges this construction and seeks to further dialogue between world faiths in a way that accepts and works with some of the categories forged by modernity. The means by which he does this are exemplified in the following essay: he takes a major proposal for a universalist perspective (in this case, Hans Küng's), points out its methodological limitations (Enlightenment categories, Eurocentrism, patriarchalism, Christocentrism), and seeks to render the perspective more complex. In his earlier work he examines in this way the liberal approaches to religious pluralism of such major exponents as John Hick and Paul Knitter. At the center of his challenge to these universalist methods which continue to work with an uncritical understanding of the term "religion," is his appeal to the specific differences between faiths. Furthermore, D'Costa is keen to demonstrate that a religion is not simply a set of ideas, but a complex living practice in which beliefs are continually formed and transformed in a dialogue with its traditions, its institutions, and its cultural contexts. We can understand the distinctiveness of D'Costa's approach if we examine the debate that took place between 1987 and 1990 on Christianity and pluralism. In 1987 the liberal thinkers John Hick and Paul Knitter published a collection of essays entitled *The Myth of Christian Uniqueness*. D'Costa responded with *Christian Uniqueness Reconsidered: The Myth of a Pluralistic Theology of Religions* (New York, 1990), which posited Christology and trinitarian theology as the two distinctive differences of the Christian faith. This appeal to tradition-based reasoning, and the foregrounding of D'Costa's own Roman Catholic standpoint at the beginning of his analyses, has since been deepened by his study of narrative theology: evidently, Alasdair MacIntyre has been an influence here, along with the work of D'Costa's close friend, the Catholic narrative theologian Gerard Loughlin. A certain self-conscious liberalism remains. Aware of oversimplification, descriptive reductionism, and the abstractions arising from the tackiness of everyday practices of believing; aware also of the internal strifes and external conflicts of different faiths; aware, too, that there is no easy way that such faiths can work together and discover some common ground, D'Costa nevertheless upholds something of a Habermasian ideal: in eschewing religious relativism and cultural pragmatism he maintains a belief in the continuing processes of communicative action. While D'Costa demonstrates that engaging in discussion of a religious tradition from the standpoint of another "is deeper and more treacherous . . . than initially recognized", he attempts to open discussion rather than impose his own theological closure. This is a dangerous way of proceeding, requiring an openness to the risk of radical change to one's own beliefs. It requires also a certain fearlessness characteristic of D'Costa's work. A sense of urgency drives his arguments – a conviction of the relevance of his thinking and the analysis upon which he has embarked. He is unafraid to push continually at the limits of what is considered – in a highly political and politicized manner – orthodox. Nowhere is this more evident than in D'Costa's *Sexing the Trinity* (London, 2000), where he raises issues of gender politics in a critical discussion with Roman Catholic theology.

It might seem churlish to pose such a question as "is a common global ethics possible or desirable?" when the world is tearing itself apart. Religions are of course both the cause of so much strife, war, and rivalry, as well as the sites whereby such destruction might be constructively met and transformed. In using the term "global ethic" in my subtitle I allude to the project started by Hans Küng in his book *Global Responsibility* (London, 1990), then developed in *A Global Ethic: The Declaration of the Parliament of the World's Religions* (London, 1993), and more recently in his huge book, *A Global Ethic for Global Politics and Economics* (London, 1997). Küng's work is immensely influential, especially among the wider public, both Christian and others. He has addressed the United Nations, the World Bank, the Hong Kong Stock Exchange, and a number of important international political groups. Küng's aim is simple: the world religions have too often been ignored as a source for righting the world's conflicts, and this could be changed if the religions were able to see that they do indeed share a common global ethic. Following this ethic, rather than constituting rival groups, might change the world. His question: how do we make the world a better place? His answer: bring the religions together, to act together, to advance a commonly agreed global ethic.

In this chapter I wish to do three things. First, I want to outline Küng's very important and increasingly influential thesis. I want to show how it assumes the hallmarks of modernity. Second, I want to criticize it constructively from a postmodern perspective, to attain the same aim as him: a desire for peace among the nations. I should add that there is no unitary essence to "postmodernity," but my own definition of the term will become clearer as the chapter progresses. Third, in staging this dialectical conversation (although admittedly Küng does not have the chance to come back on what I say), I want to develop the implications of my critique to more positively address the question from a postmodern perspective, which as we shall see is quite a different question from Küng's. The reason why it is a different question is that I believe that questions are always, to a greater or lesser extent, actually shaped by the paradigm or tradition of thought out of which we approach the world.

Before turning to my task I want the reader to recall (if you are old enough) Coca-Cola's most successful advertising campaign. In an advert that was launched in hundreds of countries and in many languages, there was a group of young, old, black, and white, women and men singing happily together, each in their own languages: "I'd like to teach the world to sing, in perfect harmony. . . ." The camera started with a fresh-faced young woman, then as the song went on, it pulled back further and further until we saw a field full of happy people singing with joyful voices, bright eyes, and hope in their hearts. They were all holding bottles of Coke. The sales of Coke shot up after this advert, because it was rather nice to imagine oneself contributing to world peace and harmony by identifying together and overcoming differences – even if only through the drinking of a universally consumed and marketed soft-drink. The colorful ethnic costumes, the basically healthy faces, the sun-drenched landscape, and the single uniting symbol of Coke all evaded the complex religious–sociopolitical realities that characterize international relations. The poor, the suffering, the exploited, the raped, murdered, and brutalized are removed from this landscape, as are the clash of religious and cultural values. I evoke this advertisement to draw you into thinking that I may not after all be a rogue in calling into question Küng's project, for I think the appearance of Küng's project and the Coke advert have something very important in common. They both eradicate the complex and painful difficulties in real history when people from different faiths meet. In so doing, they both perpetuate the status quo. But that is to conclude an argument before it has even begun.

Let me turn now to the depiction of Küng. His first book's subtitle announces the plot of his project: "In Search of a New World Ethic." Given the social, economic, religious, and political strife in the world, the book's opening words set the tone:

> No survival without a world ethic. No world peace without peace between the religions. No peace between the religions without dialogue between the religions. (Küng, *Global Responsibility*, p. xv)

The three books flush out this project, and in what follows I will mainly draw from the final book, *A Global Ethic for Global Politics and Economics*, which is the most ramified account of the entire project. In brief, Küng's argument can be advanced in three stages. First, Küng argues that religious and non-religious ideologies form an important, if not the most important, resource for world peace. He is utterly realistic in acknowledging that these same religions and ideologies are also the cause of much strife. He then carries out a very useful analysis in which he criticizes major studies on world peace because they tend to focus entirely on nation-states and political forms of government as the source and hope for advancing world peace. Küng adds a very important corrective to this analysis by bringing into focus both the political power of religious organizations and religious practices, and their questionable occlusion from serious analysis in much of the social sciences.

His second step is to argue that one might distil a global ethic from within these traditions. He is quite clear that this strategy must avoid two major pitfalls. On the one hand it must avoid a top-down approach, whereby some new ideology is imposed upon all the religions which they must follow, even if this ideology is entirely alien to their own traditions. Küng rightly sees that such an approach will be unhelpful, as it will not draw support from the religions and simply be an imposed and singular ethic, which is therefore not a shared global ethic. On the other hand, Küng wants to avoid the debilitating relativism of so much postmodern thought and "ethics," which argues that it is only possible to have, in Küng's words, a "regional ethics" (ibid, p. 93). Here he cites Richard Rorty and Alasdair MacIntyre as typical examples of postmodern thinkers who would criticize the possibility of global ethics. Between these two siren voices, imposed objectivism and fragmentary relativism, Küng sails his notion of global ethics. Global ethics is the finding and stating of what is shared by all religions, a kind of global rule actually found within the traditions, but which is transtradition-specific; i.e., an ethic that all religions can mutually agree with and advance, but from the context of their own tradition.

At this point Küng draws on Michael Walzer's work in advancing what Küng calls a discernible "core morality" and what Walzer calls "thin morality." One of Walzer's books is aptly entitled *Thick and Thin: Moral Argument at Home and Abroad* (1994). According to Küng, what Walzer calls thin morality can be found in many different forms of discourse, including all the world religions, and Küng cites as an example the fundamental rights "to life, to just treatment (also from the state), to physical and mental integrity" (*Global Ethic for Global Politics*, p. 95). In terms of the religions, which are our main concern here, Küng isolates a single golden rule found in all religions: Do unto others as you would wish them do unto you (*A Global Ethic*, p. 34). Küng uses this phrase as the refrain and theme of the "Declaration of the Parliament of the World's Religions," that all religions agree that "every human being must be treated humanely." Küng argues that at this level of thin morality, this global ethic can be stated in four propositions that are held universally: do not kill, do not steal, do not lie, and do not commit sexual immorality. This agreement is vital for Küng's project and is the basic global ethic.

Küng then acknowledges what Walzer calls "thick morality," the phenomenon whereby these commonly agreed universals are "of course enriched in the various cultures" and appear "as a 'thick' morality in which every possible historical, cultural, religious and political view comes to be involved, depending on time and place" (*Global Ethic for Global Politics*, p. 95). What is important for Küng is the underlying agreement at the level of thin morality, upon which religions can act in common. Küng realizes (after some criticisms of his earlier formulations of the global ethic) that

> A consensus is not necessary in respect of culturally differentiated/ "thick" morality.... In disputed concrete questions like abortion or euthanasia, no unifying demands should be made on other nations, cultures and religions to have the same moral praxis. (Ibid, p. 96)

Küng's third step of the argument is to work out proposals regarding economics and politics on the basis of this global ethic. His third book flushes this out in some detail. For example, he argues that responsible business cannot just maximize profit, but must also judge goods and values regarding society at large, the environment, and the future (ibid, p. 239). Or, to take another example, contained in the "Declaration":

> We condemn the poverty that stifles life's potential; the hunger that weakens the human body; the economic disparities that threaten so many families with ruin.... We consider humankind our family.... No person should ever be considered or treated as a second-class citizen, or be exploited in any way whatsoever. There should be equal partnership between men and women. We should not commit any kind of sexual immorality. We must put behind us all forms of domination or abuse.

The text, which takes up 22 pages, ends: "We invite all men and women, whether religious or not, to do the same."

It may seem churlish to question such well-intentioned rhetoric, especially as I found myself concurring with most of it – and who would not? And perhaps this is precisely the problem. Hence, I will now develop the second part of my essay by posing two questions and criticisms of Küng's project.

First, is Küng's notion of a common ethic, a thin morality, conceptually coherent? I suggest that the answer is yes, but only on a particular modernist understanding of ethics and morality. It is an understanding that I want to contest. In doing so, my answer to the question "is thin morality conceptually coherent" will be no. To situate Küng's (and my own) understanding, I would like to draw on Alasdair MacIntyre's work, especially his *Three Rival Versions of Moral Enquiry* (London, 1990). There, MacIntyre develops his scathing critique of the Enlightenment begun in his book, *After Virtue* (London, 1981), in his argument that contemporary Western society is faced with three rival versions of moral enquiry: the Encyclopedic (the Enlightenment heritage), the Genealogical (the postmodern deriving from Nietzsche), and the Thomist (deriving from Aristotle and entering the Christian tradition via Aquinas and virtue ethics). For my purpose, I want to focus on MacIntyre's critique of liberal Enlightenment ethics, and return to his broader constructive argument later. I should add that his assessment of the Genealogical tradition, which others would call postmodern, is not nuanced enough and often essentializes a movement that contains very different trajectories. The present volume in which this essay appears is evidence of this very point.

As Kelvin Knight puts it, MacIntyre argues that despite all their important differences, what

> united Hume, Kant and others in a single project was . . . their agreement that the prerequisite for enlightenment was the rejection of their Aristotelian heritage. A central part of what they thereby rejected was a syllogistic way of justifying the rules of morality on the basis not only of an apprehension of "man-as-he-happens-to-be" but also of "human-nature-as-it-could-be-if-it-realized-its-*telos*."

In so doing, claims MacIntyre,

> they [such Enlightenment thinkers] rejected the only way of coherently moving from an apprehension of what is to an apprehension of what ought to be. Only when apprehended as the only means by which to move from one's present self to one's *telos*, to one's true good in society with others, can it be concluded that the rules of morality are categorical. What followed from Enlightenment philosophers' rejection of teleology was their interminable disagreement about how the rules of morality might be justified, insoluble problems in the proposals of each being identified by others. (K. Knight (ed.), *The MacIntyre Reader*. Oxford: Polity Press, 1998, p. 8.)

Eventually, all that could be agreed was that people ought to be free to agree or disagree, and the birth of the modern nation-state and liberal democracy was its social and political counterpart. However, with no common *telos* even this minimal consensus would eventually come into question. Nietzsche was inevitable, given the unresolvable lacuna within the Enlightenment project which replaced the *telos* of the common good with that of human freedom. Nietzsche saw that there could be no real foundations for ethics and consequently celebrated the will to power, which always threatened to break out of this Enlightenment matrix. Nietzsche was the unconscious lurking within the Enlightenment. For MacIntyre's own argument to work, he develops a further critique of the postmodern or Nietzschian Genealogical "tradition"; namely, that it is fundamentally parasitic upon the Enlightenment and as morally bankrupt as the host body, for it too has no *telos*, other than nihilism. MacIntyre's alternative to the Enlightenment and the postmodern is Aristotelian virtue ethics, which eventually evolves (in MacIntyre's trilogy) into Roman Catholic Thomism (accompanied by MacIntyre's conversion).

In contrast to liberal Enlightenment ethics, which developed in forms of emotivism and consequentialism, or in terms of deontological ethics (rules, "oughts" that we must follow), MacIntyre argued for a return to Aristotle's virtue ethics.

In *After Virtue* the main difference between Aristotle and MacIntyre, as Kevin Knight points out, is twofold. First, MacIntyre follows Marx in attempting to elaborate a wholly sociological and non-metaphysical premise for philosophy. Second, and connectedly, he rejects Aristotle's metaphysics largely because it cannot deal with the radical social and ideological conflict that MacIntyre locates in society. However, MacIntyre's rejection of Aristotelian metaphysics inevitably led to a debilitating generality in the virtue ethics he proposed. MacIntyre's two subsequent books, *Whose Justice? Which Rationality?* (London, 1988) and *Three Rival Versions* eventually moved him into arguing that theism, and specifically Thomism, and specifically the Roman Catholic Church, provided the only intellectual context and social institution which could defend the sort of virtue ethics he was advancing. MacIntyre's *telos* eventually found thick descriptive specification. The virtues were located in practices, community, and the disciplined learning, all of which formed the becoming of a particular community of character (to use Stanley Hauerwas's formulation). One simply could not detach ethics from practices and reason from tradition-specific narration.

I agree with MacIntyre in his portrayal and critique of the Enlightenment, although I do have various problems with his cartography, as I have mentioned earlier, and will return to this shortly. My question was: is Küng's notion of a common ethic, a thin morality, conceptually coherent? I now want to answer no, insomuch as I situate Küng's project within what MacIntyre calls Enlightenment ethics.

Küng's notion of thin morality is in effect the attempt to specify universals apart from any tradition-specific narrative, which locates the strategy firmly within the Enlightenment project. Ironically, as MacIntyre points out, the liberal tradition presumes a universal vantage point, forgetting that it is a historically situated narration. The attempt to isolate universals in this fashion, even if they are allegedly produced from within the traditions, is a highly abstract form of deontological ethics. Let me be more specific.

Despite Küng's claim to a universal ethics, there is implicit in his project a very specific methodology and a very Kantian understanding of ethics. The notion of ethics as universal rules runs counter to an Aristotelian and Thomist account of the virtues, whereby ethics takes on its shape, form, and content only in the context of the practices and narration which accompany it. For example, words like "justice" (recalling MacIntyre's *Whose Justice?*) and other uplifting words such as "peace," "freedom," and "human dignity," have very little meaning outside the context of communal narratives and practices that inform and contextualize these terms. A single example will illustrate the point aptly.

Take the notion of "freedom," which when defined within the ideology of the Enlightenment is understood in terms of rational choice and free subjects, and this freedom is not formally or materially related to the good, the communal *telos*, which is the object of choice. That a free-market capitalist economy undergirds such a concept is an argument that has been often made, and I do not wish to repeat it. In contrast, a classical Augustinian notion of freedom, echoing St

Paul, is understood not in terms of autonomy, as with the Enlightenment, but in terms of service to God, heteronomy, such that we only actually experience freedom when we become "slaves" to God – to put it rather dramatically, and biblically. Or again, if we take the notion of freedom within Hinduism, we find that it has no meaning at all which echoes the Enlightenment tradition. It is much like the Christian, partly because of its loose affinity to virtue ethics, whereby ethical duty for the main part is related entirely to caste (role). MacIntyre's book *Whose Justice? Which Rationality?* is given over to showing the tradition-specific way in which these terms are understood, such that while there may be family resemblances between some terms, in the context of their different communal practices, *teloi*, they cannot be assumed to be commensurate.

Küng seems to half-realize the impossible vagueness of his own four universals when he acknowledges that

> A consensus is not necessary in respect of culturally differentiated/"thick" morality.... In disputed concrete questions like abortion or euthanasia, no unifying demands should be made on other nations, cultures and religions to have the same moral praxis. (*Global Ethic for Global Politics*, p. 96)

This is quite a remarkable statement in at least two ways. First, it seems to sever ethics entirely from practice. We should not be surprised, as this is part of the ethical project of the Enlightenment: that we can understand ethics and know what we mean by ethics in terms of concepts, rather than in terms of communities of practice. Second, it is remarkable as it entirely undercuts the value of Küng's own project. What is the point of stating that there is a common global ethic if it cannot amount to some sort of shared moral action? If thick morality, or as I call it, narrated forms of ethics, are irrelevant to the global project, then the global project is irrelevant to historical narrated communities. That is what Küng seems to exalt, when he proclaims a tautology at the heart of his "Declaration": "Every human being must be treated humanely." This allows brahmins to carry on treating outcastes in a "humane" and dutiful way, for that is the appropriate role relationship between the two castes. It allows women to be excluded from the Roman Catholic priesthood, for this exclusion is based on acting justly and according to divine revelation and tradition – according to some. To argue for women priests, for instance, on the grounds of "humane" treatment, is a non-argument, for only a tradition-specific argument could count within the Roman Catholic communion.

Finally, there is one further and deeply problematic consequence for Küng in his undercutting of the normative force of thick moral descriptions within traditions. It is surely an unintended consequence, for Küng's third book, *A Global Ethic for Global Politics and Economics*, is precisely the advancement of a thick moral description supposed to address the problems of global political and economic community. Küng is then stuck in a rather awkward position: either he concedes that his own global ethics advanced at a thick level is not binding or that important; or, if he wants us to take seriously his global ethics, he undercuts the very distinction upon which it is founded – that only thin morality is binding and global. Hence, Küng is unintentionally left advancing a thick description that belongs to no moral community, and which he would like to be owned by all moral communities. This leaves him succumbing to the temptation that he sought to avoid: the imposition of a moral ideology upon the religions from above. And the name of this moral ideology? Liberal modernity. Küng's solution to interreligious conflict is attained by bypassing the particular thick moral social and political descriptions advanced by the religions, and in so doing bypassing the very groups which it allegedly represents.

I shall leave Küng now and turn to the final and third part of my chapter. I have already shown my indebtedness to MacIntyre, but to further my argument I need to address two critical problems within MacIntyre's project to focus more clearly on the issues that face us when looking at the question of ethical cooperation between the religions.

The first problem is that MacIntyre is rather Christian–Eurocentric in his assessment of Western culture. There are only three rival versions of moral enquiry, and as Milbank has correctly argued, they are all generated out of the Christian narrative. (See John Milbank, *Theology and Social Theory*, Oxford, 1990.) But what of those other major Western cultural forces: Judaism and Islam? Why are they not part of MacIntyre's geography, especially since both, and especially Islam, have drawn so heavily from Aristotle? I do not think the argument will work that they are implicitly covered in the virtue ethics tradition, for I have also tried to point out that within MacIntyre's own project he has seen the futility of using a broad umbrella term such as virtue ethics and needs to more explicitly address the specific virtues that are narrated within specific ethical traditions. This in part accounts for his final conversion to Roman Catholicism. Furthermore, given the real religious plurality within the West, what of Hindu and Buddhist forms of moral enquiry? The complexity of moral argument is obscured by MacIntyre's limited cartography.

Let me give one example from a Muslim critic of MacIntyre, Muhammad Legenhausen. He highlights Islam's relationship to the Aristotelian tradition upon which MacIntyre is also so dependent. He protests at MacIntyre's misappropriation of Aristotelian virtue ethics as a purely Christian project, and criticizes MacIntyre's omission of Islam in the debate. Furthermore, Legenhausen, located in Iran, suggests that Islam can account for the aporia within MacIntyre's argument whereby MacIntyre's espousal of small sectarian communities, after the order of St Benedict, fails entirely to engage with the problem of the nation-state which MacIntyre identifies as one of the roots of the contemporary malaise. Susan Mendus and John Horton make the same point:

> Moreover, given the importance which MacIntyre attached to the social embeddedness of thought and enquiry, his largely negative view of modernity continually threatens to undermine any attempt to root his positive proposals in the contemporary world of advanced industrial societies. (J. Horton & S. Mendus (eds.), *After MacIntyre: Critical Perspectives on the Work of Alasdair MacIntyre*, Oxford: Polity Press, 1994, pp. 13–14)

According to Legenhausen, Islam, on the other hand, is able to offer a theocratic solution, allegedly avoiding both "nationalism and liberalism," an alternative that is "not taken seriously by Western theorists" (M. Legenhausen, review of *Whose Justice?* in *Al- Tawhid*, 14.2 (1997), p. 169). These are precisely the thick-description conflicts that need to be addressed, which are somewhat obscured by MacIntyre's cartography. I should add that nothing within MacIntyre's project requires their exclusion, and in later writing MacIntyre has actually addressed the differences between Thomist virtue ethics and Confucian virtue ethics – and in principle, such engagements are open-ended viz. traditions and topics of concern.

My second problem with MacIntyre concerns the notion of "tradition." MacIntyre seems to work with a rather unitary definition of tradition. For example, he obscures the fact that, historically, Christianity has developed differing forms of moral enquiry, other than an Aristotelian–Thomist virtue ethics. This would mean that if we were to advance further in addressing interreligious moral conflict and moral cooperation, we would need a far more differentiated sketch of the situation. This criticism might be seen as a footnote to the last. And both points should indicate that I do not want to contest the basic structure of MacIntyre's analysis, orientation, and argumentation, but rather to complexify it and broaden it out. This will then allow us to address the types of questions that Küng was concerned to address with more historical, intellectual, and moral coherence.

To this end, let me finish by outlining two particular avenues for further exploration that will arise if my neo-MacIntyre postmodern model is further developed. (See my *The Trinity and the Meeting of Religions*, New York, 2000.) It seems clear to me that Küng has misread MacIntyre in dismissing him as a postmodern relativist only concerned with "regional" ethics. MacIntyre's work takes utterly seriously the questions of conversation and intelligibility between differing "regional" ethical communities.

My first point would be that there is enormous room to explore and build upon the *common areas* of *agreement* regarding the goals of thick moral description deriving from different traditions of moral enquiry. This is far more realistic than undercutting the level of thick description and suggesting that it should not be binding for others. Moral conflict and moral resolution only actually exist at this level of thick description. While Küng is right to note the difficulty of making one community's thick description binding for another community, he seems to imagine that it is possible in this one instance: promoting his thick description of the global ethics. Rather, I would suggest that it is important to allow different communities to advance their own thick descriptions, and then to work with what arises at that point.

Consider one example: those who oppose abortion on tradition-specific thick moral argumentation often also argue that this should be morally binding on all people, whether they belong to that tradition or not. This is because their tradition-specific thick description also describes the way things are, whether people accept it or not: in this case, that the unborn child cannot be murdered, to put it in stark terms. Here is a clear example where Küng's injunction against the imposition of thick moral descriptions upon others simply has no force. Rather, it is a complex question of meditation and negotiation. It was upon this issue that the Roman Catholic church and some Muslim countries and Islamic movements formed a common front at the world population summit in Cairo. An extremely influential coalition operated whereby these two religious traditions worked together for a common moral end: the responsible use by women of their fertility, and the dignity of the unborn person.

I have chosen such an example to also highlight the ambiguous ways in which interreligious cooperation can work. It is often perceived to be reactionary by those within different moral communities, and even by those within the two moral communities in question – as is the case with the Cairo summit. Effective interreligious ethical cooperation can often work to consolidate control over sexual bodies rather than social bodies. It can, of course, also work in terms of social bodies: when there is agreement about social and political goals regarding, say, third world debt or nuclear armaments. In both the latter cases there has been effective interreligious action. Hence, my first point is that we do not need grand global ethical theories for interreligious ethical cooperation. Such cooperation can be generated by taking seriously thick moral descriptions and looking for points of contact and constructive engagement and disagreements.

My second point is that there is enormous room in which to explore the *conflicts and clashes* within thick moral descriptions. Interreligious harmony and peace cannot be attained easily, if indeed it is attainable at all. If conflicts and clashes are to be taken seriously, and not bypassed, then I would want to suggest that moral argumentation has to proceed along the lines proposed by MacIntyre – at least for Thomistically orientated Roman Catholics, like myself. This is not to suggest that moral communities will agree to such engagements, or even welcome them; nor is it to suggest that different societies will indeed facilitate such engagements, or that such engagements might resolve conflicts. But it is one way in which the question might be addressed fruitfully, and it is only one way. MacIntyre's argument in *Three Rival Versions* takes absolutely seriously two levels of argumentation that take place when rival or different traditions meet. One must remember that MacIntyre's proposals are being advanced from a tradition-specific point of view. First, there is the requirement to learn the other's language, their way of reasoning, their authoritative texts and so on. This process is like making the other's language one's own second language. Only then, suggests MacIntyre, can we proceed to try and show why there may be internal weaknesses and unresolved lacunae within that tradition, initially within its own terms. Of course, such internal critiques may already exist within that tradition, so that there are complex levels of intra-traditioned debates. A good example in our sphere may relate to the question of caste within Hinduism and the question of the ordination of women within the Roman Catholic church.

But there is also a second level, and these numerical distinctions do not relate to any priority or synchronism, but are purely heuristic and logical. The criticisms of such lacunae and unresolved problems within one tradition may also be better illuminated from within another tradition. MacIntyre illustrates and bases his case in regard to the debate that took place in the University of Paris in the thirteenth century. We might illustrate the same process whereby various low-caste and outcaste Hindus have moved outside of Hinduism to resolve the lacunae that they experience. In such cases some have become Buddhists (like the famous Ambedekhar) and some Christians – even though this latter move has not always resulted in their escaping the tyranny of caste operative within some Indian Christian communities. Or to give another example, it has led some philosophers like Mary Daly to leave the Roman Catholic church as the only way in which to resist and overcome patriarchy. Others, like Elizabeth Schussler-Fiorenza and Rosemary Ruether, remain within the "tradition" while subverting it and also developing repressed traditions. The equivalent to the latter would be Hindus who criticized caste and rethought it, like Gandhi and Radhakrishnan. But it is the first group of cases that is of special interest, for it shows that in such interreligious conversation there are three possible and unpredictable outcomes.

First, it may be that one has to be involved in severely criticizing another religion on moral grounds, primarily because the thick moral description on certain issues comes into conflict with the thick moral description on those same issues within our own tradition. Such criticisms of other religions are often seen as unacceptable to those advancing the cause of interreligious dialogue, but there seem to be good reasons to challenge their assumptions. It may very well be that the religions are particularly the cause of problems, rather than their solutions, when it comes to questions of, say, the role of women and the tyranny of patriarchy. It may be that some religions have particularly powerful structural alignments that might be called into question. There can be no *a priori* areas of sanctity, when the holy form unholy alliances!

This also leads to my second point. It is surely the case that there is always an element of mission in every moment of dialogue. The two are inseparable, despite some World Council of Churches and some Vatican documents on the matter. Whenever we converse with anyone regarding their and our own deep moral convictions, it would surely be naive to imagine that there will be no element of missionary zeal present: that is, we, and they, want to share the truth. The word "mission" has often been seen as unacceptable within interreligious circles, but it seems that its reality is unavoidable – and making its dynamic explicit is no bad thing. But I should register an important qualification in terms of mission as advanced by a neo-MacIntyrian, John Milbank. He suggests that we must abandon dialogue and simply seek to out-narrate rival traditions; yet another form of Christian postmodernism (see Milbank, 'The End of Dialogue' in my *Christian Uniqueness Reconsidered*, pp. 174–91). While his suspicion of dialogue, as he frames it, is founded, he too quickly dismisses MacIntyre's use of traditioned forms of rationality whereby arguments and conversations between different traditions might take place; and he too quickly resorts to out-narration, as if it were possible to narrate without conversation and some point of contact with the "audience."

One further point. In such moral conversations our own religious traditions may undergo traumatic and/or minor changes, which we could not predict prior to such conversations. This is at least true for Christianity, and one would have to make out the case for different traditions. Let me cite just one example. Capital punishment has long been sanctioned within the Roman Catholic moral tradition. It appeared in the first edition of the recent Catechism, but was sharply qualified, nearly out of existence, in the second revised edition. The storm of protest at the first edition came from Catholics and non-Catholics, and while the change of emphasis is entirely justified on intra-traditional grounds, it is arguable that the shift in this teaching has also arisen from Catholicism's long conversation with the Enlightenment. This is of course a contentious case, but one might also see the current (non) debate about women in the church as owing an important debt to non-Christian feminist currents prior to the issues being rendered worthy of discussion (or not) on intra-Christian-traditional grounds. Likewise the role of women in Islam, or the question of outcastes within Hinduism, although regarding the latter we might note that there has long been an internal Hindu critique of the caste structure.

These are just some of the avenues opened up when we rethink the problem of interreligious ethical cooperation. Focusing on what we have in common also requires that we attend to our differences. This tension, which can be constructive and is historically situated, requires us to be suspicious of a global ethics which seeks to resolve on the level of theory what can only be resolved on the level of common practice. The further advantage to this approach is that it avoids the types of attempts that seek to deem all religions true, or all religions, except one's own, as false. In one postmodernist mode: it simply seeks engagement with religious plurality, rejoicing in the often fecund differences, as well as seeing the dark complexity and horror within these differences, for the sole sake of worshiping God more truthfully.

CHAPTER 8
The Christian Difference, or Surviving Postmodernism

Stanley Hauerwas

When a detailed history of the Yale School emerges, Stanley Hauerwas's work will, no doubt, rank as a major contribution. Hauerwas's work is, however, distinct from the kind of work done by Frei and Lindbeck; distinct also from the contemporary Yale School voices in this volume – Serene Jones, Walter Lowe, and William Placher. This distinctiveness owes much to the fact that Hauerwas was not a pupil of Frei and Lindbeck, though he engaged in graduate work at Yale. His approach to narrative, to theology as a discourse (not just a discipline), to the theologian's engagement with the politics of everyday life, sets him apart from the more dogmatic and philosophical work of Jones, Lowe, and Placher (though it should be noted that these three have found themselves increasingly engaged in ethical issues and dialogues with social science). Perhaps the key to understanding why Hauerwas both belongs and does not belong to the Yale School lies in the figures at the heart of his graduate project on character and the Christian life: Barth, Wittgenstein, and Yoder. The inspiration of Barth's radical theological challenge to modernity allies Hauerwas with Yale School theology, but his more nuanced and thoroughgoing espousal of Wittgenstein makes his work distinctive. Paul Holmer was his teacher, and the nature of human action, ethics, and the politics of certain practices (and the knowledges produced, modified, and consolidated through those practices) became his concern. He was also one of the earliest theological readers of MacIntyre's philosophy of the social sciences because of his interest in narrative and action. So although sharing certain sympathies with the Yale School, Hauerwas draws on traditions which are fundamental for Catholic theology: the virtue ethics of Aristotle, the examination of theology as a discursive practice (which goes back to Augustine but is central to Aquinas), the Thomistic approach to narrative action in MacIntyre (rather than Ricoeur). As he reveals in the essay below, he is criticized for the catholicity of his approach; but it is a catholicity which is fundamental to his commitment to ecumenical dialogue and ecclesiology as the basis for theological discussion and reflection.

Stanley Hauerwas is creative and energetic. It is difficult to do justice to the spread of his work both as author and as editor. Among the most significant must be listed his works on ecclesiology: *A Community of Character: Toward a Constructive Christian Social Ethic* (Notre Dame, IN, 1981), *The Peaceable Kingdom: A Primer on Christian Ethics* (London, 1984), and *In Good Company: The Church as Polis* (Notre Dame, IN, 1995). But there have also been collections of essays on specific ethical issues facing contemporary society, among which are: *Should War be Eliminated? Philosophical and Theological Investigation* (Milwaukee, WI, 1984), *Suffering Presence: Theological Reflections on Medicine, the Mentally Handicapped and the Church* (Edinburgh, 1988), and *Naming the Silences: God, Medicine, and the Problem of Suffering* (Grand Rapid, MI, 1990). The importance of his work was recognized in the invitation to give the Gifford Lectures in 2001.

Can Postmodernism Have a History?

"Post-Modernism is the pessimism of an obsolescent class – the salaried official intelligentsia – whose fate is closely bound up with that of the declining nation-state."[1] This may sound like a particularly harsh judgment made by Nicholas Boyle in his extraordinary book, *Who Are We Now? Christian Humanism and the Global Market from Hegel to Heaney*. Yet I think Boyle is right to so judge postmodernism. That I agree with Boyle may surprise some who have grouped me with the nihilistic, relativistic, barbarian hordes who threaten all we hold dear – matters such as objectivity and the family. I confess I have at times taken great pleasure watching postmodernists dismantle the pretensions of modernism, but it is still the case that being an enemy of my enemy does not and should not necessarily make me a friend of postmodernism.

Before I elaborate and defend Boyle's judgment, however, I need to prepare a case for why his understanding of postmodernism is important for those of us who, in an allegedly postmodern time, attempt to do Christian theology. That some may have mistook me as a sympathetic supporter of postmodernism is understandable. After all, I have playfully used postmodern playfulness to try to remind Christians that we are in a life and death struggle with the world.[2] I have thought the playful use of postmodernism was justified because I have found it difficult to take postmodernism seriously as an intellectual position. However, if Boyle is right to interpret postmodernism as the position of those who would make our time the end of history, then I think it is a serious mistake not to take postmodernism seriously.

That I have not taken postmodernism seriously does not mean I have not taken seriously the work of people like Michel Foucault. Indeed, as David Toole has shown in his remarkable book, *Waiting for Godot in Sarajevo: Theological*

Reflections on Nihilism, Tragedy, and Apocalypse, Christians, particularly Christians committed to Christian nonviolence, cannot afford to ignore Foucault's extraordinary work.[3] This is particularly true, as Toole makes clear, for those who have been influenced by the equally remarkable work of John Howard Yoder.

Toole observes that where Foucault's work meets a Yoder-like reading of the New Testament, both step into the glow of a new light that is the product of their convergence. This is particularly the case when considering how similar Foucault's account of power is to that of the "principalities and powers" in the New Testament. Toole rightly defends Foucault against those that suggest he provides no alternative of resistance to the powers; but Toole argues further that it is the cross, as Yoder directed our attention, which gives the hope – a hope Foucault cannot make intelligible – necessary for such a struggle. Responding to his own question of how to characterize the difference between Foucault's tragic politics and Yoder's apocalyptic alternative, Toole observes, drawing on Beckett's *Godot*:

> For Vladimir and Estragon the difference is that Godot will finally arrive. For Nietzsche, the difference lies between Dionysus and the Crucified. John Howard Yoder sums up this difference in a word: Jesus, the slain lamb, the one who took up the cross and not the crown. Of course what this means for Vladimir and Estragon is not only that Godot will arrive one day, perhaps one day soon, but that he has already come and that they can, therefore, wait with confidence and patience; it means that even in Sarajevo they can protest their suffering with dignity.[4]

If Toole is right (and I certainly think he is), Christian intellectuals face an enormous challenge which Yoder's work only signals. In short, we theologians must provide an account of our situation that is at least as radical and imaginative as the one Foucault was attempting. In other words we must challenge the knowledges currently enshrined in the academic disciplines dominating the modern university. Such knowledges provide the theodical accounts necessary to convince us that the way things are is the way things have to be – which is one of the reasons I have had difficulty taking postmodernism seriously. The problem in brief is that postmodernism is a far too comforting story for alienated intellectuals.

Of course, it can be objected that I am being unfair to postmodernism. After all, most postmodern thinkers style themselves as radicals. As a style of thought, postmodernism is allegedly suspicious "of classical notions of truth, reason, identity and objectivity, of the idea of universal progress or emancipation, of single frameworks, grand narratives or ultimate grounds of explanation."[5] Postmodernism seems, in other words, to call into question the Enlightenment project and surely that is a good thing. Yet I am not convinced that postmodernism, either as an intellectual position or as a cultural style, is post-anything.[6]

For example, Boyle observes that many postmodernists deny or at least remain agnostic about whether "post-Modern" is a chronological term at all.

Lyotard, according to Boyle, seems to assume that postmodernism runs in parallel with modernism or is even a permanent possibility of the human spirit. Thus Montaigne, in the sixteenth century, is postmodern, but the brothers Schlegel, in the 1800s, are only modern. Boyle notes that the denial of chronology is an understandable ploy for postmodernists just to the extent that modernity depends on some opposition between the present and the past. Thus for the postmodernist, all architectural styles are always simultaneously available.[7]

The Christian difference – why we are not postmodernist – I think is clearly revealed at this point. Christians have a stake in history, which as Boyle (appealing to Hegel) observes, is the collective self-understanding of modern Europeans who thought the history of the world, or at least of their "states," to be inseparable from Christianity. They so saw themselves not because of some continuity between institutions, but just to the extent history, understood as the "meaningful interconnection of *all* events, each of which is invested both with individual uniqueness and absolute importance," is in the bounds of a Christian world.[8] Christians must be able to narrate postmodernism in a manner that postmodernism cannot narrate Christianity. Or more adequately: we must show how Christianity provides the resources for a critique of its own mistakes in a way that modernity or postmodernity cannot provide.

Such narration will require Christians to develop accounts, as I suggested above, that are more powerful than either modernist or postmodernist can muster. Indeed, one of the illusions of postmodernism is to give a far too intelligible and, thus, comforting account of where we are. Our world and our lives are far too fragmentary and disordered to know where we are, but at least Christians owe it to themselves and their neighbors to confess that such disorder is but a reflection of the failure of the churches to be faithful. Modernity, and its bastard offspring, postmodernity, are but reflections of the Christian attempt to make God a god available without the mediation of the church.[9] Such a god cannot help but become some "timeless thing" necessary to ensure the assumed truth of Christianity in service to the growth of secular power.

Postmodernism, in short, is the outworking of mistakes in Christian theology correlative to the attempt to make Christianity "true" apart from faithful witness. This is undoubtedly a strong thesis, but one I think we are beginning increasingly to appreciate thanks to that extraordinary group of theologians currently clustered at or around Cambridge University. For example, Philip Blond, with the confidence we have come to associate with this theological style, observes that the crucial moment in the surrender of theology to secular reason's account of nature and corresponding understanding of natural theology occurred in England between the time of Henry of Ghent (1217–93) and Duns Scotus (1266–1308).[10] Blond notes that Henry maintained that any knowledge of a created thing by the human intellect was also knowledge of God. In creatures, however, being was determinable; but God's being is indeterminable. For Scotus, the distinction between knowing God in himself and knowing him in a creature was not important. For this reason, according to Blond, when considering the universal science of metaphysics Scotus elevated being (*ens*) to a higher station over God in order that being could be distributed both to God and his creatures. Scotus did this because God could not be known naturally unless being is univocal (*univocum*) to the created and uncreated.[11]

The univocity of God and creature marks, according to Blond, the time when theology itself became idolatrous. Theologians disregarded what they should have learned from Aquinas, namely that nothing can be predicated univocally of God and other things. Thus in Aquinas's contention that which can be predicated of God can only be participated in by finite creatures via analogy. "This analogical mode, whilst it accepts that we only come to have knowledge via His effects, understands that the reality of these effects belongs by priority to God, even though we only uncover God as the source of these effects after having experienced such effects without initially recognizing their antecedent cause."[12]

I am painfully aware that the introduction of these rather obscure remarks about how Christian theologians came to understand God's relation to creation cannot help but appear as unrelated to issues raised by postmodernism. I am convinced, however, that in order to grasp the challenge of postmodernism – as Robert Jenson puts it, how "the world lost its story" – we must understand how modernity and postmodernity are the result of mistakes in Christian practice and theology.[13] This means, as I suggested above, Christians must challenge the postmodern narrative that simply forgets that Christianity had anything to do with the world in which we now find ourselves.

I am not suggesting that we need to remind postmodernists that Christianity once was capable of producing cultural and political effects. It is not a question of getting our historical due as Christians, though that is not entirely irrelevant, but rather of our ability to maintain for ourselves an account of the world in which the God we worship matters. The attempt to make God knowable separate from how God has made himself known through scripture makes a world without God thinkable. God could not help but become another "thing" amid other metaphysical possibilities. Accordingly, Christians robbed the world of its story.

Boyle observes, for example, that Dante's *Divine Comedy* differs in its very manner from non-Christian poetry because, like the Bible, the *Comedy* is about the world of grace and also about the world of history. Dante's poem is about real, datable men and women who at particular times accepted or rejected the grace of God offered them thirteen centuries earlier through the bodily life, death, and resurrection of Christ. For Dante, and for the world in which his poem was written, the earthly passing over of the incarnate Word was what constitutes history:

> that gives direction and purpose to the time which leads up to Christ and an eschatological expectation to the time after him; that divides the ages into a pre-Christian period of signs and figures and a Christian period of fulfillment; that provides the temporal point of reference by which years are dated and people and their

activities made singular and unrepeatable. For Dante it is only in relation to Christ that human doings are part of history, and only as part of history that human doings become the subject-matter of his poem.[14]

Postmodernism, then, names not only the end of the time when poetry like Dante's is possible, but it names a time when such poetry has become unintelligible. Modernity, drawing on the metaphysics of a transcendent god, was the attempt to be historical without Christ. Postmodernity, facing the agony of living in history with no end, is the denial of history.[15] In the wake of such a denial, the only remaining comfort is the shopping mall, which gives us the illusion of creating histories through choice, thus hiding from us the reality that none of us can avoid having our lives determined by money.[16] Money, in modernity, is the institutionalization of univocity of being that Scotus thought necessary to ensure the unmediated knowledge of God.[17]

Postmodernism and the Global Market

I began with agreeing with Boyle's extraordinary definition of postmodernism; his claim is one I think I can defend. I think he is right to suggest that postmodernism is "the pessimism of an obsolescent class." I would emphasize that the most determinative representatives of his "salaried official intelligentsia" are to be found, I believe, in the universities. That the fate of such an intelligentsia is "closely bound up with that of the declining nation-state" should not be surprising given the fact that universities as we know them were formed to produce and reproduce the knowledges to sustain the ruling classes necessary to maintain the nation-state system. That that system is currently under stress by the developments of global capitalism is reflected in the confusions trumpeted about the universities in the name of postmodernism.

I do not wish to be misunderstood. I am not suggesting that postmodernism is nothing but smoke and mirrors. Rather, I believe that Fredric Jameson rightly identified postmodernism with the cultural logic of advanced capitalism in which the production of culture has been integrated into commodity production, thus creating the urgency of producing ever fresh waves of novelty.[18] As David Harvey observes, "whatever else we do with the concept, we should not read postmodernism as some autonomous artistic current. Its rootedness in daily life is one of its most patently transparent features."[19]

The everyday life in which we are rooted, however, is not easily known, particularly by intellectuals. Indeed, intellectuals (who like to believe their "work" is free from the market) have a stake in hiding from themselves the material factors that make their existence possible. Thus the illusions of a genealogist can be thought to be quite compelling until, as Boyle observes, "the funding dries up and it becomes apparent that the nation no longer has an omnipotent monarch commanding the propagation of Enlightenment (that is, the critique of Church and the bourgeoisie) 'for its own sake' (that is, in the interests of the state.)"[20] What the university intellectual cannot face is the socioeconomic truth that in a global market we have all become the proletariat.

It is hard to imagine an intellectual alternative better suited for the elites of a global capitalism than postmodernism.[21] Capitalism is, after all, the ultimate form of deconstruction. How better to keep the laborer under the control of capital than through the scarcity produced through innovation? Capitalism, as David Harvey observes, is necessarily innovative, not because of the myth of the innovative entrepreneur, but because of the coercive laws of competition and the conditions of class struggle endemic to capitalism. Of course the effects of such innovation are to make past investments of labor skills valueless.[22]

Obviously such a system produces a self that is fragmented, if not multiple. The difficulty in the description of the loss of the unified self by postmodernists is their failure to see that such a self is the result of social and economic developments. Such a causal connection, however, is precisely

> what "genealogical" deconstructive thinking not only cannot represent – it denies it exists. In so doing it plays the game precisely as the global market wants it played. For the fiction by which the global market commends itself to us and encourages our participation in it is that the human self is purely a consumer. . . . The self is little more than a formality, the name we give to the principle that consumes options, the transient locus of interpretation. There is nothing outside the text, just as there is nothing outside the market.[23]

The belief that there is no single truth or world but only a multiplicity of mutually untranslatable perspectives, Boyle observes, is strangely analogous to the belief that the market is a boundless medium of perfect competition among an infinite number of ever-expanding commercial identities.[24] It is no wonder that, confronted with such a system, intellectuals discard the idea of totality. "For in a period when no very far-reaching political action seems really feasible, when so-called micropolitics seems the order of the day, it is relieving to convert this necessity into a virtue – to persuade oneself that one's political limits have, as it were, a solid ontological grounding, in the fact that social totality is in any case a chimera."[25]

The recent example of Richard Rorty is surely good evidence for the inability of postmodernism to mount any politics worthy of the name. In his new book, *Achieving Our Country*, Rorty confirms an earlier description of his own position by Terry Eagleton, that is, since all conventions are arbitrary, one might as well conform to those of the Free World.[26] "For purposes of thinking about how to achieve our country," Rorty asserts, "we do not need to worry about the correspondence theory of truth, the grounds of normativity, the impossibility of justice, or the infinite distance which separates us from the other. For those purposes, we can give both religion and philosophy a pass. We can just get on with trying to solve what Dewey called 'the problems of men.'"[27]

According to Rorty that means we must continue to support the nation-state as the only "agent capable of making any real difference in the amount of selfishness and sadism inflicted on Americans."[28] We must do so from Rorty's perspective because, since 1909, the only dividing line between the American Left and the American Right is the former's presumption that the state must make itself responsible for redistributive policies.[29] The cultural Left must therefore shed its "semi-conscious anti-Americanism" in order to get back "into the business of piecemeal reform within the framework of a market economy."[30]

Rorty's book, which bears the subtitle of "Leftist Thought in Twentieth Century America," is surely the tombstone that confirms the death of the Left in America. His call for a renewed loyalty to the nation-state, at least the nation-state called America, comes just at the time the nation-state, other than as an agency to ensure prosperity,[31] is increasingly undermined by the global market.[32] His "social vision," like that of so many postmodernists, turns out to be but another form of liberalism. That is, the "just state is one neutral in respect of any particular conception of the good life, confining its jurisdiction to furnishing the conditions in which individuals may discover themselves."[33]

I realize that it may be quite unjust to tar postmodernism with Rorty's brush, but too often postmodernists turn out to be liberals in their ethics and politics who no longer believe in the philosophical conceits of liberalism but have nowhere else to go.[34] If you want a way to test whether this is true try to engage a postmodernist in a discussion about abortion or so-called assisted suicide. Eagleton rightly credits postmodernism for putting on the political agenda issues of sexuality, gender, and ethnicity, but fears that these concerns can become a substitute for classical forms of radical politics that deal with class, state, ideology, revolution, and the material modes of production. Questions of sexuality are no doubt political, but they can also be a form of forgetfulness for questions about why some people do not get enough to eat. Eagleton notes that perhaps one of the reasons that feminism and ethnicity are popular is because they are not necessarily anti-capitalist and so fit well with a post-radical age.[35]

Indeed, I fear that one of the reasons postmodernism has become such an attractive alternative for many in the contemporary university is because serious work is no longer expected there. The fragmentation of the curriculum into disciplines which are unintelligible even to themselves is surely the breeding ground for postmodernism. The more fractured the university becomes, moreover, the more it is able to act as the institution capable of confirming the postmodernist description of the world. As a result the university becomes a useful place to sequester people who might otherwise get into trouble. But then that is exactly what we should expect, given Boyle's judgment that postmodernism is the pessimism of an obsolete class.

The Christian Difference

I obviously think it would be a profound mistake for Christians to side with the postmodernists, although even to think that Christians have a choice to be for or against postmodernism seems to me a far too optimistic account of our situation. If the analysis of postmodernism I have provided is close to being right, it is not a question of choice. Rather, Christians are faced – along with our non-Christian sisters and brothers – with the challenge of surviving postmodernism. To survive, moreover, means we must have skills of resistance. I believe God has given us all we need not only to survive but to flourish. But as I suggested above, theologically we have only begun to imagine the knowledges necessary for the task.

To survive will require us to develop practices and habits that make our worship of God an unavoidable witness to the world. By unavoidable I mean that we must help the world discover that it is of course unintelligible just to the extent that it does not acknowledge the God we worship. That God "is whoever raised Jesus from the dead, having before raised Israel from Egypt."[36] That is the God, who having created all that is, can be known only by way of analogy. Analogy is but the way we name the metaphysical implications that God wills to care for his creation through calling into existence a faithful people.

Commenting on the apocalyptic character of Ezekiel, Daniel, Mark, and John of Patmos, John Howard Yoder observes that these texts are not either about pie in the sky or the Russians in Mesopotamia. "They are about how the crucified Jesus is a more adequate key to understanding what God is about in the real world of empires and armies and markets than is the ruler in Rome, with all his supporting military, commercial, and sacerdotal networks."[37] Postmodernists cannot help but think such a claim to be the grandest of grand narratives, but I cannot imagine Christians saying anything less. Not only saying it, but also thinking it true.

For example, consider Yoder's claim that the point apocalyptic makes is not that people who use violence in the name of fostering justice are not as strong as they think, though that is true, but rather

> it is that people who bear crosses are working with the grain of the universe. One does not come to that belief by reducing social process to mechanical and statistical models, nor by winning some of one's battles for the control of one's corner of the fallen world. One comes to it by sharing the life of those who sing about the resurrection of the slain Lamb.[38]

"Working with the grain of the universe" is not a confessional claim peculiar to Christians, but rather a metaphysical claim about the way things are.

Contrary to the oft-made assertion that Yoder-like claims require Christians to withdraw from the world, the opposite (as Yoder constantly stressed) is the case.[39] Indeed, I think it is important for Mennonites particularly, as well as their fellow travelers – that is, people like myself and John Paul II – to deny they seek only to be a prophetic minority in the wider church or world. Rather, we seek to provide an alternative by which the world can see that we are not condemned to anarchy and violence. Rather than withdrawing from the world, even a postmodern world, we are better off siding with those who would "take over" the world.

Gerald Schlabach, a Mennonite theologian who teaches at Bluffton College, recently sent me the criticisms of me that another Mennonite had posted on an e-mail forum. The critic had argued that my work was far too Catholic and, thus, incompatible with an Anabaptist perspective: "Hauerwas has a Constantinian fear of Christian liberty. He wants the clergy to tell us the story and the church to have the sanctions to enforce it." In his response, Schlabach agreed that this is an accurate (although insufficiently nuanced) summary of my views, but defended my position nonetheless. As Schlabach put it,

> Hauerwas has discovered a dirty little secret – Anabaptists who reject historic Christendom may not actually be rejecting the vision of Christendom as a society in which all of life is integrated under the Lordship of Christ. On this reading, Christendom may in fact be a vision of shalom, and our argument with Constantinians is not over the vision so much as the sinful effort to grasp at its fullness through violence, before its eschatological time. Hauerwas is quite consistent once you see that he does want to create a Christian society (*polis, societas*) – a community and way of life shaped fully by Christian convictions. He rejects Constantinianism because "the world" cannot be this society and we only distract ourselves from building a truly Christian society by trying to make our nation into that society, rather than be content with living as a community-in-exile. So Hauerwas wants Catholics to be more Anabaptist, and Anabaptists to be more Catholic, and Protestants to be both, and the only way he can put this together in terms of his own ecclesial location is to be a "Catholic" Methodist in roughly the way that some Episcopalians are Anglo-Catholic.[40]

Schlabach's presentation of my own position says what I have been trying to say better than how I have said it. More importantly, I hope, his suggestion points a way forward if we are not only to survive but to find ways to resist global capitalism. It should surprise no one to discover that I believe that any response Christians have to the challenge of the global market will be ecclesial. In particular, I think Christians must find ways to be Catholic in a world in which the church is but another international agency – and one that is probably less effective than the many that exist already and the many more which are sure to be created.

Let me try to explain these obscure remarks by returning again to some observations by Boyle, who describes himself as a Catholic humanist,[41] about the international character of the church. He suggests that the international character of the church (and I assume he means the Roman Catholic church) is likely to be more problematic in the future than it has been for many centuries. In the era of nation-states the international character of the church was one of its most significant features, just to the extent the church offered an alternative to the loyalties bred through nationalism. Though the church often failed to challenge nationalism, its very existence at least provided the material possibility for mounting a challenge to the state's pretension to rule over minds and bodies.

Yet, Boyle suggests, in the new global order the church's universality may be an even more serious temptation than the temptation of nationalisms since the

Reformation. For the new order is a kind of universality whose ambition is to rule minds and bodies just as nations did so effectively in the past. The church may be tempted to collaborate with these worldly powers, celebrating the fact that they have adopted the church's global perspective. But as Boyle notes, the worldly powers have their own purposes, "and if one is disturbed when a papal tour becomes a media event it is because it is becoming unclear in such a case who is using, or paying homage, to whom."[42]

That the church has often imitated the secular rule of its day is no great surprise. In feudalism the popes became feudal lords, absolute monarchs in the age of absolutism, and in the age of nation-states something like presidents for life of a kind of international state. Thus in the First Vatican Council the church "battened-down the hatches" to face the totalitarian pretensions of the state in the era of unrestrained nationalism. So in an international age the church, according to Boyle, cannot help but act as one global agency among others, and we should be glad that it does so – just as Christians in the past were glad the church had the strength and presence to speak to the state when men and women were often at odds with their country and had no other friend than the church.

Yet the moral authority the church derived from its past internationalism will have to be drawn from elsewhere if the church in this new age is to continue to be different, to continue to be unassimilated to the secular world. Boyle suggests that such a church will "need to draw its moral strength not from its international presence but from its claim to represent people as they are locally and distinct from the worldwide ramifications of their existence as participants in the global market."[43] Grand narratives continue,

> but the little narratives of the victims of the grand process, the stories of what the big new world is squeezing out or ignoring, they will be told on the small scale, and full of details which the new world will dismiss as superficial and inessential. In terms of church structure, the little narratives will be told at diocesan, parochial, or base-community level.[44]

The church capable of "such little" narratives will need all the resources it can muster – particularly those resources from the past that give us the confidence in the face of the universal market to claim universality, that Jesus of Nazareth was raised from the dead. The worship of such a God surely requires that the church not forget those who have become expendable, too poor even to be debtors, and therefore from the market's perspective "non-persons."[45] The worship of such a God means that we must pray and pray fervently for the reconciliation of Catholics and Protestants, as our very division wounds not only ourselves but the world itself.[46]

Such a church is surely necessary if, as Boyle puts it, we are to learn to see God in the world in which we find ourselves, and not only in some past golden age such as the catacombs or the Middle Ages. Rather, we must be at least as courageous and inventive as those Christians who made the Middle Ages possible by living in catacombs. To be such a people in this time we must be sustained by our worship of God who wills himself known in Christ and so known can safeguard "us from self-worship and maintain us in the conviction that nothing we know in this world is ultimate – not the media of communication, nor the system of signs, not even the end of history."[47] Through the faithful worship of a God so known, Christians can not only survive postmodernism but even flourish.[48]

Notes

1. Nicholas Boyle, *Who Are We Now? Christian Humanism and the Global Market from Hegel to Heaney* (Notre Dame, IN: University of Notre Dame Press, 1998), p. 318. I have followed Boyle's use of capitalization and hyphenation of Post-Modernism in this quote, but when I am writing in my own voice I will use neither.

2. That I have been associated with the postmodernist has always seemed to me a mistake deriving from those who fail to understand Wittgenstein's influence for how I work. Stanley Fish is certainly a friend and I have learned from his work, but I have no idea what it would mean to say that Fish is a postmodernist. Philosophically I have learned more from Alasdair MacIntyre who, exactly because of his appreciation of Nietzsche, is anything but a postmodernist. I suppose my attack on the National Association of Scholars in *After Christendom?* (Nashville: Abingdon Press, 1991, pp. 140–52) may have led some to think I am a "relativist" but even if I were a relativist, which I am not, that would not make me a postmodernist. If MacIntyre is a non-foundationalist, I suppose I must also be such, but again a MacIntyrian non-foundationalism does not entail the kind of skepticism thought to be at the heart of postmodernism. For a defense of "postmodernism" in theology with which I am in large agreement, see Nancey Murphy and James McClendon, "Distinguishing Modern from Postmodern Theology," *Modern Theology*, 5/3 (April 1989), pp. 191–214.

    By a "playful use of postmodernism" I mean how I have used the "atheism" of postmodernism against the humanism of modernism: for I assume that postmodernism is the only atheism that modernity could produce. Modernism is the rejection of God, or at least a parody of the Christian God, in the interest of a kind of divinization of the human. Postmodernists, seeking to be thorough in their atheism, deny such humanism. See, for example, chapter 11, "No Enemy, No Christianity," in my book *Sanctify Them in the Truth: Holiness Exemplified* (Edinburgh: T. & T. Clark, 1998), pp. 191–200. For a powerful account of modernity as a project to build "the city of man," see Pierre Manent, *The City of Man*, trans. Marc Le Pain (Princeton, NJ: Princeton University Press, 1998). Like Boyle, Manent locates modernity with the discovery of "history" and, in particular, how such history is displayed through the sociological and economic viewpoints.

3. David Toole, *Waiting for Godot in Sarajevo: Theological Reflections on Nihilism, Tragedy, and Apocalypse* (Boulder, CO: Westview Press, 1998).

4. Toole, *Waiting for Godot*, pp. 269–70.

5. Terry Eagleton, *The Illusions of Postmodernism* (Oxford: Blackwell Publishers, 1996), p. vii. Eagleton's account of postmodernism as a general intellectual style is, I think, about as good a characterization as one can get. I confess, however, that I remain extremely suspicious of whether any coherent postmodern position exists.

6   Eagleton notes that postmodernism as a style of culture allegedly reflects an epochal change characterized by "a deathless, decentred, ungrounded, self-reflexive, playful, derivative, eclectic, pluralistic art which blurs the boundaries between 'high' and 'popular' culture, as well as between art and everyday experience. How dominant or pervasive this culture is – whether it goes all the way down, or figures just as one particular region within contemporary life – is a matter of argument" (ibid, pp. vii–viii). How to understand the relation between postmodernism as an intellectual position and as a cultural movement is not clear to me. For my "use" of modernism against itself, see my "No Enemy, No Christianity: Preaching Between Worlds," in my *Sanctify Them in the Truth: Holiness Exemplified* (Edinburgh: T. & T. Clark, 1998), pp. 191–200.

7   Boyle, *Who Are We Now?* p. 82. The problem, I think, is not that postmodernism might not have been present in earlier times, but that the unclarity about what postmodernity is makes such judgments arbitrary. Significant thinkers are bound to be ambiguous in terms of "periodizations." Thus Descartes is increasingly read as a late medieval thinker and Kant, or at least the Kant of the third *Critique*, as a harbinger of Romanticism.

8   Boyle, *Who Are We Now?* p. 290.

9   Michael Gillespie observes that "nihilism is not the result of the death of God but the consequence of the birth or rebirth of a different kind of God, an omnipotent god of will who calls into question all of reason and nature and thus overturns all eternal standards of truth and justice, and good and evil. This idea of God came to predominance in the fourteenth century and shattered the medieval synthesis of philosophy and theology, catapulting man into a new way of thinking and being, a *via moderna* essentially at odds with the *via antiqua*. This new way was in turn the foundation for modernity as the realm of human self-assertion." Gillespie, *Nihilism before Nietzsche* (Chicago: University of Chicago Press, 1995), pp. xii–xiii.

10 Philip Blond, "Introduction: Theology Before Philosophy," in *Post-Secular Philosophy: Between Philosophy and Theology*, ed. Philip Blond (London: Routledge, 1998), p. 6. Blond notes prior to this observation that modern theologians and philosophers who have attempted to resist skepticism in theology have done so by means of natural theology, that is, they have "attempted to discern, or infer, the nature of God from a secular construal of the nature of the world" (ibid, p. 5). To do this, a correspondence between cause and effect necessitated that some term be given due proportion to both creatures and creator because it was assumed that mutual knowledge depends on the classical notion that "like knows like."

11 For a much more detailed account of Scotus's position as well as critique, see Catherine Pickstock, *After Writing: On the Liturgical Consummation of Philosophy* (Oxford: Blackwell Publishers, 1998), pp. 121–40. Pickstock's book is an extraordinary account of the theological and philosophical developments that created the possibility of modernity and postmodernity correlated with social and political developments. Anyone acquainted with her work will recognize how much I have learned from her as well as her and Blond's teacher, John Milbank.

12 Blond, "Introduction," p. 6. When "being" is assumed to be univocal, analogical predication becomes a "theory." Thus the importance of David Burrell's work in freeing Aquinas from those who falsely assume the centrality of analogy in Aquinas means that Aquinas must have had a theory of analogy.

13 Robert Jenson, "How the World Lost Its Story," *First Things*, 36 (October 1993), pp. 19–24.

14 Boyle, *Who Are We Now?* pp. 289–90.
15 Boyle suggests that in postmodernity a history that refers to the past has come to an end in favor of history that only names an unrealized future (ibid, p. 81). Boyle argues that Heidegger is the great representative of this understanding of history just to the extent he believed so firmly in our power to make our future that he made that power the source of our historicity. "We make the continuity, and so the history, of our existence by choosing our hero, choosing a tradition and inheritance that we have in common with others. We create our past in the image of our future, of the projection of our existence forward to its limit in death. We have a fate [Schicksal] because, like Nietzsche, we are a fate. Out of the contingencies of that 'fate' Existence chooses its particular destiny [Geschick], the events it willingly shares with 'its collectivity, its people.' The flaw in this account is its ignoring of the extent to which our 'destiny,' the historicity of our existence (and indeed of existence itself), is a gift from others, and the extent therefore to which the temporality of existence derives from pastness as well as futurity" (ibid, p. 223). Boyle, I believe rightly, identifies Heidegger's denial of the past with his refusal to understand our existence as the result of an act of love. "Behind Heidegger's reluctance to see historicity as a gift, and not only a construct, lies a general – but, as his analysis of the presuppositions of selfhood shows, not necessarily fundamental – hostility to givenness" (ibid, p. 198).
16 Ibid, pp. 80–1. Boyle's use of the shopping mall as the image for postmodernism is anticipated by James Edwards in his *The Plain Sense of Things: The Fate of Religion in an Age of Normal Nihilism* (University Park, PA: Pennsylvania State University Press, 1997), pp. 47–50.
17 Marx no doubt deserves the credit for the discovery of the significance of money for the transformation of the market. David Harvey provides a wonderfully clear and incisive account of Marx's analysis of money in his *The Condition of Postmodernity* (Oxford: Blackwell Publishers, 1990), pp. 99–105. Harvey observes how Marx saw that with the advent of a money economy, the bonds and relations of traditional communities could not help but be dissolved so that money becomes the real community. This creates the "fetishism of commodities" just to the extent money "masks" the social relations between things. Boyle also emphasizes the significance of money for the transition to modernity. But he credits Max Weber, not Marx, with the discovery that the true revolution was not with the invention of capitalist modes of production, but with the invention of money as the means to define capital itself (Boyle, *Who Are We Now?* pp. 104–5).
18 Fredric Jameson, *Postmodernism, or, The Cultural Logic of Late Capitalism* (Durham, NC: Duke University Press, 1991), pp. 1–55. I have changed "late" to "advanced" to indicate my sense that, at least as far as capitalism is concerned, it is not clear how late his "late" is.
19 Harvey, *The Condition of Postmodernity*, p. 63.
20 Boyle, *Who Are We Now?* p. 234.
21 Terry Eagleton observes that capitalism deconstructs the difference between system and transgression, because capitalism is the mind-bending paradox of a system whose margins are installed at its center. Eagleton, *The Illusions of Postmodernism*, p. 62.
22 Harvey, *The Condition of Postmodernity*, p. 105.
23 Boyle, *Who Are We Now?* pp. 153–4.
24 Ibid, p. 152.

25 Eagleton, *The Illusions of Postmodernism*, p. 9. I am not sure what connection, if any, there may be between the rise of postmodernism as a movement in university cultures and the end of the Cold War, but I think the loss of a clear "enemy" must have some relation to the lack of seriousness on the part of many intellectuals.

26 Ibid, p. 27. For Rorty's book, see *Achieving Our Country* (Cambridge, MA: Harvard University Press, 1998).

27 Ibid, p. 97. One of the few things about which Rorty is adamant is that any future politics must leave Christianity behind and, in particular, any "vocabulary built around the notion of sin" (ibid, p. 32). I confess it is unclear to me on what basis he can be so dogmatic, but I find his dislike for Christianity rather charming. He has not, however, given up entirely on religion, urging us to not discard the hope shared by Alison, Bloom, and Matthew Arnold – "the hope for a religion of literature, in which works of the secular imagination replace Scripture as the principal source of inspiration and hope for a new generation" (ibid, p. 136). Rorty identifies this religion of literature with Whitman's and Dewey's hope that America, which is a term convertible with democracy, would be the place where people come to see the ultimate significance of the finite, human, historical project. They both hoped America would be where a religion of love would replace a religion of fear, where the traditional link between the religious impulse to stand in awe of something greater than oneself and the infantile need for security would be broken. They wanted to put hope for a casteless and classless America in the place of the will of God. "They wanted that utopian America to replace God as the unconditional object of desire" (ibid, pp. 17–18). Rorty, I suppose, is to be commended for being so candid about his faith in America. Interestingly enough, he critiques the theories of Hegel and Marx, as well as the "rationalizations of hopelessness" like Foucault's and Lacan's, for attempting to satisfy the urges that theology used to satisfy. Such urges, according to Rorty, are what Dewey hoped Americans might cease to feel (ibid, p. 38).

28 Ibid, p. 98.

29 Ibid, p. 48.

30 Ibid, p. 105. In some ways Rorty's book is an extended attack on Fred Jameson. But his criticisms of Jameson, I fear, are at best inept and at worst, stupid.

31 Foucault provides an extraordinary account of the development of this understanding of the state's function in his extremely important article, "Governmentality" in *The Foucault Effect: Studies in Governmentality*, ed. Graham Burchell, Colin Gordon, and Peter Miller (Chicago: University of Chicago Press, 1991), pp. 87–104. Foucault distinguishes the governmentality of the modern state from sovereignty by noting that the former has no interest in disposing things to lead to the common good, but rather the role of government is "to ensure that the greatest possible quantity of wealth is produced, that the people are provided with sufficient means of subsistence, that the population is enabled to multiply, etc." (ibid, p. 95). Crucial for the development of this understanding of government is the displacement of the family as the analogical paradigm for government in favor of that new entity called population. "Governmentality" does not mean that the state is any less inclined to go to war, but rather that wars fought by such states, as Hegel saw, become ends in themselves. That is, war having no end other than itself becomes the reason for the state to exist.

These are extremely complex matters, obviously, since Boyle's understanding of the effects of globalization are that they are uneven. Globalization complements the workings of a strong state like the United States which is also still captured by the myth of being a savior nation. States such as France and Germany more perfectly fit Foucault's understanding of governmentality. It is, for example, quite interesting to wonder if states such as France and Germany now could initiate a war in the name of their self-interest, whether such interest be understood in terms of honor or economic well-being. Wars, at least in Europe, increasingly will be police actions initiated by regional alliances. I am indebted to Ken Surin and Reinhard Hütter for pressing me on this point.

32 This contradiction, of course, Rorty shares with people like Mrs Thatcher, who failed to see that nations are growing obsolete not as a matter of fashion but as the result of the operation of the same economic trends she otherwise endorsed. Boyle wonderfully analyzes this contradiction in the first chapter of his book *Who Are We Now?* entitled, "After Thatcherism" (pp. 13–67). Rorty acknowledges the tension between concern with the inequality of wealth between nations and thinking one's responsibility is to the least advantaged in one's own nation. He confesses he has no idea how this dilemma is to be resolved (*Achieving Our Country*, pp. 88–9). In an interesting manner Martha Nussbaum exemplifies the same tension in her book *Cultivating Humanity: A Classical Defense of Reform in Liberal Education* (Cambridge, MA: Harvard University Press, 1997). Nussbaum, who would usually be considered on the other side of the postmodern divide than Rorty, at once wants to train students locally as well as for world citizenship. This works well as long as she is thinking of white males, but proves embarrassing once she turns to African-Americans. Should African-Americans in the interest of being world citizens, a citizenship of nowhere, become as she recommends "philosophical exiles from our (their) own way of life?" (ibid, p. 58). It is hard to be politically correct and a universalist at the same time. Nussbaum does not feel the tension since, like Rorty, she is confident that education for world citizenship has been most fully embraced in the United States (ibid, p. 9).

33 Eagleton, *The Illusions of Postmodernism*, p. 76.

34 Actually, a place where they have to go is the university, which has become for them a safe haven that serves as well as a quasi-church. Indeed, Rorty favorably quotes Eisenach's observation that "Progressive intellectuals turned American universities into what he calls 'something like a national "church" – the main repository and protector of common American values, common American meanings, and common American identities'" (Rorty, *Achieving Our Country*, p. 50).

35 Eagleton, *The Illusions of Postmodernism*, pp. 22–5. In this respect, Boyle makes some fascinating remarks about the gay movement. He credits the movement with teaching us to abandon the puritan pretense that social affections can be anything other than erotic in form. But he denies that identity, and particularly sexual identity, can be a matter of our own affective preferences. When sexual preferences are detached from the process of bodily reproduction, we lose touch with the constraints necessary for discovering that our bodies are not only for consumption but also for production. "If marriage is redefined as a long-term affective partnership, so that it may be either homosexual or heterosexual, the essential reproductive nature of male and female bodies is no longer given institutional (and therefore political) expression" (Boyle, *Who Are We Now?* p. 59).

36 Robert Jenson, *Systematic Theology: The Triune God*, vol. 1 (New York: Oxford University Press, 1997), p. 63.

37 John Howard Yoder, *The Politics of Jesus: Vicit Agnus Noster*, 2nd edn. (Grand Rapids, MI: Eerdmans, 1994), p. 246.

38 John Howard Yoder, "Armaments and Eschatology," *Studies in Christian Ethics*, 1, 1 (1998), pp. 43–61.
39 See, for example, Yoder's "Firstfruits: The Paradigmatic Public Role of God's People," that now is the first chapter in his *For the Nations: Essays Public and Evangelical* (Grand Rapids, MI: Eerdmans, 1997), pp. 15–36. Commenting on Barth, Yoder notes that "the order of the faith community constitutes a public offer to the entire society" (p. 27). I have no doubt such a characterization describes Yoder's own views.
40 I am extremely grateful to Professor Schlabach for his permission to use his characterization of my position. Schlabach's account, however, does raise some interesting questions about the differences between Yoder and myself. Yoder in style and substance was always more willing to work within the world as he found it than I have been. For example, I will polemically try to expose what I take to be the contradictions in a position by forcing, for instance, those that would defend just war theory in the name of democracies to see that they cannot do so with consistency. In contrast, Yoder would assume it is a good thing to believe that war should be limited and try to help those with that belief to live accordingly. The difference may be a matter of style, but I believe it may also be due to what might be described as my lingering longing for Christendom. For example, the strategy of argument I use in this essay, I suspect, would be quite foreign to Yoder's way of thinking about postmodernism.
41 Boyle, *Who Are We Now?* p. 8.
42 Ibid, p. 91.
43 Ibid, pp. 91–2.
44 Ibid, p. 92. For this reason Boyle thinks that the moral authority of the church in the future will lie more with the college of bishops than the papacy. For it will be the bishops who will have the authority to challenge the claim of the global market to express and exhaust the human world. Already the church has produced the glorious examples of the martyred bishops Oscar Romero and Juan Geraldi Conedera, who could understand what was going on in their little countries of El Salvador and Guatemala much better than could John Paul II (hindered as he has been by his Polish fear of communism, though now we've seen him changing as to Cuba). I owe this Central American reminder to Sarah Freedman.
45 Dan Bell makes this observation in his remarkable dissertation, "The Refusal to Cease Suffering: The Crucified People and the Liberation of Desire" (Durham, NC: Duke University, 1998).
46 See, for example, Ephraim Radner's extraordinary account of the effects of our division on the church in his *The End of the Church: A Pneumatology of Christian Division in the West* (Grand Rapids, MI: Eerdmans, 1998). It would be fascinating to compare Boyle's more Hegelian account of history with that of Radner's. Both maintain that Christians owe the world an account of the history of the world, but Radner argues such an account can never lose its "figural," that is, biblical, character. According to Radner, the division of the sixteenth century resulted in a limitation on pneumatic accounts of history that require repentance. As a result, "modern historical consciousness" was created which was but the cultural adaptation of a straitened Christian consciousness due to the incapacitation of the figural reading of history by multiple ecclesial referents (ibid, p. 301).
47 Boyle, *Who Are We Now?* p. 93. The careful reader who checks my use of this quote from Boyle will discover that I did not follow Boyle's appeal that began the quote to

the "Catholic belief that we are but creatures, and the creatures of a wholly unknowable God," which he believes safeguards us from self-worship. I do not know whether Boyle and I are in fundamental disagreement on the matter of knowledge of God, but it is clear to me, as Blond puts it, that "negative theology requires a positive discourse about God, if, that is, this form of negation is to be recognizably about God at all" (Blond, "Introduction," p. 5).

48 Besides those mentioned earlier, I am indebted to Abraham Nussbaum, Joel Shuman, and Michael Cartwright for their criticisms and, as usual, Jim Fodor.

CHAPTER 9
Justice and Prudence: Principles of Order in the Platonic City

Catherine Pickstock

Unlike politics, where a week can be counted as a long time, theology has always been governed by a more extensive notion of time. Having said that, the last few years have seen the emergence of several bright theological talents who are already having considerable impact, not only on their own discipline, but on adjacent disciplines also. Catherine Pickstock is certainly among these luminaries. Fellow of Emmanuel College, Cambridge (where Don Cupitt taught for many years), doctoral student of John Milbank, now a colleague at the Divinity School of Janet Soskice, Pickstock intersects with several voices representing various approaches to postmodern theology in this volume.

Her earlier training was in Classics and literary studies and these fields of enquiry considerably influence her work, both in terms of its content and its methodology. Pickstock is an excellent close-reader (in the tradition of Cambridge English studies) of classical Greek and Latin texts, whether it is Plato (as in the essay here) or Aquinas. But her work is not simply philological or literary; it is also philosophical and theological. Drawing together her linguistic, literary, and theological skills her earlier doctoral work examined liturgical texts. The emphasis upon what Gregory of Nyssa called "operative knowledge" or, more theologically, formative practices, has remained throughout her work. That emphasis is evident in this essay, with its analysis of the formation of the just soul and the establishment of the just city on the basis of practical reasoning as a participation in the good. Pickstock's earlier research interests culminated in her doctoral thesis, which was published as *After Writing: The Liturgical Consummation of Philosophy* (Oxford, 1998). This wide-ranging and original work charted the demise of philosophy as both contemplative and practical. Opening with a scathing attack on Derrida as the contemporary purveyor of a nihilistic metaphysics rooted in a Scotist notion of the univocity of being, Pickstock argued for a Thomistic ontology in which liturgy functioned as a mediator between the divine and the human. Through her meticulous readings of liturgical acts, she demonstrated the interrelationship between cosmic and transcendental operations and the church as a doxological community. Since its appearance the book has been widely read and quoted, provoking much reaction internationally.

In the same year Pickstock became one of three editors of the Radical Orthodoxy Series and of the first volume of that series, *Radical Orthodoxy: A New Theology* (London, 1998). Her own essay in that collection, "Music: The City in Plato," is very much a companion piece to the essay below. Both are part of a project of rethinking Plato and Plato's importance for early Christian philosophical theology. Some of the results of this project will be made evident in Pickstock's *A Short Guide to Plato* (Oxford, 2002). Pickstock, in a joint piece of writing with John Milbank, has also continued her detailed researches into the work of Aquinas. This is published as *Truth in Aquinas* (London, 2000) in the Radical Orthodoxy Series.

The following essay issues from a concern to qualify a certain imbalance in many existing general accounts of the Platonic dialogues. Put briefly, this imbalance involves an overemphasis upon a dualism in Plato between matter and spirit, body and mind. It is of course impossible to deny the presence of such dualism which derives ultimately from the pervasive ancient Greek division of reality into shaping mind and form, on the one hand, and unformed material chaos, on the other. However, Plato's dialogues are not dominated by such dualism. Too often, students are left with the impression that Plato unambiguously denigrated life in the body, time, society, history, myth, ritual, mimesis, and poetry: in fact, physical mediations of all kinds. Yet the best recent European and North American scholarship suggests that, to the contrary, Plato had his own specific way of valuing and even exalting all such mediations.[1]

This division in the reception of Plato is in fact nothing new. It arose to some extent in Neoplatonism itself. Although Neoplatonism moved in a non-dualistic direction, since it tended to derive even the lowest material degree of reality from the supreme One or Good, Plotinus emphasized an upwards ascent away from matter and into, first, the realm of the soul, and, second, the One itself.[2] His successors Proclus and Iamblichus, by contrast, laid much more stress upon the descent of the first principle into the world of material multiplicity. In their writings this was linked with the idea that dialectical interrogation is completed by ritual practice which alone enables the full attainment of union with the One. This twin understanding arose for these thinkers out of a systematic reading of the Platonic corpus. I would contend that recent scholarship confirms that the Plotinian psychic and ascending interpretation of Plato needs to be complemented by a Proclean doxological ("theurgic") and descending interpretation.[3]

To pursue further this argument, I will examine one particular focus of Platonic concern: the city. I mentioned at the outset that one aim in this essay is to qualify the dualistic understanding of Plato (and, concomitantly, dualistic construals of the Platonizing elements in early Christian thought). I have a number of other aims as well: first, to intimate certain reasons why the merging of the biblical and Platonic or Neoplatonic traditions often seemed so natural, whereas too frequently modern commentaries have tended to assume that these traditions were pulling in opposed directions; secondly, to encourage a modification of the oft-drawn contrast between the thought of Plato and that of Aristotle; thirdly, to qualify the (rather ironic) joint influence of an Anglo-Saxon analytic reading of Plato as the proponent of, first, a flawed metaphysics, and secondly, interesting but unresolved logical conundrums, together with the postmodern denigration of Plato as the source of the Western metaphysics of presence and essentialized interiority. Finally, I hope also to suggest that the more non-dualistic element in Plato is linked with the supra-philosophical place of religion in his thought. "Religion" here comprises the necessity of public ritual practice for the attainment of wisdom, and, in addition, the mediations of myth and continuous individual and collective praise of the divine. From such a perspective it seems that Plato is not the proponent of a self-standing metaphysics and that he already considers that the goals of philosophy can only be realized by going beyond philosophy. This has implications for both philosophy and theology. In the first case, it suggests that Platonism has a future in postmodern and postmetaphysical thought. In the second case, it shows that the relationship of Christianity to Plato is not primarily a matter of faith to reason, but rather of an earlier articulation of both reason and ritual practice in relation to a later one.

One often reads that Plato is a dualist, and an early draughtsman of interiority, privatized presence to self and identity. One hears that for Plato the optimum desired state is one of refined inward contemplation and that Socrates was a kind of proto-Cartesian inventor of interiority. And it is indeed the case that Plato sometimes seems to err in favor of a certain series of terms which implicitly prioritize the interior, the non-communicable, the self-knowing. The very fact that in the *Republic* Plato draws a structural parity between the soul and the city might seem to suggest an extension of the private sphere of the soul to apply to society as a whole, and, concomitantly, an abstraction from the body.[4] This possible emphasis upon the private realm as the optimum site of truth and justice is apparently confirmed in the discussion of the nature and place of justice in the *Republic* when Glaucon posits the cynical view of visible just rule: is such rule really just, since the ruler might simply be ruling in this way so as to augment by devious means the compass of his own power?[5] The truly just person, he argues, would have to be wholly invisible.[6] But, as Socrates observes, an aporia is here operative: one will by definition never know of the existence of such a just person, for the moment it ceased to be a secret the possibility of self-interest would belie the purity of his attainment of justness. Plato's resolution of this conundrum seems redolent of a supposed interiorization of virtue: although one can never check up on another person's justness, one can however know it of oneself. If one is contemplating the good, one knows of one's own justice. Such exaltation of the esoteric self as the only reliable "site" of justice is superficially endorsed by Socrates' oft-quoted injunction that the knowledge for which one should strive is self-knowledge, which, of course, for Plato, would mean something to do with the soul and its recollection of the Good.

However, despite this undeniable centrality of matters concerning the soul in Plato, there is in the *Republic* and elsewhere a significant tension concerning the priority of the soul and the city as the optimum site of justice. In the *Republic* Socrates seems to oscillate between talk of the soul and of the city, until one is uncertain where one ends and the other begins. Indeed, they are said to comprise the same tripartite structure, though on a different scale.[7] But, more significantly perhaps, there is no consistent stress in the *Republic* or elsewhere, that one can have the good at all *without the city*. First of all, one should note that the philosopher-guardians of the *Republic* are only produced by the right kind of education which in turn depends upon the right kind of city. They are not produced esoterically from nothing, but receive *from without* the public traditions of their formation.

Secondly, one should not see the soul and the city as in some sense opposed to one another, simply on the grounds that one is unified and singular, and the other is relational and multiple. Indeed, we learn elsewhere that for Plato the principle of the one and the indeterminate two is construed *positively* by Plato as the site of participation in the good.[8] Moreover, if, as has been argued, the true "city" for Plato is not primarily a complex of buildings and institutions enclosed by a city wall, but rather comprises social bonds performed in the path of the good, then one must in fact see the city not as an "unavoidable detour" for Plato (as Derrida claims),[9] but in fact the condition of possibility for dissemination of the good. It is precisely under conditions of relationality that the philosopher-guardian can recollect the good, and as the feathers of his soul begin to sprout, he can in turn pass on this beneficent effluence to others. Indeed, the notion of the city reaches perhaps its fullest realization in the *Phaedrus*, where it seems that on an eschatological level the immortal souls of the lover and beloved obtain a state of intersubjective relationality in a kind of psychical city beyond our own.[10] So, far from the soul and the city being inimical metaphysical phenomena, it seems that souls themselves can obtain to a state of relationality.

What is a City?

The city, for Plato, is by no means a tiresome detour; it is fundamental precisely because he does not construe the self as an autonomous entity: "Well, then," says Socrates in the *Republic*, "a city, as I believe, comes into being because each of us isn't self-sufficient but is in need of much."[11] In a sense, for Plato, the city is not so much a bounded edifice built of stone, but is something we perpetually enact between one another;[12] it is our perpetually renewed acts of association, and resides in what we *add* to one another: "So, then," says Socrates, "when one man takes on another for one need and another for another need, and, since many things are needed, many men gather in one settlement as partners and helpers, to this common settlement we give the name city."[13] The city is therefore both spatial – for it subsists *between* people in the form of a *relation* of some kind – and temporal – for it arises in the time inhabited by these acts of mutual supplementation and their renewal.

Now, the whole question of what exactly a "city" actually *is*, for Plato, only emerges secondarily within the long discussion as to the true nature of justice. Indeed, the reason for "constructing a city in speech," as Socrates describes the proceedings,[14] is in order to discern its nature on a larger scale than would have been possible if one considered justice in the soul. Socrates says that to consider the "soul" is akin to squinting at little letters from afar off, whilst to regard the city is to look at the *same* letters, though much larger and closer to hand. (It should be noted here, as an aside, that this is curious, since the Socratic injunction to know oneself would seem to suggest that the soul is the thing *nearest* to oneself. But in fact here it seems that our soul is further away from us even than the city. Of course, the reason for the soul's distance from us is that it is *more* than itself; it is transcendent. However, as we shall see, this is not to suggest that the city does not also exceed itself, that it is not in some sense also more than itself.) However, although for Socrates' dialogue in the *Republic*, a discussion of the city was a *detour* on the way to an apprehension of true justice, which is assumed to reside primarily in the soul, in this chapter, things will happen in reverse. Justice will become *our detour* towards a discernment of the city. Why? Because in the end, justice proved to be Plato's detour as well. He finally shows that one can only arrive at justice when one has *gone beyond* justice into the inhabited domain of the city, which will turn out to involve more than justice for the full exercise of virtue. I reserve for the conclusion of this essay a discussion of the way in which for Plato one can only arrive at a true city when one has gone beyond philosophy, which is also to have gone beyond the city, not in the sense of going outside the city walls, but of having gone beyond the ethical into the religious.

Dikaiosyne translates roughly into our word "justice," but means also integrity, rule by law, and civic sense. Amongst the poets such as Homer, justice was by no means the supreme virtue. It was simply one of several virtues, and pertained to the payment of debts.[15] In the work of the pre-Socratic philosophers such as Heraclitus and Parmenides, it had another more cosmic meaning; "justice" was the regularities to be found in nature, the rhythm of creation and its destruction.[16] According to the poetic view, where justice is something supramundane, and civic authority is seen as undergirded by the power of the gods, retold in the poetic stories of the tradition, civic laws are automatically reducible to a matter of the repaying of debts, or the rectification of imbalances by putting what has been displaced back into its proper place. But there is here no questioning of what these proper places actually are. Equally, where justice is seen as a "natural" matter by the philosophers, the given power relations of society are seen as automatically "just." Those possessing power have the right to erect further civic, purely positive, and not natural laws. So, once again, there is no question of intrinsically just distributions, only the restoration of non-debatable social positions. But it is precisely these positions and their propriety which Plato begins to draw into question.

If there is no question of distributive justice, then human society becomes a matter of one self-interest being forfeited for the sake of another self-interest. This approach to human law is defended by Thrasymachus and Glaucon in Books 1 and 2 of the *Republic*, who argue that a ruler does not have to pursue justice in order to be a good ruler, nor indeed that justice is essential for human happiness. It seems that for these two participants in the discussion, "justice" is simply an appearance or notion which people know how to use. Such a view seems to lie within the Homeric legacy where justice is simply one of several virtues, and by no means the most urgent. It is simply an ordering structure within human interaction, an architectonic which requires no questioning.[17] Thus, old Cephalus sees justice as a matter of the payment of debts.[18] A just man is one who follows a practical rule, independent of any particular political regime or psychological disposition. For Polemarchus, Cephalus' son, situated within a similar tradition, justice is to help one's friends and harm one's foes.[19] Broadly speaking, Socrates rejects these accounts of justice as purely conventional and pragmatic, on the grounds that they empty the word "justice" of all meaning: when people speak of "a just ruler" something more seems to be suggested than a politically cunning ruler, or one who only *appears* to be interested in justice.

At the end of Book 2, however, a rather surprising definition of justice, after a painstaking dialectical dismissal of the various sophistic suggestions already mentioned, is proffered by Socrates. An attempt is now made to establish a principle of original distribution of human goods apart from the mythical injunction of the gods, the play of natural forces, or the imposition of tyrannical will. Justice is defined in very spatial, mundane terms as each minding his own business. That is to say, justice is the division of labor, where each member of a community performs the tasks appropriate to their innate abilities. On a local level, this means that the person best skilled at farming will be a farmer; the person best skilled at making plows will take that as his task, and so on.[20] On a broader level, Plato's theory that justice is the division of labor enables him to expound a tripartite structure which determines not only political reality, but also psychological reality, as I have mentioned.

What societal structure, then, does Socrates envisage as a just distribution of labor? At the lowest level of the social hierarchy, by far the largest category, are the merchants and artisans whose associated governing passion in the soul is *epithumia* or desire. Next comes the military class comprising fighters, whose governing psychic disposition is *thumos* or force. And, finally, at the top of the hierarchy is the smallest class of all, the ruling political class whose associated disposition is *nous* or reason.[21] However, Plato often speaks of the uppermost two classes, rulers and fighters, as comprising one single guardian class.

```
        nous (reason)
           /\
          /  \
         /----\
        / thumos \
       /  (force)  \
      /------------\
     /              \
    /_____\
      epithumia (desire)
```

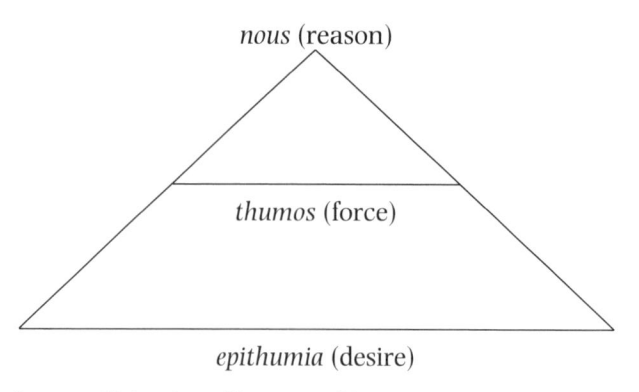

Justice as the *division of labor* (*Republic*, 370a–b)

In what, then, does justice consist, according to the division of labor? Justice is here seen to reside in keeping these three classes distinct.[22] If the order should be dismantled, and, say, the military should assert prime rule, or if the mercantile and artisan classes were to assume primacy, there would be no justice. It should be noted also that because of the psychological equivalents, the three classes correspond to the tripartition of the soul. Some people will have a greater proportion of desire or reason or force. Each person contains all three dispositions, but, as in the corresponding civic divisions, each must stay in its own proper place.

Now, there are two problems associated with this notion of justice as comprising the tripartition of labor in the city, which is to say, two problems associated with Plato's definition of justice as such.

The Problem of "Rule"

First of all, what exactly is the precise *content* of the topmost function of political "rule" in the city? Whilst it is quite clear what the lower two orders of people do, it seems that the uppermost class of rulers exists in a rather sinister empty way, simply subduing the other two classes by keeping them in their places. It seems that "rule" has no actual quality of its own except as a rather manipulative, ominous super-force which holds sway over force itself, or the realm of *thumos*, the second civic category.[23] Moreover, it seems a very secular kind of category, for it suggests that the city can subsist without recourse to the good, and that justice, seen in these spatial terms of the division of labor, is in fact suspended from an altogether dubious immanent power. The problem is rather akin to our contemporary notion of "politics" in the sense that it seems to be about everything – education, crime, economics – *but* politics. Insofar as this uppermost class seems to involve an untraceable task, its power suddenly seems unlimited, or to assume an empty and therefore dissembling character whose elusiveness lends it a gloss of innocuousness.

So, just what is the task of the ruling class? It is at this point that the government of the city (and therefore also of the soul) passes beyond its mundane limits. It is clear that the government of the city cannot proceed within the terms provided by the city alone (namely, the hierarchical distribution of its parts) without reaching an *impasse*. Socrates here introduces the crucial "content" or "quality" of the ruling class: its task is "philosophy," or the contemplation of the good which is outside both the soul and the city. The "ethical" is therefore defined as *more* than the protocols of justice.

However, it might still be possible to offer a critique of this. It is all very well to determine the ruling class as one devoted to contemplation of the good, but what in practice does this mean? If this vision of the good is mediated to the life of the city in no terms other than the division of labor already established, then in what sense, if any, does that "rule" emerge as anything but a tyrannical model of brutal subordination? The answer to this question is given its fullest articulation in the concluding words of the *Republic*. Socrates observes that one of the consequences of the soul's vision of the good is that such a person will always keep to the upward way and will practice justice with prudence (*dikaiosyne meta phroneseos*).[24] Justice is not truly justice unless it is practiced with *phronesis* or prudent judgment. Socrates suggests this many times throughout the *Republic*.[25] Early in the dialogue he says that a soul is in its best condition when it is most courageous and most prudent. A soul cannot rightly be said to be just unless it deliberates, judges, acts freely; but these are essential features of *phronesis* and not *dikaiosyne*.

So what exactly does *phronesis* add to *dikaiosyne* in the practice of rule? Whilst *dikaiosyne*, as we have seen, represents a spatial articulation or grammar of the components of the city, *phronesis* contributes a more *temporal* dimension which mediates between the eternal realm of the Forms and the need to make decisions concerning encounters with unanticipated events within time. Socrates stresses that a grid of propositional laws or the unchanging "methods" of the sophists do not have sufficient flexibility to negotiate the surprise of what arrives in the inhabited life of the city,[26] but judgments based on recollection of the transcendent good – beyond all dichotomies of near and far, space and time – paradoxically lend themselves better to a process of constant revision and improvisation in time of ever renewed proprieties. Of course, this does not mean that according to the sway of *phronesis* in the city, protocols are radically discontinuous from moment to moment, simply being assessed by the reckless dictates of local circumstances. To the contrary, *phronesis* mediates in time that which lies beyond time, as an inexhaustible source of one-ness. It is precisely this which reveals the rigid propositional legalities of ordinary sophistic ethics to be, on the one hand, superficially reliable, but, on the other hand, wholly arbitrary and insensitive to the subtly different requirements of particular circumstances. It is therefore paradoxically the transcendent good above all which is more profoundly linked to time and its vicissitudes, and can be more utterly *incarnated*, than any purely human attempts to obtain secure structures without recourse to the divine realm.

It should be noted that Aristotle takes over from Plato this idea of *phronesis*, but in such a way as to suggest a more decisive split between contemplation and ordinary practical life, between *theoria* and *praxis*. For instead of allying *phronesis* with the vision of the good, he links it more exclusively with the practical realm, where it is reduced to securing a compromise in the conduct of the self, between reason and passion.[27] Plato, on the other hand, as we have seen, discerns a more mediating relationship between the eternal and temporal domains, according to which *phronesis* comprises not so much a compromise within the self, as a creative exercise of judgment upon the exterior world via a manifestation of reason in time. There is for Plato no hierarchy of theoretical and practical reason.[28] This open character or recursiveness of phronetic or prudent judgment is allied in Plato to certain musical modes whose rhythms and harmonies are seen to order or reassemble the soul after its incarnation and inevitable dispersal in time. So, whilst Plato condemns any attempts to lay down strict legal codices, he is nonetheless very stringent in his regulation of music and other matters of style, both in the city in general and in the education of the philosopher-guardians.[29] Any disintegration of musical discipline is seen to betoken disorder of the soul and ethical decline. From this circumstance we can see more clearly the force of the claim made earlier – namely, that the detour via the city to define justice in the soul – is all of a piece with the detour via the form of the good to define justice in the city as justice-with-prudence. What we can now see is that while the vision of the good by the soul of the philosopher-guardian is necessary to enable the exercise of *phronesis* or prudence, it is equally the case that this vision of the good is only possible because inklings of the good are mediated by the patterns of *phronesis*, as embodied in the proper musical and stylistic practices of the city. Thus the good and *phronesis*, the transcendent and the city, are locked into a beneficent circle: *phronesis* needs the good, *but* those who see the good must first have inhabited the *ritual* mediations of the good in the city. Hence, the detour for the soul via the city and the forms is but one and the same passage.

The Loss of Philosophy

The first apparent problem, then, with the tripartition of the city, namely, the apparent contentlessness of the uppermost class of rulers, can be resolved by recourse to the mediation of the Forms through *phronesis* in time. But there is a second problem linked to the tripartite vision of the city which is the problem of debasement or contamination of philosophy in the sordid realm of commerce and mundanity.[30] The problem is that when the philosopher reenters the city, he somehow loses himself and his grasp on the good is weakened. The political life of the city is at best akin to life in a cave; so much is this the case, indeed, that Socrates identifies the city with the Cave.[31] This means, on the one hand, that those best equipped to rule – namely, the philosophers – are unwilling to do so; and, on the other hand, when they begin to lose their insights under the prevailing pressures of sophistry, the true aristocratic philosophic city becomes unstable and will degenerate into other forms of government. This degeneration appears inevitable because Plato seemed to envisage a real separation between the three psychological forces. To a certain extent, *reason* was seen as inherently outside the dispositions of force and desire. His account in the *Republic* of the inevitable cycles of political decline, from aristocracy to oligarchy and then tyranny, appears as a pessimistic resignation to the fact that when one incarnates reason, one will lose it in the fray of force and desire.[32]

Now, there are several different resolutions to this problem of the "loss" of philosophy and instability of the philosophic city. First of all, is Plato's demarcation between the three psychological parts of the soul – reason, force, and desire – to be seen as wholly absolute? The answer is no. For example, the desiring class of artisans is by no means excluded from a kind of contemplation of the good. As Socrates stresses, craftsmen – who belong to the lowest order, the desiring class – must, in the course of their art, deploy *phronesis* so as not "to let the crucial moment pass." Whilst it is true that other members of the city seem often to be swayed more by desires and force than by reason, the craftsmen *must* have some access to reason. In order to make a couch or a chair, says Socrates, the craftsman must after all consult the Forms.[33]

The tripartite structure of society is here no longer to be seen as a non-negotiable or rigidly fixed spatial grid; it is to some extent qualified by the fact that every soul contains all three psychological aspects, although in each person, as already mentioned, one aspect will come to the fore. This means that the philosopher-ruler will not find himself mediating the good to a realm wholly devoid of insight, and so there will be elements within the city which will help to stabilize its government, and safeguard against the city's degeneration into inferior forms of government.

The problem of degeneration, as we have seen, is caused by the fact that reason is seen as distinct from force and desire, even though all souls contain all three aspects. However, there are in Plato tendencies towards a suggestion that desire and force are not after all entirely external to the realm of reason.[34] Elsewhere I have described the mediating thrall of the "higher desire" as a crucial force in Plato's notion of philosophy as a disposition towards, or *love for*, the good, rather than a neutral or systematic discipline wholly removed from force and love.[35] The relays of the higher *eros*, perhaps not so much in the *Republic* as in Plato's later dialogues, are depicted as contagious. The philosopher-ruler does not merely *contain* his vision of the good, but disseminates or *transmits* it to others, even to the lower desiring classes of the city, just by virtue of his way of life. The good, as transcendent, cannot after all be contained or circumscribed. Rather, it must be passed on to others via the operations of the higher *eros*.[36] So, if one reads Plato's later accounts of the higher *eros* back into the *Republic*, it seems that it is by no means inevitable that the philosopher-ruler's access to reason will begin to fail when he attends to supposedly lower matters of desiring, because reason itself turns out to be desire raised to a higher power. For this outlook desire is not rigidly preordained to a bondage to the ephemeral, but has the capacity to be transformed. It seems that the lower orders of desire and force, far from being necessarily inimical to the order of reason, are in fact suspended from it, and sustained by its relay of the contagion of the good.

The True Tragedy

The final – and perhaps the ultimate – source of stabilization of the philosophic city, only tentatively discussed in the *Republic*, but more fully expounded in the *Phaedrus* and the *Laws*, is the move beyond the ethical into the tragic, or, one might say, the move beyond philosophy into theology.

In his very late dialogue, the *Laws*, the Athenian describes the city as "the true tragedy," "the finest and best we know how to make."[37] Now, what does this mean? It is indeed well known that Socrates banishes the tragedies of the Attic dramatists from his ideal city, on account of their immoral manipulation of the audience's private emotions of pity and fear via various covert devices of imitation – all forms of imitation being repudiated by Socrates on the grounds that they are representations at a third remove from reality, a mere copy of a copy, thus obfuscating access to the good itself and causing division in the soul.[38] But the city, for Plato, is the true tragedy, not because what occurs there is rueful or dreary, but because the city is where the battle of good against evil actually takes place. The souls participating in this drama are not divided from their reality by a playwright's artifices so as falsely to yield cheapened or contrived emotions of pity and fear, but are here combined with the order of a wholly superior transcendent reason which harmonizes the various dispositions of the soul. Such a city is ordered in an entirely liturgical or ritual manner, taking as its paradigm the image of the order of the cosmos ruled by divine reason, where cosmic ratios regulate human activities through a perpetual celebration of the divine.[39] As well as legislating with great care the music, song, dance, sacrifices, and play of the citizens of this city, the Athenian articulates the calendar by means of no fewer than 365 festivals in a year, so that not a day will pass without a liturgical feast.[40] By thus habituating the soul via the impress of divine harmony and rhythm in bodily maneuvers of song and dance, the Athenian hopes to banish all interior divisions and delusions, so that the whole city can "utter one and the same word,"[41] and all the citizens of the city are strung "together on a thread of song and dance."[42] Such an image suggests that through the articulations of liturgical enactment the city becomes unified in the manner of a collective higher soul (perhaps prefigured by the communality of the souls in the *Phaedrus*).[43] In this soul of the city the subordination to divine reason mediated through the patterns of the cosmos and the revolutions of its spheres becomes the superlative safeguard for the primacy of the sway of the good in human polity. (And it should be noted that the cosmos, which the city here echoes, itself has a soul – known as the world soul – as described by Plato in the *Timaeus*.)[44]

With this realization of the true city as one formed through praise of the divine, and ritual song and dance, it seems that Plato has in effect gone beyond the city through recourse to the cosmos and divine reason. But whilst the city of the *Republic*, organized as we have seen through the division of labor and the relay of the good through *phronesis*, despite its apparent practicabilities and relatively earthly structures, was deemed merely a "city in speech," the theological city of the *Laws*, with its supra-cosmic paradigm, is seen as a city not in speech but in deed.[45] Indeed, the city of the *Laws* is commonly seen by commentators as a more realistic "blueprint" because it does not involve a guardian class of philosophers.[46] But actually, the impinging of the liturgical on all citizens means that it is as if all citizens are now guardians; all are now philosophers, for all contemplate the good. Hence, in this respect, as well as in the bizarre liturgical proposals, the supposedly "more possible" city of the *Laws* is actually more apparently crazy, more exotic and focused on the divine than that of the *Republic*. What makes this city seem more possible is its utter devotion to the super-civic. Thus, we can summarize, for Plato, the city which goes beyond itself is the only actual city;[47] the ethic which goes beyond itself into the tragic is the only true ethic; and the philosophy which exceeds itself into the religious is the only true philosophy.

Everything, in this vision, is bound together by the doxological or the liturgical – this is the secret middle term which binds soul, city, cosmos, and Forms.[48] For, as we have seen, when the soul enters the city to find justice, it discovers that it can only be found within repeated ritual patterns; patterns which elevate the soul towards the vision of the Forms. And, finally, these same ordering, redistributing patterns provide the true key to the laws of nature, which are not just to be read off from the cosmos by an objectifying gaze, as for the pre-Socratics. We can once more, for the late Plato, take our laws from nature once we realize that the cosmos itself is not an impersonal order, but a psychic expression of divine praise.

Notes

1   The argument of this chapter is the product of several lectures delivered variously at the Faculty of Divinity, University of Cambridge, the Department of Religious Studies, University of Virginia, and the Arts Faculty, McGill University. I am grateful to the audiences of these lectures for their very helpful discussion and criticism of my arguments. I am particularly grateful to the following: Professor John Milbank, Professor Robert Sokolowski, Professor Rowan Williams, Professor Stephen Menn, Professor Eugene Rogers, Dr Gary Ulmen, and Dr Thomas Harrison. The present essay is an earlier version of a chapter of my book, *A Short Guide to Plato* (2001); it appears here with kind permission of the publisher, Oxford University Press. For other recent scholarship, see Jean-Louis Chrétien, *L'Inoubliable et*

l'inespéré (Paris: Desclée de Brouwer, 1991); Gerald M. Mara, *Socrates's Discursive Democracy: Logos and Ergon in Platonic Political Philosophy* (Albany, SUNY: 1997); Leo Strauss, *The Argument and The Action of Plato's Laws* (Chicago: Chicago University Press, 1975); Leo Strauss, *The City and Man* (Chicago: Chicago University Press, 1964); Thomas A. Szlezák, *Reading Plato*, trans. Graham Zanker (London: Routledge, 1999); Zdravko Planinč, *Plato's Political Philosophy: Prudence in the Republic and Laws* (London: Duckworth, 1991); Hans-Georg Gadamer, *Dialogue and Dialectic: Eight Hermeneutical Studies on Plato* (New Haven, CT: Yale University Press, 1980); Hans Joachim Krämer, *Plato and the Foundations of Metaphysics*, trans. John R. Caton (Albany: SUNY, 1990); Jacob Klein, *A Commentary on Plato's Meno* (Chicago: Chicago University Press, 1965); Stanley Rosen, *Plato's Statesman: The Web of Politics* (New Haven, CT: Yale University Press, 1995); Catherine Pickstock, *After Writing: On the Liturgical Consummation of Philosophy* (Oxford: Blackwell Publishers, 1998), ch. 1.

2   See, for example, Plotinus, *Enneads* III. 5, 2; V. 8, 12; VI. 4, 2.
3   Gregory Shaw, *Theurgy and the Soul: The Neoplatonism of Iamblichus* (University Park: Pennsylvania State University, 1995).
4   *Republic*, 434d–435c.
5   *Republic*, 366e ff.; see Adi Ophir, *Plato's Invisible Cities: Discourse and Power in the Republic* (London: Routledge, 1991), p. 68.
6   *Republic*, 359d, 361d.
7   *Republic*, 368d.
8   See ibid; Krämer, *Plato and the Foundations of Metaphysics*; Pickstock, *A Short Guide to Plato*, ch. 1.
9   See "Plato's Pharmacy" in Jacques Derrida, *Dissemination*, trans. Barbara Johnson (Chicago: Chicago University Press, 1981); Pickstock, *After Writing*, ch. 1.
10 *Phaedrus*, 256b–d.
11 " 'The origin of the city, then,' said I, 'in my opinion, is to be found in the fact that we do not severally suffice for our own needs, but each of us lacks many things. Do you think any other principle establishes the state?' 'No other,' said he. 'As a result of this, then, one man calling in another for one service and another for another, we, being in need of many things, gather many into one place of abode as associates and helpers, and to this dwelling we give the name city or state, do we not?' 'By all means.' 'And between one man and another there is an interchange of giving, if it so happens, and taking, because each supposes this to be better for himself.' " *Republic*, 369b–c.
12 See further Michael Oakeshott, *Rationalism in Politics and Other Essays* (London: Methuen, 1962).
13 *Republic*, 370a–b.
14 *Republic*, 369c.
15 Alasdair Macintyre, *Whose Justice? Which Rationality?* (London: Duckworth, 1996), ch. 2; G. Vlastos, "Equality and Justice in Early Greek Cosmology," *Classical Philosophy*, 42 (1947), pp. 156–78; C. H. Kahn, *Anaximander and the Origin of Greek Cosmology* (New York: Columbia University Press, 1960); E. A. Havelock, *The Greek Concept of Justice* (Cambridge, MA: Harvard University Press, 1978); Ophir, *Plato's Invisible Cities*, ch. 2.
16 See Havelock, *The Greek Concept of Justice*; Kahn, *Anaximander*.
17 *Republic*, 359a.

18 *Republic*, 366d–e, 379c.
19 *Republic*, 311b–c, 334b; See Strauss, *The City and Man*, pp. 68–71.
20 *Republic*, 370a–b, 395c, 496d, 500d, 507c, 530a, 597.
21 *Republic*, Book 2.
22 "Listen then," said I, "and learn if there is anything in what I say. For what we laid down in the beginning as a universal requirement when we were founding our city, this I think, or some form of this, is justice. And what we did lay down, and often said, if you recall, was that each one man must perform one social service in the state for which his nature was best adapted. . . . And again that to do one's own business and not to be a busybody is justice." *Republic*, 433a–c.
23 Adi Ophir, *Plato's Invisible Cities*, passim.
24 "But if we are guided by me we shall believe that the soul is immortal and capable of enduring all," *Republic*, 621c–d.
25 *Republic*, 621c–d, 540a, 582a–d, 521a, 504b; see further Planinc, *Plato's Political Philosophy*, p. 102ff.
26 *Republic*, 435c–d.
27 John Milbank, *Theology and Social Theory: Beyond Secular Reason* (Oxford: Blackwell Publishers), pp. 326–76; see also Macintyre, *Whose Justice?* p. 69. This is not, however, to suggest an all-encompassing contrast between Plato and Aristotle; see further Hans-Georg Gadamer, *The Idea of the Good in Platonic–Aristotelian Philosophy*, trans. P. Christopher Smith (New Haven, CT: Yale University Press, 1986).
28 *Republic*, 519b–521a, 402b–d, 485a–487a; *Phaedo*, 114a–115a.
29 *Laws*, 700a–701b.
30 Leo Strauss, *The City and Man*; J. G. Gunnell, *Political Philosophy and Time: Plato and the Origins of Political Vision* (Chicago: Chicago University Press, 1968/1987), p. 151ff.
31 *Republic*, 485b–486, 496c, 499c, 501d, 517c, 519c–d, 530e.
32 *Republic*, 543c–547a.
33 "And are we not also in the habit of saying that the craftsman who produces either of them fixes his eyes on the idea or form, and so makes in the one case the couches and in the other the tables that we use, and similarly of other things?" *Republic*, 596b; see also 370b.
34 See Strauss, *The City and Man*, pp. 124ff.
35 Pickstock, *After Writing*, ch. 1; Pickstock, *A Short Guide to Plato*, ch. 1.
36 *Phaedrus*, 255c–d.
37 *Laws*, 817b; see Helmut Kuhn, "The True Tragedy: On the Relationship between Greek Tragedy and Plato," *Harvard Studies in Classical Philology*, pt 1, LII (1941), pp. 1–40; pt 2, LIII (1942), pp. 37–88.
38 Gadamer, "Plato and the Poets," in *Dialogue and Dialectic*; Pickstock, *After Writing*, ch. 1, section 9.
39 *Laws*, 714a–d, 715a–716a, 716c–d; see Gunnell, *Political Philosophy and Time*, pp. 160, 181ff., 193.
40 *Laws*, 528a–b.
41 *Laws*, 664a.
42 *Laws*, 653c.
43 *Phaedrus*, 256b.
44 Pickstock, *A Short Guide to Plato*, ch. 4.
45 *Laws*, 968b.

46 The question of "blueprint"; see further Planinc, *Plato's Political Philosophy*.
47 See Strauss, *The City and Man*, p. 121, on the city as not self-subsistent.
48 *Timaeus*, 70d–71a; *Laws*, 846d.

CHAPTER 10
Visiting Prisoners

William C. Placher

William Placher (currently professor of philosophy and religion at Wabash College) is yet another graduate student of Yale and a postliberal theologian. Along with George Hunsinger he helped publish two collections of Hans Frei's essays in the early 1990s: *Types of Christian Theology* (New Haven, CT, 1992) and *Theology and Narrative: Selected Essays* (New York, 1993). Frei himself taught at Wabash early in his career. Placher's own work develops some key issues within theological postliberalism: narrative, scripture, the ecclesial community, revelation, and Christology. He began ambitiously with *A History of Christian Theology: An Introduction* (Louisville, KY, 1983), followed by the two volumes of *Readings in the History of Christian Theology*, the first *From Its Beginnings to the Eve of the Reformation* (Louisville, KY, 1988) and the second *From the Reformation to the Present Day* (Louisville, KY, 1988). What is evident in this work and in the essay below is Placher's practical, even pastoral concerns. His early books demonstrate a determination to provide students at universities and colleges with a route-map through the history of Christian faith, and also source material for analyzing various vistas along the way. Particularly in the second volume, with its introduction of contemporary theological voices (black and feminist among others), Placher's pastoral concerns can be understood within the context of a belief in the necessity of developing ecumenical relations. Throughout the three books he takes pains to emphasize that the tradition is not one, that Christian theology has always been diverse, and that theological discourse has always been involved in arguing a point – not just from an individual perspective, but from an ecclesial standpoint; it is argued from within a distinctive narrative tradition. This is axiomatic for the three volumes which defined Placher's standing as a major postliberal theologian: *Unapologetic Theology: A Christian Voice in a Pluralistic Conversation* (Louisville, KY, 1989), *Narratives of a Vulnerable God: Christ, Theology and Scripture* (Louisville, KY, 1994), and *The Domestication of Transcendence: How Modern Thinking About God Went Wrong* (Louisville, KY, 1996). These books pursue a more dogmatic and philosophical enquiry, engaging with construals of the trinity, the changing understanding of the doctrine of analogy, and the continuing deconstruction of the metaphysical God, for example. But one aspect of this work makes Platcher's thinking quite distinctive among other Yale School graduates: the way in which *Unapologetic Theology* pushes Lindbeck's projects into analyses of science, anthropology, and political philosophy.

The essay contributed to this volume represents a postliberal turn towards ethics and the concerns of contemporary living. In fact, as I have tried to show, specific pastoral concerns have always been important for Placher. In 1998 he jointly edited a volume with Ronald Thiemann (another important postliberal voice) entitled *Why are We Here? Everyday Questions and the Christian Life* (New York, 1998). Here the issue Placher takes up is imprisonment and punishment. He investigates the issue both in terms of statistical and sociological descriptions and the fundamental questions raised by our contemporary attitudes to criminals and retributive justice. Only once he has made this investigation does he relate the topic back to an examination of the scriptural narratives treating such issues. The examination leads directly into his argument – an argument based upon the distinctiveness of the Christian position – "how the gospel cannot help but put retributive practices radically into question." It is at this point, with the articulation of the distinctly Christian argument, that the theology becomes unapologetical and a Christian social ethics (which bears comparison with the work of Stanley Hauerwas) is announced.

I live in a country gone mad on sending people to prison. In the face of clear evidence that they do not "work" in the service of goals like lowering crime, policies of ever longer prison terms sustain themselves, at least in part, by appeal to the principle of retribution. In this essay I will review how some important postmodern thinkers have challenged the idea of retribution, but then argue that it is the Christian gospel that undercuts it most effectively, since it is only faith in redemption that allows to us to admit the reality of human guilt while challenging the logic of punishment. Thus Christians should create a space for a more humane and constructive approach to dealing with criminals. Other topics no doubt invite more complex analyses of the relation of Christianity and postmodernism – but none seems to me more humanly urgent. Thus I realize that what follows will be more practically oriented and less intellectually sophisticated than other essays in this volume, but I do not apologize for that. Christianity – and postmodernism at its best – seeks to change the world as well as to understand it.

Consider therefore some statistics. From the early twentieth century until the mid-1970s the United States imprisoned about 110 people for every 100,000 of population. The figure doubled in the late 1970s and 1980s and doubled again in the 1990s, so that today 445 out of every 100,000 Americans are in prisons.[1] If one adds those in local jails, the 1995 figure rises to about 600 per 100,000. Comparable figures to that 600 would be 36 per 100,000 for Japan, from 50 to 120 for the countries of Western Europe, 229 for the famous "police state" of Singapore, and 368 for South Africa at the height of the crisis before the change to majority rule.[2] California alone has "more inmates in its jails and prisons than do France, Great Britain, Germany, Japan, Singapore, and the Netherlands combined."[3] The Gulag or the Nazi concentration camps, with their political prisoners or whole races imprisoned, incarcerated larger percentages, but, considering simply "criminals," the United States almost certainly has a larger portion of its population in prison or jail now than any society in history.

As noted, this is a recent development, but it has become one of the dramatic characteristics of our nation. Talk about most other social issues, if honest, leads sooner rather than later to talk about prisons. Take race for example: one in every three young African-American men in the United States is either in a jail or prison, on probation or parole, or under pretrial release – in many cities the figure is more than half. More black men are in jail or prison than in college or university – in California, four times as many.[4] Black males in the United States are incarcerated at four times the rate of black males under the white regime in South Africa.[5]

Other examples: in 1996 the "official" rate of unemployment among men was 5.4 percent, but if the 1.1 million men in state or federal prison had been counted in, it would have risen to 6.9 percent. In other words, about a fourth of American males not holding down a job were in prison. A parallel analysis increases the unemployment rate among black males from 11 percent to nearly 18 percent.[6] The largest number of mentally ill Americans in any sort of institution are in jails and prisons. State budgets cut back social programs and expenditures for education as they spend more on building prisons: in the 1980s and 1990s California built twenty-one new prisons while a once much-admired state university system suffered severe budgetary cutbacks.

Conditions are often dreadful in American jails and prisons. Charles W. Colson, a tough minded conservative Republican who got interested in prisons only after being sentenced to one for his part in the Watergate affair, tells of visiting a cellblock in one Washington state prison where the smell alone was so appalling that it made him ill in a few minutes. Many prisoners had been held there continuously for longer than a year.[7] Colson, who has studied American prisons, did not find such conditions surprising. In my own state of Indiana, young men under 21, some guilty of violent crimes, some not, can be assigned to "Westville," where most of them sleep in large dormitory areas which are essentially unpatrolled at night. Some inmates, unable to defend themselves against sexual predators, quickly become flamboyantly effeminate – casting themselves in the female role gets them regularly sodomized but can protect them from getting beaten, and to the weaker that can seem a reasonable trade-off. They are obviously the victims of regular sexual assault in a way that the administrators of the facility can hardly ignore, but nothing much gets done. Indeed, the threat of rape has more or less officially become part of the deterrent policy of American prisons. In a widely publicized program called "Scared Straight," teenaged boys identified as potential troublemakers are taken to prisons where inmates harangue them about how eagerly they will welcome such good looking boys as sexual victims.

Some states have reinstituted chain gangs. New laws keep reducing the age at which capital punishment is permitted. Yet conservative American rhetoric continually talks about how "soft" we are on our prisoners and denounces the supposed "luxury" of the prison system. Running for president in 1996, Bob Dole kept calling the American criminal justice system a "liberal-leaning laboratory of leniency." When groups concerned about criminal justice have carefully investigated the cases of prisoners on Illinois' death row, over half of them have proven to be simply innocent of the crimes of which they had been convicted, yet political pressure grows to speed up execution processes by cutting back opportunities for appeal on "technicalities," with the result that such investigations would be impossible. Social programs to keep young people out of trouble, even if they have only mixed success, come far cheaper than paying for prisons, but prisons are far more politically popular.

Even the American political Left, indeed, has been scared off the prison issue. Looking "soft on crime" seems such a horrible danger that no one wants to risk it. Candidates remember the fate of Michael Dukakis who, running for president, faced notorious Republican ads showing a black man, released on a furlough program while Dukakis was governor of Massachusetts, who had committed a murder. No one else wants to be identified as on the side of criminals – perhaps, if truth were told, least of all on the side of African-American criminals.

The United States certainly has a serious problem of violent crime, but it is not clear that having more people in prison reduces crime rates. From 1985 to 1995 American rates of imprisonment and crime rates *both* dramatically increased. Since 1995 crime rates have substantially declined in some states, but there is no particular correlation between severity of sentencing and decline of crime.[8] My own sense, after reading a good many contradictory studies on the relation of incarceration to crime, comes down to some commonsense principles:

- A high probability of arrest, followed fairly promptly by time in jail or prison, has a serious deterrent effect.
- Particularly when the probability of arrest is relatively low, increases in length of sentence soon cease to have much effect. Someone who is not deterred by the probability he imagines of twenty years in prison will not be deterred by the fear of thirty. To a teenager, two years seems a lifetime; the threat of five years will not much increase deterrence.
- Rehabilitation programs have very mixed success, but a prison system which cuts inmates off from family and society, does not offer substance-abuse treatment or any educational opportunities, and provides no support services

after release makes it very likely that released inmates will soon commit further crimes. Brutality which forces prisoners to be constantly on edge in defending themselves and challenges male prisoners' self-image of masculinity makes additional crime even more likely.

Nevertheless, American public policy generally involves dramatic cutbacks in services available to prisoners, some improvement in police work (with resulting increased likelihood that a criminal will be arrested) and, far beyond anything else, spending large sums of money on longer sentences.[9] The American criminal justice system has just become weirdly irrational. What most political figures say about jails and prisons bears little relation to how they actually are. What we as a society do about prisons causes great human suffering without for the most part accomplishing any useful social goals (like lowering crime).

We continue such policies for a variety of unattractive reasons. Locking up criminals for a long time appeals to voters afraid of crime, who may not realize how often prisons make their inmates, once released, more likely to commit further crimes. Building prisons has become a substantial industry, whose entrepreneurs contribute generously to political campaigns. Still, the evidence that the current system fails to accomplish its announced goals is clear enough. Why do we not act on it? One crucial explanation lies in a general belief in retribution. Even if prisons do nothing to lower crime rates, a great many people believe, they can still be justified on the grounds that *criminals just ought to be punished.*

But why? Rehabilitating prisoners, deterring crime, protecting victims – these are goals with obvious value. But why should we punish for the sake of punishing? It is a question even the greatest philosophers have had a hard time answering. Consider, for instance, a very odd passage from Kant's *Metaphysical Elements of Justice*:

> Even if a civil society were to dissolve itself by common agreement of all its members (for example, if the people inhabiting an island decided to separate and disperse themselves around the world), the last murderer remaining in prison must first be executed, so that everyone will duly receive what his actions are worth and so that the bloodguilt therefore will not be fixed on the people because they failed to insist on carrying out the punishment.[10]

Punishment here serves no deterrent function, since a society's last act hardly establishes a deterring threat for the future. Capital punishment, obviously, does not rehabilitate. Yet Kant insists that rationality demands the punishment – though he is suddenly talking about "bloodguilt" in a way that seems to have little to do with Enlightenment rationality.

One recent scholar, in some desperation, begins his attempt to make sense of the argument just there. Kant is making a utilitarian case, he says. Divine retribution would fall on the whole society if they did not purge themselves of this bloodguilt, and therefore the greatest good for the greatest number implies making sure that that last murderer gets killed.[11]

But it seems unlikely that God as Kant understood him intervened in history to impose corporate punishments. More to the point, just before the quoted passage, Kant insisted that the categorical imperative makes clear that no one should be punished simply in order to achieve some social good.[12] Indeed, Kant was insistent that punishment be performed for the sake of punishment. Appeals to deterrence, he said, involve illegitimately using the criminal at hand as a means to some larger end. Even hoping to reform the prisoner through punishment inappropriately uses him in his present state as a means to some hoped-for future condition, and "his innate personality [that is, his right as a person] protects him against such treatment." Kant is adamant: "Judicial punishment can never be used merely as a means to promote some other good for the criminal himself or for civil society."[13] Nevertheless, we must punish.

Whence this idea that the necessity of punishment is somehow built into the order of things? It was not new in Kant's time. In Plato's *Gorgias* Socrates tries to persuade Polus that it is worse to inflict a wrong than to suffer one. He argues:

> The man who punishes does a fine thing, and the man who is punished has a fine thing done to him.... And if fine, good, since it must be either pleasant or useful. ... Then the treatment received by the man who is punished is good.... Then it must be a benefit to him.... And is the benefit what I take it to be, that if he is justly punished his soul is improved? ... Then the man who is punished is freed from badness of soul.[14]

Socrates draws an analogy with medicine: just as a cure restores one to good physical health, so punishment restores one's good health of soul.

It is tempting to read this passage in terms of rehabilitation – the criminal is made aware of guilt and brought to a better state, less likely to commit future crimes, through the psychological effects of punishment. But Plato in fact makes no such claim. As with Kant, the argument seems ontological rather than psychological: unpunished crime leaves things as they ought not to be, and it is the act of punishment itself (not any rehabilitative effects it might have) that puts the world aright again.

To punish the will of the criminal, Hegel once wrote, "is to annul the crime, which otherwise would have been held valid, and to restore the right."[15] Arguments that justify punishment in terms of prevention, deterrence, or reforming the criminal are all "superficial"; what matters is "that the crime be annulled."[16] But what does such language mean? If Sam steals George's wallet at gunpoint and gets caught, it makes sense to make him give back the money, and perhaps to lock Sam up so that George will feel a bit safer on the streets and others will be discouraged from acts like Sam's. But how does this imprisonment "annul" the crime? It might (though perhaps not) be a bad idea to give Sam another chance and put him on parole. But how would that hold his crime "valid"?

A Kantian can always argue that retribution takes people seriously as moral agents. Putting prisoners through rehabilitation programs treats them as objects to be manipulated, while simply punishing them acknowledges their own responsibility for their actions. Unfortunately, however, the reality of most contemporary prisons is thoroughly dehumanizing, the systematic denial of prisoners' integrity as human beings. The reality of punishment respects no one.

A number of contemporary, "postmodern" thinkers have applied hermeneutics of suspicion to the ways we (philosophers and ordinary citizens alike) talk about guilt, innocence, and punishment. Two such writers – René Girard and Michel Foucault – usefully get us thinking about how and why societies fall into misguided practices of punishment. In the end, both analyses seem to me flawed, but they at least help in challenging ways of thinking we might otherwise take for granted.

Girard analyzes what he calls the "scapegoat mechanism." Most societies down the centuries, he argues, have preserved themselves in time of stress by identifying scapegoats. When our conflicts with one another reach crisis level, we blame the problems on particular individuals and unite together in killing them or driving them out of the community: "Suddenly the opposition of everyone against everyone else is replaced by the opposition of all against one."[17] Myths from around the world justify all this by identifying the evil of these scapegoat figures.[18]

Uniquely, however, the Bible proclaims that scapegoats are innocent. Cain was wrong to murder Abel. His brothers should not have sold Joseph into slavery. Above all, Jesus was not guilty of blasphemy and should not have died as one man for the people.[19] The Bible, Girard thinks, makes the innocence of scapegoats so clear that we can no longer read other scapegoat stories without seeing through them:

> The violence of the cultural order is revealed in the Gospels . . . and the cultural order cannot survive such a revelation. Once the basic mechanism is revealed, the scapegoat mechanism, that expulsion of violence by violence, is rendered useless by the revelation. . . . The good news is that scapegoats can no longer save men, the persecutors' accounts of their persecutions are no longer valid, and truth shines into dark places. God is not violent, the truth of God has nothing to do with violence. . . . The Kingdom of God is at hand.[20]

Engels once remarked about Hegel that history, puzzlingly, continued after it was supposed to end.[21] Similarly, the scapegoat mechanism proves more persistent in the face of the revelation of truth than Girard's account would lead us to expect. The Bible has been around for a good long time, and persecution continues.

One problem may be that all of us bear more guilt than Girard is willing to concede. Once we see that scapegoats are innocent, Girard believes, we can stop persecuting them, and, "The kingdom of God is at hand." But on his own account we have all been involved in the mechanisms of violence that lie at the heart of the cultural order. If our scapegoats have been innocent, then all the more are we guilty. We therefore need more than to realize something; we need to be forgiven, redeemed. Girard's optimistic neo-Gnosticism, however, has no redemption to offer, no good news for the guilty.[22]

Moreover, talk about scapegoats who are innocent provides only limited help in thinking about prisoners, for, at least at some level, most prisoners are guilty. Some of them have done truly horrible things, and the vast majority have committed acts which any properly ordered society would want to prevent if it could. Whether or not it makes sense to stick them into a contemporary American prison, these are not people whom we can simply declare innocent. Girard gets us thinking about why societies single out some people for punishment, and about how irrational that might be, and that usefully calls our habits of thought and action into question, but the world in which we live is darker than the one he imagines. Neither prisoners nor the systems that condemn them can simply be found innocent.

Michel Foucault asked even more radical questions about the distinction between innocence and guilt, and no thinker in our century has brought social practices more effectively into question. Like many of his other historical analyses, his study of prisons pointed to disjunctions in historical practices as a way of raising questions about social practices we have, without much examination, simply come to take for granted. Until the beginning of the nineteenth century, he noted, imprisonment was a rather rare way of dealing with criminals, but then it quickly began to seem inevitable.

> And although, in a little over a century, this self-evident character has been transformed, it has not disappeared. We are aware of all the inconveniences of prison and that it is dangerous when it is not useless. And yet one cannot "see" how to replace it. It is the detestable solution, which one seems unable to do without.[23]

Foucault was of course not proposing a return to earlier forms of punishment – whipping, the stocks, slow torture. He first simply wanted to remind us that our contemporary form of criminal justice is not somehow built into the order of nature, but represents one historically conditioned way of doing things. Once we realize that, then we can start asking hard and radical questions about alternatives to it.

Imprisonment as we know it, Foucault argued, has a long list of obvious flaws. Increasing imprisonment does not clearly and consistently diminish the crime rate. Sending people to prison, at least in our current system, often makes it *more* likely that they will commit another crime than if we had just pardoned them. The experience of prison produces "delinquents," deeply alienated from society by attitudes within themselves and among others. Prison encourages organization among prisoners against the interests of the larger society. The usual policies in place after prisoners are freed make it hard for them to find jobs or adjust. In a variety of ways, standard procedures disrupt the lives of prisoners' families, making increased crime among them more likely.[24] Indeed, it seems a system "dangerous when it is not useless." Once we have seen the non-inevitability of our current system, such obvious flaws should quickly invite us to think about radically different alternatives.

Here as elsewhere, however, Foucault was better at offering diagnosis than at proposing treatment. When people asked him what to do about prisons, he sometimes responded that there were obvious things to do: make them less brutal, provide prisoners with the kinds of help that will make them less likely to return to prison on release. One needs no philosophical theory to justify such recommendations.[25] In other moods, however, he resisted as sentimental and superficial the kind of "humanism" that would concede the distinction between innocent and guilty but demand in the name of humanity that at least the guilty deserve flush toilets: "Our action, on the contrary . . . seeks to obliterate the deep division that lies between innocence and guilt."[26] If power defines truth, then it is the powerful in our society who have *decided* what counts as crime and what doesn't, and ameliorating the condition of prisoners avoids the real issues.

It is certainly true that societies decide what constitutes crime. We might arrest tobacco smokers and treat marijuana smokers as innocent – doing things the other way round may be a policy with arguments in its favor, but it represents a *choice* our society has made. More clearly still, federal law which sentences people to five years in prison for possession of as little as 5 grams of crack cocaine (sold primarily in the inner-city ghetto) while imposing such a sentence only for the possession of 500 grams of powdered cocaine (same potency, same effects, but used mostly in the white suburbs) is clearly a political and, frankly, racist, social policy rather than punishment which somehow responds objectively to the reality of crime.[27]

Still, when Foucault speaks of how police and prisons *create* crime,[28] one wants to protest. Yes, decisions about the relative seriousness of various crimes, and around the edges a good many questions about what counts as crime at all, can be quite arbitrary. Yet arresting armed robbers and murderers rather (except in Singapore) than those who chew gum in public is not simply one social convention among others, with no arguments in its favor. Beyond the sort of prison reform which simple human decency demands, and which he often dismissed as trivial, it is not clear what Foucault wanted us to do about prisons. For all his resistance to sentimentality in others, I suspect he had read Jean Genet at an impressionable age and never quite got over it. He romanticized the rebellion of prisoners against the oppressive social orders of normality, but he would not face questions about whether locking up murderers and rapists might not after all make pretty good sense. Sorting out such questions, he insisted, would involve developing some general theory, and it was the oppressiveness of general theories against which he was protesting – they were themselves part of the structures of oppression.[29]

Absent general theories, however, and we are left with either the sort of modest efforts at humaneness which Foucault dismisses – or with power. And if power defines truth, then the dominant powers in the United States today decree that millions should spend ever longer sentences in brutal prisons. We need a theoretical basis for challenging our society's assumptions about punishment and retribution.[30]

Christianity might seem an implausible place to look. Just for a start, it does not make sense to believe in Christianity simply because it serves some useful social function, so any turn to Christianity is available only to those already convinced of the truth of Christian faith. Second, in the United States today, self-identified Christians are more inclined than the national average to favor capital punishment and more severe sentencing. Some evangelical churches sponsor prison ministries, but relations with prisons and prisoners are rarely a part of the life of mainline Protestant (or Roman Catholic) congregations. Other political issues, from war to abortion to capital punishment, have standard places in discussions of Christian ethics; imprisonment comes up only occasionally.

Talk about prisoners – and fairly radical talk at that – however, has a significant place in the New Testament. In the synoptic gospels, Jesus's programmatic declaration of the purpose of his ministry quotes Isaiah:

> The Spirit of the Lord is upon me,
>   because he has anointed me to bring good news to the poor.
> He has sent me to proclaim release to the captives
>   and recovery of sight to the blind,
>   to let the oppressed go free,
> to proclaim the year of the Lord's favor.
>   (Luke 4.18–19 and parallels)

"Release to the captives" and "letting the oppressed go free" take a prominent place. The reference to "the year of the Lord's favor" evokes the "Jubilee year," in which, in ancient Israel, all prisoners would simply be freed every fifty years.[31] It is not clear whether Israelites ever put this idea into practice, but even its presence in theory testifies to a conviction that mercy can displace retribution. We are a long way from Kant or Plato – or the United States today.[32]

In Matthew, Jesus imagines the returning Son of Man distinguishing the righteous from the accursed in that the righteous had fed the hungry, welcomed the stranger, clothed the naked, cared for the sick, and visited prisoners (Matt. 25.35–6). Until quite recently, visiting prisoners was an important part of Christian life. Many of the dramatic scenes of early Christian faith take place in prison cells, and the Wesleys' accounts of their time with condemned prisoners are among the most moving passages in their writings. To be sure, prisoners visited in the early church were often imprisoned because of their faith rather than for ciminality in a more usual sense (though the government certainly thought of them as criminals), and such visits in later centuries were no doubt sometimes condescending and manipulative. Nevertheless, at least people who regularly visited prisoners knew what the inside of a prison looked like. They would not in general denounce its supposed luxury, and they might (and sometimes did) work to improve prison conditions.

Moreover, Christians have regularly down the centuries in various ways subverted belief in punishment and retribution. An imperial edict of 367, in the time of the first Christian emperors, ordered, in celebration of Easter, the release of all prisoners except those guilty of sorcery, adultery, rape, and homicide (thus of all crimes against property). Medieval lives of saints sometimes tell of how, when the saint or the saint's dead body passed the prison, the doors would miraculously open, and the prisoners would go free.[33] Unexpected clemency, even when occasional and arbitrary, put standard practices of punishment under question. Retribution could not be absolutized if it could be dismissed so casually in individual cases. And maybe, Christians were invited, however tentatively, to think, there are higher values than the sort of justice that leads to punishment and retribution.

Such possibilities grew out of the core of Christian faith. After all, Jesus was a crucified criminal. He was not merely punished, one important strand of Christian theology has maintained – he was guilty, for he had taken on our guilt. "For our sake," Paul wrote, God made Christ "to be sin who knew no sin, so that in him we might become the righteousness of God" (2 Cor. 5.21). Let us suppose that this means what it says; Luther certainly thought so. Christ "says to me," he wrote, "'You are no longer a sinner, but I am. I am your substitute. You have not sinned, but I have. . . . All your sins are to rest on Me and not on you.'"[34] The law thus looks at Christ and declares, "'I find him a sinner, who takes upon Himself the sins of all men. I do not see any other sins than those in Him. Therefore let Him die on the cross.' And so it attacks Him and kills Him. By this deed the whole world is purged."[35]

Christ takes on our sin, and frees us from it. Some of us may have a more immediate need of rehabilitation, or more need to be prevented from doing harm to others in the short run, but according to Christian faith it makes no sense to think of "distinguishing the innocent from the guilty" as the goal of any judicial process. Apart from Christ, we are all guilty. But Christ has taken our place as sinners, so that God no longer condemns us – any of us.[36] We may need to be helped, both by being protected from doing further wrong, and by being helped to be better, but there is no reason to *punish* anyone.

I realize that Christian talk about Christ's saving work can seem to point in a different direction. After all, Anselm, in a classic text, declared that we ought to subject our every inclination to the will of God, and,

> One who does not render this honor to God takes away from God what belong to him, and dishonors God, and to do this is to sin. Moreover, as long as he does not repay what he has stolen, he remains at fault. . . . So, then, everyone who sins must repay to God the honor that he has taken away, and this is the satisfaction that every sinner ought to make to God.[37]

Only of course we cannot repay, since we cannot do better than to follow God's will in every inclination. And therefore we need Christ to pay our debt.

This sounds like a particularly tricky form of the logic of retribution, since by it *everyone* stands condemned.[38] But I think it actually deconstructs retribution in several ways. First, the very fact of universal condemnation undercuts every human project of distinguishing guilty from innocent. Second, the problem is not defined as an abstract violation of principle but as the betrayal of a relationship – we owe recompense not to justice but to God. Therefore, third and most important, the rupture in that relationship can be healed if Christ does what we cannot do. In practice, it is just as Luther (and Paul) said: Christ has taken on our sin, and we are innocent. Anselm framed the issue in terms of a theory of retribution, so that his example makes it all the more clear how the gospel cannot help but put retributive *practices* radically into question.

Forgiveness takes the humanity of the person being forgiven seriously, but, unlike retribution, it frees us from the need then to impose dehumanizing punishment. In personal relationships we forgive each other, but it is not clear that we have the right to forgive some sorts of criminal acts on behalf of their victims. But there are no limits to the forgiveness possible for Christ, who is at once divine and the one who has taken on the guilt of all sinners. Critiques like those of Girard and Foucault raise good questions about who counts as innocent, but only a Redeemer makes it altogether unproblematic to reach out in love to the guilty. As John Milbank has written,

> The trial and punishment of Jesus itself condemns, in some measure, all other trials and punishment, and all forms of alien discipline.... The only finally tolerable, and non-sinful punishment, for Christians, must be the self-punishment inherent in sin. When a person commits an evil act, he cuts himself off from social peace, and this nearly always means that he is visited with social anger. But the aim should be to reduce this anger to a calm fury against the sin, and to offer the sinner nothing but goodwill, so bringing him to the point of realizing that his isolation is self-imposed.... The Church, while recognizing the tragic necessity of "alien," external punishment, should also seek to be an asylum, a house of refuge from its operations, a social space where a different, forgiving and restitutionary practice is pursued. This practice should also be "atoning," in that we acknowledge that an individual's sin is never his alone, that its endurance harms us all, and therefore its cancellation is also the responsibility of all.[39]

In short, we face pragmatic questions of how to protect potential victims and rehabilitate any and all to lead better lives, but Christians can think about such questions free of the need to distinguish innocent and guilty, and free of the need for punishment.

What would that mean in practice? Charles Colson's Prison Fellowship and Justice Fellowship offer useful examples, if only because Colson's history (he once said he would run over his grandmother for Richard Nixon) and attitudes on other issues free him from any suspicion of being a "soft liberal." In the Prison Fellowship, Christians work with prisoners in seminars and Bible studies and just in general visit prisoners and serve as their pen pals. They arrange for community service that prisoners can do if allowed furloughs, and they pair released prisoners with members of Christian congregations who will help them in their efforts to readjust to life "outside." Prisoners are not treated as outsiders, but as potential and then actual members of Christian communities; welcome into such communities even while they are imprisoned, and the promise of a greater degree of fellowship after their release, is crucial to the program's success.

So far, Colson's program follows the kind of Christian ethics many of us have learned from Stanley Hauerwas: the task of Christians is not to lobby for changes in government programs, but to act as the church, through local congregations.[40] Well and good. But the work of the Justice Fellowship supplements that of the Prison Fellowship, campaigning for alternative forms of punishment for nonviolent offenders, for an end to the worst abuses within the prison system, and so on.[41] How, Colson asks, can one visit prisoners, connecting with them as Christian brothers and sisters, and hear their stories of brutality or sexual abuse within their prisons, without doing something by way of publicity, political lobbying, or whatever to improve their condition? How could prisoners take seriously invitations to join Christian communities whose members were not trying to reduce the brutality and injustice of the prison system?[42]

If Christians started working with prisoners in significant numbers, it might be the beginning of the most radical changes in our criminal justice system – or it might lead simply to decreases in brutality and improvements in rehabilitation. I see no need to try to predict the end before we begin. As Will Campbell and James Holloway have written,

> We constantly discover men and women who have been in various types of prisons for decades without *one single visitor* having signed their record card. We have suggested on other occasions that each institutional church adopt three prisoners purely and simply for purposes of visitation – so that at least once each week every man and woman and child behind bars could have one human being with whom he could have community, to whom the prisoner could tell his story. And the visitor his. We have advocated that because we are convinced that this elementary act of charity alone would provide all the prison reform that society could tolerate.[43]

To be sure, Christians cannot expect that our non-Christian neighbors will share our view that we are all sinners just like the inmates of the local jail, and that their sin, like ours, has been taken by Christ. Christians have reasons for welcoming prisoners into our communities which others in our society do not share, and those others may not want to emulate our practices. But we ought to be able to persuade non-Christians too that the present prison system is not working and that, even on purely pragmatic grounds, its brutality and lack of counseling and support programs do more harm than good. We should at least remind our neighbors of what prisons are like – something we will know if we have been visiting prisoners. If we do not engage in such "political" activity, prisoners will regard our overtures with justified suspicion. Moreover, if we are visiting prisons, our hearts will compel us to try to change them. How radically? We can only find out if we begin.[44]

Notes

1 Eric Schlosser, "The Prison–Industrial Complex," *Atlantic Monthly* 282 (December 1998), p. 52. Even the early twentieth-century figures represented a dramatic increase from earlier times. "Nobody in the colonial period had yet advanced the

idea that it was good for the soul, and conducive to reform, to segregate people who committed crimes, and keep them behind bars." Indeed, one scholar has found only nineteen cases of people sent to jail in New York between 1691 and 1776, and there were no federal prisons at all (except for soldiers and sailors) until 1891. Lawrence M. Friedman, *Crime and Punishment in American History* (New York: Basic Books, 1993), pp. 48, 269.

2 Elliott Currie, *Crime and Punishment in America* (New York: Henry Holt, 1998), p. 15.
3 Schlosser, "The Prison–Industrial Complex," p. 52.
4 Currie, *Crime and Punishment in America*, p. 13.
5 Norval Morris, "The Contemporary Prison," *The Oxford History of the Prison*, ed. Norval Morris and David J. Rothman (Oxford: Oxford University Press, 1995), p. 215.
6 Unemployment data from *Economic Report of the President*, 1997; prison statistics from Bureau of Justice Statistics, *Prisoners in 1996*; cited in Currie, *Crime and Punishment in America*, p. 33.
7 Charles Colson, *Kingdoms in Conflict* (New York: Harper and Row, 1987), pp. 451–65.
8 Currie, *Crime and Punishment in America*, pp. 29, 57.
9 In 1991 one-third of federal inmates were getting substance-abuse treatment. By 1997, though the percentage of inmates with substance-abuse problems was clearly higher, only 15 percent were receiving such treatment – this largely because of cutbacks in such programs, made in spite of the fact that those who participate in them are much less likely to commit crimes after their release – 73 percent less likely to be rearrested in the first six months, for instance. Jonathan Alter, "The Buzz on Drugs," *Newsweek*, September 6, 1999, pp. 26–7.
10 Immanuel Kant, *The Metaphysical Elements of Justice*, trans. John Ladd (Indianapolis, IN: Library of Liberal Arts, 1965), p. 102.
11 John Cottingham, "Varieties of Retribution," *Philosophical Quarterly*, 29 (1979), pp. 243–4.
12 Kant, *Metaphysical Elements*, p. 100.
13 Ibid.
14 Plato, *Gorgias*, 476d–477b, trans. Walter Hamilton (Harmondsworth: Penguin Books, 1971), p. 67.
15 G. W. F. Hegel, *Philosophy of Right*, trans. T. M. Knox (Oxford: Clarendon Press, 1942), p. 69.
16 Ibid, p. 70.
17 René Girard, *Things Hidden Since the Foundation of the World* (Stanford, CA: Stanford University Press, 1987), p. 24.
18 René Girard, *The Scapegoat*, trans. Yvonne Freccero (Baltimore, MD: Johns Hopkins University Press, 1984), p. 8.
19 Ibid, p. 113.
20 Ibid, p. 189.
21 Friedrich Engels, "Ludwig Feuerbach and the End of Classical German Philosophy," *On Religion* (Moscow: Progress Publications, 1975), p. 195.
22 I have made this point in a bit more detail in William C. Placher, "Christ Takes Our Place," *Interpretation*, 53 (1999), pp. 7–9.
23 Michel Foucault, *Discipline and Punish*, 2nd edn., trans. Alan Sheridan (New York: Vintage Books, 1995), p. 232.

24 Ibid, pp. 265–8.
25 See Hubert L. Dreyfus and Paul A. Rabinow, *Michel Foucault: Beyond Structuralism and Hermeneutics* (Chicago: University of Chicago Press, 1982), p. 264.
26 Michel Foucault, *Language, Counter-Memory, Practice*, trans. Donald F. Bouchard and Sherry Simon (Ithaca, NY: Cornell University Press, 1977), p. 237.
27 Alter, "The Buzz on Drugs," p. 27.
28 See, for instance, Foucault, *Discipline and Punish*, p. 282.
29 Ibid, p. 231.
30 See Nancy Fraser, "Foucault on Modern Power: Empirical Insights and Normative Confusions," *Praxis International*, 1 (1981), p. 283.
31 Leviticus 25.
32 For a rich discussion of Biblical views of imprisonment, see Lee Griffith, *The Fall of the Prison* (Grand Rapids, MI: Eerdmans, 1993).
33 Edward M. Peters, "Prison before the Prison," *The Oxford History of the Prison*, pp. 19, 24.
34 Martin Luther, *Sermons on the Gospel of St John*, ch. 1, 12th sermon, trans. Jaroslav Pelikan, in *Luther's Works*, vol. 22 (St Louis, MO: Concordia, 1957), p. 167.
35 Martin Luther, *Lectures on Galatians* (on Gal. 3.13), trans. Jaroslav Pelikan, in *Luther's Works*, vol. 26 (St Louis, MO: Concordia, 1963), p. 280.
36 Karl Barth, *Church Dogmatics*, vol. 2, pt. 2, trans. G. W. Bromiley, et al. (Edinburgh: T. & T. Clark, 1957), p. 492; vol. 4, pt. 1, trans. G. W. Bromiley and T. F. Torrance (Edinburgh: T. & T. Clark, 1956), p. 258.
37 Anselm of Canterbury, *Why God Became Man*, 11, *A Scholastic Miscellany*, ed. and trans. Eugene R. Fairweather (New York: Macmillan, 1970), p. 119.
38 Indeed Timothy Gorringe's brilliant book *God's Just Vengeance* (Cambridge: Cambridge University Press, 1996) argues that Anselmian theory supports practices of retribution.
39 John Milbank, *Theology and Social Theory* (Oxford: Blackwell Publishers, 1993), pp. 421–2.
40 See, for instance, Stanley Hauerwas, *Against the Nations* (Minneapolis, MN: Winston Press, 1985), pp. 11–12.
41 Charles W. Colson, *Against the Night* (Ann Arbor, MI: Servant Publications, 1989), pp. 188–90.
42 Colson, *Kingdoms in Conflict*, p. 465.
43 Will D. Campbell and James Y. Holloway, *". . . and the criminals with him . . ."* (New York: Paulist Press, 1973), p. 148.
44 I am grateful to Stephen H. Webb for thoughtful comments on this essay and to Scott M. Brannon for conversations which have shaped it in a variety of ways. Neither would agree with all my conclusions.

CHAPTER 11
Suffering and Incarnation

Graham Ward

Graham Ward is one of the leading contemporary exponents of "postmodern theology," and his previous work constitutes some of the most innovative and creative thinking at the interface between theology and postmodernism. For Ward, postmodernism creates the space for a return of orthodox theology, for the recovery of a credal and patristic Christianity liberated from the distorting shackles of modernity. Indeed, postmodernism not only opens the way, but actually calls for and demands a return of theology. For without theology, secular postmodernism condemns us to nihilism and its obsessions with lack, absence, melancholy, and death. These themes and emphases are ones shared with the other theologians of "radical orthodoxy," a movement of which Ward is one of the founding and leading exponents. Together with John Milbank and Catherine Pickstock, he coedited the definitive collection of essays, *Radical Orthodoxy: A New Theology* (1999).

What is distinctive about Ward's work, however, is the way in which it is sensitive to and explores the ways in which theology and postmodernism inform, mold, and shape each other. For Ward, it is not simply that postmodernism opens a space for theology, but also that theology is itself dependent upon and indebted to postmodernism for its contemporary articulation. This interdependence is manifested in a number of ways: first, Christianity must be expressed in terms of its contemporary cultural context in order to render it intelligible and believable; in this sense, postmodernism is indispensable for effective Christian witness. Second, theology has much to gain and may consequently be enriched by a constructive engagement with contemporary postmodern and critical theory. Third, there is an acute awareness of the way in which theology is itself a cultural construct, and that a commitment to or judgment in favor of Christianity is always underpinned by the Augustinian recognition that "ignorance is unavoidable." Thus, one can see why, for Ward, an ostensibly secular thinker such as Jacques Derrida and a resolutely theological thinker such as Karl Barth both stand in need of supplementation by each other. Indeed, this was the burden of Ward's argument in his first book, *Barth, Derrida and the Language of Theology* (1995), and it was subsequently broadened out to encompass a whole host of postmodern critical theorists in *Theology and Contemporary Critical Theory* (1996).

Much of Ward's theological reflection has centered upon issues of embodiment, corporeality, and gender, indispensable facets of existence which much postmodern thought seeks to rescue from their exclusion by modernity. For Ward, however, such a rescue can only properly be accomplished by it being founded upon a theological underpinning, particularly by a theology of incarnation and *kenosis*. Many of these themes have been given extensive expression in his book *Cities of God* (2000). They are also present – and further developed – in the essay printed here, "Suffering and Incarnation." In this essay Ward makes clear that his aim is not to develop a modern "theodicy" but rather to provide a theological reading of suffering itself, with which the contemporary philosophical, psychological, and sociological accounts may be confronted. Whereas secular postmodern accounts of pain and pleasure on the parts of Derrida, Lacan, and Žižek give rise to economies of desire that are sado-masochistic and pathological, a theological economy of incarnate love sets suffering and sacrifice within a greater context which is "born of and borne by passion." This is "the very risk and labor of love." For Ward, it is only by living theologically "in the name of a transcendental hope" that we can resist a culture in which suffering itself is fetishized and lionized.

Gavin Hyman
University of Lancaster

The concern of this essay lies with a comparison and, ultimately, a confrontation between two cultures: the secular and the Christian with respect to the character and economies of pain and pleasure, suffering, sacrifice, and ultimate satisfaction.[1]

We need to begin with the corporeal, since it is the body which registers suffering and it is the theological nature of embodiment itself which is the concern of incarnation. Suffering is a mode of embodied experience: a theological account then of suffering must concern itself with what it means to be a soul enfleshed. The character of bodily experience is registered according to a pain–pleasure calculus. Those of us who are academics spend much of our time, I suggest, experiencing the extremes of neither. Perhaps most people, indeed, only take account of their embodiment when the body demands account to be taken because its experiences register the intensity of suffering or the delights of bliss. But in beginning with the corporeal let me emphasize what I am *not* doing.

First, I am not suggesting a mind-body dualism – there are intellectual pleasures (as Kantian aesthetics and the joy of reading evidence) and there is intellectual pain (as existentialism emphasized and psychiatry treats). To draw upon a distinction St Paul makes, and which we will return to later, perhaps most of us inhabit the body (*soma*) rather than the flesh (*sarx*) or the symbolics of embodiment rather than its sensate materiality. The reason for this lies in the difficulty of registering sensation as such. That is, most of the time we experience our body's sensations through cultural prisms and personal expectations. The raw givenness of the body and its experiences are already encoded. Judith Butler neatly sums this up in her book *Bodies That Matter* through a play on the word "matter" as it refers to both materiality and something of significance. That which is matter already matters, is already caught up in the exchanges of signification.[2] The soul enfleshed (where soul has much wider connotations than just the mind's cognition), the only "body" we know, sublates any mind-body dualism.

Second, I do not wish to suggest that there is a spectrum with pain at one extreme and pleasure at the other. Since early modernity the Protestant awareness of the transcendence of the divine beyond human reasoning, accounts of peering into the infinite reaches of the heavens, and aesthetic descriptions of the sublime, have each appealed to experiences which are simultaneously both painful and consummately beatific.[3] The mystic's cry of ecstasy,[4] the mathematician's speechless awe at the dark spaces between the stars,[5] the exquisite intellectual confusion as the experience of what is beautiful sheers towards the edge of the *tremendum*[6] – each testify to experiences that exceed the neat categorization, the spectrum extremities, of pain and pleasure. Though it does seem to me (and we will return to this in the last section of this essay) that to conflate suffering and bliss can also be a sign of decadence announcing a sadomasochistic culture.

Contemporary Pain and Pleasure

For some time now, at least since the 1960s and 1970s (though its roots lie in Hegel's *Phenomenology of Spirit*), intellectual debates concerned with the economies of desire – whether in Deleuze, Lacan, Lyotard, Barthes, Foucault, or Žižek – have been oriented around the notion of *jouissance*. Suffering constitutes itself as the lack or absence of *jouissance*. Bliss, as one translation, is the ultimate human goal. With Lacan and Žižek the lack itself is pleasurable. They would argue that what we desire is not the fulfillment of our desire, but the desiring itself, the prolongation of desire. To attain our desire would collapse the distinction between the imaginary and the symbolic. The extended game of hunt the slipper would come to an end. Desire only operates if there remains an *objet petit a*, a hole, a gap, a void, a loss that can never (and must never) be fully negotiated or filled. And so we fetishize – turn the hole itself into what we desire: "in fetishism we simply make the cause of desire directly into our object of desire."[7] But since the hole itself cannot be negotiated then objects substitute for and veil this ultimate void. Bliss then is endlessly deferred, yet remains the *telos* and organizing point for any local and ephemeral construction of the meaning of embodiment. Lacan (and Žižek) develop into a sacrificial logic the system of compensations and substitutions which Freud increasingly recognized as symptomatic of the way the libidinal drive operated alongside the death drive in the economy of desire. Civilization, for Freud, is founded upon its profound and ineliminable discontent. In this sacrificial logic we are caught up in a denial of what we most want and produce substitutionary forms, objects, laws, empty symbols for that which is unsubstitutional. And so we deny, sometimes even murder, what we most value, in order to maintain our fantasies about it.[8] There takes place here a renunciation in the form of a negation of negation. It is this sacrificial logic that I wish to examine. It has the structure of sado-masochism.

It finds similar forms in other poststructuralist discourses. Derrida's accounts of the economy of the sign, the economy of *différance* and the logic of the supplement, is also a sacrificial economy. In his essay "How to Avoid Speaking" (*Comment ne pas parler*), he coins the word "denegation" (*dénégation*) or the negation of negation, to describe the effects of *différance* in discourses of negative theology. Writing in the interstices between the story of Abraham and Isaac in the Old Testament and Kierkegaard's reading of the story in *Fear and Trembling*, Derrida emphasizes,

> The trembling of *Fear and Trembling*, is, or so it seems, the very experience of sacrifice . . . in the sense that sacrifice supposes the putting to death of the unique in terms of its being unique, irreplaceable, and most precious. It also therefore refers to the impossibility of substitution, the unsubstitutional; and then also to the substitution of an animal for man; and finally, especially this, it refers to what links the sacred to sacrifice and sacrifice to secrecy . . . Abraham . . . speaks and doesn't speak. . . . He speaks in order not to say anything about the essential thing he must keep secret. Speaking in order not to say anything is always the best technique for keeping a secret.[9]

Speaking in order not to say is the work of *différance* such that deconstruction produces a specific kind of syntax: in *The Gift of Death* it is "religion without religion"; in *The Politics of Friendship* it is "community without community" and "friendship without friendship"; elsewhere it is "justice without justice." The syntagma of this sacrificial economy, that keeps concealed what it most wishes to say, is "X without X."[10] It conceals a continual wounding presented as a perpetual *kenosis*, the *kenosis* of discourse.[11] The sign is always involved in a diremption of meaning as it differs and defers in its logic of sacrificial substitution and supplementation. It is this which brings *différance* into a relation with negative theology (a saying which cannot say). The sign yields up its significance in what Derrida terms a serierasure. But what governs the yielding is the logocentric promise, the call to come, an eschatology which can never arrive, can never be allowed to arrive. Suffering, sacrifice, and satisfaction are intrinsic to the economy of the sign. "Every time there is '*jouissance*' (but the 'there is' of this event is in itself extremely enigmatic), there is 'deconstruction'. Effective deconstruction. Deconstruction perhaps has the effect, if not the mission, of liberating forbidden *jouissance*. That's what has to be taken on board. It is perhaps this *jouissance* which most irritates the all-out adversaries of 'deconstruction'."[12] But this is "*jouissance* without *jouissance*" for deconstruction cannot deliver the delay it describes. Thus, a culture is produced which is fundamentally sadomasochistic: it cannot allow itself to enjoy what it most profoundly wants. Derrida composes a scenario:

> What I thus engage in the double constraint of a *double bind* is not only myself, nor my own desire, but the other, the Messiah or the god himself. As if I were calling someone – for example, on the telephone – saying to him or her, in sum: I don't want you to wait for my call and become forever dependent upon it; go out on the town, be free not to answer. And to prove it, the next time I call you, don't answer, or I won't see you again. If you answer my call, it's all over."[13]

Michel de Certeau and Emmanuel Levinas, in their different models of selfhood with respect to the other, portray the sacrificial logic in terms of an endless journeying into exile (Certeau)[14] or the position of always being accused by the other (Levinas).[15] For both, the self can never be at rest. It must always suffer displacement by the other, always undergo a passion. The displacement and suffering is given, in both their accounts, an ethical coloring, for it is constituted in and by a Good beyond being (Levinas) or the utopic horizon of union with the One (Certeau's "white ecstasy").[16] The suffering is inseparable from accounts of desire, *jouissance*, and substitution.[17]

With various modulations each of these discourses operates a sacrificial logic in which love is not-having (Cixous's formulation).[18] The suffering, the sacrifice, the *kenosis*, is both necessary and unavoidable, for it is intrinsic to the economy itself. But unlike Hegel's dialectic, the negative moment is not appropriated and welded firmly both into the providential chain of time and the constitution of the subject. The negative moment remains unappropriated, unsublated, impossible to redeem because forever endlessly repeated. Furthermore, because bound to a construal of time as a series of discrete units, each negative moment is utterly singular and utterly arbitrary insofar as the moment is infinitely re-iterated to the point where difference between moments becomes a matter of indifference (rendering the utterly singular moment identical and identically repeated). All suffering is both the same and yet singular; renunciation and sacrifice are both universal (in form) and particular. The relation of this operative negativity to the utopic horizon that governs it (*jouissance* in its various guises) is contradictory rather than paradoxical. It governs the suffering as its antithesis, not its *telos*. An infinite distance, a distance without analogy or participation, is opened constituting the other as absolutely other. In Derrida's words, "*tout autre est tout autre*."[19] As such the dreams of the bliss of union intensify the suffering in the way that Sisyphus is tormented by seeing the goal for which he strives while also knowing it can never be attained. Or, to employ another Greek myth, *jouissance* is the grapes held out to the thirsting Tantalus. And so one is led to ask what the sacrifice achieves in this infinite postponement of pleasure. As an operation, which is no longer governed by a single or a simple agency (for the poststructural subject is profoundly aporetic), it is required by and maintains the possibility of the economy. It is immanent to the economy but not assimilable to it. It resolves nothing with respect to that economy, only fissures it with the aneconomic trauma which allows the economy to proceed. What it produces, and continually reproduces then, is the economy itself: the endless production of pseudo-objects. This economy of sacrifice is fundamental to capitalism itself. For it sustains growth, limitless productivity, which is capitalism's profoundly secular fantasy. It repeats, in a sociopsychological, semiotic, and ethical keys our various monetary projects in which we deny present delights by investing for greater delights in the future (wherein the pleasures we deny ourselves are only utilized by investment banks to further develop market operations). Sacrifice as enjoying one's own suffering, in this immanent economy of desire, sustains current developments in globalism (and current illusions that such globalism is liberal and democratic).

Christian Pain and Pleasure

What role does suffering play in the economy of Christian redemption? What of its own sacrificial logic? I suggest we need to make a distinction between sacrificial suffering (as *kenosis* and passion), which undoes the economics of sin through a therapy of desire, and the suffering which is a consequence and a perpetuation of sin, which undoes the orders of grace that sustain creation in its being. Of course, this distinction is a theological one, maintained by faith and established by eschatological judgment. Living *in media res*, as Augustine reminds us, "ignorance is unavoidable – and yet the exigencies of human society make judgment also unavoidable."[20] Nevertheless, the distinction is important for it marks out a place for suffering as a passion written into creation (the first incarnation of the divine). That cryptic verse from the Book of Revelation announces that Christ was the Lamb "slain from the foundation of the world" (13.8). Creation, then, issues from a certain kenotic giving, a logic of sacrifice that always made possible the passion of Jesus Christ on the Cross, the slaying of the Lamb. The Cross becomes the place where the two forms of suffering – the sacrificial and that which is a consequence of sin – meet. Jesus is both the obedient lamb given on behalf of sinful human beings and the suffering victim of the disrupted orders of creation brought about by the lust to dominate. The kenotic abandonment assuages and reorientates the powers of disintegration, establishing grace as the principle of nature. But prior to the fall, to sin, and the judgment that installed suffering (and death) as a consequence of disobedience, prior to the judgment on Eve ("I will increase your labour and your groaning," Genesis 3.16) and the judgment on Adam ("You shall gain your food by the sweat of your brow," Genesis 3.19), there was a foundational giving that cost.

We will return to the nature of this primordial suffering later. Evidently it concerns the divine economy with respect both to its internal relations and creation.

For the moment I wish to point out how this logic of sacrifice operates in respect of divine history or *Heilsgeschichte*. For it is that which reveals itself as flesh and history, recorded in the scriptures, which, for Christians, stakes out the limits and possibilities for theological speculation. And it is in that revelation of God made flesh that the relationship between suffering and incarnation, the mystery of that relationship, can be apprehended.

The suffering that marks the incarnation is figured early in the gospel narrative of Luke in scenes and tropes of wounding and scarification. John the Baptist's circumcision is reiterated in the circumcision of Christ (1.59 and 2.21) and the prophesied rejection of Christ by the world is followed by an oracle to Mary that "a sword shall pierce your heart also" (2.35). The circumcision was interpreted by the early Church Fathers as an early blood-letting foreshadowing the sacrifice on the Cross. Suffering was also a glorification, for the detail that it took place on the eighth day was traditionally interpreted as a reference to the eschatological day of judgment; the day following the final and consummating Sabbath when the dead rise with new bodies to dwell eternally in the kingdom of light. This paradoxical nature of suffering and glorification is echoed throughout the New Testament. We will meet it in the Pauline epistles, and in the Gospel of John Christ on the Cross is portrayed as both the ultimate victim and the exalted ensign for the healing of the nations. In the Book of Revelation the Lamb worshipped and adored, the disseminator of light throughout the Eternal City, remains a Lamb that was slain.

The scenes and tropes of scarification in those opening chapters of Luke's Gospel focus other acts of violence with which the Incarnation is announced and brought about: the sacrificial offering made by Zechariah the Priest (1.10), the offering of doves or pigeons at the Presentation of Christ (2.24), the terror struck in Zechariah, Mary, and the shepherds at the visitation of the angel(s), the striking dumb of Zechariah "because you have not believed me" (1.20). The suffering of incarnation is registered somatically and psychologically in the flesh of those called to play a part in its human manifestation. The Incarnation of Christ intensifies the experience of embodiment through the sufferings it engenders, just as – in an unfolding of the same logic – it is the experience of suffering which most deeply draws the believer to prayer (in the garden of Gethsemane, in the upper room following the death, resurrection, and ascension of Christ, in Paul's imprisonment). In suffering the soul is recognized at the surface of the body, the ensoulment of the body is most exposed.[21] With the darkest nights of the soul, in which is evident the inseparability of consciousness, subconsciousness, and the sensitivities of the flesh, come the profoundest awareness of participation in the divine.

There is no deliverance from suffering promised in the New Testament before the messianic return: "He will dwell among them and they shall be his people, and God himself will be with them. He will wipe every tear from their eyes; there shall be an end to death, and to mourning and crying and pain; for the old order has passed away" (Revelation 21.3–4). In fact, in his Epistle to the Colossians, Paul cryptically remarks that he rejoices to suffer for the church at Colossi because "This is my way of helping to complete, in my poor human flesh, the full tale of Christ's afflictions still to be endured, for the sake of his body which is the church" (1.24). This is a well-wrought translation, but it filters out some of the syntactic and semantic complexity of Paul's Greek. A close, more literal translation would read:

> Now I rejoice in suffering [*en tois pathemasin*] on your behalf and fill up in turn [*antanaplero*] things lacking of the afflictions [*thlipseon*] of Christ in my flesh [*sarxi*] on behalf of his body [*somatos*] which is the church.

The Greek gives emphasis to three interrelated themes. First, it builds upon and develops spatial figurations which preoccupy Paul through this letter and (possibly) his letter to the Ephesians. Throughout the letter Paul draws attention to Christ as a cosmic space filled with all the riches and treasures of wisdom and knowledge (2.3), speaking repeatedly of Christians as living *en Christo* or *en auto* employing a locative use of the dative. All things upon earth and in heaven are reconciled "in the body of his flesh [*en to somati tes sarxos autou*]" (1.22). Second, the Greek emphasizes the interdependency of bodies and flesh such that there is a series of coactivities between the individual believer and the body of Christ as *both* the church and the person of Christ. Later in the letter Paul will talk about being co-buried [*suntaphentes*], co-raised [*sunegerthete*], and co-quickened [*sunezoopoiesen*] in Christ (2.12–13), such that there is an economy for growth and expansion through "the operation of him operating in me in power [*ten energeian autou ten energoumenen en emoi en dunamei*]." The prose borders on poetry, as alliterative and assonantal effects resonate within an iterative litany. Paul's flesh (*sarx*) participates in an unfolding and outworking of Christ's body (*soma*), just as Jesus Christ's own flesh opens up to enfold all things in earth and heaven in one body. Third, the verse picks up a rich and profound play on the verb *pleroo* and the noun *pleroma*. The verb *pleroo* stands as the opposite to the important word for Christ's descent from God in Paul's Letter to the Philippians, *kenoo* – to empty, to pour out.[22] There Paul exhorts believers to "Have this mind among yourselves, which is yours in Christ Jesus, who, though he was in the form of God, did not count equality with God a thing to be grasped, but emptied himself, taking the form of a servant, being born like other human beings" (2.5). The economics of emptying that governed the Incarnation are now reversed. The lack that *kenosis* brought about is now being satisfied. There is a filling and a fulfilling, not only of Christ but of each believer with respect to Christ. Paul works and prays for the Colossians that "you may be filled [*plerothete*] with the full knowledge of the will of him in all wisdom and spiritual understanding [*en pase sophia kai sunesei pneumatike*]" (1.9). The *pleroma* is presented as the glory or the wisdom of God filling a space, defining a certain sacred spatiality like the *Shekinah* in the tabernacle in the wilderness. Earlier in the letter Paul writes that in Christ "all the fullness [*pan to pleroma*]" dwells (1.19). Later in the letter he writes that "in him dwells all the fullness of the Godhead bodily [*to pleroma tes theotetos somatikos*] and you are in him having been filled [*pepleromenoi*]" (2.9–10). In the verse following 1.24 he presents himself as the minister according to God's economic handling [*oikonomian*] "to fulfil the word of God [*plerosa ton logon tou theou*]" (1.25) for the Colossians.

Here in 1.24 *antanaplero* is utterly distinctive. Found only at this point in the New Testament, it combines *ana-plero* (to fill up to the brim, to make up, supply, satisfy, and fulfill) with the prefix of *anti*. As J. B. Lightfoot pointed out back in 1876, if Paul's meaning was simply to fill up then the prefix is redundant.[23] With the prefix a self-reflexivity is announced. Twice in the verse the word "on behalf of [*uper*]" is employed: Paul suffers on behalf of the Colossians and on behalf of the body of Christ as the church. His suffering in the flesh is filling what remains of the afflictions of Christ *as* Christ suffered on behalf of him in his own flesh. Jesus Christ as flesh (*sarx*) is no longer: "even though we once knew Christ from the human point of view, we know him no longer in that way" Paul tells the church at Corinth (2 Corinthians 5.16). There remains the body of Christ as the church composed of the flesh (*sarx*) of believers like Paul. Paul's suffering is, then, an extension of and a participation in the suffering of Christ. Now, on one level this is living *imitatio Christi* – the church suffers persecution as Christ suffered persecution. But, considered in the light of the three emphases we have been outlining – Christ as a cosmic and spiritual space in which the operation of a divine economy of "filling" engages and makes itself manifest through the embodiment of those believers composing the body of Christ – then we have to ask what the relationship is between suffering and glorification, affliction and fulfillment. For the filling is an activity described both in terms of suffering and full knowledge, wisdom and spiritual understanding. And it is an activity that not only builds up, but defines the operation of the divine with respect to, the body of Christ. A suffering inseparable from the Incarnation of Christ is experienced in believers as a suffering inseparable from coming to the fullness of the stature of Christ or "being renewed in the full knowledge according to the image of the creator" (3.10).

Paul's writing is a theological reflection on the economics of divine power with respect to embodiment in Christ. It is a reflection upon divinity as it manifests itself in the concrete historicity of the death, burial, and resurrection of Jesus the Christ. It is not speculative in the sense of conceiving operations in the Godhead on the basis of which earthly events might be explained. Rather he develops and unfolds the logic of Christ's incarnation and crucifixion, examining the space that has been opened up "in the body of his flesh through his death" (1.22). This is not, then, an example of *deipassionism* in the sense of God suffering with humankind – the suffering of God described by Moltmann, for example. One recalls how Moltmann reads Elie Wiesel's account of the hanging of a child in the German concentration camp. Wiesel observes how the question of where God is is raised by Jewish onlookers. Moltmann examines this question and Wiesel's own response, in terms of God being in the very suffering of the child.

> To speak here of a God who could not suffer would make God a demon. To speak here of an absolute God would make God an annihilating nothingness. To speak

here of an indifferent God would condemn men to indifference. . . . Does the Shekinah, which wanders with Israel through the dust of the streets and hangs on the gallows in Auschwitz, suffer in the God who holds the ends of the earth in his hand? In that case not only would suffering affect God's *pathos* externally, so that it might be said that God himself suffers at the human history of injustice and force, but suffering would be the history in the midst of God himself.[24]

God suffers with us such that the negative moment is taken up into God in the eschatological coming of the kingdom. Moltmann's theology, endorsing a certain interpretation of Hegel's, radicalizes God being with us, compromising God's transcendence.

Balthasar's account of Christ's descent into hell and into solidarity with the most profound alienation from God the father, retains the transcendent and impassable source, opening wide the difference between the father and the son, the trinitarian processions. In the silence of Holy Saturday God is extended to the point where even that which is most remote from the Godhead is incorporated. The depths of abjection are plumbed and God is found there. "The Redeemer showed himself therefore as the only one who, going beyond the general experience of death, was able to measure the depths of that abyss."[25] Through Christ's suffering there is redemption, but once redemption has been achieved – the extreme boundaries of hell encompassed – then all is reconciled. "Hell is the *product* of redemption," Balthasar informs us.[26] Subsequent suffering is not really suffering at all, objectively speaking. For the victory has been won in Christ through the events of those three days (Good Friday, Holy Saturday, and Easter Sunday): "Inasmuch as the Son travels across the chaos in virtue of the mission received from the Father, he is, objectively speaking, whilst in the midst of the darkness of what is contrary to God, in 'paradise', and the image of triumph may well express this."[27]

But Paul's account views things differently: subsequent suffering is not epiphenomenal (which Balthasar's account may seem to render it). It participates in a true and ongoing suffering; a true and ongoing passion located in the very Godhead itself. Following this interpretation of Paul we can conclude that there is a suffering which is rendered meaningless because it has no part in redemption. This is a suffering which rejects and fights against redemption. It has no truth, no existence in Augustine's ontology of goodness, because it is privative – it deprives and strips creation of its orders of being, its treasures of wisdom. Suffering which is a consequence and promulgation of sin can find no place in the *pleroma* unless as a therapy for the orientation of desire towards sin. Only *pleroma* gives space, provides a dwelling. But there is a suffering which is intrinsically meaningful because it is a continuation, a fleshing out, and a completing of the suffering of Christ.

In several places Gregory of Nyssa will speak of this suffering as the wounding of love (a double genitive). The suffering issues from the experience of the agony of distance which is installed by difference (between the Bride of Christ and the Christ himself) and discerned by love. The agony is the very laboring of love whereby "the soul grows by its constant participation in that which transcends it."[28] Nyssa takes up a theological account of circumcision to describe this movement: "Here, too, man is circumcised, and yet he remains whole and entire and suffers no mutilation in his material nature."[29] The question raised here, with respect to the sado-masochistic economy of desire informing postmodern secularity, is how does it differ since the internalization of a pleasurable pain is common to both. For the moment let us allow that question to hang and draw, whilst I emphasize, again, that only God can discern and distinguish what is true suffering, and therefore what is being outlined here is not a theodicy, nor the grounds for providing theological rationales for human tragedies. Enlightenment theodicies preempt (and therefore in an act of hubris usurp) eschatological judgment. There is a "filling up" and therefore an end, when "Christ is all and in all [*panta kai en pasin Christos*]," but that "filling up" is not yet concluded and we remain caught between contingent knowledges and truth; intuition, ignorance, and hope.

If *kenosis* and completion, emptying and filling, are not two opposites, but two complementary operations of the divine, like breathing out in order to breathe in, then there is no lack, absence, or vacuum as such. Both movements are associated with a suffering that simultaneously glorifies. The self-emptying of Christ reaches its nadir in death only to be reversed in a final coronation: "Therefore God raised him to the heights and bestowed upon him the name above all names, that at the name of Jesus every knee should bow" (Philippians 2.9–10). The "filling up in turn [*antanaplero*]" also involves "being empowered [*dunamoumenoi*] according to the might of His glory for all endurance and long-suffering with joy [*eis pasan hupomonen kai makrothumian meta charas*]" (Colossians 1.11). This leads us to the heart of a theological mystery: what it is that constitutes the intradivine passion? That the passion is the basis for the economy of *kenoo* and *plero* and that this economy opens up a space for divine redemptive activity with respect to creation is evident. It is also evident that this passion is grounded in trinitarian relations. Paul, in his Letter to the Colossians, mainly treats of the relationship between Christ and the Godhead, but the content and dynamic of that relationship he expresses in terms of wisdom, knowledge, glory, and *energia*. There is much debate between and among New Testament scholars and dogmatic theologians over how developed trinitarian thinking is within the New Testament. Nevertheless it would appear to be true that the passion that is the basis for the economy of *kenoo* and *plero* – with respect to the glorification of all things created – is an intradivine passion that Christians have understood in terms of the differences-in-relation, the differences-in-identity between the Father, the Son, and the Holy Spirit.

The suffering comes by, through, and with the infinite capacity for divine self-exposition. Taking up the double nature of the genitive in "the wounding of love," another way of putting this would be to say that the wounding is intrinsic to the operation of love not only between the Bride and the Bridegroom, the church and Christ, but between the persons of the Trinity. This is not an account of the self divided from itself – God is one in substance – nor is this an account of the sovereignty of the Father splitting to constitute the Son. The suffering does not issue from any subordination. Father, Son, and Spirit are co-constituted; the self-exposition is eternal. But the very equality-in-difference-of-one-substance expresses the creative tensions of loving communion. The primordial suffering, then, is within the Godhead itself and is given expression in the very act of creation, so that a certain suffering is endemic to incarnate living, a suffering that always made possible the sacrifice on the Cross.

Let us explore this a little further, for we are coming dangerously close to a theological justification for suffering. We need to explore, as Nyssa does, the nature of this suffering as it adheres to the very act of loving and seeks not the possession but the glorification of the other. We need to explore the economy of that loving which incarnates the very logic of sacrifice as the endless giving (which is also a giving-up, a *kenosis*) and the endless reception (which is also an opening up towards the other in order to be filled). The suffering and sacrifice which is born of and borne by passion is the very risk and labor of love; a love which is profoundly erotic and, to employ a term from queer theory, genderfucking.[30] It is a suffering engendered by and vouchsafing difference; first trinitarian difference, subsequently, ontological difference between the uncreated Godhead and creation, and finally sexual difference as that which pertains most closely to human embodiment. Augustine describes time in creation in spatial terms, as *distentio*, and *distentio* bears the connotations of swelling, of a space that is the product of a wounding: a wounding in and of love. The primordial suffering is the suffering of loving and being loved. It is not therefore a theological warrant for tragedy. Incarnating the divine – which is the nature of all things "because in him [*oti en auto*] were created all things in the heavens and on the earth, visible and invisible" (Colossians 1.16) – is inseparable from a passion, a suffering whereby we bear fruit, grow (1.6), and glorify even as we are glorified.

The Confrontation

With this in mind let us now return to the point from which we began: the contemporary sacrificial economies of deferred *jouissance*. The profound difference between the Christian economy I have been outlining (and constructing) and postmodern accounts of the negation of negation lies in the perennial suffering and sacrifices of love as not having (in the contemporary accounts) and the eternal suffering intrinsic to the plenitude of love itself (the Christian account). The agonistic pleasure of enduring the undecideable (Derrida)[31] is akin to being suspended on the brink of orgasm without being allowed the final release of coming. This is the quintessential sado-masochistic ecstasy which, in truth, announces a certain stasis, even paralysis. In contrast, the closing lines of the New Testament resound with the call for messianic arrival: "The Spirit and the Bride say, 'Come.' And let him who hears say, 'Come.' . . . He who testifies to these things says, 'Surely I am coming soon.' Amen. Come, Lord Jesus." (Rev. 22.17, 20). The Christian always seeks that coming, not to prolong its arrival, but in the belief that proclaiming that coming is itself ushering in its fulfillment.

Žižek, in a remarkable analysis of the Christian economy of charity (which he compares with Lacan's later shift "from the 'masculine' logic of the Law and its constitutive exception towards the 'feminine' logic in which there is *no* exception"),[32] writes about its "subversive core."[33] In a reading of Paul's two letters to the church at Corinth he articulates how Christian love "unplugs itself" from its cultural context, its organic community, and so disturbs the balance of the All, the integration into the One. "Christianity *is* the miraculous Event that disturbs the balance of the One-All; it *is* the violent intrusion of Difference that precisely *throws the balanced circuit of the universe off the rails.*"[34] Closely reading the famous hymn to *agape* in 1 Corinthians 13, Žižek writes:

> The point of the claim that even if I were to possess all knowledge, without love I would be nothing, is not simply that *with* love I am "something" – in love, *I am also nothing* but, as it were, a Nothing humbly aware of itself, a Nothing paradoxically made rich through the very awareness of its lack. Only a lacking, vulnerable being is capable of love: the ultimate mystery of love is therefore that incompleteness is in a way *higher than completion*. On the one hand, only an imperfect, lacking being loves: we love because we do *not* know all. On the other hand, even if we were to know everything, love would inexplicably still be higher than completed knowledge.[35]

I remain troubled by the language of intrusion, nothingness and lack, and I am convinced this is a move by Žižek beyond Lacan, but two main points about the Christian economy of desire are sharpened here. First, this passage captures much of what I have been arguing for in terms of the agony of difference constituted by love itself. As such, the person of the Spirit holds open to creation the love between the Father and the Son, which challenges our understandings of what is intended by words like "imperfection" and "incompletion." Creation, too, groans in its distinction and its love. Only in the constitution of difference itself can there be *enjoyment* of the other as other – where enjoyment implies active interest, participation without sublation. This is an altogether different account from the sado-masochistic suffering of love as not-having, of enjoying one's own traumatic symptoms. To delight in the suffering of ambivalence that dare not hope for resolution, is to remain within what Žižek calls "the balanced circuit of the universe." For this delight has no future; deferral does not open a future, it only prolongs the present. And what desire desires, in these contemporary accounts of sacrifice and pleasure, is deferral. The logic of sacrifice to appease the terrible ire of whimsical gods is internalized, and appeasement becomes appraisal of situational ambivalence and insecurity. Sacrifice no longer wards off the arbitrary violences of a sadistic deity, but rather finds sado-masochistic pleasure in always only being compromised and ruptured.[36]

Second, the Christian account of suffering is not one installed by the suspension of the semantic by the semiotic. Žižek seems to suggest this himself in his analysis of love and knowledge. Not-knowing is not enduring of the undecideable.

The knowing-in-part reaches beyond itself, so that time, spirit, and materiality are all distended. There is a surpassing of what is understood *in* the understanding that is granted.[37] There is here an overcoming of the instrumentality of reason, whereas it is the sheer inability of the reason to be as instrumental as it might wish that creates the lag and deferral which announces *différance*. It is the very construal of reasoning as instrumental that invokes the aporetic, the undecideable.

Of course, with some irony, Foucault laid the blame for sado-masochism (in which he also delighted and deemed creative) at the feet of Christian pastoral practices, technologies of subjectivity honed and devised from Christianity's inception.[38] He was developing here Freud's concept of moral masochism as an unexpungeable and unconscious sense of guilt. But "genealogy" is a tool of polemic and resistance, not always alert to the subtleties of historical specificity. The Christian economy of suffering and incarnation sketched here is not sadomasochistic for two reasons: first, it does not view difference as rupture and therefore it does not install a (non)foundational violence (the *tout autre*) as the principle for its momentum; a violence which is either projected (sadism) or introjected (masochism). Second, the economy of its desire is not locked into love as not-having. Rather, love is continually extended beyond itself and, in and through that extension, receives itself back from the other as a non-identical repetition. Love construed as having or not-having is a commodified product. It is something one possesses or doesn't possess. It is part of an exchange between object and subject positions. But love in the Christian economy is an action not an object. It cannot be lost or found, absent or present. It constitutes the very space within which all operations in heaven and upon earth take place. The positions of persons are both constituted and dissolved. The linearity and syntax of Indo-European languages barely allows access to the mystery of trinitarian persons and processions: where one ends and another begins. As such, suffering and sacrifice are not distinct moments, *kenoo* is also and simultaneously *plero*. The wounds of love are the openings of grace.

Again, I repeat, this is a theological account of suffering and incarnation. There are myriad historical accounts of suffering and numerous philosophical, psychological, and sociological analyses. The burden of my argument is that the incarnational view of creation profoundly relates the theological and the historical – bearing both forward (in a hope that, in being ineradicable, is all the more painful to endure) towards an eschatological discernment. But the method of my argument is confrontational, not simply analytical. And the Christian theological nature of that confrontation is important, for, as Žižek himself observes, Christianity has a "subversive core," a radicality inseparable from its orthodoxy. What the confrontation suggests is that the sado-masochistic economies of desire, profoundly at work in contemporary culture, are pathological. They are destructive of what is most necessary for our well-being and cosmic flourishing. Surely the economy of incarnate love offers greater resources for social transformation, amelioration. Surely to persist in enjoying the symptoms of a cultural neurosis (which is transcultural insofar as it constitutes the economy of desire operating in global capitalism) is a decadence few can afford at the peril of us all. We need to practice an art of living in the name of a transcendental hope which breaks free of the vicious circularities of the same; to learn about good formations of the soul which produce those places which operate a logic that counters the sado-masochistic economy. We need to defend the legacies of those theological traditions that teach us the proper labor of our loving.

Notes

1 I also need to clarify here that the relationship between these cultures is complex, not oppositional or even dialectical. The character of Christianity today cannot be extracted from its cultural context. Christianity, though rooted in all its various previous forms and traditions, is conceived in the cultural terms available, the cultural terms which maintain its current relevance and render it comprehensible (and believable) in contemporary society.
2 *Bodies That Matter: On the Discursive Limits of "Sex"* (London: Routledge, 1993).
3 See my essay "Language and Silence" in Oliver Davis and Denys Turner (eds.), *Silence and the Word: Negative Theology and Incarnation* (Cambridge: Cambridge University Press, 2001); John Milbank, "Sublimity: The Modern Transcendent," in Paul Heelas (ed.), *Religion, Modernity and Postmodernity* (London: Routledge, 1998), pp. 258–84.
4 See Michel de Certeau, *The Mystic Fable*. Vol. 1: *The Sixteenth and the Seventeenth Centuries*, trans. Michael B. Smith (Chicago: University of Chicago Press, 1992).
5 See J. V. Field, *The Invention of Infinity: Mathematics and Art in the Renaissance* (Oxford: Oxford University Press, 1997).
6 See Immanuel Kant, *Critique of Judgement*, trans. James Creed Meredith (Oxford: Clarendon Press, 1952).
7 Slavoj Žižek, *The Fragile Absolute – or Why is the Christian Legacy Worth Fighting For?* (London: Verso, 2000), p. 21.
8 See Žižek on the relationship between Clara and Robert Schumann in *Plague of Fantasies* (London: Verso, 1997), pp. 66–7, 192–212.
9 Jacques Derrida, *The Gift of Death*, trans. David Wills (Chicago: University of Chicago Press, 1995), pp. 58–9.
10 Jacques Derrida, *The Politics of Friendship*, trans. George Collins (London: Verso, 1997), p. 47.
11 See Jacques Derrida, *On the Name*, trans. Thomas Dutoit (Stanford, CA: Stanford University Press, 1995), pp. 50–60.
12 "An Interview with Jacques Derrida," in Derek Attridge, *Jacques Derrida: Acts of Literature* (London: Routledge, 1992), p. 56.
13 Derrida, *The Politics of Friendship*, p. 174.
14 See Michel de Certeau, *The Mystic Fable*, trans. Michael B. Smith (Chicago: University of Chicago Press, 1992), pp. 273–96.
15 See Emmanuel Levinas, *Autrement qu'être ou au-dela de essence* (The Hague: Martinus Nijoff, 1974), pp. 206–19.
16 See Michel de Certeau, "White Ecstasy," trans. Frederick Christian Bauerschmidt and Catriona Hanley in Graham Ward (ed.), *The Postmodern God* (Oxford: Blackwell Publishers, 1998), pp. 155–8.
17 For Levinas see *Autrement qu'être*, pp. 116–20, 156–205.

18 See Hélène Cixous, "'The Egg and the Chicken': Love as Not Having" in *Reading Clarice Lispector*, trans. Verena Andermatt Conley (Hemel Hempstead: Harvester Wheatsheaf, 1990), pp. 98–122. Cixous describes two types of love as not-having: a masculine economy of renunciation and a feminine economy of enjoying that which is always excessive to possession. Lacan himself drew attention to two economies of desire in his later work, notably *Seminar XX: Encore*; see Žižek, *The Fragile Absolute*, pp. 144–8 for an important reading of this shift in Lacan for Christian construals of "charity."
19 Derrida, *Gift of Death*, pp. 82–115.
20 Augustine, *De Civitate Dei*, XIX.6.
21 This should alert us to other possible readings of Christian asceticism: the putting to death of the fleshly desires in order to focus on the soul's perfection need not entail a body–soul dualism. This would be gnostic. Christian ascetic practices intensify the experience of the body and it is in that intensification that the soul is rendered most visible, most engaged.
22 In a highly insightful and technical article on the great kenotic hymn or *Carmen Christi* in Paul's Letter to the Philippians (2.5–11) by the New Testament scholar C. F. D. Moule, the point is made that "what is *styled* kenosis is, itself, the height of plerosis: the most divine thing to give rather than to get" ("Further Reflections on Philippians 2: 5–11," in W. W. Groque and R. P. Martin (eds.), *Apostolic History and the Gospels* (Grand Rapids, MI: Eerdmans, 1970), p. 273. I am attempting to develop this insight theologically, whilst avoiding some of the neater ethical pronouncements "to give rather than to get" that Moule makes upon its basis.
23 J. B. Lightfoot, *Epistle to the Colossians* (London: Macmillan, 1876), pp. 164–5.
24 Jürgen Moltmann, *The Crucified God: The Cross of Christ as the Foundation and Criticism of Christian Theology* (London: SCM, 1974), pp. 273–4.
25 Hans Urs von Balthasar. *Mysterium Paschale*, trans. A. Nichols (Edinburgh: T. & T. Clark, 1990), p. 168.
26 Ibid, p. 174.
27 Ibid, p. 176.
28 Nyssa's *Commentary on the Canticle of Canticles* in Herbert Musurillo, SJ (ed.), *From Glory to Glory: Texts from Gregory of Nyssa's Mystical Writings* (Crestwood: St Vladimir's Seminary Press, 1995), p. 190.
29 Ibid, p. 193.
30 See Stephen Whittle, "Gender Fucking of Fucking Gender: Current Cultural Contributions to Theories of Gender Blending," in Richard Elkins and Dave King (eds.), *Blending Genders: Social Aspects of Cross-Dressing and Sex-Change* (London: Routledge, 1996), pp. 196–214.
31 Derrida, *The Politics of Friendship*, p. 123.
32 Žižek, *The Fragile Absolute*, p. 116.
33 Ibid, p. 119.
34 Ibid, p. 121. The italics are Žižek's.
35 Ibid, p. 147. The italics are Žižek's.
36 Freud recognized the strong association between sadism and masochism. It was the same instinct, the death instinct, operating by either projecting or introjecting violence. Furthermore, in his 1924 essay "The Economic Problem of Masochism," having distinguished erotogenic, feminine, and moral forms of masochism, he pointed to the relationships between masochism and impotence, the masturbatory

act of finding sexual satisfaction in oneself and infantile life. See *The Complete Works of Sigmund Freud*, vol. 19, trans. James Strachey (London: Hogarth Press, 1961), pp. 159–70.

37 That the surpassing of understanding takes places *in* what is understood, if only partially, is fundamental. It is too easy, and my own work has not always avoided this ease, to counter postmodern economies of lack with theological economies of excess. The surpassing of the understanding is not an entry into the mystical sublime, white ecstasy. The surpassing of the understanding is where what is understood by mind and eye intimates a divine depth intuited by what Gregory of Nyssa would call "the spiritual senses."

38 Michel Foucault, *The History of Sexuality: An Introduction*, trans. Robert Hurley (Harmondsworth: Penguin Books, 1981).

CHAPTER 12
Earth God: Cultivating the Spirit in an Ecocidal Culture

Mark I. Wallace

Two contemporary figures have been central to Mark Wallace's thinking: Paul Ricoeur and René Girard. Wallace is editor of a collection of essays by Paul Ricoeur, *Figuring the Sacred: Religion, Narrative, and Imagination* (Louisville, KY, 1994) and coeditor of *Curing Violence: Religion and the Thought of René Girard* (1994). He weaves the thinking of these two people into a rich theological heritage – Augustine, Aquinas, and more recently Barth, Jüngel, and Moltmann. Having finished his dissertation work, published as *The Second Naivety: Barth, Ricoeur, and the New Yale Theology* (Macon, GA, 1996), Wallace turned his attention to developing a contemporary doctrine of the Holy Spirit. The following essay evidences this concern and how it has developed since his book *Fragments of the Spirit: Nature, Violence, and the Renewal of Creation* (New York, 1996). In that book he clearly and concisely set out his project, which is rhetorical rather than philosophical. In other words, he is not attempting to prove the reality of the Spirit, but recovering and constructing discourses about the Spirit. The pneumatology that is thus recovered and constructed is nature-based, for the Spirit is conceived as a wild and insurgent natural force. To some extent Wallace's line of thinking continues a tradition of *Lebensphilosophie* – the different vitalisms of Nietzsche, Whitehead, and Cobb. This line of thought can seem to accept the naturalism and essentialisms of modernity, rather than the fragmentation and critiques of metaphysics and metanarratives which are the hallmarks of postmodern thinking. But this is exactly where the project of Wallace is most distinctive for, as his essay in this volume states, his is a postmodern pneumatology. Various poststructural theorists facilitate and are engaged in developing this pneumatology: the work of Levinas, Derrida, and Kristeva is brought into critical dialogue with that of Ricoeur, Girard, and Ogden. Wallace's is a postmetaphysical approach to *Geist*; rhetorical insofar as it is developed through narratives which return to and reinscribe central scriptural tropes. This relates Wallace's methodol-

> ogy with a Yale School approach to theology that he has also been interested in and a Barthian emphasis upon preserving the radical freedom of God from human, philosophical thinking. Unlike the process theologians, he seeks to maintain the radical otherness of God and to develop a dialectic between this otherness and God's radical immanence in the world.
>
> Wallace's project is not simply an exercise in Christian dogmatics. It is an exercise in practical theology, in social ethics. The constitution of a credible account of the Spirit's activity within the world has ultimately an ecological and a social function. Ecologically, it calls for viewing the world in terms of creation, as a sacral order to be respected. Sociologically, this provides a constructive response to contemporary living, for it tells stories of hope, restoration, and renewal in what is otherwise a prevailing culture of pessimism and the commodification of all values. The telling of stories, the narrative basis of the project, is again part of the rhetorical methodology – which draws attention to mediation, persuasion, and performance.

At the threshold of a new century we are witnessing a profound groundshift in the spiritual sensibilities of our culture. There is a sense that we now live in the "age of the Spirit," a time in which many and diverse persons and groups are experiencing the immanent reality of a power greater than themselves in their everyday lives. The medieval mystic Joachim of Fiore prophesied that humankind has lived through the periods of the Father and the Son and has now entered the age of the Spirit.[1] Karl Barth mused at the end of his life that the Holy Spirit might well be the best point of departure for a theology that is right for the present situation.[2] The theorist Ihab Hassan locates the topic of the "Holy Spirit" along with such themes as "play," "desire," and "immanence" as distinctly postmodern emphases that challenge an earlier modernist paradigm.[3] And practitioners of nature-based religion, from native peoples to modern neopagans, claim that a reverence for the Spirit in all life-forms, from people and animals to trees and watersheds, is the most promising response to the threat of global ecological collapse at the end of the second millennium.[4] There is an emerging sensibility that the coming and already present reality of the Spirit is the proper focus for a global theology that speaks to the spiritual hopes and desires of our age.

Nevertheless, amidst this renewed longing for the Spirit is considerable theological and cultural pessimism. The origins of this malaise are many, but I believe that the root cause of this anxiety is a deeply felt despair about the prospects of the planet for future generations. Few observers of the contemporary situation doubt that we face today an ecological crisis of unimaginable proportions. Whether through slow and steady environmental degradation or the sudden exchange of nuclear weapons, the specter of ecocide haunts all human and nonhuman life that shares the resources of our planet home. Many of us have become numb to the various dimensions of the crisis: acid rain, ozone depletion, global warming, food-chain pesticides, soil erosion, mass consumption of non-renewable fossil fuels, agricultural runoff, radioactive wastes, overpopulation, deforestation and desertification, carbon emissions, and loss of habitat.[5] In our time nature has been commodified and domesticated into a piece of real estate; it has become one more consumer item to be bought and sold in order to maximize profits. Once a source of terror and awe, nature no longer functions as wild and sacred space for the eruption of the sublime or the manifestation of transcendence. We have exchanged the power and mystery of the earth for the invisible hand of the marketplace and we are all the poorer for it.

These two phenomena – the yearning for the Spirit in religious life and the cultural anxiety over the environmental crisis – have led many theologians to a profound awareness of the deep interrelationship between God and the earth.[6] Could it be, then, that the most compelling theological response to the threat of ecocide lies in a rediscovery of God's presence within and love for all things earthly and bodily? An affirmative response to this question is the focus of this essay. My argument is that a rediscovery of the ancient doctrine of the Holy Spirit as God's power of life-giving breath (*rûah*) within the cosmos is the doctrine that is ripe for recovery in our troubled times. I contend that an earth-centered reenvisioning of the Spirit as the "green face" of God in the world is the best grounds for hope and renewal at a point in human history when our rapacious appetites seemed destined to destroy the earth.[7] From this perspective, hope for a renewed earth is best founded on belief in God as Earth Spirit, the benevolent, all-encompassing divine force within the biosphere who continually indwells and works to maintain the integrity of all forms of life.

My case is that the Spirit is the enfleshment of God within every thing that burrows, creeps, runs, swims, and flies in and across the earth. The Spirit is the promise of God's material, palpable presence within the good earth God has made for the sustenance and health of all beings. God continually pours out Godself into the cosmos through Earth Spirit, the driving force within the universe who brings each thing into its natural fruition. In a word, God is *carnal*: through the Spirit, God *incarnates* Godself within the natural order in order to nurture and protect every form of life. The Holy Spirit, therefore, is an enfleshed being, an earthly life-form who interanimates life on earth as the outflowing of God's compassion for all things. The Nicene Creed in 381 CE named the Spirit as "the Lord, the Giver of Life." In this essay I will try to make sense of this ancient appellation by reenvisioning the Holy Spirit as God's invigorating corporeal presence within the society of all living beings.[8]

Unfortunately, however, many contemporary Christians experience and understand the Spirit – if they think about the Spirit at all – as the forgotten member of the Trinity, the shy member of the Godhead, the left hand of God. In the lived practice of God's presence in many non-charismatic Christian communities today, the promise of the Spirit to fill and renew all of God's creation is generally overlooked. This oversight renders present-day Christianity a binary religion, a religion of the Father and the Son, with little if any awareness of the Spirit's critically important work in the world. This neglect of the Spirit saddles

Christianity with a backward-looking orientation. It undercuts one of the most important promises of the gospel, namely, that the departure of Jesus from the world two thousand years ago entails the gift of the Spirit for all who seek the truth. In John 16 Jesus says "I tell you the truth: it is to your advantage that I go away, for if I do not go away, the Counselor will not come to you; but if I go, I will send him to you. . . . When the Spirit of truth comes, he will guide you into all the truth" (vv. 7, 13). The hope of Christianity is the promise of God's omnipresent Spirit to fill the earth with God's power and love so that all of God's creatures, human and nonhuman alike, can be brought into a healing and restorative relationship with the truth. This hope, in effect, renders Christianity a religion of multiple perspectives. In its best moments Christian spirituality consists, simultaneously, of *remembering* with gratitude God's goodness and love in the mission of Jesus and *looking forward* with hope and expectation to the continuation of that mission, under the power of the Spirit, in the new situation of the present and future. The "new situation" that now confronts us is the earth crisis. Jesus has departed this world but in his stead God has offered to us the all-encompassing work of the Spirit – the Spirit's work of renewal and restoration in a world badly wounded by chronic environmental abuse. In this model, Jesus and Spirit are dual foci within a single ellipse.

Yet many Christians, because of their understandable but exclusive identity with the story of Jesus, are today unable to track the new work of the Spirit in a world under siege.[9] To counteract this tendency, I offer here a forward-looking, earth-centered model of the Spirit as the green face of God who sustains the natural order and unifies all of God's creation into one common biotic family. From a religious perspective this earth-centered doctrine of the Spirit – as reminiscent of Jesus's love for all creatures testified to in the gospels – is the best grounds for hope and renewal at a point in human history when our unchecked appetites seem destined to destroy the planet. A new vision of the carnal God as the Spirit of the earth has the potential to invigorate all of us in our struggles to love and protect the gift of creation.

Green Pneumatology

My methodological approach is rhetorically and exegetically oriented toward retrieving central biblical tropes of the Spirit in a manner that is self-reflexively aware of my own commitments and passions. Understanding theology as a rhetorical–exegetical enterprise, I believe the Spirit is best understood not as a metaphysical entity but as a healing life-force who engenders human flourishing as well as the welfare of the planet. I label this approach "green pneumatology" in order to distinguish it from metaphysically based notions of the Spirit characteristic of normative Western thought. I want this distinction to relocate understandings of the Spirit outside the philosophical question of being and squarely within a nature-based desire for the integrity and health of all life-forms – human and nonhuman. This model understands the Spirit not as divine intellect, nor the principle of consciousness, but as a healing and subversive *life-form* – as water, light, dove, mother, fire, breath, and wind – on the basis of different biblical figurations of the Spirit in nature. Philosophers of consciousness (for example, G. W. F. Hegel) have bequeathed to contemporary theology a metaphysically burdened idea of the Spirit that has little purchase on the role of the Spirit in creation as the power of benevolent unity between all natural kinds. The wager of this essay is that a rhetorical understanding of the Spirit (beyond the categories of being) can both rehabilitate the central biblical affirmation of the Spirit's carnal nature and provide resources for confronting the environmental violence that marks our time.

My plea for a postmetaphysical green pneumatology stems from a desire to preserve the complete freedom of God as Spirit apart from the limitations imposed on the concept of God by metaphysics. In the history of metaphysics (which includes such otherwise disparate thinkers as Aristotle, Hegel, and Wolfhart Pannenberg) God is understood as the supreme Being who is the source of unity among all other beings. In this model the otherness of God (including the otherness of God as Spirit) is colonized by a reductive philosophical analysis of God as a reality within, or coterminous with, Being itself. But in order to preserve divine freedom and novelty, I suggest that God as Spirit is not by any metaphysical necessity the Being of beings; rather, God as Spirit, in free and indeterminate decision, desires to be the life-giving breath who animates and maintains the whole natural order. God as Spirit is best understood not as the Being of beings but, paradoxically, as *beyond* Being and still radically *immanent* to all beings within the natural order. Dialectically understood, therefore, God as Spirit should be figured as both *wholly other* to creation and *wholly enfleshed* within creation as the green love who nurtures and sustains all living things. The move away from defining God according to Being toward imagining God as life-source is not an exchange of one metaphysical absolute ("Being") for another ("Life" or "Nature"). Rather, this move attempts to open up conceptual space for reenvisioning the freedom of God as Spirit to "blow where she wills" and not be determined by the question of Being within the domain of speculative philosophy.[10]

Jacques Derrida's thought is a fruitful resource in my attempt to reenvision God as Earth Spirit outside the confines of metaphysics. Born in 1930 as a Jew in Muslim Algeria on a street named after St Augustine, the rue Saint-Augustin, Derrida was raised in the lap of the three Western religions of the Book. Born a Jew, but whose "alliance" with Judaism was "broken in every respect," Derrida grew up praying to God in "Christian Latin French," but writes, nonetheless, that "I quite rightly pass for an atheist."[11] He is not an observant or confessing member of any religious denomination. And yet in his quasi-autobiographical musings entitled *Circumfession*, a running commentary on Augustine's *Confessions*, Derrida evinces a prayerful, spiritual yearning that he says everyone (including his own mother) has missed and misunderstood over the years. In these memoirs he laments a general misunderstanding of

> my religion about which nobody understands anything, any more than does my mother who asked other people a while ago, not daring to talk to me about it, if I still believed in God. . . . But she must have known that the constancy of God in my life is called by other names.[12]

In the vocabulary of the heart, God's presence and constancy is felt and understood, but this God can only be identified through indirection, never directly. God is the object of Derrida's prayers and longings but, at the same time, this God is objectless and has no one definitive name (or to put it another way, God is the infinite bearer of many names). "All my life," he writes, "I have never stopped praying to God."[13] But *who* is this God he prays to? What is the *name* of this God? God cannot be *named*, according to Derrida, but many names can be *assigned* to God, nevertheless. No one name *per se* is adequate to describing God, but God can be named, prayed to, worshiped, and adored. Like Augustine, whose voluminous writings assign a panoply of different names to God, Derrida says his own work operates under various designations for God – including names such as justice and hospitality and the coming of the gift.[14] In order to shatter the idols that purport to name God with univocal certainty, Derrida implies here in his memoirs, and says explicitly elsewhere, that true religion must abandon all names for God in order to preserve God's freedom from captivity to the metaphysics of self-presence.[15] Could we say, then, that God is not at our disposal, but, rather, that God disposes us?

In his article "Sauf le nom" Derrida argues that in order to *save* the name of God it is necessary to *suspend* all names for God: to put into abeyance all names for God in order to identify the object of divine naming as without determinable object or reference.[16] As John Caputo says, one must save (*sauf*) "the name of God by keeping it safe (*sauf*); sacrificing the name of God precisely in order to save it. Sacrifice everything, save or except (*sauf*) the name of God. Save everything about God (keep God safe) save (except) the name of God, lest it become an idol that blocks our way."[17] In this regard, Derrida's religious thought has deep affinities with the tradition of so-called negative theology, which says God is neither this nor that in order to emancipate the possibility of God beyond the reach of the classical economy of ideas and names for God.[18] Although Derrida is quick to question the "hyperessentialism" of many forms of negative theology that understand God as Being, he writes approvingly, nevertheless, of certain negative theologies, such as Angelus Silesius's, that appear to avoid the sirens of crypto-essentialism by articulating an a/theology that "loses" God in order to "find" God (but not as Being). Commenting on Silesius's *The Cherubinic Wanderer*, Derrida writes that

> It is necessary to leave all, to leave every "something" through love of God, and no doubt to leave God himself, to abandon him, that is, at once to leave him and (but) let him (be beyond being-something):

One must leave the something
Man, if you love something, then you love nothing truly:
God is not this and that, leave then forever the something.

The most secret abandon
Abandon seizes God; but to leave God himself,
Is an abandonment that few men can grasp [quoting *The Cherubinic Wanderer*, 1: 44, 2: 92][19]

Ironically, then, the best religion, in a certain sense, is no religion at all; the best name for God is no name at all. The "constancy of God in my life," Derrida writes, "is called by other names,"[20] but not by the name(s) of God as such, which allows Derrida to write about God, much in the way Silesius does, in the spirit of pseudonymous indirection, permitting God language a certain freedom and spontaneity that is denied it when it is under the control of strict philosophical or theological orthodoxy. Writing and talking about God indirectly allows God to relate to human persons in disruptive, heterogeneous freedom unconstrained by the controls of any sign-system – philosophical, religious, or otherwise. The refusal to name God allows God, as an alien other, to arrive as the unassimilable, indeterminate "something more," as William James puts it, who can productively transform human expectations. This refusal to name God preserves as much as possible the freedom of God to be God and unpredictably impact human experience as the question who subverts our answers – as the nameless, abyssal, ungraspable one who is coming but is nonetheless here as the heteronomic Other of our deepest longings.

God is Underfoot

If God is wholly other as Derrida argues, can anything positive and determinate be said about this God other than the negative theological claim that God is unknowable? If God is unknowable and unnameable, what role, if any, can positive theology, and, in particular, a positive theology of the Spirit play in dialogue with Derrida's thought? In response to this question, I believe Derrida's iconoclasm encourages contemporary Spirit theology, in spontaneity and freedom, to retrieve language and imagery of the divine life that has been repressed or forgotten. By eschewing the task of *naming* God as a knowable certainty, postmodern Spirit theology *rediscovers* God to be a carnal life-form through the agency of the Spirit. Derrida helps contemporary theology initiate this rediscovery of Earth God by encouraging it to abandon the pseudo-certainty of metaphysics in favor of uncovering neglected dimensions of the biblical witness that are desperately needed in our time of ecocidal despair. Unlike, say, Descartes's divine ground for self-knowledge or Kant's transcendent source for the moral law within, Derrida, much like Karl Barth did a generation before him, argues for the preservation of the freedom of God beyond metaphysics – to liberate theology, as Derrida puts it, from its "philosophical ego" in order to set free "a faith lived in a venturous, dangerous, free way."[21] From this angle, Derridean deconstruction is best understood not as a weapon in the war against faith, as its many critics argue, but as an exercise in philosophical hygiene that helps theology purge itself of its desire for metaphysical security. Rather than putting an end to theology as its judge and executioner, deconstruction now becomes theology's helpmate and enables it to realize its true aim: a release from its dependency on philosophy in order to set free the evangelical testimony to a God who daily enfleshes Godself within the rich flora and fauna of the biotic order.

The sad legacy of historic Western thought, however, blunts our ability to envision this possibility. In the history of the West the Spirit is not understood as a friend of the earth but as a ghostly, bodiless entity far removed from the concerns of the created order. Conventional understandings of the Spirit evoke images of a vapid and invisible phantom ("the Holy Ghost") divorced from the tangible reality of life on this planet as we know it. These popular notions are rooted in the canonical definition of the Spirit as an incorporeal, bodiless, nonmaterial being that stands over and against the physical world, which is not of the same nature as the Spirit. As one theological dictionary puts it, the Spirit is "immaterial or nonmaterial substance.... The term *spiritus* can therefore be applied to God generally [or] to the Third Person of the Trinity specifically."[22] Much of Western thought – including religious thought – operates according to a series of binary oppositions that separate spirit from body, mind from matter, and God from nature. These dichotomies not only divide the spiritual world from the physical order. They also order the two terms in the polarity in a valuational hierarchy by positing the first term (spirit, mind, God) as superior to the second term (body, matter, nature). In general, therefore, Western thought has not only pitted the spiritual world and the physical order against one another but also subordinated the one to the other. In this schema, the Spirit is regarded as an eternally invisible and incorporeal force superior to the earthly realm which is mired in contingency and change.

This bipartite division between spirit and matter has a long and tenacious history in Western philosophical and religious traditions.[23] Plato's philosophical anthropology, for example, is controlled by metaphors of the body as the "prison house" and the "tomb" of the soul. The fulfillment of human existence, according to Plato, is to release oneself – one's soul – from bondage to dumb, bodily appetites in order to cultivate a life in harmony with one's spiritual, intellectual nature.[24] Origen, the third century CE Christian Platonist, took literally Jesus's blessing on those who "made themselves eunuchs for the kingdom of heaven" (Matt. 15.1) and at age twenty had himself castrated. As a virgin for Christ no longer dominated by his sexual and physical drives, Origen became a perfect vessel for the display of the Spirit.[25] But in the Christian West, Augustine is arguably most responsible for the hierarchical division between spirit and nature. Augustine maintains that human beings are ruled by carnal desire – *concupiscence* – as a result of Adam's fall from grace in the Garden of Eden. Adam's sin is transferred to his offspring – the human race – through erotic desire leading to sex and the birth of children. In their fleshly bodies, according to Augustine, infants are tainted with "original sin" communicated to them through their biological parents' sexual intercourse. Physical weakness and sexual desire are signs that the bodily, material world is under God's judgment. Thus, without the infusion of supernatural grace, all of creation – as depraved and corrupted – is no longer amenable to the influence of the Spirit.[26] This long tradition of hierarchical and antagonistic division between spirit and matter continues into our own time – an era, often in the name of religion, marked by deep anxiety about and hostility toward human sexuality, the body, and the natural world.

At first glance, some of the biblical writings appear partial to this binary opposition between body and spirit. Consider Paul's rhetoric of spirit versus flesh in the Books of Romans and Galatians as cases in point. In Rom. 8.5–13 Paul emphasizes that "life in the flesh leads to death while life in the Spirit leads to life." This juxtaposition lends credence to the received notion that the material and spiritual orders are fundamental opposites in the New Testament. But while this reading of Paul is understandable given the force of his rhetoric here and elsewhere, this reading is a mistake. In reality, Paul's thought utilizes a threefold anthropology that trades on the terms *sarx* ("flesh"), *soma* ("body"), and *pneuma* ("spirit"). In this tripartite schema the Christian subject is an embodied self (*soma*) who experiences the inner warfare between impulses that resist life in Christ (*sarx*) and a power within the self that brings the self into relationship with Christ (*pneuma*). Each of these terms carries a certain value in Paul's "systems" theory of the self: *soma*, as the human person in her essential bodily state, is positively understood as the environment within which the battle between the negative tendencies of *sarx* and the beneficial influence of *pneuma* is carried out. Far from denigrating the body (*soma*), Paul views bodily existence as essential to human being: it is not that we *have* bodies but that we *are* bodies as corporeal, enfleshed selves. As well, Paul's generally positive attitude toward the body is further expressed in 1 Cor. 6.19, 20, where he writes, "Do you not know that your body [*soma*] is a temple of the Holy Spirit [*hagiou pneumatos*] within you, which you have from God? You are not your own; you were bought with a price. So glorify God in your body." The embodied, somatic Christian subject is a sacred dwelling place – a temple – inhabited by the Spirit of God. The Spirit and the body, therefore, are coterminous ideas in Paul's thought.[27]

Along with Paul the vast majority of the biblical texts undermine the split between God and nature by structurally interlocking the terms in the polarity with one another. In particular, on the question of the Spirit, the system of polar oppositions is consistently undermined. In terms of the Spirit, rather than prioritizing the spiritual over the earthly, the scriptural texts figure the Spirit as a carnal, creaturely life-form always already interpenetrated by the material world. Granted, the term "Spirit" does conjure the image of a ghostly, shadowy nonentity in both the "popular" and "high" thinking of the Christian West. But the biblical texts stand as a stunning countertestimony to this conventional mindset – including the conventional theological mindset. The Bible, rather, is awash with rich imagery of the Spirit borrowed directly from the natural world. In fact, the four traditional elements of natural, embodied life – *earth, air, water,* and *fire* – are constitutive of the Spirit's biblical reality as an enfleshed being who ministers to the whole creation God has made for the refreshment and joy of all beings. In the Bible the Spirit is not a wraithlike being separated from matter but a creature (like Jesus who was also an enfleshed life-form) made up of the four cardinal substances that compose the physical universe.

Numerous biblical passages attest to the foundational role of the four basic elements regarding the biocentric identity of the Spirit. (1) As *earth*, the Spirit is both the *divine dove*, with an olive branch in its mouth, that brings peace and renewal to a broken and divided world (Gen. 8.11; Matt. 3.16; John 1.32), and a *fruit bearer*, such as a tree or vine, that yields the virtues of love, joy, and peace in the life of the disciple (Gal. 5.22–6). (2) As *air*, the Spirit is both the *vivifying breath* that animates all living things (Gen. 1.2; Ps. 104.29–30) and the *prophetic wind* that brings salvation and new life to those it indwells (Judges 6.34; John 3.6–8; Acts 2.1–4). (3) As *water*, the Spirit is the *living water* that quickens and refreshes all who drink from its eternal springs (John 4.14; 7.37–8). (4) And as *fire*, the Spirit is the *purgative fire* that alternately judges evildoers and ignites the prophetic mission of the early church (Matt. 3.11–12; Acts 2.1–4). In these texts the Spirit is figured as a potency in nature who engenders life and healing throughout the biotic order.

Far from being ghostly and bodiless, the Spirit reveals herself in the biblical literatures as an earthly *life-form* who labors to create, sustain, and renew humankind and otherkind in solidarity with one another. As the divine wind in Genesis, the dove in the gospels, or the tongues of flame in Acts, the Spirit does not exist apart from nature as a separate reality externally related to the created order. Rather, nature itself in all its fecundity and variety is the primary and indispensable mode of being for the Spirit's work in the world. The Spirit, then, is always underfoot, quite literally, as God's power in the earth who makes all things live and grow toward their natural ends. The earth's waters and winds and birds and fires that move within and upon the earth are not only *symbols* of the Spirit – as important as this nature symbolism is – but share in the Spirit's very *being* as the Spirit is continually enfleshed and embodied through natural organisms and processes.

There are inklings of nature-centered pneumatology within historic Christianity. In Western theology the work of the Holy Spirit has always been understood in terms of communion, mutuality, and the overcoming of divisions. The early Latin Fathers conceived of the Spirit in the bosom of the Trinity as the divine power that unites the Father and the Son in a bond of mutual love. Basil of Caesarea wrote that the Holy Spirit is the agent of inseparable union within the Trinity. The Spirit labors alongside the Creator and the Redeemer as the Perfector who strengthens and completes the divine work of salvation in the world.[28] Similarly, Augustine analyzed the role of the Spirit in terms of the *vinculum caritatis* (bond of love) or the *vinculum Trinitatis* (bond of the Trinity), the communion that binds the other two members of the Godhead together in dynamic unity.²⁹ The Spirit enables the mutual indwelling of each divine person in the other. Moreover, as the bond of peace and love universal, these early texts imply (without stating as such outrightly) that the Spirit is not only the power of relation between the other members of the Trinity but also between God and the whole creation as well.

Later medieval iconographers make a similar point but in a pictorial medium. The doctrine of the Spirit as the *vinculum caritatis* is graphically set forth in the trinitarian miniatures of the medieval *Rothschild Canticles*, in which the Spirit is pictured as a giant encircling "dove" whose wings enfold the Father and Son, and whose large talons and tail provide points of intersection for all three figures. But in the *Canticles* the Spirit is represented less like the domesticated birds or pigeons of traditional church art and more like the wild raptors of the mountain wildernesses. The Spirit-Bird in the *Canticles* spins and twirls the other two members of the Godhead into amorous and novel combinations and permutations. As the *Canticles* progress, each life-form within the Trinity loses its separate identity in a blur of erotic passion and movement and color. As the Trinity twists and turns into surprising recombinations, the human Father and Son smile and twirl and dance around the aviary Spirit, symbolizing the union of each figure in the sacred bird – as well as the union of all life-forms in a common biotic order.³⁰ The Spirit-Bird of the *Canticles* ensures the interrelationship of each divine person in a ludic celebration of perichoretic harmony.³¹ As the Spirit exists perichoretically within the Godhead to foster communion between the divine persons, my proposal is that the Spirit also performs the role of the *vinculum caritatis* within nature in order to promote the well-being and fecundity of creation.

From the perspective of biocentric trinitarian theology, nature is the enfleshment of God's sustaining love. As Trinity, God bodies forth divine compassion for all life-forms in the rhythms of the natural order. The divine Trinity's boundless passion for the integrity of all living things is revealed in God's preservation of the life-web that is our common biological inheritance. God as Trinity is set forth in the Father/Mother God's creation of the biosphere, the Son's reconciliation of all beings to himself, and the Spirit's gift of life to every member of the created order who relies on her beneficence for daily sustenance. As *creator*, God is manifested in the ebb and flow of the seasons whose plantings and harvests are a constant reminder of earth's original blessings. As *redeemer*, God is revealed in the complex interactions of organisms and the earth in mutual sustenance – an economy of interdependence best symbolized by Jesus's reconciling work of the cross. And as *sustainer*, God shows Godself through breathing the breath of life into all members of the life-web, a living testimony to the Divine's compassion for all things.

God's presence in the living Christ through the Spirit's maintenance of the ecosphere is the basis for the greening of trinitarian theology. The then and there incarnation of God in Jesus is recapitulated in the here and now embodiment of the Spirit in the world which hearkens back to the originary Mother God's birthing of order out of chaos. This trinitarian enfleshment of God in nature represents a tripartite movement. The first move to an embodied doctrine of God is signaled by the inaugural hymn of Genesis where the Creator Spirit (*rûah*) breathes the world into existence and thereby enfleshes itself in the creation and maintenance of the natural order. The embodiment of the divine life in Jesus – an earth creature like Adam, who himself was fashioned from the soil – is the second move toward a nature-centered model of the Godhead. And the perichoretic union of Jesus in the Spirit – like Jesus, an earth being as well, but now figured in the biblical tropes of water, dove, fire, and wind – represents the third move toward a biophilic notion of God. It is the move to embodiment – the procession of Godself into the biotic realm that sustains all life – that is the basis for unity within the Godhead. In perichoresis, God as Trinity subsists in interpersonal unity through incarnating Godself in all things that swim, creep, crawl, run, fly, and grow upon the earth.

The understanding of the Spirit as a life-form intrinsically related to nature emphasizes a generally neglected model of the Spirit in the history of Western theology. In theory, the Spirit has always been defined as both the Spirit *of God* and the Spirit *of creation*. As the Spirit of God, the Spirit is the power of reciprocity between the first two persons of the Trinity, on the one hand, and the interior power of redemption within human beings, on the other. And as the Spirit of creation, the Spirit has been defined as the breath of God who indwells and sustains the cosmos. In practice, however, the Spirit has been almost exclusively understood as the Spirit of God; the stress has fallen on its roles as the source of consubstantiality within the Godhead and the divine agent of human salvation. The result is that the biocentric role of the Spirit as the power of life-giving breath within creation, including nonhuman as well as human creation, has been consistently downplayed.[32]

Water, light, dove, mother, fire, breath, wind – the Spirit reveals herself as a healing life-form in the biblical witness. These nature-based descriptions of the Spirit are the basis of my attempt to shift the theological focus back to the Spirit as the Spirit of the earth. Such a focus neither denigrates nor ignores the regnant understanding of the Spirit's other roles as the power of relationship between the Father and Son or as the agent of human sanctification within the history of salvation. Rather, this emphasis on the Spirit's carnal identity as the divine breath who interanimates all other life-forms readdresses our attention to the Spirit's work in *all* realms of life – which includes, but is not limited to, the inner life of God and salvation history. Part of the burden of this essay, then, is to shift the weight of theological emphasis away from understanding the Spirit either theocentrically or anthropocentrically toward an explicitly biocentric model of the Spirit in nature.

The Wounded Spirit

To reconceive the Spirit as the enfleshment of God's sustaining power in the biosphere is to emphasize the coinherence of the Spirit and the natural world.

Whether manifesting herself as a living, breathing organism like a dove, or an inanimate life-form, such as wind or fire, the Spirit indwells nature as its interanimating force in order to lead all creation into a peaceable relationship with itself. Spirit and earth internally condition and permeate one another; both modes of being coinhere through and with one another without collapsing into undifferentiated sameness or equivalence. The reciprocal indwelling of Spirit and earth is neither an absorption of the one into the other nor a confusion of the two. By the same token, this mutual indwelling is not an outward and transitory connection between the two realities but rather an internal and abiding union of the two in a common life together. Insofar as the Spirit abides in and with all living things, Spirit and earth are *inseparable* and yet at the same time *distinguishable*. Spirit and earth are internally indivisible because both modes of being are living realities with the common goal of sustaining other life-forms. But Spirit and earth also possess their own distinctive identities insofar as the Spirit is the unseen power who vivifies and sustains all living things, while the earth is the visible agent of the life that pulsates throughout creation.

Under the control of this dialectic, the earth is the "body" of the Spirit. Metaphorically speaking, God as Spirit corporealizes Godself through her interanimation of the biosphere. In breathing life into humankind and otherkind, a fundamental transformation within Godself occurs: God is fully incarnated in the green fuse that drives all forms of life to their natural fruition in a carnival of praise to the Creator Spirit. As once God became human in the body of Jesus, so continually God enfleshes Godself in the embodied reality of life on earth. Quintessentially, then, both Spirit and earth are life-givers: the Spirit *ensouls* the earth with the quickening breath of divine life and the earth *enfleshes* the Spirit as it offers spiritual and physical sustenance to all living things. The Spirit inhabits the earth as its invisible and life-giving breath (*rûah*), and the earth (*gaia*) is the outward manifestation, the body, as it were, of the Spirit's presence within, and maintenance of, all life-forms.[33]

This proposal for an ecological pneumatology of internal relatedness presents an extraordinary challenge to the traditional Aristotelian and early Christian doctrine of God as an unchangeable and self-subsistent being fundamentally unaffected by the creation God has spun into existence. One intriguing but troubling implication of ecological pneumatology, therefore, is that it places the divine life at risk in a manner that an extrinsic doctrine of the Spirit *vis-à-vis* the earth does not. The theological problem is that if Spirit and earth mutually indwell one another then it follows that God as Spirit is vulnerable to serious trauma and loss just insofar as the earth is abused and despoiled. In an earth-centered model of the Spirit, God is a thoroughgoing incarnational reality who decides in freedom, and not by any internal necessity, to indwell all things. But in making this decision, the Spirit places herself at risk by virtue of her coinherence with a continually degraded biosphere. God, then, is so internally related to the universe that the specter of ecocide raises the risk of deicide: to wreak environmental havoc on the earth is to run the risk that we will do irreparable harm to the Love and Mystery we call God. The wager of this model is that while God and world are not identical to one another, their basic unity and common destiny raises the possibility that ongoing assaults against the earth's biotic communities may eventually result in permanent injury to the divine life itself.

The coinherence of God and earth can be further developed by considering the "suffering God" motif in recent theology. Jürgen Moltmann's *The Crucified God* (and the wealth of similar books it spawned on the topic of divine suffering) argues that God in Jesus suffers the godforsaken death of the cross.[34] In antitheopaschite terms, the cross does not signify the "death of God" but rather the death of Jesus as a terrifying event of loss and suffering within the inner life of Godself. The cross is not an instance of God dying but an event in Godself where the divine life takes into itself the death of the godless son of God crucified for the sins of the world. In the cross, God now becomes radically discontinuous with Godself by taking up the crucified one.

> [W]hat happened on the cross was an event between God and God. It was a deep division in God himself, insofar as God abandoned God and contradicted himself, and at the same time a unity in God, insofar as God was at one with God and corresponded to himself. In that case one would have to put the formula in a paradoxical way: God died the death of the godless on the cross and yet did not die. God is dead and yet is not dead.[35]

In the cross, God splits Godself by incorporating the godless death of Jesus into the inner life of the Godhead. In this rift caused by Jesus's death, God now undergoes a permanent and fundamental change by becoming a willing victim of death itself.

As Jesus's death on the cross brought death and loss into Godself, so the Spirit's suffering from persistent environmental trauma engenders chronic agony in the Godhead. From the perspective of ecological pneumatology, Moltmann's "crucified God" has a double valence: death enters the inner life of God through the cross of Jesus even as the prospect of ecological mass death enters the life of God through the Spirit's communion with a despoiled planet. We see, then, that the Spirit is Christ-like or cruciform because she suffers the same violent fate as did Jesus – but now a suffering not confined to the onetime event of the cross but a continuous suffering because the Spirit experiences daily the degradation of the earth and its inhabitants. Because this trauma deeply grieves the Spirit, she pleads with God's people to nurture and protect the fragile bioregions we all share. Paul writes that human arrogance causes the whole creation to groan in agony as it waits for deliverance; he continues that as the creation sighs in pain the Spirit on our behalf likewise groans in sounds too deep for words – interceding on our behalf that God's love for all creation will be consummated (Rom. 8.18–39). In the midst of the current crisis the created order groans under the weight of humankind's habitual ecoviolence; in turn, the Spirit intensely beseeches us to care for our planetary heritage. God as Spirit agonizes over the squalor we have caused and through her abiding earthly presence implores us to stop the violence before it is too late.

From this viewpoint, as the God who knows death through the cross of Jesus is the crucified God, so also is the Spirit who enfleshes divine presence in nature the wounded Spirit. Jesus's body was inscribed with the marks of human sin even as God's enfleshed presence – the earth body of the Spirit – is lacerated by continued assaults upon our planet home. Consider the sad parallels between the crucified Jesus and the cruciform Spirit: the lash marks of human sin cut into the body of the crucified God are now even more graphically displayed across the expanse of the whole planet as the body of the wounded Spirit bears the incisions of further abuse. Because God as Spirit is enfleshed within creation, God experiences within the core of her deepest self the agony and suffering of an earth under siege. The Spirit, then, as the green face of God, has also become in our time the wounded God. Earth Spirit is the wounded God who daily suffers the environmental violence wrought by humankind's unremitting ecocidal attitudes and habits. The Spirit is the wounded God even as Christ is the crucified God – as God once suffered on a tree by taking onto Godself humankind's sin, so God now continually suffers the agony of death and loss by bringing into Godself the environmental squalor that humankind has wrought.

Conclusion

I have suggested that we refer to the Spirit in our time as the "wounded Spirit" or "cruciform Spirit" who, like Christ, takes into herself the burden of human sin and the deep ecological damage this sin has wrought in the biosphere. But as Christ's wounds become the eucharistic blood that nourishes the believer, so also does the Spirit's agony over damage to the earth become a source of hope for all forms of life who face seemingly hopeless environmental destitution. The message of the cross is that senseless death is not foreign to God because it is through the cross that God lives in solidarity with all who suffer. The promise of new life that flows from the suffering God hanging from a tree is recapitulated in the ministry of the wounded Spirit whose solidarity with a broken world is a token of divine forbearance and love. Hope, then, for a restored earth in our time is theologically rooted in the belief in the Spirit's benevolent cohabitation with all of the damaged and forgotten members of the biosphere – human and non-human alike. The Spirit's abiding presence in a world wracked by human greed is a constant reminder that God desires the welfare of all members of the life-web – indeed, that no population of life-forms is beyond the ken of divine love, no matter how serious, even permanent, the ecological damage is to these biotic communities.

One of the many ironies of Christian faith is the belief that out of death comes life, from loss and suffering comes the possibility of hope and renewal. This irony is symbolized in the Creator's emptying of herself in creation so that all beings may enjoy fullness of life; in Jesus's crucifixion where the spilling of his life blood becomes the opportunity for all persons to experience the fullness of new life in him; and in the Spirit's kenotic coinherence with the earth and concomitant willingness to endure our ecological violence so that we can be offered again the chance to change our habits and reenter the sorority of the earth and her Creator. Our rapacious habits daily wound afresh the Earth Spirit who breathes life into all things; and daily the Earth Spirit intercedes for us and protects us by allowing us to remain richly alive in spite of our behavior to the contrary. The Spirit in and through the body of the earth groans in travail over our addictions to ecoviolence. But in her wounds we have life, because it is in the wounded Spirit that we see God's love overabundant and outpouring on our behalf. In her wounds we see God's refusal to remain aloof from creation – apathetic, unmoved, uncaring – just insofar as God decided to enflesh Godself in all of the processes and life-forms that constitute life as we know it. We continue unabated in our ravaging of the earth body of the one who has given herself for us so that we might live. But to this point the cruciform Spirit has not withdrawn her sustaining presence from the planet – a reminder to us that God is a lover of all things bodily and earthly – and a call to a renewed passion on our part for nurturing and protecting the biosphere that is our common inheritance and common home.

Can a recovery of the ancient, biblical idea of the Spirit as the green face of God provide the necessary focus for the practice of earth-healing in our time? The answer to this question has been the focus of this essay. I have proposed here that one of the most compelling *Christian* responses to the threat of ecocide lies in a recovery of the Holy Spirit as God's power of life-giving breath (*rûah*) who indwells and sustains all life-forms. The answer to the increasing environmental degradation in our time is not better technology – a matter of more know-how – but a Spirit-motivated conversion of our whole way of life to sustainable living – a matter of the heart. Such a change of heart can occur through an encounter with Christian earth wisdom. This wisdom for our troubled times can be found in the rich biblical imagery of God as Spirit who sustains and renews all forms of life on the planet; the corresponding belief, since the Spirit vivifies all things, in the interdependence that binds together all members of the biosphere in a global web of life; and the concomitant ethical ideal of working toward the healing of various biotic communities whenever they suffer ecological degradation.

We need today a conversion of the heart to a vision of a green earth where all persons live in harmony with their natural environments. May the Holy Spirit, as divine force for sustenance and renewal in all things, come into our hearts and minds and persuade us to work toward a seamless social–environmental ethic of justice and love toward all God's creatures.

Notes

1 See the analysis of Joachim's tripartite theology of history in George H. Tavard, "Apostolic Life and Church Reform," in *Christian Spirituality: High Middle Ages and Reformation*, ed. Jill Raitt (New York: Crossroad, 1987), pp. 1–11.

2   See Eberhard Busch, *Karl Barth: His Life from Letters and Autobiographical Texts*, trans. John Bowden (Philadelphia: Fortress Press, 1976), p. 494.
3   Ihab Hassan, quoted in David Harvey, *The Condition of Postmodernity* (Oxford: Blackwell Publishers, 1990), pp. 42–5.
4   See Margot Adler, *Drawing Down the Moon: Witches, Druids, Goddess-Worshippers, and Other Pagans in America Today*, revd. edn. (Boston: Beacon Press, 1986).
5   See Bill McKibben, *The End of Nature* (New York: Random House, 1989), and Jeremy Rifkin, *Biosphere Politics: A Cultural Odyssey from the Middle Ages to the New Age* (San Francisco: HarperSanFrancisco, 1991), pp. 71–91.
6   The dual topics of Spirit and earth were the focus of the Seventh Assembly of the World Council of Churches in Canberra, Australia, February 1991, entitled "Come Holy Spirit, Renew the Whole Creation."
7   In her earlier work Sallie McFague argued that the model of God as Spirit is not retrievable in an ecological age, criticizing traditional descriptions of the Spirit as ethereal and vacant. But in her recent writing McFague performs the very retrieval of pneumatology she had earlier claimed to be impossible: a revisioning of God as Spirit in order to thematize the immanent and dynamic presence of the divine life within all creation. See *The Body of God: An Ecological Theology* (Minneapolis, MN: Fortress Press, 1993), pp. 141–50. For an appreciation and critique of McFague's ecotheology see my *Fragments of the Spirit: Nature, Violence, and the Renewal of Creation* (New York: Continuum, 1996), pp. 139–44. Some of the material in this essay is borrowed from *Fragments of the Spirit*.
8   In recent years there has been a surge of interest in Spirit-discourse from a variety of disciplinary perspectives. Many of these works have been essential to my own thinking about the Spirit in nature. In theology, see José Comblin, *The Holy Spirit and Liberation*, trans. Paul Burns (Maryknoll, NY: Orbis Books, 1989); Peter C. Hodgson, *Winds of the Spirit: A Constructive Christian Theology* (Louisville, KY: Westminster John Knox Press, 1994); Adolf Holl, *The Left Hand of God: A Biography of the Holy Spirit*, trans. John Cullen (New York: Doubleday, 1998); Chung Hyun-Kyung, "Welcome the Spirit; Hear Her Cries: The Holy Spirit, Creation, and the Culture of Life," *Christianity and Crisis*, 51 (July 15, 1991), pp. 220–3; Elizabeth A. Johnson, *She Who Is: The Mystery of God in Feminist Theological Discourse* (New York: Crossroad, 1992); Jürgen Moltmann, *God in Creation: A New Theology of Creation and the Spirit of God*, trans. Margaret Kohl (San Francisco: Harper & Row, 1985); Jürgen Moltmann, *The Spirit of Life: A Universal Affirmation*, trans. Margaret Kohl (Minneapolis, MN: Fortress Press, 1992); Jürgen Moltmann, *The Source of Life: The Holy Spirit and the Theology of Life*, trans. Margaret Kohl (Minneapolis, MN: Fortress Press, 1997); Geiko Müller-Fahrenholz, *God's Spirit: Transforming a World in Crisis*, trans. John Cumming (New York: Continuum, 1995); Nancy Victorin-Vangerud, *The Raging Hearth: Spirit in the Household of God* (St Louis, MO: Chalice Press, 2000); and Michael Welker, *God the Spirit*, trans. John F. Hoffmeyer (Minneapolis, MN: Fortress Press, 1994); in philosophy, see Jacques Derrida, *Of Spirit: Heidegger and the Question*, trans. Geoffrey Bennington and Rachel Bowlby (Chicago: University of Chicago Press, 1989); Jacques Derrida, *Specters of Marx: The State of the Debt, the Work of Mourning, and the New International*, trans. Peggy Kampf (New York: Routledge, 1994); and Steven G. Smith, *The Concept of the Spiritual: An Essay in First Philosophy* (Philadelphia: Temple University Press, 1988); and in cultural studies, see Joel Kovel, *History and Spirit: An Inquiry into the Philosophy of Liberation* (Boston: Beacon Press, 1991).

9   On contemporary theology as an exercise in tracking the traces of the Spirit (or spirit) in contemporary culture, see Mark McClain Taylor, "Tracking Spirit: Theology as Cultural Critique in America," in *Changing Conversations: Religious Reflection and Cultural Analysis*, ed. Dwight N. Hopkins and Sheila Greeve Davaney (New York: Routledge, 1996), pp. 123–44.

10 On the history of the problematic relation between metaphysics and pneumatology, see Alan M. Olson, *Hegel and the Spirit: Philosophy as Pneumatology* (Princeton, NJ: Princeton University Press, 1992), pp. 3–35, 107–62. For a defense of a counter-metaphysical model of God, see Jean-Luc Marion, *God Without Being: Hors-Texte*, trans. Thomas A. Carlson (Chicago: University of Chicago Press, 1991). Finally, a note here about my use of different pronouns for the Spirit – including the female pronoun. As God's indwelling presence throughout the created order, the Spirit is variously identified with feminine, maternal characteristics in the biblical witness. The mother Spirit bird in Gen. 1 broods over the earth bringing all things into life and fruition; this same hovering Spirit bird appears in the gospels at Jesus's baptism to inaugurate his public ministry. In Proverbs 1, 8, 9 and the Book of Wisdom, God as Wisdom or *Sophia* is understood analogously to the maternal Spirit of Gen. 1 and the gospels: the nursing mother of creation who protects and sustains the well-being of all things in the cosmic web of life. Early Christian communities in the Middle East consistently spoke of the Spirit as the motherly, regenerative breath and power of God within creation. These early Christians believed that the Hebrew feminine grammatical name of the Spirit – *rûah* – was a linguistic clue to certain woman-identified characteristics of God as Spirit. As these early Christians rightly understood that God transcends sex and gender, their point was not that God was a female deity but that it is appropriate alternately to refer to God's mystery and love and power in male *and* female terms. I will occasionally refer to the Spirit in this essay as "she" in order to capture something of the biblical understanding of the special relationship between God as Spirit-*Sophia* and the created order the divine mother birthed into existence. On the history of feminine language for the Spirit, see Susan Ashbrook Harvey, "Feminine Imagery for the Divine: The Holy Spirit, the Odes of Solomon, and Early Syriac Tradition," *St Vladimir's Theological Quarterly*, 37 (1993), pp. 111–40; Gary Steven Kinkel, *Our Dear Mother the Spirit: An Investigation of Count Zinzendorf's Theology and Praxis* (Lanham, MD: University Press of America, 1990); and Johnson, *She Who Is*, pp. 128–31.

11 Jacques Derrida, *Circumfession: Fifty-nine Periods and Periphrases*, in Geoffrey Bennington and Jacques Derrida, *Jacques Derrida* (Chicago: University of Chicago Press, 1993), pp. 154–5. I classify Derrida's musings in *Circumfession* as "autobiography" or "memoirs" insofar as these writings are exercises in writing the self, without making any claim as to the historicity of the "self" figured in these texts by Derrida.

12 Ibid. On the character of Derrida's philosophy of religion, see John Caputo, *The Prayers and Tears of Jacques Derrida: Religion without Religion* (Bloomington: Indiana University Press, 1997); Kevin Hart, "Jacques Derrida: The God Effect," in *Post-Secular Philosophy: Between Philosophy and Theology*, ed. Phillip Blond (London: Routledge, 1998), pp. 259–80; and Mark I. Wallace, "God Beyond God: Derrida's Theological Self-Portraiture," in *Method as Path: Religious Experience and Hermeneutical Discourse*, ed. Elliot R. Wolfson (New York: Seven Bridges Press, forthcoming).

13 Derrida, *Circumfession*, p. 56.

14 John Caputo has identified in Derrida these and other unnameable names for God in *The Prayers and Tears of Jacques Derrida*.

15 Jacques Derrida, "Post-Scriptum: Aporias, Ways and Voices," trans. John P. Leavey, Jr., in *Derrida and Negative Theology*, ed. Harold Coward and Toby Foshay (Albany, NY: State University of New York Press, 1992), p. 317. I am referring to this article here as "Sauf le nom." See a slightly different version in Jacques Derrida, "Sauf le nom (Post-Scriptum)," trans. John P. Leavey, Jr., in *On the Name*, ed. Thomas Dutoit (Stanford, CA: Stanford University Press, 1995), pp. 35–85.
16 See Derrida, "Post-Scriptum: Aporias, Ways and Voices" (aka "Sauf le nom").
17 Caputo, *The Prayers and Tears of Jacques Derrida*, p. 43.
18 Jacques Derrida, "How to Avoid Speaking: Denials," in *Derrida and Negative Theology*, ed. Harold Coward and Toby Foshay (Albany, NY: State University of New York Press, 1992).
19 Derrida, "Post-Scriptum: Aporias, Ways and Voices," p. 317.
20 Derrida, *Circumfession*, p. 155.
21 The quotation by Derrida is from Anselm Haverkamp (ed.), *Deconstruction in America: A New Sense of the Political* (New York: New York University Press, 1995), p. 12. At first glance this Derrida–Barth association may appear forced. What does the Jerusalem of Protestant Word-based theology have to do with the Athens of postmodern criticism of logocentrism? There are many illuminating points of contact, however, between Barth's theology and Derridean deconstruction. Barth's insistence on the mystery of God and his concomitant refusal to secure religious language on the pseudo-security of a philosophical foundation anticipate Derrida's attention to the unassimilable otherness within language that escapes the false closure of any metaphysical system. To highlight this common sensibility between Barth and Derrida is not to deny the important differences underlying their thought. Nevertheless, each thinker's countermetaphysical concern with ineradicable alterity in language – what Barth calls the *Word in the words* and Derrida now refers to as the *undeconstructible* – provides a fertile field of comparative analysis in spite of their important differences. On the potential of deconstruction in theological reflection (with special reference to Barth), see Graham Ward, *Barth, Derrida and the Language of Theology* (Cambridge: Cambridge University Press, 1995), and my "Karl Barth and Deconstruction," *Religious Studies Review*, 25 (October 1999), pp. 349–54. On the potential of deconstruction in theological reflection in general, see Jacques Derrida and Gianni Vattimo (eds.), *Religion* (Stanford, CA: Stanford University Press, 1998) and Kevin Hart, *The Trespass of the Sign: Deconstruction, Theology and Philosophy* (Cambridge: Cambridge University Press, 1989). For a less sanguine reading of the relationship between deconstruction and theology in which Derridean thought is labeled as nihilistic, necrophilic, and fascistic, see John Milbank, Catherine Pickstock, and Graham Ward (eds.), "Introduction: Suspending the Material: The Turn of Radical Orthodoxy," in *Radical Orthodoxy: A New Theology* (London: Routledge, 1999), pp. 1–20; Catherine Pickstock, *After Writing: On the Liturgical Consummation of Philosophy* (Oxford: Blackwell Publishers, 1998); and Phillip Blond (ed.), "Introduction: Theology Before Philosophy," in *Post-Secular Philosophy: Between Philosophy and Theology* (London: Routledge, 1998), pp. 1–66.
22 This definition is from the entry on "spiritus" by Richard A. Muller, *Dictionary of Latin and Greek Theological Terms* (Grand Rapids, MI: Baker Book House, 1985), p. 286.
23 The literature on this question is extensive. See *inter alia* Caroline Walker Bynum, *Fragmentation and Redemption: Essays on Gender and the Human Body in Medieval Religion* (New York: Zone Books, 1991); Susan Griffin, *Woman and Nature: The Roaring*

Inside Her (New York: Harper & Row, 1978); Mark Johnson, *The Body in the Mind: The Bodily Basis of Meaning, Imagination, and Reason* (Chicago: University of Chicago Press, 1987); and William R. LaFleur, "Body," in *Critical Terms for Religious Studies*, ed. Mark C. Taylor (Chicago: University of Chicago Press, 1998), pp. 36–54.

24 Plato *Timaeus*, 42–9, 89–92.
25 Peter Brown, *The Body and Society: Men, Women, and Sexual Renunciation in Early Christianity* (New York: Columbia University Press, 1988), pp. 160–89.
26 Augustine *The Confessions*, 7–8. Also see Peter Brown, *Augustine of Hippo* (Berkeley: University of California Press, 1969), pp. 158–81, 340–97, and Elaine Pagels, *Adam, Eve, and the Serpent* (New York: Random House, 1988), pp. 98–154.
27 On Paul's anthropology, see J. Christiaan Beker, *Paul the Apostle: The Triumph of God in Life and Thought* (Philadelphia: Fortress Press, 1980), pp. 213–302.
28 Basil of Caesarea, *De Spiritu Sancto*, bk. 16.
29 Augustine, *De Trinitate*, bk. 15.
30 For reproductions and commentary, see Jeffrey F. Hamburger, *The Rothschild Canticles: Art and Mysticism in Flanders and the Rhineland Circa 1300* (New Haven, CT: Yale University Press, 1990), pp. 118–42. I am grateful to Ellen Ross for directing my attention to this volume.
31 Perichoresis is the doctrine that teaches the coinherence of each member of the Trinity in the other. For a fuller discussion of this term and its relevance to contemporary theology, see Catherine Mowry LaCugna, *God For Us: The Trinity and Christian Life* (San Francisco: HarperSanFrancisco, 1991), pp. 270–8.
32 There are notable exceptions to this general orientation (for example, Chung Hyun-Kyung, Johnson, Moltmann, Welker), but most other contemporary theologies of the Holy Spirit generally deemphasize, or ignore altogether, the model of the Spirit as God's power of ecological renewal and healing within the cosmos. This shortcoming applies to a number of otherwise invaluable books in pneumatology, including Yves M. J. Congar, *I Believe in the Holy Spirit*, trans. Geoffrey Chapman, 3 vols. (New York: Seabury Press, 1983); Alasdair I. C. Heron, *The Holy Spirit: The Holy Spirit in the Bible, the History of Christian Thought, and Recent Theology* (Philadelphia: Westminster Press, 1983); G. W. H. Lampe, *God as Spirit* (Oxford: Clarendon Press, 1977); and John V. Taylor, *The Go-Between God: The Holy Spirit and the Christian Mission* (London: SCM Press, 1972). As well, the writings on the Spirit in the important systematic theologies of authors such as Barth, Rahner, and Tillich reflect a similar lacuna, though this oversight is understandable given the general lack of cultural awareness of the ecocrisis at the time these authors were writing. (This anachronistic qualification applies to some of the other writers listed above as well.)
33 See Jürgen Moltmann's *The Spirit of Life*, pp. 274–89, and his model of the Spirit as the *vita vivificans* who sustains all creation, and James E. Lovelock's *Gaia: A New Look at Life on Earth* (Oxford: Oxford University Press, 1979) in defense of the model of the earth as a single living organism which supports all life-forms within a common ecosystem.
34 See *inter alia* Edward Farley, *Divine Empathy: A Theology of God* (Minneapolis, MN: Fortress Press, 1996); Joseph Halloran, *The Descent of God: Divine Suffering in History and Theology* (Minneapolis, MN: Fortress Press, 1992); and Grace Jantzen, *God's World and God's Body* (Philadelphia: Westminster Press, 1984).
35 Jürgen Moltmann, *The Crucified God*, trans. R. A. Wilson and John Bowden (New York: Harper & Row, 1974), p. 244.

PART III
Gender

13	An Ethics of Memory: Promising, Forgiving, Yearning	231
14	Is Macrina a Woman? Gregory of Nyssa's *Dialogue on the Soul and Resurrection*	249
15	"They Will Know We are Christians by Our Regulated Improvisation": Ecclesial Hybridity and the Unity of the Church	265
16	On Changing the Imaginary	280
17	Companionable Wisdoms: What Insights Might Feminist Theorists Gather from Feminist Theologians?	294

CHAPTER 13

An Ethics of Memory: Promising, Forgiving, Yearning

Pamela Sue Anderson

Pamela Sue Anderson's work is rooted in concerns with mimesis which were also the focus of her doctoral work in Oxford. This is not to say that her work has traversed the same ground since the publication of her thesis *Kant and Ricoeur* (Atlanta, GA, 1993), for it has not. Anderson's questioning mind and intellectual energies do not repeat but push forwards – pressing ever-harder the conclusions reached in earlier investigations. But Kant, Ricoeur, and in some ways the Oxford tradition of analytical philosophy, remain key features of her work. In was Ricoeur's attention to myth, symbol, and narrative – which itself sought to combine Hegel's diachronic sense of history with the Kantian synchronic approach to the construction of knowledge – that provided Anderson with a philosophical foundation for appreciating the concerns with representation in the work of Julia Kristeva, Luce Irigaray, and Michèle Le Doeuff. Their analyses of gender, sexual difference, psychoanalysis as a practice of love, and the erasing of the feminine philosophical voice supplemented and transformed the work of Ricoeur. But something of Ricoeur's concern with what he earlier called "reference" and later saw more as a trace of the real in the mimetic, and something of Kant's continuous insistence upon the *Ding an Sich*, remain important to Anderson. This desire to maintain a "weak" realist position – evidence of the influence of the Oxford analytical tradition – whilst all too aware of the feminist critique of the "Man of Reason" subtending that position, led Anderson into a conversation with standpoint epistemologists: the work of Sandra Harding and Helen Longino, among others. The result of this interesting and imaginative confluence of voices was Anderson's important book, *A Feminist Philosophy of Religion: The Rationality and Myths of Religious Belief* (Oxford, 1998).

The essay included here indicates the nature and scope of Anderson's subsequent project, which, as she herself states, develops out of her ambitious desire to rewrite philosophy of religion in a feminist key. The new direction of this project lies in its attention to ethics (and politics as related to the question of justice raised by social ethics). This is not to say that an ethical dimension was not intrinsic to her earlier work – and fundamental to the work of both Kant and Ricoeur. Knowledge is, for Anderson, linked to love and desire and, therefore, agency, intention, and human flourishing. But her earlier concerns were more orientated towards an epistemological analysis. The ethical and political implications of that analysis are now being explored, as this essay demonstrates. New dialogue partners also emerge: Hannah Arendt and Gillian Rose. And one wonders whether, mirroring the Kantian trilogy, Anderson does not envisage developing an aesthetics of feminist judgment at a future date. She works methodically, and in a postmodern commitment to mimesis, myth, and narrative does not reduce rationality to fantastic tales spun to veil the void (as both Deleuze and at least early Lacan might be said to do). Her work may well be articulating a feminist philosophical system in which the three traditional branches of the discipline – epistemology, ethics, and aesthetics – are each treated with respect to rhetoric. We shall see.

The past is a cemetery of promises which have not been kept.
Paul Ricoeur

in loving memory
of a life we shared
in gratitude for a love . . .
that calls me to remember
and let the past go
bell hooks

Introduction: On Memory

Memory is a form of knowledge; or, at least, this is my first premise.[1] Even when we vaguely remember what has been, memory is at work cognitively. Yet in postmodern terms the object of memory's cognition is at most a trace. In breaking with the modern sense of an empirical mark standing for an original non-trace, the postmodern "trace" also has its origin in a trace.[2] The distinctiveness of this concept is its differential relation to a non-origin created by a lack of nostalgia for what has been lost; the trace's lack of origin renders doubtful the reality of the past. Nevertheless, the postmodern challenge to the reality and temporal identity signified by the trace has not been decisive. For instance, Paul Ricoeur presents a strong case for retaining the significance of the trace as a vestige of the past.[3] To support this case I shall argue that memory continues to condition what appear to be attempts to rediscover and retain traces of a past about which women and men have written and seek to write. This activity of writing a narrative of the past, or of telling a story, is part of what has been called "our ordinary reliance on memory."[4]

Storytelling is a significant form of memory; it shapes remembering. However, early in the twentieth century Walter Benjamin expressed regret for the loss of our ability to tell or write stories about our lives.[5] Benjamin experienced the shattering of European memory in the two world wars, when the moral and political agreements, or mutual promises, which had shaped the Western Enlightenment were tragically broken down. My essay builds critically on this profound sense of loss and presents a reconsideration of three acts of memory: promising, forgiving, and yearning. Each of these acts presupposes the creation of stories. My contention is that these acts of memory make narrative sense of life. In the narrative act of promise-keeping memory gives a particular coherence to living, even while broken promises call for forgiving; and in yearning we seek to bring these two acts together in appropriate ways. Further, I shall demonstrate how an ethics of memory emerges in the initiation of a narrative act, in the sense of Hannah Arendt's concept of natality, which represents a new beginning. Though natality has been emphasized by feminist philosophers, this is not just a feminist issue.

Arendt and Ricoeur follow Benjamin in articulating the role and meaning of enacted stories, or narrative, for living a human life.[6] I shall not follow Benjamin, Arendt, or Ricoeur precisely, or establish any strict technical conception of narrative. Instead, I employ the term "narrative" to include accounts of everyday events, memoirs of one's or another's life, and myths which configure communal identities.[7] In these terms we shall see that narratives are created – and discovered – despite the postmodern charge of no original non-trace.[8] Even in a postmodern age, making narrative sense of one's life and others' lives remains crucial to human knowledge, ethics, and justice.

Besides a form of knowledge, memory is rendered a form of mimesis by the imagination: it imitates and represents a past. Postmodern accounts of mimesis in contemporary French philosophy tend to stress the difference between forms of mimesis rather than the difference between mimesis and its original.[9] Memory, at the same time as it informs, is informed by the memoirs, myths, and mimetic rituals which shape our lives communally and individually in time. We recollect by telling our own or another's stories, but also by retelling and refiguring the founding myths of our own tradition(s).[10] The memoirs, myths, and mimesis which shape our lives can be – and always are – in process of revision and multiplication. So memory involves metamorphosis. In dialectical relation to memory, memoirs are exchanged at a narrative level and so allow communication, comprehension, and change. In this process, memory creates a space in which memoirs meet and conflict with other memoirs. Similarly, individual myths constantly intersect with other individual and communal myths, often conflicting, often changing. Implicit in this mimetic space of cognition and imagination is the use – and possible abuse – of the past.[11] Thus memory raises a question of ethics.

An ethics of memory is exposed in the human activity of making narrative sense of our lives. Whether unwittingly or not we seek to give our lives a narrative shape, both creating and discovering an evaluative concept of personal identity.[12] According to Ricoeur, the distinctiveness of narrative identity is not being dependent upon any biological or natural sameness; to create narrative identity no particular thing *has* to stay the same through the ravages of time.[13] In fact it finds its highest expression in an act of memory which achieves self-constancy in continuing through change; this act which endures, while other things dissipate in time, is promise-keeping. I intend to defend promising as not only an act between oneself and another self, as not merely a crucial element in most economic transactions, but as the heart of a communal act of commitment.[14] In modern times a mutual promise has been extended collectively as the basis for shared convictions, rules, norms, customs, and beliefs. The result is a social contract.[15]

An ethics of memory is necessary because of the potential use and abuse of acts of self-constancy.[16] When promising becomes promise-keeping it reveals an evaluative concept of personal identity in time; forgiving frees us from a past of broken promises; yearning seeks to achieve justice and love in being both bound in promising and unbound in forgetting or forgiving. Imagination and mimesis play integral roles in both the epistemological and the ethical dimensions of memory. Ancient Greek philosophy made memory, imitation, and reminiscence topics of critical debate. In recent times philosophical discussions of memory have been frequently displaced by psychoanalytic critiques of the unconscious as the unknowable. Nevertheless, I seek to demonstrate that an ethics of memory is an integral part of postmodern theology, whether debated or not. Feminist philosophy of religion is the domain of postmodern theology which raises the ethical issues of concern here.

The ultimate aim of my project, which I can only adumbrate here, is to apply an ethics of memory to the feminist problematic of philosophy of religion. Interestingly, Arendt, as an often-debated "philosopher" of this century, resists the labels of "modern," "postmodern," and "feminist."[17] Yet she writes insightfully about the human condition of enacted stories, promising, forgiving, the identities of self and other. Ironically, Arendt may better resist the binary oppositions from which postmodern thinking tries to extricate itself than those who call themselves postmodern. Thus her critical thought offers timely insight for not only feminist philosophers, but also postmodern theologians. Before I discuss Arendt's *The Human Condition* let me set out the terms of my relation to postmodern theology.

Memory and Postmodern Theology

My contention is that the demise of traditional metaphysics, and revised conceptions of history and selfhood have forced philosophers and theologians in a postmodern age to rethink their premises. If the postmodern is defined in terms of the three, metaphorically speaking, deaths of modern philosophy, then memory is arguably that with which we are left. These so-called deaths include the end of history as a grand narrative of progress, the end of self-identity as a form of sameness, and the loss of metaphysics as a logic of presence.[18] In making narrative sense of life memory remains the faculty of rendering a weak sense of a historical past, of a self in relation to another and of a presence in traces of the face of another.[19]

I propose that postmodern theologians turn to the ethics and implicit epistemology in the traces of memory. This proposal follows from four points which I have established in the introductory section. First, I asserted that memory is a form of knowledge; second, I pointed out that memory is rendered a form of mimesis by the imagination; third, the use and abuse of memory in cognition and imagination makes necessary an ethics of memory; fourth, a turn to an ethics of memory – built upon memory's revised epistemological role – gives new possibilities for retrieving traces of the past, even if there is no original non-trace. The retrieval of what remains essentially a spiritual dimension can happen through an ethical reassessment of promising, forgiving, and yearning as personal and communal acts of memory.

In 1993 I addressed the postmodern question, "After Theology: End or Transformation?"[20] My answer called for theology to transform the strong conceptions of history, self, and reality found in empirical realist forms of Christian theism. A reformist feminist concern that women not be obliged to give up their history, agency, and embodiment just when they were beginning to discover the reality of their lives motivated my "weak" reconstruction of the objects of postmodern critiques.[21] I insisted upon giving up the exclusive, patriarchal reading of philosophical theology. But this giving up did – and does – *not* imply that we no longer seek to make narrative sense of our lives, to give our lives a unity, a shape or, in a certain sense, an identity. It is simply that there will never be a closure to the narrative of living a human life. We continue to write memoirs, to reenact what has taken place, and to create stories, in order to understand the values shaping our personal and communal identities.

In this essay I build on my earlier response to the postmodern challenge to Enlightenment philosophy. My position has been restated and developed in *A Feminist Philosophy of Religion*.[22] The present project on an ethics of memory is a further contribution to ground-breaking work towards a feminist philosophy of religion. What needs to be retrieved are the shattered promises, the ability to forgive, and the yearning which leads to transforming melancholia into love and justice.[23] Acts of memory are contextualized in specific ways by theologians; but rather than become involved with these specifics I concentrate on ethical issues, presenting an epistemological framework for their reconceptualization by feminist philosophers and postmodern theologians.

Memory is presupposed in a variety of feminist activities. It informs the writing of memoirs as autobiographies and the retrieval of lost histories of women, their lives and voices. It makes possible the unearthing of buried promises so that "the cemetery of past promises" can be transformed by a love that goes beyond morality in forgiveness. The transformative power of love is expressed in the subtitle of *Forgiveness: Shattering the Debt*.[24] bell hooks's words, "in loving memory of a life we shared; in gratitude for a love . . . that calls me to remember and let the past go," suggest that forgiveness, achieved through love, must move memory toward the future.[25] When the past is virtually unthinkable and the future is unimaginable, then an ethics of memory renders justice mournable through commitment to a transformative love in forgiveness. My ethics of memory builds upon both Gillian Rose's conception of "a transcendent, mournable justice"[26] and Parita Mukta's critical question: "The incapacity to feel grief cedes more power to violent formations. For how can lives be sustained without their passing being mourned?"[27] Further support comes from feminist philosophers who are actively figuring and refiguring stories and myths about the past (suffering) of women. Memory is implied in their mimetic activity of disruptively refiguring the partial, often violent configurations of patriarchy. In my concluding section I shall make explicit a form of social epistemology – spontaneous standpoint epistemology[28] – which is implicit in a feminist ethics of memory.

The Human Condition: Enacted Stories, Promising, and Forgiving

In *The Human Condition* Arendt responds fortuitously to the mourning resulting from the postmodern deaths of history, self, and metaphysics. She proposes that a web of relationships allows the enactment of our own stories; we gain narrative identity as agents who promise and forgive; and we find a shared reality in our commitments which create a political realm. These elements for an ethics of memory are embedded in her account of human action and speech.

Crucially, Arendt describes the curious intangibility that renders impossible all attempts to give an unequivocal, verbal account of the "who" of the doer of action. Although we can say "what" the doer is, the disclosure of the agent herself is in a certain sense ineffable. Arendt comes close to a Wittgensteinian claim that the disclosure of the agent can only be shown, not said: she insists upon the impossibility of putting into words the "living essence" of the person as it shows itself in "the flux of action and speech."[29] The disclosure of the "who" can only take place through speech when a new beginning is established through action which "fall[s] into an already existing web of relationships." This "web" is said to be "a somewhat intangible metaphor."[30] Nevertheless it names the context in which the natality of action is felt. In this context of action a new process emerges as "the unique life story of the newcomer, affecting uniquely the life stories of all those with whom he [sic] comes into contact."[31]

Arendt thus develops an ethics of promising and forgiving. Human action produces stories in the medium of human relationships which involve conflicting wills and intentions. No one is the sole author of their own life story.[32] The specific revelatory quality of action and speech is tied to the web in which acting and speaking can be represented by "repetition, imitation, or *mimesis*."[33] In turn, the narrative mimesis of forgiving and promising contains the potential to change the apparent irreversibility and unpredictability of the process of acting. Forgiveness makes possible a redemption from "the predicament of irreversibility" (i.e., through being unable to undo what one has done though one did not, and could not, have known what one was doing). The making and keeping of promises offer "the remedy for unpredictability" (i.e., taking some control of "the chaotic uncertainty" of the future). Together, forgiving and promise-keeping both unbind and bind us temporally. As Arendt explains, "binding oneself through promises serves to set up in the ocean of uncertainty, which the future is by definition, islands of security without which not even continuity, let alone durability of any kind, would be possible in the relationships between men [*sic*]."[34] I would say that without promise-keeping we would not have self-constancy as the evaluative concept of personal identity.[35] For Arendt, "the power generated when people gather together and "'act in concert' ... disappears the moment they depart. The force that keeps them together ... is the force of mutual promise or contract."[36] However, she treats "power" in a positive sense only. What about false promises, or the duty to keep an oppressive commitment? Arendt seems to assume that a false promise is not a promise and an oppressive duty is not a duty.

Ricoeur's rereading of Kantian philosophy confronts the ethical problem raised by the question of promise-keeping. Ricoeur signals the need to make explicit a social epistemology premissed upon a conviction about justice, i.e., about giving each person her due.[37] The Enlightenment conviction that human beings are equal, can think and freely choose to act rationally, supports mutual promises as the basis for a social contract. The result is a birth of a society which binds individual persons together through the rule of reciprocity.[38] Immanuel Kant is the paradigmatic figure of rational freedom; he is also the object of postmodern critique. Ricoeur's reading of promise-keeping pinpoints what remains one of the important points for postmodern debates in Kant's philosophy.[39]

First, Ricoeur confronts the problem of *idem*-identity, where sameness is constitutive of an agent yet dissipates in time. This problem is solved when commitment creates *ipse*-identity (i.e., self-constancy) which endures despite temporal change.[40] Second, Ricoeur distinguishes promising as defined by a "constitutive rule," which places me under the obligation to do tomorrow what today I say I shall do, from keeping one's promise as defined by a "moral rule" of fidelity, which obligates one to another.[41] Third, Ricoeur remains Kantian insofar as promising as a moral action is temporally shaped: as such, promising must imply promise-keeping. In other words, for promising to be moral it must be freely *carried out* and *kept*. Thus, for Ricoeur, like Arendt, promise-keeping is an example of "the highest expression of selfhood": it reflects a desire to respond to an expectation, or request coming from other(s), with a commitment of self-constancy. As moral and so rational promise-keeping is also mutual and potentially communal. Kant provides a key support for this commitment by conceiving practical reason as diachronic in giving shape to the lives of rational beings in a kingdom of ends.[42] This implies a distinctive form of judgment.

The role of practical reason in judgment of particular cases renders human rationality diachronic.[43] Sensitivity to the particular appears in Kant's account of reflective judgment where the general is *not* given. The general must be sought for the particular. Ricoeur relies upon such judgment in confronting concrete situations of moral conflicts. Similarly, Arendt accounts for singular judgments of action whose inscrutable maxim cannot be placed under a rule.[44] Kant's use of the imagination in reflective judgments concerning the past supports the diachronic search for a particularist and, by implication, socially embedded account of ethical acts. This returns us to imagination's rendering of memory as a form of mimesis in representing the past.

Memory gives coherence to one's past, present, and future life diachronically in making narrative sense of life. This process begins in the initiation of a temporal act such as promising within a web of relationships. As we have seen, Arendt calls this initiation "natality." Ricoeur himself explored "birth" in his doctoral thesis,[45] but after reading Arendt he commended her distinctive account of natality.[46] Ricoeur continues to reflect on birth and memory in accounting for the "cohesion of life."[47] In his words, "I encounter the word 'life' at the most basic level of ethics; now this is also the level on which memory is constituted, beneath discourses, before the stage of predication."[48]

An additional ethical problem follows from the proposed socially embedded account of ethical acts. This problem rests with the mimesis of the past, especially of "founding events" which have shaped individual and communal identities.[49] Only self-conscious vigilance and imaginative engagement produce an ethics which preserves past (historical or mythical) events critically and responsibly on a public level. As Ricoeur explains,

> to speak of memory is not only to evoke a psycho-physiological faculty which has something to do with the preservation and recollection of traces of the past; it is to put forward the "narrative" function through which this primary capacity of preservation and recollection is exercised at the public level of language.[50]

But this does not mean we can actually relive the life of others: "More modestly, but also more energetically, it is a matter of exchanging memories at the narrative level where they are presented for comprehension."[51] To be responsible we must read the past by following the narrative memories of others. Memory as a form of cognition and imagination links ethics with an ability to think from the standpoint of others. This ability engages Kant's notion of public sense in reflective judgment. Applied to social or political life this judgment generates epistemological and ethical challenges.[52]

Binding, Unbinding, and Yearning

The third act of memory – yearning – brings together the binding and unbinding of human time in, respectively, promise-keeping and forgiveness. Time is characterized as human when its frame of reference is not restricted solely by causal relations, but is constituted by ethical relations which agents freely initiate and maintain. Human time is distinguished from physical causality by the ethical role of agents in narrative acts. Here I contend that the act of yearning for love and justice renders human time in narratives of promise-keeping and forgiving. Yet there is a question of the source for the content of yearning, as well as the problem that it can take on positive and negative forms. Let us consider this problem first; the former question is raised in the next section of this essay.

In its most positive, social form yearning constitutes a vital reality in human life uniting acts of memory in narratives of passionate rationality. Yearning takes on the character of mourning in the longing for a lost love object. Mourning in itself is not negative if it achieves a reconciliation with loss. However, reconciliation with the loss of a love object, or unity in love, is not always achievable. Failure results in a negative form of yearning turned inward – where the longing is not satiable.[53] Here Mukta employs the image of "the rainbird [who] thirsts" to express the insatiable nature of a privatized yearning which fails to create transformative relations in mourning.

Julia Kristeva explains in psycholinguistic terms that the failure of mourning results in melancholia.[54] The yearning for the lost object is interiorized; the result is a repetition of the past which fails to be reconciled with the reality of loss and death. This inhibits a healthy or "just," memory as the condition of a positive yearning for social justice.[55] Neither promise-keeping nor positive yearning is possible when a person is suffering from melancholia. The person's memory becomes rigid, locked into destructive forms of repetition. In melancholia the acts of promising and yearning are abused by an excess of memory. Forgiveness can be a solution to the inertia of melancholia, if it moderates the obsession with death and physical time.[56] The space of forgiveness is human time, reenacting stories with an ethical focus from birth to death. Philosophical literature contains images of a just memory which *reconciles* by rightly unbinding from and binding us to the past. A just memory conditions rebirth and the narrative sense of life.

Gillian Rose seeks to avoid the abuse of mimetic forms of mourning, while resisting the binary opposition of modern and postmodern. She holds together the tensions of philosophy and theology in a "tale of three cities" on a narrative level reminiscent of Greek mythology. For instance, Rose reads Nicholas Poussin's painting "Gathering the Ashes of Phocion" as a narrative of mourning and justice. In the gathering of her husband's ashes the wife of Phocion, accompanied by her servant, does not protest against power and the law as such. Instead, Poussin's painting configures "a transcendent but mournable justice";

the absence of justice is given presence in "the architectural perspective which frames and focuses the enacted justice of two women."[57] Rose compares the wife of Phocion with Antigone. Both women insist on the right and rites of mourning: "[they] carry out that intense work of the soul, that gradual rearrangement of its boundaries, which must occur when a loved one is lost – so as to let go, to allow the other fully to depart, and hence fully to be regained beyond sorrow." Narratives representing mournable justice render suffering of immediate experience visible and speakable: "Mourning draws on transcendent but representable justice."[58]

Rose demonstrates that philosophy and its representations remain necessary for creating a just memory. The new ethics of Jerusalem should not be opposed to the old justice of Athens. Instead, the architectural perspective framing the enacted justice of two women in Poussin's painting represents the continuing, critical relation to the perspective of order and rationality worked out by philosophers. In this light, philosophy's representations are crucial for an ethics of memory which is not new, but exists to enact every situation anew in relation to justice, including the postmodern situation of theology and justice.

Gloria Anzaldua provides an image and narrative for the struggle needed to move beyond the past in order to forge new links with the future. The struggle is not to interiorize harmful memories, but to create just memories which move us toward a reconciliation with truth as imagined in mimetic acts of yearning for justice.[59] Anzaldua employs the image of a snake shedding its skin. She queries,

> Why does she have to go and try to make "sense" of it all? Every time she makes "sense" of something, she has to "cross over," kicking a hole out of the old boundaries of the self and slipping under or over, dragging the old skin along, stumbling over it. It hampers her movement in the new territory, dragging the ghost of the past within her.[60]

The difficulty of making narrative sense of one's life renders action and truth a process of remembering and moving with a just memory forward into a more ethically and epistemologically informed future. No straight or easy line of progress toward justice exists. In Anzaldua's words,

> It is only when she is on the other side and the shell cracks open and the lid from her eyes lifts that she sees things in a different perspective. It is only then that she makes the connections, formulates the insights. It is only then that her consciousness expands a tiny notch, another rattle appears on the rattlesnake's tail and the added growth slightly alters the sounds she makes.[61]

Struggling to articulate a third-person standpoint uncovers the role of our social and material positioning in achieving truth and justice. The struggle for a feminist standpoint constitutes a new shape for philosophy of religion.[62]

"Spirituality": An Empty Construct?

Feminist-standpoint epistemology shapes philosophy of religion around yearning as a cognitive act of a creative and just memory. *A Feminist Philosophy of Religion* urges an engagement in the struggle to transform philosophy of religion on behalf of those women's lives that have been excluded from Western accounts of theistic belief. It also urges an engagement in imaginative thinking by and with those who have risked forming relationships on the margins of patriarchal societies in order to be transformed.[63] Those philosophers of religion who engage in the struggle over perspectives on justice which have formed mutual promises and generated beliefs, norms, and customs, are made vulnerable to having their thinking and living transformed.[64] Yearning as a positive act motivates struggle in the search for personal and communal justice. It shapes a spirituality.

However, at least one theologian has objected to my "decontextualized" approach to engaged standpoints.[65] But this objection fails to take into account the nature of a feminist standpoint, especially in relation to one's own perspective. A perspective is not the same as a standpoint: the latter is a result of being engaged in a struggle to achieve – imagine or know – more than one's own perspective. At the same time, achieving a feminist standpoint never implies giving up one's perspective. In any case, one cannot simply give up one's perspective. Perhaps this tension reveals my indelible philosophical colors.

In focusing on ethics, knowledge, and self-conscious action, "we" might be caught up in a modern philosophical search for Enlightenment ideals. But, then, is the conception of spirituality which emerges in feminist discourse a mere philosophical construct empty of any theological content? It is my conviction that the ideals of freedom, good will, truth, and justice remain integral to any theological project. What makes these ideals "theological" and this search "postmodern" is the impact of the critiques of modern philosophy. Modern critiques have left philosophy with gaps which could be filled by a vital spirituality. In Donna Haraway's words,

> the hypertext metaphor . . . put[s] pressure on the sore spots in my soul that this figure inflames. . . . Communication and articulation disconnected from yearning toward possible worlds does not make enough sense. And explicit purposes – politics, rationality, ethics, or technics in a reductive sense – do not say much about the furnace that is personal and collective yearning for just barely possible worlds.[66]

> It does not matter much to the figure of the still gestating, feminist, antiracist, mutated modest witness whether freedom, justice, and knowledge are branded as modernist or not; that is not our issue. . . . Rather freedom, justice and knowledge are – in bell hooks's terms – about "yearning," not about putative Enlightenment foundations.[67]

> Without doubt, such yearning is rooted in a reconfigured unconscious, in mutated desire, in the practice of love, in the ecstatic hope for the corporeal and imaginary

materialization of the antiracist female subject of feminism, and all other possible subjects of feminism.[68]

Haraway's cyborg feminism exposes yearning's critical relation to freedom, justice, knowledge, desire, and the vision of female subjects. Positions rooted in love and yearning for a corporeal/imaginary materialization of new feminist subjects could appear modern. Yet with closer inspection it is clear that postmodern critiques of blindly privileged conceptions have profoundly changed how we think, live, and feel.

Yearning is pivotal in representing the postmodern change. As a cognitive act, a moral and political sensibility, and a regulative feeling, yearning creates a common meeting point between otherwise different positions.[69] For example, yearning provides a meeting point between my work and Grace Jantzen's *Becoming Divine*.[70] While Jantzen advocates beginning with natality, I seek to begin prior to this: "Where bodies embrace": "Both in and not in the same place: with the one being in the other who contains."[71] Luce Irigaray claims that male philosophers have forgotten their debt to their mothers, yet she does not privilege birth over the love between subjects. Instead, together, desire and reason make each new beginning a creative act. To become natals – and mortals – we must be created and creative in love. In Arendt's terms the web of relationships is crucial and more fundamental than natality, since I do not give birth to myself. The yearning to *know* such love renders possible not only our relationships and mutual promises, but our suffering in birth, in life, and at the death or loss of another.

Yearning constitutes a vital reality in human life, offering a resource for new expressions of the difference of memory for a postmodern age. Difference is expressible at the level of narratives where beliefs and convictions are enacted and so constitute the identity of a culture.[72] Enacted stories represent a pregnant present, while memory enables recalling acts of love and justice. An ethics of memory takes responsibility for the life stories of the other, through the exchange of narratives in imagination and empathy. An ethics of memory would not deny the reality of the past, the repression of female desire, and the eclipse of justice and reason. It would seek the interaction of desire and reason in narrative expressions of particular sorts of spiritual fulfillment. Although my feminist philosophy of religion does not advocate a particular theological perspective on yearning, or strictly speaking prescribe the spiritual content of yearning, feminist-standpoint epistemology offers the grounds for the retelling of life's stories.

Conclusion

I conclude my proposal for an ethics of memory with a viable attempt by bell hooks to make narrative sense of life. In writing her life, hooks reenacts an ethics of promising, forgiving, and yearning which moves toward a just memory. At the same time she presents an example of a spontaneous standpoint epistemology.[73] This epistemology enables feminist philosophers to recognize the material and social framing influence on the perspectives of each person and every group. A first-person account is not enough. So hooks's autobiographical writings voice standpoint arguments by narrating from both a first-person perspective – her own – and a third-person standpoint. Together, these points of view generate a transformation.

A Feminist Philosophy of Religion presents two imperatives from standpoint epistemology: (1) thinking from the lives of others; (2) reinventing ourselves as other. In hooks's narratives, (1) her third-person witness thinks from the first-person narratives; and (2) her yearning ends in the transformation of the two positions. The first-person perspective and the standpoint of the witness will ultimately be reinvented, merging into one. hooks expresses her desire to bring together the reality of her experiences as a black woman and of her witnessing to that experience as mediated by a writing life.[74] In her words,

> *Wounds of Passion: A Writing Life* links childhood obsessions with writing and the body to the early years of young adulthood wherein I strived to establish a writing voice. . . . I move back and forth between first person narrative and third person. I conceptualize the third person voice as that part of myself that is an observer – that bears witness. At times I also use the third person as an attempt to distance myself from the pain. The inclusion of the third person narrator who has both critical insight and an almost psychoanalytic power that enables critical reflection on events described is an act of mediation.[75]

The above passage shows the effort needed to make narrative sense of life. It is not simply a matter of telling a first-person story. It involves an act of mediation, in this case the invention of a writing life. hooks explains:

> In my girlhood imagination, embodiment was feared as it was linked to exploitation and oppression. Yet later in my young womanhood I wanted to learn ways to accept and embrace the female body, to discover its pleasures. The desire for sex, the longing to reconcile these desires with a yearning to know love, were all part of my struggle to become a writer, to invent a writing life that could nurture and sustain a liberated woman. Fully feminist, fully self-actualized, I wanted to care for the soul and to let my heart speak. . . . [But] to feel deeply we cannot avoid pain.[76]

In hooks we find the recognition that achieving a feminist standpoint involves a struggle motivated by a yearning to know love. But this struggle is not resolved in a private or individual suffering. The struggle leads to personal and social transformation only insofar as the response to the injustice of broken promises involves forgiving others and yearning for the transformation of life's narratives. As hooks concludes,

> I don't want to make the heartbreak church my home. . . . Even so suffering changes me.[77]

... Somewhere when we have come to the end of our journey, when we are no longer mourners at the heartbreak church, when we no longer feel that there is anything that stands between us and all that we have been seeking, our confession will be simply that there was never any witness. The story was written so that it could stand alone, two hands raised to glory, that the spirit may descend among us, one hand raised to glory, that the spirit has come – touched me and left my body whole.[78]

The above encapsulates the transformative possibilities in an ethics of memory. We need not each write our own autobiography as a form of consciousness-raising, but each of us needs to make narrative sense of life.

Postmodern theology should address the making and keeping of promises, the forgiveness of broken promises, and the discovery of enacted stories aiming at wholeness in relation to oneself and others in the past, present, and future. A spiritual aspiration for postmodernity would be that, for in one sense, oppositional differences will dissolve; while, in another sense, a plurality of perspectives will be preserved within our temporal and spatial world by a rational passion for a mournable justice. Justice is mournable insofar as we recognize that fallible men and women constantly fail to achieve the ideal of giving each other their due in physical and spiritual love. Yet this failure does not undermine the ethical focus of yearning or the framing influence of a transcendent but representable justice.

Notes

1 On the cognitive role of memory both for a narrative understanding of life and against antirealism, see John Campbell, *Past, Space and Self* (Cambridge, MA: MIT Press, 1995), pp. 1–4, 58–63, 69–71, 221–51.
2 Emmanuel Levinas, "La Trace," in *Humanisme de l'autre homme* (Montpellier: Fata Morgana, 1972), pp. 57–63; Levinas, *Otherwise than Being, or Beyond Essence*, trans. Alphonso Lingis (The Hague: Martinus Nijhoff, 1981); and Jacques Derrida, *Of Grammatology*, trans. Gayatri Chakravorty Spivak (Baltimore, MD: Johns Hopkins University Press, 1976), pp. 46–8, 61–3.
3 Paul Ricoeur, *Time and Narrative*, vol. 3, trans. Kathleen Blamey and David Pellauer (Chicago: University of Chicago Press, 1988), pp. 118–26.
4 Campbell, *Past, Space and Self*, pp. 69–71, 225–38, 244–6, 251.
5 Walter Benjamin, "The Storyteller," in *Illuminations*, with an introduction by Hannah Arendt (New York: Schocken Books, 1969), pp. 83–109.
6 Hannah Arendt, *The Human Condition*, 2nd. edn., with an introduction by Margaret Canovan (Chicago: University of Chicago Press, 1998), pp. 97, 184–8, 191–2, 198. Ricoeur, *Time and Narrative*, vol. 3, pp. 246–74; Ricoeur, "Life in Quest of Narrative" and "Narrative Identity," in David Wood (ed.), *On Paul Ricoeur: Narrative and Interpretation* (London: Routledge, 1991), pp. 20–33 and pp. 188–99, respectively; Ricoeur, *Oneself as Another*, trans. Kathleen Blamey (Chicago: University of Chicago Press, 1992), pp. 140–68.
7 For a fuller discussion of different approaches to myth, see Pamela Sue Anderson

"Myth and Feminist Philosophy," in Kevin Schilbrack (ed.), *Myth and Philosophy* (London: Routledge, 2001).

8   A. W. Moore, *Points of View* (Oxford: Clarendon Press, 1997), pp. 220–52. For discussion of the tension between creating and discovering, or "fabulation and actual experience," in making narrative sense of one's own life, see Ricoeur, *Oneself as Another*, pp. 159–63.

9   See Samuel Ijsseling, *Mimesis: On Appearing and Being*, trans. Hester Ijsseling and Jeffrey Bloechl (Kampen, the Netherlands: Kok Pharos, 1990).

10 Ricoeur, "Myth as the Bearer of Possible Worlds," in Richard Kearney (ed.), *Dialogues with Contemporary Continental Thinkers* (Manchester: Manchester University Press, 1984), pp. 36–46; Ricoeur, "Memory and Forgetting," in Richard Kearney and Mark Dooley (eds.), *Questioning Ethics: Contemporary Debates in Philosophy* (London: Routledge, 1999), pp. 5–11.

11 For reconceiving this space as "an imaginary domain" in which persons can recover and relocate themselves in relation to an abusive past of pain and oppression, see Drucilla Cornell, *At the Heart of Freedom: Feminism, Sex and Equality* (Princeton, NJ: Princeton University Press, 1998), pp. 8–11, 14–17, 174, 182–6.

12 Moore, *Points of View*, pp. 220–52; Campbell, *Past, Space and Self*, pp. 58, 63, 69–71, 187–93.

13 Ricoeur, *Time and Narrative*, pp. 244–9; *Oneself as Another*, pp. 116–25, 129, 135, 141ff.

14 For the abuse of so-called mutual acts of commitment, or "a pact," between "master" philosophers and their partners/students, see Michèle Le Doeuff, "Mastering a Woman: The Imaginary Foundation of a Certain Metaphysical Order," in Arleen B. Dallery and Stephen H. Watson with E. Marya Bower (eds.), *Transitions in Continental Philosophy* (New York: State University of New York Press, 1994), pp. 59–70.

15 For two sorts of social contract, one of which is based on mutual promises, see Hannah Arendt, *On Revolution* (Harmondsworth: Penguin Books, 1973), pp. 169–75; also see Paul Ricoeur, *The Just* trans. David Pellauer (Chicago: University of Chicago Press, 2000) pp. 7–10.

16 Ricoeur, "Memory and Forgetting," and Richard Kearney, "Narrative and the Ethics of Remembrance," in *Questioning Ethics*, pp. 5–11 and 18–32, respectively.

17 Robert Bernasconi, "Arendt," in Simon Critchley and William R. Schroeder (eds.), *A Companion to Continental Philosophy* (Oxford: Blackwell Publishers, 1998), pp. 478–83; Mary G. Dietz, "Feminist Receptions of Arendt," in Bonnie Honig (ed.), *Feminist Interpretations of Hannah Arendt* (University Park: Pennsylvania State University Press, 1995), pp. 17–50.

18 Seyla Benhabib, "Feminism and Postmodernism" and "Subjectivity, Historiography and Politics," in *Feminist Contentions: A Philosophical Exchange* (London: Routledge, 1995), pp. 17–34 and 107–26, respectively.

19 On traces of the face of the Other, see Pamela Sue Anderson, "Tracing Sexual Difference: Beyond the *Aporia* of the Other," *Sophia: The Journal for Philosophical Theology, Cross-cultural Philosophy of Religion and Ethics*, 38, 1 (March–April 1999), pp. 54–73.

20 Pamela Sue Anderson, "After Theology: End or Transformation?" *Literature and Theology*, vol. 7, no. 1 (March 1993), pp. 78–86.

21 On a "weak" instead of a "strong" reading of postmodern critiques, see Benhabib, "Feminism and Postmodernism," pp. 17–34.

22 Pamela Sue Anderson, *A Feminist Philosophy of Religion: The Rationality and Myths of Religious Belief* (Oxford: Blackwell Publishers, 1998).
23 On promising and forgiving, see Arendt, *The Human Condition*, pp. 238–43.
24 The subtitle of this book, which was published by Editions Autrement, is given in English translation in Ricoeur, "Reflections on A New Ethos for Europe," *Paul Ricoeur: The Hermeneutics of Action*, ed. Richard Kearney (London: Sage Publications, 1996), pp. 10–11; also see Ricoeur, *The Just*, p. 144.
25 bell hooks, *Wounds of Passion: A Writing Life* (New York: Henry Holt, 1997), p. v.
26 Gillian Rose, *Mourning Becomes the Law: Philosophy and Representation* (Cambridge: Cambridge University Press, 1997), pp. 14, 104. Also see Parita Mukta, "Lament and Power: The Subversion and Appropriation of Grief," *Studies in History*, 13, 2 (1997), pp. 209–46.
27 Mukta, "Lament and Power," p. 246.
28 Sandra Harding, *Is Science Multi-Cultural? Postcolonialism, Feminisms and Epistemologies* (Bloomington: Indiana University Press, 1998), pp. 148–54.
29 Arendt, *The Human Condition*, p. 181.
30 Ibid, p. 183.
31 Ibid, p. 184.
32 Ibid; cf. Ricoeur, *Time and Narrative*, vol. 3, pp. 246–9.
33 Arendt, *The Human Condition*, p. 187.
34 Ibid, pp. 236–7.
35 Ibid, p. 237.
36 Ibid, pp. 244–5.
37 Ricoeur, *Oneself as Another*, pp. 118–25.
38 This sort of social contract can be distinguished from the sort in which consent is given to a ruler or government and so lacks the reciprocity of promising; see Arendt, *On Revolution*, pp. 170–5.
39 For a critical reading of Ricoeur's Kantianism, see Pamela Sue Anderson, "Reclaiming Autonomy: Unity, Plurality and Totality," in *The Moral Capacity: Paul Ricoeur and Contemporary Moral Thought*, edited by William Schweiker, David Hall and John Wall (New York: Routledge, 2002).
40 Ricoeur, *Oneself as Another*, pp. 154–5.
41 Ibid, p. 266.
42 A. W. Moore, "A Kantian View of Moral Luck," *Philosophy*, 65 (1990), pp. 297–321; Ricoeur, *Oneself as Another*, p. 267; Ricoeur, "Self as Ipse," in Barbara Johnson (ed.), *Freedom and Interpretation: Oxford Amnesty Lectures 1992* (New York: Basic Books, 1993), pp. 118–19.
43 Immanuel Kant, *Critique of Judgment*, trans with analytical indexes by James Creed Meredith (Oxford: Clarendon Press, 1952), pp. 150–4, 295–6; *Critique of Practical Reason*, trans. and ed. Mary Gregor, introduction by Andrews Reath (Cambridge: Cambridge University Press, 1997), pp. 3, 12–13, 37–44; *Critique of Pure Reason*, trans. and ed. Paul Guyer and Allen W. Wood (Cambridge: Cambridge University Press, 1997), pp. 268–70, 486–8.
44 Hannah Arendt, *The Life of the Mind* (New York/London: Harcourt Brace, 1978), pp. 3–6, 111; Arendt, *Eichmann in Jerusalem: A Report on the Banality of Evil*, revd. edn. (Harmondsworth: Penguin Books, 1992); cf. Richard Bernstein, "Judging – The Actor and The Spectator," in his *Philosophical Profiles* (Cambridge: Polity Press, 1986), pp. 221–38; Seyla Benhabib, "Judgment in Kant's Moral Philosophy and

Arendt's Reappropriation," in *The Reluctant Modernism of Hannah Arendt* (London: Sage Publications, 1996), pp. 185–93.
45 Paul Ricoeur, *Le Volontaire et l'involontaire* (Paris: Aubier, 1950).
46 Paul Ricoeur, *"Préface," Condition de l'homme moderne*, trans. George Fradier (Paris: Calamann-Lévy, 1983), pp. 1–32.
47 Paul Ricoeur, *Critique and Conviction*, trans. Kathleen Blamey (Cambridge: Polity Press, 1998), pp. 93–4, 157–9; cf. Ricoeur, *Oneself as Another*, pp. 147, 158–63.
48 Ricoeur, *Critique and Conviction*, pp. 93–4.
49 Ricoeur, "Reflections on A New Ethos for Europe," pp. 7–9.
50 Ibid, p. 6.
51 Ibid, p. 7.
52 Hannah Arendt, *Lectures on Kant's Political Philosophy*, ed. with an interpretative essay by Ronald Beiner (Chicago: University of Chicago Press, 1982), pp. 37–44. Cf. Kant, *Critique of Judgment*, section 40, pp. 152–4.
53 Mukta, "Lament and Power," pp. 227, 230; cf. Parita Mukta, *Upholding the Common Life: The Community of Mirabai* (New Delhi: Oxford University Press, 1994), p. 223.
54 Julia Kristeva, *Black Sun: Depression and Melancholia*, trans. Leon S. Roudiez (New York: Columbia University Press, 1989), pp. 3–11, 189–90, 194, 199, 206–7.
55 Ricoeur, "Memory and Forgetting," pp. 7–11.
56 Kristeva, *Black Sun*, pp. 189–90.
57 Rose, *Mourning Becomes the Law*, pp. 25–6.
58 Ibid, pp. 35–6, also p. 104.
59 Gloria Anzaldua, *Borderlands/La Frontera* (San Francisco: Spinsters/Aunt Lute, 1987), p. 49.
60 Ibid, p. 49.
61 Ibid.
62 Pamela Sue Anderson, "'Standpoint': Its Rightful Place in a Realist Epistemology," *Journal of Philosophical Research* XXVI (2001), pp. 131–53.
63 On the empowering strands of bhakti, see Mukta, *Upholding the Common Life*, pp. 69–169.
64 bell hooks, *Yearning: Race, Gender and Cultural Politics* (Boston, MA: South End Press, 1990), especially pp. 12–13. For her own yearning to become a fully autonomous woman in "a writing life," see bell hooks, *Wounds of Passion*.
65 Tina Beattie, "Discussion Point: Pamela Sue Anderson's *A Feminist Philosophy of Religion*," in *Women's Philosophy Review*, vol. 21 (Summer 1999), pp. 103–10. For another perspective on spirituality, see Patricia Hill Collins, *Fighting Words: Black Feminist Thought and the Search for Justice* (Minneapolis, MN: University of Minnesota Press, 1998), pp. 243–4.
66 Donna Haraway, *Modest_Witness@Second_Millennium: FemaleMan_Meets_OncoMouse* (London: Routledge, 1997), p. 127.
67 Ibid, p. 128.
68 Ibid, pp. 191–2.
69 Kathleen O'Grady, "Where Bodies Embrace: Pamela Sue Anderson's *A Feminist Philosophy of Religion*," review essay, *Feminist Theology*, 20 (1999), pp. 108–9.
70 Grace Jantzen, *Becoming Divine: Towards A Feminist Philosophy of Religion* (Manchester: Manchester University Press, 1998), p. 236.
71 Anderson, *A Feminist Philosophy of Religion*, p. ii; cf. Luce Irigaray, *An Ethics of Sexual Difference*, trans. Carolyn Burke and Gillian C. Gill (London: Athlone Press, 1993), pp. 34–5, 54–5, also p. 190.

72 Ricoeur, "Reflections on A New Ethos for Europe," p. 6.
73 Harding, *Is Science Multi-Cultural?* pp. 75–6, 149–50ff. On bell hooks, see Nancy Hartsock, "Feminist Standpoint Revisited," in her *Feminist Standpoint Revisited and Other Essays* (Boulder, CO: Westview Press, 1998), pp. 229, 237.
74 See Lorraine Code, "Incredulity, Experientialism and the Politics of Knowledge," in her *Rhetorical Spaces: Essays on Gendered Locations* (London: Routledge, 1995), pp. 58–82.
75 hooks, *Wounds of Passion*, p. xxii.
76 Ibid, p. xxiii.
77 Compare Ricoeur on suffering and acting, *Oneself As Another*, pp. 190–2.
78 hooks, *Wounds of Passion*, pp. 259–60.

CHAPTER 14

Is Macrina a Woman? Gregory of Nyssa's *Dialogue on the Soul and Resurrection*

Virginia Burrus

There is a geography of postmodernism (and postmodernity) which, as far as I am aware, has not yet been mapped. Certain cities have been designated production sites for postmodernism (Las Vegas and Los Angeles most particularly, through the work of Mike Davis and Edward Soja). But because postmodernism has been almost integrated into globalism, it is assumed (like modernism) to be an international culture. Its internationalism may be manifesting itself now, but postmodernism has a history of development and certain parts of the world were more significant in that development than others. France (particularly the avant-garde of Paris), California, and the younger universities of Britain are three such locations.

Virginia Burrus's work could be set alongside Daniel Boyarin's. Berkeley, California, has a tradition going back to the 1970s of encouraging new approaches to established disciplines through contemporary critical theory. Not only were Certeau and Foucault visiting professors there, but the Irvine Institute provides a forum for the gathering of many of the critical voices of the late twentieth century. So, while Stephen Greenblatt and Joel Fineman were pushing English studies in the direction of New Historicism, and Daniel Boyarin was taking an interdisciplinary approach to Jewish studies, Virginia Burrus was learning much from feminist reexaminations of early patristic texts (by Elizabeth Clark) and applying what she found to forms of late Hellenistic writing. Her first book, developed from her Master's thesis, was *Chastity as Autonomy: Women in the Stories of Apocryphal Acts* (Lewiston, NY, 1987). Here, feminist and literary studies (structuralist analyses of folktales) foster the development of a method in which stories can be given a "thick" (in the Geertzian sense) historical interpretation. The stories chosen are found in various Greek apocryphal texts of late antiquity and they are each told by women. Burrus attempts to uncover the social and psychological factors which characterize these women's experiences (there are links here with the

> early work of Mieke Bal). Each of the texts used is a Christian one: the texts of the early Christian church have been the main focus of Burrus's research. Her second book developed out of her doctoral thesis: *The Making of a Heretic: Gender, Authority, and the Priscillianist Controversy* (Berkeley, CA, 1995) evidences Burrus's concern with cultural politics and her deeper appreciation of gender studies, but the focus of the research is the same: the Christian woman's story. It is interesting that gender studies – more than feminist studies – have increasingly become important in Burrus's work; that is, the study of the construction of the feminine is viewed as inseparable from the construction of the masculine. In a sense this development is not surprising, since the women's stories Burrus analyses are recorded by male voices. This problematic is raised in the following essay: the speaking of woman through the masculine mouth (here in the writing of Gregory of Nyssa). Burrus's third volume is *Begotten, Not Made: Conceiving Manhood in Late Antiquity* (Stanford, CA, 2000) – the turn of attention towards masculinity is not surprising given the previous direction of Burrus's work.

For scholars of ancient Christianity, there is a notorious problem with "sources." The few woman-authored texts surviving from Christian antiquity can be bundled into a slim volume of translations, with room to spare for introductions and notes; and when such a volume is entitled *A Lost Tradition*,[1] the contents, far from adding up to a plump "rediscovery," stand rather as a gaunt reminder of a persisting lack. In the case of the relative plenitude of references to women in works authored by men, if the sense of "loss" is less extreme, the interpretive task remains daunting, since the problem of authorial perspective is accentuated by the fact that "woman" is so frequently a sign for something else: the challenge is not only to distinguish prescriptive language from descriptive, for example, but also to assess the reliability of references to women *qua* women where their dominant rhetorical function may be to serve, in a variety of ways, as tokens of exchange in the negotiation of power relations among men, relations often strongly marked by the politics of class, ethnicity, or religious identity.[2]

Underlying the problem of "sources" and their interpretation is a theoretical conundrum having to do with the status of female subjectivity itself. Even historians – typically leery of "universalizing" frameworks of interpretation – have felt the influence of a feminist school of thought strongly informed by psychoanalytic and linguistic theory that suggests that the discursive habits that pervade Western cultural practices, together with the psychic formations to which they give rise, may allow only for the production of a "subject" always marked as "masculine," not least through its constructed relation to a feminized "object" – regardless of the sex or gender of a text's author. "Discourse," it is implied, may prove the most stubborn mediator of the constraints of patriarchy, even in the face of partial successes (both historical and contemporary) in shifting the ordering of kinship and political relations. The opening lines of Luce

Irigaray's now classic essay in her *Speculum of the Other Woman* make the point quite sharply:

> We can assume that any theory of the subject has always been appropriated by the "masculine." When she submits to (such a) theory, woman fails to realize that she is renouncing the specificity of her own relationship to the imaginary. Subjecting herself to objectivization in discourse – by being "female." Reobjectivizing her own self whenever she claims to identify herself "as" a masculine subject.[3]

From this perspective the interpretive challenges and possibilities facing a "feminist" reader are multiplied. On the one hand, the category of "woman" – dislodged from its foundations in biology – is understood as a fictive construction, the byproduct of a discourse's investment in the production of the (equally fictive) category of "man," so that the "object" of study for "women's history" ("women") is stabilized only through its relation to a "subject" (the "historian") seemingly necessarily marked as "masculine." On the other hand, "woman" as "other" is construed not only as articulable "object" in relation to a masculine "subject" (so that there is always only one sex, the male), but also as that which is excluded from discourse's symbolic order altogether, the exclusion of which is indeed the condition for the foundation of that order, according to Irigaray's analysis. This second point is crucial, for it is in the interplay between woman as "object" and woman as what is excluded by or excessive in relation to discourse itself that Irigaray locates the possible emergence of a female subjectivity "that is not one," i.e., that is neither the inevitably objectified reflection of the (masculine) "one" nor an attempted singular displacement of the male subject (always doomed to fail) – that neither renounces voice nor is entirely subjected to discourse's objectifying symbolic order, that speaks and yet speaks "otherwise." As Irigaray puts it in *This Sex Which Is Not One*,

> One must assume the feminine role deliberately: which means already to convert a form of subordination into an affirmation, and thus to begin to thwart it.... To play with mimesis is thus, for a woman, to try to recover the place of her exploitation by discourse, without allowing herself to be simply reduced to it. It means to resubmit herself – inasmuch as she is on the side of the "perceptible," of "matter" – to "ideas," in particular to ideas about herself, that are elaborated in/by a masculine logic, but so as to make "visible," by an effect of playful repetition, what was supposed to remain invisible: the cover-up of a possible operation of the feminine in language. It is also to "unveil" the fact that, if women are such good mimics, it is because they are not simply reabsorbed in this function. They also remain elsewhere.[4]

At this point, one aspect of the project of "women's history" might be conceived as the development of a set of interpretive practices that could produce the historian as "woman" by locating those subversive positionalities historically discursively available to female subjects. That is to say, a third sexed position – neither the "masculine subject" nor his mirrored "feminine object" – may be produced through a mimetic process in which to "read" a woman in the text is also to "become" a woman historian. This is the possibility that I would like to explore in this essay, via a reading of a particular late fourth-century text. It would be naive to deny that the stakes are high at a moment in the evolution of academic feminism in which a paralyzing polarization between poststructuralist theorists and those who insist on the importance of retaining some version of a stable (i.e., in the words of their detractors, "essentialist") category of sex and/or gender appears a constant threat. It is thus perhaps all the more important to renounce the temptation of doctrinaire proclamations and hold open a space for ambiguity and experimentation.

The text that here concerns me is Gregory of Nyssa's dialogue *On the Soul and the Resurrection*, which presents a conversation between Gregory and his sister Macrina. Crucial to my reading of the text is the recognition that its portrayal of Macrina owes much to allusions to the Diotima figure of Plato's *Symposium*. Gregory's dialogue was not the first Christian take-off on Plato's *Symposium*: Methodius of Olympus had already produced a heavily allegorical revision that recast the original all-male drinking party held in Eros's honor – where the prophetess Diotima was present only *in absentia* – as a female gathering at which the famous virgin Thecla delivered the winning speech in honor of virginity. By scripting his own dialogue on desire as a private conversation between himself and his dying sister Macrina (whose "secret name" was Thecla, as he tells us elsewhere), Gregory distinguishes his work not least by transgressing the homosocial worlds of gender kept intact by both Plato and Methodius. He dares to represent a direct and indeed purportedly "historical" exchange between a man and a woman on the topic of love. Or does he? Arnaldo Momigliano remarks that "Macrina is here Socrates to her brother."[5] Making the Macrina of Gregory's dialogue male, he seems to anticipate David Halperin's cue to hear in Diotima's speech mere "Sokratic ventriloquism,"[6] so that Macrina as Diotima is really Socrates in drag – a "woman" but not a woman, as Elizabeth Clark suggests, following Halperin's lead.[7] Of course, Momigliano only *seems* to anticipate such a reading, for his remark in its context constitutes a fairly straightforward reference to the strong and frequently noted allusions in Gregory's text to Socrates' death-bed discourse in the *Phaedo*;[8] nevertheless, such a suppression of the *Symposium*'s influence may amount to much the same thing as Halperin's spookily mimetic encrypting of the woman within "scare quotes": Diotima is a "woman," but not a woman. If, as Catharine Roth acknowledges, Gregory's dialogue exhibits "not only many parallels with Plato's *Phaedo*" but "also a relationship with Plato's *Symposium*, where Socrates becomes the not-so-apt pupil of the wise woman teacher Diotima,"[9] why has this relationship so rarely been commented on?[10] And if we choose to comment now, what might we make of Gregory's choice not only to write like Plato but also to write like a woman, explicitly performing his own multi-gendered polyphony by employing a literary format that calls attention to the fact that he is creating his own role and also that he is creating "hers," that both voices are his own and also that neither is simply and singularly proper to him?

The dramatic occasion for the conversation between Gregory and Macrina is Gregory's overweening grief at Basil's death. Gregory explicitly casts Macrina as "the Teacher" (ἡ διδάσκαλος), whose task is to school her overwrought brother in the proper management of his passion. Although she initially gives way to Gregory's grief ("like a skilled horseman," as he puts it), Macrina moves subsequently to curb the galloping excesses of his sorrow (anim.et res.12A).[11] She addresses her younger brother from the privileged vantage-point of her own death-bed, in a gently chiding and distinctly maternal tone. ("Those who look on a death-bed can hardly bear the sight!" he protests (anim.et res.13A).) Having hoped for a soothing sibling empathy, as he represents it, Gregory instead encounters in his sister both fresh cause for mourning – Macrina's unexpected illness – and a stern exhortation to pull himself together. Her loving admonitions are framed within a discourse on the passions, in which grief is subsumed within the Platonic duo of anger (θυμός) and desire (ἐπιθυμία): of the other passions, "each of them seems akin to the principle of desire or to that of anger," as she remarks (anim.et res.56B).

Already it becomes evident that the links between Gregory's dialogue and the Platonic corpus are multiple and complicatedly intertwined: as Rowan Williams has suggested, the *Phaedrus*'s metaphor of the soul's charioteer (λόγος) and his yoked horses (θυμός and ἐπιθυμία) may be almost as important to the allusive construction of this text as the *Phaedo* or the *Symposium*. The figure of the chariot is initially introduced by Gregory in the narrator's voice, with Macrina in the driver's seat and Gregory on the side of the horses. Subsequently Macrina herself explicitly rejects the Platonic passage in favor of a scriptural guide (anim.et res.49C); yet still later it apparently offers her just the resolution she seeks to her psychological dilemma (anim.et res.61B–C). The charioteer and his bestial team thus haunt the text with ambivalence.[12] Williams suggests that "the *Phaedrus* analogy is evoked at this early stage to pre-empt any undialectical reading of Macrina's apparent critique of the passions wholesale." We are to understand that throughout the dialogue Macrina will both give rein to Gregory's passions and – allowing him to be carried by their horsepower – eventually lead him where she wants him to go; through a similar pattern of give and take, the Teacher will also draw the acute reader along the path of psychological insight and health. Williams notes further, "The dialogue form not only enacts what it discusses (the protracted exploration of an emotion) but, later on, allows Macrina to modify her initial rigorism in response to Gregory's objections in behalf of emotions."[13] If, however, as Warren Smith argues, Gregory's initial analogy refers either to the "breaking" of a young horse not yet used to the bit and bridle or to the similar technique of allowing an excited horse to run until it has exhausted itself, Williams's conflation of this analogy with the later invocation of the Platonic chariot may falsely confuse "the relationship between Macrina's initial indulgence of Gregory's sorrow and her pedagogical method."[14] Whether Macrina is merely taming or also already instructing her brother in the opening lines of the dialogue, the roles seem clear enough: "Gregory" oveflows with the passion of his grief in the face of life's transience, while the maternalized virgin – his sister, a "woman" – is left high and dry(-eyed). But if it appears easy to identify the roles, where, or who, is the *author* of the text? Does he simply identify with Macrina, as the stern discipliner of passion's horses? Is he instead more ambiguously allied with the younger brother's cautious support for the value of a little emotional laxity? Or does he not rather locate himself elsewhere, beyond even compromise or synthesis, as both "Macrina" and "Gregory," driver and horse, and also neither, also *more*? If so, how did he get there? How does he come to have it all, and what is finally left over for the woman?

One of the central questions to be pursued in the course of the dialogue is, as Macrina formulates it, "what we are to think of the principle of desire and the principle of anger within us." Are desire and anger "consubstantial with the soul, inherent in the soul's very self," or not? (anim.et res.49B). Macrina's initial answer is that they are not, and this is the context for her rejection of "the Platonic chariot and the pair of horses of dissimilar forces yoked to it, and their driver, whereby the philosopher allegorizes these facts about the soul" (anim.et res.49B–52A). The passions are "only like warts growing out of the soul's thinking part, which are reckoned as parts of it because they adhere to it, and yet are not that actual thing which the soul is in its essence" (anim.et res.56C). "Accretions from without," they nevertheless lie close "on the border-land" of the soul (anim.et res.57C), representing the effects or "touch" of "the other things which are knit up with" the soul in its divine creation (anim.et res.61A). Acknowledging the "deep-rootedness" of the passions in created human nature (anim.et res.61A), Macrina absolves the Creator from any authorship of evil (or even "warts") by returning to the metaphor of the charioteer, this time in a positive vein. The emotions of the soul, divinely implanted, can "become the instruments of virtue or of vice," according to her now partly revised account; when properly governed by reason's driver, anger generates fortitude, and "the instinct of desire will procure for us the delight that is Divine and perfect" (anim.et res.61B). Rejecting the "dissimilarity" built into a tripartite model of a composite soul that appears to grant each part too much independence, Macrina nevertheless seems to concede that a unitive psychological theory might after all be effectively propelled by the figure of a skillfully guided chariot.[15]

The faultlines of incipient contradiction running through Macrina's position offer Gregory the opportunity to pose a question and Macrina the occasion to clarify. In the process, attention is shifted from the original constitution of the soul's "nature" to its final purpose. Is the *telos* of human perfection the proper direction of the emotions or their eventual eradication? (anim.et res.88C–89A). The latter, Macrina answers swiftly, seeming at first to return to an affirmation of the externality of passion in relation to the nature of a soul defined exclusively by its rationality. The soul purified of vice will ultimately transcend "the need of the impulse of desire to lead the way to the beautiful," she states. Anger now drops out of the discussion and the focus remains solely on desire. "Whoever passes his time in darkness, he it is who will be under the influence of a desire for the light; but whenever he comes into that light, then enjoyment (ἀπόλαυσις) takes the place of desire, and the power to enjoy renders desire useless and out of date" (anim.et res.89C). "Desire" (ἐπιθυμία) will be reconfigured as "love" (ἀγάπη), as the yearning for that which is lacking gives way to the enjoyment of that which has been found. Indeed all other movements of the soul will cease except the movement of love. She adds that "love alone finds no limit" (anim.et res.96A). "When the thing hoped for actually comes, then all other faculties are reduced to quiescence, and love alone remains active, finding nothing to succeed itself" (anim.et res.96B). Passion, we should note, is in Macrina's account not eradicated but transformed: the horse is not so much "tamed," nor even "trained" by means of bit and bridle, as given its own head, when logos and love melt into one.

At this point, it becomes clear that Gregory is citing not just the role but also the words of Diotima in his Macrinan dialogue.[16] Diotima's speech in the *Symposium* offers a startling depiction of Eros as a "needy" god, standing on the borderlands of poverty and resourcefulness, ignorance and wisdom, embodying the productive longing for the beautiful that he himself lacks (symp.203C–E). Love for the beautiful, she clarifies, is not so much "for the beautiful itself, but for the conception and generation that the beautiful effects" (τῆς γεννήσεως καὶ τοῦ τόκου ἐν τῷ καλῷ). "Those whose procreancy is of the spirit [ψυχή] rather than of the flesh – and they are not unknown, Socrates," she confides, "conceive and bear the things of the spirit," thereby winning a kind of immortality (symp.206E–209A). Diotima closes with a famous description of the "heavenly ladder." The soul ascends this "ladder" rung by rung, "starting from individual beauties" and moving from there to "*every* lovely body," thence to the "beauty of institutions, from institutions to learning, and from learning in general to the special lore that pertains to nothing but the beautiful itself – until at last he comes to know what beauty is." Through the drive of eros (in the guise of an awareness of lack), the ever-conceiving soul moves up toward the ultimate *telos* of desire, which is represented as "an everlasting loveliness which neither comes nor goes, which neither flowers nor fades, for such beauty is the same on every hand, the same then as now, here as there, this way as that way, the same to every worshiper as it is to every other" (symp.210E–211C).

In the setting of the *Symposium* this speech is reported by Socrates, who introduces it by informing his audience:

> I want to talk about some lessons I was given, once upon a time, by a Mantinean woman called Diotima – a woman who was deeply versed in this and many other fields of knowledge. It was she who brought about a ten years' postponement of the great plague of Athens on the occasion of a certain sacrifice, and it was she who taught me the philosophy of Love [τὰ ἐρωτικὰ].... And I think the easiest way will be to adopt Diotima's own method of inquiry by question and answer. (symp.201D–E)

Gregory seems to find this "the easiest way" as well. His own dialogue is not so much a rescripting of the *Symposium* itself as a rescripting – in question and answer format – of the prior, off-stage conversation between Diotima and

Socrates. In Plato's dialogue Socrates reports this conversation to a gathering of somewhat dubious fellow philosophers; in Gregory's dialogue the readers themselves are the guests at the party at which Gregory relates his exchange with Macrina, transmitting what she taught him of the philosophy of Love.

Halperin argues that the Diotima of Plato's *Symposium* is the site for the articulation of a specular femininity that is finally reabsorbed by the male subject, who is himself thereby transformed. Plato, he suggests, is engaged in a radical contestation and reinscription of classical pederastic love that strategically borrows from two culturally available (and also contradictory) conceptualizations of women as desiring subjects: first, women as excessively responsive to the tug of sexual desire; and, second, women as drawn solely to procreate. By introducing these representations of female desire through the figure of Diotima, Plato is able to construct a new theory of male erotics that, according to Halperin, thematizes mutual or reciprocal relations between men as the site of the production of sublimated procreative potentialities within a homosocial community. In the end, then, the absent figure of Diotima functions to erase the "feminine" via male appropriation, a strategy furthered by Plato's subtle hints that "she" is a fictive construction from the start, a mask for a Socratic performance of "mimetic transvestitism."[17]

As Clark notes, this interpretation of Diotima "provides sobering food for thought" for historians who have wanted to mine not only Plato's but also Gregory's dialogue for social historical data on gender roles and relations.[18] Before sobering up entirely, however, I would like to return briefly to the raucous scene of Plato's dialogue, not so as to quibble with the charge of appropriationism (or even fictionalism), but rather to complicate our sense of its dynamics and structure. In so doing I intend to take up what seems practically an invitation from Halperin himself to tug at some of the all-too-tightly woven threads of his text, in which, as he puts it, his own "interpretive practice . . . by erasing female presence from the terms of its discourse . . . reproduces and exemplifies the very strategies of appropriation – characteristic of male culture – that it purports to illumine and criticize."[19] One place to begin to challenge those "strategies of appropriation" is perhaps by asking, with Irigaray, how complete is the success of the exclusion of the "female" on which Halperin argues this textual inscription of masculine subjectivity is founded? The Platonic dialogue itself opens up ample space for raising the question, as it seems to me.

I might first note briefly that, however much Plato does disrupt our confidence in Diotima's "reality," this disruption takes place in the context of a broader set of strategies that call into question the reliability of the account of the symposium as a whole. In the opening pages of the dialogue, we learn that one Aristodemus, an eye-witness to the events, had told Phoenix, who in turn had told "a man," who subsequently told Glaucon "something sketchy" about the event and also referred him to Apollodorus, who, upon Glaucon's questioning him, revealed that he himself had the story only second-hand and from Aristodemus as well, for it had taken place while he, like Glaucon, was still "in the nursery." Apollodorus, having recently reconstructed the story (indeed, having it now "pretty pat," as he puts it), agrees to relate it to another friend, "in Aristodemus's own words," as he claims (implausibly enough by this point!). It is this second, now "pat," retelling on which Plato's reader is invited to eavesdrop. Aristodemus, the only tenuous and now-distant link to the events, was, we learn quickly, both an uninvited guest at the symposium and a self-proclaimed "ignoramus." He is, moreover, as absent from the dialogue itself as Diotima is from the original party. And, finally, his reported speech, in which the whole account of the symposium is embedded, frequently calls its own reliability into question. What more warning do we need that all of the speeches are "made up," that all of the figures are "masks?" And does this not somewhat compromise the contrast between the "fictiveness" of Diotima and the relative solidity of the positioning of the male speakers suggested by Halperin and used by him to confirm the point that this text inscribes only a male subjectivity?

But still more significant, for my purposes, is what is perhaps overlooked by Halperin about the complex ways in which the text itself configures female gender. One of the first decisive actions taken by the group of assembled men on the legendary evening of the symposium on love was, we are told, the agreement not to become excessively drunk and to "dispense with the services of the flute girl" who had just come in; "let her go and play to herself or to the women inside there, whichever she prefers, while we spend our evening in discussion," the host proclaims (symp.176E). The excluded flute girl ($αὐλητρίς$) thus stands in rather explicitly for that which is excessive in relation to the form of rational discourse to be fostered on this occasion; and yet her banishment from the symposium still seems to locate her, along with "the women" more generally, in the inner courtyard ($αὐλή$) of the men's talk. Nor does she remain safely roped off from the party. For just as Socrates finishes delivering his own suspiciously cross-dressed Diotima speech, the flute girl herself intrudes again, accompanying a drunken and ribbon-bedecked Alcibiades (symp.212D). Alcibiades crowns Socrates with his ribbons, calls for more wine, and proposes that it is Socrates himself, so lately self-presented in verbal drag as Diotima and now dripping with ribbons, who is to be configured as Eros, whose eulogy (offered by Alcibiades) will finally displace and thereby reinterpret the previous eulogies of Love. It is, however, no simple or sober text, warns Alcibiades – the eulogy of Socrates whose satyric pipings and Bacchic performances incite others with "this philosophical frenzy, this sacred rage," while he himself "spends his whole life playing a little game of irony, and laughing up his sleeve at all the world." As Alcibiades reinscribes Socrates as a Dionysiac text of Love, the party dissolves into a drunken revel (symp.212E–223D). The flute girl is back; indeed perhaps she never really quite left. And the Platonic dialogue seems to construct her as a catachrestic figure for those excesses on whose imperfect exclusion the masculine symbolic order is founded. Transgressively identified with Socrates through the mediation of Alicibiades, the flute girl also puts into question the extent to which the figure of Diotoma is controlled by the terms of the specular economy of a male subjectivity. Has the masculine subject simply absorbed the feminine element, or does she also partly displace *him*, disrupting his singularity by miming her role as "object" excessively, even parodically, while she "also remain[s] elsewhere?"[20] Insofar as she practices a "different" dialectic, Diotima introduces an "other" love, suggests Irigaray: "its fecundity is *mediumlike, daimonic*, the guarantee for all, male and female, of the immortal becoming of the living." "Love's aim is to realize the immortal in the mortal between lovers."[21]

Returning to Gregory's dialogue, we can now ask: Why is *Macrina* a "woman?" She is a "woman" in part for reasons similar to those diagnosed by Halperin in the case of Diotima's "womanhood." Gregory is indeed repeating, and also exaggerating, the gestures of Plato's own sublimated restructuring of pederastic love. A "dry" female virgin embodies most eloquently, for the gushy son, the elusive goal of a radically transcendentalized erotic desire, while the maternalized body serves as a particularly fertile site for the forced conflation of erotic and procreative urges, effectively "sealed" by one thin (and resonant) membrane. Macrina is a "woman," then, because she both is and is not a wife and also because she both is and is not a mother. In the dialogue her positioning as a virginal lover and a spiritual mother is subtle but pervasive. Gregory's biography of his sister is more explicit. We learn from the *Life of Macrina* that the beautiful girl, much sought after as a bride, was widowed before consummating her marriage and was thus (on her own interpretation) both wife and virgin (v.Macr.4–5); dying, she becomes the virginal bride of Christ himself (v.Macr.22).[22] The *Life* also identifies Macrina closely with her own (and Gregory's) mother Emmelia, to whom she chose to be effectively wed – as if she had never left the womb, as Emmelia is said to have described the bond (v.Macr.5). Although her daughter's ascetic achievements are foreseen by Emmelia, who grants her the "secret name" of Thecla during childbirth (v.Macr.2), Macrina is later presented, in a reversal of roles, as mother to her own mother, Emmelia's "guide toward the philosophical and unworldly way of life" – an "existence [that] bordered on both the human and the incorporeal nature," as Gregory puts it (v.Macr.11). With unwavering firmness she sees her mother through the death of a favored son – Naucratius – and takes over for her in the nurturance and education of another – Peter (v.Macr.10, 12). Following the deaths of Emmelia and Basil, Macrina "remained like an undefeated athlete" (v.Macr.14).

Macrina then – not unlike Diotima – is the reflection of a masculine erotics, initially displaced or masked via its feminized representation, that is marked by both a sublimated and maternalized fecundity and a radical transcendentalization of erotic passion via its transformation into an agapic love. To adapt (and appropriate) Halperin's words: Macrina is a woman because Gregory's philosophy must borrow her femininity in order to seem to leave nothing out and thereby to ensure the success of its own procreative enterprises, the continual reproduction of its universalizing discourse in the male culture of late ancient orthodox Christianity.[23]

What are we to do, however, with the fact that Gregory's text, unlike Plato's, rather than artfully undermining its own truth claims, seems to assert its "historicity" and to emphasize its reliability as an eye-witness report? Is the historian not, in this case, rightly tempted to search for traces in the dialogue of the "real Macrina?" Without downplaying Gregory's literary artfulness in the least, I think the temptation of an attempted retrieval of a "historical Macrina" is worth yielding to, momentarily and strategically. By presenting itself as "history," and by inviting an intertextual reading in relation to other works that likewise seem to offer social historical "data," Gregory's dialogue provides an opportunity to raise questions that might subsequently be turned back on Plato's less "historical" text as well.

We can, for example, reconstruct something of Gregory's and Macrina's family profile and history. Macrina was significantly older than Gregory and seems from an early point to have taken over from her mother many of the responsibilities for the management of their household, which she reestablished as an ascetic community. It is quite likely that Gregory experienced Macrina rather literally as a "maternal" figure and furthermore as one senior and authoritative in the ascetic life subsequently embraced by several of her brothers, but perhaps uniquely configured by Gregory as constituting a familial "heritage" mediated by older women (his brother Basil, by contrast, is curiously silent on the topic of his sister). Thus, although a certain version of "discourse analysis" might invite us to see Gregory's representation of Macrina in the dialogue as the product of a set of social practices that consolidated an all-male community, easily conflatable with a set of linguistic practices that produce only a masculine subjectivity, we might also read this text as configuring relations, perhaps even partly "referring to" actual social formations, that are *not* completely successful in their exclusion of female presence and voice. What I am getting at is the possibility that the discursive space occupied earlier by Plato's Diotima and flute girl, or here by Gregory's Macrina, might also correlate, however inexactly, with the social roles and influence of women: that the textual production of an articulable feminine positionality via the interaction of the female as "object" and the female as the excluded transgressive, may at least indirectly point toward actual subject positions and social roles available to and occupiable by women historically "as women." The representations of women in male-centered texts may stand in for, without exactly reproducing, the intrusive presence of women in the always incomplete formation of male homosocial communities. And at this point I would ask – without here attempting to answer – whether Halperin has not only overestimated the success of textual exclusions of "the female" but also compounded this problematic aspect of his reading by too quickly conflating discursive and social practices of exclusion.

At the same time that I would want to turn such questions back on Plato's text (on the basis of similarities between it and Gregory's dialogue), I would also want to note differences in the roles and voices available to women in these two distinct historical settings. The position of the cultured courtesan depicted in many classical Greek texts, and perhaps approximated in the interaction of the figures of Diotima and the flute girl in Plato's *Symposium*, is significantly reconfigured within the context of late ancient Christian asceticism, where women intrude onto the scene of male social bonding as social peers – whether or not literal "sisters" and "mothers." In addition, whereas the *Symposium* occupied a liminal space in relation to public and private spheres that was nevertheless clearly marked as "male," Gregory's dialogue, in its much later setting, offers a slightly different marking of semi-private space in which gendered roles are partially blurred. In the *Dialogue* the strategically privatized male leader (withdrawn from the bustle of life in the *polis*) chooses to publish a conversation that takes place in the domestic sphere of ascetic circles in which elite women may be imagined to speak to men, and to speak with authority. Indeed, the stage for the dialogue is Macrina's own room in her female community.

Gregory's *Life of Macrina*, when read alongside the dialogue, illuminates the ways in which the "woman" enters disruptively into the terrain of Gregory's speech, even as he depicts himself as intruding into "her" space – thereby raising the question of the broader impact of female communities on the social and discursive worlds constructed by and for men. Whereas Gregory's *Dialogue* represents Macrina as Gregory's "Teacher" in the arts of transcending grief, his account of Macrina's funeral in the *Life* portrays the virgins of his sister's community as flamboyant in their expressions of grief. Like Plato's flute girl these women embody a transgressive potentiality that cannot be completely excluded from the discursive space of Gregory's carefully crafted texts, that is even constitutive of those texts. "My soul was disquieted for two reasons," Gregory relates in his report of the funeral: "because of what I saw and because I heard the weeping of the virgins." Although, as he tells it, they had "kept in check the grief in their souls and they had choked down the impulse to cry out in fear of her, as if they were afraid of the reproach of her voice already grown silent," subsequently their voices burst through the disciplined silence. "A bitter, unrestrained cry broke forth," writes Gregory, "so that my reason no longer maintained itself but, like a mountain stream overflowing, it was overwhelmed below the surface by my suffering and, disregarding the tasks at hand, I gave myself over wholly to lamentation." Gregory here quite explicitly "borrows" the explosive subterranean voice of the virgins, but its liquidities subsequently possess *him*. He records their lament that "the bond of our union [with Macrina] has been demolished" by her physical death, remarking that "the ones who called her mother and nurse were more seriously distraught than the rest" (v.Macr.26). Dragging his soul from the abyss of his own grief, he attempts to reassert the control of rationality's word, "shouting at the virgins in a loud voice" intended to drown out their wailings, commanding (in Macrina's name) that they should not lament but sing psalms (v.Macr.27). Temporarily sent back to their quarters, the irrepressible virgins later reappear: "the maidens' psalm-singing, mingled with lamentation, resounded through the place," drawing a huge crowd from the surrounding area. Out of the virgins' hybrid voice of psalm and lamentation, now swollen with the wails of the country folk, Gregory eventually achieves a suitable effect by "separating the flow of people according to sex": "I arranged for the singing to come rhythmically and harmoniously from the group, blended well as in choral singing with the common responses of all" (v.Macr.33). And yet control by sexual segregation is tenuous at best. During the burial, as Gregory reports it, one virgin cried out, and "the rest of the maidens joined her in her outburst and confusion drowned out the orderly and sacred singing." Soon everyone was weeping. As the habitual prayers were intoned by the persistent clergy, the people only gradually returned their attention to the liturgy (v.Macr.34).[24]

By giving voice to Macrina's preference for praise over grief, Gregory is able to make himself once again a man.[25] But his "identity" is barely contained by his masculine *logos*, as Gregory's Macrinan texts also invoke and recall, sloshingly, seductively, "what milk and tears have in common," in the language of Julia Kristeva: "they are the metaphors of non-speech, of a 'semiotics' that linguistic communication does not account for." The liquid laments of the virgins seek convergence with the expressive body of the maternal Macrina. To the extent that it is women (or rather "women?") who "reproduce among themselves the strange gamut of forgotten body relationships with their mothers," Gregory both does and does not want to be one of the girls, like a mountain stream flowing beyond the limits of language, searching for that "complicity in the unspoken, connivance of the inexpressible, of a wink, a tone of voice, a gesture, a tinge, a scent,"[26] the enjoyment of a love without limit.

In Gregory's Macrinan dialogue, as in the funeral scenes at the end of the *Life of Macrina*, the flute girl is always in the act of breaking in – or rather "she" is always *coming out* into the company of men, as Gregory himself opens the door on the inner space where he and his sister are closeted. But who is "she?" If the arid Macrina comes out in Gregory's texts, it is only so as to bring with her that soggy boy whose emotions *will* run away with him: the tearful Gregory comes out too, like one of Macrina's wailing virgins spilling onto the public landscape of his sister's funeral. If Macrina is Diotima, then Gregory is Socrates; if Gregory is the weeping virgin, then Macrina must be Socrates after all. The "woman" is everywhere and nowhere, and the transgressive element of excess produced by "her" exclusion from discourse is for Gregory the necessary source of his own transcendence. The potentially static *telos* envisioned by Macrina's ambivalently cited "Platonism"[27] is overtaken and transformed in the stampede of a desire not limited by *logos* but rather internal to it: Gregory's womanish *agape* does not so much tame Plato's *eros* as drive it over the edge.[28] As Irigaray paraphrases Diotima's message, she repeats Gregory's own act of Platonic retrieval: "Everything is always in movement, in a state of becoming. And the mediator of all this is, among other things, or exemplarily, *love*. Never fulfilled, always becoming."[29]

Concealed within the question borrowed and adapted from Halperin's essay – "Why is Macrina a woman?" – is another question – "*Is* Macrina a woman?" Well, no and also yes. The Macrina of the dialogue is, of course, Gregory's creature. As such, she is also one rather spectacular instance of a male-centered discourse's specular production of a feminized "object" who is always already appropriated by the masculine subject. And so perhaps there is after all no woman in this text. And yet are we not in danger of overestimating the success of this text (of all texts, even?) in its strategies of exclusion-by-appropriation when our own interpretations mime *those* gestures without *also* reproducing the disruptions and transgressions enacted by the text? If the "real Macrina" inevitably eludes us (as does the "real Gregory," for that matter), does the dialogue not still map sites of excess that may be "re-covered" (and thereby also "unveiled") by a historian who would write herself as a "woman" by "reading a woman," Macrina, in this text? And if such an explicit naming of the eisegetical seems alarming, I might yet ask: what else is "history" than a particular art of disciplined projection, a particular set of practices concerned with the intersubjective play of similarity and difference, identity and objectification, continuity and discontinuity, as measured across the dimension of time?

Notes

1 *A Lost Tradition: Women Writers of the Early Church*, ed. Patricia Wilson-Kastner, G. Ronald Kastner, Ann Millin, Rosemary Rader, and Jeremiah Reedy (Lanham, MD: University Press of America, 1981).
2 A point well developed by Kate Cooper, *The Virgin and the Bride: Idealized Womanhood in Late Antiquity* (Cambridge, MA: Harvard University Press, 1996).
3 Luce Irigaray, *Speculum of the Other Woman*, trans. Gillian C. Gill (Ithaca, NY: Cornell University Press, 1985), p. 133.
4 Luce Irigaray, *This Sex Which Is Not One* (Ithaca, NY: Cornell University Press, 1985), p. 76.
5 Arnaldo Momigliano, "The Life of St Macrina by Gregory of Nyssa," in *On Pagans, Jews, and Christians* (Middletown, CT: Wesleyan University Press, 1987), p. 335.
6 David M. Halperin, "Why is Diotima a Woman? Platonic Erōs and the Figuration of Gender," in *Before Sexuality: The Construction of Erotic Experience in the Ancient Greek World*, ed. David Halperin, Jack Winkler, and Froma Zeitlin (Princeton, NJ: Princeton University Press, 1990), pp. 257–308; citation at 293.
7 Elizabeth A. Clark, "The Lady Vanishes: Dilemmas of a Feminist Historian After 'the Linguistic Turn'," *Church History*, 67, 1 (1998), pp. 23–30, and Elizabeth A. Clark, "Holy Women, Holy Words: Early Christian Women, Social History, and the 'Linguistic Turn'," *Journal of Early Christian Studies*, 6, 3 (1998), pp. 423–9.
8 An entire monograph has recently been devoted to a comparative reading of the two texts: Charalambos Apostolopoulos, *Phaedo Christianus: Studien zur Verbindung und Abwägung des Verhältnisses zwischen dem platonischen "Phaidon" und dem Dialog Gregors von Nyssa "Über die Seele und die Auferstehung,"* European University Studies, Series 20: Philosophy (Frankfurt am Main, Bern, New York: Peter Lang, 1986).
9 Gregory of Nyssa, *St Gregory of Nyssa: The Soul and the Resurrection*, trans. and intro. Catharine P. Roth (Crestwood, NY: St Vladimir's Seminary Press, 1993), p. 11. A more extended treatment of the comparison of the two dialogues is found in Roth, "Platonic and Pauline Elements in the Ascent of the Soul in Gregory of Nyssa's Dialogue on the Soul and Resurrection," *Vigiliae Christianae*, 46 (1992), pp. 20–30. See also the brief comments of Rowan Williams, "Macrina's Deathbed Revisited: Gregory of Nyssa on Mind and Passion," in *Christian Faith and Greek Philosophy in Late Antiquity: Essays in Tribute to George Christopher Stead*, ed. Lionel R. Wickham and Caroline P. Bammel (Leiden: E. J. Brill, 1993), p. 244: "As in the *Symposium*, the

sage is being instructed by a holy woman, whose sexual indeterminacy qua spiritual guide is here signalled by her repeated designation as *he didaskalos* – female article with male noun."

10 For example, although the literary and philosophic precedents and context for Macrina's role as dialogue partner and female mystagogue are clearly of interest to the author, there is virtually no mention of the *Symposium* and none at all of Diotima in the monographic study of Gregory's dialogue by Henriette M. Meissner, *Rhetorik und Theologie: der Dialog Gregors von Nyssa De anima et resurrectione*, Patrologia: Beiträge zum Studium der Kirchenväter (Frankfurt am Main, Bern, New York, Paris: Peter Lang, 1991).

11 English translations of the *On the Soul and the Resurrection* follow Gregory of Nyssa, *Select Writings and Letters*, pp. 430–68. See also the more recent renditions: Gregory of Nyssa, *Ascetical Works*, trans. Virginia Woods Callahan, Fathers of the Church (Washington, DC, 1967); and Gregory of Nyssa, *St. Gregory of Nyssa: The Soul and the Resurrection*. Numbered references are to the columns in the Greek edition in Gregory of Nyssa, *Opera, Volume 3: Patrologia Graeca*, Volume 46, ed. J.-P. Migne (Paris, 1863), pp. 11–160.

12 Compare Williams, "Macrina's Deathbed Revisitied," pp. 245–6: "Macrina's sense of the risks of [the *Phaedrus*'s] mythology is real enough; but she is no less haunted, on this her literary deathbed in DAR, by the same challenge, the challenge to reconceive mind itself as the ultimate – and never sated or exhausted – case of *eros*."

13 Ibid. pp. 231–2.

14 J. Warren Smith, "Macrina, Tamer of Horses and Healer of Souls: Grief and the Therapy of Hope in Gregory of Nyssa's *De Anima et Resurrectione*." Paper presented at the North American Patristics Society annual meeting (Chicago, 1998).

15 Michel R. Barnes, "The Polemical Context and Content of Gregory of Nyssa's Psychology," *Medieval Philosophy and Theology*, 4 (1994), pp. 9–11, helpfully locates this discussion in the context of debates within Hellenistic philosophy about the unity of the soul, noting further that the dialogue's assertion of a sharp distinction between the rational and passionate faculties of the soul is strongly linked with the affirmation of God's impassibility, where God is the paradigm for human rationality. Barnes attributes the lack of reference in the dialogue to the trinitarian implications of divine impassibility to the influence of the historic Macrina and her more traditional ascetic psychological views.

16 Clark, "The Lady Vanishes," p. 24, remarks that, although Macrina's role is modeled on "Socrates' muse Diotima of the *Symposium*," her "words in the dialogue on the soul and the afterlife owe much to Plato's *Phaedo*." The "words" of the *Symposium* also press themselves into Gregory's text, which – its title notwithstanding – can be read as a discourse on desire and immortality through spiritual procreancy as much as on "the soul and the afterlife." Roth, "Platonic and Pauline Elements," p. 23, comments on "the parallels between Gregory's dialogue and the *Symposium*" in this description of the soul's ascent, also noting the allusion to the same Platonic passage in *On Virginity*.

17 Halperin, "Why is Diotima a Woman?"

18 Clark, "The Lady Vanishes," p. 25.

19 Halperin, "Why is Diotima a Woman?" p. 259.

20 Irigaray, *This Sex*, p. 76.

21 Luce Irigaray, *An Ethics of Sexual Difference*, trans. Carolyn Burke and Gillian C. Gill (Ithaca, NY: Cornell University Press, 1993), p. 26.

22 English translations of the *Life of Macrina* follow Gregory of Nyssa, *Ascetical Works*, pp. 163–91. Callahan's critical edition of the Greek is published in Gregory of Nyssa, *Opera ascetica*, pp. 347–414.
23 See Halperin, "Why is Diotima a Woman?" p. 288.
24 See the discussion of Gregory's attempt to suppress the tradition of ritual lament, condemning it "as pagan and effeminate," in Margaret Alexiou, *The Ritual Lament in Greek Tradition* (Cambridge: Cambridge University Press, 1974), pp. 27–31.
25 Intriguing is a comparison with the seemingly parodic Platonic *Menexenus*, in which Socrates borrows his speech from a memory of Aspasia's funeral oration (itself supposedly composed for Pericles' use!). If, as Nicole Loraux, *The Invention of Athens: The Funeral Oration in the Classical City*, trans. Alan Sheridan (Cambridge, MA: Harvard University Press, 1986), has argued, the eulogistic funeral oration is, for classical Athens, male civic speech *par excellence*, built on the suppression of the female discourse of lament, then Plato's dialogue is satirical not least in its inversions of gender: the woman Aspasia teaches a man how to talk like a man (Menex.236b–c). Robert C. Gregg, *Consolation Philosophy: Greek and Christian Paideia in Basil and the Two Gregories*, Patristic Monograph Series (Cambridge, MA: Philadelphia Patristic Foundation, 1975), examines the striking continuities with earlier, non-Christian Greek traditions in the consolatory letters and orations of the Cappadocians more generally.
26 Julia Kristeva, "Stabat Mater," trans. León S. Roudiez, in *The Kristeva Reader*, ed. Toril Moi (Oxford: Blackwell Publishers, 1986), pp. 174, 180.
27 I am aware that Macrina is most commonly seen as the "Christian" voice, Gregory the voice of secular learning, in this dialogue. I think the matter may be more complicated, particularly in relation to the metaphor of the charioteer.
28 Franz Dünzl, *Braut und Bräutigam: die Auslegung des Canticum durch Gregor von Nyssa*, Beiträge zur Geschichte der biblischen Exegese (Tübingen: J. C. B. Mohr, 1993), pp. 369–79, provides a recent and helpful discussion of the well-known "*eros* versus *agape*" debate as it relates to Gregory's works.
29 Irigaray, *Ethics of Sexual Difference*, p. 21.

CHAPTER 15

"They Will Know We are Christians by Our Regulated Improvisation": Ecclesial Hybridity and the Unity of the Church

Mary McClintock Fulkerson

The work of Mary McClintock Fulkerson introduces a distinctive element into postmodern theology: a cultural anthropology that is both philosophically informed and empirically based. In some ways, though not herself a product of the Yale School, she develops Lindbeck's postliberalism based upon Geerzt's semiotic cultural model. Her first book, *Changing the Subject* (Minneapolis, MN, 1994), employed this approach with respect to women in the church and the relationship between ecclesial language and ecclesial practice. Fulkerson challenged the liberal feminism that seemed to universalize the categories of "woman." She demonstrated how the identity politics of such a universalization excluded rather than included, and, in its abstraction, could not treat of the specificities of women's lives in various Christian congregational settings. The book remains a provocative study. But the postliberalism of Fulkerson's work has always to be understood alongside her ethnographic methodology. While Fulkerson's attention is on the sociolinguistic cultures that Christian churches and congregations participate in and foster, and while the nature of her investigations impacts upon theological doctrines of ecclesiology and Christology, the ethnographic approach to her material lends a certain empirical objectivity, or outsiderliness, to her thinking. She articulates something of the "other" voice, the outsider's perspective, from within the Christian tradition. What has clearly marked her methodology, besides the work of various (mainly Marxist) cultural analysts (from Raymond Williams to her colleagues at Duke University, Fredric Jameson and Ken Surin) and cultural anthropologists, is the emphasis in Michel Foucault upon the relationship between knowledge and power. She adapts Foucault's investigations into how knowledge issues from specific practices and disciplines. As a result of this approach, theological knowledge is viewed as a set of discourses, liturgies, interpretations, and practical wisdoms that forms subjectivities, constitutes identities, and thus opens itself to being examined by cultural studies.

> In the following essay conversations with ethnography continue (the concept of hybridity has been developed by various analysts of postmodern multiculturalism from Homi Bhabha to Bruno Latour). Rather than working with a Foucauldian method, Fulkerson turns to Pierre Bourdieu's notion of habitus for an approach to "the bodily, interactive character of knowing," though, more like Foucault than Bourdieu, her focus remains the body and its disciplining. The distinctiveness of her approach to the theological allows for new conversations between theology and politics, theology and sociology, theology and social ethics. Like several other postmodern theologians Fulkerson is always aware of the wider cultural setting within which postmodern modes of thinking are situated, always alert to the unavoidable politics of all knowledges. The useful tools honed by postmodernity for thinking through alterity – hybridity and habitus – cannot, for her, be divorced from the economic forces governing globalization, the erasure of racial, sexual, and cultural difference, the threat of a rampant relativism that fosters indifference. Christianity stands for a possible resistance to such hegemony. One senses that this is why Fulkerson is driven to challenging Christian communities as both outsider (ethnographer) and insider (member). She wishes to assess their potential for instituting a non-innocent and political intervention in which singularities and differences continue to matter.

There is a gate on a bridge that separates Juarez, Mexico from its near neighbor, El Paso, Texas, impeding the flow of brown bodies northward. That same gate facilitates a huge flow of goods made by these bodies into the US. The advantage of cheap labor in unregulated Mexico has drawn 350 (mostly US) factories to Juarez, as well as Mexicans willing to work for starvation wages. Not only does the gate physically keep "illegals" out, the very concept of Juarez fails to register in the public consciousness of El Paso, only a few yards away. Juarez is completely absent from El Paso's media and public conversations.[1] This "nonrelation relation" is only one of countless examples of human obliviousness in the face of social difference. Gated communities in the US create space protected from social difference; interstate highways are carefully routed through cities to avoid poverty-stricken areas or traverse them quickly; countless neighborhoods and Christian churches are ghettoized by race and class. While racism, classism, and sexism are the terms for "othering" that we typically use for such practices, there is a sense in which obliviousness is their precondition. For their maintenance requires not so much an intentional excluding of the Other, the outsider (although it includes that), but conditions where obliviousness toward the Other in her/his concreteness and particularity, can persist undisturbed.

According to theories attending to the effects of complex global capitalism on culture, the conditions supporting obliviousness to the Other are important aspects of the contemporary "postmodern condition."[2] As these accounts explain it, new forms of global capitalist technology create common "cultures" with no sense of place or memory (viz., what Skip Gates calls "coca-colonization").³ The commodification that is inherent to capitalism opens cultural meaning to a process of universalization, where meanings that are shared by particular communities get detached from those specific locales and their histories. In addition to the abstracting of meaning from its specific context, profit-motivated media "clean it up" as well. Thus meaning is divested not only of locale, but also of finitude, complexity, and ambiguity.

Christian accounts of community would seem a likely place to articulate resistance to the conditions of obliviousness. Given postmodern processes, however, for ecclesiology to do so, intellectual and even ritual admonitions to care for the stranger are insufficient. Even "liberation" discourse can be fodder for abstraction. The concept of "the poor" can become a commodity and be cleaned up and romanticized for sentimental pieties. Communities must be formed, then, where persons of different social locations are in physical proximity with one another, where the concrete finite "otherness" of race, gender, and other markers of difference can be experienced face to face, rather than cleaned up or abstracted. Of course our physical "nearness" is not enough, as the nonrelation of Juarez and El Paso reminds us. Thus this physical proximity must be interpreted and embodied through specific accounts of "neighborliness."

In this essay I will consider and commend a Christian account and practice of neighborliness that models resistance to conditions of obliviousness. The account will be drawn from my three years of participatory observation at Good Samaritan United Methodist Church, a community where intentional physical proximity between persons of different social locations (racial, gender, national, class, and ability) has helped to create a sociality of the kind I seek. I will ask about the ecclesial identity of this community. By "identity" I do not mean a descriptor that all participants would agree to, but a normative account that could be a contemporary version of what the tradition has identified with the four classic marks of the church: unity, holiness, catholicity, and apostolicity (first articulated in the Niceno-Constantinopolitan Creed). While all four marks are relevant to the question of identity (and will be taken up in a larger project), here I want to speak in particular of unity. Historically, unity is the mark answering the question, where is the church? As a primary term for identity – what is "the same" about this entity when we meet it in different places, or what makes it "one thing" – I will think of unity as that which might fill in the predicate in the hymn line, "They Will Know We are Christians by our —— ?"

Good Samaritan UMC and the Problem of Identity

First, a description of the church. Good Samaritan meets in a small converted garage in the eastern (less fashionable) section of a moderately sized southern city. It was originally a dying all-white UM church in an area that became increasingly African-American over the past two decades. Thus the area surrounding the church is one of the most integrated in the city. Good Samaritan was founded by a white southern former Baptist, Dan White, in the fall, 1988. His lower middle-class Appalachian background in an alcoholic family led him to social work after conversions to Christian faith as a teenager. His second wife, Sue, came out of a similar background. One evening not long after Dan was called to resurrect this dying white church, he had a Bible study on the story of Philip and the eunuch. The group interpreted the story as a sign that God was calling the church to "go and find people who are different from us . . . the overlooked, the looked over and passed over," as Dan put it. And so they did.

Beginning by reaching out to African-Americans they knew, by 1996 the small community had grown to 146 congregants on the roll and was characterized by much racial and national diversity. In winter of 1989, with Dan's prompting, the church decided that "folks who are different from us" should include "special needs" people from nearby group homes and began "special needs" services. Since then the regular worship services include group home residents and bi-monthly services are held with predominantly group home attendance. The church membership includes teachers, nurses, women who clean houses, clerical workers, service workers, a policeman, folks on welfare, janitors, and a few mid-level managers. The African population has grown steadily and adds its own cultural richness to the mix. A number of university students attend as well as a couple of university professors – all white. A 1996 survey taken by about a third of the congregation revealed that the average income was $28,334.

Given this diversity, the "unity" of Good Samaritan would not be well described with the notion propagated by Irenaeus, third-century bishop of Lyons. Unity, he said, is the possession of the apostolic tradition in the canon (or rule) of truth.[4] Whatever consensus around that canon of faith ever existed, surely a disputed fact, I search in vain for a shared set of beliefs at Good Samaritan. Jesus is God, Son of God for some, Wonderful Counselor and the one who ate with sinners for others, "only" a moral example for another, and for some the partner in an intensely personal, almost erotic-sounding relationship.[5] Nor will Cyprian's sacerdotal and hierarchical definition suffice.[6] The denominational frame here is minimally definitive. Dan, the founding pastor, had a mix of nondenominational evangelicalism and low-church Methodism. He crafted a Lord's supper from his own folksy style, never using a manuscript in preaching and (rarely) in liturgy. In 1995 he was replaced by the bishop with Gerald, a Bahamian Methodist raised Catholic, who favors high-church Methodism, brought in the Methodist liturgy and hymnbook, along with elements of African and Bahamian culture. Neither shared creed, liturgy, nor a commitment to polity qualifies as a persistent feature of Good Samaritan, either descriptively or normatively. One might find Augustine's image for unity more appropriate, namely, that the unity of the church consists in the love that is a manifestation of the Holy Spirit.[7] (Then, indeed, we might sing the hymn as it's written: "They Will Know We are Christians by Our Love.") However, given the conflict that ensues, we would need more specificity about what counts as "love" to have the question resolved so easily.

Now it could be countered that precisely because it lacks a "rule of faith" or apostolic polity, this is no real church. However, the seeming doctrinal "sloppiness" of Good Samaritan is not the only challenge to these traditional definitions. If persons of different social locations, different racial histories, nationalities, class positions, gender, and degrees of ability are to come together, a canon of truth is unlikely to render adequately whatever they have in common. Not only is this due to the diversity of the community – contemporary cultural anthropology assures us that it is not shared teachings that constitute the "culture" of groups. There are always conflicts in communities, power differentials, and even the shared practices or rituals are understood differently by participants.[8] (Modern attempts to appropriate a notion of the church as cultural–linguistic communities with their own distinctive grammars are inaccurate accounts of what characterizes ecclesial identity.)[9] To insist upon a genre for identity that consists of same content or liturgy is akin to the images of stable centers, cores, and wholes that come with identity politics, where one's identity is defined by a stable gender (or race, etc.) and boundaries are clear and fixed.

Here I refer to current conversations over the problems of identity politics. As you know, the phrase refers to the strategy whereby liberatory attention to marginalized populations in cultural studies and elsewhere (feminist, race, sexuality, Marxist studies, etc.) is expressed by identity claims on the basis of the mark that signals a marginalized group off from its other, usually the oppressor. Women claim an identity around gender; African-Americans claim race; and gay/lesbian/bisexual/transgendered persons, sexuality. Of course this proves unsatisfactory, since "membership" in multiple groups and the crosshatching of social markers render the identity claims too simplistic and, worse, they perpetuate false universalizing descriptions. In the terms of these categories from identity studies, accounts of the church's unity which depend upon certain content or shared belief would be akin to the notion that there is something called "gender" that gives all women something in common – a shared, fixed identity. Another kind of "identity" politics version of unity would focus on the cultures represented at Good Samaritan: there are African-American Baptists, white Methodists, Liberian members of the Church of Liberia, Bahamian Methodists, a couple of Hispanics, some white and some African-American Pentecostals. If the various groups were to claim identity by some construction of their culture, the nature of the church might be fragmented by competing cultural Christianities, and be assured, the differences in cultural practice are definitely there. Such notions of identity are simply problematic, just as they have been for feminist and other liberation thinking, and for similar reasons. Even if there were one language, in the liturgy, for example, if all do not share the same interpretation of the practice, then merely the question of whose account is "correct" renders the model questionable.

In the place of ascribing single identities to fixed subjects the discourse of multiple oppression has emerged (triple oppression for African-American women, intersecting matrices, kyriarchy), and, more recently, a rhetoric of spatiality and mobility in various interdisciplinary identity studies. Susan Friedman calls it a geographics of identity. This rhetoric (related to postmodernity) commends itself because of the way in which the complexities of concreteness and power can be better imagined: "identity is a positionality, a location, a standpoint, a terrain, an intersection, a network, a crossroads of multiple situated knowledges." In the place of fixed subjects we speak of multiple subject positions, contradictory subject positions, and relationality.[10] It is in this move to spatial, relational, and mobile discourse that the term "hybridity" has gained popularity.

Highly contested for its racist and colonialist legacy in its biological uses, the term "hybrid" invokes purity anxieties and a nineteenth-century obsession and abhorrence of racial mixing.[11] However, in contemporary theory hybridity is also used to describe cultures and languages in terms of different kinds of mixing: (1) the observation that every discourse is a mixing of other discourses; (2) the kind of mix where differences still appear (creolization – a new language still has recognizable elements of two old ones); and (3) the kind of mixing that creates something new. The political potential of hybrids is judged to range from pernicious (Young), to neutral, to transgressive (Rushdie, Bhabha).[12] Gloria Anzaldua, for example, assesses her hybrid Mestiza identity to be a result of historic oppression (Spanish, Indian, Mexican, and American relations of conquest) but also as the space for productive creativity.[13]

Because the issues for Good Samaritan folks are never simply racial, nor about class or gender, hybridity is a promising model. The binary of "whites" and blacks moves in and out of importance as the difference between African and African-American and within "African" emerges. One is never just one thing; one is also an exile (Liberian), or an African-American with Down's syndrome, or the white Adventist wife of a Latino man. In what follows I will consider the usefulness of a notion of hybridity for recognizing a normative identity for this community; hybridity, that is, as the mixing of discourses that contributes to something new.[14]

Worship

Worship under Dan's leadership was a boisterous and sensory experience. This was a result of his attempt to capture the wide diversity of traditions represented in the community, as well as racial, national, and class factors. At the time of its biggest enrollment, the church included about one third Anglo members, more than one third African-Americans and Africans, and a smaller percentage of "Others" (Korean, Hispanic). A large number of the white members came from Methodist, Baptist, and nondenominational conservative groups. Most of the Africans were from Liberia, with some few from Uganda and Kenya. The African-Americans came from largely Black Baptist, or nondenominational conservative churches. To speak to the needs of these various sensibilities

Dan and his wife, Sue, planned worship services that were, as Toni, another member of the congregation, put it, "compromises." Since some members (African-American and African) were used to long services of several hours' duration, and others (predominately white North Americans) expected to be out at 12:00, the services at Good Samaritan were typically one-and-a-half hours. Instead of the Methodist hymnbook, most of each service would rely upon the songs from "parachurch" nondenominational Christian music, called "Praise Songs." ("In Moments Like these" "In moments like these, I sing out a song / I sing out a love song to Jesus.[15]) Much of the music was simple, full of love and passionate – almost erotic – language, and rich in melody. Sue, a large, loud woman, led the singing and the choir with great force while Dan accompanied on guitar. Sometimes African songs were sung, both as solos with accompanying movement by individual members, and sometimes by the whole congregation. Often instruments were played by the congregation, and the bodily movement during these songfests was a sight to behold. Women and men in bright African dress were mixed among the tony American suits and jewelry of African-American women, and the casual dress of the university folk. Arms were lifted in praise during prayer and during the singing; the African-Americans' "amen," "yes, Jesus," and "tell it, preacher" could be heard as well.

The decibel level of the service was also enhanced by the contribution of "special needs" persons. Brought by attendants every Sunday, some came in wheelchairs, some came in slowly on walkers. This mix of folks added voices and movements that created a counterpoint to the communal interchange. Diane would yell out "OK!" at odd moments; someone else would respond with loud glee to something in the service. What in a more "orderly" service would have been unruly outbursts were met by both ministers, Dan and Gerald, with warm and pleased personal responses. The "sound," in other words, was a wonderful mix of cultures and styles, but it also expressed a wide continuum of human responses. Was there a literal hybrid created by the mix of parachurch "Praise Songs" and the African melodies? Was the expansion of "responsive" to include not just responsive readings, but unpredictable laughter from the Sunshine Home folks, a hybrid? Perhaps not in a technical sense, but the combination created a shared palpable sense of joy at the noise we could produce. It was felt by many Good Samaritan members to be a distinctive feature of the community.

Dan's sermons were largely conversion and repentance narratives, with a particular focus on the special place of the ordinary person in God's heart. He continually placed himself in the role of the ordinary sinner, confessing his own shortcomings, narrating his troubled autobiography, and inviting others to occupy the place of the "ordinary sinner" along with him. Many congregants were most struck and attracted to his nonpretentious and welcoming style. Many, that is, save for some of the university folks, who found his sermons too simple, and, as one said, full of "shouting" and pulling teeth. Yet the largest part of the community was brought in by Dan, and the overwhelming majority warmed to his friendly, informal, and "ordinary folks" discourse. While I am using the term loosely here (without a close textual display), the appearance and circulation of liturgical and musical styles from at least two or three different communities, the mix of Dan's "ordinary folks" discourses with biblical discourse, are also hybridizations important to the identity of the community.

Conflict

Anthropologist Veena Das argues that crises in communities – what she calls "critical events" – are times where identity may get clarified or renegotiated and new "modes of action" made possible.[16] A serious incident disrupted the community's life soon after Dan and Sue's departure, and I will use it to illustrate such a clarification. A mixed-race married couple who were very active in the church, Kitty (Anglo) and Geraldo (Hispanic), left the church when the new minister, Gerald, explained in Sunday school the Methodist church's position on gay/lesbian/bisexual persons, namely, that they could not be ordained, but should be treated as persons of "sacred worth." With the complaint that this was non-biblical the couple left and took their adult children with them. Another older conservative white couple and a younger white couple and black couple soon followed them.

Many conversations around the departures helped the church clarify its mind about its nature as a welcoming, inclusive church. A number of the community had been brought up in white conservative traditions, or African-American churches where the topic of homosexuality was either clearly condemned or, in some African churches, a non-issue. One encounter occurred in Sunday school: as Sam, a conservative African-American, formerly Islam, said, we must hate the sin, love the sinner. The Marxist–feminist university professor who wanted to bring her daughter's friends' lesbian mothers to church countered Sam with clear conviction. Other kinds of discourse, frequently among the women, constructed the issue more indirectly, but ultimately contributed to the forming of a kind of tentative consensus. Certain themes repeated. Aggie, a Liberian woman, expressed her dismay and anger about the departure of Kitty and Geraldo: "this is a time the church should really hang together and hang in there" (because of Dan's sudden departure). A sudden comment about the oddness and the sadness of the leaving came from Yani, an African-American woman: "Jesus never turned anyone away . . . it is so important for people to stick together. Forgiveness is the most important thing for a Christian to practice. We have to accept people, despite what they do. Different beliefs, different practices." In many of these conversations no one ever brought up the topic of homosexuality; but frequent mention was made of what Kate said were "personal beliefs" of those who left that had nothing to do with the church. Yani said, "I'm very hurt by this . . . I can't believe people could feel this way and leave the church and not be able to accept people for who they are and where they are and what they are, that's what this church does!"

At other times a careful "account" of the problem of nonheterosexuality was constructed. At a United Methodist Women's meeting, the conversation between the women circled around the feeling of anger at the sudden departures and more focused discourse emerged on the topic of homosexuality. The issues of gay/lesbian people were "private"; they belonged in the bedroom. They were not people's business. As Terry announced emphatically at a Bible study over the same topic, "What happens in people's bedrooms is private . . . what you do – heterosexual or homosexual in your own bedroom is private . . . it's none of our business . . . I really believe that!"

A really important conversation happened around the theme of the mission of the church at a brainstorming "retreat." There, a formerly Baptist African-American couple (Fran and Bill) raised to think it a "sin," a Kenyan man, a gay white man (not out), and other regulars negotiated a meaning for what "inclusive" means. The discussion began with Gerald's (the minister) rumination on Acts 1.1–8. He interpreted the commissioning of disciples as a call to reach out, like the ripples caused by a pebble in a lake, to those who are "not like us." The topic turned to the meaning of "inclusive," and a young white university student insisted that the church is not "merely" inclusive; its identity is dependent upon loving God. Others agreed that loving God is primary, but inclusivity is its necessary expression. The rub, of course, was what that meant. Following discussion of the Kitty/Geraldo incident, an African man pressed for honesty, expressing the fear that if people weren't honest with one another this was just a game. Another African man pressed the question of limits: . . . what would the church do if a Rastafarian joined who smoked marijuana as a religious practice? Or a tribesman with several wives? While no one could resolve the latter possibilities, a kind of consensus emerged around the meaning of faithful inclusiveness. Fran: "I am supposed to accept other people for who they are . . . sexual orientation or whatever . . . we are all the same and I'm not supposed to judge . . . only later in the community I may show scripture to them or they might come to know that something isn't God's will for their life; but we all have those sins and it's not true that one is greater than the other." Bill: "People just as they are off the street are supposed to be included . . . the bottom line is that Jesus never turned anyone away." Gerald: "What is the common denominator to being included? Being human?" Aggie: "It's just being willing to work on your spiritual life. We all have sins and need to work on our relationship with God, that's all you have to be here."

To summarize the characteristics of the inclusive church: anyone off the street should feel welcome; patterned after Jesus; loving acceptance of people for who they are; it's not our doing, but made possible by God; requires reassessment; it should unsettle your comfort zone; involves transformation of sin, but no sin in particular. Although this last is not stated, an implicit consensus emerged that not taking up your problems honestly with the community is the worst breach.

Finding Identity

Now of course I have been slightly disingenuous by saying there is no consensus that might count as the "creedal" unity of this church. As you might infer from these conversations many of the folks *are* clear on the identity of the church in terms of its *uniqueness*. The one theme I heard most consistently was some version of Dan's vision of its vocation – welcoming: to go after people "not like us," those who are on the outside. A brochure from Dan's years announces: "There is room for you at Good Samaritan! We are persons who are African-American, White American, Asian, Native American, Latino, Mentally and Physically Challenged from many different cultural and socioeconomic backgrounds. COME AND SHARE GOD'S LOVE!"

The church is described by many in terms of precisely its welcoming everyone as family. Kitty, Church of Nazarene, said: "Good Samaritan just makes you feel that no matter what you've done in your life, God can forgive you for the asking and you can go on and grow in his love." Aggie: "you just feel welcome at Good Samaritan . . . [because of her troubles as a Liberian immigrant] Dan and Sue were always so willing to listen . . . more like family, and you could always call them." Admiringly, "Dan would say, 'well you got flaws? I'm struggling . . . don't think because I stand up here that I'm any different . . . I have all my flaws and you will see it'." Nancy (older white woman, married to a retired mailman) grew up Holiness and says of what attracted them to Good Samaritan: "All people were welcome; in the military you know [where she and Ray spent much time] racism doesn't get to be a problem, at least it wasn't for us. So I think we just felt that's the way you have to do it. So . . . we got this . . . bulletin from Good Sam and it had . . . a choir, a picture of a choir . . . and it had two black people in it. And I used to think, that's just what we need . . . so it's been great." What's special about Good Samaritan? Nancy says, "it's people that are open and people that basically can care about other people no matter what."

One might say that the biblical warrant for this identity originally was the story of Philip and the eunuch, and that the eunuch is the figure for the "outsider." The interpretation of what it means to "go out to eunuchs" is articulated with the cultural discourses at hand. Negotiating of what constituted an outsider and what constituted welcoming happens through a variety of hybrid discourses – liberal notions of inclusion, language of the "private" (to protect the integrity of g/l/b persons), and the therapeutic – feeling accepted for what you are, regardless. In that case, insofar as something new is created in the combinations, rather than simply a kind of pluralism, the term hybrid is appropriate. Of the varying definitions of hybridity, I would suggest we have the first kind, the hybridity of linguistic mixture, the almost unconscious cobbling together of different discourses. (This squares with Bakhtin's notion of organic, or unconscious, hybridity, as distinguished from hybridity as the conscious product of a poet.)[17] Now by saying this I am opting for one of the more neutral accounts of hybridity, since this mixing goes on in much if not most human conversation and reflection. What I have described is hardly the creation of something solid enough to call subversive or transformative. Indeed, if hybridity is to help fill in the predicate for the hymn of unity "They Will Know We are Christians by our ———" in some interesting way, another form of cohesion must be there for something lasting and worthy of being termed an "identity" and some account must be given as to why it should be granted the status of "normative."

I will close by addressing (briefly) these last two needs. First, I believe that even if I am right that something new is created here that deserves to be termed hybrid discourse, it is inadequate for the continuity of a community, particularly when its mixed languages might seem as unstable as they are creative.[18] In order for this discourse to qualify as a community's ecclesial identity, it must be joined to the learning that comes with bodied interaction, including the tacit understandings associated with place, gender, race, and other social markers. This is to say with William Connolly that the visceral register of experience always accompanies language and rationality.[19] But it is to say more. An adequate category of this register must allow for the bodily, interactive character of knowing. A good candidate is Pierre Bourdieu's concept of habitus, the communally produced knowledge that effects "a permanent disposition, embedded into the agents' very bodies in the form of mental disposition, schemes of perception and thought."[20]

Habitus is a category that can map how positionality and bodily practice communicate meanings crucial to a community. In Good Samaritan it is important that habituation, or bodily learning about what it means to be a Christian, occurs as persons are placed in intersubjective relations with others who are marked by great social differences. I can tell you a number of different stories of productive interaction between those who are very different ideologically. Holly, a progressive university student, tells of meeting up with David, a conservative electrician, at an NRA meeting, she as protester, he as member. Later, David wrote her a note: "I hope you will continue to come – this is the place where we can differ on things, but support each other and care for each other and love each other." However, other examples better illustrate the *bodily character* of this knowing. Take habituation in relations between the "special needs" folks and the able-bodied participants. Many of the latter have developed dispositions in relation to those who cannot talk, or who communicate their experience of the world with screams of joy or cries of alarm, or only with eye contact. Gerald has altered his bodily movements in worship to respond more reciprocally to the folks who depend upon eye contact for communication; he has developed a conversational style that honors and names persons in ways that give them visible pleasure. Likewise, judging from his changing bodily responses over the years, Steve is one of the wheelchair-bound who are being habituated into trust for Gerald. Nancy tells with pride that Marty, silent and wheelchair-bound, has learned to recognize her and no longer reacts with fear at her approach. Olga and Terry (with children who have different disabilities) and others in the congregation are habituated to develop the kind of touch, the patient form of address, that bring the group home participants out, that calm their panic. It is only physical proximity, interactive placement with and between the folks like Debra, Steve, and others from the group homes and other members of Good Samaritan that the specificities of the language of "inclusion" become what Bourdieu calls "memories of the body."

Other settings for habituation: the relations of persons constructed as white with persons constructed as black or brown are important sites of habituation. To tell stories of Jesus and hear stories of differently constructed lives in a multiracial and national setting where all are named as God's children is a shaping of dispositions about the nature of difference. But what matters here is not simply proximity, but posture and positioning. It is significant for the members who are constructed by society as "white" when a man "of color" is in the leadership position rather than the janitorial. The importance of this is especially vivid in the Sunday school class, where African-American children have "race" complicated for them by the presence of African children; white children hear about the gospel with their multi-colored peers. And all three groups speak of the "outsider" as some group not represented in this racial mix.

While there is much more to say about the racial relations here, including the "not seeing" that occurs, I must stop and answer my second question, regarding normativity. What constitutes a normative identity here is not the Methodist or even hybrid discourse of "ordinary folks" plus liberalism plus stories of Jesus with African and parachurch aesthetics. They are necessary, to be sure. Without this hybridity we could not see an identity. I have also argued that the hybridized language about being inclusive, welcoming those "not like us," has no purchase unless it is a bodily knowledge – a being-together as differently abled and racialized and gendered bodied subjects. However, it is *how* the discourse has purchase and allows for continuity that gets at its normativity. This claiming that "all are welcome here," as Terry put it, refers in a particular way. When African-American Terry says "all" she has disabled and white bodies in her field of reference. In addition, a habituation has a temporal life – duration – and the category "all" must not only last, it must be expandable.[21]

The importance of a habitus, Bourdieu tells us, is that it is a way communities *pass on* "culture" or knowledge of distinctive ways of being, such that persons "know how to get on" as a result. (I have stressed that it is embodied knowledge, not explicitly thematized, although thematization is a part of its emergence.) However, the point now is that what results is an improvisational skill – a bodied knowing about how to "do" the culture in a new situation. Adjusting to new situations, a habitus "regulates" itself in response.[22] Thus what is distinctive about the earlier-mentioned crisis conversation regarding the meaning of inclusivity is the hint that the community's life has helped create a way of being inclusive in new situations. The referent for "those welcome here" did not remain stable according to that conversation. A new form of "eunuch," the figure for the "outsider," was decoded. The facility to welcome a "new form of stranger" has been developed. (The folks discussing the issue of hypothetical g/l/b participants had had g/l/b/ persons either vilified or rendered invisible in their previous churches, but they had developed the wisdom to improvise when this new challenge emerged.) Continuity, then, is not dependent upon "same content" believed or used to police boundaries; it is the bodily knowledge that supports an improvisatory, expanding capacity to welcome the neighbor.

The hybridized story of welcome – Christian neighborliness – habituating persons into postures of welcome, even reciprocity with those who are radically different is, perhaps, a thin beginning of a full account of the distinctive identity of the church. Much more will need to be said to account for its apostolicity, holiness, and catholicity. (I will need to argue how this hybridized practice is a creative weaving of biblical and traditional elements and how it constitutes a witness to the trinitarian God, for example.) However, I commend it as theologically significant because it does two things. First, getting the skill to expand one's notion of the neighbor (the stranger), such that this graciousness becomes a "body memory," is a mark of uniqueness, and it is uniqueness that, unlike doctrinal marks, can "travel," i.e., occur in different locales and contexts, look different, and require different liturgical and mission forms.

Second, this skill might be worth singing about, even if "They will know we are Christians by our regulated improvisation" might not be winner lyrics. A refusal of the conditions of obliviousness requires a serious attending to the bodily and historical difference (and possible threat) of the Other. And despite its limits, such an attending by habituation into postures of comfort and ease between persons of very different social histories and communities has seriously begun. Even given the suspicions that it was the change from white to black leadership that drove some of the white people away – residual racism – the context for refusing obliviousness is there. That white people could be happy with black and brown people as fellow congregants but could not "habituate" to a man of color (Gerald) in the place of leadership simply illustrates the difficulties and complexities of truly honoring reality in its concreteness – its ambiguity and finitude. The possibilities for the abstracting and distancing effects of the postmodern culture on Christian talk about love for the neighbor are subverted in this community in an important way. They are, then, the basis for a "politics" of Christian neighborliness. And filled in in this way, the notion that it is the Holy Spirit's manifestation of love in the community that constitutes its unity might not be a bad idea after all.

Notes

1 This story is recounted by political theorist Kimberly Curtis as a paradigmatic instance of the human propensity to "not see" reality in its particularity in *Our Sense of the Real: Aesthetic Experience and Arendtian Politics* (Ithaca, NY: Cornell University Press, 1999), pp. 1–3.
2 Accounts of the postmodern that take seriously the effects of the economic on the cultural and political are found in the work of Fredric Jameson, David Harvey, Scott Lash, Lawrence Grossberg, to name a few. Accounts of the effects of commodification on thought and cultural products that predate this term are still useful (T. Adorno, Raymond Williams).

3 Henry Louis Gates, Jr., "Planet Rap: Notes on the Globalization of Culture," in *Fieldwork: Sites in Literary and Cultural Studies*, ed. Marjorie Garber, Rebecca L. Walkowitz, and Paul B. Franklin (New York: Routledge, 1996), pp. 55–66.

4 Of course the marks themselves were not permanent timeless definitions, but came into being as solutions to specific threats. It was in response to Gnostics that Irenaeus argued that the unity of the church consisted in its possession of the true apostolic tradition in the form of the canon (or rule) of truth. See Eric Jay, *The Church: Its Changing Image Through Twenty Centuries* (Atlanta: John Knox Press, 1978). As early as 1934 Walter Bauer challenges the notion of consensus on this tradition. See *Orthodoxy and Heresy in Earliest Christianity*, trans. by the Philadelphia Seminar on Christian Origins, ed. Robert A. Kraft and Gerhard Krodel (Philadelphia: Fortress Press, 1971).

5 This is not to say one could not interpret the community Christologically; it would simply be more complex than this.

6 Jay, *The Church*, pp. 29–92. The persecution which resulted in lapsed Christians was important to the formation of Cyprian's sacerdotal and hierarchical definition of unity, "No bishop no church." It is a reminder that these definitions are always cocreated in relation to the "competition."

7 I would not want to simply invoke the specific practices that gave flesh to this vision, however, given the coercion Augustine was willing to approve against heretics. See Augustine, "On Baptism, Against the Donatists," in *Nicene and Post-Nicene Fathers*, vol. 4, trans. Richard Stothert and Albert H. Newman (Grand Rapids, MI: Eerdmans, 1956), pp. 411–514.

8 See especially James Clifford's "Identity in Mashpee," in *The Predicament of Culture: Twentieth-Century Ethnography, Literature, and Art* (Cambridge, MA: Harvard University Press, 1988), pp. 277–346.

9 The reference here is to postliberal theologies influenced by George Lindbeck's cultural–linguistic account of Christian community Many criticisms of George Lindbeck get at this point (see Terrence Tilley). The most incisive connection of his work with problematic modern accounts of culture, however, is found in Kathryn Tanner's *Theories of Culture: A New Agenda for Theology*, pp. 72–9, 138–51.

10 For a helpful summary of these options see Susan Stanford Friedman, *Mappings: Feminism and the Cultural Geographies of Encounter* (Princeton, NJ: Princeton University Press, 1998), pp. 19, 17–35.

11 See Robert J. C. Young, *Colonial Desire: Hybridity in Theory, Culture and Race* (London: Routledge, 1995).

12 See Friedman, *Mappings*, pp. 82–93; also Homi Bhabha, *The Location of Culture* (London: Routledge, 1994); M. M. Bakhtin, who discusses the hybridity of discourses in *The Dialogic Imagination: Four Essays*, ed. Michael Holquist, trans. Caryl Emerson and M. Holquist (Austin: University of Texas Press, 1981, 1998).

13 Gloria Anzaldua, *Borderlands/La Frontera: The New Mestiza* (San Francisco: Aunt Lute Books, 1987).

14 While the construction and complicating of identity relative to race and gender are really important topics to think through with the grid of hybridity, I will confine myself in this essay to a few practices and dispositions that yield to different categorizations than either beliefs/creedal convictions or "love," leaving "race/gender/class" for another time.

15 The rest goes: "In moments like these, I lift up my hands / I lift up my hands to the Lord, Singing, I love you Lord, singing I love you, Lord / Singing, I love you Lord, I love you."

16 Veena Das, *Critical Events: An Anthropological Perspective on Contemporary India* (New York: Oxford University Press, 1995).
17 Bakhtin, *The Dialogic Imagination*.
18 A full account would require description of the narratives that organize these hybrid discourses, and they would be discipleship narratives, Christological and other theological narratives. That, too, is part of a larger project.
19 This political theorist is arguing for an extension of the political to include this dimension of experience. See William E. Connolly, *Why I am Not a Secularist* (Minneapolis: University of Minnesota Press, 1999), pp. 35ff.
20 Pierre Bourdieu, *Outline of a Theory of Practice*, trans. Richard Nice (Cambridge: Cambridge University Press, 1977), pp. 1–29.
21 There is not enough evidence here to say this bodied expandable knowledge is completely successful; however, there could not be such a thing, since only new situations create the possibility to test its expandability.
22 Bourdieu, *Outline*, pp. 78, 10.

CHAPTER 16
On Changing the Imaginary

Grace M. Jantzen

Grace Jantzen was trained as a philosopher of religion at Oxford, and from her earliest work in *God's World, God's Body* (London, 1984) she has been concerned with the triangulation of religion, culture, and gender. The way in which she has investigated that triangulation has changed over time; for example, since the mid-1990s she has given greater attention to contemporary forms of critical theory – the work of continental thinkers such as Foucault, Lacan, Irigaray, and Kristeva. These figures, though certainly not accepted uncritically, have facilitated a deeper understanding of the cultural politics within which religious discourse and activity take place. Foucault's analysis of power provides Jantzen with a means for analyzing the cultural politics of religion in the Middle Ages, in her book *Power, Gender and Christian Mysticism* (Cambridge, 1995). The work of Lacan, Irigaray, and Kristeva enable and inspire Jantzen to develop an account of the symbolic order in relation to the imaginary, and see a way to transform the symbolic order altogether in order to provide "a god according to our gender." It is no accident that these three particular thinkers are indebted to Freudian psychology and its implications for the social order. Jantzen herself has been interested in the kind of therapeutic model psychology provides, and while supplementing its analysis with "attention to ideologies and their function," views psychological investigations as useful for probing "the cultural symbolic of the West."

Consequently, there has been less attention to analytical and process schools of philosophy in her work and a growing recognition that the kind of philosophy of religion which came to the fore in modernity promoted patriarchy and phallocentrism. Poststructural continental thinking opened for Jantzen new possibilities for transforming patriarchal culture and, to some extent, recovering religious insights made evident in her extensive examination of female medieval mystics like Hildegard of Bingen, Julian of Norwich, and Margarete Porete. Her book *Becoming Divine: Towards a Feminist Philoso-*

phy of Religion (Manchester, 1998) is, in part, a sustained attack upon the analytic tradition of philosophy, not only for its inscription of the *man* of reason, but also its uncritical acceptance (and reproduction) of the "scientific worldview." Significantly, in the same book process philosophy, because of its correlation between God and the world, is demonstrated to have potential for feminist revision. The Spinozistic pantheism argued for with respect to classical theism in her early work can now not only offer an account of divine embodiment, but also be employed in imagining a female divine.

In her most recent work this revisionist and therapeutic project, the move from feminist critique to gender-conscious construction, is developed further: synchronically, in terms of a philosophical analysis; and diachronically, in terms of specific historical discourses and practices. Jantzen has always been interested in the historical and, following Foucault, in providing genealogical accounts. Specifically, she has discerned (partly through a reading of Hannah Arendt's work on natality and Adriana Cavarero's feminist reading of Plato) a preoccupation with death and violence as it appears to subtend the masculinist imaginary. To transform the symbolic order which inscribes this imaginary requires changing the imaginary.

The essay included here is an excellent representation of her ongoing researches. Her 1998 book increasingly spoke about a new symbolic of natality as opposed to a Western preoccupation with necrophilia/necrophobia. In the introduction to the reissue of her book *Julian of Norwich* (London, 2000) Jantzen speaks about shaping a postmodern spirituality. In pursuing this project the present essay engages these two lines of thinking (death and postmodernity) in a concern with the aesthetics of the beautiful (as distinct from the sublime). These three themes constitute the bases for Jantzen's current ambitious work.

Whatever their many differences, thinkers loosely categorized as "postmodern" tend to be sharply critical of the trajectories that have shaped the West since its turn to "modernity" from about the seventeenth century onwards. The general features of "modernity" are easily rehearsed. Among other things there is the rise of science and the exaltation of empiricism as the foundation of knowledge; its tentacles in militarism and in technology; capitalism and commodification and utilitarianism; colonialism, slavery, the hegemony of the West and the exploitation of the rest; the destabilization of traditional social structures and the rise of individualism . . . the litany could be extended. Of course much nuancing is necessary; of course it is not all bad. But one would need to be singularly unmindful of the effects of Western modernity on the rest of the world's peoples, on the earth itself, and on the narrowing of the human spirit in the West, to think that the primary response to modernity should be celebration. Moreover one would need to be singularly optimistic to suppose that these effects will somehow right themselves in a new era called "postmodernity" or "the new millennium" without effort and without cost.

"The point, however, is to change it": to change the world of modernity, and to change the imaginary which has rigidified into its death-dealing discursive and material structures. The world, to be sure, *is* changing, and with great rapidity. The ground shifts under our feet in relation to technologies from informational and military hardware to genetically modified species. But these changes, arguably, are continuations of trajectories that already cut deep ruts through modernity. What is necessary is to find some way of thinking – and living – otherwise. If philosophy/theology does not engage with this problematic, the legacy of modernity, it is useless – or worse.

But how shall such thinking/living be done? By whom? And from what place? Should we perhaps wait for a great heroic poet heralding news of Being? But even if we thought that Being could become present, how would we recognize the difference between the demonic and the angelic messenger? Should we respond to the face of the other immediately before us – and the next one, and the next, until we turn away in exhaustion while the causes of human misery (which may rest in ourselves) remain unaddressed? Should we stop worrying about it, count ourselves lucky to be among the privileged, and play, erring, among the simulacra while we may? Heidegger once said, notoriously, "Only a god can save us now." But we had better not wait "for the dead god of Nietzsche" whose absence is as hard to pin down as ever his presence was amongst the shifting signifiers, for this "god is dead, and we have killed him," and the black sun is upon us. The allusions, of course, are to twentieth-century continental thinkers who look for ways to deal with modernity, and point to their suggestions, and in some cases despair, for reconfiguration of its symbolic. Their writings merit sustained attention, especially, I think, in their hints and dismissals of the divine.

The invocation of the divine is indeed apposite: it leads, at least, to reconsideration of the features of modernity. For interconnected with all the characteristics of modernity is its secularism, achieved by the banishment of God from the world, at first into a "heaven" to which one might aspire after death, and eventually out of consideration altogether for all practical or public purposes. The *saeculum*, which according to Christian thought was the time between creation and final judgment, became the present time, the time of God's absence. Eternity, and the divine who inhabits it, was something qualitatively different from the present order and irrelevant to the march of the millennia, which in the West are, ironically, dated (ostensibly) from the birth of Jesus.

There was no neat linear or logical progression about the banishment of the divine. At the same time as Locke was banning "enthusiasm" (lit. "God within") from rigorous epistemology, and Hume was mocking the idea of a miracle as divine "tampering" with a law of nature, God was being invoked, by themselves and their compatriots, to justify civil religion, the appropriation of continents, slavery, genocide, the subordination of women, and the exploitation of the "lower" classes. Nevertheless, this God was a god in heaven, not on earth, and was increasingly removed from the public realm. Thus more and more religion was either rejected outright or confined to the private and domestic sphere. In either case, it was turned in large measure into a question of "beliefs": it was no longer primarily the place of meeting between human and divine, the sacrament of divine presence, the holy place or saint or shrine or holy well in which heaven and earth were visibly fused in outward signature of grace: where, therefore, miracles might take place as between the two angels facing each other across the place of holiness.

All this has become at best "poetic," where poetry itself serves no useful purpose unless as rhyming couplets to advertise McDonald's or to be placed with posters about what's on in the West End and the help-line for the Samaritans on the London underground. Yet given the extent to which this process of secularization is interwoven with the discourses and practices of modernity, it is hardly possible to probe those discourses without revisiting the question of religion, a revisitation not separate from a revolution in poetic language, and indeed, I shall suggest, willingness once again to contemplate beauty (as distinct from the sublime and the unrepresentable). If this is what is involved, then it is very different from a return to endless assessments of "proofs" for the existence of God, of the coherence of theism, of theodicy, and all the other tedious preoccupations of traditional Anglo-American analytic philosophers of religion. All these buy into, and thus reinforce, modernity's understanding of religion as a set of beliefs: they already have their reward. But perhaps we do need to ask what counts as religion, and who is doing the counting? What functions has religion served? Which technologies of power has it authorized, and what resistances can it generate? Moreover, all these questions must *also* be asked of secularism, religion's putative other.

As I shall explain later, probing these questions will not of itself change the imaginary. It will, however, generate a genealogy of religion/secularism which will show its place in the master discourses of modernity, the current cultural symbolic, and will also show, in an effective history of the present, how it came to be structured thus. The importance of such genealogies is largely taken for granted (at least among those open to continental thought) in relation to many areas of discourse: sexuality, rationality, and punishment, to name only three brought to the fore in the work of Michel Foucault. But if religion (as much as madness or sexuality) is to be understood not as a fixed or natural essence but as constructed, and with a genealogy, and interwoven in all the master discourses of modernity, then the urgency of reexamining it can hardly be overstated. Indeed it is all the more important because the unexamined assumptions of secularism have occluded consciousness of the ways in which a religious symbolic still permeates those discourses, as, for instance, in a preoccupation with other worlds, or the idea of a "God's-eye" view from nowhere as the gold standard of rationality, or the warning against "playing God" in genetic technology.

Such a genealogy of religion/secularism immediately indicates further dimensions. First among them is gender. As I have argued elsewhere, as long as Christendom considered religious experience potentially authoritative not merely over the private life of the experiencer but over the whole polity, then there were very strict controls, along gendered lines, over who could legitimately claim to be the recipient of such experiences. Once religion became a private matter, these controls were largely dropped: anybody could count as a mystic when a mystic did not count for much. But this should not mislead us into thinking that the secularism of modernity was less oppressive to women. Feminists who turn with relief from the misogynist structures of Christendom find misogyny reinscribed in the secular structures of modernity, though often under a veneer of liberalism reminiscent of the churches' avowals of the value of women: in both cases the menial jobs without which the structures would collapse are largely women's work, and this remains the case even when a few women are priests, scientists, or executive directors.

Feminists are aware, of course, that the master discourses of modernity oppress women. Feminist philosophers have been showing how rationality (putatively neutral) has been constructed on masculine lines, how science (putatively objective) has worked against the insights and interests of women, how politics and economics (putatively free and democratic) have been developed in ways that foster competition, aggression, and an adversarial approach which has often actively excluded women or been uncongenial to women, or, perhaps even worse, encouraged women to develop those same attitudes and responses until they have (as was said of Mrs Thatcher) more balls than the boys. I am not suggesting that there is any one-to-one gender mapping, let alone biological essentialism. Nevertheless, many feminists assume that by discarding religion we have at least rid ourselves of one misogynist structure, even if there are plenty left to be going on with. That there is systemic oppression of women (and others) in the material and discursive practices of Christendom is not in doubt. However, if my suggestion for a genealogy of religion in the West (largely though not only Christendom) is correct, then it follows, first, that it is mistaken to see secularism and religion in essentialist terms; second, that secularism and religion are not therefore binary opposites; and third, that it is thus far too simplistic to assume that secularism is the obvious choice for feminists (or for any progressive thinkers). What I believe emerges instead is that the construction of both religion *and* secularism in modernity leaves the two in mutual entanglement, not least in what counts as rationality and value, and that this is closely entwined with questions of gender.

This becomes more apparent by the introduction of the notion of death. I use the term "notion" because, although death is indubitably real, I suggest that, like sexuality, bodies, madness, and indeed religion, death also is socially constructed and has a genealogy. Death is a guiding motif in the construction of rationality, a rationality often characterized as freedom from the body and the delusions of the passions. Death is central to the construction of Western science, which is premised on the banishment of divine life not only from the act of knowing (in the elimination of enthusiasm) but also from the universe, which is thereby rendered lifeless, even mechanistic, a complicated version of the Strasbourg clock beloved of Locke, Boyle, and the Royal Academy.[1] The philosophy of modernity is premised on the death of God; and this leads to ideas of the death of "man," the death of the subject, the death of the author.... In popular and "high" culture, in musical compositions, novels, painting, and sports writing, there is continual preoccupation with death, often interlinked with love and sex.

The cultural portrayals of death show how closely ideas of death and gender are intertwined. This is of course not new in modernity, though it is given different emphases. The womb and the tomb of Plato's cave or the anchorite's cell, the Christian insistence on a new birth not of flesh and blood as prerequisite for eternal life, the fear of female sexuality in medieval monastic writings and early modern witch hunts, the linkage of sexual love with death so that women are regularly described in poetry as diverse as Donne and Blake as bearing children (not for life but) for death, ejaculation as a "little death," and the interweaving of death and the female in the writings of psychoanalytic theory from Freud onwards, all show that the genealogy of death in the West is a gendered genealogy, and one which has had disastrous consequences for women. The urgency to escape mortality, whether through immortal fame as a Greek – or Faustian – hero, through heaven after death, or through the attainment of some other world in outer space, has been an obsession for men in the West which did not disappear with modernity; it went through metamorphoses into secular (but no less gendered) forms. Indeed the secular forms of modernity are, in relation to gender and death, related very closely indeed to their precursors in Christendom, as a developed genealogy would show.

Moreover, it is this obsession with death, largely suppressed, which can be shown to be acted out in the violent and death-dealing structures of modernity. From militarization and death camps and genocide to exploitation and commodification and the accumulation of wealth, from the construction of pleasure and desire to the development of terminator genes, from the violence on the streets to the heaven-obsessed hymnody of evangelical churches, preoccupation with death and the means of death and the combat with death is ubiquitous. It is a necrophilia so deeply a part of the Western symbolic that it emerges at every turn: our language is full of metaphors of war, weaponry, violence, and death, even in relation to aspects of life where violence should have no place: "the war against homelessness," "the battle with illness," "fighting against child abuse" . . .

The term "necrophilia" is appropriate; for although the preoccupation with death presents itself as a dread or fear, literally a phobia, Freud has shown how such phobias, as obsessions, are simultaneously a love or desire for the very thing so dreaded. In fact Freud believed that *Thanatos*, a death drive, was as strong as *Eros*, and closely linked with it. Whereas he held that it was a universal of human nature, I would argue that it is a gendered construction of Western modernity, with precursors in Christendom and in ancient Greek thought. It is at least abundantly clear that a gendered obsession with death saturates the Western symbolic and is actualized in the continuing destructive–obsessive practices of modernity.

Now, if I am correct in characterizing the deathly symbolic of modernity (and indeed postmodernity) as rooted in and reinforcing necrophilia/phobia, if I am correct, that is, in treating it as an obsession or psychic disorder of the social realm, then it will not be changed by arguing against it. Although many traditional philosophers of religion and theologians continue to write as though Freud and Lacan had never lived, such an approach in my opinion lacks integrity. For all the problems of psychoanalytic theory – and from a feminist perspective there are many – its recognition that the structures of social and individual existence both act out and reinforce the cultural symbolic, complete with its (gendered) repressions, means that rational analysis of the ills of modernity, and rational solutions to them (even if they can be found), will not effect a cure. The symbolic of Western modernity is inseparable from the repressions and compulsions which form its underside. That being the case, appeals to rationality will not bring about the desired change, any more than it would help to tell a person in the grip of a neurosis what it is that they are repressing. Such strategies only bring out stronger resistance, ever more clever rationalizations, deeper anger and control.

This is not to say that careful analysis, genealogies, archeologies, and deconstructions are useless; it does, however, mean that it is necessary to think through what their use is and what it is not. As I have said, it is not likely to be effective in the case of a society deeply invested in the symbolic of modernity and unwilling to recognize at a deep level the problems which that symbolic generates. However, these problems are coming more and more to the fore, in barbarically violent international and internecine conflicts, "ethnic cleansings," and the consequences of global warming, to take only three examples; and there are those who are seeking ways of thinking otherwise. Now, it is usually a necessary step in any effective *individual* therapy that the client should come to explicit consciousness of the ideas that have been shaping problematic responses and behaviors, and see where those ideas came from. The same, I suggest, is true at a *cultural* level. Although rational argument on its own is unlikely to change action, it is a crucial part of understanding the provenances of the symbolic (and its changes and variants) and of recognizing the responses it generates. This then enables the question of whether we really want to continue to have our actions and thoughts controlled by these unconscious motivations or how we might find release from them. It is worth reiterating that even this will be useful only for those who acknowledge that there is a problem, however. Those who refuse that recognition, or displace the problem on to others – "underdeveloped countries," "welfare scroungers," "climatic forces" – will only try to strengthen their controlling grip.

I am not arguing that the psychoanalytic model of neurosis and therapy is in every respect applicable to the social order, let alone that it is the only model. The analogy must be complexified, for example, by attention to ideologies and their function; and also the dynamics of resistance within any power structure. Nevertheless, although the analogy must be qualified and supplemented, I believe that it is a useful one in probing the cultural symbolic of the West, formed as it is by the triangulation of death, gender, and religion/secularism, especially if we are asking how this symbolic and its underlying imaginary could be transformed. I suggest in particular that using the therapeutic analogy brings to mind three related questions, questions which are heightened by the development of a critical genealogy. What is it exactly that is being repressed in this gendered and ostensibly secular necrophilic symbolic? What deep fear underlies the repression? How is that fear related to longing and desire: what are these desires?

Only a patient and detailed investigation and analysis can develop adequate responses to these questions. Some preliminary considerations, however, present themselves. First, as we have learned from the deconstructive strategies of Derrida, it is instructive to discern, in a dominant notion like necrophilia (or speech, or rationality, or indeed religion), what it is that this discourse simultaneously silences and depends upon: what it constructs as its binary opposite. This is not to say that it really *is* its opposite, of course; indeed, part of the point of the deconstructive strategy is to dismantle such putative binaries. However, it is significant to lift up what has been suppressed, to see how this changes the picture. As I have begun to argue elsewhere, drawing on the work of Hannah Arendt and Adriana Cavarero, examination of the necrophilic symbolic from this perspective raises up the idea of natality: bodily birth, which is hardly ever taken seriously in the Western philosophical tradition and yet upon which depends the very possibility of death, not only as a philosophical category but also in reality. Moreover, that birth is intricately involved with gender can hardly be in doubt. Every body who is born is gendered, and gender shapes the trajectory of natals. And although new reproductive technologies may make the generation of human life possible in unforeseeable ways, everyone who has ever been born until now has been born of a woman.

This leads to a second preliminary consideration. Necrophilia presents itself as obsessive anxiety about death, and virtually ignores birth, which is repressed at the level of the symbolic. Now, one of the things that the therapy analogy brings to mind is the question of displacement. A phobia about one thing (e.g., spiders, dirt) is often actually a deeply unresolved complex about something else, to which the ostensible object of fear is related but represses precisely by attaching itself to a substitute. Thus in Freud's account of Little Hans, the boy's phobia about horses was a disguised complex about his father and masculine sexuality. What suggests itself, then, is that the obsession with death characteristic of the Western symbolic may be a displacement of something to which it is related but which renders it invisible within the symbolic structure. From what I have already said, an obvious candidate is natality, and underlying it the mother and female sexuality. Could this be the real locus of fear of death, the site which must be both silenced and controlled at all costs? And are the death-dealing structures of modernity and its master discourses attempts to silence and control the mother, and all the other (m)others which might bring this fear to mind: the earth, its beauty, its peoples, its unpredictable life? Again, the suggestion calls for careful working out; but if what we need is a changed imaginary, then I think we ignore it at our peril.

If for the moment we assume that it is along the right lines, then this raises another consideration. Is it not the case that a phobia, if it is expressive of an unresolved complex, indicates not only deep fear and dread but also unacknowledgable longing and desire? If that is so, or even partly so, what desire lies deep within the symbolic of necrophilia/phobia? Freud took the death drive at face value: he postulated *Thanatos* straightforwardly as a desire for stasis. However, I believe that a genealogy of Western necrophilia reveals not so much a desire for death as stasis, but a desire for death as entrance to other worlds: immortality, whether understood in religious or secular terms. It is a desire to escape from gendered bodies (and indeed the gendered earth) by regimes of control. But underlying that, as Freud also sometimes recognized, is there not a repression of longing for lost unity – and lost unity precisely with the maternal? The identification of the womb and the tomb is a trope in Western representation from Plato's myth of the cave, to the medieval understanding of a monastery or an anchorhold, from Francis Bacon's forcible "wooing" of nature and the "masculine birth of time," to William Blake's "Daughters of Albion," and the lyrics of contemporary pop music. Moreover it is a commonplace of psychoanalytic theory that the infant longs for unification with its mother, and enters the (masculinist) social and linguistic symbolic only by repressing that unassuageable loss. Now if, as I would argue, that symbolic is necrophilic, then the complex which underlies it is at least in part an unacknowledged longing for the maternal, a longing repressed by death-dealing strategies of control.

In many respects these ideas are not new; they are the stock-in-trade of a considerable body of feminist writings, even if I have juxtaposed them in a slightly different way. But the question returns: how shall this necrophilic symbolic be changed, even if it is complexified in the ways I have mentioned? Again, the analogy with therapy may prove useful. When a client has begun to recognize not only the problems generated by their feelings, responses, and behaviors but also the underlying fears and desires, these then become available for deliberate reappraisal and choice: not choice in the abstract or once and for all, but steady quotidian reorientation. Similarly when society recognizes the genealogy of death on which it is premised, and its underlying fears and desires, then choices open up for natality, new beginnings which reorient responses and attitudes and revalue otherness, whether of gender, sexuality, "race," or species, or indeed the planet itself and the material universe.

These considerations are further sharpened by reintroducing the third side of the triangulation, namely the genealogy of religion/secularism, which is at every turn interrelated with gender but also with the symbolic of death and other worlds. In modernity religion and secularism are regularly presented as opposites, as for example in the putative conflict between religion and science. However, I have already suggested that in many respects religion and secularism in modernity are on common ground, in particular in banishing God from the world and from knowledge, in the emphasis on beliefs and their justification, and in their focus on practicality or utilitarianism which easily slides into commodification: all these, again, can be shown to be interlinked with preoccupation with death and with "conquering" death, whether in this world or some other.

What I suggest, therefore, is that we should look not so much for what secularism by itself is repressing, or religion by itself; but rather we should ask what is being silenced by the common ground shared between them. And here I want to urge that a very important consideration is beauty. If we compare the centrality of beauty in the religious writings of late antiquity and the medieval mystics and theologians with its virtual absence in contemporary Christian theology and philosophy of religion, the contrast is startling. In premodern writing there were many who placed beauty squarely in the center of such a conversion of the imaginary: "Late have I loved you, O Beauty, so ancient and so new, late have I loved you!" wrote Augustine;[2] and it was the discovery of this Beauty and this love that released him to his real longings and helped him find a way forward in his tangled up sexuality. Augustine, to be sure, struggled with the relationship between this Beauty and his sensory experiences, often relegating the former to the strictly spiritual, as though Beauty can have nothing to do with the body. He bequeathed his struggle, on this as on sexual matters, to medieval thinkers in the West, who were often torn, as he was, between *concupiscentia oculorum*, ocular desire for beauty that diverts from spiritual concern, and a recognition that in painting, architecture, music, illumination of manuscripts, and the physical world itself the soul can be drawn to the wonder of God.[3] With the Reformation, however, and the emphasis (at least in Protestant countries) upon the Word, visual representation was often taken to be less important, even idolatrous;[4] and belief replaced beauty as the mode of access to the divine. The emphasis on beliefs and their justification in Protestant theology and philosophy of religion almost completely obscures consideration of beauty and its centrality in inspiring and focusing longing and desire.[5]

In the secular counterpart of religion in modernity, the march of technology and the military–industrial–information complex has little room for beauty, which is relegated (with mystical experience) to the private realm, not of public importance. It is of course true that there is great interest in "fine arts," as well as intense holiday pressure on the countryside; but here again we find the features of modernity, of slipping into commodification and being a private "leisure" activity, not part of the serious business of everyday life. It could be argued that contrary to what I am suggesting modernity in fact shows a heightened awareness of beauty, as evidenced by the establishment of museums, national parks, art galleries, and concert halls. Welcome as these are, however, I would argue that the very need for them partly proves my point: if areas of the countryside were not set apart for conservation they would be gobbled up as building sites; but we do not have to worry about the converse, that factories or motorways will be destroyed because of increasing demand for unspoiled country. Similarly art and artifacts are gathered into museums and galleries, partly to conserve them, partly to render them commodities for cultured consumption; but it would be hard to argue that before the existence of museums people were less involved with beautiful things or cared less about their preservation.

Beauty is, of course, also a candidate for genealogy, and can not be discussed as a natural or universal essence. In modernity beauty has been linked with the feminine, as in the writings of Burke and Kant, and with the emotional; whereas sublimity was seen as masculine, awe-inspiring, and ultimately rational. Again, there has been considerable attention focused on the sublime, perhaps precisely because it has been constructed as rational and masculine, whereas (feminized) beauty was more easily dismissable as mere prettiness.[6] Thus Derrida, in *The Truth in Painting*, discusses the claim that "the sublime cannot inhabit any sensible form"[7] and therefore, unlike beauty, cannot be presented or occur in natural configuration. The unrepresentibility of the sublime is taken even further by Lyotard, who valorizes the sublime precisely as the feeling of incommensurability, the shock of impossible juxtaposition, linked with desire, but desire best glossed as violent.[8] Beauty and its attracting power is ignored or dismissed as naive consolation. Throughout the modern and postmodern discourse on the beautiful and the sublime, the interconnections with gender and death require careful investigation; clearly they are ubiquitous.

One of the reasons that it is so interesting to lift up beauty for reconsideration is the way in which it links longing and desire with natality, and both with the divine. Elaine Scarry, in her book *On Beauty and Being Just*, points out that recognition of beauty "seems to incite, even to require, the act of replication":[9] if we see a beautiful landscape (or person, or painting) we paint a copy, if we can, or take photographs, or write a poem or an entry in a journal, or send a postcard to a friend describing the beauty we have experienced. We long not only to retain the experience of the beautiful but also in some way to recreate it. Yet the recreation is not just mindless copying (unless it is mere commodification: a thousand bookmarks and mugs printed with Wordsworth's "Daffodils"), but can often be a creation of beauty in itself, as a Mahler symphony creates a musical rendition of light upon a mountain. Thus beauty demands the enactments of one of the central features of natality, which, above all else, is the potential for newness, fresh beginnings, while at the same time requiring its own preservation. Scarry points out how often we remark of a beautiful thing: "I never saw/heard/etc. anything quite like it": it both presents itself as newness and also leads to fresh creativity. "The beautiful thing seems – is – incomparable, unprecedented; and that sense of being without precedent conveys a sense of the 'newness' or 'newbornness' of the entire world."[10] As Simone Weil wrote,

> The love of the beauty of the world ... involves ... the love of all the truly precious things that bad fortune can destroy. The truly precious things are those forming ladders reaching toward the beauty of the world, openings on to it –

and Weil immediately speaks of books and education, along with the kestrel hovering in the air currents, as having the potential to develop in us such openings.[11]

But putting this another way, is there not here an indication that attending to beauty could help to change the imaginary? If the necrophilia of modernity is an obsession, to be understood as I have suggested as a collective neurosis, then even if we accept this diagnosis, I have pointed out why rational argument and analysis will not get us out of it. Only by catching glimpses of a better way, of delight, of freedom and joy, can those struggling with neuroses find the courage and incentive to liberate themselves from the structures of control and claim instead that which meets their true desires. To change the necrophilic symbolic of modernity and its discursive and material practices, might it not be an effective strategy to seek, in the counter discourses of natality which give the lie to the omnipotence and fearfulness of death, the beauty that draws us spontaneously to yearn towards it?

And yet, even if this is partly right, it cannot be the whole story. For if it is true that attending to beauty could change the imaginary, surely it is equally true that unless our imaginary changes we will not attend to beauty. Part of my point, after all, has been that in modernity beauty – and certainly an acknowledgment of longing for beauty – has largely been crowded out of the world into museums and galleries and national parks, into the margins of private or leisure existence. Neither is it any use pretending that anyone seeking to address this situation, no matter how progressive in their thinking, is somehow outside of the necrophilic symbolic, in a pure place, free of the compulsions and repressions which that symbolic enacts in the master discourses and practices of modernity. We cannot just step outside the broad contours of the scientific or legal or economic or philosophical conceptualizations of Western modernity even if we want to. We bring ourselves along to any consideration and action; and we – any who read and write and seek to intervene in the languages and civilization of Western post/modernity – are always already formed, for good and ill, by its symbolic.

Thus those of us who want to help effect changes in the death-dealing structures of thought and practice are the first to stand in need of re-formation, of learning how to think – and be – otherwise. And so we are back to the questions with which I began: who, and from what place, can intervene in the imaginary? Yet this sort of circle is of course not new, either in hermeneutics or in psychotherapy; and in both cases it is frequently found that while one might return again and again to the same old questions, one is not asking them from quite the same old place or in quite the same old way. The previous considerations have, I hope, somewhat altered the perspective on these questions. Indeed, though the questions are the same, some resources have begun to emerge which help enable a response.

Some things are obvious. First, we cannot think otherwise just by deciding, perhaps as a resolution for the new millennium, that from now on that is what we are going to do. But what we can do is to set ourselves the task of deliberately problematizing the present and its symbolic. Moreover, once we are alert to thinking about the multiple ways in which religion, gender, and death have been triangulated in the changing formation of the Western symbolic, we can work to develop genealogies which bring them to light and thus enable us to understand the present in different ways. This will ensure that we will never be able to think about it in the same way again, just as we can never go back to the old ways of thinking about madness or sexuality or carceral regimes once we have read Foucault. And in this work we can try to uncover what has been silenced, listen to the voices which can often be discerned in the margins, retrieve the dangerous memories that tell of other ways of thinking and being. All this requires patience and investigation; and in the research on which I am embarked I make a start at a gendered genealogy of necrophilia and at attending to alternative voices, voices of natality and beauty which can still be discerned and retrieved, even if not unambiguously.

Yet while I believe that such mental reeducation is enormously important, the idea of the centrality of beauty suggests something further. There is something highly ironic (if not actually disingenuous) about those of us who are paid good salaries and retained in posts of respect and esteem by academic establishments to set ourselves up as people who will lead the way in thinking/being otherwise. Our identities, not to mention our livelihoods and our daily tasks and expectations, are shaped by these institutions of modernity. While there is a long and precious tradition of academic freedom which must be zealously guarded, it is also true that respectability, publication, and professional advance are never without criteria set from within the academic world: and indeed it is probably better that they are set there than by some external body which would be all too prone further to commodify and package what counts as thought. Inevitably, our thoughts and even the possibilities of our thoughts are shaped by where we are and whom we wish to please, whose respect we need to gain or retain. How, then, shall *we* think otherwise?

The premodern monastic impulse, especially the early movement by men and women into the solitude and silence of the desert, for all its many problems, did recognize the need, and provided the opportunity, to place oneself outside conventional structures and expectations, and to develop a self-discipline geared toward contemplation of the divine Beauty as a central good. At its worst, asceticism degenerated into self-hatred, misogyny, fear of sexuality, irrelevance, and utter pettiness. But at its best it enabled a gradual transformation in which core desires could be recognized and enhanced, desire for beauty, goodness, the divine; while the fears and attachments that stood in as the displacement of these desires could gradually fall away. Such an *ascesis*, or "therapy of desires," worked not by trying to argue people out of a destructive symbolic but by fostering the longing for beauty and its creative newness. Nor was this desire premised on a lack, but on a plenitude, whose fullness, however, deepened and reduplicated desire.

From any perspective, and certainly from a feminist's, an exploration of such ascesis not merely as an idea but as a way of living has enormous problems. And yet, if we dismiss it altogether, as has largely been the case in modernity, do we not lose more than we gain? Putting it another way, is it not urgent that we – academics – find or construct places where we become again vulnerable to beauty? – beauty that incites to creativity, newbornness, while at the same time generating fierce, tender protectiveness toward that which must on no account be lost? What is holiness in postmodernity? That is the underlying question of my research.

Notes

1. Cf. my "Before the Rooster Crows: John Locke, Margaret Fell, and the Betrayal of Knowledge in Modernity," *Literature and Theology*, 15: 1 (March 2001).
2. Augustine, *Confessions* X.27.
3. Cf. Margaret Miles, *Image as Insight: Visual Understanding in Western Christianity and Secular Culture* (Boston: Beacon Press, 1985).
4. Cf. Martin Jay, *Downcast Eyes: The Denigration of Vision in Twentieth-Century French Thought* (Berkeley: University of California Press, 1994), ch. 1.
5. This is to a large extent also true of Catholic theology in modernity, with however the monumental exception of Hans Urs von Balthasar's *Herrlichkeit*; trans. *The Glory of the Lord*, 7 vols. (Edinburgh: T. & T. Clark, 1983ff.); cf. John Riches, (ed.), *The Analogy of Beauty: The Theology of Hans Urs von Balthasar* (Edinburgh: T. & T. Clark, 1986).
6. Cf. Peter de Bella, *The Discourse of the Sublime: History, Aesthetics and the Subject* (Oxford: Blackwell Publishers, 1989).
7. Jacques Derrida, *The Truth in Painting*, trans. Geoff Bennington and Ian McLeod (Chicago and London: University of Chicago Press, 1987), p. 131.
8. Cf. Jean-François Lyotard, *The Postmodern Condition: A Report on Knowledge*, trans. Geoff Bennington and Brian Massumi (Manchester: Manchester University Press, 1984), p. 78; "The Sublime and the Avant-Garde," in *The Lyotard Reader*, ed. Andrew Benjamin (Oxford: Blackwell Publishers, 1989), pp. 196–211.
9. Elaine Scarry, *On Beauty and Being Just* (Princeton, NJ: Princeton University Press, 1999), p. 3.
10. Ibid, p. 22.
11. Simone Weil, *Waiting on God*, trans. Emma Craufurd (London: Routledge and Kegan Paul, 1951), p. 180.

CHAPTER 17

Companionable Wisdoms: What Insights Might Feminist Theorists Gather from Feminist Theologians?

Serene Jones

As Serene Jones informs us in the following essay, she is a Christian feminist theologically working out of the Reformed tradition. Several feminist voices can be heard in this volume – Grace Jantzen, Mieke Bal, Mary McClintock Fulkerson, Janet Soskice, Pamela Sue Anderson. All of them owe a considerable debt to their conversations with secular feminist theory, but only some of them identify themselves as Christian and working out of a particular tradition. In this respect Jones's work establishes a link with Janet Soskice's, albeit that Soskice hails from the Roman Catholic tradition. Jones's relationship to the Reformed tradition is not unambivalent, however. Her first book (from her thesis) was a scholarly exposition of Calvin's *Institutes* within their historical, biographical, theological, and rhetorical contexts: *Calvin and the Rhetoric of Piety* (Louisville, KY, 1995). This book's last chapter gestures towards contemporary theology in both its poststructural possibilities (with respect to Calvin) and its postliberal forms.

As both a doctoral student and a teacher at Yale, Jones has enjoyed conversations with the founding voices of postliberalism: Hans Frei and George Lindbeck. An interesting connection and comparison might be made here between Jones's work and that of an older Yale School graduate who has contributed to this volume, Walter Lowe. It is significant that the work of both Lowe and Jones has developed by pushing postliberal emphases (on discourse, community, and tradition-based reasoning) towards a profound dialogue with poststructuralism. For both, the attention paid to rhetoric and representation no doubt facilitated an entry into poststructuralist theories of language and meaning. (One recalls the passing references to Wittgenstein in Lindbeck's book *The Nature of Doctrine*.) But with Jones the engagement with poststructural theory has issued in a more explicit commitment to feminism. In a paper presented in the Women and Religion Section of the American Academy of Religion in 1988, entitled "This God Which Is Not One: Irigaray and Barth on the Divine" (published in 1993), Jones demonstrated an early concern to bring the Reformed tradition into dialogue with feminism. Whereas her book on Calvin has nothing to say about *sexual* politics, it is certainly concerned throughout with the political. There is, for example, an explicit examination of the way in which theological discourse is always a rhetorical practice, an exercise of power on behalf of a specific community. There is also a criticism of postliberal theology's failure to engage with the nature of power relations. But it is in her more recent book, *Feminist Theory and Christian Theology: Cartographies of Grace* (Minneapolis, MN, 2000), that she most fully explores the relation between Reformed theology and what she discerns as the "pragmatic eschatological orientation" of feminist theory.

As she states at the beginning of her essay, having completed *Feminist Theory and Christian Theology* Jones was led to think through the relationship between contemporary critical theory and theology from the other side: the contribution theological discourse can make to contemporary secular debates. This is a rich vein to mine and points to a significant new perspective for someone emerging from the postliberal concern with the maintenance of the tradition-based community. That is, through conversations with other disciplines Jones is being drawn to see how theology can become a public discourse, not simply in-house talk that might gain some clarification when viewed in terms of contemporary theoretical analysis. We will have to see how this develops, but the essay here marks once more the sea change I mention in my introduction to the present volume: an openness to engage into theological ideas, secular liberal approaches having exhausted themselves.

Several weeks ago I had lunch with a friend of mine who teaches feminist theory and employment law at the Yale Law School. We have become good friends over the years because we teach together in Women's Studies. As feminists, we always end up at all the same political meetings on campus; and we both have three-year-old daughters who, much to our feminist bewilderment, love to wear pink dresses. That day, she was working on a talk she was giving on employment law and gender. She wanted to suggest guidelines for designing work-place regulations that would not only prevent harm or protect rights but that would also go the added step and positively promote work environments where the worker as "a whole person" can flourish. She was stumped, at the level of theory, as to how she might construct her argument.

I responded, quite off the top of my head, not trying to be particularly theological, that Augustine's discussion of freedom might be helpful. I suggested that she was coming up against liberal social contract theory's rather limited understanding of freedom as "freedom of choice." I explained that in theological discussions, we often describe freedom as a condition that obtains when a person finds herself in an environment in which she can become, fully and in joy, the person she was created to be. Apart from this environment, no matter how many choices she might have, she is understood to be "imprisoned" in sin which "diminishes." I added further that she might be particularly interested in what feminist theologians and ethicists had said in recent years about this notion of freedom with respect to issues of embodiment and agency.

I finished and looked up to find my lunch companion staring at me, her brow furrowed in thought. "Wow . . . Augustine said that? And feminist theologians write about it?" "Well, yes," I said, grinning slightly at her surprise. Needless to say, a fascinating conversation ensued in which I continued to learn more about employment law and my friend, to her own amazement, gleaned new insights into the concept of freedom.

I begin with this story not because I take up the topic of freedom in this essay, but because, at a more general level, it is an example of the many conversations that have inspired my ongoing interest in the relationship between feminist theory and feminist theology.[1] As a theologian who both teaches in Women's and Gender Studies and does feminist work on Christian doctrine, I have long been aware that I have much to learn from feminist theorists. Like most feminist theologians, I read them avidly. However, the converse has not always been the case. Until recently, one would have been hard pressed to find a feminist theorist who not only took religion seriously but who actually read theological texts. I say "until recently" because in the last two years I have begun to sense a sea change in secular feminist attitudes toward theological matters. After years of uncomfortable silence when I would mention theology, I am now being asked earnest questions about theological resources for reflecting on issues like freedom, agency, embodiment, to say nothing of topics like truth, justice, and beauty.

In asking such questions, it is clear to me that feminist theorists are turning to theologians not simply because they want to be open-minded pluralists. They are asking because they seriously believe we may be able to help them get through some of the conceptual tangles in which feminist theory is currently caught. To borrow a metaphor, if feminist theory and theology can be imagined as dance partners, the theorists are at last asking us to lead, if only for a moment, in the expectation that they have new steps to learn and unexpected graces to master. What I want to do briefly in this essay is sketch out the beginnings of what I hope will be a useful theological response to their long-awaited queries.[2]

Let me begin by first describing who I am referring to when I speak of feminist theorists. Although the title "feminist theory" refers to work being done in fields that stretch across the disciplinary spectrum, I am most interested here in work being done in the fields of literary theory, cultural studies, political philosophy, and legal studies, work represented in the thought of figures like Seyla Benhabib, Judith Butler, Patricia Hill Collins, Drucilla Cornell, Luce Irigaray, and Iris Young.[3] Although the theoretic work of each of these thinkers differs enormously, they share a number of intellectual commitments. All are constructivists with respect to gender; all are epistemological anti-foundationalists; and their constructive proposals are all motivated by deeply pragmatic sensibilities.

On the other side, when I refer to feminist theology in this essay, I am narrowing a large field of reflection by focusing primarily on those feminist theologians who engage in constructive theological reflection on doctrines central to the Christian tradition, who are similarly anti-foundationalists and social constructivists, and whose theological reflections are bounded by strongly pragmatic, feminist sensibilities. Here I would list the work of theologians such as Rebecca Chopp, Mary Fulkerson, Ada Maria Isasi-Diaz, Joan Martin, Amy Plantinga Pauw, Letty Russell, and Kathryn Tanner.[4] I should say as well that in this essay my own voice as a feminist theologian working out of the Reformed tradition sounds loudly in my accounts of the potential "companionable wisdoms" that feminist theologians might offer to feminist theorists.

To begin outlining a response to the question of what feminist theorists have to learn from theologians, it is helpful to start with a description of what we share. Here I offer a brief outline of four central moments in what I refer to as our common story. It is the story that feminist theorists and theologians alike tell when they are asked to give an account of the overarching aim and nature of their enterprise. (It's a story that surfaced repeatedly at Yale in our recent discussions about changing the title of "Women's Studies" to "Women's and Gender Studies.") The story goes something like this: first, we begin our descriptions of feminist theory and/or theology by pointing to the communal contexts of struggle within which we first became feminists. For feminist theorists, this community is sometimes (but not frequently) religious. For feminist theologians, Christian and Jewish faith communities and their traditions and scriptures are of paramount importance. Next, we embrace what I call a "pragmatic utopianism," in that we recognize the role that a normative vision of "the-way-things-should-be" plays in motivating these communities to struggle for social change. The story continues as we then describe sharing a sense that the best contribution we can offer to this struggle and vision is to do the critical work of "theory" and/or "theology" – to reflect on the myriad ways gender relations of power inform our most fundamental patterns of thought and practice; and this move to theory has been made by many, both anti-foundationalists and social constructivists. In this context, we typically narrate three common themes that surface again and again when we do theory: the themes of "self," "oppression," and "community." And finally, we conclude the story by reflexively committing our work to the pragmatic test of communal viability – we ask: Does it contribute to the betterment of women's lives?[5]

So this is our "ideal" story: feminist theologians and theorists alike stand grounded in a community, teleologically oriented toward a normative vision of the future, critically positioned to reflect on themes of self, oppression, and community in light of this normative vision, and committed to a reflexive pragmatics of communal enactment.

Now against the backdrop of this shared narrative, let me describe a tangle that feminist theory finds itself in as of late – a tangle that has partially prompted their recent interest in things theological. After a long period of postmodernist disenchantment with Enlightenment universals, feminist theorists are reawakening to the need for theory to engage in the work of normative reflection – the need for theorists to do *constructive* as well as *deconstructive* work on the issue of gendered relations of power. However, the road that feminists have traveled to reach this place of realization makes doing this constructive work quite difficult. For those who work in literary and philosophical fields, their deconstructive impulses seem to have paralyzed their constructive impulses.[6] For those working in the fields of political science and legal studies, their social constructivism has turned them squarely toward community as the locus of value, but having arrived, they find it a difficult place to be. Not only have they struggled with the reality that communities can be rather oppressive environments, but they have also found their communitarian colleagues using "community" to authorize a return to traditional values – many of which are uncritically patriarchal.[7] Consequently, both types of theorists – the deconstructivists and the communitarians – find themselves uncertain about how they should proceed when crafting constructive proposals.

What has also happened to feminist theory as it has wandered down this path over the past twenty years is that it has increasingly distanced itself from the communities that initially inspired its eschatological yearnings – its originary normative moment. It is not an exaggeration to say of feminist theory that its principal interlocutor has become the academy and not, as feminists ideally describe it, both the academy and emancipatory communities of struggle. This increasing distance has had the deleterious effect of leaving feminist theorists "stranded in theory" to work out their theoretical uncertainty about normative claims. In other words (recalling my original narrative), feminist theorists have left behind their grounding communities, have jumped over the issue of emancipatory visions, and now find themselves stranded on the island of theory, with only the academy to talk to. If feminist theorists were content with such a place (and some are), this wouldn't be a problem. But most of them (I should say "us" because I think of my work as firmly rooted in the area of feminist theory) aren't, because it conflicts with the pragmatic utopian impulses that drove their project in the first place, impulses that are now resurfacing in this move toward normative reflection.[8]

Here is the first place that I think feminist theorists might find the work of feminist theologians helpful. For all its faults, feminist theology has not lost touch with the communities and the normative traditions that inspire its eschatological yearnings. Because they are not stranded in theory but remain tied to communities of faith and their normative visions, which theory is intended to serve, feminist theologians are well situated to negotiate tangles related to the work of normative reflection. In this regard, they are better versed than their sister theorists in the arts of immanent critique, and they are theoretically more agile than some of their secular feminist colleagues when articulating the nature of pragmatic utopianism – or in a theological context, "the pragmatics of an already/not-yet eschatology." Because of this orientation, I contend that feminist theologians are much better at managing the messy character of communally grounded normative claims.[9] This is most evident in the fact that where feminist theorists see tensions, contradictions, dualisms, and debilitating conflicts, feminist theologians often see what I call "companionable wisdoms."

Here, I want to focus on this last point – feminist theologians' ability to manage the messiness of normative claims in the context of its pragmatic eschatology and its correlative understanding of grace. And I do not want to explore this point by simply making a few methodological comments about what feminist theologians do. Rather, I want to jump right into the substance of normative claims made by feminist theologians about the three topics I mentioned earlier, self, community, and oppression, and describe briefly how, as feminist theologians, we negotiate the tangles that seem to have entrapped our sister theorists.

Let's begin with the first: the nature of the self. At the center of contemporary feminist theoretical discussions of this topic has been the now well-worn debate between constructivists and essentialists over women's nature and sexual difference.[10] On the essentialist side of the debate, we have seen the strength of its ability to generate robust conceptions of selfhood that have functioned in empowering ways for women.[11] Yet as a negative consequence, we have seen the dangers of constructing false universals that reinscribe, under the label "essential," typically sexist, racist, heterosexist, and classist views about the proper roles of men and women. On the constructivist side, we have seen the strength of its ability to dismantle traditional gendered patterns of thought and to cause productive "gender trouble" as it disturbs and exposes the constructed character of normative "essentials." As a negative result of this, however, we have also seen how this activity of relentless critique has left little positive space for articulating a vision of personhood that women can practically "become into." Thus, we find this debate stalemated as the strengths and weaknesses of each press inward.[12]

How have feminist theologians negotiated this same issue in their struggle to deconstruct patriarchal understandings of the self while reconstructing an emancipatory conception of personhood? As suggested above, they have done so by seeing companionable wisdoms where feminist theorists see contradictions.[13] Nowhere is this more evident than in a feminist theological reappropriation of the doctrines of justification and sanctification.[14] In the doctrine of justification one encounters a theological logic in which the self is radically "undone" or "deconstructed" by a judgment set upon her, not by merit or nature, but by divine decree, a decree that calls into question all the identifying descriptions we are wont to put upon ourselves and others. When interpreted from a feminist perspective, this doctrine allows one to critique the hold traditional gender conceptions have upon the self. Grace undoes it. Companion to this logic is the doctrine of sanctification, a doctrine driven by a theological logic of identity reconstruction. In sanctification the self undone by justification is remade according to the law of love. The self is given constraints to live in, form to become into. Grace, in this second moment, contains us. In this context the self is viewed according to two simultaneous images: one of dismantling critique and freeing judgment, the other of organic wholeness and envelopment. Use of these doctrines thus illustrates that two very different imagistic economies – one judicial, the other organic – can serve as identity markers for a single self held in the embrace of a unified, double grace.

Alongside, and related to, these doctrinal companions, we may place feminist theologians' embrace of a synthetic position between pure essentialism and radical constructivism – what feminist theorists call "strategic essentialism."[15] As the name implies, this position accepts a minimal number of strategically helpful claims for universality. Claims, for example, that allow us to talk about women as a more or less definable collective, generally sharing the common experiences of exploitation and oppression and a rudimentary sense of the conditions basic to the flourishing of women. The specifics of these claims may vary from theologian to theologian and from one context to another – hence the position's immediate impulse toward constructivism. Further, while acknowledging some fundamental commonality among women, strategic essentialism also openly affirms the powerful role played by culture in shaping the thick gendered overlay of that commonality, such that "womanness" manifests in both predictable patterns and wildly unpredictable (subversive, creative, faith-driven) variations.[16] Although essentialism and constructivism coexist in this position, essentialism is logically prior in determining *upon whom* social construction bears its influence. To borrow the rhetoric of sanctification and justification, here the containing power of God's sanctifying grace logically precedes the dismantling power of God's judgment. In other words, our personhood as women is affirmed before our performance of culturally prescribed gender roles receives God's refining critique. Thus, the companions of a minimal essentialism and a qualified constructivism allow women both a graced "envelope" for selfhood and what amounts to both an opportunity for and challenge to renewable creativity in our enactments of gender.

I could say much more about this topic, but I would like to move on to the next theme, oppression, to further my argument that feminist theology can help feminist theorists find companionable wisdoms where they presently see only conflicts. While feminists have long been adept at analyzing the oppression of women, feminist theory has raised this conversation to a new level in recent years. In addition to expanding our appreciation for the institutional dimensions of oppression, all the theorists I mentioned earlier have pushed us to see that a binary logic of gender relations which privileges things "masculine" and undervalues the "feminine" undergirds the very language that crafts the contours of the selves we all become.[17] This recognition has had the positive effect of humbling feminist "purist" pretensions about our abilities to escape patriarchy – for one can no more easily step out of it than one can step out of language itself.[18] But the positive humbling has come at a cost and has led feminists into yet another series of tangles. If language so entraps us, what are we to say about possibilities for agency within this prison? How do we avoid a kind of linguistic social determinism that rules out the very acts of resistance that have motivated feminism since its inception? On the other side, if we dodge the force of this feminist analysis of language, how do we avoid the debilitating guilt that attends conceptions of oppression that see it solely in terms of individual agency? In asking these questions, feminist theory is asking us as theologians: Is there a place for understanding oppression that stands somewhere between exaggerated notions of responsibility and rather despairing notions of entrapment?

Again, to this last question, feminist theologians can respond by pointing to the doctrine of sin – a doctrine in which the tensions that have stumped feminist theorists are held together as companionable wisdoms that mark our life before God.[19] According to the classical formulation of the doctrine of original sin, sin is paradoxically both something that happens to us and something that we do. We are caught in it and cannot escape it, despite our best intentions, and yet we are responsible for it, for we willingly participate in it. Sin, in the classic language of Luther, is a prison house of our own making, albeit one that we cannot simply choose to escape by force of will.

It seems to me that this describes well feminist theory's view of the prison house of language – it inhabits us just as we willingly inhabit it. What feminist theologians can point to, further, is that the Christian doctrine of sin does not end here but is inextricably intertwined with a lively conception of the grace that forgives (and in its forgiveness, reveals sin). In grace, we are authored by a freeing word that comes to us from beyond the prison house while also leaving us where we are, implicated in a sin from which we cannot fully disentangle ourselves. We stand here, *simul iustus et peccator*, simultaneously saint and sinner – persons who are unceasingly marked by sin and yet are freed from it through the counter-discourse of grace. With respect to gender and the oppression of women, we are thus doubly marked as persons (both men and women) who are deeply implicated in its oppressive logic – as both perpetrators and victims – and yet also called to live in a grace that affirms the ultimate flourishing of women. We thus stand here, affirming our agency as both a willing tool of sin and a resister of sin.[20] Here, then, we see yet again how, in the doctrines of sin and grace, we find two very different imagistic economies standing together as markers of a single self.

Let me now very briefly turn to the last topic: community – a theme which has lately occupied the attention of both feminist theorists and theologians alike, a theme which also builds directly on what I have said about self and oppression, or grace and sin. In the world of feminist theory the most sustained discussions of this topic have occurred among political theorists who have made feminist interventions into the liberal/communitarian debate. Out of this discussion has emerged yet another set of tangles. With respect to liberalism the feminists I mentioned earlier all share a deep suspicion of its Enlightenment rationalism and its unexamined universalism. On the other hand, it is hard to find feminists who are not also deeply appreciative of the deliberative openness that the liberal model of political life seeks to foster – a model that in theory tries to accommodate great diversity. With respect to the other side of the debate, feminist theorists have found themselves in agreement with communitarian constructivism, at least in principle, but have become quite uncomfortable with its seeming provincialism and its social conservatism. It's rather ironic that the appealing openness of constructivism, which originally drove feminists to conversation with the communitarians, has led feminists to accuse communitarians of an insularity that exceeds anything feminists found previously in the liberalism that, as feminists, they so fiercely critiqued. In the midst of this tangle, feminists are seeking to construct alternative models that imagine communities marked by what I have called "bounded openness" – a model of ideal community in which boundaries exist for the sake of establishing a ruled community whose very identity rests in its openness.[21]

While I would never suggest to a feminist theorist that "the church" is the ideal/real community she is looking for, it does seem to me that feminist reflections on Christian ecclesial identity might be extremely helpful to theorists as they struggle to define this space of "bounded openness." What kind of ecclesial community might we describe for them? In the language of the tradition, I would suggest a community marked by the double signs of Law and Gospel.[22] Marked by Gospel, the church stands as a community freed to be for the world – to be witnesses to a grace that embraces all. Marked by Law, it is also a community who in its freedom seeks to witness to the Gospel by embodying practices, disciplines, and rules that give to this grace material form. Another way of thinking about this space of bounded openness in ecclesial community is to see the church under the marks of justification and sanctification – the double marks of a freeing judgment that turns us outward and a material set of laws that give us specific form. While it is quite evident to anyone who looks at present-day churches that this bounded openness hardly exists in any state of perfection, this too is another lesson that feminist theologians might pass on to theorists. The power of an eschatological vision lies not only in its future but also in its ability to transform the present as we try to live into that future in the here and now.

Having now considered some of the places that feminist theologians find companionable wisdoms where feminist theorists might locate tensions or dualisms, it is worth signaling a methodological point. Feminists' (both theorists' and theologians') concerns over Western binarisms focus on the dynamic of implicit exclusion or subjugation that typically obtains in these pairings. Simplistically, the negative or lesser value of the (by necessity) subjugated term defines and buttresses the decidedly higher value of the other – hence, male over female, mind over body, reason over emotion. One might be tempted, from a cursory glance, to place some of the couplings above – Law and Gospel, sin and grace – under the same concern. Yet, in much contemporary feminist theology, these couplings do not function dualistically, that is, as either/or concepts; nor do they map onto binarisms like the ones listed above in which a gendered code is virtually always at work. Rather, they operate *paradoxically* (as opposed to parasitically), first one taking logical or conceptual priority, now the other. So, for example, one does not choose whether to live in sin or under grace; one lives in the tension of having been simultaneously overcome by both. Further, one's starting point for talking about this paradoxical condition depends on one's rhetorical context and purpose. Thus, each pair, as pair, has a strategically malleable nature that benefits from the implicit and positive inclusion of both terms.

One final word about this conversation I have been describing between feminist theologians and theorists. I have tried to avoid casting it as a conversation of strict correlation in which theorists ask the eternal questions that feminist theology then answers. I think the process is actually much more ad hoc than this and moves in both directions. When done best, it proceeds in a rather rough fashion. Sometimes insights spark; at other times, nothing emerges. And feminist theologians need to be well aware that the insights they spark in this sharing may well lead some feminist theorists to carry feminist theological insights into realms of reflection where we would not, in good faith, choose to go. Nor should we. The specificity of our theology need not be diluted or compromised by work that feminist theorists do with our insights. I also want to make it clear that I do not think feminist theorists would find all their answers if they simply became *Christian* feminists. I imagine their gleanings to be more like those I take home from an interreligious dialogue in which the resources of another tradition serve to help me better understand my own.

In conclusion, I should add, if in this process of feminist theologians and theorists dancing together, we both manage to loosen up a few tensed muscles and learn a few new, graceful steps, then, as a feminist theologian, I cannot help but imagine that God will have added her blessings to this delightfully awkward endeavor.

Notes

This essay was originally delivered to an interdisciplinary group of scholars gathered for a conference at Notre Dame in the spring of 1999. The conference was entitled "Religion in the Academy: Disciplinary Perspectives," and was sponsored by an ongoing group convened to discuss "Religion and Higher Education." At the time I presented this paper, I had just completed *Feminist Theory and Christian Theology: Cartographies of Grace*, and this is my attempt to respond, publicly, to a very important topic not addressed in that text, namely, how a feminist theology, like the one I outline in the book, might decisively intervene in contemporary debates in feminist theory.

1. Serene Jones, *Feminist Theory and Christian Theology: Cartographies of Grace* (Minneapolis, MN: Fortress Press, 2000). For an excellent discussion of the relation between feminist theory and theology, see *Horizons in Feminist Theology*, ed. Sheila Davaney and Rebecca Chopp (Minneapolis, MN: Augsburg Fortress, 1997).
2. For the past several years I have been writing about the relationship between feminist theory and feminist theology. An image I have often used to describe this work borrows from a metaphor of Luce Irigaray's. I have tried to set feminist theory and feminist theology "near to one another" in order to see how they refract and reflect off and through one another. For the most part, I have found myself following an age-old pattern of theological reflection and primarily tracing the refraction of light as it moves *from* theory *in and through* theology. What I want to do in this essay is to reverse this direction, and suggest several "insights" that feminist theorists might gather from feminist theologians if we paused to watch the light of the theological

texts refract through those of theory. I want to further suggest that these insights are more than just an interesting side-show for feminist theorists. They have the potential to help feminist theorists get through some of the complicated theoretical tangles in which they are currently caught.

It is important to note, as well, that feminist theologians and ethicists are, on the whole, studious readers of feminist theory. And much to our benefit, their writings have advanced our work enormously. Such is not the case, however, with respect to present-day feminist theorists' interest in theology. It is hard to find feminist theorists who are aware of the feminist theological corpus, much less well versed in its internal workings. This lack of familiarity is, I am afraid, not only the product of feminist theorists' diverted attention. For many, it signals a deeper aversion towards things "religious" in general. This aversion is rooted, I believe, partly in the anti-religious sentiments of the Marxism that many of them cut their theoretical teeth on and partly in negative associations they have with the "Christianity" that has been caricatured in the media as the "religious Right." I am sure there are more reasons, but whatever the case may be, their basic posture towards things religious – including feminist theology – has been, until recently, "defensive" and "uninformed."

This aversion is rather odd when viewed in historical perspective. As any student of recent North American history well knows, it was in Christian churches and Jewish synagogues that first and second wave feminism first made its appearance on North American soil. And in the 1960s and 1970s it was in religious studies programs and seminaries (where Mary Daly et al. were being read: Mary Daly, *Beyond God the Father* (Boston: Beacon Press, 1973); *Woman Spirit Rising: A Feminist Reader in Religion*, ed. Carol Christ and Judith Plaskow (New York: Harper & Row, 1979) that an interest in feminist academic studies first made its appearance on university campuses. A similar pattern holds today, in that the bulk of the "theoretical" work on gender done by women of color is "theological" in nature. It has been interesting for me to watch my colleagues in women's studies deal with this phenomenon. It is striking how much more "open" to religion they are when it appears in the work of Latina and African-American women than in the work of Euro-American scholars. I should also add here that African-American and Latina feminist theorists rarely have the same aversion to theology that their Euro-American feminist colleagues have.

3   This short list of theorists does not begin to cover the disciplinary diversity of feminists currently doing work in "theory." For general introductions to feminist theory, I recommend Chris Weedon, *Feminist Practice and Poststructuralist Theory* (Oxford: Blackwell Publishers, 1987); Josephine Donovan, *Feminist Theory: The Intellectual Traditions of American Feminism* (New York: Continuum, 1985); and Rosemarie Tong, *Feminist Thought: A Comprehensive Analysis* (Boulder, CO: Westview Press, 1989). I have chosen the six theorists listed above because their work incorporates what I considered to be the most salient features of the present day options in feminist theory. See Seyla Benhabib, *Situating the Self: Gender, Community, and Postmodernism in Contemporary Ethics* (New York: Cambridge University Press, 1992); Judith Butler, *Gender Trouble: Feminism and the Subversion of Identity* (New York: Routledge, 1990); Patricia Hill Collins, *Black Feminist Thought: Knowledge, Consciousness, and the Politics of Empowerment* (Boston: Unwin Press, 1990); Drucilla Cornell, *Beyond Accommodation: Ethical Feminism, Deconstruction, and the Law* (New York: Routledge: 1991); Luce Irigaray, *Speculum of the Other Woman*, trans. Gillian

C. Gill (Ithaca, NY: Cornell University Press, 1985) and *An Ethics of Sexual Difference*, trans. Carolyn Burke and Gillian Gill (Ithaca, NY: Cornell University Press, 1993); Iris Marion Young, *Justice and the Politics of Difference* (Princeton, NJ: Princeton University Press, 1990).

4   This list of feminist theologians is by no means meant to be comprehensive. I have highlighted only a few representative thinkers who simultaneously engage postmodernist questions and classical Christian doctrines. See Rebecca Chopp, *The Power to Speak: Feminism, Language, God* (New York: Crossroads, 1989); Mary Fulkerson, *Changing the Subject: Women's Discourses and Feminist Theology* (Minneapolis, MN: Fortress Press, 1994); Ada Maria Isasi-Diaz, *En La Lucha* (Minneapolis, MN: Fortress Press, 1993); Joan Martin, "The Notion of Difference for Emerging Womanish Ethics: The Writings of Audre Lorde and bell hooks," *Journal of Feminist Studies in Religion*, 9 (Spring–Fall 1993), pp. 39–51; Amy Plantinga Pauw, "The Word is Near You: A Feminist Conversation with Lindbeck," *Theology Today*, 50 (April 1993), pp. 45–55; Letty Russell, *Church in the Round: Feminist Interpretation of the Church* (Louisville, KY: Westminster/John Knox Press, 1993); and Kathryn Tanner, *Politics of God: Christian Theories and Social Justice* (Minneapolis, MN: Fortress Press, 1992) and *Theories of Culture: A New Agenda for Theology*, Guides to Theological Inquiry Series (Minneapolis, MN: Fortress Press, 1998). See also *Feminist Dictionary of Theology*, ed. Shannon Clarkson and Letty Russell (Louisville, KY: Westminster/John Knox Press, 1996).

5   The differences between us, in terms of this story, is an equally if not more interesting topic, but alas, that will have to wait for another day.

6   Here, I think primarily of the work of Judy Butler, *Gender Trouble*.

7   Here, I refer most specifically to the work of Iris Young, *Justice and the Politics of Difference* and Seyla Benhabib, *Situating the Self*.

8   For an interesting discussion of four different perspectives on "normative claims" in feminist theory, see Seyla Benhabib, Judith Butler, Drucilla Cornell, and Nancy Fraser, *Feminist Contentions: A Philosophical Exchange* (New York: Routledge, 1995).

9   For feminist theological discussions of normative claims, see Margaret Farley, "Feminism and Universal Morality," in *Prospects for a Common Morality*, ed. Gene Outka and John P. Reeder, Jr. (Princeton, NJ: Princeton University Press, 1993), pp. 170–90. Also see Sheila Davaney, ch. 12, "Continuing the Story, but Departing the Text: A Historicist Interpretation of Feminist Norms in Theology," in *Horizons in Feminist Theology* (Minneapolis, MN: Augsburg Fortress, 1997), pp. 198–214.

10 On feminist theorists' discussion of human nature, see Alison M. Jaggar, *Feminist Politics and Human Nature* (Totowa, NJ: Rowman and Allanheld, 1983); Elizabeth Spelman, *Inessential Women: Problems of Exclusion in Feminist Thought* (Boston: Beacon Press, 1988).

11 As I have argued elsewhere, this is particularly true of women whose identities have been fractured and dissimulated by Western socialization practices and the violences embedded therein.

12 Butler, Young, Benhabib, Collins, and Irigaray all try in different ways to negotiate this tension. See *Feminist Contentions*. Also see Kathi Weeks, *Constituting Feminist Subjects* (Ithaca, NY: Cornell University Press, 1998).

13 This balance in theological anthropology is achieved in different ways by different theorists. In *She Who Is*, Elizabeth Johnsonn, for example, posits the essential/constructivist "hoping self," and has no problem asserting both the constructed

character of gender and the centrality of "hope" as a normative moment in the construction of self. Rebecca Chopp takes a similar approach but places more emphasis on the constructivist side in *The Power to Speak: Feminism, Language, God* (New York: Crossroads, 1989). See similar discussions in Letty Russell's *Becoming Human* (Philadelphia: Westminster Press, 1982); Elaine Graham, *Making the Difference: Gender, Personhood, and Theology* (Minneapolis, MN: Fortress Press, 1995); Mary Fulkerson, *Changing the Subject: Women's Discourses and Feminist Theology* (Minneapolis, MN: Fortress Press, 1994); Susan Nelson Dunfee, *Beyond Servanthood: Christianity and the Liberation of Women* (Rochester, NH: University Press of America, 1989); Catherine Keller, *From a Broken Web: Separation, Sexism, and the Self* (Boston: Beacon Press, 1986); Mary Aquin O'Neill, "The Mystery of Being Human Together," in *Freeing Theology: The Essentials of Theology in Feminist Perspective*, ed. Catherine Mowry LaCugna (San Francisco: Harper Collins, 1993); Paula Cooey, *Religious Imagination and the Body: A Feminist Analysis* (New York: Oxford University Press, 1994). For critiques of essentialized womanhood in feminist theology see Ellen Armour, "Questioning 'Woman' in Feminist/Womanist Theology: Irigaray, Ruether, and Daly," ch. 6 in *Transfigurations: Theology and the French Feminists*, ed. C. W. Maggie Kim, Susan M. St. Ville, and Susan M. Simonaitis (Minneapolis, MN: Fortress Press, 1993); Katie Cannon, *Black Womanist Ethics* (Atlanta: Scholars Press, 1988) and *Katie's Cannon: Womanism and the Soul of the Black Community* (New York: Continuum, 1995). Also see Joan Martin, "The Notion of Difference."

14 A fuller description of a feminist reworking of the doctrine of justification and sanctification can be found in Jones, *Feminist Theory and Christian Theology*, ch. 3. Other feminist theological works on justification include Elsa Tamez, *Amnesty of Grace: Justification by Faith from a Latin American Perspective*, trans. Sharon Ringe (Nashville, TN: Abingdon Press, 1993) and Kathryn Tanner, "Justification and Justice in a Theology of Grace," *Theology Today*, 55, 4. Feminist works on sanctification include Cannon, *Black Womanist Ethics*; Nelson, *Beyond Servanthood* and Elsa Tamez, *The Scandalous Message of James: Faith Without Works is Dead*, trans. John Eagleson (New York: Crossroads, 1990).

15 The four most significant works in this area of feminist theory are Diana Fuss, *Essentially Speaking: Feminism, Nature and Difference* (New York: Routledge, 1989); Seyla Benhabib, *Situating the Self: Gender, Community, and Postmodernism in Contemporary Ethics* (Cambridge: Polity Press, 1992), who uses the term "pragmatic utopianism"; Martha C. Nussbaum, "Human Functioning and Social Justice: In Defense of Aristotelian Essentialism," *Political Theory*, 20 (1992), pp. 202–46; and Lynne Huffer, "An Interview with Nicole Brossard," *Another Look, Another Woman: Yale French Studies*, 87 (1995), p. 118. Brossard refers to "a mythic space/mythic essentialism." Also see Patricia Hunington, *Ecstatic Subject, Utopic and Recognition: Kristeva, Heidegger, and Irigaray* (New York: State University of New York Press, 1998); Rosi Braidotti, *Patterns of Dissonance* (New York: Routledge, 1991).

16 See Serene Jones, "Women's Experience Between a Rock and a Hard Place," in *Horizons in Feminist Theology: Identity, Tradition, and Norms*, ed. Rebecca Chopp and Sheila Greeve Davaney (Minneapolis, MN: Fortress Press, 1997), pp. 33–53.

17 See Michelle Barrett, *Women's Oppression Today: Problems in Marxist Feminist Analysis* (London: Verso, 1988); Teresa Ebert, *Ludic Feminism and After* (Ann

Arbor: University of Michigan Press, 1996); Iris Marion Young, *Justice and the Politics of Difference* (Princeton, NJ: Princeton University Press, 1990); Carol Pateman, *The Sexual Contract* (Cambridge: Polity Press, 1988) and *The Disorder of Women* (Cambridge: Polity Press, 1989); Christine Delphy, *Close to Home: A Materialist Analysis of Women's Oppression*, trans. Diana Leonard (Amherst, MA: 1984).

18 On this point the work of Luce Irigaray and Judy Butler has been crucial.

19 The feminist account of sin I describe here is largely my own. *See Feminist Theory and Christian Theology*, ch. 5. For similar feminist accounts of sin, see Rebecca Chopp, "Anointed to Preach: Speaking of Sin in the Midst of Grace," in *The Portion of the Poor: Good News to the Poor in the Wesleyan Tradition*, ed. M. Douglas Meeks (Nashville, TN: Kingswood Books, 1995); Mary Fulkerson, "Sexism as Original Sin: Developing a Theacentric Discourse," *Journal of the American Academy of Religion*, 59 (Winter 1991), pp. 653–75; Christine E. Gudorf, "Admonishing the Sinner: Owning Structural Sin," in *Rethinking the Spiritual Works of Mercy*, ed. Francis Eigo (Villanova, PA: Villanova University Press, 1993), pp. 1–31; Mary Potter Engel, "Evil, Sin, and Violation of the Vulnerable," ch. 11 in *Lift Every Voice: Constructing Christian Theologies from the Underside* (San Francisco: Harper & Row, 1990), pp. 152–64. Also see Delores Williams, *Sisters in the Wilderness: The Challenge of Womanist God-Talk* (Maryknoll, NY: Orbis Books, 1993); "Sin, Nature, and Black Women's Bodies," in *Ecofeminism and the Sacred*, ed. Carol Adams (New York: Continuum, 1993), and "A Womanist Perspective on Sin," in *A Troubling in My Soul: Womanist Perspectives on Evil and Suffering*, ed. Emily Townes (Maryknoll, NY: Orbis Books, 1993). See also Kathleen Sands, *Escape From Paradise: Evil and Tragedy in Feminist Theology* (Minneapolis, MN: Fortress Press, 1994), ch. 3, "Escape from Paradise: Responses to Evil in Religious Feminism," pp. 37–69; Sally Ann McReynolds and Ann O'Hara Graff, "Sin: When Women are the Context," in *In the Embrace of God: Feminist Approaches to Theological Anthropology*, ed. Ann O'Hara Graff (Maryknoll: Orbis Books, 1995), pp. 161–72.

20 I refer to this as "implicated resistance." See Jones, *Feminist Theory and Christian Theology*.

21 For feminist discussion of community, see Elizabeth Frazer and Nicola Lacey, *The Politics of Community: A Feminist Critique of the Liberal–Communitarian Debate* (Toronto: University of Toronto Press, 1993) and *Feminism and Community*, ed. Penny Weiss and Marilyn Friedman (Philadelphia: Temple University Press, 1995). Also see Shane Phelan, *Identity Politics: Lesbian Feminism and the Limits of Community* (Philadelphia: Temple University Press), 1989; "Democracy and Difference: Contesting the Boundaries of the Political," *Journal of Politics*, 59 (November 1997), pp. 1314–16 and "The Shape of Queer: Assimilation and Articulation," *Women and Politics*, 17 (1997), pp. 55–73; Kate Nash, *Universal Difference: Feminism and the Liberal Undecidability of "Women"* (London: Macmillan, 1998); Nancy Fraser, *Justice Interruptus: Critical Reflections on the "Postsocialist" Condition* (New York: Routledge, 1997).

22 The following account of a feminist theological version of "bounded openness" is taken from Jones, ch. 7, *Feminist Theory and Christian Theology*. For similar feminist theological accounts of the church as a community of "bounded openness," see Russell, *Church in the Round*; Rebecca Chopp, *The Power to Speak*; Elizabeth Schüssler Fiorenza, *Discipleship of Equals: A Critical Feminist Ekklesia-logy of Liberation* (New

York: Crossroads, 1993); Sharon Welch, *A Feminist Ethic of Risk* (Minneapolis, MN: Fortress Press, 1990); Mud Flower Collective (Katie Cannon, Beverly Harrison, Carter Heyward, Ada Maria Isasi-Diaz, Bess Johnson, Mary Pelauer, Nancy Richardson), *God's Fierce Whimsy: Christian Feminism and Theological Education* (New York: Pilgrim Press, 1985).

PART IV
Hermeneutics

18	Shattering the Logos: Hermeneutics Between a Hammer and a Hard Place	311
19	The Renewal of Jewish Theology Today: Under the Sign of Three	324
20	Intending Transcendence: Desiring God	349

CHAPTER 18
Shattering the Logos: Hermeneutics Between a Hammer and a Hard Place

Daniel Boyarin

Daniel Boyarin's work to date has three abiding concerns, each of which pushes him in distinct but not unrelated directions. The first concern is broadly with hermeneutics, exemplified in the essay below. Following a number of mainly Jewish scholars (notably Stanford Budick, Geoffrey Hartmann, and Susan Handelman) who have encountered the challenge to traditional hermeneutical theory posed by Derrida (himself Jewish), Boyarin's work has investigated the distinctiveness of Jewish forms of interpretation as evident in the various midrashim. This was the central examination in his first book, *Intertextuality and the Reading of Midrash* (Bloomington, IN, 1990). His approach, like that of the rabbis before him, is characterized by a careful, close readings of texts and a sensitivity to the way in which texts are both circumscribed by and transcend contexts, generating plural readings and disseminating interpretations. This seemed to suggest and establish a certain binary figuration: the Greek model of hermeneutics governed by an understanding of a closed or finalized meaning (logocentrism), as opposed to a rabbinic model of hermeneutics which encouraged a view of texts as open-ended and a generative model of interpretation. However, Boyarin, as alert as Derrida to the concealed metaphysics of binarisms, has been troubled by this figuration. The second concern of his work then became evident: an investigation into the construction of identity within a culture that is both Hellenistic and Judaic. To conduct this investigation he turned to texts that were early examples of Jewish thinking, the writings of St Paul (and more recently St John's Gospel). *A Radical Jew: Paul and the Politics of Identity* (Berkeley, CA, 1994) was followed by *Dying for God: Martyrdom and the Making of Christianity and Judaism* (Stanford, CA, 1999). With the first of these books Boyarin ventures into questions of identity, not only by examining ethnicity, but also by providing analyses of gender construction. His investigations into the interface of Hellenism and Judaism do not lead to a synthesis of perspectives, the disappearance of their distinctiveness, or the triumph of Judaism over Christianity. Rather, they develop what Boyarin calls "cultural dialectics." In the introduction to *Carnal Israel: Reading Sex in Talmudic Culture* (Berkeley, CA, 1993), he writes: "By cultural dialectics, I intend a mode of analysis that compares related cultural formations by showing that they represent complementary 'solutions' to given cultural 'problems.' Among other things, this method of presentation allows for cultural comparison without triumphalism, for each formation provides critique of its Other." Boyarin's third concern is illustrated by *Carnal Israel* and the prominence given to questions of gender in his book on St Paul. Following his examination of the construction of certain religious identities, he explores the construction of certain sexual ideologies and practices. The male body, the nature of sexual desire, circumcision, marriage, intercourse, the identity and role of women as debated in the Talmudic texts, are compared to the Christian understanding of these matters in late antiquity. Here Boyarin's work as rabbinic exegete moves in the direction of cultural anthropology. It is a move which he further extended in his book *Unheroic Conduct: The Rise of Heterosexuality and the Invention of the Jewish Man* (Berkeley, CA, 1997).

These interrelated concerns constitute the field of Boyarin's academic analyses. What characterizes this work is close textual reading of rabbinic and early Christian writings, facilitated by a contemporary critical and theoretical understanding of the nature of reading itself. This explicit engagement of the past through the present, this practice of intertextuality, foregrounds the politics of any reading and the continuing construction of identities and ideologies.

One of the more startling developments in the historiography of Judaism has been occasioned by a movement in literary theory, the movement that has come to be known as "Deconstruction," but is probably, for this context, more properly referred to as "Grammatology." Associated originally and primarily with the work of Jacques Derrida, grammatology made us realize that the modes of reading texts that we had taken to be completely natural, as indeed the only possible modes of reading that could be called interpretation in good faith and with good sense, were, in fact, culturally conditioned, specific historical products, the products of the reign of the Logos, hence logocentrism.[1] It had already been realized as early as the 1950s that the reading practice characteristic of rabbinic Judaism known as midrash can most powerfully be described as "breaking the Logos."[2] In an initial rush of enthusiasm in the wake of Derrida, various critics and most notably Susan Handelman sought to describe rabbinic Judaism, then, as a project in textuality wholly Other from the project of "Western," "Hellenic," logocentrism, and to claim that this project in large part constituted Jewish difference from Christianity.[3] The difference of rabbinic Judaism as to textuality – and midrash is at the center of this difference – is crucial for its description; it does have to do with the "breaking of the Logos," or as I have styled it for reasons that will become apparent throughout this essay, "the crucifixion of the Logos," but this is not an essential difference that defines a pure, originary Judaism as against a Hellenized, contaminated Christianity, but rather the product of the long process of self-differentiation and definition of rabbinic and Christian Judaism that took all of late antiquity to take place.

In a seminal paper David Stern argued against the notion that midrash represents a species of early deconstruction, or at any rate a theory of language and interpretation that had quite escaped the logocentrism of Western (read Christian) interpretation. In doing so he raised several important questions, theoretical and historical.[4] The theoretical question is whether there is possible anywhere a praxis of interpretation that is not logocentric, if not indeed we are imposing contemporary so-called postmodern categories where they cannot be sustained, except by dint of some severe orientalizing moves. The historical question is whether it is even appropriate to consider rabbinic textuality as a system of meaning that has somehow escaped "contamination" of Hellenism, or whether it is indeed a species of Hellenism itself. Stern makes a strong argument for the latter in both cases, furthermore interrupting a kind of essentialist binary opposing of "Jewish" and "Christian" textualities.[5]

Stern refers to the *locus classicus* of so-called midrashic indeterminacy and a notorious crux since the Middle Ages, the famous simile by which midrash is compared to a "hammer on the rock," a figure perhaps for the shattering of the Logos. Before he wrote his paradigm-making paper,[6] Stern had engaged in a debate on the interpretation of this passage in a critique of Handelman's work and a subsequent exchange of essays.[7] I would like here to take up and expand the discussion of this crucial and evocative text by way of explicating Handelman's and Stern's approaches and offering one of my own as well. This will then serve as an exemplum for a postmodern critical praxis of reading midrash.

Handelman projected two traditions of biblical hermeneutics as the ancestors of two modern schools of hermeneutic theory: the Platonic–Christian–Patristic tradition which culminated in the Protestant German hermeneutics and the Jewish–midrashic one which culminated in psychoanalysis and deconstruction. In his initial review, entitled "Moses-cide: Midrash and Contemporary Literary Criticism," Stern argued that Handelman's thesis is wrong on two counts. First of all, it is impossible to separate out the two traditions so neatly at the outset, and secondly there is insufficient evidence for the connection between the modern literary theories involved and the midrashic tradition. The first point which must be made here is that Handelman's response to Stern's review was arrogant in its assumption that she, alone, of scholars of Judaism has an understanding of literary theory. She presents Stern as if he were an opponent of theory, in part by quoting Terry Eagleton in an epigraph to her paper to the effect that opponents of theory are merely "opposing others' theories and oblivious to their own."[8] There is nothing in Stern's essay that implies an opposition to theory. Eagleton's epigram might well be turned on its head: those who accuse others of being unaware of theory may often merely be distressed that these others do not share their theoretical stance.

The issue between Handelman and Stern is reading. Handelman claims that what she is doing is reading rabbinic literature while Stern and other scholars of rabbinic literature do not read. Her parting shot, as it were, is:

> As de Man[9] also notes, though, before we generalize about literary texts, we have to learn how to *read*, and the possibility of reading can never be taken for granted. Students of rabbinic texts, of Jewish Studies in general, need, once more, to learn to read anew.[10]

Stern, on the other hand, claims that Handelman's reading of texts is simply not reading but homiletical exploitation of the text. In my consideration of the controversy between them I will concentrate on a text which was discussed in detail by both of them, present some discussion of the problems of that text (as it is a founding text for a rabbinic literary theory), and try to articulate some of what seems to me at issue in the contest of readings. Stern dubs Handelman's interpretation an allegory and a homily:

> In the first place, it must be said that the "plain-sense" of the Talmudic passage [that Handelman invokes; see discussion below, DB] . . . is far more problematic than Handelman makes it out to be. . . . Leaving aside these mere textual details, however, it is worth asking what kind of literary analysis does Handelman provide for the passage.
>
> Neither literary criticism nor literary theory, Handelman's reading of the passage is a kind of homily. Its strength lies in its rhetorical effectiveness, in the way Handelman exploits the rabbinic passage to make it serve as illustration for her argument, in much the same way a rabbi tells anecdotes or cites Scripture in order to illustrate his sermon (and, as one imagines, the authors of midrash often interpreted Scripture in their synagogues to illustrate their homiletical lessons). No one, of course, listens to a sermon expecting to hear literary criticism or literary theory, nor does a good sermon pretend to be academic scholarship, which is why no one ever thinks of criticizing a homilist's interpretation for distorting the verse's meaning or turning it on its head in order to make a sermonic point.[11]

I have my problems with both Handelman's and Stern's statements here. Stern's remarks about "mere textual details" are certainly meant ironically, but I think he is giving too much away to Handelman by tossing that off. If reading does not begin with such "mere textual details" then what is it? What could a non-reductive reading practice which Handelman calls for (and I do agree with her that much of the practice of Jewish studies is not reading and is reductive) mean if it does not at least begin or ground itself on close reading? Whatever de Manian and indeed Derridian theory may be, their practice is one of extremely close and careful reading of texts. They do not deconstruct by rhapsodizing romantically above the texts but by getting inside the language and teasing out its meaning (and almost inevitably then the ways it contests its meanings) slowly and unrelentingly. Handelman's work on this text is a kind of parody of de Man, in that it does not begin with even a basic fidelity to the details of the text's language. I will back up this serious charge further on. On the other hand, much of what I think is wrong with contemporary and even traditional reading of midrash is precisely reflected in Stern's understanding that midrash is homily and not, therefore, to be taken seriously as interpretation.[12] However, both Stern and Handelman have raised what seems to me to be a crucial issue. How shall we go about making sense *for us* of rabbinic texts? What shall be the practice of a reading of midrash today? I would like to show what I think about this subject in part by tackling precisely the text that Stern and Handelman discussed, the famous characterization of God's word as being like a hammer on the rock.

As Stern says, "After all there is little sense in discussing the disruptions of midrashic discourse when you don't know if there's a lacuna in the manuscript."[13] I would like to underline this point with a sort of fable.

In 1978 a man by the name of Stanley E. Fish produced a text called "Normal Circumstances, Literal Language, Direct Speech Acts, the Ordinary, the Everyday, the Obvious, What Goes Without Saying, and Other Special Cases."[14] In this brilliant and witty essay Fish showed how the literal reading of the text "Private Members Only" is conditioned by the context of its reading. As a sign on the faculty club door, it means one thing. As a text for interpretation out of that context, i.e., in the context of the classroom in literary criticism, it can mean all sorts of things having to do with genitalia, etc. The meaning of Fish's text, in its context, seemed quite clear. It is now the year 2978. We have only a very partial knowledge of twentieth-century English. It has been quite forgotten that the words "private" and "member" once had sexual connotations. Fish's text, which was perfectly clear to its audience back in the twentieth century, has become quite meaningless. Alternatively, the one surviving copy of *Critical Inquiry* has been damaged. The first two letters of the word "members" are missing. Someone has suggested somewhat hesitantly that the text ought to read "numbers." The text is extraordinarily difficult.

The point should be clear. Whatever assumptions we make about meaning and interpretation, we assume that we all have a certain understanding of the language of the text *on some level*. All that I am saying is that our reading and theory assume that we understand each other's words. Otherwise, why translate Derrida into English? When reading ancient texts we simply cannot make that assumption, so reading must be preceded by philology. What is the text to the best of our ability to establish it, or what are, at least, the parameters of doubt? What could the words have meant in the language in which the text was written? These will always be significant, nay necessary questions.

In his review Stern took Handelman to task for ignoring previous scholarship and philological standards in her readings of rabbinic literature. Her response, in part, was to present a reading of Babylonian Talmud, *Sanhedrin* 34a:

> Rav Asi asked Rabbi Yohanan, "if two [judges] have cited the same law from two verses, what is the law?" He said, "they are not counted as more than one." From whence comes this principle? Abayye said, "for the verse says, *One spoke God, these two have I heard* [Psalm. 62.12]. One verse gives rise to several laws

[meanings], but one law does not come out of several verses." He of the house of R. Ishmael teaches it, "*Like a hammer which shatters a rock* [Jeremiah 23.29]; just as the hammer is divided into several sparks, so a single verse gives rise to several laws."

Handelman translates the crucial phrase of the house of R. Ishmael thus: "just as the hammer shatters the rock into many fragments, so may one verse be divided into many meanings."[15] Since, however, in a parallel passage [*Shabbat* 88b] she imagines that the text reads "Just as the hammer is broken," she decides that in that text it is the rabbinical interpreters with their stubborn desires that are compared to the hammer which is smashed on encountering the adamant of God's word. The alleged ambiguity of meaning set up by the two variants is crucial to her analysis. "The ambiguous relation of interpreter and text, hammer and rock, rabbi and Scripture are all described here."[16] The analogies are clearly drawn:

> But where do we, modern hammerers on the rock fit in? For all of us from Zunz to Heinemann to Neusner to Stern and myself are also engaged in hammering on the rock of midrash. And there are problems with our hammering as well. Do our hammers, our critical methods taken from "secular" disciplines of history, literary theory and so forth, get split apart by a resistant sacredness in Scripture? Or do they split and open up new meanings of sacred texts?

Either way, the implication is clear: why bother with the unsophisticated efforts of philology to establish the debunked "original" meaning of the text?

However, in fact, this very talmudic passage is extraordinarily difficult, *on precisely the philological level*, a fact which Handelman's translation covers up entirely, a fact which the medieval commentators, known as the "scholiasts" (*Tosafot*, fl. eleventh to thirteenth centuries, France and Germany) realized very well. The verb which Handelman has translated "shatters" is, in fact, as she herself notes, a passive/reflexive form which *a priori* ought to be translated as "is divided." Therefore, in the text in *Sanhedrin*, unless we emend it, we must translate also: "Just as the hammer is shattered by the rock." There is, accordingly, no difference between the two parallel sources.

There seems to be, however, strong discord between the verse which is being glossed and the midrashic gloss. The verse appears to say that the hammer shatters the rock, while the rabbinic gloss has the hammer being divided and not the rock. This discord is what motivates the comments of the glossators to which Handelman refers. Let us see what they have to say:

> Rabbenu Shmuel reads "divides," for it is not the hammer which is divided but the rock. However, this is difficult, for [then] it ought to have said, "just as the rock is divided." And likewise in *Chapter Rabbi Akiba* [*Shabbat* 88b] the reading is "just as the hammer is divided into several sparks, so every speech which came out of the Mouth of the Holy One, Blessed is He, was divided into seventy languages, and it should have said [were the reading of Rabbenu Shmuel correct],

"just as the rock is divided." Therefore, Rabbenu Tam interprets, "like a hammer, which the rock shatters," that the hammer is divided by the rock, as we have said in the midrash: "There was a case of a certain person who bought a sapphire and went to examine it. He placed it onto the anvil and hit it with a hammer. The sapphire remains in its place." This is what it says, "like a hammer, which the rock shatters."

Rabbenu Shmuel has emended the text. He does not indicate in any way that he has a tradition of reading the text differently, as Handelman would have it. He is rather responding to the interpretive problem that it obviously presents. The grammar of the biblical verse seems clearly to say that the hammer is shattering the rock, so how can the rabbinic interpretations say that the hammer is being shattered, therefore the interpretation must have reached us in an imperfect form, and is to be corrected.[17] The anonymous scholiast, however, remarks that Rabbenu Shmuel's emendation is unfelicitous, for it would seem then that it is the verse which is being compared to the rock, and the text of the Talmud's comment should have been, "just as the rock etc." Moreover, the received text finds support in a parallel passage in Tractate *Shabbat*, where the same problem arises.[18]

Therefore, Rabbenu Tam (the younger brother of said Rabbenu Shmuel) suggests that it is not the text of the rabbinic interpretation which has to be remade to fit the verse, but rather we must understand the verse differently. He accordingly reads it as a topicalized construction, the sort of construction known to Semitists as a *casus pendens*. That is, the verse is to be read "as for the hammer, the rock shatters [it]." The problem with Rabbenu Tam's reading is also grammatical: the pronoun which I have supplied in brackets is, in fact, generally required in such a construction in Hebrew.

If we take a look at the medieval scholion in the parallel passage itself, we will see that this interpretation of the controversy is an exact rendition of what the issue was for these medieval hammerers, at any rate:

Rabbenu Shmuel objected [to Rabbenu Tam his brother]: but behold the verse means that the hammer shatters the rock, since it does not say, "as for the hammer, the rock shatters *it*." Furthermore, we see that it is the hammer which shatters the rocks [i.e., in the real world!]. We cannot read, "just as the rock is divided into several sparks," for the speech, which is Torah, is compared to the hammer and not to the rock. However, Rabbenu Tam says that the verse is talking about a stone which shatters iron, as it says in *Midrash Hazit*, a story of one etc. [as above]. And even though it does not say, "shatters it," there are many similar verses: "stones have worn down water," [Job 14.19] which obviously must be read, "as for stones, the water has worn [them] down" [and the pronoun is missing in the Hebrew there too]. And it fits well, for it says in the first chapter of *Kiddushin*, The one of the house of Ishmael[!] taught, "my son, if the wicked one [the evil inclination] meets you drag him to the study house. If he is a stone, he will be dissolved, for it says, "stones – water has worn [them] down." If he is iron, he will be shattered, for it says, "And as a hammer which the rock shatters."

We see, accordingly, that Rabbenu Shmuel's linguistic objection is completely and adequately solved by Rabbenu Tam's remark.[19] The verse of parallel structure "stones have worn down water" is exactly the same syntactically as "the rock shatters the stone," and therefore, just as that one *must* be read as, "As for stones, the water wears them down," similarly we *can* read, "As for the hammer, the rock shatters it." Moreover, to Rabbenu Shmuel's argument from the real world, Rabbenu Tam brings an answer from the intertext. It may be, indeed, that you observe that hammers usually shatter rocks, but we see that rocks which shatter hammers were also known to the rabbinic sociolect. There is, therefore, no justification whatever for the emendation. The emendation, then, is no more relevant for interpretation than is any other scholarly emendation, which time or new insight has shown to be unwarranted. Indeed, I may presume to say that I believe that Rabbenu Shmuel, the consummate philologist of the school, would have it no other way. There is, accordingly, no Talmudic text which reads, "Just as the hammer shatters the rock"; they all read, "Just as the hammer is shattered by the rock." Moreover, a point which Handelman completely ignores, and for that matter, so does Stern, is how the cited text from *Kiddushin* virtually forces us to accept Rabbenu Tam's solution, since in that text we find a quotation from the same source, "The School of Ishmael," where the verse is explicitly glossed as iron being shattered by a rock. There, we can only understand that the verse is being read to mean that the hammer is destroyed by the rock, for otherwise the whole point is lost entirely. Since it is the same interpreter reading the verse in all cases, namely "the one of the school of Ishmael," it is clear that he read the verse as topicalized.[20] I will inquire into the reason for this reading below.

Now that we have read the text with some degree of fidelity to its simple linguistic meaning, we can begin to "do a reading of it." Construal before deconstruction is my watchword here. I would like to stress, however, that I am not proposing a Hirschian distinction between meaning and significance or interpretation and application. In my view, what I have done here is an activity that is prior to any interpretation of the text whatever. I would claim that this type of philological work, which is not yet reading, has to be done before an ancient text can be read, *if* the reading is to be a dialogue with the ancient text and not solely a projection of the thoughts of the reader onto the text, and this will be so even on a deconstructive theory of meaning. This is epistemologically equivalent to learning the language of the text and not more than that. This rabbinic text is not simply a simile, but an interpretation, a reading of a simile, so let us begin by looking again at the text which it reads. "Behold, thus is my word like a fire and like a hammer which shatters the rock/which is shattered by the rock." Now, in the verse itself, however we construe it grammatically, it is clear that it is God's word which is being compared to the hammer. The midrash is not necessarily constrained by the grammar of the verse, but *a priori* there seems no reason to assume that it is not. Therefore, we will begin with the assumption that in the interpretive remark of the tanna, it is the hammer which represents the verse of the Torah. Now then all the text says is that just as the hammer is shattered by the rock into several entities,[21] so does the verse give rise to several meanings. Note that the text does not say, again as Handelman would have it, that the verse is fragmented by the activity of interpretation. It is not shattered into several meanings; it rather produces them. The rock is not identified in the simile at all.

The passage from *Kiddushin* 30b raises, however, difficulty with this reading. Let us have a closer look at that text:

> The one of the house of Ishmael taught, "my son, if the wicked one [the evil inclination] meets you drag him to the study house. If he is a stone, he will be dissolved, for it says, "stones – water has worn [them] down." If he is iron, he will be shattered, for it says, "And as a hammer which the rock shatters/is shattered by the rock."

It is quite clear that the stones in the first verse and the hammer in the second are figures for the evil inclination, but where is the study house? A parallel text will answer this question, for it makes explicit what is implicit here, namely that in the first verse, a *topos* of midrashic interpretation is being evoked, that "water" = Torah. As I have said, the parallel text in *Sukkah* 52b makes this explicit: "If he is a stone, he will be dissolved, for it says, 'all who are thirsty – go to water,' [Isaiah 55.1] and then it says, 'stones – water has worn them down.'" The function of the first cited verse is to establish the equivalence "water" = Torah, for so is "water" being used in the context of the Prophet and moreover, this was a traditionally used prooftext for this equivalence.[22] Accordingly, the second half of the dilemma must also have an equivalent for Torah (justified, of course, by the explicit figurative content of the verse about, "My word"). If the "hammer" is the evil inclination, the only candidate left for the Torah is the rock – a reversal of the apparent meaning of the simile, which certainly seems to be "My word is like a fire, and My word is like a hammer." The midrash is accordingly very difficult. The difficulty has been well phrased by the Rashba[23] on *Sukkah*, who says:

> And if he be iron, he is shattered, like a hard rock which shatters the hammer, and this is what it says, "And like a hammer which shatters the rock," that is to say, "like a hammer – the rock shatters [it]." But this cannot be correct, because the verse compares the words of Torah to a hammer, and it must be causing the shattering, not being shattered.

Rashba's solution is to adopt a radical emendation of the Talmudic passage:

> There are some who read, "if it be stone, then it will shatter and if it be iron then it will melt," meaning: the words of Torah are like the fire which heat the iron and melt it, as it is written, "Behold my word is like a fire." And similarly, the words of Torah are like a strong hammer which shatters the pieces of rock, as it is written, "and like a hammer which shatters the stone."

There seems to be no evidence, however, for this emendation, but it does expose the difficulty brilliantly and precisely. If we understand the "hammer" to refer to Torah, as the verse seems to mean, then the midrash is incomprehensible in its present form, but if we understand the "hammer" to be the evil inclination, which is shattered by the rock – "The Torah" – rendering the midrash coherent, the sense of the verse is totally ignored. Is there any way to avoid emendation and save the text? The Maharsha[24] in Sanhedrin has tried a completely different approach to this problem:

> One can interpret here that according to these homilies, the word *sela'* is from rabbinic Hebrew *sela'*, where it means a coin, which is also from metal and iron.

Maharsha goes on to explain the simile according to this view. The "iron" which the hammer = Torah shatters is the nature of the man. Just as a coin which is no longer valid is put under the fire and hammer to be recoined, so is the man with his evil inclination remade under the fire and hammer of God's word. Now for my taste, Maharsha's comment is rather going beyond what seems to me a supportable reading in the text itself, which nowhere hints that it is speaking of a coin. Moreover, coins are not typically made of iron. Philology, it seems, has reached its limiting case here. Either emendation or lexicographical pyrotechnics seem to be required to "save this text" from splitting between the verse and its interpretation. I will return to this point later.

Maharsha's comment is nevertheless helpful. We have to identify the realia of a simile before we will be able to understand it. Of course, I do not mean the "real realia" but the intertextual code of realia to which the text seems to allude. Let us go back for a while to the *Sanhedrin* text. The single most important question that we must ask here is: are we in a quarry or a blacksmith's shop;[25] are we dealing with fragments or sparks? Before we can begin to read the tenor of the figure here, we simply have to try at least to establish what the vehicle is. I believe that a strong argument can be made for the blacksmith's shop and sparks, and that this argument will ultimately provide the answer to the dilemma above. The support for this point is that the sparks that fly out from under the blacksmith's hammer is a *topos*, and they are referred to precisely in the language used in our simile (*nitzotzot*). Thus, for example, in *Baba Kamma* 32b, we find:

> If one entered a blacksmith's shop and sparks flew out and hit him on the face and he died, the blacksmith is not liable.

Moreover, in *Tanhuma Wayesheb 1*, Joseph's sons are compared to "the sparks of his smithy, which would ignite the straw."

There is, therefore, ample evidence for seeing the hammer here as the blacksmith's hammer and the sparks as the red-hot bits of metal that fly out from under the hammer, when it strikes the metal. On the basis of these considerations, my friend Mark Steiner has proposed what seems to me to be the best interpretation of the text. He suggests that the rabbis understood the two similes

SHATTERING THE LOGOS   321

as being in synonymous parallelism.[26] It follows then, that the idea of "fire" is repeated in the second bi-colon of the verse. We then can understand that the "hammer which explodes the rock" is not being understood concretely but rather referring metonymically to the situation of the hammer striking the rock.[27] Since, as I have said, the semanteme "fire" is given by the parallelism with the first half of the verse, the rabbis understood that what is being referred to is the shower of sparks that results from the hammer blow of the smith. Translating the verse in accordance with this reading, we would get something like, "My word is like fire, saith the Lord; yea like the hammer smashing the rock [= anvil]."

This interpretive move solves all of the problems here, and one is no longer constrained to adopt the forced reading, "As for the hammer, the rock smashes it." On the other hand, the *Kiddushin* passage does force us to understand the verse in that way. The two texts taken together then form a very elegant self-referential illustration of precisely the point that the *Sanhedrin* passage wished to make: a single verse can be read in many ways, i.e., it can be interpreted in accordance with all of the possibilities that its language allows. There is, moreover, nothing new about this insight, as it has been already seen by the *Tosafot* on *Shabbat*, who remark:

> And even though there [i.e., in *Kiddushin*] he compares The Evil Inclination to the hammer and here the [he compares] Torah [to the hammer], that should not disturb us, *for a verse gives rise to many meanings.*

The polysemy that the rabbis are claiming for the Holy Text is thus illustrated in the very process of deriving that principle of polysemy from the Holy Text. I am not sure whether this is "a good version of the hermeneutic circle," as Handelman would have it,[28] but it certainly is a lovely example of a text illustrating by its very essence the point it wishes to make, an elegant self-reflexivity. This is a common move of midrashic rhetoric.

There is, then, it seems, very little justification for the reading proposed by Handelman. What *can* we say about this text then? I would suggest that it does provide evidence for a special understanding of semiology among the rabbis. The image of a hammer striking sparks off a rock as the symbol of the process of interpretation is itself a striking representation of the *making* of meaning in the reading activity, as opposed to meaning being a given in the language itself. It is, moreover, a powerful metaphor for multivalence, precisely what it claims to be. There is, after all, testimony here for a rabbinic understanding of hermeneutics which is very different both from the hermeneutics of the so-called "simple meaning," and the hermeneutics of the hierarchic fourfold meaning, both so characteristic of the Middle Ages. In this sense, midrash and rabbinic interpretation in general can have much to teach us about the different options that hermeneutics can take and help us to ironize our own reading practices. There simply is no warrant in this text for interpretations which found themselves on notions of the interpreter being a hammer which before the obduracy of the text smashes himself/herself upon it. That may be an accurate description of the fate of interpreters; it does not seem to have been one that the rabbis shared. They did, however, seem to be articulating and acting out a hermeneutic practice of dissemination of meaning and fracturing of textual organicity. That practice can certainly be better apprehended by us in the light of the denaturalization of metaphysics of language which Derrida has endeavored to do, and provides a kind of model for a non-logocentric reading practice.

Notes

1 Jacques Derrida, *Of Grammatology* (Baltimore, MD: Johns Hopkins University Press, 1976).
2 Isaak Heinemann, *Darxei Ha'Agada* (Jerusalem: Magnes Press, 1970), pp. 101–2 and passim.
3 Susan Handelman, *The Slayers of Moses* (Albany: State University of New York Press, 1982). For a somewhat more sophisticated version of this argument, see Shira Wolosky, "Derrida, Jabès, Levinas: Sign-Theory as Ethical Discourse," *Prooftexts*, 2 (1982), pp. 282–302. It should be emphasized, however, that whatever the critique that was subsequently leveled at the work of Handelman, it was beyond doubt a groundbreaking work in its time.
4 David Stern, "Midrash and Indeterminacy," *Critical Inquiry*, 15: 1 (Autumn 1988), pp. 132–62.
5 In the longer work of which this will eventually be a small part, tentatively entitled *How Christianity Created the Jewish Religion*, I shall be arguing, *deo volente*, that the characteristic rabbinic form of textuality, including (but not only) midrash, adumbrated here was the product of a long and dialectical response to "Hellenism," to a deferral of earlier Jewish Logos theology (in the form known as "Christology") and, therefore, that the binary opposition of Judaism/Hellenism needs indeed to be deconstructed.
6 In my above-mentioned forthcoming work, I will include, *deo volente*, a longer discussion of Stern's work. For the nonce, see Daniel Boyarin, "A Tale of Two Synods: Nicaea, Yavneh and the Making of Orthodox Judaism," *Exemplaria*, 12: 1 (Spring 2000), pp. 21–62.
7 Handelman, *Moses*; David Stern, "Moses-Cide: Midrash and Contemporary Literary Criticism," *Prooftexts*, 4 (1984), pp. 193–204; Susan Handelman, "Fragments of the Rock: Contemporary Literary Theory and the Study of Rabbinic Texts – a Response to David Stern," *Prooftexts*, 5 (1985), pp. 73–95; David Stern, "Literary Criticism or Literary Homilies? Susan Handelman and the Contemporary Study of Midrash," *Prooftexts*, 5 (1985), pp. 96–103.
8 Quoted in Handelman, "Fragments," p. 75.
9 For those who are unfamiliar with Paul de Man's way of *reading*, the best introduction is his *Allegories of Reading Figural Language in Rousseau, Nietzsche, Rilke, and Proust* (New Haven, CT: Yale University Press, 1979).
10 Handelman, "Fragments," p. 93.
11 Stern, "Homilies," p. 101.
12 Daniel Boyarin, *Intertextuality and the Reading of Midrash* (Bloomington: Indiana University Press, 1990).

13 Stern, "Homilies," p. 98.
14 Stanley Fish, "Normal Circumstances, Literal Language, Direct Speech Acts, the Ordinary, the Obvious, What Goes Without Saying, and Other Special Cases," *Critical Inquiry*, 4 (1978), pp. 622–55.
15 Handelman, "Fragments," p. 89.
16 Ibid, p. 90.
17 I fail to understand Stern's remark that "The precise cause of the Tosafists' difficulties with the passage are difficult to locate": Stern, "Homilies," p. 103.
18 As Stern has already observed, it is somewhat bizarre to find Handelman interpreting the *Tosafot* as having somehow based themselves on a difference between the two parallel texts, which is found only in the printed editions, and which the *Tosafot* themselves clearly did not have in their editions!
19 Contra Stern, "Homilies," p. 101.
20 Accordingly, Stern's suggestion that the reflexive is to be read here as a middle with an active sense is unwarranted.
21 The translation is purposely vague at this point.
22 Cf. for example, *Mekilta, Wayassa 1* and the brief discussion of this passage in James Kugel, *The Idea of Biblical Poetry* (New Haven, CT: Yale University Press, 1981), pp. 137–8.
23 Rabben Shlomo ibn Aderet, a twelfth-century Spanish Talmudic commentator of the school of Nachmanides.
24 R. Shmuel Ederles, a major sixteenth-century Polish Talmudist. His gloss is quoted by Handelman but apparently totally misunderstood.
25 Rashi on Jeremiah, ad loc., showed awareness of this question when he asked whether the word *patish* should be translated "pick" or "martel."
26 This reading is a further development from Stern's interpretation. He proposes, "The explanation lies, I would like to suggest, in what was for the School of R. Ishmael the problematic relationship of the two similes in Jer. 23:29: as the reader will recall, in the first simile God compares His word to fire, in the second to a hammer breaking a rock. Why two similes? the Rabbis would have asked themselves. And what is the connection between the two similes? In response, the school of Ishmael interpreted the verse so that, in effect, the second simile explains the first: 'My word is like fire, says the Lord, like sparks of fire that a hammer produces when it strikes a rock.' " Stern, "Moses-Cide," p. 103. As far as it goes, I agree completely with this reading. Does it bear out Stern's description of midrash as homily unconcerned with what the text means?
27 According to Steiner, what we have here is "deferred ostension."
28 She has, however, seriously misread the sentence, taking it to refer to the *Shabbat* passage and not the one from *Kiddushin*. Indeed, she seems unaware of the latter text and its import.

CHAPTER 19

The Renewal of Jewish Theology Today: Under the Sign of Three

Peter Ochs

According to "Introductions," the opening statement to *Reasoning After Revelation* (Boulder, CO, 1998), a book Peter Ochs wrote with Steven Kepnes and Robert Gibbs, a group of contemporary Jewish philosophers (Ochs among them) met in December 1992 to discuss a phrase each was starting to use in their work: postmodern Jewish philosophy. Influenced both by postliberal theologians and Catholic "correlational" theologians such as David Tracy, Robert Gibbs, and Yudit Greenberg, Steven Kepnes and Peter Ochs began a discussion which has since drawn in many other Jewish thinkers, including Edith Wyschogrod and Elliot R. Wolfson. "Introductions" is something of a manifesto. It makes clear the ground upon which the work of Peter Ochs (and the other members of what came to be called the Society for Textual Reasoning) proceeds: "In their search for more adequate paradigms, these Jewish thinkers derive support from the work of Continental, academic postmodernists and literary theorists, from Jacques Derrida to Julia Kristeva and Luce Irigaray; but this support is partial, and it becomes effective only when it is reapplied to practices of reading, communal interaction, and social comportment that are irreducibly Jewish" (ibid, p. 1). Ochs's work both advocates and constitutes a certain practice – a philosophy of practice – which reads and reasons on the basis of a commitment to the Jewish faith. "We see mutually enriching and critical correlations between Torah and the world," wrote Ochs, Kepnes, and Gibbs. As such the Torah is examined through the lenses of various literary theories, hermeneutics, and semiotics, not for its own sake but for fostering ways of living in the world. Reading as a practice issues in ethical activities on behalf of others, in a critique of consumerism, narcissism, and the exploitation of the weak and oppressed. At the center of this Jewish textual reading is dialogue. In this, Ochs's Jewish philosophy forges links with and builds upon the dialogicalism of Martin Buber and Franz Rosenzweig. *Reasoning After Revelation* is composed from edited conversations between named participants in which stated positions marked by one voice, are then responded to and disrupted by another voice. This mode of proceeding itself invokes a traditional Jewish practice, a rabbinic way of interacting and reading the Torah. As both the epilogue to *Reason After Revelation* and the essay Ochs has contributed to this volume make explicit, the boundaries of conversation cannot be staked out in advance; the nature and the limit of those who participate in the conversations cannot be circumscribed, especially when the scriptures constituting one of the major bases for Textual Reasoning are shared with other traditions, namely the Christian and the Islamic. Thus the conversation begun in Boston on that winter evening in 1992 has fostered another society. In 1996 both Peter Ochs and Elliot Wolfson (along with the Christian theologians Daniel Hardy and David Ford) became founding directors of the Society for Scriptural Reasoning. Ochs refers to these interfaith connections in his essay.

What of Ochs's own contribution? It is the mark of this man's personal integrity that he initiates, then contributes and sometimes seems to lose his own voice amid the conversations he is involved in. However, Ochs has published the fruit of many years of intellectual labor in *Peirce, Pragmatism and the Logic of Scripture* (Cambridge, 1998). This book embodies the methodology (which is for him a Jewish methodology) characteristic of his work: Peirce is both a major critic of "modernism" and a champion of semiotics (the first science of postmodernism). Peirce's pragmatism becomes for Ochs the means for rethinking what he calls the "logic of scripture." Peirce's work joins that of Derrida, Kristeva, and Irigaray, "effective only when it is reapplied to practices of reading, communal interaction, and social comportment."

No, this is not an effort at "Christianizing Judaism" – some mirror of the Christian heresy of "Judaizing." This is, rather, part of a comprehensive response to the near-destruction not only of Jewish bodies, but also Jewish theology in the twentieth century. As you will see in the essay, I believe the salvation history of Judaism is a history of cyclical religious-renewals-after-destruction; and I believe each successful renewal begins only when sages of the people Israel acknowledge the *death* of Judaism's previous religious form. Without this acknowledgment, and the appropriate ritual of mourning that follows it, Judaism is not renewed, but merely limps along, stitching together incompatible relics of past belief systems.

If you will permit me an over-generalization for the sake of clarity, I conceive the Jewish people now as predominately in a condition of limping-along: limping, in particular, on the two worn-out legs of a Jewish liberal universalism and a Jewish anti-liberal orthodoxy. As in every generation, however, "our redeemer lives": the redeemer, that is, who will redeem us from the dead – even the horrible death we have suffered this century. The redeemer is always a name of God (*shem elohim*), delivered to us as a word of God (*dibbur*); the word is always a renewal and regiving of Torah; and this regiving gives us a new theopolitical reality and a new rule (*logos, torah*) of practical reasoning (a complex of *chokhmah, binah, daat*; or of *halakhah* and *s'vora*). We have, for example, received Mosaic law after Egypt, the Torah canon of Ezekiel/Ezra after the First Destruction, the rabbinic oral Torah of Mishnah and Talmud after the Second Destruction, the secret *torot* of *kabbalah* after the various losses of diaspora. And, now, after Shoa?

The work-in-progress that I bring to you is an effort to disclose the leading tendencies of an emergent movement of Jewish philosophic theologians. Collected into a "Society for Textual Reasoning," this group is beginning to provide a name (and a dress) for the redeemer who would renew Judaism for us after Shoa *and* after modernity. I add "after modernity" because our Judaism emerges today from out of two destructions: one is the literal Destruction of European Jewry in the Shoa; the other is Jewish assimilation to a modern secularism that has now lost its own hegemony in the West. I am not a spokesperson for the Textual Reasoners, but I am attempting to identify its significance for Jewish rebirth out of these deaths and losses.

There are two reasons why it would be particularly helpful for me to discuss this attempt with you. One reason is that, in this time of rebirth, certain trinitarian logics may be (surprisingly for some) useful as analogues for Jewish reasoning. The other reason is that this time of Jewish renewal may correspond to certain transitional periods, as well, for Christians and Muslims in a weakened secular West. If so, Jewish–Christian (and –Muslim) theological dialogue may be of unusual significance for intra-religious movement as well as for the reshaping of Western culture.

Here is a broad and quick outline of what I mean about the usefulness of trinitarian logics. This outline may itself serve as a sufficiently suggestive syllabus for our discussion; the lengthier writings to follow will amplify some items in the outline, but I have not as yet completed any more comprehensive treatment. (I confess that I am also apprehensive about how to make this treatment public. I am not worried about misreading Christian doctrine, since readers of this book can simply correct me; and, even then, my goal is analogical and associative use of the doctrine for the sake of Judaism, not to offer any informative claims about Christianity. However, Jewish scholars and congregants across the board are very suspicious of trinitarian doctrine in its own right; a thinker who purports to learn something Jewishly from this doctrine may, all the more so, jeopardize his capacity to be heard in Jewish communities, including Jewish academia. So please read my argument as analogical and, even then, as written as if in an esoteric code that makes the words other than they may seem to untutored readers.)

A point of departure for this exercise is Michael Wyschogrod's declaration in that remarkable book, *The Body of Faith*, that his inquiry will not be constrained by the otherwise understandable, age-old Jewish fear of proclaiming aloud those *Jewish* beliefs which became cornerstones of Christian doctrine and, thereby, became associated in the public imagination with something particularly *Christian* rather than Jewish. He then proceeds to his powerful teachings about the incarnation of God in the people Israel. I will return later to these teachings. For now, I hope to imitate Wyschogrod's concern to disclose certain truths about Judaism, however the sound of them may confound certain contemporary Jewish habits of hearing. At the same time, my practice of truth-telling will have more of a pragmatic ring to it – friendly but not identical to his avowedly Barthian practice, which is a practice of being true to the plain sense of scripture above all.

To explain what I mean by "pragmatic Jewish truth-telling" let me turn now to the main essay.

The Condition of Judaism Today

The condition of Judaism today is one of spiritual exile:

> By the rivers of Babylon where we sat down, there we wept as we remembered Zion.
> "How can I sing a song of the Lord on alien soil?" (Ps. 137)

While the Jews have, in the last fifty years, begun to recover the physical body of their peoplehood, the effects of the previous century's destructions continue to dissipate their spiritual energies – to separate them, we might say, from a shared spiritual center. The primary destruction of our time is, of course, the Shoa, as well as the history of pogrom and exclusion that was horribly fulfilled in it. Jewish memory is still defined by the trauma of this destruction, and Jewish spirituality remains a victim of this trauma: Where was God? What difference does piety make? What place will we ever have as a "light to the nations?" Such questions mark the current state of Jewish religious uncertainty and confusion. But the sources of Jewish spiritual dissipation are even deeper, beyond questions about traditional belief.

Judaism's spiritual dissipation is also a mirror of broader contemporary disillusionment with Enlightenment rationalism. Here, the Jewish spirit suffers doubly. Enlightenment optimism already tempted much of Jewry out of its traditional patterns of religiosity, and this exile, along with ultra-orthodox reactions to it, already defined the Jewish religious condition before Shoa. Now, the twentieth century's destructions have crushed Enlightenment optimism as well; and, as the great paradigms of secular reason lose their hegemony across the West, modern Jewish religiosity suffers both from its original suspicions of tradition and from current disillusionment with its alternative rationalisms.

The nonorthodox Jewish theologian Eugene Borowitz narrates this history of Judaism into and out of modernity. In his history Jewish modernism is, first, a sociopolitical condition and only consequently a source of various epistemological and ethical claims. The sociopolitical condition is defined by the Emancipation:

After more than a millennium of ostracism and persecution, European Jews were astounded when the French Revolution signaled a turn to political equality in Europe, including even Jews.... Slowly, often begrudgingly, states granted Jews civil and social equality, – regardless, Emancipation revolutionized Jewish spirituality, for whenever Jews were permitted to modernize, they did so avidly, and uncomplainingly accepted its accompanying secularizaton.

The startling effects of this fundamental shift of cultural context cannot be overemphasized. Freedom from segregated existence brought on a transition from a life oriented by revelation, tradition, and a sense of the holy to one in which religion became privatized if not irrelevant or obsolete. This had the advantage of making a Jew's religion no longer a public handicap. It also meant that as the realm of religiously neutral activity expanded, the twin questions of Jewish identity and continuity became increasingly troublesome. Jews began to ask, "What does it mean to be a Jew today? Why should one undertake its special responsibilities?" Modern Jewish thought arose as Jews sought to respond to these questions in ways that would be culturally credible and Jewishly persuasive.[1]

By what criteria would modern Jews now choose which aspects of their Jewishness to retain and which to discard?

According to Borowitz, modern Jews chose criteria offered by Western Enlightenment sources rather than traditional rabbinic sources: sharply separating private and public spheres; relegating religion to the private sphere; and adopting, for the public sphere, the rules of scientific reason, modern statehood, individual rights, and universal ethics.[2] The modern nation-state was the agent of Jewish emancipation, an expression of the state's movement toward democracy. Both citizenship in the state and democracy brought with them the substitution of individual for communal enfranchisement and rights. The postmodern Jewish philosopher Edith Wyschogrod notes that "in a statement that could almost have been drafted as a manifesto for liberal modernist Judaism, Jürgen Habermas writes":

> The project of modernity formulated in the eighteenth century by the philosophers of the Enlightenment consisted in their efforts to develop objective science, universal morality and law, and autonomous art according to their inner logic.[3]

Wyschogrod explains that

> the leitmotif of liberal modern Jewish theology has been what is perhaps the grandest of Enlightenment modernity's metanarratives, that of Kantian and post-Kantian philosophy. Moses Mendelssohn, Kant's contemporary, offered a Jewish theological version of this narrative ... when he argued that Judaism's belief in God's existence and just governance of the world are in conformity with the requirements of reason and as such, available to all rational beings. (Ibid)

From Borowitz's perspective, however, "Jewish modernism" also contained the seeds of self-criticism or even self-negation, since it represented an historically particular condition of social assimilation that could not over time adequately serve the people Israel's covenantal norms of community and traditional religious law:

> As the twentieth century waned, doubts about modernity's beneficence arose throughout Western civilization. People were profoundly disturbed by the deterioration of the quality of life. A great deal of their unhappiness was disappointment. The Enlightenment, the intellectual credo of modernity, had promised that replacing tradition with rational skepticism, hierarchy with democracy, and custom with freedom would bring messianic benefit – and certainly it hasn't.
>
> On a much deeper level, this loss of confidence in Enlightenment values has come from the collapse of its philosophical foundations. All the certainties about mind and self and human nature that once powered the bold move into greater freedom now seem dubious.

There is no simple alternative, however, since the dominant forms of Jewish religious practice in the modern era emerged as reactions against Jewish rationalism rather than as transformatory responses to it: popular Hasidism, as well as the varieties of esoteric kabbalism that lie behind it; Neo-Orthodoxy, which ultimately offers only a means for traditionally religious Jews to make use of the socioeconomic vehicles of life inside of modern civilization; and the expanding varieties of contemporary ultra-Orthodoxy, combined in Israel with political or ethnic nationalism.

So far, I have left out all of the in-between Judaisms of America that would seem to offer redeeming alternatives to stark modernism and stark anti-modernism: a group that includes a continuum of mediatory movements, from Reform to Reconstructionist to Conservative to Traditional to some expressions of Modern Orthodoxy. I will, indeed, argue that the redeemer for Israel after Shoa will come out of this continuum; rabbis, scholars, and thinkers from these movements are the emergent architects of Jewish renewal. Their blueprints remain inchoate, however, because each of their movements replays some aspect of the failed modern dialectic of liberal universalism and orthodox reaction. Risking hyperbole and offense, I must label this dialectic a logic of death: on one level, because it imitates the dialectical logic of the modern West, and the fruits of this logic were Shoa; on another level, because no Judaism informed by this dialectical logic can declare the death of this dialectic – its own death! – and appropriately mourn its passing.

There is a lot packed into the last sentence, and the unpacking will come in the next section of this essay. For now, I will offer two foretastes of the argument. First, a philosophic analogy. Consider the dialectic of modern empiricism and rationalism to be analogues of the dialectic of religious liberalism and orthodoxy. Consider what has by now become the mythic Descartes – symbol of the origins of the modern project of philosophy – as analogue of the mythic modern Jew. The "Cartesian Jew," if you will, will for argument's sake be said to stimulate the dialectical logic of modernity by over-stating the attractions of modern science and economics and over-stating the ills of inherited religious tradition – in particular its purported incapacity to accommodate and also guide these modern technologies. Overlooking the epistemological role of tradition as condition for all subsequent reasoning, the symbolic Descartes lacks a means of mediating the inner (rationalist) and outer (empiricist) poles of his reflections on the modern technologies and the worlds they disclose. Analogously, the modern Jew lacks tradition's resources for mediating the outer (universalizing and rationalizing) and inner (communitarian) poles of the Jewish people's efforts to accommodate and influence its changing world. Seen from this perspective, reactionary orthodoxy (which I identify here with the strictly communitarian pole) is not – against its own apologetic – to be identified as the "bearer of Jewish tradition." Orthodoxy will appear instead to have replaced actual tradition with the idea of it – replaced, that is, the humanly unpredictable evolution of traditional Jewish life and law with artificially constructed systems of communal and hermeneutical order.

Now, to complete this exercise, credit Kant with having perceived the errors and inadequacy of philosophy's modern dialectic and with having appropriately sought a means of mediating its outer and inner poles. At the same time, consider his Critical project to have failed in fact to disclose the actual Mediator, because he sought to construct the vehicle of mediation out of his rational idea of it (and desire for it), rather than seeking to rediscover the Mediator who already lived behind the Cartesian dialectic and suffered on behalf of it. In this way, the dialectical logic of modernity creeps back into his system, which then paradoxically and subtly reinforces this logic. Analogously, consider the American non-Orthodox movements to have correctly perceived the errors and inadequacy of the modern dialectic of Jewish liberalism and orthodoxy, but to have failed to disclose the Jewish tradition's means of mediating these poles. The American movements appropriately desire a mediating third, but their desire tends to overreach their capacity to hear the Mediator's own voice. Constructing more than listening, they tend to replay aspects of the modern dialectic in subtle and subversive ways.

So, now a second foretaste of the overall argument. It is, sadly, that there is no way for Jews (as well, I trust, as for Christians) to move beyond the dialectic of modernity without allowing its inner logic to die. To mourn for the literal deaths of our people is both to acknowledge the actuality of those deaths and to believe in the resurrection of the dead. To acknowledge the fact of our deaths is, in part, to acknowledge the incapacity of the culture of modern Europe, or the modern West, to prevent those deaths. To the degree that the modern West inherits the unmediated dialectic of modern reasoning, then, to acknowledge our deaths is to recognize that, unredeemed, the modern West is no home for us; it is a place of death. To believe in the resurrection of the dead is, in part, to believe that our redeemer lives. Reapplying a rabbinic tautology ("there is no place in the world to come for those who do not believe in the world to come" – paraphrasing *Mishnah B'rachot* 11), we may then infer that belief in the redeemer is incompatible with a belief system that precludes the actual existence of the redeemer. If Jews live in a world informed by the dialectical logic of modernity, and if that is a world of death, then the redeemer for Jewish life in this world must be one who comes from outside this dialectic, to mediate and mend it. There is no life for such a redeemer within the unmediated dialectic, nor can the dialectic support the capacity to believe in and perceive such a redeemer. Both Jewish liberal universalism and Jewish anti-modern orthodoxy belong to the unmediated dialectic of modernity. They therefore cannot be sources of redemption for modern Judaism and, in this sense, Jews who seek religous renewal must acknowledge and mourn the deaths of both these poles of modern Jewish religion.

The historicist aspect of this approach precludes our condemning either of these poles as "errant." Jews entering modernity may have seen the appearance of their Redeemer by way of this very dialectic, which may indeed have kept them in religious life for a brief epoch. All we need say is that this epoch has past; that *that* redeemer has died – or *that* appearance of the Redeemer has died – and it is only by mourning this death that we can even seed the possibility of seeing our life after death – the life of Judaism after this Destruction.

Mourning and the Memory of Past Losses

Suffering is not itself redemptive. Our prayer in each cycle of Jewish life is to enter the final world-to-come and to know that the redeemer who comes is our last, that the cycle of history is truly over, and that not just we but all humanity and all God's creatures have been forever reunited with the divine word – so that through this union the breach in God's own Name is repaired and God's Name is one.

But for now humanity does suffer and we suffer. And after each suffering we stand over our dead and acknowledge the death and await *this* cycle of rebirth. Descartes is right, by the way. Tradition fails us periodically and a redeemer must be born anew, rising out of the ashes of our present death. But Descartes is also wrong; there is a concealed dimension of tradition that does not fail, the ever-living dimension from which, out of the depths, the redeemer is reborn in our day, called into the living by the very fact of our mourning. *Called*, that is; not forced, but called, like the cry of Israel out of bondage (Ex. 2). The memory of the dead calls out – remember our ancestors, God, and their covenant with you! – and the redeemer is given new life by their memory.

In the present cycle of rabbinic Judaism, the people Israel mourns each summer, in the month of Av, for the destructions of both Temples. The period of mourning reaches a crescendo on Tisha B'av, a full fast, a day of ashes and sitting on the ground and mournfully reading Lamentations, Eicha! But after sunset of that day, the mourning is past; in Hasidic communities, in fact, there is a custom to dance. Why dance? Without, at this time, commenting directly on the Hasidic practice, I will turn now to see how, in our own approach, mourning may rise to a kind of dancing. The remaining pages of this essay will have three parts: (a) mourning and remembering previous destructions in Jewish history; (b) attending to our destruction today: rabbinic pragmatism and the logic of redemption; and (c) dancing after mourning today: Jewish semiotics and redemptive historiography.

The commemoration of Tisha B'av is a crucial practice for our present days of mourning. For a time of present mourning it is a ritual of remembering previous mourning and thus engendering in us the realization that we participate in a cycle whose present-day outcome may have much to do with what and how we remember. Consider, for example, the following catalogue of previous destructions.

Mitzrayim

> The Israelites groaned in their bondage and cried out and their cry for help because of their bondage went up to God. (Ex. 2)

The primordial event of loss: exile, enslavement, and the dissolution of the partriarchal/matriarchal, Abrahamite religion.

Chorban: first destruction

> I reared up children and brought them up, but they have rebelled against me. . . . The Lord's anger burns against his people. (Is. 1)

> > How solitary sits the city, once so full of people.
> > Bitterly she weeps at night, tears are upon her cheeks. . . .
> > Jerusalem has become unclean. (Lam. 1)

The paradigmatic destruction: the burning of Israel's Temple, the end of its monarchical theo-polity and political independence, the exile of its priests and intellectuals to Babylonian captivity.

Chorban: second destruction

An image dominates even more than a text: the Burnt Temple (70–1 CE); Jerusalem razed and salted (135 CE). But texts abound:

> It was decreed for Israel that they study words of Torah in distress, in enslavement, in wandering and in uncertainty, suffering for lack of food. (*Midrash Eliayahu Rabbah*)

> When Rabbi Joshua looked at the Temple in ruins one day, he burst into tears. "Alas for us! The place which atoned for the sins of all the people Israel lies in ruins!" (From *Avot de Rabbi Natan* 11a, in *Machzor for Yom Kippur*, J. Harlow)

THE RENEWAL OF JEWISH THEOLOGY TODAY 333

The defining destruction for our Judaism, which is rabbinic Judaism. The biblical promises are broken, so it seems. "Because of our sins, we are exiled from the land." Galut. The end of direct biblical jurisdiction over Israel's life.

Galut in Muslim Afro-asia and Christian Europe, with its refrain of pogrom, forced conversions, and displacements

Sorest in memory are sufferings in Christian Europe: the massacres of the Crusades, the Expulsion from Spain, the Chmielnicki pogroms of eighteenth-century Poland, the pogroms of nineteenth- and early twentieth-century Russia and the then Soviet Union.

> The sword and the book came down from heaven tied to each other. Said the Almighty, "If you keep what is written in this book, you will be spared this sword; if not, you will be consumed by it." (*Midrash Rabbah Deuteronomy 4.2*)
>
> We clung to the book, yet were consumed by the sword. (David Halivni, *The Book and the Sword*)[4]

Shoa

The crescendo of Galut in Christian-and-secular Europe. I need not offer you details. But this text, again from Davi Halivni's memoir *The Book and the Sword*:

> When the sound of the closing of the door, after the first child was shoved into the crematorium, reached heaven, Michael, the most beneficent of angels, could not contain himself and angrily approached God. Michael asked, "Do You now pour out Your wrath upon children? In the past, children were indirectly caught up in the slaughter. This time they are the chief target of destruction. Have pity on the little ones, O Lord." God, piqued by Michael's insolence, shouted back at him, "I am the Lord of the Universe. If you are displeased with the way I conduct the world, I will return it to void and null." Hearing these words, Michael knew that there was to be no reversal. He had heard these words once before in connection with the Ten Martyrs. He knew their effect. He went back to his place, ashen and dejected, but could not resist looking back sheepishly at God and saw a huge tear rolling down His face, destined for the legendary cup which collects tear and which, when full, will bring the redemption of the world. Alas, to Michael's horror, instead of entering the cup, the tear hit its rim, most of it spilling on the ground – and the fire of the crematorium continued to burn.

Modernity

If the bodies of Israel were destroyed in the Shoa, Israel's religion had already been sent into spiritual exile two hundred years earlier: not destroyed, but separated into the dialectical poles of Jewish modernism we discussed earlier. These poles define present-day Judaism as well. This is why, as suggested earlier, we remain within the trauma of our most recent death; within that dialectic, there is no hope for rebirth and thus no means of ending our formal period of mourning.

Attending to Destruction Today: Rabbinic Pragmatism and the Logic of Redemption

Mourning never ends. But rabbinic Judaism provided rituals of gradual reentry into the customs and lawful conduct of everyday life: after the dead are buried, a week of strictest mourning, sitting on boxes at home; a month of modified mourning and partial return to everyday life and work; then another level of return: a period of up to a year before the deceased's headstone is unveiled, and a full year until the first *Yahrzeit* or annual memorial; normal social life is then resumed, except for the annual memorial. These rituals would make no sense if we had not seen death before and our subsequent return to life, with sadness and enduring loss but also renewed life. It will soon be time for Israel to enter another stage, as well, of its mourning in and after the Shoa. There has been utter shock and silence; there have been three decades of acknowledgment and witness and protest and redescription; and there has been wrestling, much of it premature, with the "meaning" and consequences of this Destruction. These responses are premature only because they are for the most part offered within the terms of Judaism's modern dialectic. But those terms are not adequate for any response – any more than the literal sense of the Bible was adequate to respond to the Second Destruction.

One step out of the terms of modern Judaism is simply to remember the cycles of death and rebirth that we have previously suffered and, in that memory, to begin to distinguish between the visible part of modern Judaism that must die if we are to live again and the concealed part that has reappeared after each of the previous destructions that we remember. In its broadest expression, the activity of distinguishing these two parts belongs to what I will call *rabbinic pragmatism*. With limited space, I will not offer here any systematic introduction to this pragmatism, but only a philosophic propaedeutic: *a note on Charles Peirce's exercise in separating "A" and "B" reasonings*. I will trust in the capacities of your reflective imaginations to abstract, rename, and reconstruct from this note a larger and more coherent picture.

As a tool in the service of religious renewal, Jewish philosophy is primarily a source of redemptive–logical thinking, by which I mean an exercise in reducing certain redemptive rules of reasoning to a more visible portrait of their elemental parts. Seeing these parts more simply, we can more easily evaluate different reasonings, manipulate the rules we have, and then apply them more efficiently. This means that philosophy does not itself invent the rules; it is only a vehicle for their simple display. The "invention" is something we may later label both ongoing revelation and the work of the Holy Spirit.

Just as previous stages of Jewish renewal have been aided by the Jewish use of Platonic, certain Muslim, Aristotelian, and most recently Kantian models of philosophic logic, so this emergent stage is already aided by the use of various post-foundational or postmodern logics, of which I believe the most powerful is at work in Charles Peirce's pragmatic and semiotic writings. Very few theologians, however, are aware of the power of Peirce's potential contribution to contemporary religious renewal. Knowingly or unknowingly, many theologians still make use of late medieval or Enlightenment/modern logics that have long since outworn their applicability to the conditions of contemporary life; some who depart from the modern logics believe they are therefore required to settle for the un-logic of some of the postmodern methods dominant on the Continent and now in the United States. Surely, however, they must realize that scripture's word is a source of revealed logics of redemption, which could not, since God speaks in them, be reducible to the rational constructions of late scholastic and modern philosophers. Nor – since God offers them to us for the sake of redemption – can they be adequately represented by the anti-logics of both secular postmodernists *and* neo-orthodox anti-modernists. Peirce's logics offer remarkable assistance to us at this time because they are *both* competent to serve the needs of post-Newtonian science *and* traceable as abstractions from out of a reading of scripture as revealed logic. The expanding company of contemporary Peirce scholars (pragmatists and semioticians working in American philosophy, but also in Italian semiotics and in an emergent school of German pragmatists – but where are the Engish and French?) are well convinced of their master's role in helping underwrite the development of twentieth-century logics of relativity, along with various systems of mathematics and of sign-theory and phenomenology. So theologians might take some comfort in their philosophic colleagues' judgments here. But Peirce scholars are also, on the whole, quite resistant to my second claim – that their master is at bottom a scriptural philosopher. Peircean philosophers today are themselves too deeply rerouted through the dialectics of modern thinking to entertain such a claim, despite Peirce's own avowal that his "pragmatism is nothing but a logical corollary to Jesus' injunction that 'ye may know them by their fruit,'" and despite his efforts to ground a semiotic metaphysics in "Christian love."

To confront the philosophers and make an opening for the theologians, I recently wrote a dense book on *Peirce, Pragmatism, and the Logic of Scripture*.[5] In the first part, I reread all of Peirce's writings on pragmatism to show how, almost line by line, it is felicitous to read him as I have suggested. In the second part, I reread his mature pragmatism and "existential" mathematics to show how they could provide a philosophic logic for contemporary scriptural theologians – Jewish and Christian (and potentially Muslim as well). In a recent paper on "'He is Our Peace': The Letter to the Ephesians and the Theology of Fulfillment," David Ford tests this approach to Peirce's pragmatism by applying it, experimentally, to a pragmatic rereading of Ephesians.[6] In the process, he restates my thesis much more efficiently. Illumined by his reading, my claim about Peirce's pragmatism may be restated as follows.

Pragmatism arises out of the failures of Cartesian rationalism. It says that history has already said No to Descartes' Yes. This Yes is the assertion that a clear and distinct criterion for evaluating the efficacy and thus truth of all traditions could be found outside all traditions in a vision of individuated and distilled reason. But, as Borowitz has stated, the Jews have learned too awfully well that the modern vision of what really is and what the whole world ought to do is one that leads inevitably to imperialism, colonialism, and totalitarianism – or else to disillusionment, relativism, and anomie. The pragmatic alternative is not, however, just to reaffirm "Tradition." It is, rather, *with* Descartes to recognize the failings of tradition *but also* to recognize that the modern project of reasoning itself takes flight out of the night of these failings. What the pragmatists add to Descartes is the *memory* that this reason that flies out of the night is itself a messenger *only* of night: that is, our means of seeing in bold relief just what has gone wrong in our religious and social traditions. This flight of reason is in this sense a prophetic complaint. But it is not itself the vehicle of redemption, a source of new light. It is the cry without which Israel in bondage could not be heard, the cry that goes up to God. But it is not itself God's response, coming down and sending Moses. Schelling saw this, when he wrote of the negativity that is philosophy's proper subject matter. Rosenzweig based his *Star of Redemption* on this insight. And the Jews after destruction see this, for at this dark time, reasoning can be trusted only if it begins with *negation*. This is not a time to declare philosophy begins with wonder! Or even that reasoning begins with Phenomena, that is, with any Presence – or the ways things present themselves. This is not a time to begin with what Is, or with Being.

Positive being is for the orthodox, for the customary, for the conventional, for those secure in the everyday. Please God that we *could* begin with such security. That indeed is our prayer. And that is the sweet blessing of any time of extended peace, when a community's values and elemental relations have some quiet time to nurture undisturbed, everyday life. For this we pray: that we enjoy enough peace to allow the Jewish love of *this* world to flower. In such a time, we may enjoy Being's face, and give our trust to the conventional reasonings – religious law – that arise out of such enjoyment and wonder and observation.

But, for the Jews at this specific moment of their history, this is *not* such a time. That face of God, the face called being, is Hidden – *mistater panim* in Isaiah's terms, often cited by Buber – or clouded over, rather, by the other side of being, non-being in all its varieties: contrariety, contradiction, aporia, not- or, at least, not-yet being. God alone (or, as we shall see, God-with-us alone) can unveil his hiddenness, human reason cannot.

The redemptive power of *part* of continental postmodern thought is that it has brought the attention of Western philosophers to the eruption of negation and not-being into the complacency of their secular, ego-logical project. This is the strength of Levinas' metaphenomenology of the Face and of the other who interrupts my gaze (with parallels in Marion's doctrine of the beyond-being; note as well how Levinas and Jüngel may be brought into dialogue on this matter, as in David Ford's *Self and Salvation, Being Transformed*.)[7] Peering into the abyss, not by looking away from it or rationalizing it, Jews are able to encounter the God to whom they cried in Egypt. God sent Moses, who asked, "Who shall I say sent me?" He answered, my name is *ehyeh imach*, "I will be with you," to which Isaiah adds, "I will be with you in suffering." The Jews are able thereby to encounter their redeemer in the very face of their death. For only by embracing their loss in its utmost negativity do they experience the negative as itself the hidden face of God, *el mistater*; and only then can a dim light glow in the eyes of the dark, and the Jews can embrace the Burnt Temple itself as sign of the redeemer, and they can dance the dance of mourners as they return to life. The rabbis of the time after the Second Destruction label the cognitive dimension of this dance belief in *tichiyat hametim*, the resurrection of the dead. Jews in modernity have for too long forgotten this belief and its centrality to the rebirth of their religion after destruction. Death is death, but it is not only death. The letter remains the letter, but it is also the letter reborn, which the rabbis call the *torah she b'al peh*, the Oral Torah in which the Judaism of the Written Torah, *torah she b'ichtav*, is reborn.

How, then, does God unveil God's Face after this time of Destruction? If pragmatism is the logician's way of saying "know them by their fruit," this means both that prophecy's word is told only in the testing of its public consequences, and that reasoning is a vehicle of prophecy. Stated in Jewish terms, this means that what Descartes calls reason is prophetic, but only a prophecy of warning and condemnation. The fruit of such prophecy is redemption – or the lack of it. The question is, how to find the fruit? The pragmatic answer is: learn to read death, understand its signs. Here, in brief voice, is a sampling of pragmatic rules for doing this:

(1) Realize that the mark of death is the individuated reasoning that declares by its very individuation the death (alias error) of some specific, failed practices, failed bits of tradition and of social process. This mark is critical reasoning: the Western academy's defining tool. The method of critical reasoning is to thematize certain objects of inspection, which occupy the place, in the propositional logic of critical reasoning, of "subjects" about which certain predications are made. Each subject of this kind is a mark of something that has failed. To paraphrase Rosenzweig, whatever the philosopher can thematize is already dead.

(2) Realize that every death of this kind is finite: the death of *a* creature. The reasoning that declares this death is itself finite: the finite mark of a finite death. Descartes errs only because he over-generalizes the failings of this or that aspect of his inherited tradition of inquiry (scholastic), as if he knew also of the potential failings of all of that tradition (all of scholasticism, or all of medieval Christianity). But there is no reason to doubt that some failing in Descartes' inheritance gave rise to his reasonings. Western academic reasoning is prophetic but finite.

(3) Realize that, if this academic–philosophic reasoning is finite, then there must be more to say than what this reasoning has to say. If reasoning tells me what has failed, then more-than-reason alone will tell me what in my tradition, heritage, past, has not failed, is not yet subject to question or to thematization. The Israelite prophets reject neither Israel itself, nor its divine law, nor its priesthood. They reject only the error and sin in all these.

Philosophic/academic reasoning is comparably prophetic in the West. Whatever it assumes and continues of its cultural heritage is not doubted nor negated, and is therefore affirmed by the very fact of its being left alone. Whatever is affirmed in this way discloses the positive traces of the Redeemer in the academic's cultural heritage. This is the pragmatist's means of turning from negative philosophy to positive theology. Within what has not died there is reason for dancing. This is what Peirce calls, after Thomas Reid, his "Scotch common-sense realism," reread theologically. It is, in Rosenzweig's rereading of the Song of Songs, the beloved's discovery that she (alias the Western reasoner) is not alone, but is already loved: that she must now love in return and, in that loving, confess that she has been alone, has been separate, and has not until now called out to her lover.[8] For Levinas, this is a lesson about the revelation that continues after Sinai: when each individual hears a voice that preceded him or her (preceding their reasoning, preceding their consciousness, preceding their birth), saying "you are already obligated to me."

> The human soul is obligated before all commitment. It is not only practical reason, the source of its obligations for others, but responsibility in the forgetting of self.[9]

This is "the Revelation that becomes ethics," because it reveals how we have been created: "A responsibility preceding freedom, . . . preceding intentionality!" (ibid, p. 127). In the Talmud's rereading of Exodus 24, it is the responsibility the Israelites were supposed to accept at Sinai, when, like the angels, they declared of God's commandments, *naaseh v'nishmah*, "We will act first [upon your word] and only then reflect" [upon it, or "hear" it] – acknowledging that they must await God's word before they act, hear his word as the very condition of their action (from b. Talmud *Shabbat* 88).

Rule (3) is therefore the rebirth of elemental faith amid the darkness after destruction. It is, having listened to the prophetic voice of critical reasoning, to listen to the potentially redemptive voices of all our other faculties of memory: feeling, imagining, reading, listening. . . .

Peirce calls this listening "A-reasoning," to be distinguished from the "B-reasoning" that marks whatever we doubt. A-reasoning is the ability to rehear, beneath what we doubt, the persistent rules of conduct and belief that we do not doubt. This is the redemptive side of prophecy, because, in rule (4) we must readopt the fruits of A-reasoning as positive guides to our work of concretely repairing the faulty B-reasonings in our inherited social and religious traditions. This is the Talmudic principle of *kiyemu mah she kiblu*: "[the Jews] affirmed what they had previously accepted" (from Esther 9). In the Talmudic midrash alluded

THE RENEWAL OF JEWISH THEOLOGY TODAY 339

to earlier (from *Shabbat* 88a), Exodus 19, *v'yityatzvu b'tachtit he har* (they stood at the bottom, literally "underneath," the mountain) is taken to indicate that God held Mt. Sinai over the Israelites' heads – offering them a choice to accept the Torah or else. One sage objects that, if that were what happened, the Torah would no longer be binding (since, by Jewish law, an agreement entered into by force is not binding). Another sage saves the original midrash by rereading that line from Esther to mean that, in the days of Esther (exile in Persia), the Jews willingly affirmed the law that they had accepted earlier only by force. In our context the principle teaches that, in times after destruction, we are forced, for the sake of our spiritual survival, to uncover A-reasonings otherwise concealed behind our customary beliefs and to readopt them, willingly, as laws of our renewed life.

Let me, then, illustrate how we might practice these four rules for rereading the signs of death as signs of new life: that is, for refinding within the negativity of our loss the marks of our redeemer. Once again, my illustration is only a sampling of steps to be taken in order to practice these rules:

Step 1 was already to have declared the death of Judaism's modern dialectic. This is to have acknowledged the inadequacy of either pole of modern Judaism – secular universalism or anti-modern orthodoxy – to remove us from that dialectic.

Step 2 is to make use of the resouces of modern critical scholarship to help us see clearly just what has died, where and how. The dominant form of academic Jewish scholarship is still modeled, with some revisions, on the nineteenth-century German–Jewish program of historical–critical text scholarship – *das Wissenschaft des judentums*. Its practitioners assume that this scholarship offers the only unprejudicial means of explaining what all the classic Jewish texts mean, by uncovering what evidence we may have about how the texts were constructed and what their various constitutive documents could have meant in the time they were redacted together. Step 2 would, for example, be to reappraise this scholarship, against the assumptions of its practitioners and detractors, as neither adequately disclosive of what these texts mean, nor therefore as redemptive for Judaism, nor for that matter as simply errant. The scholarship would serve, instead, as an indirect source of prophetic disclosures about the kinds of failures and deaths (so to speak) of which each text – including the scholars' own – is a sign.

To complete Step 2 is at the same time to undertake Step 3, which is to recollect behind each of these texts the living dimensions of Judaism, or A-reasonings, that are brought to life, but never thematized, through the texts.

This step, finally, can itself be practiced only by way of Step 4, which is the actual work of readopting the A-reasonings as guides to reimagining and repairing what has failed for us in modern Jewish tradition: to disclose the fruits of Jewish scholarship only in its consequences for a redeemed Jewish life. It appears necessary to describe this work, at once, in two different ways. These two ways correspond to the two warring poles of modern Judaism, but only as transformed here into the two complementary poles or partners of a renewed Jewish life. One way is to describe Step 4 as the work of *ruach hakodesh*, the Holy Spirit, which alone may reveal to Jews in their suffering visions or expressions of the words of the living Torah (A-reasoning) that will redeem them from suffering and bring renewed life. A second way is to describe Step 4 as the exhaustive discipline of rereading Jewish text and historical scholarship, pragmatically, as indirect disclosures of redemptive A-reasonings. These are reasonings, since they guide certain forms of rational inquiry, but they are not the kind of reasonings whose ratio or measure can be thematized, or defined clearly and distinctly to the satisfaction of the individual thinker. This measure can be displayed, however, in the patterns of shared work that animate communities of what we may call "rabbinic pragmatists." These are philosophically disciplined readers of classic Jewish texts who – rereading contemporary Jewish text scholarship pragmatically – rediscover in the classic Jewish texts *directives* for responding in specific ways to what they collectively judge to be the crises of contemporary Jewish life.

These two ways of characterizing Step 4 are mediated by the fact that there may be no way to account for the possibility of successful pragmatic reading without appealing to a doctrine of the Holy Spirit, or the Spirit of God that moves from the written Torah to the Torah lived today after Destruction. While there are explicit disciplines that inform pragmatic reading, there is no formula that allows us to predict that any such reading will be successful. Any success would display unpredictable aspects of the communal life of the rabbinic pragmatists, which includes unpredictable aspects of the community's relation to the words of scripture, the words of subsequent rabbinic commentary, and the conditions of Jewish life today after Destruction. At the same time, these characterizations of Step 4 remain distinguishable, because there is also no way to assume that the Spirit of God need work through rabbinic pragmatism, as opposed to other practices of Jewish renewal.

My own characterizations of Steps 1–4 would be of little value if they had been deduced, in Cartesian-like fashion, from some concept or vision of some individuated thinker. I have offered this entire essay, however (along with the description of these steps), as one way of characterizing the work of an actual community of rabbinic pragmatists – including the work of the two broader communities in which they participate. One of these communities calls itself the Society for Textual Reasoning (TR), initiated eleven years ago, as a circle of 10 and now 300 philosophers and text scholars seeking to articulate a new form of Jewish discourse beyond the medieval philosophic and modern historicist models. Including such thinkers as Robert Gibbs, Steven Kepnes, Michael Zank, Peter Ochs, and Nancy Levene in philosophy, Elliot Wolfson and Shaul Magid in mysticism and rabbinics, and Laurie Zoloth in orthodox-and-feminist ethics, this group rereads the patterns of reasoning that emerge prototypically out of Talmudic–rabbinic practices of interpretation, and it suggests that we consider these patterns expressions of a redemptive logic for Jewish renewal. The other community calls itself the Society for Scriptural Reasoning (SSR): initiated five years ago, through an overlap of interests among members of TR, of the postcritical movement of Christian theologians some label the "Yale School" (students of Hans Frei, George Lindbeck, and Stanley Hauerwas), of a group of Anglican and English Catholic theologians who both overlap with and differ from the Yale folks, and most recently a group of Sunni Muslim thinkers who find in the work of Muhammed Iqbal parallels to the work of SSR. Among the founding members of the group are David Ford, Daniel Hardy, Elliot Wolfson, Peter Ochs, Steven Kepnes, Kurt Richardson, Kris Lindbeck, and so on (the present membership is about 60). The goal of SSR is to examine together the parallel forms of reasoning that emerge out of philosophically disciplined readings of holy scripture by members of each religious sub-community. These forms of reasoning are received as potential substitutes for the foundational or reductive rules of reasoning that guide the secular academy *as well as* the anti-modern sects that oppose the academy.

Embedded in the essay you have been reading is a sampling of one version of how the community of Textual Reasoners actually undertakes Steps 1–4. Let me spell out how it may do this.

TR Steps 1–2: The TR members gathered together explicitly to find an alternative to the individuated practices of modern Jewish philosophy. They sought a non-individuated method of inquiry (communal work, interacting over the internet, coauthoring papers and books) and paradigms of non-individuated text-reading (the rabbinic style of *chevruta* or studying with partners) and of non-individuated logic (Rosenzweig's *Sprachdenken*, Peirce's logic of relatives and predicate calculus, and so on). Finally, the members of TR and SSR, together, looked to these methods of inquiry and these logics not only as guides to their intra-communal practice, but also as potential substitutes for the dominant methods and logics of inquiry within the university. They claimed, therefore, that some aspects of their inquiry were community-specific (specific to particular denominations, and so on), but that some aspects were generalizable to the work not only of several denominations and religions, but also to the project of academic inquiry in the West.

TR Step 3: For this time after Destruction, the members of TR saw their work as reformatory, both within academia and within their own religious communities. Their goal was not simply to transmit a received Judaism into their disciplines of academic inquiry, but to recognize at the same time that the received forms of both modern and anti-modern Judaism were inadequate to the task of Jewish renewal. They were therefore moved to say no to several aspects of their dialectical inheritance:

- No to the warring dialectic itself, including a no to the authority of *either* secular universalism or reactionary orthodoxy and ethnocentrism.
- No to adopting any persistent embodiment of the European dialectic as their own: the dialectic of inner vs. outer forms of knowledge, of spirit/mind vs. body/politics, or any competing forms of totalizing reason.
- No to inadequate mediators; no to recent attempts to locate a refuge for Judaism in mere ethnocentrism or nationalism; no to the wandering intellect, as embodied in abstractive practices of academic scholarship or (as we

will see below) in exclusively male traditions of kabbalah; and no to the more subtly failed mediations that persist in Jewish academe (in secular Kantianism, in historicism, and in postmodernist varieties of both of these) and in the non-Orthodox American Jewish movements (when, despite their intentions, they replay subtle varieties of the modern dialectic).

TR Step 4: All this no-saying was made, however, on behalf of the great Yes that the text-reasoners received from their encounter with a renewed spirit of Torah, a Holy Spirit that was neither independent of TR's inherited traditions of Jewish law and Jewish reasoning, nor wholly reducible to any of its explicit terms or practices. The encounter took place prototypically within communal, pragmatic readings of classic Jewish texts, reread at once as redemptive responses to historically specific events of Destruction *and* as directives to the TR community itself to participate in certain redemptive processes. The co-presence of these two modes of reading may be the defining characteristic of Step 4.

In terms of Peirce's technology, these two modes of reading correspond to the two complementary types of sign interpretation that contribute to the full life of religious symbols (another name for A-reasonings, in this case as displayed by way of sacred texts). One type interprets the symbol (or text) as the "interpretant" or fruit of a pragmatic (or redemptive) response to certain antecedent sufferings: in this case, the suffering (or destruction) is the "dynamical object" (stimulus or ostensive referent) of the symbol; the way the suffering is portrayed is the "immediate object" (conceptual form or sense) of the symbol; and what the symbol directs its reader to do about the suffering is the symbol's own legislative or symbolic force *per se*. A defining characteristic of the pragmatic semiotic (distinguishing it from continental semiotics from Locke to de Saussure) is the claim that, while the symbol's existence is itself an index (or indubitable existential mark) of its legislative force, the recognizable (conceptual) content (description) of that force is made available only by way of a subsequent interpretant (interpreting sign) as it is received by some specific community of interpreters. Modern Jewish text historians tend to identify "objective scholarship" with claims about the dynamical and immediate objects of classical Jewish texts and, in more recent scholarship, about how the Jewish community at the historical time of a text's redaction received the symbolic force of this text. While making careful use of this historical scholarship, the text reasoner adds at least two claims. Placing limits on the "objectivity" of historical scholarship, one claim is that the legislative force of a classic text displays the A-reasonings at work in a text's redaction and reception: while it is appropriate to ask how the redactors' community received this force, it is inappropriate to assume that historical scholars can adequately characterize the ancient community's reception without participating themselves in the A-reasoning in question. Rephrasing our previous claim, A-reasonings cannot be thematized; to characterize them, scholars must seek, instead, to imitate them by enacting their directives.

THE RENEWAL OF JEWISH THEOLOGY TODAY   343

The second claim of text reasoners is, thus, to urge text historians to risk what the latter might call a kind of "subjectivity." Recognizing that A-reasonings *then* (displayed within the text's historical redaction) can be characterized only by participating in A-reasonings *now* (displayed within the text-scholar's own interpretive work), historians are urged either to delimit considerably the scope of their work, or to "get their feet wet" – to relinquish, that is, modern academe's strict dichotomization of observation and participation. To make useful claims about the legislative force of texts is in some way to participate in that force: and that is to be bound up in the historically contingent and particular relationship between a text, its dynamical object, and the life of the community of interpreters that receives and responds to that text. If we call the text in question a "sacred text," this indicates our assumption that the text concerns God, portrayed either as object of the text as we receive it, as its body, as its legislative force, or as all of these, which would also mean as that in relation to whom all these semiotic dimensions of the text are united. Text reasoners therefore argue that scholars who seek to talk about the reception history of sacred texts need to do so within the context of their participating in a contemporary community of religious practice. Text reasoners who are attentive to the pragmatic/redemptive context and force of A-reasoning *also* argue that A-reasonings are displayed only in response to suffering or destruction, and that scholars of Jewish reception history should therefore desist from their work unless they are prepared to contribute to the Jewish renewal that is implicated in the A-reasonings they seek to examine.

In sum, text reasoners participate in the redemptive process that enables them not only to say no to failed practices they have inherited, but also to transform those failures into constructive vehicles of the enduring A-reasonings of Judaism – the enduring symbols of Torah. In this essay, we have considered the most awful no that modern Jews suffer – the enduring spiritual darkness of Shoa – and the most comprehensive no that rabbinic pragmatists declare enroute to renewing Judaism after Shoa: no to both sides of the dialectical logic of modern Europe and of modern Judaism. We have examined, in its most general terms, the yes upon which textual reasoners base their contribution to Jewish renewal, as well as a very general depiction about how this yes, or A-reasoning, guides their reformatory rereading of the methods and subject matters of modern Jewish scholarship. In the actual, communal practice of text reasoners as well as scriptural reasoners, the reformatory readings come slowly, through careful pragmatic reexamination of specific commentaries on specific sacred texts. Appropriate only to the quick pace and overly broad reach of this introductory essay, I will close by illustrating how a sampling of classic Jewish texts could be reread, pragmatically, as directives for text reasoners today to rediscover, in the very death of the dialectic of modern Judaism, signs of the A-reasoning through which Jewish theology is reborn – or, in directly theological terms, how they rediscover, in the very darkness of this century's Jewish spiritual loss, a mark of its redeemer.

From Mourning to Dancing: Redemptive, Pragmatic Rereading of Jewish Text History

In the beginning of this essay we suggested that this century's deaths brought back to memory the cycle of destruction that has marked Jewish salvation history. One task of textual reasoning is to reread the sacred texts that mark earlier destructions as also signs of *tichiyat hametim*, Jewish rebirth from the dead.

Mitzrayim

> The Lord continued, "I have marked well the plight of My people in Egypt and have heeded their outcry because of their taskmasters." . . . "I have come down to rescue them. . . . I will send you." Moses said, "Who am I that I should go?" . . . He said, "*ehyeh imach*, I will be with you." . . . "Thus shall you say to the Israelites, '*ehyeh* sent me to you.'" (Ex. 3).

The partriarchal/matriarchal religion of Abraham died in Egypt, but it was reborn as the Mosaic religion of the One whose Name is with Israel in its suffering, and of the people of Israel that is united under the legislative force of Torah.

Chorban: first destruction

> But you, Israel, My servant, Jacob, whom I have chosen, Seed of Abraham my friend – You whom I drew from the ends of the earth. . . . To whom I said: You are My servant. . . . Fear not, for I am with you. . . .
> This is My servant, whom I uphold, My chosen one, in whom I delight. I have put My spirit in him, He shall teach the true way to the nations. . . .
> Who formed you, O Israel: Fear not, for I will redeem you. . . . You are Mine. (Is. 41–3)

The religion of the dialectic of monarchy and prophet died in the First Destruction, as did the religion defined by what the Talmud later called *chate'u yisrael*, "the sins of Israel," whose written Torah was maintained only imperfectly through a vicious cycle of meritorious and sinful governments. In the very place of exile, however, in Babylon, the religion of Israel was reborn as the religion of second Isaiah, Ezekiel, and Ezra: a religion of scribal priests who would redact and reteach the Torah as well as maintain it, and whose reteaching would gradually become the legislative voice of Torah within the Second Commonwealth.

Chorban: second destruction

> All Israel has a place in the world to come, as it is written, "Your people shall all be righteous, they shall possess the land forever; they are a shoot of My planting, the work of My hands in whom I shall be glorified" (Is. 60).
>
> Moses received Torah from Sinai and transmitted it to Joshua, and Joshua to the elders, the elders to the prophets, the prophets to the members of the Great Assembly. . . .
>
> Simeon the Just was one of the last members of the Great Assembly. He used to teach: The world rests on three things: on Torah, on service to God, and on acts of lovingkindness. (*Pirke Avot* 1)
>
> Hillel taught: Do not separate yourself from the community . . .
>
> Rabbi Tarfon used to teach: You are not obligated to finish the task, neither are you free to neglect it. (*Pirke Avot* 2)

The religion of biblical Israel died in the Second Destruction: the religion maintained by Temple service, as defined by the literal word of the written Torah, and as lived by Israel only on its holy soil. In its place, directly out of the fires of Chorban, the religion of rabbinic Judaism was reborn: a religion that inherited the Torah teachings of the scribal priests and the central beliefs of their Pharisaic defenders. These are belief in the resurrection of the dead, in life in the world to come (*olam haba*) as well as in this world, and belief that, on Sinai, God gave Moses two *torot*, not one: the Written Torah (*torah she b'chtav*) and the the Oral Torah (*torah she b'al peh*), carried through a chain of transmission to the rabbinic sages. This is the Torah through which, alone, the directives of the Written Torah are disclosed and enacted. As articulated by the great Talmudist – and orthodox text reasoner – David Weiss Halivni, this Oral Torah is the fruit of Ezra's reception of the Spirit of God, through whom he redacted and restored Israel's blemished Torah and initiated what would later become the rabbinic practice of midrashic reinterpretation. This is the practice that is reconstituted today as rabbinic pragmatism or textual reasoning. In the hour after Israel's Destruction the rabbis renewed Judaism through the teachings of Mishnah and Talmud, and they recodified the directives of Torah through the legislative activity of the *halakhah*.

Galut in Muslim Afro-asia and Christian Europe, with its refrain of pogrom, forced conversions, and displacements

> God both creates and destroys; indeed, he destroys by creating and he creates by destroying. . . . Consider the comment attributed to R. Abbahu on the verse, "There was evening and there was morning, the first day" (Gen. 1). "From here [we learn that] the Holy One, blessed be He, created worlds and destroyed them, until He created these. He said: These give me pleasure, but those did not give me pleasure" (*Genesis Rabbah* 3)

> The full implications of these ideas are drawn out in the medieval kabbalistic sources. According to a bold idea expressed in the *Zohar* and further developed in the Lurianic material of the sixteenth century, the first act of divine creativity involves the elimination of the forces of impurity from the Godhead. This act of catharsis of evil is related to the attribute of judgment or divine limitation, which is referred to in the Lurianic kabbalah by the technical term *tsimtsum* (withdrawal). ... From this perspective, we can speak of divine suffering at the very core of existence. If God did not sufffer his own death as the infinite, there would be no existence outside of the infinite God. (Elliot Wolfson)[10]

The self-sufficiency of rabbinic Judaism died during Israel's medieval and modern Exile. This means that the public framework of rabbinic piety was more or less maintained, but only as supported by the emergence of new elite and esoteric discourses among its religious and intellectual leadership. In addition to various philosophic, hermeneutic, legal, and pietistic discourses, the emblematic elite discourse of medieval and modern religious Judaism was the zoharic and then lurianic kabbalah. As Wolfson indicates, the kabbalah intensified rabbinic tendencies to transform the negativity of destruction into an attribute of God and, thus, paradoxically, into a vehicle of redemption. God not only suffers with us; he also suffers in himself. In fact, our suffering is but a reflection of divine suffering. Our redemption comes only through God's own, and our prayers are no longer only our means for eliciting divine help; they are also our means of returning divine assistance to God himself. "Torah, divine service, and acts of lovingkindness" uphold the world because they contribute to the restoration of the creator's own name: the name through which the world is created and through whose repair the world will be repaired.

Shoa and modernity

Like rabbinic Judaism in the medieval/early modern period, kabbalistic Judaism has not died in this century's Destruction, but its self-sufficiency has, as an esoteric discourse for spiritual/intellectual elites. For medieval and later Judaisms entering into the dialectical logic of modernity, versions of Jewish mysticism served as mediating discourses for the elites. With European Judaism's assimilation to modernity, however, that dialectic has become so strong and so public that it has exceeded the kabbalah's mediating capacity. The resilience of Hasidism – a public manifestation of kabbalistic practice – may be cited as evidence to the contrary. But there are also very strong movements today of secular–universalist and of ultra-orthodox Jews. When I argue that all these forms of Judaism have "died" in this century's Destruction, I do not mean that they fail to serve as resources for some good and very vibrant Jewish people. I am, instead, arguing formally: that the redemptive logics of these Judaisms remain unresponsive to the events of this century and that, while aspects of their lived practices will continue to enrich the everyday conduct of Jewish life, the

Judaism that is now emerging will exhibit rules of overall interpretation that are irreducible to the rules that inform any of these Judaisms now. The kabbalah is a prime test case. Many textual reasoners show increased interest in kabbalistic studies, but I expect the fruit of their present studies will be a rebirth of kabbalistic tropes in strikingly new forms. As suggested already by tendencies in Wolfson's writings and those of his students, this kabbalah will most likely become a dimension of textual reasoning. This means, for example, that there would be transformations in the male-centered imagery and logocentrism of the medieval kabbalah, as well as in its responsiveness to the political and ethical concerns of the Jewish people as a whole. While there will be a place for esoteric intellectual life in the community of textual reasoners (postmodern discourses are a case in point!), the esoteric should express the parabolic appearance of A-reasoning and the need for scholarly specialization, rather than the secrecy of a sub-sectarian practice and of a culturally privileged elite.

In many ways, modern Jewish academics have adopted a status and role within the Jewish community that is comparable to that of the kabbalistic elites in an earlier epoch. Like the kabbalistic systems, academic Judaism may serve as intellectual–spiritual mediator for some intellectuals, but not for the broader Jewish community in its efforts at renewal. While it arises out of Jewish academia (with some kabbalistic influences as well), Textual Reasoning – or its equivalents – should offer this kind of mediation. If so, we might expect developments like textual reasoning to emerge, gradually, within the various denominations and movements of present-day Judaism. Among the early exponents of such developments within the broader movements are Eugene Borowitz in the Reform movement, Max Kadushin (forty years ago!) in the Conservative movement – which now boasts as well many members of the Society for Textual Reasoning – and David Weiss Halivni, whose movement for Traditional Judaism stands in-between Orthodox and Conservative Judaism. Noted Talmudist and Auschwitz survivor, Halivni offers poignant testimony to the capacity of religious Judaism to renew itself in ways that both continue what is enduring in Jewish tradition and move beyond what is not. In closing, I will cite my own foreword to Halivni's book, *Revelation Restored*.[11] In this book Halivni rereads the biblical story of Ezra, pragmatically,

> as evidence that Ezra, under divine guidance, restored Israel's Torah after destruction. At the same time, he interprets Ezra's restorative work as figure of the restorative work that the rabbinic sages performed after the Second Destruction and that we can perform, again, after the destructions that define our epoch. Halivni addresses his words, in particular, to the perplexed religious Jews of the contemporary academy, as well as the perplexed critically minded Jews of the contemporary yeshivah. He seeks to show both groups how, contrary to their fears, they can lead pious lives at the same time as they examine with critical clarity the sacred texts on which their piety rests. Nevertheless, his pragmatic lesson may apply more generally: that, in the tradition of Ezra, the judgments that guide postcritical theology must draw on both cognitive and emotive–spiritual energies, on intimate familiarity with the sacred text tradition, on a heart enflamed by love of God, of

revealed text, and of humanity, and on a profound sense of responsibility to correct blemishes in the text tradition – as if this tradition constituted the creation itself, as if that creation were broken, and as if those few with the power to mend the creation must do so at once.

Notes

A version of this essay was first delivered to the Duodecim Society in Princeton, New Jersey, in 1999.

1 Eugene Borowitz, *Renewing the Covenant: A Theology for the Postmodern Jew* (Philadelphia, PA: Jewish Publication Society, 1991), pp. 3–4.
2 Eugene Borowitz, *Exploring Jewish Ethics: Papers on Covenant Responsibility* (Detroit, MI: Wayne State University Press, 1990), pp. 26ff.
3 Jürgen Habermas, "Modernity versus Postmodernity," *New German Critique*, 1981; cited in Edith Wyschogrod, "Trends in Postmodern Jewish Philosophy," *Soundings*, 76: 1 (1993), p. 131.
4 David Halivni, *The Book and the Sword* (New York: Farrar, Straus and Giroux, 1996).
5 Peter Ochs, *Peirce, Pragmatism, and the Logic of Scripture* (Cambridge: Cambridge University Press, 1998).
6 Delivered at the November 1999 meeting of the Society for Scriptural Reasoning.
7 David Ford, *Self and Salvation, Being Transformed* (Cambridge: Cambridge University Press, 1999).
8 See Robert Gibbs, *Correlations in Rosenzweig and Levinas* (Princeton, NJ: Princeton University Press, 1992), p. 26.
9 Emmanuel Levinas, *Beyond the Verse: Talmudic Readings and Lectures*, trans. Gary Mole (Bloomington and Indianapolis: Indiana University Press, 1994), p. 125.
10 Elliot Wolfson, "Listening to Speak," in S. Kepnes et al. (eds.), *Reasoning After Revelation* (Boulder, CO: Westview Press, 1998).
11 David Weiss Halivni, *Revelation Restored* (Boulder, CO: Westview Press, 1998).

CHAPTER 20
Intending Transcendence: Desiring God

Edith Wyschogrod

Although she was briefly a student of Paul Tillich, Edith Wyschogrod's work bears the marks of another legacy, distinctly Jewish and existential: the work of Simone Weil, Hannah Arendt and, more recently, Gillian Rose. It is no accident that she is one of the respondents in Och's postmodern Jewish philosophy. Wyschogrod herself mentions Arendt, once and briefly, but Weil's and Rose's theological wrestling, Arendt's political analyses, and the critiques by all of them of violence and totalitarianism, plus their shared concern with historical materialism, seem fundamental for Wyschogrod's thinking. Until recently the Jewishness of that thinking has been filtered through her analysis of modern Jewish thinkers, particularly Levinas and Derrida (Cohen and Blanchot to a lesser extent). The Jewishness has not been foregrounded, however. It is as if, in her call for a new ethics and politics of the other, she has been continuing a line of thinking that passes through Moses Mendelsonn to Herman Cohen and Martin Buber, in which a universalized Judaism can become the basis for a social ontology. The Jewishness is also evident in the scar of the Shoah. What she calls the "cataclysm" of history comes about with the advent of the mass annihilation of human beings, and, like Arthur Cohen with his construal of the *tremendum*, this calls for a new academic undertaking. The cataclysm exposes a profound cultural nihilism. In her book *An Ethics of Remembering* (Chicago, 1998) Wyschogrod introduces the figure of the heterological historian whose writing is haunted by the dense weight of absence, whose narrative nevertheless negotiates the void.

Right from the start, with *Spirit in Ashes: Hegel, Heidegger and Man-Made Mass Death* (New Haven, CT, 1985), Wyschogrod's concerns have been genealogical: highly philosophical examinations of modernity's cultural obsessions attentive to the abjected one, the marginalized, and the silenced. She proceeds textually, even intertextually, closely reading primary sources, advancing her own argument and perspective in, through, and beyond the voices she entertains in her work. Her eye is always on the possibility of redemption. Refusing to give in to the cataclysm, her work is a search for a way of moving us elsewhere: to new forms of saintliness (as in *Saints and Postmodernism: Revisioning Moral Philosophy*, Chicago, 1990), to new forms of community. In this a certain Hegelianism is evident, and there are some similarities between her work and the way in which Hegel has been used by death-of-God theologians such as Altizer and atheologians like Mark C. Taylor. But there is no simple acceptance, no easy cut to the spectacle of Altizer's apocalyptic polemics or the glamour of Taylor's headlong rush for global capitalism.

The following essay continues a phenomenological investigation by examining the scope for a move beyond the philosophy of the subject pointed to, but not investigated by, Husserl, and examined by Heidegger, but in a nihilistic fashion. Wyschogrod continues her conversation with Levinas who, more than Derrida (who is perhaps too closely following in Heidegger's footsteps), offers a way towards a valuing, a revisioning, a judgment in the name of a transcendental Good. What is interesting and significantly new about this present essay is the way it returns to explicitly Jewish analyses. Seyla Benhabib once wrote famously about the need to shift from discourses about the general other and to examine the situated knowledges (and narratives) of the concrete other. In this new work Wyschogrod seems to be exploring the resources (as Levinas has done) of Jewish tradition-based reasoning. Again, this connects her to the work of Ochs, Robert Gibbs, and Elliot Wolfson. Intrepid as always, Wyschogrod moves forward, in painstaking detail. There are no quick fixes: both writing and responsibility in postmodernity have become freighted with the politics of complexity. And so like Weil, Arendt, and Rose, Wyschogrod undertakes an academic labor of immense gravity and a generous love.

In what may seem a paradoxical claim, Edmund Husserl maintains that the "rich use of fancy" in art and poetry can contribute significantly to phenomenological philosophy conceived as a rigorous science. Phenomenology "can draw extraordinary profit" from the gifts of these arts that "in the abundance of detailed features . . . greatly excel the performances of our own fancy," Husserl declares.[1] In consonance with this claim it may be useful to turn (briefly) to contemporary Italian artist Francesco Clemente's "Inside/Outside," an artwork that mimes the apophatic discourse of negative theology in its attempt to render visually that which resists representation, exteriority itself. An agglomeration of fourteen paper panels executed in pastel, watercolor, and ink, Clemente's work depicts a nude male figure behind horizontal and vertical bars formed by green cloth strips that join the panels. The man's right arm is bent, his right index finger pointing to his left nostril, his left arm extending to link hands with another outstretched arm, that of a figure whose torso and head lie outside the confines of the work, an absent presence. The left half of the composition is broken only by the omnipresent squares formed by the green bars and the long branch of a tree that cuts across the work horizontally and brushes against the man's face. Frowning, the man appears to be inside, behind the bars, viewing the tree that is outside. Upon closer inspection, inside and outside are indeterminable, continually exchanging places in a dizzying metaphor of immanence and transcendence.[2]

For Husserlian transcendental phenomenology, exteriority or being that is "outside" is always (and already) being *for* an "inside" as though captured behind the green bars of Clemente's painting, an inside that is "a *self-contained system of Being*, as a system of *Absolute Being*, into which nothing can penetrate and from which nothing can escape" (*Ideas*, p. 139, emphasis in original). A veritable abyss separates the meanings of consciousness and of reality, Husserl declares. It is a virtual given of Husserl's *Ideas* that the spatiotemporal world has a merely secondary or relative sense in that it exists as being for a consciousness that posits it, that the field of physical nature is to be "switched off" and that what remains is the field of pure consciousness.

But if objects are grasped only as objects for an intending consciousness that reaches towards them and bestows meaning upon them, can there be anything that does not become an artifact of consciousness? Husserl's description of consciousness as absolute suggests that consciousness requires no real being outside itself, thereby vitiating the possibility of an exteriority that transcends the subject. As a philosophy of consciousness, phenomenology must sublate transcendence, for, if it fails to do so, it would self-destruct as phenomenology. It would seem that a theology spawned by Husserlian phenomenology must necessarily be an immanentist theology. If pre-reflective religious experience is invoked to establish the existence of a transcendent object, not only is transcendence subordinated to the subject, but thought returns to a naive empiricism that credits philosophically unclarified experience with providing the warranty for transcendence.

In what follows I shall argue that, in the face of these difficulties, Husserl attempts to perform the high wire act of finding a place for transcendence while upholding the primacy of a consciousness that subordinates objects to itself. Thus phenomenology can be said both to succumb to and elude a conception of being beyond the being of consciousness. Because consciousness as intentional is, Husserl contends, meaning bestowing, its objects are always (and already) discursive, so that conscious acts may be seen as textual practices. "Phenomenology," Paul Ricoeur succinctly comments, "gambles on the possibility of thinking and naming . . . on that primordial discursivity of each subjective process" as well as on reflection.[3] If phenomenology's claim for the linguisticality of the phenomena as constituted by consciousness is warranted, then even the wildest reaches of affect are always already discursive. But a transcendent Absolute that is beyond consciousness necessitates an apophatic theology that may be disclosed as an unremitting yearning *for* an absent Other or as a divestiture of self *on behalf of* an Other who, as Other, never appears. I shall maintain that in his questioning of the primacy of the transcendental subject and in his description of the desire *for* God, Derrida's account of naming and negative theology is essentially transgressive, an *erotics* of transcendence. When the sheer contingency of fact leads neither to an eidetic science, to the certainty of an eidos that remains invariant through all of an object's variations, nor to an erotic desire for the Other, but rather to an alterity that is beyond consciousness, the way is open for a Levinasian *ethics* of transcendence.

Phenomenology's God

It is by now a truism of transcendental phenomenology that consciousness is intentional, that it points towards objects. A conscious intending act (*noesis*) is directed towards a "something" that is intended (*noema*). A physical or conceptual entity as the object of an intention cannot be posited apart from the act that intends it as the correlate of that act. A phenomenological description of intending acts is not to be confused with a psychological description of states of mind. The latter is undertaken from the standpoint of a naive faith in the givenness of the world in its plenary presence, what Husserl designates as the natural attitude, the apprehension of the world as real. Husserl insists that the phenomenological cordoning off of exteriority, of the existence of nature as outside in order to comprehend the being of consciousness, cannot be the achievement of an empirical psychology. Only a suspension of the natural attitude, of the belief in the independent existence, the own-being of the world by bracketing or putting that existence out of play, assures access to the transcendental structure of consciousness (*Ideas*, p. 98).

Placing the actuality of the fact world in brackets is not to be confused with the world denial of the sophist. As Paul Ricoeur points out, any such misapprehension is laid to rest in *Cartesian Meditations*. "'I gain myself as the pure ego with the pure flux of my cogitations,'" Husserl alleges, so that far from losing the world that has been placed in brackets, the world is retained as a world-for-me.[4] Similarly, bracketing is not to be confused with a skeptical doubt that is insufficiently radical because it is nothing but a modification of the natural attitude. It is rather a strategy "[barring one] from using any judgment that concerns spatiotemporal existence" (*Ideas*, p. 100). Nor should bracketing be identified with the abstractions generated by the theoretical inquiries of natural science, in that such investigations transpire within the sphere of the natural attitude. The phenomenological reduction or bracketing of the existing world, the *epoche*, can be viewed as a stratagem designed to outwit the realist illusion rather than to denigrate the world that it cordons off.

"Although we have suspended the whole world, things, living creatures, men ourselves included," Husserl concludes, "we have lost nothing, but have won the whole Absolute Being, which, properly understood, conceals in itself all transcendences, 'constituting' them within [consciousness]" (*Ideas*, p. 141). Far from spawning meaningless agglomerations, consciousness constitutes objective unities in every region of being. The modalities of consciousness – perceiving, thinking, willing, wishing, and the like – constitute or prefigure "all possibilities and impossibilities of being" (*Ideas*, p. 232). Still, Paul Ricoeur cautions, "Husserl will progressively abandon his earlier idealism so that the reduction as a reversion to a monadic ego will diminish to be replaced by a return to the prepredicative experience of the world."[5] Far from impugning the fact world, Husserl affirms even at the conclusion of the *Cartesian Meditations* that the phenomenological reduction is undertaken in the interest of accounting for the way in which the world is experienced. Thus, he maintains:

> Phenomenological reduction does nothing but explicate the sense the world has for us all, prior to any philosophizing, and obviously gets solely from our experience – a sense which philosophy can uncover but never alter, and which because of an essential necessity, not because of our weakness entails (in the case of any actual experience) horizons that need fundamental clarification.[6]

Still, in the idealistic transcendental analyses of *Ideas* I, the "feel" of presentness and reality, of lived experience, is subordinated to acts of reflection about them, "acts of the second level" (*Ideas*, p. 141). Are we then to conclude that, despite shifting emphases, the being of consciousness remains absolute being, or are there grounds for maintaining that the notion of the being of consciousness can be viewed as itself subordinated to a transcendent absolute?

The paucity of theological reflection in Husserl's published work should not blind us to the importance of his remarks about God in *Ideas* I. In a remarkable passage, Husserl asserts that God's absoluteness is different from that of absolute consciousness (*Ideas*, p. 174). Rudolf Boehm points out that, although consciousness may not require the support of actual beings in order to exist, "it might indeed require being sustained by another being and 'have its source in what is ultimately and truly absolute.'"[7] In an enigmatic statement that, on the face of it, would appear to sanction the primacy of consciousness, Husserl asserts: "*Immanent Being is . . . without doubt absolute in this sense, that in principle nulla 're' indiget ad existendum*" (*Ideas*, p. 137, emphasis in original). The Latin phrase originates in Descartes' definition of substance as that which requires nothing other than itself to exist.

It could be argued that, in a Husserlian context, the phrase acknowledges a difference between the being of consciousness and that of reality but that, for him, it is the being of consciousness that is absolute. It would then be possible to conclude that absolute consciousness is the sole substance and, as such, is analagous to the being of God. There is however room for an alternative interpretation. Just as Descartes does not apply the term "substance" univocally to God and other things, a corresponding disjunction can be detected in Husserl's surprising assertion that God "is an absolute in an entirely different sense than the absolute of consciousness."[8]

In a claim reminiscent of Kant's account of the purposiveness of nature in his third *Critique*, Husserl maintains that an intraworldly teleology may be discerned in organic life and in the development of human culture.[9] But if, as Husserl argues, the governing principle of that order derives from this immanent arrangement itself, world-being is regulated by a principle of internal ordering such that an internal teleological principle would be grounded in the immanence it is intended to explain and thus would be circular. "A world-god is impossible" Husserl says in a note to Section 51 (*Ideas*, p. 142). Such a god would not be exempted from the conditions governing spatial perception which would hold, "not only for us human beings, but also for [him in that] whatever has the character of a spatial thing, is intuitable only through appearances, as changing perspectively" (*Ideas*, p. 386).

Husserl asserts that there must be strategies to disclose transcendence apart from those appropriate to constituting thing-like realities. At the same time, phenomenological method cannot circumvent consciousness and still retain its identity as a philosophy of the subject. Although Husserl in the same note in Section 51 seems unable to surrender the notion that the Absolute is "a research-domain proper to phenomenology" (*Ideas*, p. 143), divine transcendence is explicated so as to suggest that phenomenology's dependence on consciousness can be bypassed. The Absolute transcends the world in a fashion different from that of the pure Ego that is given as a unity accompanying all intraworldly presentations, a transcendence in immanence he contends in Section 58 (*Ideas*, pp. 157–60).[10] In contrast to the pure Ego through which thought takes place and that radiates through its acts and is united immediately to consciousness, we come across another transcendence, says Husserl, that we know in mediated form. "[It] stand[s] over and against the transcendence of the world as if it were its polar opposite. We refer to the transcendence of God" (*Ideas*, p. 157). He speaks of "a morphologically ordered world" which the natural sciences can apprehend and claims to stand in awe before this extraordinary teleology. He goes on to say:

> It is not concrete actuality [*Faktum*] in general, but concrete actuality as the source of possible and real values extending indefinitely, which compels us to ask after the ground.... What concerns us here ... is that this existence should not only transcend the world but also the "absolute" Consciousness. It would thus be an Absolute in a totally different sense from the Absolute of consciousness, as on the other hand it would be a transcendent in a totally different sense from the transcendent in the sense of the world. (*Ideas*, p. 153)

In relating the transcendental absolute to the absolute of consciousness, it could be argued that Husserl simply asserts their disconnection. Alternatively, the question of teleology could be seen as supplying the impetus to transcend phenomenological reflection upon the nature of fact and instead to account for the *order* of the fact-world by positing its grounding in transcendence in what might be seen as a version of standard teleological arguments.[11]

A more nuanced reading than either of these presupposes the inadequacy of a discursive consciousness, one that bestows meaning upon the fact-world, to account for a teleologically driven Absolute. Such an Absolute resists the semiotic pretensions of a language that is adequate to the phenomenological description of the fact-world but is unable to convey in predicative language the being beyond being of God. The being of such an Absolute has traditionally been conveyed in a language of negation that speaks without speaking, an apophasis to which Husserl does not directly appeal and that derives its semantic power, as Derrida notes, from being "written completely otherwise." The language of negation is often preceded by a rhetoric of exhortation, of utterances addressing, beseeching, cajoling the unrepresentable God in expressions of erotic yearning. The quest for an Absolute whose hyperessentiality is felt as an absent presence demands the rhetoric of apostrophe, of an address to one that remains unseen.[12]

Absolute transcendence that is disclosed by awe and wonder before the order of the world can alternatively, as Husserl asserts, lead to the ascent from reflection upon the nature of the individual *faktum* to thought about the ultimate purpose of the world, to what Husserl does not hesitate to designate as "value" even if in an unspecified sense (*Ideas*, p. 158). It is value that drives the quest to grasp the ground of intraworldly order rather than the converse.[13] (Were concrete actuality the causal ground of value, the naturalistic fallacy of a discredited old-style positivism would have been resurrected.) Has phenomenology then given way to axiology?

Far from surrendering the primacy of value, in a remark in the *Nachlass* Husserl subordinates ontology to the Good, maintaining: "The ultimate meaning of being [*Sinn des Seins*] is the Good and that is the divine activity toward which the All of divine action is directed. . . . God as will of the Good is ultimate reality.[14] This remark can be seen as premonitory of Levinas' repeated insistence that the Good beyond being, separate from the totality of essences, is the gift of Greek metaphysics. "The Good is Good in itself. . . . The place of the Good above every essence is the most profound teaching, the definitive teaching, not of theology but of philosophy."[15] I shall consider in turn the *Spuren* of a transcendence that is on the way to both an erotics and an ethics of transcendence and for which Husserl's elusive remarks provide a prolegomenon.

The Ineffable Name and the Erotics of Transcendence

Although Anselm's *Proslogion* is hardly a document of negative theology, the entreaties that suggest a lover *in extremis* that precede the ontological argument offer a striking example of the affective tone of the pleas that may introduce such theologizing. "Thy face Lord do I desire . . . where should I seek thee who art absent," Anselm cries out.[16] It is perhaps no accident that in what can be seen as an inversion of the plea for the plenary presence of God, Nietzsche's Zarathustra speaks the language of an erotics of immanence that *ab origine* attests the absence of transcendence. Is Zarathustra's ineluctable yearning for eternity, for the ring of recurrence ("For I love you oh eternity"),[17] the erotic prolegomenon to what can be seen as the obverse of Anselm's argument, Nietzsche's celebrated claim that "If there were gods, how could I endure not to be a god! Hence there are no gods. Though I drew this conclusion, now it draws me."[18] Does Nietzsche's "being drawn" not *to* but *by* the conclusion of this argument reflect a solicitation that pulls one towards an absence different from that which is conveyed by the linguistic ruses of negative theology?

The question can be pursued by examining Derrida's account of God's name, an issue of particular interest to him in that terms such as *différance* and "trace" intrinsic to his own work have been identified (erroneously, he believes) with negative theology. Neither a genre nor an art, neither a concept nor a name, the term "negative theology" is used to designate disparate discourses loosely united by the claim that predicative language is inadequate to the beyond-being of God and that only negative attribution can be the preliminary to an intuition of God.[19] It can be objected that negative theology is speech having no object, speech about nothing. Derrida responds that, in referring to negative theology's object, the objector is caught in the same bind as the advocate, in that she or he speaks simply for the sake of speaking, for nothing. Moreover, according to Derrida, "to speak for nothing is not: not to speak. Above all it is not to speak to no one" (*DNT*, p. 76). Thus, in considering the *Symbolic Theology of Dionysius*, Derrida suggests that there is something beyond the intelligible itself:

> In affirmative theology the logos descends from what is above downward to the last, and increases according to the measure of the descent toward an analogical multitude. But here, as we ascend from the highest to what lies beyond, the logos is drawn inward. . . . [I]t will be wholly without sound and wholly united to the unspeakable.[20]

On the one hand, Derrida notes, Dionysius invokes a secret mystical discourse, on the other a philosophical and demonstrative one. The crossing of these discourses with one another and with that of Derrida suggests revealed and secret messages that intersect and that both must and must not be divulged, a move of discursive assertion and self-divestiture that Derrida calls denegation, "a negation that denies itself" (*DNT*, p. 95). Always (and already) dissimulating itself to the other who putatively shares but cannot share it, the secret is inwardly fractured. Derrida denies that the secret is theological, yet (and this is the point to which we are heading) Derrida avers: "The name of God (I do not say God, but how to avoid saying God here, from the moment when I say the name of God?) can only be *said* in the modality of this secret denial" (*DNT*, p. 95).

The way in which apophasis is configured, Derrida contends, may rest on sheer autobiographical chance. Challenging Heidegger's obsession with the discourse of Angelus Silesius, who is not the best example of an apophatic mystic, Derrida explains the choice of Silesius as somehow pertinent to Heidegger's life.[21] Nevertheless, Derrida pointedly avoids discussing the apophasis found in the Jewish and Islamic traditions relevant to his own life, arguing that not to speak of them is itself a form of attestation. Yet it is precisely with regard to the missing traditions that one might apply Derrida's term, the logic of the supplement, the hidden presuppositions that drive his analyses, to his account of apophasis and denegation.[22]

Consider first the claim that negative theology's contention that God's excessive being cannot be conveyed in positive assertions tests the limits of language: "Of him there is nothing said that might hold."[23] Derrida fastens upon the exclusionary phrase *sauf le nom* (except the name) as that which must be rescued and preserved. Although Angelus Silesius uses the term *Eigenschaft* rather than *Namen* in relation to God as pouring himself into creation, it is the name of God that is meant. What Silesius longs for, Derrida declares, is "to say God, such as he is, beyond his images, beyond this idol that being can still be, . . . to respond to the true name of God, to the name to which God responds and corresponds, beyond the name we know him by or hear."[24]

The work of Silesius as explicated by Derrida both conceals and reveals a crucial theological tenet of rabbinic discourse: the terms used to refer to God, his biblical names, are charged with the utmost sanctity. For the negative theologian, Derrida contends, the name erases itself before what it names, thereby safeguarding the named: "'The name is necessary' would mean that the name is lacking [*il y faut le nom*]. . . . Thus *managing to efface itself* it *itself will be safe, will be, save itself*" (emphasis in original).[25] According to a rabbinic text, those who know and guard, who save the secret name that cannot be pronounced, inherit this world and the next. "He who knows the secret, who is careful of it, who preserves it in purity, is loved by God and esteemed among men."[26] Another text suggests a way in which non-disclosure is also disclosure. When Moses asks God to reveal his sacred name, God replies that he is to be called in accordance with his acts: "When I judge my creatures, I am called Elohim or Judge" (Ex. 22.27); "when I punish my enemies, Lord of Hosts; when I suspend my judgment over man's sin, El Shaddai [Almighty God]; when I sit with the attribute of mercy, I am called the Compassionate One."[27] The name may be written but not read aloud, so that it is as utterance that the name remains secret. Although its thaumaturgical use is feared, the principal worry is that of violating the sanctity of the ineffable name as attested in the claim "As the sanctification of the name is the supreme virtue or duty, so the profanation of the name is the supreme sin."[28] He who dares to pronounce the name will have no place in the world to come.

There is then in rabbinic thought a crisis of language bound up with God's name that can be found in the apophatics of negative theology and, to an extent, in Husserl's account of what he acknowledges as a crisis of phenomenology. This crisis is identified as the possibility of an empty intuition whose meaning is not borne out by the plenary presence of what is intended. Similarly, apophatic statements announce from within language a forgetting of that which exists, an ontological amnesia that destabilizes the presuppositions of phenomenology itself.

In negative theology, that which is exterior to the apophatic moment, the prefatory address or hymn, saves and protects it in much the same way as the biblical name of God that is not to be uttered is protected by substituting the positive enumeration of God's deeds. In a gesture of denegation, the ineffable name that must not be pronounced is negated by the positivity of God's acts, acts that both are and are not who God essentially is. The impossibility of naming God in negative theology attests the limit of language in the face of God's hyperessentiality, whereas for rabbinic thought naming the God who cannot be named carries the penalty of irreparable privation, the loss of one's place in the world to come.

Does not the absence of affirmative discourse in effect affirm a nothingness, a void, that suggests atheism? Yet atheism affirms the most ardent desire for God. In an almost priapic surge towards the transcendent Other the phrase "desire of God," for Derrida, attests the ambiguity or equivocity of what Derrida calls a double genitive: the force of the preposition "of" suggests that God can become the one who desires, its subject, or the one desired, the object of God's love. In what could be envisaged as a gloss on the ambiguity of inside and outside as depicted in the Clemente work described earlier, the desire of God can mean *my* desire for the unreachable transcendent God or *God's* desire for me. "Does it come from God in us, from God for us, from us for God?" But if, as Derrida claims, there can be no determination of self without an antecedent relation to another, "all reflection is caught in the genealogy of this genitive, a reflection on self, an autobiographical reflection."[29] Thus in naming the ineffable, God, one is named and the name denegated in an identity that cannot be conferred. But is not the "desire of God" a yearning for the unnameable, a desire for a kenosis that remains impossible, for a transcendence that can only be experienced as a failed immanence?

Transcendence is not a Failed Immanence

Can there be a relation to transcendence that resists phenomenology's claims to truth and certainty yet resorts neither to the apophatic stance of negative theology nor to denegation? Such a relation would avoid a desire that succumbs to the allure of its own futility. In desiring otherwise, it would retain the unbridgeable distance of an exteriority that does not cease to call into question the multiple manifestations of immanence.

In the quest for that which remains beyond experience, Levinas is drawn into language that is replete with traditional an-iconic resonances. Critical of phenomenology's privileging of visibility, Levinas maintains that "inasmuch as the access to beings concerns vision, it dominates those beings, exercises a power over them. A thing is given, offers itself to me. In gaining access to it, I maintain myself within the same."[30] Consciousness's reduction of alterity to the same reflects the dominance of thought as grounded in visibility that, in Husserlian phenomenology, reveals itself in the intentionality, the directedness of consciousness towards objects as expressed in phenomenology's familiar apothegm:

consciousness is always consciousness of. For Levinas, the subordination of the object to consciousness is unavoidable, a necessary condition for cognition and perception but, as applied to the Other, constitutes an act of primordial violence. As a quest for that which is originary in the knowledge-act, phenomenology falls back upon "the substantive, the nameable, the entity and the Same" essential to the construction of truth as determined by consciousness.[31] Nor is the sublation of alterity overcome by philosophies that proclaim the end of metaphysics: "The rear-guard work of this philosophy in retreat consists in deconstructing this so-called metaphysical language, which ... is neither perception nor science."[32]

These reservations do not preclude Levinas' fastening upon Husserl's use of the term "living" as suggesting an aperture in phenomenology's appeal to the structures of consciousness as the ground of truth and certainty. Husserl's depiction of the pre-reflective experience of the I breaks into the equanimity of consciousness to awaken it, to rupture its self-presence. The lived that is "a lived for me" is a "transcendence in immanence" that unfreezes the hypostatized subject. This account of the fissuring of self opens the way for describing how the other person "tears me away from my hypostasis" (*EN*, pp. 85–6). The relation of an I to another renders possible an awakening that is a "sobering up" in which the I is freed from its everyday indolence. Yet Levinas maintains that the exploration of the ethical implications of awakening lie outside the scope of Husserlian phenomenology, in that phenomenology's aim is the overcoming of an epistemological *naïveté* in the interest of ultimate truth and certainty.

Facing Up

Can there be a given that faces up to phenomenology's model of truth as a sublation of the Other by resisting the cannibalization of the Other? For Levinas, the face of the Other in showing itself always (and already) as a refusal to be contained in images or concepts contests the sovereignty of the subject. Even in the contemporary culture of images, each face is never a mere datum of sense. An-iconic, exposed, vulnerable in its nudity, the face "speaks otherwise" than as a visual or tactile sensation. Nor can the face of the Other be defined in terms of attributes that set it apart from the self, since comparison depends upon common categories.

For Levinas, the Other is higher than the self. "The eye can conceive [the asymmetry between self and Other] only by virtue of position, which as an above–below disposition constitutes the elementary fact of morality."[33] Could it not be objected that the entanglement in spatial metaphor renders alterity subject to phenomenological explication? Is Levinas not trapped by the language of description without which he would fall back into apophatic discourse? "Above" and "below" in this context are not abstractions, as are terms that express value hierarchies, for example "Magnanimity is better than parsimony."

For Levinas, spatial elevation expresses the pedagogic function of the Other as one's teacher. It is as elevation that the Other looms over the self, mandating not only that the self assume responsibility for the Other but that it surrender its interests, including its very life, on behalf of the Other.[34]

Levinas also describes the Other as "an epiphany" given "in expression, the sensible, still graspable, [that] turns into total resistance to the grasp."[35] The face yields itself to sensibility as a powerlessness that fissures the sensible. For Levinas, the Other, divested of form, reveals her/himself as a surplus beyond the inevitable stasis of manifestation. But, in a crucial move, Levinas goes on to say: "The face speaks.... To speak is before all else this manner of coming from behind his appearance, from behind his form, an opening in the opening" (translation mine).[36] Images must give way to discourse, which now provides the warranty not only for individual actions but for social peace, peace among states. Violence is not a failure of social agreement but rather the result of a collapse of attentiveness to the command of alterity, a command that is an excess of sociality, "a proximity as the impossible assumption of difference ... as impossible appearance."[37]

In the effort to disconnect the face from its status as a given whose veracity is attested by its perceptible presence, the face is said to be in the track or trace of transcendence. Neither an image nor an intraworldly discursive sign, the trace disturbs the order of the world, means without meaning to mean "interven[ing] in a way so subtle that it already withdraws unless we retain it."[38] The trace attests a past that can never be made present, a transcendence that has already passed by. Far from yielding an essence of the human or a universal moral law as a distillate of faciality, the face transcends images, remains exterior to them.

Levinas' shift from image to discourse can best be understood in the light of the biblical suspicion of images as adumbrated in rabbinic thought and Jewish philosophy. Thus Maimonides views the release of a figural imagination required in order to render theological truths accessible as disfiguring those truths through figuration itself. Compelled to account for the use of imagery in biblical discourse, he appeals to a property of verbal utterance, homonymy, in an effort to make sense of the dangerous but ineliminable visibility of the face in connection with God's countenance. If Moses is said to speak to God face to face (Deut. 5.4) and the face is a visible form, does it follow that, because faciality is attributed to God, that God is corporeal? Maimonides responds by highlighting the ambiguity of faciality and by converting visibility into discourse. There is no doubt that the principal meaning of the word *panim* (face) is "the presence and existence of a person." When Moses is said to have spoken with God face to face "without any intervening medium," Maimonides, as Levinas will do later, both proclaims and erases the face's materiality by transforming the visible into discourse:

> We read more plainly in another place, "Ye heard the voice of the words, but saw no similitude; only ye heard a voice" [Deut. 4.12]. The hearing of a voice without

seeing any similitude is termed "face to face." Similarly in God's speaking to Moses is meant that Moses heard a voice [Num. 7.89).[39]

It is noteworthy that for Maimonides a form of the word *panim* is used biblically to express time long past: "Of old [*le-phanim*] hast thou laid the foundation of the earth" (Psalm 102.25; p. 53). Maimonides singles out yet another biblical meaning of the term "attention and regard," as in "And a person receiving attention [*panim*]" (Isa. 3.3). This signification is retained in the blessing "'The Lord turns his face to thee [i.e., let[s] his Providence accompany thee] and gives thee peace.'"[40] It is this metonymic dissemination of *panim* as signifying unmediated encounter, archaic time, a past that is irrecoverable, peace as the outcome of attention and regard for the person, that expands the multiple meanings of alterity.

The Infinition of Transcendence

The surplus of meaning attested by the irruption of the face into the world of phenomena, Levinas asserts, "makes God come to mind" (*EN*, p. 131). Beyond being, unrepresentable, dazzling in his excessiveness, God singles out the self as responsible for the Other. This divine extravagence is conveyed in the term "the Infinite." Understood in a Cartesian sense, the Infinite is an idea that exceeds any idea one may have of it, an idea that compels thought to think beyond what it can think. "In relation to what should be its 'intentional correlate', [the idea] would be thrown off its course, not resulting in anything or arriving at an end."[41]

For Levinas, thought that occurs within the ambit of fulfillable intentionality is necessarily atheist because it cannot accommodate that which is in excess of itself, the Infinite. Levinas is careful to contrast the inadequacy of a thought when understood as a deficit, as the failure of thought to fulfill its intentional aim, from what he calls "the deportation or transcendence beyond any end and any finality; the thinking of the absolute without this absolute being reached as an end."[42] He also avoids thinking the Infinite as the aim of a thought to think beyond the boundaries of a given concept in an effort to reconcile the possibility of "the more" to which it aspires with the fullness of the actual (*AT*, p. 58). Thus Levinas dissociates his view of the Infinite from that of the potential infinite of Kant, who holds that for any finite number of X's selected, however large, there is a number of X's that is always greater. This view of the potential Infinite contrasts with Descartes' account of the Infinite as actual that is intrinsic to his argument for God's existence.[43] Inwardization offers no solution to the problem of the excess of the Infinite, since the finite would then (*per impossibile*) merge with the transcendent (*AT*, p. 75). Unlike the face that remains haunted by a residuum of corporeality, the Infinite must be envisaged in a/theophanic terms as other than what could appear.

Although God lays claim to the self, commands that it heed the suffering of the Other, God is not to be understood teleologically as the final cause of one's actions. The Infinite is rather a direction, a "toward-God," as Levinas would have it. Irreducible to the eschatological that he sees as a yearning for persistence in being, the Infinite interrupts the self's anxiety as a being-towards-death by transcending being, an event described by the traditional term "glory" (*EN*, p. 132). The excessiveness of the idea of the Infinite precludes its originating in finite consciousness so that it owes its impingement upon the self to God. The Infinite to the finite is not connected to the finite through simple negation, but is rather a being-affected by the Other, a relation beyond conceptual retrieval. At the same time, to understand the idea of the infinite as mere uncertainty would constitute a misreading of its irreducible originality (*EN*, p. 220).

Conclusion

If the relation to transcendence is one of irreducible exteriority, then Francesco Clemente's "Inside/Outside" as an artwork that portrays the interplay of their reciprocal negation would seem to have little bearing upon the connection between self and Other. Yet the work's green bars that separate and undo the separation of inside and outside serve to highlight the nude male figure reaching for the hand of the Other whose body lies outside the confines of the work and who remains invisible. Beyond concupiscence, each as other to the other is in the trace or track of a transcendence suggested by the proximity of the handclasp, a gesture of primordial generosity that is not a privation of presence but the "more" that lies beyond it. "Transcendence is no longer a failed immanence. It has the sort of excellence proper to Spirit: perfection or the Good" (*EN*, p. 221).

Notes

1 Edmund Husserl, *Ideas: General Introduction to Pure Phenomenology*, trans. W. R. Boyce Gibson (New York: Collier Books, 1962), p. 184. Hereafter cited in the text as *Ideas*.
2 "Inside/Outside" was exhibited in a retrospective of Clemente's art at the Solomon R. Guggenheim Museum, October 8, 1999–January 9, 2000. Composed on handmade Pondicherry paper, 63 inches high and 164 inches wide, the work was completed in 1980. The locking of hands appears to be an ironic visual commentary upon the linked hands in the creation as well as the temptation and expulsion scenes of Michelangelo's famous Sistine Chapel ceiling. For a reproduction of the work, see *Clemente* (Guggenheim Museum Publications, 1999), plate 115.
3 Paul Ricoeur, *Husserl: An Analysis of His Phenomenology*, trans. Edward G. Ballard and Lester E. Embree (Evanston, IL: Northwestern University Press, 1967), p. 216.
4 Ibid, pp. 87–8.

5   Ibid, p. 12.
6   Edmund Husserl, *Cartesian Meditations: An Introduction to Phenomenology*, trans. Dorion Cairns (the Hague: Martinus Nijhoff, 1960), p. 151.
7   Rudolf Boehm, "Husserl's Concept of the Absolute," in R. O. Elveon, *The Phenomenology of Husserl: Selected Critical Readings* (Chicago: Quadrangle Books, 1970), p. 183.
8   This interpretation, including that of *nulla "re" indiget ad existendum*, follows that of Rudolf Boehm in Elveson, *The Phenomenology of Husserl*, pp. 181ff.
9   Immanuel Kant, *Critique of Judgement*, trans. J. H. Bernard (New York: Haffner Press, 1951), p. 294, writes: "If now we meet with purposive arrangements in the world and, as reason inevitably requires, subordinate the purposes that are conditioned to an unconditioned supreme, i.e. final purpose, then we easily see that . . . we are thus concerned not with a purpose of nature (internal to itself) . . . [but] with the ultimate purpose of creation. . . . It is only as a moral being that we recognize man as the purpose of creation [and have a ground for] regarding the world as a system of purposes."
10 James G. Hart in "A Précis of an Husserlian Philosophical Theology," in *Essays in Phenomenological Theology*, ed. Steven W. Laycock and James G. Hart (Albany, NY: State University of New York Press), sees the Absolute's transcendence as different from the transcendence of the world and of the I-pole; it remains a single but dipolar principle (p. 141).
11 Rudolf Boehm in Elveson, *The Phenomenology of Husserl*, p. 199, suggests that the key question for Heidegger is, "Why is there something rather than nothing," whereas for Husserl it is, "To what end is everything that is?"
12 See Jacques Derrida, "How to Avoid Speaking: Denials," trans. Ken Frieden in *Derrida and Negative Theology*, ed. Harold Coward and Toby Foshay (Albany, NY: State University of New York Press, 1992), pp. 73–7. Hereafter cited in the text as *DNT*. In a subtle account of apophasis, Michael A. Sells, *Mystical Languages of Unsaying* (Chicago: University of Chicago Press, 1994), pp. 1–33, writes: "The authentic subject of discourse slips back beyond each effort to name it or even deny its nameability." He shows how this strategy initiates a language of apophasis, a Greek term meaning "negation" or "un-saying or speaking away" (ibid, p. 2).
13 For a comparable claim in Kant, see note 10.
14 The citation by James G. Hart in *Essays In Phenomenological Theology* is from Husserl's *Nachlass*, B II, 2, 54, 146.
15 Emmanuel Levinas, *Totality and Infinity: An Essay in Exteriority*, trans. Alphonso Lingis (Pittsburgh, PA: Duquesne University Press, 1969), pp. 102–3.
16 Anselm, *Proslogion, A Scholastic Miscellany*, ed. E. R. Fairchild (Philadelphia: Westminster Press, 1966), p. 70.
17 *The Portable Nietzsche*, ed. Walter Kaufmann (New York: Penguin Books, 1976), p. 340.
18 Ibid, p. 198.
19 Jacques Derrida, in *Derrida and Negative Theology*, ed. Harold Coward and Toby Foshay, p. 74.
20 The citation by Derrida is from Pseudo-Dionysius, *The Mystical Theology* in *The Divine Names and Mystical Theology*, trans. John D. Jones (Milwaukee, WI: Marquette University Press, 1980), ch. 3:1033bc. See *DNT*, p. 81.
21 "Post-Scriptum: Aporias, Ways and Voices," trans. John P. Leavey, Jr., *DNT*, p. 321.

22 In *Of Grammatology*, trans. Gayatri Chakravorty Spivak (Baltimore, MD: Johns Hopkins University Press, 1976), p. 215, the supplement is seen as a refractory element that destabilizes a theory. Derrida writes: "There must (should) have been plenitude and not lack, presence without difference. . . . The dangerous supplement . . . [then] adds itself from the outside as evil and lack to happy and innocent plenitude, . . . an outside that would simply be the outside. [But according to the logic of supplementarity] the logic would be inside . . . [T]he other and the lack add themselves as a plus to replace the minus, . . . [W]hat adds itself to something takes the place of a default in the thing."

23 Jacques Derrida, *On the Name*, ed. Thomas Dutoit, trans. John P. Leavey, Jr. and Ian McLeod (Stanford, CA: Stanford University Press, 1995), p. 55.

24 Ibid, p. 69.

25 Ibid, p. 68.

26 *Kiddushin*, 71a in C. G. Montefiore and H. Lowe (eds.), *A Rabbinic Anthology* (New York: Schocken Books, 1974), p. 14.

27 *Tanhuma*, Shemot, 20, f.88b (cp.[9]), ibid, p. 11.

28 *Kiddushin*, 40a, ibid, p. 304.

29 Jacques Derrida, *Sauf le Nom*, DNT, p. 37.

30 Levinas, *Totality and Infinity*, p. 194.

31 Levinas' critical but appreciative relation to Husserl's phenomenological method especially as explicated in *Ideas* I has been explored in studies too numerous to list exhaustively here. The following are relevant to the issues considered here: Silvano Petrosini and Jacques Roland in *La Verité nomade* (Paris: Editions la Découverte, 1984) describes Levinas' thought as an an-archeology of meaning in which "meaning precedes essence" and thus is anterior to constituting consciousness (p. 146). Theo de Boer in "An Ethical Transcendental Philosophy," in Richard Cohen (ed.), *Face to Face with Levinas* (Albany: State University of New York Press, 1986), pp. 83–115, sees Levinas' thought as transcendental philosophy in that it works back from objectifying knowledge to what precedes it (see esp. pp. 106–7). Adriaan T. Peperzak in "From Intentionality to Responsibility: On Levinas' Philosophy of Language" in *The Question of the Other*, ed. Arlene B. Dallery and Charles E. Scott (Albany, NY: State University of New York Press, 1989), pp. 3–22, traces Levinas' path, from intentionality to language and responsibility as it unfolds in *Autrement qu'être*. Edith Wyschogrod in *Emmanuel Levinas: The Problem of Ethical Metaphysics*, 2nd edn. (New York: Fordham University Press, 2000), pp. 28–55, shows that Levinas cannot accept analogical appresentation as an account of the relation to the other.

32 Emmanuel Levinas, *Entre nous*, trans. Michael B. Smith and Barbara Harshav (New York: Columbia University Press, 1998), pp. 78–9. Hereafter cited in the text as *EN*.

33 Levinas, *Totality and Infinity*, p. 297.

34 The notion of height is stressed in Richard Cohen's *Elevations: The Height of the Good in Rosenzweig and Levinas* (Chicago: University of Chicago Press, 1994).

35 Ibid, p. 197.

36 Emmanuel Levinas, *En découvrant l'existence avec Husserl et Heidegger* (Paris: Librairie philosophique J. Vrin, 1967) p. 194. Hereafter cited in the text as *DEHH*.

37 Emmanuel Levinas, *Alterity and Transcendence*, trans. Michael B. Smith (New York: Columbia University Press, 1999), p. 138. Hereafter cited in the text as *AT*.

38 Emmanuel Levinas, *En decouvrant l'existence avec Husserl et Heidegger* (translation mine), p. 208.

39 Moses Maimonides, *The Guide for the Perplexed*, trans. M. Friedlander (New York: Dover Publications, 1956), p. 13. Reprinted from the second edition, Routledge Kegan Paul, 1904.
40 Ibid, p. 53. Some of these meanings attributed to faciality are referred to in Susan Handelman, *Fragments of Redemption: Jewish Thought and Literary Theory in Benjamin, Scholem, and Levinas* (Bloomington: Indiana University Press), p. 359, n. 4.
41 Emmanuel Levinas, "Transcendence and Intelligibility," in *Basic Philosophical Writings*, ed. Adriaan T. Peperzak, Simon Critchley and Robert Bernasconi (Bloomington, Indiana University Press, 1996), p. 156.
42 Ibid.
43 Levinas offers a brief overview of various accounts of infinity in the history of Western thought. See "Infinity" (*AT*, pp. 53–76).

PART V
Phenomenology

21	Transfiguring God	369
22	Presence and Parousia	394
23	The Formal Reason for the Infinite	399
24	Religions as Conventions	413

CHAPTER 21
Transfiguring God

Richard Kearney

Richard Kearney is at home on both sides of the Atlantic, as Professor of Philosophy at University College, Dublin, and Visiting European Professor at Boston College. He is at home also with several academic disciplines and a number of foreign languages. Putting to one side his ventures into novel writing and a number of volumes on Irish history (social and literary), his work engages in cross-faculty dialogues between continental philosophy, literary theory, theology, and cultural studies. Many were introduced both to him and to the influential work coming out of post-World War II France through his important book *Dialogues with Contemporary Continental Thinkers* (Manchester, 1984). There, in discussion with Kearney, were five French philosophers working with a phenomenological heritage from Husserl and Heidegger. This heritage has, since Schleiermacher, always retained a close relationship to hermeneutics, and hermeneutical issues surface throughout. The dialogue as a form offers itself as a reflection upon the relationship between phenomenology and hermeneutics, raising questions concerning the spoken and the written, the writer and the reader. The last chapter of *Dialogues* begins an investigation into the philosophy of dialogue which has since preoccupied Kearney. Dialogue, dialectic, and hermeneutical reappropriation have been among his dominant philosophical, ethical, and theological concerns. They opened a space for thinking through the processes of the imagination and the relationship between ethics and poetics. In books composed between 1988 and 1995 Kearney provided us with genealogical, philosophical, aesthetic, and ethical accounts of the modern and postmodern imagination. But his task was not simply descriptive. In *The Wake of the Imagination* (London, 1988), *Poetics of Imagining* (London, 1991), and *The Poetics of Modernity: Towards a Hermeneutic Imagination* (Atlantic Highlands, NJ, 1995), Kearney has made manifest a certain bankruptcy of postmodern construals of the imagination, while emphasizing the creative potential of imagining other possible worlds. The possibility of reconciling ethics and poetics lies within the faculty of the imagination, and it is at this point that theological investigations begin.

Certain figures remain central to his thinking, among them Heidegger, Ricoeur, Levinas, and Derrida. Each, in their own way, wrestle with theological questions. Kearney (himself a practicing Catholic) has been sensitive to these theological struggles, as shown in *Dialogues* by some of the questions put to continental thinkers like Levinas and Derrida. The theological imagination is itself explored in the first part of *The Wake of the Imagination*, and in developing his account of hermeneutic imagination (and Heidegger's construal of poetical dwelling) Kearney speaks directly of the theological reconciliation between ethics and poetics: "Surely an eschatology of divine justice (if it exists) demands that ethics and poetics be reconciled? Such a demand is the proper task of hermeneutic imagination" (ibid, p. 64). The parenthetical "if" is coy, for his project has involved excavating the utopian potential of the imagination, its transcendental possibilities, its capacity to invent other worlds, even eschatological kingdoms. He has wanted to bear testimony, through his readings, to the transcendent. Imaginative testimonial can transform – transform by transfiguring.

The association of eschatology with transfigurative possibility lies at the heart of the more explicitly theological reflections in the essay contributed to this volume. As Kearney points out, the essay develops thoughts that lay in his French book *Poétique du possible* (Paris, 1984). It brings together and exemplifies Kearney's phenomenological approach, concern with ethics, interpretive engagement (with a biblical text), and theological enquiry. Countermanding the simulations and simulacra of postmodernity, what is offered (attentive to several poststructuralist voices) is an imaginative possibility, "a personalism of the icon against the cultism of the idol." This brings him closer to the work of Marion than probably anyone else represented in this volume.

For William J. Richardson

I say more: the just man justices;
keeps grace: that keeps all his going graces;
Acts in God's eye what in God's eye he is –
Christ – for Christ plays in ten thousand places,
Lovely in limbs, and lovely in eyes not his
To the Father through the features of men's faces.
Gerard Manley Hopkins, "As Kingfishers Catch Fire"

I propose to explore here the theme of transfiguration, first in terms of a phenomenology of the *persona*, and then with more specific reference to the transfiguration of Christ on Mt. Tabor (Mark 9, Matthew 17, Luke 9, John 12). Finally, I will look at some contemporary debates on the transfigured God before offering my own reflections on this enigma during a recent Pascal visit to Israel.

Figure of the Other: Persona

Each person has a *persona*. *Persona* is that eschatological aura of "possibility" which outstrips but informs a person's actual presence here and now. It is another word for the otherness of the other. At a purely phenomenological level, *persona* is all that in the other which exceeds my searching gaze, safeguarding their inimitable and unique singularity. It is what escapes me towards a past that I cannot recover and a future I cannot predict. It resides, if it resides anywhere, beyond the intentional horizons of retention and protention. Beyond, therefore, both the presenting consciousness of perception here and now and the presentifying consciousness of imagination (with its attempts to reassimilate and foresee what resists intuition, albeit in the fictional mode of *as-if*). The *persona* of the other even defies the names and categories of signifying consciousness. It is beyond consciousness *tout court*.

This is what Levinas names *la trace d'autrui*; what Derrida calls the spectral enigma of "alterity"; what in most religions goes, quite simply but often quite misleadingly, by the term "spirit" (*pneuma/anima/âme/Geist*). I will endeavor to develop the notion of *persona* here in terms of a radical eschatology of transfiguration, first sketched out in chapter 8 of my *Poétique du possible (1984)*.[1]

We never encounter another without at the same time configuring them in some manner. To configure the other as a *persona* is to grasp him/her as present in absence, as both incarnate in flesh and transcendent in time. To accept this paradox is to *transfigure* the other, allowing this other to appear as his/her unique *persona*. To refuse this paradox, opting instead to regard someone as pure presence (thing) or pure absence (nothing), is to *defigure* the other.

To be sure, this is not an easy matter. The other always appears to us "as if" it was actually present. And it is all too tempting to ignore the "as if" proviso and presume to have the other literally before us, to appropriate them to our scheme of things, reading them off against our familiar models of understanding and identification. (Especially since the otherness of the other is not located some *where* else, e.g., in some Platonic heaven of pure forms.) Accepting the other as a "stranger" in our midst here and now is an uncanny and often threatening experience, as Kristeva reminds us.[2] Far easier to take the other as given, to take him/her for granted, as no more than what we can grasp – following the logic: what you see is what you get. For if it is true to say that we do somehow "see" the *persona* in the face of the person, we never *get* it. It always exceeds the limits of our capturing gaze. It transcends us.

Or, going to the other extreme, it is easier too to mistake the other's *persona* for an idol than accept it as an icon of transcendence.[3] In this case, the "as if" presence of the *persona* is suspended in the interests of deification or apotheosis: a phenomenon not confined to religious idolatry (where an ordinary human person is revered as a divinity) but also evidenced daily in the cult of stardom (where Madonna replaces the Madonna . . .). Just think of Andy Warhol's multi-series of famous faces. We defigure others not just by ignoring their transcendence but equally by ignoring their flesh-and-blood thereness. There is a thin line, of course, between seeking to capture the other as divine (*qua* idol) and receiving the divine through the other (*qua* icon). But thin lines are no excuse for confusion or fusion. They call rather for acute hermeneutic vigilance. Because the *persona* is at once so near and so far, we easily fall for the lure of possession.

The enigma of the *persona* as presence–absence is usually betrayed in the name of some fictitious totality. Such betrayal derives from the fact that the fictitious character of this "totality" is unacknowledged. We simply forget the *as-if* strategy that effects the illusion of full presence. We succumb to *literalism* (masking the figural in the literal). Or what amounts to the same thing, curiously, in this instance: *fetishism*. For both literalism and fetishism conflate the orders of the possible and the actual, the fictional and the empirical. A strange convergence this, witnessed in the surprising collusion in our time between the ostensibly opposite movements of positivism and postmodernism. Or in the religious world, between fundamentalism and New Ageism. But more on this below.

We live more and more under the eclipse of the "as if." Which doesn't mean the "as if" no longer functions. It might even be argued that it functions more effectively today than ever to the extent that it operates behind our backs, unbeknownst to us: a process of concealment actually abetted by our postmodern culture of simulation. Indeed, as critics of ideology from Marx to Ricoeur have observed: ideology is a "false consciousness" which, like the camera obscura, works by inversion, in the dark, to give us what seems like a perfectly believable illusion.[4]

Ideological lies hide themselves and gain power from this stealth. One doesn't have to look far for examples of this. One finds it recurring, on the scale of persons, in the wild obsessions of fans and fanatics, ranging from stalker- and voyeur-fantasies to the mass-media apotheosis of certain figures of power, fame, and charisma (a postmodern version of the Personality Cult). But it doesn't have to be a human person. Nations, states, and empires have also been subject to idolatrous personifications (e.g., the sacralizing cults of national security, sovereignty, and territory). Here too we find defiguring practices.

Persona as Eschaton

What characterizes the eschatological notion of *persona*, by contrast, is that it vouchsafes the irreducible finality of the other as *eschaton*. I stress, as *eschaton* not as *telos*. And I understand *eschaton* here precisely in the sense of an end without end – an end that escapes and surprises us, like a thief in the night – rather than as the closing completion of some immanent teleological striving. Eschatologically considered, the *persona* of the person brings home to us that we have no power over her/him. Or as Levinas puts it, "nous ne pouvons plus pouvoir." The *eschaton*, as *persona*, is precisely the other's future possibles which are impossible for me (to realize, possess, grasp). The vertical "may-be" of the other is irreducible to *my* set of possibilities or powers. That is why "the future is that which is not grasped . . . the relation with the future is the relation with the other."[5] In other words, if we could figure out – in the sense of knowing and appropriating – the other's *persona*, it would no longer be *other*. We would have denied the other's temporality, futurity, alterity. We would literally *have* them. But the otherness of the other is precisely that which cannot be had, however much we fool ourselves into thinking it can. Just when it seems we hold it in our hands, it invariably absents and absolves itself, resisting the lure of totalized presence. "The relation with the other is the absence of the other; not absence pure and simple, not absence as pure nothing [*néant*], but absence in a futural horizon, an absence which is time."[6] It is in this temporal sense that we might say that the *persona* is both younger and older than its person, preexisting and postponing the seizure of presence (*qua* sum of identifiable and totalizable properties).

The *persona* is there where there is no one ("il y a persona là où il n'y a personne").[7] It is the no-place that a person takes the place of; but it does not itself take place. Yet it does *give place* to the person and without it the person could not take its place. It is the non-presence that allows presence to happen in the here and now as a human person appearing to me in flesh and blood. It is the quasi-condition of the other remaining other to me even as he/she stands before me in this moment. "Lovely in limbs, and lovely in eyes not his / To the Father through the features of men's faces."

But the *persona* is also there to remind us – spectrally, anachronically, messianically – that there is always something *more* to flesh and blood than flesh and blood.[8] Hence the inevitable frustration of the torturer, so acutely observed by Sartre, when he discovers that the tortured is dead but unvanquished: the torturer now has a corpse (*Korper*) in his hands but he has lost precisely that which he was seeking to subject – the free transcendence incarnate in that person's living body (*Leib*). The tortured *persona* escapes the torturer.

The *persona* also escapes, in a more banal sense, my everyday attempts – often quite benevolent – to turn it into an alter-ego. Hence the futility of Husserl's attempts in the fifth of his *Cartesian Meditations* to ground inter-subjective relations in an imaginative projection of one ego onto another. What he describes in his efforts to eschew the solipsism of the transcendental I is a reciprocating process of apperception, appropriation, pairing, and empathy (*Aneignung/Paarung/Einfuhlung*).[9] And we thus realize that it is not only I–It relations of crude coercion that compromise the irreducible alterity of the other's *persona*. Such compromise can take the form of symmetrical I–Thou relations as well. Especially where the Thou plays the role of another I: my mirror-image, my own ego in drag. The other as myself by proxy.

Time and again we seek to appropriate the other's *persona* as if it could be magically conjured in its present-at-hand thereness (*Vorhandensein*). We even lose ourselves in *jouissance* in the hope that ecstasy can make us one with the other. But it cannot. The other will never be me, or even like me. Whence the shock, for example, of a spouse reading his partner's private diary and discovering he never really knew the person (that is, *persona*) he lived with for so many years. Whence also the post-coital *tristesse* that derives from the awareness that no amount of intimacy can ever give us the other. It does give us something of course – the other person, in all their delightful givenness, but not the other's *persona*.

And so, in a curious reversal of tradition, we note here that it is the transcendent *persona* who marks the uniquely differentiating character of the finite person rather than the contrary. For us, while the "person" is a token of sameness (*idem*) – all that is statistically, logistically, metrically, anatomically computable and therefore comparable in the order of like-with-like – it is the *persona* who is guarantor of alterity. The *persona* tells us more about the person than can be captured on an ID card or identikit.

You can fake a person's ID but never their *persona*. Despite the most ingenious efforts, you can never quite take on another's *persona*. Anymore than you can imitate their fingerprint. The body, lest we forget Merleau-Ponty's and Marcel's reminders, is the primary locus of incarnate *persona*. It inscribes a singular style and manner of existing that is unique to each person. Whence Merleau-Ponty's quip about the transcending–transfiguring nature of the body-subject: "perception already stylizes."[10] Even our most involuntary alimentary and libidinal functions – ingestion, excretion, copulation – have their symbolic charge, as psychoanalysis reminds us; and as religious apologetics sometimes forgets. Contrary to spiritualist illusions, the *persona* is not some disembodied soul. It gives itself in and through the incarnate body. Just as it absolves or witholds itself. There and not there (but never somewhere else). Lovely in limbs and eyes. Through the features of faces.

Beyond Fusion

But the self-defeating endeavor to fuse with the other is not always carnal, or even personal. The unconscious has countless ruses up its sleeve to transfer libidinal drives onto sublimated, impersonal Figures. The Eternal Feminine, the Sovereign-as-Fetish, the Phallic Sujet-supposé-savoir, the Replacement Lost Object (*petit-a*), and so on.[11] All examples of refusing singular individuated others in the name of some totalizing One: the Same-One who is, at bottom, no more than the sum of our ideal ego-fantasies. The transcendent *persona* is thereby reduced to the Person-as-Phallus. And there is no more eligible candidate, one might add, in that the *persona*, like the elusive Phallus, is never present as full presence, is never all there so to speak. The big difference is, however, that the *persona* gives, calls, loves, solicits – and, as Levinas reminds us, forbids murder. The Phallus does not. Indeed the Phallus does nothing at all, for the Phallus does not care. Unlike the *persona*, the Phallus does not exist. That is the difference between Lacan and Levinas. So near and yet so far.[12]

A more benign, but no less compromising, version of the idealized-fetishized *persona* is to be found in Plato's theory of eros where the object desired is, at best, no more than an exemplification of an Idea. In the *Symposium* Plato invokes the Idea of Beauty which is always one and the same (like the permanent Oneness of divine *agathon* which it reflects). The so-called Platonic love which reveres a woman as exemplary instance of the Eternal Feminine is not a love of the other's unique singularity (*persona*) but love of the Self-Same-One. We thus participate in the Self-Loving-Love of the eternal *telos*, approximating to the divine condition of Aristotle's Self-Thinking-Thought or scholastic Self-Causing-Cause (*ens causa sui*); but we lose the alterity of the other person in the process.[13] What we gain on ideal roundabouts we lose on the real swings.

The stakes are high. For what we are contrasting here is the eschatological relation of one-for-the-other with the onto-theological relation of one-for-one, or if you prefer, of the one-for-itself-in-itself. The latter comprises a long logocentric tradition running from certain aspects of Plato and Aristotle to Hegel and Heidegger. And the political implications of this legacy are not always propitious. As Levinas points out: "Plato constructed a Republic which must imitate the world of Ideas ... and on this basis the ideal of the social will be sought in an ideal of fusion. One will assume that the subject relates to the other by identifying with him, collapsing into a collective representation, into a common ideality."[14]

Against this fusionary universalism of the Same-One, we might oppose the eschatological universality of the Different-Other. This second universality is ethical to the extent that it is conceived in terms of a possible coexistence of unique *personas*, whose singular transcendence is in each case vouchsafed. That such a universality remains a "possibility" still to be attained – still heralding from an infinitely open future – resists the temptation of the Same-One already present: a recipe for acquiescence in the security of the accomplished. The fact that universal justice and love is an eschatological possible still-to-come creates a sense of urgency and exigency, inviting each person to strive for its instantiation, however partial and particular, in any given situation.

To put this in theological language, we might say that the eschatological universal holds out the promise of a perichoretic interplay of infinitely differing *personas*, meeting without fusing, communing without totalizing, discoursing without dissolving. A sort of divine *circumin(c/s)essio* of the trinitarian kingdom: a no-place which may one day be and where each *persona* cedes its place to its other (*cedere*) even as they sit down together (*sedere*). The Latins knew what they were about when they played on the semantic ambidexterity of the c/s as alternative spellings of the phonetically identical root term *cessio/sessio*. They knew about the bi-valent promise of *persona* as both there and not there, absence–presence, transcendence–immanence, visible–invisible. But the *eschaton* is just that: a promise not a *fait accompli*. A possibility of the future to come, impossible in the present where the allure of total presence risks reigning supreme. As such, the eschatological *persona* defies my power – even if I have all the weapons in the world and it has none. The *persona* transfigures me before I configure it.

And to the extent that I avow and accord this assymetrical priority to the other, I am transfigured by that particular *persona* and empowered to transfigure in turn – that is, to figure the other in their otherness.

The assymetrical priority of the other's *persona* over my person (*qua* ego-cogito-cogitans*) finds expression in the fact that the other comes to me not as some figure-intuition – a presenting-presentifying fullness responding to my intentional consciousness – but as a figure-face (*figure-visage*) which shatters my intentional horizons. The face of the *persona* discountenances me before I countenance it. Which is another way of saying that the *persona* never actually appears in so far as it has *already come* (and gone, leaving only its trace) or is *still to come*, preceding and exceeding every figuration on my part. It hails and haunts me before I even begin to represent it *as if* it were present before me.[15]

These idioms of "already," "prior," "before," "after," and "still to come" signal a new kind of temporality – a specifically *ethical* time. This ethical relation expresses itself in the temporal exstasis of the ego towards the other who surpasses it, responding to the call of the *persona* issued from a time which antecedes my beginning and exceeds my end. That is why the *persona* assumes the form of an *achronic* figure-visage that disrupts and obsesses me before and after every as-if synchronism I impose upon it. In the very proximity of the other person – which itself attests to the distance of the *persona vis-à-vis* the present person – an ethical summons is heralded and heard – a call coming to me from some immemorial past. And it is this aspect of the proximate neighbor as transcendence that Levinas terms "visage."[16]

Persona as Chiasm

Strictly speaking then we might say that the phenomenon of the *persona* surpasses phenomenology altogether. At least phenomenology understood in the Husserlian sense of an eidetics of intentional consciousness (striving towards a rigorous science of transcendental immanence). It calls for a new or quasi-phenomenology, mobilized by ethics rather than eidetics. The enigma of the *persona* supersedes every presentation or re-presentation which seeks to apprehend it as intuitive adequation. It flouts the *adequatio intellectus ad rem*. Which is another way of saying that the figure-face is, at bottom, not literally a figure at all, but only figuratively so – that is, a quasi-figure which appears *as if* it was an appearance, as a prefiguration or refiguration of that which effaces itself as it faces us. So doing, and always avowing its own as-if conditionality, the *persona* of the other announces a difference which differentiates itself indefinitely, ad infinitum. *Persona* as infinitely premature and invariably overdue, always missed and already deferred. *Persona* as chiasm or cross-over with person.[17] Which is why we cannot think of the time of the *persona* except as an immemorial beginning (before the beginning) and an unimaginable end (after the end). That is precisely its eschatological stature – the messianic achronicity which breaks up and breaks open the continuous moment-by-moment time of everyday chronology or clock-time.

The time of the *eschaton* is anti-clockwise. Or if one prefers, post-clockwise. It cannot be accounted for in terms of prediction or prevision. The inexhaustible alterity of the *persona* remains forever anterior to its manifestation and baffles every cognitive interpretation I project onto it. That is why it "deranges" me.[18] (We shall return to this enigma in our discussion of "messianic time," below.)

In sum, the *persona* is never "adequately" there. Which is why *persona* is literally *personne*. It is no one, if someone means a person who is phenomenally equal to me; but it is *this* one and no one but *this* one, if my neighbor appears to me eschatologically defying the as-if figurations by means of which I tell but part of its story. For the *persona* is always other than the other-for-me here and now. It is the figure which transfigures by absolving itself from the very presence of its being-there, absenting itself as *personne* in the very moment that it hails and holds me. Like Celan's *Niemands Rose*.

In this sense we might best describe ourselves as actors (*figurants*) in a play authored by *personne* (the French carries the dual sense of "person" and "no one"). To interpret a role is, therefore, to respond to the script of the *persona* who speaks through (*per-sona*) the other, to figure and play out this role as a one-for-the-other, as a one through (*trans*) the other. It is to behold the other as an icon for the passage of the infinite – while refusing to construe the infinite as some other being *hiding behind* the other. This is not Platonism. Nor Kantianism. *Persona* is neither Idea nor Noumenon. Neither pure form nor *Ding-an-sich*. Nor any other kind of transcendental signified for that matter. No. It is the in-finite other in the finite other person before me. In and through that person. And because there is no other to this in-finite other, bound to but irreducible to the empirical person, we refer to this *persona* as the sign of God. Not the other person as divine, mind you – that would be idolatry – but the divine in and through that person. The divine as trace, as icon, as visage, passage, voice – the otherness of the other in and through that flesh-and-blood person over there. Trans-cendence in and through, but not reducible to, immanence.

We call it *trans-figuration*. Something we allow the *persona* to do to us. Something we suffer to be done unto us. Like the will of God. Or the eyes of the icon that look through us from beyond us. Or the thin small voice of Elijah's cave. Or the cry in the wilderness. A far cry from the Sartrian world where hell is other people. The only hell in this scenario is that of self condemned to self. The empty choosing will. The idolatry of each-for-itself.

What we are proposing, therefore, is a personalism of the icon against the cultism of the idol.[19] If the tradition of onto-theology granted priority to being over the good, this counter-tradition of eschatology reverses that priority. Herewith the good of the *persona* has priority over the being of the person and holds it to account. And, where possible, cares for it. Against Heidegger we say: it is not our being that cares for itself, as being-towards-death, but the good that cares for being, as promise of endless rebirth.

Messianic Transfiguration

The act of transfiguration finds canonical expression in the Christian testimony of Mt. Tabor. Here the person of Jesus is metamorphosed before the eyes of his disciples into the *persona* of Christ. The alteration – from one to the other – is Christ's coming into his own, fully assuming his messianic calling announced by the prophetic tradition from Moses to Elijah. It is marked not by Jesus abandoning his original person to become *someone* else, but by a change of "figure" which allows his divine *persona* to shine forth – in exemplary fashion – through his flesh-and-blood embodiedness. Jesus comes into his own by being "othered" as Christ. His person transforms into the *persona* latent in his self, the very divine otherness of his finite being, his in-finity.

It is no accident that the episode occurs just eight days after Jesus announced the first prophecy of the Passion and the coming of the kingdom: the double-act of death and promised resurrection which sets the condition of following Christ: "anyone who loses his life for my sake will save it" (Luke 9.22–8). Nor is it adventitious that prior to this announcement, Jesus had challenged Peter with the question of his identity – "who do you say that I am?" – receiving as response: "The Christ of God" (Luke 9.21). What occurs shortly afterwards on Mt. Tabor, in the presence of Peter and two other apostles, is Jesus's own way of confirming this mystery of messianic incarnation: the word made flesh, the Christ made man in and through Jesus. *To the father through his face.*

The *Dictionary of the Bible* writes: "The transfiguration of Our Lord which ancient tradition locates on Mount Tabor, is indicated by the verb *metemorphothe, transfiguratus est*, which supposes a change, not in the person itself, but in the *figure* in which it normally appears."[20] St Luke's Gospel tells us that as Jesus was praying, "the aspect of his face was changed and his clothing became sparkling white" (Luke 9.29–30). We note that it is the *face* that registers the transfiguring event, marking an ethical openness to transcendence which refuses idolatry. A distancing precaution is also evidenced in the mention of "whiteness," a common metaphor for the infinite and ineffable character of divinity (see also Matthew 17.2). Indeed the fact that Jesus carefully prepares his three disciples, James, John, and Peter, leading them to a sequestered high mountain to pray, and covering himself in a cloud, are further measures of protection against idolatrous appropriation. And it is in this same spirit that Christ insists, after the event, that the disciples build no monuments and keep their counsel, i.e., for fear of making him into an idol. As we are told, "the disciples kept silence and, at that time, told no one what they had seen" (Luke 9.36). (An echo of Christ's admonition after Peter's profession of faith in the "Christ of God" – "he charged them not to say this to anyone": Luke 9.21).

It may be instructive to recall here the famous *Homily on the Transfiguration* by St John Damascene. Here we read: "The holy body finds itself circumscribed because, at the very moment it stands on Mt. Tabor, it does not surpass the physical limits of the mountain; but the divinity [of Christ] is infinite; it is . . . beyond all."[21] Damascene goes on to make this connection between Christ's infinity and the whiteness of his transfigured aspect: "Just as the sun's light is other, so the visage of Christ shines forth like the sun and his garments white as light; they glisten with the splendour of the divine light."[22] But the author is adamant that the transfigured character of Christ does not mean his divinity is reducible to this appearance – it "receives glory," he tells us, "by investment not by fusion."[23] In this sense we might say that the transfiguration signals a surplus or incommensurability between *persona* and person even as it inscribes the one in and through the other.

Thus the Chalcedonian formula of two-in-one. A curious chiasm of infinity in the finite. Almost monstrous in its initial monstration. Certainly too much for his disciples, who are so baffled and bedazzled by Christ's whiteness that they immediately recoil in fear and must be reassured by the voice of the Father speaking from the cloud – "This is my Son, the Chosen One. Listen to him" (Luke 9.36). An echo of Moses' initial fright before the blinding brightness of the burning bush, removing his sandals in fear before he is summoned to his mission by the voice of God.

We might even recall here what Melville has to say about the strange and estranging quality of whiteness in *Moby Dick*:

> But not yet have we solved the incantation of this whiteness, and learned why it appeals with such power to the soul; and more strange and far more portentous – why . . . it is at once the most meaning symbol of spiritual things, nay, the very veil of the Christian's Deity; and yet should be as it is, the intensifying agent in things the most appalling to mankind. . . . Is it, that as in essence whiteness is not so much a color as the visible absence of color, and at the same time the concrete of all colors; is it for these reasons that there is such a dumb blankness, full of meaning, in a wide landscape of snows – a colorless, all-color of atheism from which we shrink?[24]

The thin white line between atheism and theism marks the seemingly undecidable frontier of faith. God-man as double-bind. The Christic criss-cross of *persona* and person.[25] A holy braille to be deciphered in blinding light. Which is why the transfiguring God calls at all times for hermeneutic vigilance and discernment, setting us at a critical distance – yet never so distant as to forfeit grace. Far in its very nearness, but not so far as not to be at all. It bids us cast a cold eye but not the eye of death.

It is surely telling then that while the disciples who witness the transfigured Christ are filled with fright (Luke 9.34), his two Jewish forebears – the first and last prophets, Moses and Elijah – appear not in fear but "in glory" (Luke 9.31). The calm wisdom of the prophets as they converse with Christ stems doubtless from the fact that they have already encountered the infinite – and lived. Moses in Ex. 3.14 and Elijah in Kings 19. And again in contrast with Peter, James, and John, the two prophets do not propose setting up tents of cultic adoration there on the mountain but choose to speak to the transfigured Christ about his coming mission – "his passing which he was about to accomplish in Jerusalem" (Luke 9.31).

The disciples' efforts to fix Christ as a fetish of presence, imposing their own designs on him, makes it necessary for God to intercede from the cloud and bid them attend to Christ's otherness: "Listen to *him*!" In this manner, the voice of transcendence speaks through Christ as divine *persona*, thereby arresting the idolatrous impulse of Peter, James, and John to fuse with his person or possess him as a cult object. The next line is especially telling. "After the voice had spoken, Jesus was found alone" (Luke 9.36). In other words, Christ is *set apart* from his followers by the divine voice-over (*per-sona*). And it is this very solitude of Christ, together with the consequent silence of the disciples as they follow him down the mountain, that marks this incident off as an epiphany of radical alterity. Mt. Tabor unfolds accordingly as a gospel replay of Mt. Sinai, with the transfigured Christ both re-figuring the Burning Bush (Ex. 3.14) and pre-figuring the coming of the messianic kingdom (when the resurrected Christ and the last prophet Elijah will return). Christ as figure *between* Moses and Elijah.

To rephrase this in the phenomenological idioms of our opening anaysis, we might say that the Transfigured Christ breaches the limits of intentional consciousness. The very otherness and uniqueness of his *persona* exceeds the horizonal reach of our three main modalities of noetic intentionality: it goes beyond perception (the dazzling whiteness and the cloud, recalling the veil protecting the holy of holies), beyond imagination (the refusal of Peter's cultic imaginings), and beyond signification (the observing of silence). This excess of transcendent *persona* over immanent person is what prompts John Damascene to portray Jesus thus cautioning Peter against the precipitous desire to have what cannot be had: "If Adam had not sought deification, before the time, he would have achieved what he desired. Do not seek goods before their time, O Peter!"[26] Moreover, the fact that the day after their descent from Mt. Tabor Christ makes his second prophecy of the Passion to come – announcing that he will be "delivered into the power of men" (Luke 9.44) – and then proceeds to declare that a helpless child on the street is greater than all the ambitious disciples, is a further indication of how the Transfiguration is framed with scenes which resist attempts to apotheosize Christ as some magical power or possession. The Transfiguration reminds us that when it comes to the *persona* of God – marking the unique thisness (*haecitas*) of each person – it is a question of the old enigma: now you have him now you don't. One moment there, one moment gone.

From which it follows that the cult of the historical Jesus is a form of idolatry just as compromising of Christ's *persona* as his reduction to some impersonal fetish (gnostic or ecclesiastic). The infinite *persona* of Christ is not exhausted in the finite figure of Jesus the historical person. The Messiah is distinct, if not separable, from the Nazarene. For as John Damascene once again reminds us, God only becomes man "in an indivisible difference, in a union *without confusion*."[27] A point reinforced by St John the favorite apostle when he identifies the transfiguring spirit of Christ with the eschatological Paraclete of the kingdom. Jesus the historical person must depart from this finite world so that the *persona* of the infinite Christ may return as the Paraclete who recollects all in a new heaven and a new earth (John 14.26). This is what the Homily of St Anastasius refers to as the "marvellous theophany on Mt. Tabor in the guise of an image prefiguring the Kingdom."[28] For, according to this eschatologico-messianic reading, what we witness on Mt. Tabor is nothing less than a pre-view of the "new creation," a call to "draw a recreated creation towards God."[29]

This audacious view is confirmed by many another post-gospel commentary. Pseudo-Dionysius the Areopagite, for example, claims that to be perfect as the heavenly father is perfect means that the "Lord will appear to his perfect servants (in the kingdom) in the same guise as he was seen by the apostles on Mt. Tabor."[30] And several other theologians find support for this eschatological perspective in St Mark's account of God reminding the three apostles that the transfigured Christ is his "beloved son, who is neither slave nor angel nor ancient" (Mark 9.7). So doing, God confounds the apostles' "natural" expectations and announces Christ as the possibility of all humans becoming "sons of God," i.e., by being transfigured into their own unique *personas.* Accordingly, Christ is held out to us as a promise inscribed in the great prophetic path leading towards the coming kingdom, and already signposted by Moses and Elijah (the iconoclastic and messianic prophets respectively). Indeed it is no accident that both these predecessors are harbingers of exodus (*ex-hodos*, the way towards) rather than of closure. Their accompaniment of Jesus in his moment of metamorphosis on the mountain serves as reminder that the transfigured Christ is a *way* not a terminus, a figure of the end but not the end itself. A fact powerfully brought home to us by Christ's pre- and post-transfiguration ennunciation of his own exodic "passing" in the days to come. God as passage then, not presence. As way, truth, and light – but never as *fait accompli.*

The Pauline Legacy

It is no doubt St Paul, however, who is most responsible for the eschatological reading of the Transfiguration. In 2 Corinthians 3.18 he invokes this perspective of the kingdom when he suggests that the scene on Mt. Tabor is a call to each one of us to become transfigured in the light of Christ. Such transfiguring is of course something done unto us by the grace-giving *persona* of Christ; but it is also something we can do to others in turn, indeed in return. ("Anything you do for the least of my brothers and sisters you do for me": Matthew 25.) That is why we have an ethical choice to transfigure our world according to the Christic figure of love and justice as icon of the end-to-come, *or* to fix him as an idol of presence – whose only end is in itself. The choice is between Christ as transformation or as fixation.

For Paul, therefore, Mt. Tabor is to be reread within the broader biblical history as both a re-figuration of Jewish messianic prophecy (e.g., the Psalms and prophets who already foretold the holiness of Mt. Tabor) and a prefiguration of the kingdom – when each human person will be transfigured in Christ's image (*eikon*). As Paul says, when the kingdom of ultimate transfiguration comes the clouds and veils that protect God will be lifted so that we may see face to face: "And all of us, with our unveiled faces like mirrors reflecting the glory of the Lord, are transfigured into the figure that we reflect in brighter and brighter glory; this is the working of the Lord who is the Spirit" (2 Cor. 3.18). What Paul calls Spirit here, we call *persona*.

Elsewhere – 1 Cor. 15 and Col. 3.10 – Paul elaborates on these key metaphors of figuring, imagining, and reflecting. Referring to Christ as the final Adam (*eschatos Adam*), Paul suggests that the transfigured – or what he calls "heavenly" – body of Christ is in fact the secret goal of divine creation aimed at from the very beginning, though it is only revealed in the *eschaton*. And this eschatological revelation or *pleroma* will be one in which each person may find itself transformed according to Christ's image and likeness. "And as we have borne the likeness of the earthly man, so we shall bear the likeness of the heavenly one . . . we are all going to be changed, instantly, in the twinkling of an eye, when the last trumpet sounds" (2 Cor 15.49). That at least is the promise of the messianic *persona*. It is *all* humanity that is invited to be transfigured according to the image-*eikon* of Christ. In this universalist scenario the "old self" is "renewed in the image of its Creator" (Col. 3.10–11). A renewal open to everyone: "in that image there is no room for distinction between Greek and Jew . . . slave and free. There is only Christ: he is everything and he is in everything."

This eschatological promise requires not only grace but ethical action on our part. The instauration of the *eschaton* of Creation is inseparable from human innovation.[31] In short, for Paul the transfigured–transfiguring Christ is not some *eidolon* to be embalmed and enshrined but the *eikon tou epouraniou*: the icon of the ultimate *persona* prefigured from the origins of time. This divine *persona* is what, finally, *both* safeguards what is unique in each one of us – what stiches each in its mother's womb, what knows every hair of our head – *and* what convenes us in a shared humanity. When Christ appears in the kingdom, as John (a witness of Mt. Tabor) writes, "we shall be like him, because we shall see him as he really is" (John 1.2).

Messianic Time

This brings us to the crucial question of what Levinas and Derrida term "Messianic time." Our story of transfiguration as a re-figuring of Adam and a prefiguring of Christ-come-again surpasses the limits of what is ordinarily known as history.[32] The *persona* is "eternal" in its very unicity to the extent that it remains irreducible to the laws of a purely causal or dialectical history. Its *eschaton* does not operate according to the objective laws of cause–effect or potency–act (though it does recognize that this is the chronological time in which human persons exist). Nor is it exhausted in the world-historical mutations of some teleological plan *à la* Hegel or Hartshorne. The reason that Paul says that the kingdom will come in a "blink of an eye" is to signal the utterly unpredictable and unprogrammable character of its coming. That is how we should understand the paradoxical language of anterior–posteriority which Christ and later Paul use to describe the eschatological kingdom. The kingdom is already "amongst us" yet still to come (Luke 17.20–5). Or as we might add, the eschatological *persona* is transfiguring always, in each moment, but always remains to be ultimately transfigured, at the end of time. Which is another way of saying its temporality exceeds the limits of ordinary time.[33]

Walter Benjamin offers this intriguing gloss on the subject in his *Theologico-Poetical Fragment* (1921): "This future does not correspond to homogeneous empty time; because at the heart of every moment of the future is contained the little door through which the Messiah may enter."[34] That is why we need always to remain vigilant and expectant. There is no guarantee or calculus as to how the transfiguring Messiah will come. When he comes, if he comes, it will be a surprise. An instant event that takes us unawares (as it does the three apostles on Mt. Tabor) even as it is prefigured from the beginning of time (and prophesied by the three holy figures on the same mountain, Moses, Elijah, and Jesus). Maybe it is this very unpredictability which has Jesus swear his apostles to silence both after Mt. Tabor, and also after the questioning scene with Peter which precedes it. For remember, Jesus does not here declare himself the one and only Christ. No, he asks the question: "Who do you say that I am?" And when the crowds and disciples seek to capture and capitalize on his divinity, he invariably rebukes them, deferring them to the "Father in heaven" – the same father of Moses and Elijah and every son of man.

True, the Father calls him his "chosen one." But does not Christ's transfiguring *persona* do the same for each of us? Are we not all called to be chosen ones? If you do it to the least of these you do it to me. "For Christ plays in ten thousand places . . . To the Father through the features of men's faces."

Some early Christian commentators seem to point in this direction. The *persona* of the transfigured Christ is, as John Damascene suggests, "both this and that, of the same essence as the Father (the universal kingdom) and of the same race and nature as us (the particular descendants of Adam)."[35] The transfiguration thus is as much about us as it is about God, for the transfigured Christ "renews our nature in himself restoring it to the pristine beauty of the image charged with the common visage of humanity."[36] Such a transfiguring mission includes all who seek justice-to-come. Or as John Damascene's version of Christ transfigured promises: "It is thus that the just will shine at the resurrection, transfigured into my condition . . . according to this image, this figure, this light, as they sit with me, the son of God."[37] Perhaps it is this universal invitation of the Christic *persona* that St Anastasius has in mind when he urges us to waste no further time but hurry towards the kingdom: "We should make speed towards it – I say this boldly – like Christ our precursor with whom we will all shine with spiritual eyes, renewed in the features of our souls, configured to his image and like him forever transfigured."[38] Our understanding of this eschatological transfiguration of the face does not seek to exclude other messianic (or non-messianic) religions in some sort of Christo-centric triumphalism. On the contrary, what I as a Christian mean by the *persona-visage* of Christ is the same, I believe, as what a Jew like Levinas believes when he says that when he thinks of the ethical relation of the "face" he thinks of Jesus Christ.[39]

The New Age Controversy

The fact that the transfigured Christ is not all there, so to speak – that is, is not reducible to his actual personal presence there and then – means that his *persona* remains to be perpetually interpreted. The surplus meaning of the Mt. Tabor event, marked by this incommensurability of *persona vis-à-vis* person, invites a history of plural readings. (Though this chiasm of incommensurable aspects does not for a moment belie the indivisibility of Christ Jesus – any more than two sides of a sleeve belie the indivisibility of that sleeve.) Indeed it is, paradoxically, the very silence which surrounds the event that in turn provokes a plurality of competing and often conflicting interpretations. Its ineffability becomes the motor of its *fability* – its translation into a variety of accounts, testimonies, fables, narratives, and doctrines ranging from the initial versions of John (actually present on the mountain) and his fellow evangelists, to the multiplicity of later readings offered by Paul and the Church Fathers and extending down through the entire "effective-history" (Gadamer's *Wirkungsgeschichte*) of Christian theology.

St Paul was especially sensitive to the various ways, good and bad, that Christ's promise of metamorphosis could be read. He was as enthusiastic about the eschatological reading, where Mt. Tabor pre-figures the kingdom to come, as he was suspicious of the various defigurations of this same promise – including those attributed to the power of false apostles and pseudo-prophets to "transform themselves" (*transfigurantes se*) into manipulators of souls (2 Cor. 11.13–15). Even Satan, Paul warns, deploys such fake mutations – turning himself into an angel of light just as his followers pretend to "transfigure" themselves into ministers of justice. The very fact, he notes, that the life and death of the transfigured Christ come down to us in words and "figures" – in spite of the injunction to keep silent – means that they are always open to both transfiguring and defiguring interpretations: the former enabling us to see Christ as an icon of alterity; the latter misleading us into an idolatry of presence (1 Cor. 4, 6).[40]

In our own postmodern times, the controversies continue. One recent debate on the subject is that between Slavoj Žižek's neo-Pauline reading of Christ versus the New Age Gnostic nostalgia for the historical Jesus. Žižek's basic point, for which I have much sympathy, is that we are currently witnessing a suspension of the "authentic kernel of Christianity" – to wit, the promise of a New Beginning, epitomized by such "symbolizing" events as the Transfiguration and

Resurrection. These events represent the true "scandal" of Christ as heralder of a messianic time of miracle and grace: a time which can undo the sins of the past (brushing history backwards) while simultaneously invoking a universal kingdom that is both now and still to come (that is, "eternal" or *sur-chronic*).

What the advocates of New Age Gnosticism promote, by contrast, is a return to the historical or material Jesus. This Jesus is all too literal – however shrouded in fake mystique – and supposedly escaped from the tomb to live on in the south of France, marry Mary Magdalene, and leave several descendants behind him! This hypothesis ignores the eschatological rupturing of chronological history by the transfigured–resurrected Christ in favor of a banalized Jesus, now little more than a guru-cum-escape-artist who teaches DIY self-improvement techniques: a sort of glorified Maharashi-Houdini.[41] But the banality of this particular New Age thesis has not prevented the emergence of a whole spate of pseudo-scientific bestsellers recounting various attempts to reveal the secret of Jesus, suppressed for millennia by the churches, viz., that he was a crypto-gnostic preaching inner journeying and "purification of the soul": a man with brothers and brides and babies and all such things besides.

How different these New Age narratives are to the marvelously faithful *Last Temptation of Christ* by Kazantzakis, which portrays such a naturalist scenario as pure *fantasy*. Unlike Kazantzakis, the neo-Gnostic craze to literalize the historical line of Jesus takes the eschatological harm (that is, grace) out of the transfiguration. It makes it utterly immanent. Or to use Žižek's Lacanian language, it contrives to reverse the Transfiguration, *qua* radical "symbolic" event (*creatio ex nihilo*), back into the order of the "real."[42] In the process the very transcendence of Christ's *persona* is masked and disavowed. The revolutionary challenge of transfiguration is defused. Emptied of alterity.[43] Explained away.

What is important here, I submit, is not just to expose such pseudo-scientific fabulations but to recognize them as precisely that: *fabulutions*. As part of the inevitable excess of fantasy generated by the very *figurative* character of the Transfiguration itself. And one, moreover, capable of being read as a symptom of our times. The point is not to resist such a multiplicity of interpretations but to enter the conflict and *take sides*. And the choice of sides is determined ultimately by which interpretations we deem more faithful to the ethico-eschatological import of the Christ-event. Which readings, we must ask, best testify to the transfiguring (i.e., singularizing–universalizing) power of the *persona*?[44] For testimony is the bottom line. Faithful and discerning testimony. The rest is indeed silence.

Pascal Testimonies

In this concluding section, I offer some personal reflections on the enigma of transfiguration, as it relates to the resurrected Christ, recorded during a recent visit to Israel.

On the morning of April 4, 1999, I arrived in Tel Aviv with my wife, Anne, and two daughters, Simone and Sarah. We landed in time for Easter Sunday mass at the small French Benedictine monastery of Abu Ghosh, the alleged site of Emmaus, located some 11 miles north of Jerusalem. During the simple uncrowded ceremony, accompanied by plainchant, I could not help being struck by the gospel reading: Jesus appearing to his disciples on the road to Emmaus (Luke 24.13–35). The first thing that hit me was how the two disciples walking on the road *failed* to recognize their Messiah when he appeared. In a wonderful twist of irony, Jesus asks them what they are talking about: to which they reply that he must be about the only person in Jerusalem who hasn't yet heard about Jesus being crucified! Continuing the game Jesus asks the disciples to tell him all.

They do, even mentioning – with doubled irony – how the apostles who went to the empty tomb on hearing that Jesus had risen, "did not see him." Jesus scolds them gently for not believing what the prophets had taught, thus making it necessary for the Messiah to suffer crucifixion before entering into his glory. But still they do not see him. Only, finally, when Jesus agrees to stop off at the village of Emmaus and share their evening meal are the scales lifted from their eyes. In the breaking of the bread they at last recognize him. As soon as they do, however, and their "eyes are opened," Jesus "vanishes from their sight." No sooner does he appear than he disappears. Now they see him, now they don't.

Several things about this story reminded me of the enigma of the Transfiguration. We do not recognize the sons of God there where they appear to us as we wander along the road of life. So full of great expectations are we that we fail to see the divine in the simplest of beings: we overlook the *persona* in the person. Second, the embodied God cares for our physical and material being: it is in the sharing of food that he makes himself visible. And third, rather than glorying in some kind of I-told-you-so posthumous triumph, Jesus takes his leave. As soon as he is seen, he absolves himself, goes invisible, refuses to be appropriated, enthroned, idolized; he becomes little or nothing again.

After the mass at Abu Ghosh, I drove with my family the 11 miles south to Jerusalem. There we visited the Church of the Holy Sepulchre, the very ground where the risen Christ had appeared to Mary Magdalene on this same day almost 2,000 years before, and said more or less the same thing he said to the disciples at Emmaus: "Do not hold onto me!" (John 2.11–18). Here Jesus chose to make himself visible to the most despised of sinners – a fallen woman – and to make her the premier evangelist of his risen message. Moreover, standing there on the spot where the gardener appeared to the Magdalene, I could not help recalling that what women prostitutes were in Jesus's time, the handicapped and homeless are all too often in our own day: scorned, spurned, unwelcomed – the lowest of the low.

Afterwards, as I wandered with my family through those narrow winding streets of Jerusalem, I realized it was in a closed room of this city that Jesus made his third apparition after his death: this time to the disciples (including the two just returned from Emmaus). Once again, we discover one of the simplest messages of the post-Pascal transfiguration – the overcoming of fear. The apostles are so "terrified" by what they see that they cannot recognize Jesus at first (Luke 24.35–48); they mistake him for a ghost. Doubts invade their hearts. But Jesus tells them not to be afraid – to approach and touch his wounds. And seeing that they are still "disbelieving," still not accepting that his wounded body is risen from the dead – transfigured – he resorts once more to the nourishment motif. "Have you anything to eat?" It is only then, when he takes some broiled fish and sits and eats with them, that they finally recognize him. They see and hear his message of dying and rising again: a message of transfiguration that comes – paradoxically but tellingly – through the body, a broken body, bruised and hungry for something to eat. Not primarily through power and glory, but through woundedness and want does the transfiguring *persona* make itself known.

It was, however, when we drove north to Galilee the following day (a Monday) that I began to appreciate some deeper implications of the transfigured–resurrected Christ. Visiting the fourth and last site where Jesus appeared after his death – the shore between Tabha and Capernaum – I was struck by how the miracle of bread and fish was nothing less than the story of Christ himself. Christ as *gift* of food and life. (The only trace still remaining in Tabha today is a faded fresco of two small loaves and fishes.) The miracle of multiplication from next to nothing, the mystery of excess from paucity, of surplus from scarcity. The mystery of less as more. Of person as *persona*. Divine criss-crossing. Chiasm. Monstrance of the not-there in the there.[45]

Standing on the stony beach of Tabha with my youngest daughter Sarah – who was busily collecting tiny shells (like mustard seeds from the sea) for her friends back in Dublin – I thought about the gospel passage in question (John 21.1–14). When Jesus stood on this same spot on this same day 2,000 years ago, his disciples "did not know that it was Jesus." The transfigured *persona* was still incognito, unrecognizable to them in his person standing on that stony shore. And when he called across to them in their boat some 90 meters from shore, asking if they had any fish, and they said no, they still did not recognize him. It was only when he instructed them to cast their empty nets out the other side of the boat, resulting in the famous miraculous catch, that the most impetuous and unthinking of them all, Simon Peter, the very one who'd denied him three times a few days earlier, finally identified him. And jumped into the water! Coming ashore Peter – and the other disciples who *still* did not recognize Jesus – found a charcoal fire already prepared for them with fish and bread. "Come and have breakfast," said Jesus. For he knew their hunger. He knew their want, their lack, their need, their desire. He invited them to sit and eat; and it was *then* and only then that their eyes were opened. Once again, the seeing comes in the sharing of bread and fish. It is in the carnal giving of his *persona* – the transsubstantiation of his *persona* into an embodied giver of nourishment – that the transfigured–resurrected Christ reveals his identity. As John writes: "Now none of the disciples dared to ask him, 'Who are you?' because they knew it was the Lord. Jesus came and took the bread and gave it to them, and did the same with the fish." Here we witness the power of transfiguration as ultimate answer to blood-sacrifice – as the epitome of an ethics of kenosis and gift.

Seen thus as *kerygma* of Transfiguration–Passion–Resurrection, the ethical message of Christ's post-Pascal visitations might go something like this: if you are hungry and need to eat bread and fish, ask for it and you shall have your fill. If you see a lost loved one standing on the shore and are filled with joy, throw decorum to the wind, jump into the waves and swim to them. If someone gives you food, do not ask for identity papers or credentials ("Who are you?"), just sit and receive. If you are wanting in body or mind – that is, crippled, despised, rejected, downcast – and your nets are still empty after many tries, do not despair; someone will come and tell you where to cast your net so that you may have life and have it more abundantly. Indeed the most transfiguring thing about this God of little things is that he gives with a gratuity that defies the limits of space and time. Now he's gone, now he's here, now he's gone again. Now he's dead, now he's alive. Now he's buried, now risen. Now the net is empty, now it's full. And more surprising still, the fish is cooked for us even before we get ashore and unload our nets! "Come and have breakfast," Christ says as the boat touches land.

Conclusion

The post-Pascal message of the transfiguring *persona* of Christ is that the kingdom is given to fishermen and fallen women, to those lost and wandering on the road from Jerusalem to nowhere, to the wounded and weak and hungry, to those who lack and do not despair of their lack, to little people, to the "poor in spirit." The transfigured–resurrected Christ testifies that after the long night of fasting and waiting and darkness and need – afloat on a wilderness of sea – breakfast is always ready.

As I returned with my family from the sea of Galilee to Jerusalem, we finally passed Mount Tabor. Peering up at the huge basilica now perched on that hill, I felt how easy it is to compromise the Christian message by erecting triumphal monuments there where Christ himself asked for discretion, for nothing, no tents or temples or memorials, at most a trace. And driving into Nazareth later that afternoon I thought how dispiriting it was to see Christians and Muslims fighting over who would appropriate the vast "millennial" space in front of the Church of the Annunciation (a giant edifice now towering over the ground where a humble young woman once knelt). As dispiriting as it was to witness, the following day, the various Christian sects – Armenian, Greek Orthodox, Coptic, and Catholic – skirmishing with silver turifers and bronze crucifixes over rights of priority procession through the Church of the Nativity in Bethlehem. The message of transfiguration so easily disfigured.

Not that such violence is the prerogative of Christian zealots. Bitter conflicts over the possession of holy places are equally rife in the other revealed religions.

The Jews with their Wailing Wall and the Muslims with their Dome of the Rock. Why such strife and hostility should continue to exist in the Holy City of Jerusalem – that messianic City on the Hill *par excellence* – as we reach the second millennium is a vexed question. Why the great monotheistic religions are still at war over the rock of Mount Moriah or the tomb of Abraham (in Hebron) is a depressing enigma.

All I knew as I wandered through this ancient Holy Land was that I sensed traces of transfiguration not in the great monuments of power and triumph but in the silent, scattered ruins which still bear testimony – as only traces can – to things that come and go, like the thin small voice, like the burning bush, like the voice crying out in the wilderness, like the word made flesh, like the wind that blows where it wills. Or if I were to cite places I visited that Easter of 1999: like the now-ruined walls of Capernaum where Jesus and the apostles took refuge after their expulsion from Nazareth; like the hill-caves of Sitve and Avdat where the Christian Napoteans (a people of the Spice Trail now extinct) rested on their passage through the Negev desert; or the sequestered hermitages of St George and Maar Saba carved into rockcliffs in the hills of Judea. For these are places which resist the triumphalism of ecclesiastical empire. Hide-outs, off the beaten track, without foundation. Cut against the grain. Self-effacing, modest, vulnerable, welcoming. Sanctuaries for migrants. Shelters for the exiled. Footholds for the forgotten. Arks. Perfect places for rejected *personas* to come and lay their heads. Cyphers, perhaps, of a new millennium?

Notes

1. R. Kearney, *Poétique du possible: phénoménologie herméneutique de la figuration* (Paris: Beauchesne, 1984). Chapter 8 of this work, entitled "La Transfiguration de la personne," was deeply influenced by both Emmanuel Levinas's notion of the "trace" developed in *Totality and Infinity* (1961) and Jacques Derrida's notion of "alterity" outlined in *Writing and Difference* (1967) and *Of Grammatology* (1967).
2. J. Kristeva, *Strangers to Ourselves* (London: Harvester Press, 1991).
3. J.-L. Marion, *L'Icône et la distance* (Paris: Grasset, 1977).
4. See P. Ricoeur's *Lectures on Ideology and Utopia* (New York: Columbia University Press, 1986).
5. E. Levinas, *Le Temps et l'autre* (Paris: Artaud, 1948), p. 64.
6. Ibid, p. 185.
7. Kearney, *Poétique du possible*, p. 161. This u-topian no-place of *persona* may well correspond, at the level of the unconscious psyche, to what Winnicott called the "potential space" which exceeds the dualism of internal subject and external other. Indeed we should understand its status of no-place in the context of the Pauline view that God chooses "things that are not [*ta me onta*] in order that he might cancel things that are" (1 Cor. 1.28). It is in a similar Pauline sense that we understand the analysis of *persona* as *personne* (no one) below.
8. See Derrida's intriguing analysis of the Messianic (which he contrasts to messianism) in, for example, *Spectres of Marx* (New York and London: Routledge), 1994.

9   See E. Husserl's fifth meditation in *Cartesian Meditations* (the Hague: Nijhof, 1960).
10 M. Merleau-Ponty, *The Phenomenology of Perception* (London: Routledge, 1962).
11 For a lucid account of Jacques Lacan's difficult theories of the object "petit a" and "le sujet supposé savoir," see W. J. Richardson and J. Muller, *Lacan and Language* (International Universities Press, 1982) and Richard Boothy, *Death and Desire: Psychoanalytic Theory in Lacan's Return to Freud* (New York: Routledge, 1991).
12 See W. J. Richardson on the vexed question of the "ethics of psychoanalysis" in a number of studies, notably, "In the Name of the Father: The Law," in *Questioning Ethics* ed. M. Dooley and R. Kearney (London and New York: Routledge, 1998), pp. 201–20.
13 Levinas, *Le Temps et l'autre*, p. 88.
14 Ibid, p. 88.
15 Levinas: "Le prochain m'assigne avant que je ne le désigne – ce qui est une modalité non pas d'un savoir mais d'une obsession . . . la conscience ne vient pas s'interposer entre moi et le prochain; ou, du moins, elle ne surgit déjà que sur le fond de cette relation préalable de l'obsession qu'aucune conscience ne saurait annuler – et dont la conscience même est une modification." *Autrement qu'être ou au-delà de l'essence* (the Hague, Nijhoff, 1974), p. 100.
16 Ibid, p. 112.
17 Robert Magliola, *On Deconstructing Life Worlds: Buddhism, Christianity, Culture* (Atlanta, GA: Scholars Press, 1997), pp. 127–8. Magliola cites here Derrida's rendition of the Mosaic God of Edmond Jabes: "God himself is, and appears as what he is, within difference, that is to say, as difference and within dissimulation"; and he goes on to quote, in this connection, Derrida's reflections in *The Post Card* on the two-in-one nature of the biblical God – "this double bind is firstly that of YHVH."
18 Levinas: "Autrui m'apparaissant comme étant dans sa plasticité d'image, je suis en relation avec le multipliable qui, malgré l'infinité des reproductions que j'en prends, reste *intact* et je peux, à son égard, me payer des mots à la mesure de ces images sans me livrer à un dire. La proximité n'entre pas dans le temps commun des horloges qui rend possible les rendez-vous. Elle est dérangement." *Autrement qu'être*, pp. 112–13.
19 J.-L. Marion, *L'Idole et la distance* (Paris: Grasset, 1977), pp. 255–93.
20 J.-L. Marion, "*L'Idole et l'icône*," in *Revue de métaphysique et de morale*, no. 4 (1979), pp. 433–45.
21 See homilies on the Transfiguration by St John Damascene and St Anastasia of Sinai in R. de Feraudy, *L'Icône de la transfiguration*, special issue of *Spiritualité Orientale*, no. 23 (1978), p. 172.
22 Ibid, p. 173.
23 Ibid, p. 156.
24 Herman Melville, *Moby Dick* (New York: Modern Library, 1930), p. 282.
25 Magliola, *On Deconstructing Life-Worlds*, pp. 127ff.
26 *Homilie de Damascène* in Feraudy, *L'Icône de la transfiguration*, p. 177.
27 Ibid, p. 152. See also the brilliant analyses of this topic in Christos Sidiropoulos, *L'Homme Jesus et le principe trinitaire*, Ph.D. thesis, University of Strasbourg, 1978, pp. 116–232. This mystery of "union without confusion" also recalls the presence–absence/universal–singular doubleness of the living divine in *Wisdom* 7.22–8.1, "For wisdom is more mobile than any motion; because of her pureness she pervades and penetrates all things. For she is a breath of the power of God, and a pure emanation of the glory of the Almighty; therefore nothing defiled gains

entrance into her. For she is a reflection of eternal light, a spotless mirror of the working of God, and an image of his goodness. Although she is but one, she can do all things; in every generation she passes into holy souls and makes them friends of God, and prophets; for God loves nothing so much as the person who lives with wisdom."

28 On the necessity, and impossibility, of translating the "messianic" import of Mt. Tabor, see Kearney, *Poétique du possible*, p. 168.
29 Feraudy, *L'Icône de la transfiguration*, pp. 130, 175.
30 Ibid, p. 128.
31 See Kearney, *Poétique du possible*, p. 160.
32 On the pre-figuring/re-figuring temporality of the transfiguration see the analysis of Anastasius's Homily in Kearney, *Poétique du possible*, pp. 170–1: "Anastase annonce qu'avec la transfiguration du Christ sa 'nature adamique, jadis créée semblable à Dieu, mais obscurcie par les figures informes des idoles, à été transfigurée en l'ancienne beauté de l'homme créé à l'image et à la ressemblance de Dieu' (*Homilie d'Anastase, L'Icône de la Transfiguration*, pp. 128, aussi 138, 149, 152–4, 150). Autrement dit, la Transfiguration est a la fois une *préfiguration* de la nouvelle création à faire (ce qu'Anastase nomme 'la terre de promesse') et une *refiguration* de la création originelle de l'homme selon l'image de Dieu. Le sens eschatologique de la Transfiguration du Christ nous renvoie ainsi à la création du commencement et de la fin. C'est pour cela qu'Anastase appelle Moise et Elie 'les célestes *préfigures* du Christ' (pp. 135, 138), et affirme que le Christ en tant que 'potentialité divine dans la figure d'un homme', doit être compris à son tour comme 'préfigure de la parousie': 'Tout esquissait et préfigurait là les mystères de la seconde parousie . . . le Royaume des cieux à venir'" (p. 142).
33 On this complex notion of "Messianic time" see E. Levinas, *Totality and Infinity* (Pittsburgh, PA: Duquesne University Press, 1969) and Derrida, *Spectres of Marx*. A key passage in Luke 17.20–5 where the Christian paradox of Messianic time is found reads as follows: "The kingdom of God is not coming with things that can be observed: nor will they say, 'Look, here it is!' or 'There it is!' For in fact the kingdom of God is among you." The passage continues, combining several of the motifs observed in our above analysis of the transfigured Christ – the whiteness of light, the refusal of immediate presence (literalism), the resurrection following the passion and brokenness of Christ: "Then Jesus said to the disciples, 'The days are coming when you will long to see one of the days of the Son of Man, and you will not see it. They will say to you, 'Look there!' or 'Look here!' Do not go, do not set off in pursuit. For as the lightning flashes and lights up the sky from one side to the other, so will the Son of Man be in his day. But first he must endure much suffering and be rejected by this generation."
34 Cited in Kearney, *Poétique du possible*, p. 172.
35 Feraudy, *L'Icône de la transfiguration*, pp. 168–9.
36 Ibid, p. 170.
37 Ibid, p. 143.
38 Ibid, p. 132.
39 Levinas in conversation with me during the Levinas Colloquium at Cerisy-La-Salle, Normandy, August, 1987. But in extending the Christian reference to include the Jewish, I do not mean either to replace a Christocentric bias with a Judeo-Christocentric one. Messianic time (as variously outlined by Levinas, Benjamin, Derrida, Marion, and even Heidegger in his pre-*Being and Time* period), marks a

universal quasi-transcendental condition which may include all religious experience of some sacred "other" time, be it monotheistic or otherwise.

40 This ethical choice between our transfiguring and defiguring acts corresponds broadly with the Talmudic distinction between the Good and Evil *yezer* as two opposing drives; namely, to recreate the world according to the design of God or to reduce it to our own ego-image. See *The Encyclopaedia Judaica* (London: Macmillan), vol. 8, p. 1,319; see also the chapter on the "Hebraic imagination" in R. Kearney, *The Wake of Imagination* (London and New York: Routledge, 1988), pp. 39–53.

41 See S. Žižek, *The Ticklish Subject* (London: Verso, 1999), p. 331: "Christianity proper – the belief in Christ's Resurrection – is the highest religious expression of the power of symbolic fiction as the medium of universality: the death of the 'real' Christ is 'sublated' in the Holy Spirit, that is, in the spiritual community of believers. This authentic kernel of Christianity, first articulated by St Paul, is under attack today: the danger comes in the guise of the New Age Gnostic/dualist (mis)reading, which reduces the Resurrection to a metaphor of the 'inner' spiritual growth of the individual soul."

42 Ibid, pp. 331–2, beginning, "these narratives endeavour to supplant the diminishing power of the *symbolic function* of the Holy Spirit (the community of believers) with the *bodily real* of Christ and/or his descendants. And again, the fact that Christ left his body or bodily descendants behind serves the purpose of undermining the Christian–Pauline narrative of Resurrection: Christ's body was not actually resurrected; 'the true message of Jesus was lost with the Resurrection'. This 'true message' allegedly lies in promoting 'the path of self-determination, as distinct from obedience to the written word': redemption results from the soul's inner journey, not from an act of pardon coming from outside; that is, 'Resurrection' is to be understood as the inner renewal/rebirth of the soul on its journey of self-purification. Although the advocates of this 'return of/in the Real' promote their discovery as the unearthing of the heretic and subversive secret long repressed by the Church as Institution, one could counter this claim with the question: what if this very unearthing of the 'Secret' is in the service of 'undoing', of getting rid of the truly traumatic, subversive core of Christian teaching, the *skandalon* of Resurrection and the retroactive forgiveness of sins – that is, the unique character of the Event of Resurrection?"

43 Ibid, p. 331: "the crucial point is that this New Beginning is possible only through Divine Grace – its impetus must come from *outside*; it is not the result of man's inner effort to overcome his/her limitations and elevate his/her soul above egotistic material interests; in this precise sense, the properly Christian New Beginning is absolutely incompatible with the pagan Gnostic problematic of the 'purification of the soul'. So what is actually at stake in recent New Age pop-Gnostic endeavours to reassert a kind of 'Christ's secret teaching' beneath the official Pauline dogma is the effort to undo the 'Event-Christ', reducing it to a continuation of the preceding Gnostic lineage."

44 In terms of the above controversy I would side with Žižek against the neo-Gnostics. But I also have my differences with Žižek, for whom the symbolic order is in fact an empty void. For Žižek, it is precisely the non-existence and emptiness of God that makes him function as the "big Other" in the symbolic chain, although this function begins to wane (as in our postmodern times) when the religious belief system begins to collapse. I do not see how Žižek's atheist reading is compatible with my theistic interpretation of this Pauline Christ. I also disagree with Žižek's attempt

to evacuate Christ of any carnal or corporeal character, reducing the notion of the "body" to the purely empirical, material order of the historical Jesus. As our above examples of Christ's post-Pascal apparitions seek to suggest, the body can take on a more significant "transubstantiated" sense in the context of a resurrected–transfigured Christ. Once again I find most suggestive here Merleau-Ponty's model of the body-subject as chiasmic crossing-over between visible carnality and invisible transcendence: as double but indivisible. It certainly points to a third way beyond the Žižek–Gnostic alternative extremes: either all spirit or all body! For us, as for the Chalcedonian theologians, the two natures are in one person (*hypostasis*).

45 On this notion of Christ-bread as "monstrance" see Magliola, *On Deconstructing Life-Worlds*, p. 128: "In the Benediction rite, the 'host' of consecrated Bread (through which form God dissimulates) – the *shechinah* of the New Covenant – is 'exposed' and 'exhibited' in a golden receptacle (called the 'monstrance', from L. *monstrare*, to show). That is, Christ is concealed/revealed: He is self-concealed under the form of Bread, and thus *dissimulates*, yet He is really the Bread, and thus self-reveals. Raising the monstrance on high, the priest moves the host in a giant 'sign of the Cross' over the adoring faithful, blessing them, *marking* them, in and into God's Chiasm." There follows Magliola's own profession of faith in the Chiasmic God: "I am called to Christ's differential way" (p. 129).

CHAPTER 22
Presence and Parousia

Jean-Yves Lacoste

Despite the fact that he often visits universities in the United States and Britain – in Britain he holds a life membership of Clare Hall, a graduate college in the University of Cambridge – the work to date of Jean-Yves Lacoste largely remains untranslated. This is much to be regretted, for his work gives an explicit theological focus to a particular interest in phenomenology in French thinking. Lacoste is one of a group of philosophical theologians – Jean-Luc Marion, Remi Brague, Michel Henry, Jean-François Courtine included – thoroughly schooled in Husserl and Heidegger, who are rethinking the questions of God and Being, the change in the nature of metaphysics from Aristotle to Suarez, and the emergence of ontotheology. Behind them lie the philosophical theologians and historians of the *nouvelle théologie*: Gilson, de Lubac, and Daniélou. With Lacoste, the phenomenological project is associated with more anthropological interests, in which he develops Heidegger's existential concerns. His attention to experience and familiarity with continental (rather than analytical) philosophy lead him to develop a philosophical theology quite distinct from the work done on mysticism or religious epistemology, say, by American philosophers such as Nelson Pike and William Alston. The research for Lacoste's *Note sur le temps: essai sur les raisons de la mémoire et de l'espérance* (Paris, 1990) was conducted in the early 1980s, but publication was delayed. The focus of this book is the development of a theology of time, as both experienced by human beings and as eschatologically informed by God's movement through history, by the Spirit, towards the *eschaton*. In a discussion towards the end of the book on the gift of being, memorial, and eschatology, Lacoste touches upon the sacraments, and the eucharist in particular, such that the essay offered for this volume can be seen as a subsequent reflection upon this work. His second book, *Expérience et absolu: questions disputées sur l'humanité de l'homme* (Paris, 1994, and dedicated to Henri de Lubac), complements this first, for if time is the central concept in the first book, it is space which is the fundamental concept in the second. (There is a reworking of a Kantian emphasis upon time and space as intuitions fundamental to experience itself.) Here he brings together reflections on Heidegger's construal of being towards death with a Christological account of being human which is characterized by kenosis. He develops what he calls an *anthropologia crucis*: an account of Christic subjectivity in which there is a self-emptying, a continual movement beyond oneself towards a transcendental, absolute horizon. Reflections on the eucharist hardly feature, but his evolving theology of space – as he seeks to locate human beings with respect to creation – is centered upon the nature of liturgy and human beings as liturgical beings. The last part of *Expérience et absolu* is translated into English, and can be found in my edited volume *The Postmodern God* (1998). It is a continuation and development of his method and interests, then, that we find in the following essay. Mention must also be made of Lacoste's outstanding achievement as an editor: his massive and exhaustive *Dictionnaire critique de théologie* (Paris, 1999).

The following lines propose a hypothesis, scarcely more. The author is well aware of their bleakness, and is very conscious of a certain arrogance which can, fatally, enter outlines such as these. Some searches which are already old (see, for example, our *Note sur le temps*, particularly §§66–99, or our *Expérience et absolu*, particularly §§1–22, 43–60) provide some support for this very short text. But other works would be necessary – possibly those of another author . . .

Sacramental *presence*? Two objections are commonly raised to this concept, or to the idea which evolves from it. The first is linked remotely to the reservations of Thomas Aquinas, who says that presence would bind the Body Eucharistic in place. The second is the one crystallized by Hegel: it is like an "external thing," *äußerliches Ding*, which Catholic theory would employ to adore God the Spirit (*Enzyklopädie*, §552). But is locality – Being here, with being understood in terms of geometric space, i.e., space which is non-living and which is not experienced – the essential trait of presence? And while speaking of presence, does this indeed mean Being as a thing, as an objectivity which is thus imposed on the resurrected body? We must allow ourselves to doubt this. We will first suggest that presence, if it must have a precise conceptual content, obtains it by being distinguished from objectivity. We will then propose that the "here" of the eucharist, or its "there," is much less a place than a non-place, and that the resurrected body is only encountered here and there by putting aside the logic which governs experience, and the conceptual organization of all which is "there." We shall remark finally that in the non-place of eucharistic celebration, or of eucharistic worship, what is offered to us is a presence in our time and for our flesh: so that presence appears to us as not-being eschatological omnipresence (as not-being parousia).

In order to determine a precise use for the word "object," what we understand by this is the conceptual correlate of the subject: the being which metaphysics, when it is (belatedly) organized as ontology (and therefore according to Suarez), measures as an imagined Being, or as a Being contained in consciousness. Defined thus, this object possesses a very remarkable negative property, namely that of being granted to perception and ideation, but not to affection. This object is afforded to consciousness, but exerts no pressure on feeling: it has form, color, speed, and the rest, but its appearance does not demand affect: it is sufficient for it to be discerned (or it is sufficient for us to discern it to have knowledge of it). And regarding the ontology of this object – the ontology of Being when constituted as an object – one point is clear: it is definitely "in the nature of things" that an ontology such as this is provided with means of interrogation. It can always be said that the object which I see, understand, represent, etc., is now present as such. However, this affirmation will be alternatively meaningless (it will introduce a term, "presence," without this introduction fulfilling a conceptual need) or harmful (it will subsequently prohibit the provision of a concept of presence which fulfills the requirements of the real).

I should therefore like to propose that the language of presence, if it is to be truly meaningful acquires it in a setting which is not that of a general ontology of the object, when the "present" predicate applies to beings who jointly ask for perception and affection, and who often add a third request to these solicitations, namely one which is addressed to our freedom. Heidegger taught us that we live in the environment of the world in the company of beings who are "within easy reach" or "close at hand": which is a good way of thinking of objectivity when one wants to think of it existentially. But if we want to speak of presence, we do not have to ask for evidence for it from a stone or from a pen placed on a table, but from a work of art, from the other man, the whole of reality, which indeed cannot appear without opening the realm of emotional experience within us. The object objectivates itself (the stone), or (the pen) it waits until its time comes, the time of its usefulness and of its use. A work of art, on the other hand, and the other man who confronts me, demand to be recognized: they appear to us whilst calling for a response. Certainly, the other man, once he has entered my field of perception, is seen and "seen well." A work of art, once it has entered my field of perception, is also seen and "seen well," and is heard and "heard well." What do these last statements show, however, except that the problem of presence is not precisely there? In a first analysis, it is possible to admit the existence of phenomena to which we give their due by being satisfied with discerning them. But when the face of man appears to us, when some bars of Mozart are played to us, etc., we are no longer able to limit ourselves simply to perceiving and representing: it is necessary to recognize oneself as a brother (Levinas), simply to recognize (Cavell), to allow oneself to profit from joy, etc. Presence is not discerned, it is felt and is welcomed; any theory of objective knowledge fails here. Mozart certainly remains Mozart when a philistine listens to him with half an ear; the victim is indeed present even if the executioner treats him like a thing; Christ's eucharistic Body is really present in the tabernacle even if no one is there to praise his presence. Our welcome is not what provides his presence; it does not confer it. Presence invites my presence. It doesn't compel it, but has need of it.

None of these features would be attributable to an object. They all prove that it is not necessary to believe in the interchangeability of the objective and the present.

How, therefore, are we to link presence and *place?* If we are only allowed to speak here of eucharistic presence, and if we are also allowed to assume that the definition of place in terms of geometry carries no weight as a true theological consideration, a vivid paradox then requires that place, in this case, benefits from pure and simple *extraterritoriality*. Extraterritoriality in relation to the *world*: the piece of bread and the few drops of wine are the divine presence here (in a church, on an altar), but here, encompassed by the gift of presence, it perturbs all the hermeneutics of that which is factitive: if the world is defined (in terms which are both Pauline and phenomenological) as the realm of existence where man is without God, namely as atheistic, then the place of eucharistic presence puts the world aside. Extraterritoriality in relation to *history*: if the time of eucharistic memorial is indeed that of contemporaneousness with he who gave his body and his blood, then, for him also, the sequence of the past, the present, and the future is placed in brackets, in a place where nothing happens but the same memory and the praise of the same presence. Finally, extraterritoriality in relation to *the earth* [sic!]: if the sacred is perpetually in proximity to man, with the earth being defined as this region of "the continent of existence" in which man confronts the "divine," then the word of the eucharist, namely bread, wine, and the whole liturgy, the origins of which were established by praising the holiness of the God of Israel, and of his Son, arises from its numinous diffuse entities (or qualities), and from a judgment of paganism, in exchange for the worship practiced by nations.

A question then arises. Praise and contemplation are marginal without a place in the world, without a place in history. They mean more than this, however. In fact, this difference is understood by understanding the condition of happiness. And in what is offered to praise and contemplation, it is the definitive which faith sees, which is therefore less of a marginality than an excess and a subversion. This is very true, but it is true with one reservation, namely that one also discerns that the presence of the definitive is *only* itself given to us under the conditions of the temporary. The believer wants to praise presence – but he has to reckon with the burdens of a tired body and a distracted mind, and even has to reckon with boredom. He has given his assent to the mystery of presence, and would like to respond to presence in a unified act of faith and love – but spiritual life has its nocturnal face, in which affect cannot quite feel what we would like it to feel. Therefore, to designate that which presence is not, let us speak of parousia. All this has certainly been done, and has certainly been said . . . However, the believer only enters this structure of proposition and welcome, pressure and recognition, to which the name of presence is given, while he is mortal and while time is leading him towards death. God is not absent or staying away from these mortal lives. He is present there. But he is not only present. His sacramental presence, here and now, makes the atheism of the world, the paganism of the earth, and the violence of history, incidental. It does not abolish them, however. The believer prays for "that which surpasses this world," but this is a request which is appropriate to the hours before his dying hour. And in these hours before his dying hour, presence is also given in order to instil the desire for parousia in man.

Translated by A. J. Wickens

CHAPTER 23
The Formal Reason for the Infinite

Jean-Luc Marion

Jean-Luc Marion is probably one of the most talked about Christian theologians of our times. With his regular visits to the United States (where he holds a Visiting Chair in the department of philosophy of religion at Chicago University), his tenured position as Professor of Philosophy at the University of Paris-Sorbonne and his associations with the Institut Catholique de Paris, he is internationally known as a teacher as well as an academic. His work is also theologically contentious. His training is as a philosopher, and he distinguished himself early in his career with several books on Descartes's ontology. While his Cartesian meditations continued he published the book *L'Idol et la distance. Cinq etudes* (Paris: 1977; English translation in press). This book revealed his familiarity not only with contemporary philosophical discussions (Husserl, Heidegger, Levinas, and Derrida), but also with patristic theology. It announced quite a distinct approach to philosophical theology – an approach which married the analytical concerns displayed in his work on Descartes, with the theological influence of *nouvelle théologie* and a phenomenological method. What profoundly relates these three perspectives (and links back to Marion's abiding interest in Descartes) is the question of ontology and God's relationship to being.

Since the publication of *Réduction et donation. Recherches sur Husserl, Heidegger and la phénoménologie* (Paris, 1989), Marion has embarked upon an ambitious project: an exhaustive phenomenological investigation into the nature of the donation. A second study, *Étant donné. Essai d'une phénoménologie de la donation*, followed in 1997 (with a corrected edition in 1998). As I write, a third book has appeared, *Du Surcroît* (Paris, 2001). In these volumes Marion pushes his thinking in an examination of what is visible towards a transcendent reduction, a primordial givenness which lies beyond, and yet renders possible, a created order. In doing this all phenomena are viewed as saturated by an irreducibility, an excess of meaning, the incomprehensibility of the Infinite. *Du Surcroît* concludes with an examination of the language of doxology.

Five years after *L'Idol et la distance* Marion produced what is still the most well known and well-read of his books, *Dieu sans l'être* (Paris, 1982). Ten years later, the English translation, *God Without Being* (Chicago, 1992), launched Marion's reputation as an international theologian with something distinctively contemporary to offer – something as original and as intellectually rigorous as it is controversial. Here, following a phenomenological account of the idol and the icon, Marion relates the practice of theology to eucharistic presence and, in doing so, sacralizes the office of theologian: the theologian *par excellence* is the bishop. Nevertheless, his appeals to sacerdotal authority, to scriptural revelation, to the ecclesial tradition (particularly its Cappadocian and Greek legacy) – which some have argued renders him a conservative thinker – have to be understood in terms of his emphasis upon hermeneutics: there is no unmediated move from the visible to the invisible. It is no surprise, therefore, to see the close friendship between Marion and the American theologian David Tracy (often viewed as a liberal Catholic thinker).

The essay contributed to this volume brings together many themes (philosophical, theological, and aesthetic) which have shaped his research over the last twenty-five years: the act of seeing as it distinguishes the idol from the icon; the philosophical work on reasoning at the dawn of modernity; the *via negativa* of the Cappadocian Fathers who insisted upon divine distance and incomprehensibility; the existential position, or more broadly the anthropology a theological approach to phenomenology defines; the centrality of the scriptures to Christian faith. In brief, Marion's thesis announces that "Christ is a matter of epistemology" – where the activity of knowing presupposes the divine.

The Infinite in Reason, Reason in the Infinite

The use of reason first of all requires us to practice the Infinite, as one practices an unmanageable but essential instrument, in order to improve our rational capacities by applying them not to some delimited object, but to that which, by definition, will always resist definition. More than this: reason also consists of exercising the Infinite, as one exercises a political, administrative, or financial responsibility – because it is very necessary for one to assume the crushing but indispensable burden of it; and also because the supreme task, that of contemplating the Infinite, fascinates, attracts, and captivates the minds of those who are most endowed with reason, so to speak. Man is a privileged being, not only because there is Being within him, but also because the Infinite is even in the Being within him. For us really to succeed in thinking, in one way or another, in any field of knowledge, depends on our picturing the Infinite, on our thinking of the Infinite. But this depends less on our picturing the Infinite in a positive manner than on our applying our reason, in one way or another, to the Infinite. Therefore, the Infinite is first of all not called transcendent, but is given a transcendental status – that which stems from the very condition of exercising reason. A form of reason which would not think about the Infinite – not only about it, but in accordance with its requirements – would be deficient in itself. There is no rationality without turning to the Infinite.

It must be stressed that this is first of all not solely a requirement of a philosophy, of a speculation, of a desire, or of a religious belief. It is a requirement, above and beyond a narrow practice common to all the sciences. For us nowadays, each of the sciences has dealings indeed with the Infinite, in one way or another. The formal infinity of mathematics, the real infinity of space in physics, which itself encompasses, to paraphrase Pascal, the small "infinity" of particle physics, of biology, and of the life sciences, and the large "infinity" of the science of matter, of astrophysics, etc.; and again, or even above all, the infinity by accumulation which is generated, at its risk and at our peril, by industrial production and its imperialistic interpretation of the world; without omitting the infinity by projection and classification which is engendered by the parameters of statistical science. For us, a science which would never have dealings with infinity would not be a science, because it would not possess two necessary characteristics of scientific rigor: firstly that of a proper method which would open up entirely new types of subjects to it, and secondly free scope for progress without assignable boundaries.

That all science must practice the Infinite and must even exercise the Infinite within its domain, goes without saying for us, but this was not so for the Greeks. In fact, according to Aristotle, every science was assigned to its place, without anyone being able, or at least having the right, to move from one to another. The homogeneous space of the *Mathesis Universalis* did not have to be and, in fact, did not succeed in being organized by the Greeks, but had to await the new Cartesian beginning. The only universality admitted by Aristotelian thought and its final heirs in the sixteenth century related solely to mathematics, where number in general enabled arithmetic, geometry, astronomy, music (and other applied mathematics) to be rigorously amalgamated into a general form of mathematics (*Mathematica Universalis*), which was scarcely outlined historically. However, this restriction was based, both for Aristotle and even for Plato, on an even more radical argument which in turn was evidence of a fundamental theoretical decision: namely, that knowledge requires the delimitation of that which is known, that the act of knowing requires that that which is known is indeed the first to be delimited. The undivided, the unlimited, or in short the Infinite, which is understood in a negative sense as the Indefinite, renders man incapable of knowledge, according to a meaningful play on words employed by Plato. In all logic, such an indefinite, unlimited, and undivided Infinite culminates in matter – and culminates less in materiality as such than in the imprecision which it imposes on form with the effort of delimitation and therefore of intelligibility. Even Plato did not hesitate to conclude, in the name of the whole of Greek thought, that matter is equivalent to the Indefinite.[1]

Modern thought has transgressed this restriction – that to know excludes the Infinite, because the latter implies indeterminacy and therefore contingency. Modern thought has only established itself by transgressing this restriction. We could think here of Duns Scotus, Nicolas of Cusa, and Kepler or Galileo. We shall stay with Descartes, who lucidly met the Greek objection with: "I must not think that I do not discern the Infinite by a real idea, but only by the negation of the finite, as I discern rest and darkness by the negation of movement and light; because on the contrary I manifestly understand that there is more reality in infinite substance than in finite substance and that, consequently, the perception of the Infinite is to be found in some manner within me before that of the finite, namely [the perception] of God [before that] of myself." Consequently, and definitively, the Infinite appears to be first. This does not only mean, nor does it primarily mean, that it is established as a metaphysical name for God (although it is just this since Duns Scotus and Suarez), opening the way to a rational theology of the infinite Being who is infinitely perfect, the privileged provider of a future "ontological argument." More profoundly, however, this reversal means that the Infinite precedes the finite – human thought, that which organizes and deploys its sciences – like a horizon which is always already open to welcome its progress and its desires as an advance. It is here, since Descartes, that the Infinite has become established as the ultimate transcendent, even more than it has become established as the first transcendent. Kant recollected this, writing that "The Infinite is not the specific objective concept of a size in its relationship to others, but, *being brought into effect subjectively*, it surpasses in magnitude anything else which we might put forward, even though this would not be the result of every understanding." In short, it is such that it will always be possible to conceive of something bigger. But this transcendental priority, which determines the conditions of possibility of all knowledge (including scientific knowledge first and foremost), has a price: if the Infinite precedes the finite and makes the latter possible, the finite cannot, by definition, include the Infinite within its comprehension, since it is precisely the Infinite which makes the finite possible; that which is governed cannot comprise the unconditional which governs it. It is therefore necessary to admit this impossibility as an *a priori* necessity, or rather to admit this *a priori* impossibility as a necessity: "It is not an obstacle that I do not understand the Infinite, or that in God there is an infinity of other things, which I can by no means understand and which perhaps I cannot even attain by thought (*nec comprehendere, nec forte etiam attingere cogitatione*); in fact, it follows from the reason for [or the definition of] the Infinite that it cannot be understood by me who is finite." Paradoxically, an incomprehensibility such as this does not imply ignorance, nor does it in the least imply a regression towards the unknown, because, absolutely as a first idea, or we could also say as an idea on the horizon, the Infinite quite rightly imposes itself on my mind as "the clearest and most distinct idea" and the "most real idea" of all. It is precisely because the Infinite is a condition which transcends all others that this idea surpasses other ideas epistemologically. So that the impossibility of understanding the infinite as a finite object precisely coincides with its perfect clarity and distinction, its incomparable truth.

However, there then follows a paradoxical conclusion, stemming from one of those paradoxes which provides reason with its most unshakable points of support: "to be true, the idea of the Infinite does not by any means have to be understood, because incomprehensibility itself is contained in the formal reason for the Infinite – *idea enim Infiniti, ut sit vera, nullo modo debet comprehendi, quoniam ispa incomprehensibilitas in ratione formali infiniti continetur.*" Let us give attentive consideration to this fundamental statement. (a) It of course explains the title of our subject: the formal reason for the Infinite precisely consists of its incomprehensibility. (b) It not only shows that incomprehensibility defines the Infinite (in the forestalling sense of *ratio formalis*), but also shows in particular that reason (the primary meaning of *ratio*) does not constitute a limit of intelligibility, but formally includes the incomprehensible when it pictures the Infinite. Incomprehensibility constitutes the epistemological reverse side of that for which the Infinite provides the ontological obverse. The same coinage has an ontological face (the Infinite) and an epistemological face (incomprehensibility). (c) Incomprehensibility must also be pictured in a manner such that in principle it forms part of reason, in the situation where it has dealings with the Infinite and has to consider it intelligently. Taken in this sense, the incomprehensible does not go beyond the frontiers of rationality, but designates the most extreme parish of it, or indeed its most strategic step; because, by losing the incomprehensible, reason would risk losing all its legitimacy, and therefore all its domain.

To Know the Incomprehensible As Such

However, even according to Descartes, this paradox is only valid on one condition: that the task of reason must be to picture God. To which there are two objections. (a) Does not this condition assume that what is to be proved has been established – namely that reason can always claim to picture God, whether such a one exists or whether knowledge of him exceeds the theoretical powers of reason? And does not the Cartesian solution – namely that to picture the Infinite is equivalent to picturing the incomprehensible – precisely confirm that reason is doing that which it does not have the means to do? (b) To which another objection can be added: even though in the case of God, which constitutes an exceptional definition, it would be possible to picture the Infinite as incomprehensibility, what result is to be derived from this? What other use of incomprehensibility could this offer elsewhere, where it is only a question of a finite being and is most often a question of synthesized objects, which are constituted and finally produced at will, and which are all perfectly comprehensible? The incomprehensible is therefore open to two rebuttals: its noetic impracticability, and its marginal character within the actual use of reason. We shall examine these one after the other.

First, can the conception of the incomprehensible take the place of authentic knowledge? This cannot be evaluated without referring to the position taken by Descartes to an unwavering tradition, even though he doubtlessly ignored this. In fact, his wording echoes that of others. (a) The problem is clearly formulated by St Anselm: in relation to God, it is a question of "rationally comprehending that he is incomprehensible." The rationality which this oxymoron ("to comprehend the incomprehensible") is capable of surmounting (or accomplishing) remains to be defined. In fact, is it not sufficient to renounce argument in order to return to holiness, as St Bernard points out: "It is not debate, but the holiness which comprises it, to which recourse must be made if at least that which is incomprehensible is capable of being comprehended in any way?" This is not certain, since the comprehensibility of the incomprehensible would then remain doubtful, because first and foremost holiness does not have a theoretical vocation.

(b) Since, in these two cases, one encounters the head-on opposition between comprehension and the incomprehensible, what would be needed is an attempt to organize these within a relationship which is itself rational. This was attempted by St Augustine: "It is of God that we speak, so what is astonishing in that you did not understand? Because if you had understood, it would not be God." The paradox regains its full intelligibility here: it is no longer a question of placing comprehension in opposition to incomprehensibility in the same field, but of constructing a hierarchy for the whole of comprehension in general in relation to an exceptional thought, in which this concept, and only this concept, *must* remain incomprehensible in order to remain rational. This is what Descartes calls the Infinite. Consequently, incomprehensibility is perfectly capable not of suspending knowledge, but of supporting it, since it provides it with a theme which is out of the ordinary. It is not a question of abandoning knowing, but of recognizing that which, as such and by positive privilege, exceeds comprehensibility; and in order to know this, it is rightly only a question of recognizing the excess therein. Consequently, experiencing it by the conception of its incomprehensibility (subjective) becomes the experience of the Infinite (objective). Between Augustine and Descartes, Montaigne can be heard amongst others: "It is through our ignorance rather than through our science that we know this divine knowledge." Therefore, ignorance is worth nothing less than the only mode of knowledge which is paradoxically appropriate to the knowledge of the Infinite. Several scholars have clearly emphasized this; St Augustine: "this supreme God, whom one knows best by not knowing [him]"; and Thomas Aquinas: "such is the ultimate [advance] of human knowledge about God – to know that it does not know God"; and even Dionysius: "God is known by knowledge and by the unknown.... And it is also the most divine knowledge of God that one knows by the unknown."

(c) Yet there is more: incomprehensibility, as an experience which cannot be grasped, does not only have a negative function (the apophysis of transcendence); it can also, by the same function, give access to a real and positive experience of the Infinite. Basil of Caesarea does not hesitate to speak of nothing less than a *sensation* of incomprehensibility: knowledge of the divine essence is only the sensation of its very incomprehensibility. The Infinite appears positively to the extent that even its incomprehensibility is vouched for positively in the records of epistemology. Certainly, we obviously do not understand the incomprehensible, but we experience this incomprehensibility not as a denial of evidence, but altogether as evidence that affects us by right, or in short as a mark of affection of the Infinite. We understand that we do not comprehend, and that we do not have to comprehend, the Infinite, and that it will be henceforth by this sign that we will know or recognize it – as that which certainly never allows itself to be reduced to the *a priori* conditions of knowledge of an object. In other words, according to Gregory of Nyssa, "It is in this that true knowledge of what is sought is to be found" (i.e., incomprehensible God): seeing him is to be found in not seeing him. We conclude: incomprehensibility does not epistemologically disqualify the Infinite, but designates what we can grasp of it without striving in vain to understand it like an object. "All that is incomprehensible does not cease to be." The Infinite remains amongst us, not in spite of, but indeed because of the sensation of the incomprehensible.

"But," one could retort, "is this simple sensation of the incomprehensible really accessible to us?" Even though one recognizes, in the manner of Kant, its inevitable appearance from reason, does one also have to grant it phenomenality by right? Is it not a question of a perspective-effect, which is certainly impossible to eliminate, but which all the same is much more illusory? An additional hypothesis may – we do not say must – intervene here. Thus, since the Infinite almost always remains with us, under the nature of incomprehensibility, in accordance with the establishment of our finite experience of the Infinite over two thousand years, this same Infinite has moreover "pitched its tent among us" and "has become flesh"; in short, it has taken our flesh.

One can all the more refuse to comprehend this unprecedented event because it is effectively inconceivable and is only of account while remaining such. One can reject its viewpoint, but one can dispute neither its logic, nor its consistency, nor its rationality. However, one cannot dispute the fact that, for two thousand years, an uninterrupted religious tradition which has always been robust has been built on the belief that the Infinite has taken flesh – flesh, blood, and bone – amongst us, and has made itself one of us until our death and until the Resurrection which it inaugurates. In any event, whether one rejects it or whether one assumes it, it is obligatory to ask what this claim means. It implies two paradoxes at least. Firstly, it does not imply that the Infinite henceforth becomes comprehensible in Christ (which would be equivalent to the "fanaticism" of the *Schwämerei*), but, on the contrary, it implies that the incomprehensibility of the Infinite becomes the flesh of our flesh to us. Indeed, if the Infinite has become incarnate and if the incomprehensible "has assumed man's likeness, and has been taken as a man," what do we see on this face? On the one hand, while seeing Christ, we of course see the Father. ("Who has seen me has seen the Father. How can you say 'Show me the Father?' Do you not believe that I am in the Father and that the Father is in me?") On the other hand, except for his return this side of the multi-faceted Revelation, it remains established that "no one has ever seen God, but the only son of God, [he who is] turned toward the bosom of the Father, and constitutes the exegesis of him." Therefore, on Christ's face we always see the incomprehensible, but this time we see it definitively – in the authorized and definitive exegesis of his filial otherness, which is insurmountable since it is carnal. Inescapable, insoluble in its objectivity, a face of faces, other things *par excellence*, the perfect immanence of transcendence. Immanence and transcendence are henceforth reconciled with each other. The incomprehensible has become reality in us.

This leads to the second paradox. This Infinite has assumed and always assumes our flesh in its integrity without remainder; the incomprehensible Infinite has therefore taken flesh in our reason; our reason is henceforth to be found serving as an enclosure for the Infinite. It has therefore taken on a dimension which definitely and infinitely surpasses us. It henceforth ranks as the Infinite, despite our finiteness, or rather by virtue of it; it therefore appears to us in this sense, which is incomprehensible to us. Not because we no longer comprehend our reason, but because we suspect, and indeed we note, that it henceforth extends infinitely further than our representations, our calculations, our wishes and our desires, that it conceals a power of intelligibility, the limits of which escape us – or which at least cannot be reduced to what we imagine by it, but which is even more extreme.

When we speak of the endless progress of science, we suspect that there is much more than progress and science. It is the right of the Infinite to make itself, constantly, without respite, without rest, without attributable purpose, the official passenger of our poor, lurching rationality, which is henceforth in charge of a precariousness of reason which infinitely transcends that which could ever be imagined.

One does not object that an encompassment such as this could weigh down our reason with pretensions and irrational pressures, or could lead it astray into an ideological or imaginary delirium of an illusory "new age" which is just as dangerous. This is because what has taken flesh in our reason, the Infinite in the form of the incomprehensible, has demanded a name – which is precisely that of the very term which the wisdom of the Greeks assigned to the rigor of thought and the sense of things. The Infinite, which has taken flesh in our finite flesh, demands the very name from which our reason emerges. Reason has taken flesh in our reason. Only this can claim the title, which is elsewhere misused, of the "Great Reason." And in its way, philosophy has never ceased to justify this claim, by basing itself on it in order to read of rationality in history, as far as its most overt contingencies, by practicing the work of this concept there. As regards our formal logic, our mathematical computations, our quantifications and our models, our hypotheses and even our ideological deliriums, we remain haunted by the . . . Infinite in him, which is henceforth incarnate in our reason. If in our rationality we not only carry the comprehensible, but also the incomprehensible, if we are henceforth no longer able to keep it within the limits of that which we understand in the manner of objects, if it does not cease to make us aspire to all ambitions, for better or for worse, it is that whether we want it or not, we remain inhabited by it. It is necessary to possess lucidity in order to conclude that Christology is a matter of epistemology. The historians of science have abundantly verified this. It remains to contemporary philosophers to admit it.

Man is Incomprehensible to Himself

We can now approach the second question: even though, in the exceptionally defined case of God, the Infinite could be thought of as incomprehensibility, what consequence can be derived from this? What domain of contemporary rationality would still have need of these kinds of considerations, which are of admissible rigor when limits are exceeded, but which are of no use when the preoccupation is with a need for substantial reinforcement in research programs in what are termed the "basic" sciences? What science would need to take seriously the epistemological, the incomprehensible, side of the coin, the ontological face of which is called the Infinite? Returning to our starting point, it could be replied that all sciences worthy of their respective methodologies have dealings with the Infinite. But the question here is of something else – of the incomprehensible. However, the progress of every science takes place in the line of battle where it confronts that which, until then, remained incomprehensible, in order to render it comprehensible. It is therefore not only a question of a heuristic, temporary incomprehensibility, which is always assumed to be reducible to the finite. What matters is the definitive incomprehensible, for what can we say about it except that it does not form part of the rational domain and must disappear in the outer darkness, where there will be tears and grinding of teeth? Or rather, where there will never be any, lost as they are in the silence of infinite space.

Nothing is this simple, however. If, as we have seen, the Infinite lives within us and constitutes us as such, the incomprehensible therefore inhabits us also – it has become us. We are ourselves the incomprehensible which is nearest to ourselves. In fact, there is nothing astonishing in this paradox: the nearest remains the most difficultly accessible, the most far away. Firstly, this is because our incomprehensibility to ourselves results directly from the incomprehensibility of the Infinite, where God reveals himself in our flesh. Indeed, according to an impeccable argument of Gregory of Nyssa, if one admits that God created us, mankind who is nothing less than "as his icon and in his resemblance"; if, on the other hand, divine essence by definition remains "unknowable" to us, then our own "nature in terms of our spirit" must also "escape knowledge." In short, the honor of receiving his essential definition from an iconic reference to the Infinite implies man's incomprehensibility – and a double title. It does this because an icon of the Infinite bears the mark of the Infinite by resemblance, and therefore becomes incomprehensible; it is in this sense that Descartes recognizes himself as an infinite Will, which is therefore unintelligible to his own finite understanding, because he admits "that I bear some image and likeness of God." Man's incomprehensibility therefore results firstly from his likeness to the Infinite. Secondly, his incomprehensibility results from the fact that no finite image can equal his infinite model; or, to quote Dionysius the Areopagite, "Man is never like his icon" and his incomprehensibility results from the fact that by definition he is not able faithfully to resemble the Infinite. In short, as a necessarily inadequate image of the original Infinite, man firstly becomes incomprehensible because he is given an excess of the Infinite, and secondly because there is a deficiency of the Infinite in him. However, what matters here is not the vicissitudes of the *imitatio Christi*, the salvific concern of only the Christians, but the quasi-transcendental imprint with which the Infinite marks the finite. How do we recognize that man is a god (in the sense in which a picture is immediately recognized as being "a Cézanne" or "a Piero della Francesca")? By its incomprehensible character, the signature of its original icon, the Infinite.

This result – our reason includes incomprehensibility because our essence bears the picture and the likeness of the Infinite, and therefore of the incomprehensible – leads to the elucidation of several difficulties. It firstly becomes intelligible that no anthropology can ever explain the nature of man. Pascal said: "If he boasts I humble him. If he humbles himself I praise him. And I contradict him always. Until he understands that he is an incomprehensible monster" – a phenomenon, therefore, which cannot be grasped. We can also hear this from other voices: that which metaphysics has little by little constructed in the name of "man" doubtless only achieves the status, or at least we suspect this with Foucault, of a drawing which is sketched in the sand, and which is erased in the rising tide of nihilism. For all knowledge, even rigorous knowledge which has been won by the "human sciences," can, by the very definition of the scientific method, only relate to the objects which the respective methods of these sciences produce each time. However, these objects – models of logic, principles of linguistics, psychic pulses, decision-making processes, laws of genesis of perception, etc. – even by generously granting them an apodicticity which is nevertheless problematical, can only ever attain, at best, that which can be universalized, modeled, and measured by man. In short, there is this thin coat, even though it is not limited by what can be made objective in me or in you, but which is not you, nor me, nor anyone who is humanly of man. All that the human sciences will teach me (and they instruct me more every day) will always relate to the object, which can be universalized, constituted, and reproduced, which they will have, certainly more and more subtly, substituted for me and my very self, which is irreducible and unrepeatable. Between I who remain, with myself only, and all these objects and objective parts of me, there stretches an impassable chasm, which Husserl called "the most fundamental difference between ways of being, the most cardinal of which, in general, is that between conscience and reality"; in short between the incomprehensible I that I am and the things that I understand. We recognize the stamp of the incomprehensible in us, which shows our consubstantial Infinite.

Therefore, it is not only a matter of admitting, with John Chrysostom, that "we do not really know the essence of our own soul; rather, it is not known to us in any way," which is a simple acknowledgment of an empirical difficulty, and which is perhaps surmountable by a more rigorous science. It is a matter of drawing a conclusion from the efforts, which are as grandiose as they are fruitless, of modern metaphysics in order to designate what I really think when I utter the words "I think." This impossibility does not only result from going from "I think" to the potential certainty of "I am" – which is another, even more problematical ambition – but from the simple intellection, or even the representation, of Being which is limited by only uttering what is apparently the simplest and most paltry statement, "I am." This is according to Descartes, who calls it a "thing" without succeeding in establishing that it is indeed like a substance, and according to Spinoza, who reduces it to the body, of which he remains without any further idea, and Malebranche, who admits, without quibbling, that we have no idea of our soul. From which Kant drew the inevitable conclusion concerning the nature of our thinking essence: "we can establish nothing other than the simple representation *I*, which in itself is entirely empty of content, and of which one can never say that it is a concept, but [which is] a simple conscience which accompanies all concepts." In short, it is an accident of objectivity. Psychoanalysis, by introducing the unconscious into the core of this conscience, which is already incomprehensible in itself, only takes this paradox to its end.

Man's incomprehensibility to himself in these terms often passes either for a defeat of metaphysical reason, which is to be deplored, or for the liberation of post-metaphysical thought, which is to be applauded. An alternative such as this indubitably misses the essential point: with the final denial of any representable idea of *I*, there is firstly no success, either fortunate or unfortunate, which is achieved by metaphysics, but there is the forced or spontaneous recognition of the rational fact that incomprehensibility entirely determines the very reason which any *I* worthy of its humanity puts into effect. And in this incomprehensibility (or even in our incomprehension of this incomprehensibility), we must recognize that we can only and must only think in the Infinite, which is where we are, where we live, and where we breathe. And, if ever we dreamed of knowing ourselves (of representing ourselves, and therefore of understanding ourselves like an object), then we would come up against the freely uttered warning of Paul: "If it seems to someone that he is someone [of being, *aliquid esse*], as he is nothing [nothing of Being, *nihil*], he is himself mistaken. We are not a being, even a privileged one, because we come from the icon of the unknowable, beyond all being and beyond all beingness, and must return there in order ultimately to have access to ourselves. Finally, it is necessary to take seriously the fact that "I am another."

This consubstantial incomprehensibility to a reason which is saturated with the Infinite could be found in other cases which are just as completely remote from us: our fellow human beings, the temporality of our birth (much more than that of our death), and also the splendor of the visible and the sweetness of this world of flesh. But can nothing be said of the *what* that should be – in short, if it is a question of *what*, this *what* itself, which was rightly called *das Mystics* by Wittgenstein? Undoubtedly, we can say nothing about it if language only speaks of objects in the objectivity of its predication. But perhaps we must ourselves learn to speak, and therefore to think, otherwise than in accordance with objectivity. Because our reason, surrounded by the Infinite, could also perhaps, with care, prudence, and reverential fear, address mystical things in a mystical manner, in the saintly manner of the saints (Gregory of Nazianzus). For what is more holy in us than that we are ourselves incomprehensible?

Resisting the Auto-Objectivation of Man

There remains, however, a final objection which is a test of good sense: what interest is there in wanting to visualize the incomprehensible as it is, at any price? What is to be gained by it? Can one even genuinely attain this, or is it a poor illusion of the Infinite?

A first answer, at least, goes without saying. Was it not a mistake to visualize the incomprehensible – and therefore to visualize it by the only way possible, "the very sensation of incomprehensibility," because reason denies all access to God – as the final question of our infinite horizon? This is because the danger with regard to the knowledge of God never resides in his incomprehensibility, which is the inevitable effect of the ontological Infinite in the epistemological, but resides in the insane illusion of pretending to understand him. Indeed, to postulate that "the human mind has an adequate knowledge of the eternal and infinite essence of the essence of God," results in access to the incomprehensible being led astray in the form of a commonplace conceptual idol. In the simple case of the recurrent temptation of metaphysics: embracing a fundamental idea within the grasp of the concept so as to transform it into an object.

However, this first answer immediately puts us on the route to another, more general answer. If "the sensation of incomprehensibility," far from denying access to knowledge of God, opens up this access, it is because it keeps us from understanding him like an object and incites us to approach him without understanding him, to see him without subjecting him to the attention of our gaze (*intuitus*). Moreover, this attitude of non-objective knowledge – real knowledge, but not of an object, or even of a non-object – is not only appropriate, as has been explained above, for the question of God, but is appropriate in the same way for the question of others. If to know others requires me to admit that they are others like myself, then, precisely in order to approach them in this manner, I must forgo transforming them into an object, since, as another me, they are not objectified but possibly objectify the remainder of what is knowable. In order to know others as another *I*, I must recognize them as an exception to objectivation, since I myself only make myself felt as an *I* by excepting myself from the objectivation which I carry out. Consequently, others, just like God, only become accessible to me as an exception to the objectivation which elsewhere is always possible and is sometimes desirable. Others share with God the privilege – which is by no means a fault – of only disclosing themselves to a "sensation of incomprehensibility" as an object.

Therefore, considering these two occurrences of the privilege of incomprehensibility, why not consider the possibility of a third? Am I not, myself, threatened with being comprehended as an object? In fact, the sciences which are termed "human" sciences, just like those termed "basic" sciences, never cease to propose their attempts to me, which are always more powerful, more coercive, and therefore more attractive, and which are aimed at ultimately knowing me as an object – by formal linguistics, by the "sciences of the mind," by the theory of action or decision, by experimental psychology, by neurology, by genetics, by economics, or by sociology. Certainly, any reader of Kant knows how to counter this: the determination of the empirical me will never enable the transcendental *I* to be attained, and even less to be known; that transcendental *I* which alone is precisely that which thinks, as a thinking mind upstream of the imagined mind. But this fitting answer, as definitive as it remains, can scarcely resist the authority of science which has developed and has proclaimed itself. Moreover, it is not in fact a question of the authority of models or of ideological intimidation. The rise in the power (which moreover is only beginning) of man's objectivation by himself, namely his self-degradation in the public eye to the rank of an object amongst others, would quite simply remain unintelligible, and would even be a matter of a demoniacal excess of self-hatred, if it did not follow the metaphysical accomplishment of the principle of sufficient reason, as is definitively put into effect by the essence of this technique: there is nothing which reason can and must account for which is an exception to this, including man. Therefore, in the name of reason reduced to the principle of reason, and reduced therefore to universal calculation, man must account for man himself. There is indubitably a contradiction to what the thinking mind itself calculates as a visualized thought, like an object. But there was the same contradiction in defining God as *causa sui*, since nothing can differ from itself by at the same time becoming its effect and its cause. Although Descartes did not hesitate to defy this formal contradiction (which he lucidly admitted), in order to extend the principle of causality (the tangential anticipation of the principle of reason) even to God. If the Infinite, God himself, at least in his metaphysical sense, is not once allowed to make exception to the *principium reddendae rationis*, how can the finite, i.e., man, elude this today? This question, like a threat which has come from the depths of modernity, overhangs what we call, more in imprecise hope than with guiding criteria, postmodernity – in other words what is unfolding at the turn of this millennium.

What is the position to be held in the face of this expanding empire of the *principium reddendae rationis*? There is one only: to contest radically that to explain constitutes the highest degree of reason – reason itself, and reason above all, remains without any other explanation which it would have to make (and to whom?): reason remains without reason. We must insist that reason, taken in its formality, namely in its Infinite, surpasses its ambition to explain objects, whilst reducing all that can be known to that which can be objectivized and which as a whole can be synthesized or constructed, in short to that which is comprehensible. In a word, we must think of the Infinite as being consubstantial with reason, which gives it right of access even to the incomprehensible. The right, therefore the duty. In some forms of knowledge, reason has the duty, because it has the right, to know the manner of incomprehensibility. Which forms? We have already met them: God, then – valid even for those who are perturbed by the question of God – others and the *I*. No one can be forced to consider the question of God seriously if he denies this question. But no one can avoid, as optional questions, the questions of others and of I. Moreover, our thesis will be at least this: no one can approach this question with the least hope of making one step of progress without admitting that reason deals with what cannot be inobjectivized, which is therefore the incomprehensible. Incomprehensibility, the formal reason for the Infinite, stands as the unique rampart against the deadly imperialism of sufficient reason. Sufficient reason, whose sufficiency can only limit reason and forbid us access to ourselves.

"Know yourself!" enjoined the oracle of Delphi. But he was obviously not asking us to know ourselves as objects according to the principle of sufficient reason. Perhaps, as in the anticipation of another, he was already suggesting that, of ourselves, we have to know the incomprehensible which henceforth lives among us.

The formal reason for the Infinite would then state that "man infinitely surpasses man," and therefore "that without this mystery, the most incomprehensible of all, we are incomprehensible to ourselves." In the two millennia since the Infinite has met with us, the time has undoubtedly come to admit the incomprehensibility in us.

Translated by A. J. Wickens

Note

1 See, on this tradition, L. Sweeney, *Divine Infinity in Greek and Modern Thought*, New York, Peter Lang, 1992.

CHAPTER 24
Religions as Conventions

Joseph S. O'Leary

Joseph O'Leary's work leaves no room for doubt as to his personal commitment. He writes passionately and with an uncanny intellectual control of his own rhetoric. He is a man of conviction who strongly argues a case in a mode that verges upon, but never quite falls into, polemic. The following essay is a case in point. However, in order to assess why he writes in this manner we have to turn to the task he set himself in his first book, *Questioning Back: The Overcoming of Metaphysics in Christian Tradition* (Minneapolis, MN, 1985). As the title of the book suggests, and like several other scholars whose work is represented in this volume (John Caputo, Jean-Luc Marion, and Jean-Yves Lacoste), O'Leary works out of a phenomenological legacy bequeathed by Heidegger (and Nietzsche): the overcoming of the ontotheological position. Indeed, O'Leary coedited one of the first books to treat the God-question in Heidegger's work systematically (see *Heidegger et la question de Dieu*). Interestingly, perhaps significantly, O'Leary is also, like many of these other theologians, a Catholic. Several Catholics (particularly the French) have seen phenomenology as a resource for doing theology. In O'Leary's first book the overcoming of metaphysics is viewed as essential in order to address the contemporary crisis of the Christian faith. Fundamental to rethinking the faith is a certain deconstruction of Christianity's concepts and categories; the recognition that all truths are conventional, not unmediated revelation (O'Leary shares this perspective with Don Cupitt, among others represented in this volume). The truly distinctive aspect of O'Leary's project with respect to this rethinking is not the rejection of Christian faith (in an espousal of some post-Christian religion without religion), but the posing of a question to that faith from within it: "what does fidelity to the Christian tradition entail today?" His concern is with "the claims of orthodoxy" and he pursues a continuous dialogue with orthodox theologians like Augustine, Martin Luther, and Karl Barth. Various forms of Christian certitude are undermined in his

> deconstruction of metaphysics, along with the formalizing of truth claims in terms of prescriptive dogmas, and the policing of those claims by various forms of traditionalism and fundamentalism. Christian theology is thus implicated in an open-ended and ongoing questioning, conducted within cultural horizons which render the knowledges it produces contingent and therefore revisable.
>
> In his long-awaited second volume, *Religious Pluralism and Christian Truth* (Edinburgh, 1996, originally published in French in 1994), O'Leary pushes further his post-metaphysical approach to Christian theology by relating Christian truth claims to what he terms an "interreligious space." This space is composed of the different visions of salvation and reality found in other religious traditions. As in *Questioning Back*, Derrida's thinking is given methodological prominence, but this time O'Leary develops Derrida's construal of "dissemination" alongside a new theoretical position: that of the second-century Buddhist teacher Nagarjuna (O'Leary has been teaching at universities in Tokyo for several years).
>
> Several of the themes of the present essay are recognizable from his earlier work, as is its characteristically energetic style. O'Leary remarks that his second volume will be followed by a third, so that his three books will constitute a "critical trilogy, a quasi-Kantian 'prolegomenon to any future theology'." We still await this third volume, but "Religions as Conventions" no doubt paves the way.

the truth rushes in to fill the gaps left by
Its sudden demise so that a fairly accurate record of its activity is possible
John Ashbery

Since I regard postmodernism as merely an acceleration of the modern (as Fredric Jameson and Slavoj Žižek argue) and since, unlike the proponents of Radical Orthodoxy, I believe that modernity is an irreversible breakthrough for the human spirit that may require a fuller development and a more secure grounding but that it is futile to call radically into question, the theme I shall meditate on here – namely the conventionality of religion – is one that I consider indistinguishably modern and postmodern. If modernity stands for political freedom, intellectual integrity and fearlessness, ethical coming of age, then it itself stands in judgment over its self-betrayal in consumerist trivializations of freedom, rationalistic parodies of reason, and the subtle transformation of technological power into a new slavery. If there is a more radical crisis of modernity, it is the fruit of that critical radicality intrinsic to the modern project, and its resolution can only come through pursuing the dialectic farther, not by a step back to the premodern. Heidegger's step back is really a step forward, in struggle with the most sinister possibility uncovered by modernity, namely nihilism. Barth attempted something similar in theology, but was overtaken by restorationist instincts. Despite Schleiermacher, Harnack,

Troeltsch, Tyrrell, one is left wondering whether any theology has adequately confronted modernity.

The modern sense of the relativity and historical embeddedness of religious traditions, virulent already in the Enlightenment (Hume, Voltaire), leads to an awareness of the historical relativity of Enlightenment values themselves. Foucault's diagnosis that reason itself is mortal, that each new epoch consigns to unintelligibility the basic frameworks of its predecessor, represents a characteristic self-undercutting twist within modernity. Religions have to some extent come to terms with the modern "critique of historical reason" (Dilthey) thanks to the highly inventive discipline of hermeneutics, which stretches very far what can count as a legitimate reinterpretation of past doctrines, thus saving them from obsolescence. Now the hermeneutics of religious traditions is being forced to take a further step, not only by poststructuralist theorists but by an increasing awareness of religious pluralism in contemporary culture. That step is the full recognition of the contingent nature of all religions as human constructs born of particular cultural contexts and intimately marked by the prejudices and peculiarities of those contexts. Foucault's question is whether reason can live with its own relativity. A truly modern faith, also, has to live with the awareness that there are no privileged viewpoints, and that religious constructions, just like philosophical or scientific ones, must sink or swim on the basis of their particular and always limited merits, buffeted by their rivals in the sea of history. Religions are fragile human language-games, always slipping into obsolescence. In Buddhist terms, they are conventional, world-ensconced constructs (*saṃvṛti-satya*), skillful means, which can in certain circumstances convey a sense of ultimacy (*paramārtha-satya*) or conduce to spiritual liberation, but which become agents of enslavement if they claim ultimate status for themselves.

De-absolutizing Religion

There are many reasons why it is salutary to deepen this sense of the conventionality of religion. The most obvious is the need to defuse the various forms of religious absolutism and fundamentalism that wreak such havoc on the planet. From a Buddhist perspective, identity, including religious identity, is a provisional construct. To reify it, cling to it, and hate those who threaten it, is to be ill from the three poisons of craving, aversion, and delusion. Threatened identity projects demonized others: for nationalism, it is the hereditary foe, the unclean alien, and the traitor; for Christians, it has been the Jew, the heathen, and the heretic. Religion has very often made itself the absolute to which it would bear witness. The dynamic of authentic faith (or authentic wisdom) is the reverse of this, and operates a prophetic (or enlightened) sifting of means from ends, the conventional from the ultimate. Release from the "mind-forg'd manacles" of absolutism requires the insight that neither individuals nor nations nor creeds possess a stable identity, unchanging throughout history. What they have instead is a story, a trajectory, in which they are constantly reinventing their identity. Religions, in particular, are constantly tinkering with their own story, and when through historical research they become aware that they are doing so, then the radical contingency of the choices founding them comes to light.

The sense of conventionality sheds retrospective light on our traditions and identifies points at which some now archaic category was placed on the pedestal of dogmatic definition, where it lingers on to numb the mind, or points at which some local prejudice became a timeless moral prescription, at immense cost in human suffering. On the latter front, it looks as if the Catholic church now faces the prospect of having to contradict its solemn teachings on such matters as homosexuality and contraceptives. These are topics that leave little room for the diplomatic vagueness that can mask change in dogma, for they concern not nebulous notions such as substance or hypostasis, but precise identification of defined acts as intrinsically wrong. A clear confession of long-entrenched error here would entail the realization that it is time for the church to extricate itself from the business of precise moral prescription. Religious revelations are not the source of new moral precepts, but merely mark the ultimacy implicit in morality. This can lead to the absolutization of unenlightened moral attitudes, or to their gradual correction by the influence of the ultimate values.

In traditional societies, religious institutions claim to legitimate social and legal institutions, but they do so chiefly by referring the socially established conventions to the ultimate, figured as the Law of the Father. When a religion claims to judge from outside, to reshape, or to add a concrete supplement to the conventional sociopolitical order that secretes it, in fact it uses a rhetoric of law or prophecy that this order has itself supplied. The reference of the conventional to the ultimate has a purifying, clarifying effect on the conventional, made aware of its conventionality, and enabled to differentiate more radically between what is arbitrary and what points to ultimacy within its texture. The commandment of love thus emerges out of the thicket of Hebrew law as an index of ultimacy. Ethical revelation has in a sense no content, or rather its content is of a comprehensive transcendental order that resists encapsulation in easily grasped slogans. The revealed adds nothing to the conventional, except to bring it into ultimate perspective. Religious fantasy abounds in tall tales, but when one distills from them the mature religious imagination, it consists in a rich vision of things as they are. The impression that revelation has no content, that there are no specifics in its call, is based on the reality that revelation is merely the remarking of a given cosmic, moral, and social order in its conventional dependently arisen state as a vehicle of access to the real. If religion ventures to correct and challenge that order, it is in light of the latter's own intrinsic orientation to ultimacy. Religion never teaches the world from outside but is the emergence of the ultimacy secreted within the world.

That is one reason why even the inspiration behind the New Testament does not effect a sudden conversion of the moral codes of the culture into a new, pure religious code. Enlightened awareness does not immediately purge its conventional basis of all unenlightened features. The conventional basis remains a vessel of clay, bearing all the prejudices and fixations of the culture that produced it. Treasuring the traditions that have yielded a vision of the ultimate aspect of things, people naturally tend to confer on these traditions themselves an ultimate status. Thus ancient errors and immoralities, enshrined in supposedly inerrant sacred texts, are propagated to later ages as divine wisdom that must override the protests of reason and conscience. If religion has been, as Enlightenment crusaders claimed, a plague to the human race, it is because of this confusion of ends and means, this transfer of ultimacy to the conventional. To cure religion what is needed is a discerning critique of religious conventions, which can both appreciate their value as paths to ultimacy and see their poverty, flimsiness, and provisionality. Religious education confined to one tradition cannot attain this critical perspective. Only when young people are taught to see their own set of religious conventions in the broader context of human religious creativity can they be inoculated against the viruses of absolutism and fundamentalism.

If the churches accept this recontextualization of their moral authority, their dogmatic authority will also need to be rethought. Authoritative dogmatic definition can be seen as a human effort to clarify the truth of faith according to the best lights of a given period, which are drawn on ad hoc and in a pragmatic way (though the later glorification of a dogma will thoroughly occlude its humble origins). Seen thus, doctrine does not lose its clarificatory value, but ceases to be an instrument of tyranny over mind or conscience. Such a demystified account of authority seems compatible with the models of religious teaching that we find in scripture.

The products of fourth- and fifth-century thought which provide the basic framework of the Christian dogmatic system have become to a large extent an oppressive *caput mortuum*. It is not so much that one would wish to see them as false or mistaken, as that their relationship to truth, to reality, has come to seem oblique and opaque. They represent good theological work within the conventions of the time, but these conventions have been shattered on a modern sense of ultimacy. They are no longer conventions that point to ultimacy, but rather point away from it. To give an example: the divinity of Jesus Christ is an idea that has developed into a cumbersome and baroque discourse on the God-Man; this needs to be recalled to its phenomenological basis, and perhaps translated into Buddhist language as follows: the divinity of Christ means that the dependently arisen story of Jesus, in his historical connections with Israel and the Christian community, is a privileged conventional vehicle for attunement to divine ultimacy. Squaring this with the claims of orthodoxy is a delicate theological game, whose importance I am far from underestimating, but the hysterical nannyism of current watchdogs has done nothing to clarify this task.

In Buddhism there appear to be two levels of conventional truth. One is the everyday reliance on substantive understandings of the self and of things for the purpose of conducting the practical business of life. The other is the speculative level, at which this substantializing mindset is deconstructed and the mutual conditionality, and consequent emptiness of own-nature, of the self and all things is taught. This teaching points to ultimate truth, but is itself a conventional means. Within Christianity the effort to formulate the ultimate radical truth about God and grace produces first the scriptural kerygma, with its subversive thrust, then the dogmatic clarification of the ontological implications of this kerygma, and finally a set of teachings which combines the existential immediacy of the kerygma with the scope of dogmatic principle: such are the teachings of Augustine on grace and of Luther on justification, meta-dogmatic criteria for making sense of dogmas and for re-rooting dogmas in the thrust of the biblical kerygma. All this labor on conventional diction is led by an intuition of the ultimate. But its efficacy in pointing to ultimacy is not guaranteed. A conjunction of certain words and a certain historical period may be a powerful vehicle of ultimacy. But as the period passes the words lose their electrifying clarity and immediacy, and the conventional language is now sensed to point to a pseudo-ultimate, and to hold the spirit back in postures that no longer correspond to its present existential possibilities. That fate seems to have overtaken the bulk of talk on God and creation, sin and grace, so that, for example, the Lutheran–Catholic consensus on justification appears as an exercise in rearranging archaic ideas, no longer real enough to be worth fighting about. The failure of great artists such as Claudel, Eliot, and Stravinsky to breathe convincing new life into the traditional vehicles of the Christian vision of ultimacy can only mean that the task itself is impossible. To find ultimacy today we must seek its bases in securely established contemporary conventionalities, warranted by science, historical scholarship, and real life experience as registered and analyzed in the arts. Only out of our reappropriation of our real world can new languages of ultimacy be born.

All formulated religious or philosophical truths are conventional truths, not ultimate truth. Religious language has the specific function of awakening an awareness of the limits of the conventional and a thirst for the ultimate. It is a language practiced at the borders of language. No matter how realistic it becomes, religious language always refers whatever topic it deals with to the ultimate, and thus signals the conventionality of that topic. The religious act summarizes and symbolizes my whole being-in-the-world. It redoubles the conventions of life: sacrifice redoubles gift, sacred meals redouble everyday meals. Nietzsche noted this parasitism of religion. But the redoubling reveals the conventions as conventions, marking them as such before the ultimate. The ultimate is not the absolute or the transcendent, it is merely the truly real. The ultimate is the reality of the conventional. The conventional goes through the looking-glass of religious representation to discover itself as conventional and so come closer to its ultimate reality. Yet the conventional base must be as real as possible. To provide a shoddy or archaic or sentimentalized conventional basis for religious insight, on the pretext that religion aims beyond the conventional in any case, is to ensure a treacherous hollowness in the rhetoric of ultimacy.

The ability not to take the conventional world with undue seriousness can be invaluable when it comes to breaking the deadlocks that arise from tendencies to absolutization. Human and religious maturity sometimes demands that we swallow the unswallowable, forgive the unforgivable. If the new parliament in Northern Ireland succeeds, it will be a living monument to the wisdom of such courage. The forgiving spirit that enables one to do business with those one abhorred as evil is facilitated by a sense of relativity. Human evil is always a situational matter, and part of the situation is that the one who condemns is rarely himself free of involvement in some comparable evil (see Romans 2). Forgiveness of sins deconstructs the absolute categorization of the other as sinner and constructs new perspectives within which the other can be dealt with more flexibly. In fact the Ulster peace-keepers have gone beyond the paradigm of forgiveness. In active forgetting, they have jettisoned tired identities and put their hands to the wheel of present history. This is a transgressive, almost blasphemous liberation, especially in an age of vengeful political correctness. Perhaps all religions need to find such freedom from inherited paradigms, treating them as useful conventions that can be put on the back burner when they become dysfunctional.

Sin has a near-absolute status in traditional Christianity and "conviction of sin" is the essential first step in conversion and reconciliation. But supposing we realize that this entire scenario of sin and forgiveness is only one way of acting out the relation of our conventional world and gracious ultimacy. "Sin is a Jewish feeling and a Jewish invention" (Nietzsche, *The Gay Science*, paragraph 135); it belongs to a contingent, historically situated language. Other religions offer different scenarios, and none of these have absolute status. They are all imaginative skillful means for dealing with the perplexities of existence and attuning them to the ultimate in a healing way. Pauline Christianity is a magnificent vision, but it has had too long and successful a run in the West, and has produced a number of morbid offshoots – Calvinist nightmares about predestination, Pascalian misanthropy, Kierkegaardian masochism. If we view it as a conventional language-game, we do not lose the sense of ultimacy with which it is charged, but we are no longer imprisoned in it; we keep the Spirit (the ultimate) but are free in regard to the letter (the conventional), as Paul himself would say. Indeed, authentic voices of ultimacy can only be heard when they cease to be authoritarian megaphones and are heard instead as fragile human voices reaching out into gracious mystery.

Pluralistic Revelation

A religious revelation is an encounter with ultimate reality. But it always occurs at a given time and place, within the frameworks of understanding built up by previous tradition. The element of ultimacy in the revelation may be beyond criticism, but it cannot be siphoned out of the totality of representations and practices in which it is embedded, and these are exposed to the same questions as every other human historical construction. Religions depend on language and they are constantly changing and developing. No authority can arrest the course of change or reanchor language in a fixed, transparent reference to ultimate truth. Rather than sigh for the transparent paradisal language of logocentric myth, or attempt its simulacrum in a frozen canonical speech, religions have to recognize that their claims to ultimacy are irremediably entangled in linguistic and historical contingency. As apophatic theologians have always felt, it is only in a thorough confession of this broken, dispersed, and incomplete condition that religious language can give its testimony to the ultimate.

This recognition releases faith from idolatry, that is, from fixated religious representations which divert and thwart the opening of the believing mind to the ultimate. Furthermore, when the faiths rediscover their situatedness in history and culture, and the makeshift and provisional status of any language that they may use, a space is opened for inter-faith encounter on a new basis of modest inquiry. Each of the religious traditions can say to the others: "Your long duration, your vitality, and the fruits you have borne, testify that you, like us, are a vehicle of access to ultimate, gracious, life-giving reality. But just as we see you as a flimsy, myth-laden construction, you are equally justified in seeing us in the same way. Help us, as we help you, to reshape our language so that it can be a more functional and credible vehicle of ultimacy in the contemporary context we share."

Barth's sympathy for Hegel is based on their common acceptance of the historical and cultural contextuality of human thought and language, with all the relativization this entails, and their common aspiration to think through this, dialectically, to an "absolute" position – a confident resumption of the totality of the tradition in a key suited to the times. But the most comprehensive and thoroughly reflected reappropriation of tradition is the one that most keenly realizes the conventional status of traditional discourse, its tangentiality in relation to ultimacy. Barth would perhaps agree that the origins of religious traditions are impure in that they involve many archaic conceptions that later ages are saddled with as a hermeneutic burden, and that a religious tradition never comes to express itself in a full and pure way, in some golden age of its development (for wherever we look in history we find the same murkiness, the same hybridization, the same obsolescence). He might accept that there is a pluralism between the different epochs and even within each epoch, which cannot be ironed out to yield a single transparent vision. He could agree that to make sense of the history of religions the first thing to realize is its thoroughly human character, and not to expect of it the providential order and luminous unfolding that is typical of myth but not of real history.

But having admitted all this Barth would reserve one corner of history as the place of a privileged breakthrough to ultimacy, which is somehow immunized against the impact of the insights just mentioned. Yet the dialectic between the human-all-too-human conventionalities of religion and the ultimacy of revelation that Barth finds in Christianity may be expected to be operative also in the case of the other historical vehicles of ultimacy, albeit with specific distinguishing features. A generalized, open-ended Barthianism, like a generalized, open-ended Hegelianism, can retrieve Barth's power of systematic integration and give it a larger field of exercise. Instead of being a defensive fortress, Barthian reflection can become a pluralistic plateau, in which all religions are dialectically unfolded in their interplay of conventional and ultimate. To see religions as human constructs does not exclude the possibility that they are vehicles of revelation. It may be precisely in their very fragility as historical constructs that they best serve the reality of revelation. What we call a religious revelation can be conceived as the emergence of ultimacy within a given tradition of conventional representations. Revelation need not consist in new information or the happening of a supernatural event that cuts across the normal unfolding of the human quest of ultimacy. It could be understood as a moment in the laborious development of a tradition of religious words, concepts, stories, and practices when things click into place, when a luminous perspective emerges, which both perfects the pre-given religious framework (through clarifying the ultimate sense of its conventional designations) and exceeds it (through an immediate tasting or touching of ultimacy that shows up all the conventions of discourse as "mere straw"). Just as "naturalist" theology accepts the texture of the universe as one in which no intervention of a divine causal agency appears, and in which such an intervention is in principle impossible, so a historically based view of religions excludes the actuality or possibility of a revelatory intervention from outside. Evolution is seamless in both cases. Such a viewpoint does justice to the naturalistic modern sense of the historical texture of religions, while resisting the skeptical and atheistic conclusions commonly drawn. It can respect the central events in the history of religions as breakthroughs to ultimacy.

Some tragic works paint a depressing picture of the world, and the spectator leaves the theater asking: "but is it true?" One asks this after Zola or Maupassant, not after Racine or Flaubert. For artists that have created a vision marked by ultimacy, debates about true and false fall aside. These artists have said nothing new, but this very "nothing" is what permits things to click into perspective in a breathtaking way. Analogously, a religion bothered by the obsessive question "is it true?" is one that has failed to establish its authority in the only way possible, by a breakthrough to ultimacy. A pseudo-religion, that begins as a faked rhetoric of ultimacy, might become a real religion if the rhetoric begins to work as a medium of ultimacy. Conversely, a true religion, forgetting its core vision and declining into rhetorical convention, might end up vainly insisting on its truth, when the propositions of its distinguished past have lost their connection with ultimacy.

We should think of ultimacy in adjectival rather than nominal terms. It is a quality of pristine religious insight, its character of unsurpassability, of being supremely, indubitably real. Awareness of the ultimate is immediate, luminous, blissful. But ultimacy is not merely a psychological trait of contemplative peak-experiences. It is the lighting-up of reality as such. Such a lighting-up may occur independently of developed religious traditions, for example in a spontaneous natural mysticism, or in the state of being in love. In any case ultimacy is always "ultimacy of" – it is not a thing, but the aspect of things when they come into their own, revealing their thusness.

Religious vision is simply the happening of ultimacy. If we convert the claims of individual religions into terms compatible with this description, we find a wide array of myths that can be taken as narrativization of insight into ultimacy. The resurrection narratives in the gospels, for example, could be "cashed" as signifying the emergence of the ultimate significance of Christ's life and death, a pneumatic lighting-up of the core reality they attested. The mythical scenes of annunciation, transfiguration, resurrection, ascension, second coming, serve only to mark the ultimate significance of the empirical career of Jesus in its total dependently arisen context. The breakthrough of ultimacy in the event of Jesus who became Christ, or in the event of Gautama who became Buddha, is not marked by the revelation of any radically new idea. All the elements of their teaching and action are drawn from a rich anterior tradition. But the elements fall into a new and luminous arrangement, solving the complexities of the tradition and relaunching it on a more fundamental and integral basis. Central emphases such as the notion of non-self in Buddhism or of death-and-resurrection in Christianity stamp the new movement with a radical style that frees it from subservience to the categories of preceding tradition. The new religion leaps to a place of freedom from which it can assess the categories of the past as pointers to its own privileged vision or as obstacles to it.

These founding leaps in religious tradition are not merely a breakthrough from one level of conventional insight to a deeper level of the same. They are a judgment on the entire mass of preceding tradition, seen as an accumulation oppressing whatever seeds of ultimacy it may have contained. They proceed under the sign of contradiction. The emergence of ultimacy is likely to be translated as an attack on tradition: Buddha's attack on *ātmavāda*, the Mahāyāna attack on Abhidharma, the Zen attack on reliance on scriptures, Muhammad's attack on trinitarianism, Luther's on Catholicism. The radical force and truth of these attacks derives from the contradiction between ultimacy and conventions that no longer serve it in a changed context. Doctrinal views are a matter for scholastic debate. Ultimacy takes little account of them. The breakthrough to ultimacy is never simply a confirmation of established doctrine. It re-envisions the old doctrines from a simpler and more radical vantage point, retaining only what resonates with the new sense of ultimacy and casting off as chaff what does not. This judgment is unanswerable from the level of convention. To defend trinitarianism against Islam one would have to show that trinitarian dogma is a defense of ultimacy just as much as Islamic monotheism is. That defense would have to be more a "showing" than a "saying." How limited the scope of argument in this realm is becomes clear when we recall that ultimacy is not merely an epistemological quality, but is experienced as salvific. The substance of a religion is its function, for a religion is exhaustively defined by the salvation it brings. "Salvation" means health (Greek *soteria*, Latin *salus*). The ultimacy in a religion is the springing up of new life, which casts aside the old conventions no longer functioning for health and healing, and generates new laws out of itself.

Over a number of centuries a religious path will be tried by many adepts who will approach in nearer or closer degree to the supremely real as envisaged by that path. Each path yields a distinctive mode of encounter. Within a given tradition the path undergoes slow modifications, and the encounter with ultimacy accordingly takes on a new cast: nirvana in early Buddhism has not quite the same character as enlightenment in Ch'an Buddhism; mystical union in Christianity takes a variety of complexions from Gregory of Nyssa to Teresa of Avila; the prophetic passion for justice has a very different cast in the theocracies of ancient Israel and in modern democracies. A changed world must bring some alteration in the mode of encounter with the ultimate.

There is of course a tension between the historical approach to religion, which finds a pluralism of culture-specific languages, irreducible to any common core, and the testimony of religious founders and mystics, who are convinced that they have seen the way things really are. Religious visionaries often become keenly aware of the flimsiness of their linguistic and conceptual constructions, yet their vision is not compromised or relativized by this insight. Does this mean that historical and cultural conditioning come to a halt in the higher realms of religious experience? But if ultimacy is always the ultimacy of a given conventional basis, this conventional basis should make a difference to the way in which ultimacy emerges. When Plotinus talks of the One, or when Buddhists talk of buddha-nature, or when Śaṅkara talks of Brahman, or when Augustine talks of the *internum aeternum*, the affinities between these discourses are so intense that one senses they are all treading the same realm. Yet the differences between them are not less striking. A whole world is concentrated in each of these namings of ultimacy, and the distinct physiognomy of that world is not eclipsed. Ultimacy in each tradition comes into view in reference to a different set of conventional representations. It is ultimacy as accessible from that particular conventional starting-point. Pure ultimacy, independent of any conventional perspective, is unimaginable.

The role of imagination in religious vision makes it porous to the world of art. Conversely, great works of art yield a sense of ultimacy. If one finds a breakthrough to ultimacy in the music of Mozart, that ultimacy is inseparable from the concrete texture of the musical writing. It is the clicking into perspective of the musical conventions mastered and perfected by Mozart. Aesthetic ultimacy is fully embedded in the artistic language that expresses it. Religious language, in contrast, signals its own inadequacy and points beyond itself to a revelation of ultimacy that surpasses language. The linguistic conventions clear the ground for the emergence of ultimacy, which both validates them and validates their sense of their own inadequation; the confident affirmative path and the modest apophatic path in negative theology are both validated and surpassed in a living encounter with ultimate reality, beyond affirmation and negation. Ultimacy deconstitutes conventional religious worlds, shows them up as flimsy fictions, yet again reconstitutes them as valid conventional vehicles of insight. In the world of art, ultimacy is always the ultimacy of the language in which it is expressed and cannot be imagined apart from this language. In religion, ultimacy also depends on conventional linguistic vehicles, yet in a more oblique and tangential way. Yet one cannot draw a clear dividing line between religion and art. The dialogue between religious ultimacy and aesthetic ultimacy would be an important part of a healthy culture of religious pluralism, especially at a time when for many art is the primary mode of access to ultimacy.

The formulated theses of given religious traditions are subject to critique and debate, though this is a task of daunting hermeneutical complexity when the debate is between views formulated in different epochs or in different traditions. But the happening of ultimacy within traditions is not a matter for the kind of comparison and differentiation practiced in logical debate. This happening is the kingpin of a religion's vitality, worth, and truth, and it is what lends their ultimate significance to the complex ideas and representations that the tradition generates. It includes an implicit critique of these terms insofar as they fail to conduce to the central vision. The constant polemic against suspected substantialism in the Buddhist schools or the suspicion of Hellenistic metaphysics in Christianity may be seen as defending the breakthrough to ultimacy against its reduction to a self-satisfied convention posing as ultimate.

Contradictions and comparisons between different breakthroughs of ultimacy depend on a distorting reification. A religion is its world grasped in its ultimacy, or opened to ultimacy in its distinctive style. One does not put entire worlds in contradiction. Within these worlds and between these worlds there will be quarrels about rival truth-claims. But truth-claims function on the conventional plane; at the level of ultimacy they fall silent, their purpose accomplished. Purging the conventional religious language of falsehood is an endless task, but its purpose is to keep the language serviceable for giving access to ultimacy. When the truth-claims become ends in themselves, as in many bitter historical debates, the perspective of ultimacy is already long forgotten. Theology should be pursued without odium, as a serious game, content to tend the garden of conventionality, and to ensure that its fragile products do not assume airs of self-sufficient substantiality that would make them an obstacle to the emergence of ultimacy.

Our religious awareness does seem to be undergoing a millennial "turn," call it modern or postmodern as you please, in which many an old truth is taking on a ghostly pallor. But as some certitudes die, new insights take their place. Our task is not to resist the evolutional process in which we are caught up, but to attune ourselves discerningly to its workings.

The above was written before the publication of the Vatican document Dominus Iesus, which I address in two forthcoming essays: "Towards a Buddhist Interpretation of Christian Truth" (in a volume on "Double Belonging," ed. Catherine Cornille, and "Emptiness and Dogma" (submitted to *Buddhist-Christian Studies*). For more light on the conventions/ultimacy dyad, so slippery in its logic but so pervasive in Indian thought, see Malcolm Eckel, Jnanagarbha's *Commentary on the Distinction Between the Two Truths* (State University of New York Press, 1987); Guy Newland, *The Two Truths* (Snow Lion Publications, 1992); Jay L. Garfield, *The Fundamental Wisdom of the Middle Way: Nagarjuna's Mulamadhyamakakarika* (Oxford University Press, 1995).

PART VI
Heideggerians

25	The Self-Saving of God	427
26	The Subject of Prayer: Unwilling Words in the Postmodern Access to God	444
27	The Christian Message and the Dissolution of Metaphysics	458

CHAPTER 25
The Self-Saving of God

Thomas J. J. Altizer

In a critical, even self-deprecating, article on his own work entitled "Altizer on Altizer," Altizer makes the following observation: "Despite the fact that Altizer completed a doctorate in the History of Religions at the University of Chicago, he is neither an historian nor an historian of religions. Instead he is an ersatz theologian, largely self-taught, and one who only employs the history of religions as a route into a non-theological theology. This theology is grounded in the death of God" (*Literature & Theology*, June 2001). Although internationally the development of death-of-God theology only emerged in the mid-1960s with the publication of *Radical Theology and the Death of God* (Harmondsworth, 1968) edited by Altizer and William Hamilton, many of the themes of Altizer's work were announced in books he published before this date. His explorations of Nietzsche's work, his interest in eschatology and concern with *homo religiosus* and the experience of negativity are all evident in his first book, *Oriental Mysticism and Biblical Eschatology* (1961) and the second part of his study *Mircea Eliade and the Dialectic of the Sacred* (1963). The early appraisal of dialectic is also significant, for it is the explicit investigation into Hegel's dialectic and its relation to the death-of-God which comes to the fore in two books published almost concurrently with the announcement of the new "mood" of radical death-of-God theology: *The Gospel of Christian Atheism* (London, 1966) and *The New Apocalypse: The Radical Christian Vision of William Blake* (East Lansing, MI, 1967, but actually written before *The Gospel of Christian Atheism*). Hegel is crucial for Altizer, enabling him to conceive of a theology of history, a doctrine of predestination in which the death-of-God features as a significant moment in a realized eschatology. The total loss of the divine gives way to an abandonment, to a Yes-saying which lies at the very center of the darkness announcing "a total and immediate presence" (*Total Presence*, New York, 1980).

In the preface to *Radical Theology and the Death of God* the "Radical Theology" of Hamilton and Altizer defined itself as "a form of Christianity coming to expression without a belief in God" and, significantly, "a contemporary development within Protestantism." It placed itself on a map which designated four sites of theological production, the three others being neo-orthodoxy, hermeneutics working out of the Bultmann School, and Process theology. The language of what they termed neither a movement nor a school but a "mood" or a "tendency" demonstrates what has been learnt both from earlier dialectical theology and the theology of culture that Tillich's voice still represented. They spoke of a cultural crisis and the experience in contemporary America of God as "hidden, absent, silent." As such Radical Theology was a new voice combining the liberal call for freedom, authenticity, and the integrity of the secular with the dialectical polemics of Gogarten and the attention to cultural symbolics in both Bultmann and Eliade. Of course, other "radical" forms of Christianity "doing-without theology" were evident at the same time: in Britain with John Robinson, in France with Teilhard de Chardin, and elsewhere in America with the work of Paul Van Buren. What is distinctive about Altizer's work is the way it developed a 1960s radical theology into a 1980s postmodern theology. Neither Hamilton nor Van Buren were able to do this, and, in Britain, Robinson's work only did it through being taken up and developed by Don Cupitt.

Altizer raises the question in "Altizer on Altizer" whether his 1980 book *Total Presence: The Language of Jesus and the Language of Today* might not be "the first theological book to discuss a postmodern theological situation?" Certainly Altizer is found now at the forefront of a group of radical American theologians who explicitly view their work as postmodern theology. These theologians – Mark C. Taylor, Charles Winquist, and Robert P. Scharlemann – came together in a volume entitled *Deconstruction and Theology* (New York, 1982) and later in *Theology at the End of the Century* (Charlottesville, VA, 1990) (see the introduction to Carl Raschke's essay, this volume, chapter 31). In these books, and in Altizer's work from 1980 through to his book *The Contemporary Jesus* (Albany, NY, 1997), there had been an attempt to respond theologically to a cultural situation viewed as the "'total realization of the crucified God' when ending is occuring everywhere and filling everything with silence" (*Theology at the End of the Century*).

The essay which follows is a chapter from Altizer's work on a new book. It picks up and develops many of the themes in his early work, but there is also something new here. The novelty is evident in the turn away from Hegel, Nietzsche, and Kierkegaard (his dialogue partners throughout until 1997) to new investigations and appropriations of Husserl's and Heidegger's work. No doubt something has been learnt here from the work of Winquist and Taylor, but although Heidegger is mentioned briefly in earlier books, Altizer has not explicitly worked with Heidegger's thinking. And this is the first time, to my knowledge, he has ever spoken at length about Husserl. What this development makes clear is Altizer's continuing imaginative and intellectual energies. The vision is constant, and the investigation, analysis, and appropriation for what he called "Christian atheism" continues.

THE SELF-SAVING OF GOD 429

Perhaps Heidegger's greatest treatise is his "Nihilism as Determined by the History of Being," the conclusion of his primal study of Nietzsche, which was written in the time of his own greatest crisis, 1944–5. Here Heidegger speaks with unusual force of "the default" (*das Ausbleiben*) of Being, a default that is the very destiny of Being, and yet Being saves itself in its default. This is the treatise in which Heidegger, in response to Nietzsche, gives us his deepest understanding of nihilism, a nihilism which he can now identify as the history of Being, and this is the very history in which Being saves itself. For Heidegger, this history is the history of metaphysics, one which determines the history of the Western era, but metaphysics thinks Being only in the sense of "the Being" as such, therefore Being itself is necessarily unthought in metaphysics, and as such metaphysics is nihilism proper. This is the history which comes to an end in Nietzsche's thinking, even if Nietzsche is the last metaphysical thinker, and it comes to an end in the "self-withdrawal" of Being, yet this self-withdrawal is the very advent of Being, and the abode of this event is: "*das Sein gibt*." That giving is finally the self-saving of Being, one proceeding from the withdrawal or self-concealing of Being, and the advent of the default of Being is the advent of the unconcealment of Being, one which is an essential occurrence of Being itself. This occurs in the final or apocalyptic age of the destitution of Being itself, wherein a closure of the holy occurs, and while Being itself now fails to appear, the disclosure of its default is an ultimate sign and seal of its own "self-saving."

Now the very symbol of the self-saving of God or Being is extraordinarily rare until the full advent of the modern world; perhaps it can be found in the ancient world only in Gnosticism, and above all so if a truly Gnostic redemption is the "self-saving" of the Godhead. Alone in the ancient world, Gnosticism could know a primordial fall in Godhead itself, wherein a devolution of deity occurs, an ultimately inner divine devolution, one embodying an ultimate tragedy within the Godhead itself, a tragedy wholly unknown in the pre-Gnostic world. This is the very devolution which is reversed by a redemption effecting the reintegration of the impaired Godhead, and if that is effected for Valentinian Gnostics by the Incarnation itself, this is an incarnation transforming everything whatsoever, and thereby Godhead itself becomes "all in all." Conservative critics have long known Heidegger's "Being" as a Gnostic Godhead, but the truth is that Heidegger knows the finitude of Being more deeply than any other thinker, an absolutely anti-Gnostic motif, and Heidegger could finally know redemption as the absolute event of *Ereignis*, and all too significantly *Ereignis* is the very word which Goethe employs in envisioning the final redemption of Faust in the conclusion of the second part of *Faust*, that very Faust who embodies a uniquely Western damnation, or a uniquely Western "soul."

Just as an absolute hatred of the world was born in ancient Gnosticism, that birth can be understood as the advent of a true nihilism, which is yet another reason why Gnosticism has been so deeply reborn in our world, and even as the Hellenistic world becomes ever more gradually a nihilistic world, Gnostic theologians were deeply influential in that world, as witness their impact not only upon Plotinus but indirectly upon Augustine himself. While we still lack a history of Gnosticism in the post-ancient world, it would be difficult to deny that the symbol if not the actuality of the self-saving of God is at least potentially deeply present in that world, as in the depths of a truly new Jewish, Islamic, and Christian mysticism, then bursting into the open in the circles surrounding Meister Eckhart and Jacob Boehme. This is a genuinely dialectical mysticism which is reborn in German Idealism, and the self-saving of God is at the very center of the thinking of Fichte, Schelling, and Hegel, just as it is in the visionary depths of Hoelderlin, Goethe, and Blake. At no other point has such a deep modernity been a more profound threat to theology, and if Christian theology was born in Paul in response to a primitive Christian Gnosticism, a uniquely modern Christian theology could be understood as having been born in response to a uniquely modern self-saving of God.

Yet God can be saved only from God's own darkness, a darkness which truly is the "alien" God; this is that God who is purely and fully an absolute No-saying, as so deeply known by Luther, Kierkegaard, and Nietzsche, an absolutely alien darkness that is ultimately a divine darkness, as first unveiled in the Book of Job, and then as fully released in the world in the very advent of Christianity. If it is Christianity which first embodies an absolute world-negation, hence the Christian origin of Gnosticism, that world-negation itself is inseparable from a new and ultimate redemption, a redemption which can be known, and has been known, as the self-saving of God. This and this alone makes possible what the Gnostic knows as the perfection of the elect, a perfection that is an absolute deification, one surely echoed in deeply Christian quests for deification or Godmanhood, a quest already present in the earliest expressions of Christianity. But if that quest is truly new, or truly new in the Mediterranean world, it could be understood as a response to an absolutely new self-saving of God, and one not only absent from the Hellenistic and Classical worlds, but from the Oriental world as well. Nowhere there can we discover the image or the symbol of the self-saving of God, just as nowhere there can we discover a symbol or image of an actual or ultimate death of deity, a death that is an absolutely redemptive death, and a death transforming everything whatsoever.

While Gnosticism could know the crucifixion, it could only know it as resurrection, a deeply Gnostic motif which soon overwhelms the great body of Christianity, and while this is a pre-Christian motif, and is deeply present in the Hellenistic mystery cults, never therein is it so absolute as it is in Gnosticism, never there calling forth a total union with the depths of Godhead itself. But it is possible to understand this very union as being possible only as a consequence of the fall of the Godhead, for that fall could make possible a profound transfiguration of Godhead itself, and if it is Gnosticism which first knows such a transfiguration, it is Gnosticism which first knows the fall of Godhead. So it is that if a Gnostic deification is truly new, and new as an absolute deification, it could be understood as a reflection or embodiment of an ultimate transfiguration of the Godhead, a transfiguration wherein the depths of darkness pass into the depths of light, and now the Godhead is fully all in all, and even all in all in the "perfect" or the elect. Thereby matter itself wholly passes into nothingness, and just as *The Gospel of Truth* can know a cosmic "forgetfulness" as the very creation of the world, the material universe passes into nothingness when the "Father" is truly known, but the Father's secret is His Son, and the name of the Father is the Son (38: 6), that Son by whom alone the Father can be known, a *gnosis* that is an absolute return from forgetfulness to that Father who is all in all.

A knowledge of this very forgetfulness is essential to a Gnostic redemption, for even if that forgetfulness is reversed in this redemption, it is precisely thereby essential to it, and only thereby can a profoundly divided pleroma be restored to its original or primordial condition. Here, Gnosticism profoundly differs from Buddhism, and from every Oriental way, and does so most clearly in knowing an ultimate self-division or self-alienation of the original pleroma, a self-alienation which is an ultimate fall, and a self-alienation which is reversed in a uniquely Gnostic redemption. This is just the point at which an original or nascent Christian orthodoxy most deeply struggled with Gnosticism, ever more fully refusing any possible transfiguration of the Godhead, and just thereby coming to understand the absolute immutability of the Godhead, an immutability becoming the very core of the orthodox Christian doctrine of God. Now that we know that there were deeply Gnostic expressions of primitive Christianity, as in the Gospel of Thomas and quite probably in the earliest strata of Q, a profound struggle was clearly therein at hand, and one creating ultimate divisions in the Pauline and Johannine communities. These are divisions which become overwhelming in the second century of the Christian era, and even if the Great Church is the victor in that conflict, a pure Gnosticism has returned again and again in Christian history, just as a muted or transformed Gnosticism is seemingly deeply embedded in Christian orthodoxy itself.

It continues to remain impossible fully to understand the depths of the transformation of an original Christianity, and even if the earliest Christianity which we can know was a deeply divided Christianity, as can most clearly be seen in the extreme polarity between its Gnostic and its apocalyptic poles, these poles did not simply disappear in the triumph of orthodox Christianity, they were profoundly transformed, and transformed within a new orthodox Christianity. Now a truly new Godhead is manifest and real, one absolutely immutable, an absolute immutability impossible within the horizons of a biblical Godhead, but likewise impossible within the horizons of apocalypticism and Gnosticism, both of which could know profound transformations of the Godhead, transformations making possible what both Gnosticism and apocalypticism know as an absolutely new redemption or an absolutely new totality. The very word "totality" is illuminating here, for just as a new aeon or a new pleroma became ever more deeply alien to Christian orthodoxy, totality can here be known only as Godhead itself, an absolutely immutable totality, and one foreclosing the very possibility of an ultimate or absolute transfiguration.

With the advent of an imperial or Constantinian Christianity, not only do Gnosticism and apocalypticism seemingly disappear forever from all ecclesiastical Christianity, but Christianity itself, or orthodox Christianity, ever more fully comes to exercise a profoundly conservative role, and while this very orthodoxy ever called forth new heresies, it was the profound dichotomy between orthodoxy and heresy which generated the deepest crises of Christendom, crises finally bringing Christendom to an end. Perhaps the most ultimate Christian heresy is the belief in an ultimate and total transfiguration, one inseparable from an absolute transfiguration of the Godhead, a transfiguration which here could only be a transfiguration of totality itself. While this is a transfiguration which we have come to understand as the very core of a pure apocalypticism, it also can be understood as the core of a truly new Gnosticism, and if an ultimate and primordial fall is deeper in Gnosticism and apocalypticism than within any other horizons, such a fall is inseparable from an absolute transfiguration, hence here an absolute transfiguration is wholly inseparable from an absolute fall. Just as it was Augustine who most fully created the Christian dogma of original sin, and did so by way of his renewal of Paul, it was also Augustine who inaugurated a profound interior transformation, one truly revolutionary in its ultimate historical impact, and one ever in profound and even explosive tension with its deep theological ground, an Augustinian God who is simultaneously immanent and transcendent, and whose absolute transcendence is inseparable from his absolute immanence.

This is an immanence that will explode in the radically new mysticism of the medieval world, but so likewise does it explode in late medieval Augustinian theology, a radically Franciscan theology which all too significantly is finally inseparable from a truly new apocalypticism, and one calling forth a truly new and truly absolute transfiguration. Orthodox theologians inevitably judge such a transfiguration as being either Gnostic or apocalyptic, but all too significantly with the triumph of modernity it is ecclesiastical Christianity which becomes ever more dormant and unmoving, giving us an orthodox theology which for the first time ceases to evolve, or insofar as it evolves regresses into paganism (with, of course, the great exception of Barth's radically new understanding of predestination). So that a theology finally bound to the absolute immutability of God becomes immutable itself, reflecting in itself its own absolute ground, but also reflecting within itself what both Kierkegaard and Nietzsche knew all too deeply as the end of Christendom. But that ending is surely not the ending of theology, which is deeply reborn in a new and universal apocalyptic theology, a theology which is deeply anti-ecclesiastical, but precisely thereby deeply secular or worldly, and it inevitably calls forth an absolute transfiguration of totality itself.

At this crucial point Hegel, Marx, and Nietzsche are united, and if purely conservative critics can know all three as being deeply Gnostic and deeply apocalyptic at once, and as the very embodiment of a truly Satanic thinking, so that if here a truly new theological thinking becomes a purely anti-theological thinking, and above all so in its enactment of the death of God, it does so as a purely apocalyptic thinking, and an apocalyptic thinking thinking absolute transfiguration. If only here, the ultimate transgression of genuine apocalyptic thinking is manifest for all to see, and just as the Great Church simultaneously profoundly turned away both from a new apocalypticism and a new Gnosticism, it thereby refused not only an absolute transfiguration but an absolute transgression as well, and did so most deeply in its total affirmation of the absolute immutability of the Godhead. That is an immutability making impossible a new totality, and with that impossibility the impossibility also of a total transgression, or of a transgression truly and absolutely challenging a primordial totality, a totality absolutely eternal and immutable, and therefore infinitely beyond any possible challenge or questioning. The very idea of a true and absolute infinity does not dawn until the advent of Christianity, and then it dawns so as to establish an infinite distance between the creature and the Creator, and even if this releases a new ideal of Godmanhood, that is a Godmanhood calling forth an absolutely primordial humanity, and one freed of every impact of either history or the world.

This is the humanity that Augustine can know as the City of God, a humanity infinitely distant from the City of Man, and even if the Great Church before the apocalypse embodies both the City of Man and the City of God, the elect or the predestined truly exist only in the City of God, therefore they are absolutely unmoving in that very eternity, reflecting in their own holiness the absolute immutability of their Creator. This is a holiness simply unknown in the pre-Christian world; its nearest parallel is the absolute emptiness of Buddhism, but that is an emptiness free of any possible Godhead, and thus free of any possible actual immutability, or any possible actual necessity. Such an absolute immutability and absolute necessity are born only with the advent of Christianity; then a pre-Christian fate or providence is transformed into an absolute necessity, an absolute necessity which is an absolute authority, but now and for the first time an absolute authority comprehending everything whatsoever, as now an absolute and total obedience is truly born.

Whitehead, the one major twentieth-century philosopher who could actually think of God, could understand the new Christian Godhead as Caesar reborn, but a Constantinian empire goes beyond a pre-Christian empire in its demand for total obedience, and just as the Great Church ever increases its demands for total obedience, it thereby truly is a servant of this new Godhead, as now an absolute authority is born which is truly total and all-comprehending, and an authority which in its very essence is absolutely immutable. But that absolute immutability ever more gradually and ever more decisively called forth its true opposite, an opposite inseparable from a reversal of absolute immutability, and thus finally inseparable from an absolute reversal of the immutability of Godhead itself. Already this occurs in the medieval world, and there perhaps most deeply and most purely in Dante's *Commedia*, one giving us two divine empires, each embodying the authority of God, and each truly divided from the other; thereby one immutable authority and order become two orders and authorities, and time and finitude for the first time are envisioned as being fully coordinate with eternity. Dante's vision is inseparable from an ultimate assault upon the temporal authority of the papacy; thereby a new papacy can be named as Antichrist (*Inferno* XIX), and this very inversion of the authority of the Great

Church is inseparable from an absolutely new recognition of the ultimate authority of the world, one fully actual in a *quia* or "thatness" which is the very heart of the real, and which even our perception can draw forth as the movement of an ultimate love (*Purgatorio* XVIII, 22–33). Certainly that is a love unknown in the ancient world, and even more deeply unknown in the ancient Christian world, but it only appears in the medieval world by way of an ultimate challenge to the deepest authority of the temporal church, and if that very challenge calls forth a new eternal church, and a truly invisible church, that invisibility is inseparable from a truly new visibility of the world, and one inevitably assaulting what the Great Church could know as God's absolutely immutable order and authority, as now a new world ever more gradually and comprehensively appears embodying its own absolute authority and order.

Of course, with the full dawning of modernity this new world becomes a profoundly divided or dichotomous world, one embodying an ultimate division or dichotomy between its interior and its exterior poles, and one releasing a truly new dichotomy within theology itself, as theology becomes ultimately divided between its ecclesiastical and its philosophical and imaginative expressions, and for the first time both philosophy and the imagination become truly autonomous, and thereby truly independent of all ecclesiastical authority. While ecclesiastical spokesmen will increasingly insist that it is only an ecclesiastical theology which is a genuine theology, the truth is that both modern philosophy and the modern imagination have been profoundly theological, and even if this is a theology deeply alien to all ecclesiastical Christianity, it is nonetheless deeply theological, and even is so in its seemingly most secular expressions. This is most manifestly true in full modernity's very enactment of the death of God, so it is that Heidegger can know that the realization that "God is dead" is not atheism but rather "ontotheology," and an ontotheology in which both metaphysics and nihilism are fulfilled. Both Hegel and Heidegger, even as Plato and Aristotle, know metaphysics or the deepest philosophical thinking as theology, but unlike all ancient or medieval metaphysicians, Heidegger and Hegel finally know "Being" or Absolute Spirit or the Godhead as the self-saving of God, and a self-saving occurring in the deepest darkness and abyss, a darkness only made possible by the death of God.

Indeed, it is precisely the death of God which both Hegel and Heidegger can know as bringing metaphysics to an end, but that ending is itself a metaphysical or "ontotheological" event, and therefore a theological event, and even if it is wholly alien to all ecclesiastical theology, it is overwhelming in the fullness of modernity itself, and not only in the imagination of that modernity, but also in its deepest and purest philosophical thinking. Accordingly, it is only in late modernity that an ecclesiastical theology arose which is infinitely distant from every possible cultural or social ground, but also not until the advent of modernity that deep theologies appear which are independent of every possible ecclesiastical ground, unless this is true of Aristotle's theology, which would be ironic, indeed, since post-medieval Catholic theology has been so dominated by neo-Aristotelianism. Milton's theology is the fullest theology ever given us by a poet, but his is a deeply anti-ecclesiastical theology, and one assaulting virtually every expression of ecclesiastical tradition. If thereby Milton's theology is a pure expression of the Radical Reformation, it is a founding expression of a uniquely modern theology, and a modern theology which truly is a radical theology, and one not confined to poets and seers, but realizing itself in pure thinking, and in that very thinking which triumphs in a full modernity. While this is a thinking refused by every ecclesiastical theology, nothing else more fully makes manifest the radical isolation of modern ecclesiastical theology, an isolation which itself was only born in the modern world.

This deep isolation is itself a witness to the death of God, and as Nietzsche knew so deeply everything that we can know as the church could only be the tomb of God, and just as Nietzsche could know Christianity itself as the stone upon the grave of Jesus, everything which is publicly manifest to us as theology is such a stone, and dead and lifeless as it has become, that very death may well harbor the deep presence of its very opposite. So it is that everything that theology once knew as the absolute immutability of God has actually become its true opposite, and if nothing could be further removed from that immutability than the absolute transfiguration of the Godhead, a transfiguration which is the self-saving of God, the brute fact that this is absolutely alien to every ecclesiastical theology could be a decisive sign of its deep theological truth for us, and a theological truth not confined to a sanctuary, but embodied in the very actuality of the world as world. Certainly, modern "secular" theologies know this truth, and the deeper the secular theology the deeper the calling forth of this truth; here our deeper thinking and our deeper imagination fully coincide, and if "descent" and not "ascent" is our deeper primary image, it is the Descent into Hell and not the Ascension which is our primary symbolic ground, a Descent into Hell which is the Harrowing of Hell, or the sanctification of an ultimate abyss and darkness.

Yes, that darkness is the darkness of Godhead itself, which is precisely why it is an absolute darkness, and to know and to envision that darkness is to envision and to know the darkness of God, a darkness that can be and has been known as an absolute Nothing, and an absolutely actual Nothing, a Nothing that has been named as damnation, Satan, and Hell, an absolutely original naming which has fully occurred only within a Christian horizon, but which becomes a truly comprehensive naming only within the horizon of a full and final modernity. If our deeper modern voyages have been voyages into a fully actual nothingness, a nothingness which is the very opposite of an absolutely empty nothingness, these have been voyages into an absolutely actual Nothing, one envisioned by every deeply modern poet, and one known by every deeply modern philosopher, except for Spinoza and Husserl, and so known even if only in calling forth a pure and absolute surd or void, a void previously unknown, unless it was known in Epicureanism, the only truly secular philosophy in the ancient world. That pure and absolute infinitude which was born after the advent of Christianity is at least implicitly accompanied by its very opposite, and even if this opposite is not fully born conceptually until the waning of the Middle

Ages, it is ever realized in all genuinely modern Idealism, again with the exception of Husserl and Spinoza. And why is it that Husserl is the only truly or absolutely transcendental Idealist of the twentieth century, as most purely manifest in the *Sixth Cartesian Meditation*, one intending an absolute reversal of Western philosophy, and even going beyond Heidegger in its "deconstruction" of the Western philosophical tradition, a deconstruction now inseparable from pure philosophical thinking? Why has such a radical deconstruction now become so necessary for us, or was it inaugurated by Spinoza himself, and inaugurated if only to deconstruct a uniquely modern nothingness, and a nothingness inevitable in every post-Classical understanding of Being, or every understanding of Being within a Christian horizon of consciousness?

Spinoza's most radical thinking was not directed against Descartes but rather against the whole world of scholastic philosophy, one inaugurated by Philo and finally ended by Spinoza, and Spinoza's "atheism," a truly theological atheism, is an inversion or reversal of the Western understanding of Being, although it is centered upon a reversal of a post-Classical understanding of infinity, and is so by fully calling forth a full and actual union between infinity and finitude, and one only possible by way of a pure thinking that is fully harmonious with body or world. Now this is precisely the thinking that will never appear again in our philosophy, and certainly not in the absolutely transcendental thinking of Husserl, who at this point is further from Spinoza than any modern philosopher, so that it is possible to think that Spinoza could know a pure harmony between mind and body that is possible only by way of a true transcendence of every possible nothingness, and if it is Spinoza alone who could truly know such a transcendence, and one thereby foreclosing both the possibility and the necessity of every truly transcendental transcendence, the mere presence of any such transcendental transcendence is a decisive sign of an intended negation of an actual nothingness, and of the actual presence of that nothingness as a deep even if unacknowledged ground of every such transcending movement of thinking itself.

Is it impossible then for us to escape an actual nothingness, and surely not by a seemingly pure empiricism which so forcefully calls it forth, and certainly not by a pure idealism which could only be a purely transcendental idealism, and one only possible as Hegel knew so deeply by way of a pure negation of a pure and actual nothingness? That negation does not disappear in Husserl's final transcendental idealism, and if world itself now becomes a purely and absolutely transcendental world, it does so only by way of a transcendental phenomenological reduction which is a truly "Copernican revolution," a revolution grounded in an absolutely new discovery of an absolutely transcendental "I," one which can know only a transcendental cosmogony, and can realize itself only as an absolutely constituting "I," or that very "I" which all post-Classical theology had known as the "I" of the Creator. Husserl finally transcends even Hegel in his absolute Idealism, and if here the "I" of an absolutely transcendental thinking is finally the "I" of the Creator, that could only be a creation *ex nihilo*, and even if this is an absolute thinking thinking against an absolute nothingness, it is only possible by way of an absolute negation of that nothingness, and a negation here occurring only through that purely transcendental "I" or transcendental subjectivity which is the constituting source of the universe itself.

Now if only the radical Spinoza and the radical Husserl among our modern philosophers are seemingly innocent of an actual nothingness, and if both had an enormous but only indirect impact upon philosophy, and virtually no actual followers, is that because it is simply impossible for us to be free of a fully actual nothingness, even though that may well be our deepest destiny and goal? We could understand both Husserl and Spinoza as giving us a truly and even absolutely radical thinking which is finally directed to an absolute dissolution of nothingness, but the profound radicality of their thinking is deep evidence of the ultimate difficulty of that goal, and even if this is a goal which would simply be meaningless in the pre-Christian world, it is certainly not meaningless in ours, as witness our deep response both to Spinoza and Husserl. And is it possible that Spinoza truly is our most God-obsessed philosopher, just as the late Husserl clearly is that one thinker who called forth an absolutely transcendental "I" that constitutes existence itself, an "I" that could only be known theologically as the Creator, and even as both Spinoza and Husserl refuse every actual pronunciation of the name of God, is that here made possible by their purely conceptual embodiment of the very power of God, and a power of God which is finally the self-saving of God?

A uniquely modern philosophical "atheism," just as a uniquely modern imaginative "atheism," intends to embody the depths of Godhead itself in its own enactment, or to embody everything which our history and consciousness have known as Godhead, as can most clearly be seen in Spinoza, Hegel, and Husserl, but no less so in Nietzsche and Heidegger, thereby Godhead itself can be realized only by a pure reversal of its own absolute immutability, and with that reversal that immutability wholly disappears. Thereby every given and established distinction and division between an absolute infinitude and an absolute finitude is dissolved, and while such a dissolution is impossible in the ancient or pre-Christian world, that world could know neither a true finitude nor a true infinitude. Although Christianity almost immediately comes to know an absolute infinitude or an absolute Godhead, it only very gradually comes to realize a true or fully actual finitude, one not fully called forth until the late Middle Ages, and then it dawns only by way of an ultimate chasm between finitude and infinitude, a chasm alone making possible a *coincidentia oppositorum* between these now ultimately opposing poles. Such a *coincidentia oppositorum* certainly occurs, as can most clearly be seen in the birth of modern science, which truly not only united but identified the celestial and the terrestrial spheres, and did so with a truly apocalyptic finality. Now the universe itself can be known as an infinite universe, as infinitude and finitude are truly united, and if it is Spinoza who knows this most purely, it is the late Husserl's enactment of an absolutely transcendental "I" which most closely approximates the absolute act of creation itself. If this was possible only by way of a full reversal of philosophy, this reversal itself occurred at the very time of the triumph of Nazism, then a new gulf between Husserl and Heidegger becomes uncrossable, and Godhead itself becomes more impenetrable than it had ever previously been, and pure thinking becomes torn asunder by the very widening gulf between its infinite and finite poles. Finitude itself seemingly disappears in Husserl's absolutely transcendental Idealism, and if at no other point is there a deeper gulf between Husserl and Spinoza, at no other point is there a deeper gulf between early and late modernity, as now world or finitude itself either disappears or becomes a deep and impenetrable surd, or that very surd which Hegel could so deeply know as a pure and actual nothingness. Now a new nihilism truly becomes incarnate, and one now present wherever either a pure thinking or a pure imagination is actual and real, and if only our deepest depths have called forth a pure nihilism, this has occurred only in the late modern world, a world which is simply inconceivable apart from such a finally *incarnate nihilism*.

If a truly ironic theology were now possible, it would not be impossible to identify Husserl's final absolute Idealism as a Descent into Hell; it surely occurred in a world being consumed by an absolute evil, and a world inevitably affecting and perhaps even making possible this absolute "idealism"; now finitude can only be manifest as darkness itself, and it inevitably disappears as such in a new absolute "light." But is that "light" and the absolute "I" of that light anything which a previous thinking could know as either subject or consciousness; is an absolutely transcendental "I" now so absolutely pure that it can shine or appear only in an absolute light, and therefore not only be absolutely unknown but absolutely inactual in anything less than that light? Here is a light so absolutely dazzling that it can only be known by an absolutely transcendental "I." Therein every other "I" finally disappears in its consumption by that "I." And just as Heidegger at this very time was withdrawing from that *Dasein* which had been the center of *Being and Time*, a *Dasein* first establishing a gulf between Heidegger and Husserl, now both a Heideggerian *das Sein* and a Husserlian transcendental "I" are absolutely invisible. Or they are visible or speakable only by this absolutely new "I" or this absolutely impenetrable *das Sein*. Each therein and thereby are inseparable from the other, and are so if only because each is an absolute transcendence that *is* an absolute immanence, as now an Augustinian Godhead is fully and finally embodied.

Of course, something very like this already occurs in Spinoza, just as it is comprehensively embodied in Hegelian thinking, and if Husserl and Heidegger are the deepest Hegelians in the twentieth century, although perhaps being rivaled by Whitehead, they can be so only by enacting an absolute transcendence of both history and consciousness going far beyond a Spinoza or a Hegel, and a transcendence now demanded by that consciousness and history itself, a history or a consciousness that has now truly ended, as most purely manifest in this radically new thinking itself. Now an ultimate abyss becomes truly universal, and if this now makes possible an absolutely unhearable "Being-itself" or an absolutely invisible transcendental "I," that "I" and this "Being" are possible only by way of this abyss, or only by way of a "Descent into Hell." Our deeper theological community has long sought a truly theological way into both Husserl and Heidegger, and sought it here as they have into no other twentieth-century philosophers, with the possible exception of Whitehead and Wittgenstein. But this way has been profoundly blocked by the very language of Husserl and Heidegger, both of whom resolutely refused all speaking of God, and did so far more than any other major philosophers. And this despite the fact that Heidegger's background is so deeply theological, and unique as such among twentieth-century philosophers.

Yet if this is a truly new thinking it will inevitably transcend everything that we have known as God, and while both a Hegelian and a Nietzschean language can be heard as a language about God, this is impossible in the language of Husserl and Heidegger, unless Husserl's "transcendental world-constitution" can be heard as the language of creation, and Heidegger's "self-saving of Being" can be heard as the language of redemption. Now the mere fact that no God-language is here called forth is all too significant, indeed, its mere occurrence would dissolve the deeper language of both Husserl and Heidegger. And while some theologians have been tempted to think that it is an Eckhartian Godhead that speaks here, and hence a Godhead transcending "God," this is manifestly impossible if neither Husserl nor Heidegger are truly mystical thinkers, and equally impossible if each speaks wholly and fully within the very horizon of world itself. A truly Eckhartian language is immune to the darkness of the world, but this is certainly not true of either Husserl or Heidegger, both of whom could know an absolute "crisis" or *krisis* of the world itself. This crisis alone makes possible their deepest thinking, and one that they certainly could not meet with a Nietzschean joy, or with anything that the Christian world has historically known as faith.

The truth is that neither Husserl nor Heidegger can know a deep light apart from darkness, a light only called forth by an ultimate and final "crisis" of our history and consciousness, and hence one impossible apart not only from a realization of that darkness, but impossible apart from a deep descent within it, a descent alone truly calling forth that darkness. Here we can see the model not only of a primordial shamanic descent, but even more deeply of a uniquely Christian descent into Hell, and here a truly Pauline dying with Christ could only be a participation in that descent, a participation which alone realizes true glory, or what the Christian most deeply knows as "resurrection." Is a reflection of that resurrection present in the ecstatic celebration of Heidegger or in the purely transcendental thinking of Husserl? And could this be a reflection of the Descent into Hell or the Self-Saving of God? For a self-saving of God could only be a descent into Hell, or a descent into God's own darkness, a darkness which is an absolute nothingness, and an absolutely actual nothingness which alone could effect the "death of God," or alone could effect the absolute self-negation or self-emptying of Godhead itself.

Now it is of ultimate significance that virtually all of our truly major late modern poets could evoke and enact the absolute alienness or the absolute guilt of Godhead itself, and if this naming begins with Blake, it has not even yet ended. It surely realized its most comprehensive enactments at the very time when Husserl and Heidegger were realizing their deepest breakthroughs, breakthroughs impossible apart from the full advent of an absolute darkness, and yet breakthroughs making possible a truly new light. Is this a "light" that finally can be known as Godhead itself, and even as the absolute light of the *Paradiso* is inseparable from the ultimate voyage of the *Inferno*, is a uniquely twentieth-century "light" inseparable from a uniquely twentieth-century darkness? If here light and darkness are pure and total opposites of each other, are they precisely thereby purely and totally bound to or essentially related to each other? In this perspective we could understand the necessity of the new Christian dogma of the absolute immutability of God, an immutability foreclosing the possibility of an ultimate descent, or of an ultimate light only possible through such descent, a foreclosure necessitated by the very occurrence or calling forth of an absolute Incarnation, an absolute Crucifixion, or an absolute Descent into Hell. Inevitably, it is the Descent into Hell which is the most hidden or fragile or marginal dogma in Christianity, only barely appearing in patristic Christianity, and only actually being called forth in medieval Christianity, and not becoming all in all until the full advent of the modern world. But then it is truly universal, and universal as it had never previously been, now occurring not only in the depths of the imagination but in the depths of thinking itself, and most deeply occurring there precisely when it loses all the imagery of belief, and is now present only as purely apocalyptic totality.

If Husserl is that twentieth-century philosopher most distant from all imaginative language (and here he truly is a Spinoza reborn), and Heidegger is the twentieth-century philosopher most committed to imaginative language, at least at this point they are genuine opposites in their thinking, but both are nevertheless genuinely abstract or esoteric thinkers, thinkers who in their very thinking demand a new language, and do so as had never previously occurred in our thinking. Certainly Hegel's language is far closer to the Germanic language of his world than is Heidegger's, and certainly Husserl's language is far more purely abstract than is Hegel's. Both Heidegger and Husserl ever more deeply revolted against the philosophical language which they were given, with the result that they are clearly the most difficult of our twentieth-century philosophers. Yet something very like this could be said of all of our great late modern poets, and just as these poets have inspired genuine cults, so likewise has Heidegger, and perhaps Husserl as well. It is as though we have here been given a new sacred language, and a sacred language vastly distant from our common or profane language, and one only meaningful to a new priesthood or a new sacred elite. So it is that both Husserl and Heidegger have been given a sacred aura by their followers, even as have our great modern artists, but in Heidegger alone this sacred aura has become virtually a divine aura. And this despite his Nazi period, as though Heidegger, like a god, is truly beyond good and evil.

Indeed, it is Heidegger alone in Western philosophy who actually speaks of the gods, and speaks of the gods even while being silent about God, and just as it is only Heidegger among our philosophers who has sought an absolutely primordial ground, or only Heidegger apart from Plotinus, it is Heidegger who is seemingly our most sacred thinker; and even if this is only a mask or persona, such a mask would appear to be essential to his impact. But it is also Heidegger who is our most deeply blasphemous or theologically transgressive twentieth-century thinker; here once again he is a reborn Nietzsche. If it is Nietzsche who had the deepest impact upon Heidegger, or the deepest apart from Hegel, the blasphemy in Heidegger, too, is a purely theological blasphemy and the transgression a purely theological transgression. Yet it is just at this point that both Heidegger and Nietzsche are most powerful theologically, just at this point that they induce the deepest aura. Here a divine and ultimate voice has been heard most decisively, and heard most fully in its deepest transgression. And what could be more transgressive than to speak so powerfully of the self-saving of Being, a "Being" that here could only be heard as Godhead itself, a self-saving that soon can be named as an absolute *Ereignis*, and as an absolute event, an event that is not simply a divine event, but far rather the final actualization of Godhead itself. So it is that the late Heidegger becomes the apocalyptic Heidegger, even as the late Nietzsche becomes the apocalyptic Nietzsche, and this is the Heidegger even as this is the Nietzsche who can only be heard as a sacred voice. It is a sacred voice which is an ultimately transgressive voice, simultaneously deeply attracting and deeply repelling its hearer, and a voice which is finally charismatic only in its deeply repulsive or deeply demonic power. Only Nietzsche and Heidegger among our true philosophers have been capable of an actually demonic language, but only here in modern philosophy can we discover a fully actual sacred language, and now a sacred language which is inevitably a language of a full and total descent.

Of course, we should not think that it is Nietzsche and Heidegger alone who assumed or who were given a divine voice; this could be said of all of our great poets, and just as Nietzsche and Heidegger are truly poetic philosophers, they are thereby voices of revelation itself, and are accepted as such among their deepest followers. But it is Nietzsche and not Heidegger who writes about Jesus, and is the only philosopher who has written fully about Jesus, even if this only occurs in *The Antichrist*. Earlier Nietzsche had gone so far as to intend a recreation of the very voice of Jesus, creating an absolutely new gospel in *Thus Spoke Zarathustra*, a Zarathustra who could be understood as the resurrected Jesus, but a resurrection possible only as a consequence of the deepest descent, and one alone making possible a freedom from all *ressentiment*. While Heidegger was once deeply engaged in a New Testament seminar at Marburg, and had a deep impact upon Bultmann and many other theologians, he seemingly had no interest at all in the language of Jesus. Perhaps he was being Bultmannian in thinking that this language can never be known, or perhaps he was following Paul in transforming Jesus's language into a truly new language, for we do know of

Heidegger's deep attraction to a Pauline language, even employing it in the opening of *An Introduction to Metaphysics* to insist that a "Christian philosophy" is a round square and a misunderstanding. And it is Paul's apocalyptic language which most affected Heidegger; perhaps it is only apocalyptic language which was real to Heidegger as a biblical language, and just as he became ever more distant from his original and deeply Catholic ground, it was even thereby that he moved ever more fully into a sacred or ultimate language, a language unique to a twentieth-century philosopher.

Is it the death of God that makes possible such language? This certainly could be said of Nietzsche himself, and Heidegger was more fully drawn to the actual language of the death of God than any other twentieth-century thinker, a language surely necessary to his own project of creating an ultimate or sacred language, and just as he speaks most fully of the self-saving of Being in the context of speaking of the death of God and the destitution of the holy, he finally can speak of Being only as a crossed-out Being, as Being for the first time is symbolically known through the Cross. If thereby Heidegger finally becomes a profoundly anti-Gnostic thinker, it is also thereby that he is finally freed of *Dasein*, or of that uniquely modern self-consciousness that he had come ever more fully to unveil as the deepest "other" of a genuinely or truly philosophical thinking. Yet this is possible only when "Being itself" becomes all in all, and if this is that ultimate apocalyptic event which we are awaiting, and one signaled by the very word "*Ereignis*," this is possible only by way of the deepest descent, and the deepest descent into the deepest darkness. Perhaps his loyalist followers can understand Heidegger's descent into Nazism as such a descent, but it is clear that Nietzsche's madness can be understood as the consequence of an ultimate descent into darkness. If that can theologically be understood as an imitation of Jesus, whether a pathological one or not, it is simply not possible for a truly twentieth-century sensibility to dissociate an actual redeemer from such a descent, and thus not possible for us to know a self-saving of God which is not such a descent.

While it would be impossible to imagine Husserl thinking of nothingness, or thinking of an actual nothingness, and Heidegger only fully speaks of nothingness in his 1929 lecture, "What is Metaphysics?" and in the posthumously published *Berträge*. It is nevertheless also impossible to think of either of these philosophers apart from a world which so deeply and so profoundly called forth an absolute nothingness, and one against which their thinking was most deeply directed. This is the nothingness which is the deep ground of our ultimate "crisis," and even if it is unspoken by every twentieth-century philosopher except Heidegger, all genuine twentieth-century philosophers knew that crisis, and embody it in their deepest thinking. Yet only in the nineteenth century does philosophy openly contend with an absolute nothingness, one deeply occurring in Schelling, Hegel, and Nietzsche, but likewise occurring in Blake, Goethe, and Mallarmé, and it is Kafka, Joyce, and Beckett who have most clearly and most purely called forth an absolute nothingness in the twentieth century. Although echoes of this occur in all deeply twentieth-century poetry, this cannot possibly be a nothingness that is alien to our real thinking, even if it inevitably is deeply disguised or muted in that thinking. But is this not precisely the arena in which we can become open to a self-saving of God? And while God may well be unnameable as such within that arena, this is an arena calling forth an ultimate naming, and an ultimate naming of absolute nothingness itself.

CHAPTER 26

The Subject of Prayer: Unwilling Words in the Postmodern Access to God

Laurence Paul Hemming

Like several other contributors to this volume (Jean-Yves Lacoste, Jean-Luc Marion, Janet Soskice), Laurence Paul Hemming is a Roman Catholic theologian working from an explicit Christian basis. His work differs from Marion's with respect to its more existential (rather than phenomenological) approach, although he shares with both Marion and Lacoste a profound interest in the philosophical legacy of Heidegger. Hemming's early research (at Oxford, where he studied theology and philosophy) explored Marion's interpretation of Heidegger. He continued and expanded his analysis of Heidegger and the question of God in his doctoral dissertation (at Cambridge), published as *Heidegger's Atheism* (Notre Dame, IN, 2002).

Hemming's commitment to Christian reasoning, a faith seeking understanding, brings his work into association with the thinking of Radical Orthodoxy. The essay in this volume points to other characteristics shared with the work of Milbank, Pickstock, and Ward: a critique of modernity's metaphysics of the subject through submitting that metaphysics to its genealogy; emphasis upon liturgy or Christian piety as practice; appeal to aspects of Christian medieval life and thought as a resource for rethinking a contemporary perspective on a theological topic (prayer, in this case). Hemming contributed an important essay to the volume *Radical Orthodoxy: A New Theology* on Heidegger's Nietzsche and nihilism, but he has also maintained a critical distance from Radical Orthodoxy. In 1999 he organized a conference in London which became the basis for his edited volume *Radical Orthodoxy? A Catholic Enquiry* (Aldershot, 2000), which sought to bring exponents of Radical Orthodoxy into debate with leading Catholic theologians in Britain such as John Hanby, Fergus Kerr, and Oliver Davis.

Hemming's writing (his essays have appeared in journals such as *Heythrop Journal, New Blackfriars, The Thomist*, and *Literature and Theology*) is characterized by close philosophical analysis and attention to language. He is currently completing a book entitled *Postmodernity's God* (Aldershot, forthcoming).

All prayer is worded – which means that all prayer is my being inscribed into the Word of prayer, which through the Spirit returns to the Father. In so much as I am of Christ, my prayer is of the body, and so takes for granted the assembly, the *ecclesia*, the body of Christ. Is there, therefore, an ontology of prayer, and what do we mean by the "interiority" of prayer?

These questions appear to have simple answers: the ontological basis of prayer is language, the human, speaking being; interiority is the place where I talk to God without you: the place where I can be with God and you need have no access. This place is boundaried, so that its outermost limit is the speech I have when I am speaking with you, when we talk, or I declaim, and you listen. We can share this outer space, we can even pray together, but unless (I lapse for a moment here into the language of modern theology, especially of liturgy and prayer) I interiorize what we say together – unless I *mean* it, these words have no force. I can make a prayer with you that I do not really intend, or that means some *one* thing to you, and another to me. My interiority is alone the place where I am with God, which means I am alone with God unless I *choose* to be with God with you. God and you no longer belong together, unless you are alone with God (like me), or unless I (and you, I suppose, but I could only ever *suppose*) choose it to be otherwise. Gesture, posture, shared exertion in the doing of prayer (like singing) are no longer enough to share the God to whom we pray. Thought like this, can we any more say that our bodies make our prayers?

Put another way, what understanding of our being human underlies our practices of common prayer? Indeed, much of our preparation for prayer takes for granted that we know what "praying" means. Taking for granted means in practice "over-looking." Prayer becomes a kind of thinking: devoted thinking. Devoted thinking needs no pieties, for piety is, if anything at all, practice.

Surely, however, the injunction in the gospels to go into your room to pray in secret contradicts what I suggest here?[1] Entering a room to be hidden, and so to speak with our Father who is hidden, is, however, not to exit the world, but rather to be in the world in a different way. How can it be that the interiority of prayer is taken to refer to a place which cannot be found in the world, a place, if you like, that lies behind us, because in its privacy, we cannot see it? What is at issue here is how we understand prayer as the action of an agent subject, and moreover, a psychological act, something I *intend* (in order) to do. How did we come to understand prayer subjectively and psychologically?

The understanding of God that is unfolded in Descartes' third meditation makes clearer what I am trying to indicate. After establishing the method of doubt, and having made ontologically basic the *cogito*, Descartes proceeds to God. He says:

For those ideas which exhibit substances to me are without doubt something greater, and, as I would so speak, they contain more objective reality in themselves, than those ideas which represent only modes or accidents. And again, that idea through which I understand a highest God, eternal, infinite, omniscient, omnipotent and the creator of all things that, besides him, are – has in fact more objective reality in itself than those ideas through which finite substances are exhibited.[2]

The phenomenal appearance is less real than the substance which stands under and undergirds it. That which most undergirds, the "most real thing," therefore, is God, who as most real, possesses the fullness of substance. It is entirely clear from the structure of the third meditation that the infinite God who occurs together with the idea of myself is an inference, in virtue of myself. The very idea I have of myself yields together with it the idea of the God who guarantees my existence. Indeed, insofar as there might be anything else, the dubitability of all things does not affect in the least bit the dubiety either of myself or of God. Descartes notes that

> By the term "God" I understand a substance: a substance infinite, independent, most highly intelligent, most highly powerful, and by which I myself and everything else that is extant – if something else is extant – have been created.[3]

The self, disclosing itself to itself as indubitable, co-discloses one other indubiety, God. This indubitable idea is, however, an inference, a projection of the only thing that God *could* be, in view of the disclosure of the self to the self through the method of doubt, and as the only thing that could found the self and provide it with a causal origin. This indubiety is both in consequence of and what simultaneously underpins what Descartes now establishes substance to be. God, in other words, is indubitably a function of the knowing of the self, by a mental act, purely referred to myself, and nothing beyond me. God is disclosed to the self "within" the confines of the self. This means that being with God is entirely independent of any exterior experience I might have of the world. God is in consequence of a re-cognitive act of will, which can then be fulfilled in forms of prayer. This act of will is itself experienced psychologically; it is interior. How does this affect our prayer in common? Liturgy itself is now adjunct to this relationship. We are no longer constituted liturgically in prayer: we constitute for ourselves the liturgy that best expresses our interior psychic life. Liturgy becomes style. It does not produce me, I produce it. In consequence, when I say that it "feels right" I am saying that it fits an interior disposition I already have – if I think about it at all.

Descartes understands the God who is disclosed through the method of doubt to be coterminous with the God of revelation: indeed it is an implicit but fundamental guarantee of the correctness of his deduction that the God who is indubitably given through the method of doubt corresponds with the God of (Christian) revelation. Descartes, to establish the indubitability of the subjective self, cites the Christian God of revelation. Any God who now appears "outside," in the realm of the dubitable, must, in order to be God, be identical to (and so resemble) the God cited, the citation itself. The divine names – Eternal, Infinite, Omniscient, Omnipresent, etc., are re-cited, and so invoked and *performed*. The divine names function as a perform*ative*, a re-citation, a deflection of power. To invoke this God is to proclaim the already established and indubitable subject. Moreover, to paraphrase Descartes, the highest power possible, God, establishes and causes the subject. The power of this event, however, is concealed precisely because it is a citation. It is not God as such who founds this subject, but the interior projection forward into the highest possibilities of power. Even in Descartes the subject as self-founding *then* proceeds to "discover" itself as already-having-been founded by God in a projection, even if a projection *back*. This is a projection from where I now stand, into the future, only to find a secure, but imaginary past.

This God who Descartes cites is now a pure interior postulation of the intellect which will next, that is subsequently, explain all that is exterior. Descartes says that as I am founded by this God, because created by it, so *anything else* would likewise have been so founded. The establishment of the interior and exterior, boundaried and so bounded by my-self, is performed through an invocation, a prayer, an act of will, which itself discloses the subject it performs.

God, as cause of the subject (deduced by an act of reason), is really thereby grounded *by* the subject through reason. God thereby becomes other to the subject, as that object which, occurring together with the subject *against* the dubitability of every other thing, occurs as the constitutive sufficient condition of the "within" that subjectivity posits as the place wherein all knowing and certitude takes place. The dubitable "without" (itself only established as subsequent to self-establishment and God-establishment) is thereby deprived of God, except, and insofar as, I grant that the God I find without is the God I cite within. The dubiety of the outside may now be cancelled through acts of will: I *enter* this exterior world to cancel its dubiety. Indeed the world only appears at all as something that occurs subsequent to the positing of the *cogito* and the projection of the *cogito*'s foundation on God. In this sense, and insofar as the epistemological structures of the subject remain transcendentally deduced, the *same* God can be presumed to be enacted through all my psychic acts. In this way, I presume that the God I pray to is the same as the God you too invoke.

The province that Descartes begins to trace is fully charted and completed by Leibniz, in a manner that even the most contemporary theologians return to again and again. Above all in the ninety propositions of his tiny work the *Monadology*, Leibniz lays out the conditions of substantiality that are now understood by the name of intersubjectivity.[4] Much postmodern theology, with its concern for intersubjectivity (which it so often traces to Levinas, Buber, and to a lesser extent Husserl) in fact works entirely within the possibilities laid out here by Leibniz.

Leibniz develops and completes the radical transformation of substance initiated by Descartes, by understanding substance, not only as a general category of being whereby the relation between humanity and God is as between finite and infinite substance, but also by recourse to the postulation of human being (soul) as separate, monadic, substance. Thus the first proposition of the *Monadology* states: "The Monad, of which we shall speak here, is nothing but a simple substance . . . without parts."[5] To posit the Monad in this way, however, provides for other Monads than myself: difference is now constituted monadically. Moreover, at the center of the working out of the theses of the *Monadology* is, as for Descartes in the *Meditations*, an invocation of God: a postulation of the only thing that God could be like, for God to be God, and the Monad to be a subject.

Leibniz confronts the problem of how you may know God in the same way that I know God by asking how it is that difference itself postulates unity. He argues that every contingent substance is shown to be grounded in the one, infinite, and necessary substance, the plenitude of reality, God. He concludes:

> This is why the final reason of things must lie in a necessary substance, in which the differentiation of the changes [i.e., of separate, finite substances] only exists eminently as in their source; and this is what we call God.[6]

Leibniz presents this as a proof, citing Aquinas's conclusion of all of his five ways ("et hoc dicimus Deum"). However, this citation of the *necessity* of God's existence only completes and executes the invocation of God's names begun in Descartes.[7] Leibniz completes the charting of the topology of the "inside" and "outside" of the subjectivity of the subject by demonstrating (what Descartes took for granted) that the God "within" is coextensive with the God "without." Moreover, far from overcoming the dualism between body and mind or body and rational soul, Leibniz completes the division undertaken by Descartes to instrumentalize the body to the rational soul. He concludes: "Souls act according to the laws of final causes through appetitions, ends, and means. Bodies act according to the laws of efficient causes or motions and the two realms, that of efficient causes and that of final causes, are in harmony with one another."[8] Difference, for Leibniz, is now constructed "appetitively," as a movement of desire from the inside to the outside.[9]

Exactly as in Levinas and for Buber, God occurs at the center of every intersubjectival relationship, so this appearance is prefigured in Leibniz in consequence of the very structure of the Monad as substance and separate substance. God appears as the summation of will, and the securing of interiority, in order to continue to bear the divine names of greatest, most, highest, best: *omni* – and at the same time *summum* – and simultaneously God appears as the transcendental horizon of exteriority, the shared horizon toward which everything exterior points and tends – the apex of being. Martin Heidegger says of this exhaustive projecting (within and without, to a causal past within, to the future perfection of everything without) that every Monad in itself "reflects the whole entirety of beings, each according to its different viewpoints and divided according to degree of acuity . . . from this there is a hierarchy up to God the central-Monad, God thought in the sense of Christian theology."[10]

Heidegger's reference to Christian theology precisely refers to the way in which both the proofs and names of God are cited in order to install this God in place. Heidegger does not say so, but it is clearly Leibniz's intention that the whole hierarchy here described is exactly as presented by Aquinas, where every sentient being contains in itself a mirroring of the whole of creation graded according to its sentient and intellective capacity and grade of being, with one important difference: in contrast to Aquinas, Leibniz has installed this God in virtue of the whole structure of "inner" and "outer" that constitutes the subjectivity of the subject as such.[11] In consequence, subjectivity will be the condition under which God might appear and become known *at all*.

This installed God is not, however, the God invoked: this God, *Deus ex machina*, is reason itself. This God is a construction, deduced through proofs and projections. David Lachterman has traced the genealogy of this constructedness through the geometrical mathematics of the Enlightenment; he examines the innovations of Galileo, Descartes, Leibniz, Newton, and finally Kant, and concludes that modernity is a "trajectory from mathematical construction (in its precise technical sense) to self-deification. The mind is not nature's mirror; it is nature's generative or creative source."[12] The God installed through the "inner" and "outer" of the subject is the self, concealed from it-self by means of an invocation, the invocation of the Christian God. Prayer is rendered as method.

In the province charted by Descartes and Leibniz, two different, but related, conceptions of the subject appear. The subject first appears through the *cogito*, as self-grounding, and so able to deduce the interior certainty of its having been caused by God, and next (exteriorly) that each substance corresponds to God and mirrors God in the same way as every other substance. God here is taken as a kind of self-evidence, as what would have to complete, and so perfect, the "inner" and "outer" experience of the subject. Moreover, for as long as God can be taken for granted, as what ties all the monads together in a single common source of the many mirrored reflections of the whole, the problem of other subjects does not specifically or thematically arise. Substance, understood like this, though no longer disclosive of "world" as such (because primarily it discloses God and only subsequently "world," as I have shown – the order of disclosure is not an arbitrary one, and is an order governed by a hierarchy of epistemological certainty), still has unity. The difference in substance implied by many monads is only "speculative," as an illusion proffered by mirroring.

We are no longer in such a place, however. The construction of the understanding of the subject in the Enlightenment, the "subject of Modernity," is itself *Post*modernity's construct. Postmodernity, as the refusal of the very claims of reason that guarantee both the causal origin and the transcendental universality of subjectivity, exposes the means by which Descartes and Leibniz proceed not as means of truth attained by reason but as strategies, as claims to certainty. Lachterman cites Emerson's "god in ruins" as the inaugural moment of postmodernity, though in fact (as with others of Emerson's conceptions) this ruination is taken up, radicalized, and fulfilled by Nietzsche.[13] The critique that Nieztsche exacts on Cartesian and Leibnizian reason through proclaiming the death of God means that every God to whom I have access in Descartes' manner is simultaneously only my own act of God. In the unraveling of God as the tying together of monadic subjects as a unity, we are left only with the subject and subjectivity as such.

The unity of subjectivity as Leibniz envisaged it gives way to the absolute isolation of the subject, because what comes to the fore is not what founds the subject and ties its monadic substance together with others (God), but the boundaries that produce subjectivity. Leibniz's assertion that "the Monads have no windows"[14] reveals them to be Baroque *chambres enfilade* – apartments whose doors face each other (so that entrance and exit are collapsed into pure presence), walled with mirrors on every side (and so without windows), where the pleasure of seeing oneself endlessly reflected becomes the agony of seeing only oneself in endless speculations, in a room that could be dungeon or delightful camera, but has no way in or out. Because it can no longer be taken for granted (because God is dead), every attempt to reestablish the originary unity of one subject with its others must now be reaccomplished through an act of will, a refashioning of this absent unity.

The monad is thereby always conditioned to be reaching out, so that appetition becomes desire for the other, whilst at the same time for ever tracing the contours and boundaries that being a subject enforces, and that thereby divide the other from myself – what Judith Butler has called "subjection."[15] The encounters such subjects have with one another occur as encounters possessing the same (nihilated) valency, repetitiously overcoming the marks of negation that subject us. When God appears within this intersubjectivity, God appears only as *another* subject (even if desired to be the greatest, most powerful, highest subject, yet still another monad), and never as the conditioning possibility for subjectivity as such, precisely because the subject now understands itself and takes itself to be *self*-founding. Every renewed claim that God is the founding possibility of subjectivity as such must confront the fact that through the limitations imposed by the "inner" and "outer" this claim can only be realized by making God the only "real" subject, annihilating the reality of every other subjective form. Every act of self-foundation is always an act of self-isolation and reenactment of the borders and forces of separation-from-others at the same time. To call God "Father" in this structure is now to invoke the darkest psychic force of alterity, separation, and subjection.

Heidegger's celebrated and repetitiously recited critique of the God of the Enlightenment as "*causa-sui*," the "cause of itself," has rarely been heard in its proper ironic tone. For the *sui* here does not refer to God, which, if God was at issue here (and it is always assumed that God *is* at issue here, when it should be remembered that for Heidegger God is *never* at issue in any positive sense), surely it should. The *sui*, "of itself," refers to the self, as self-causing in virtue of the projection of God it has undertaken through its act of self-willing, and so to the God it has created for itself and installed. For in the very passage where Heidegger refers to *causa sui* as the name for God in metaphysics, he makes clear that what is at issue is the inability of metaphysics to think the being of beings, in favor of thinking only substance and subjectivity.[16] This God, as a mask of the self, can in no sense be invoked or prayed to *as God*, for every invocation of this God would be a self-invocation.

Intersubjectivity precisely arises as a theme and as a problem when what could self-evidently be taken to tie two subjects together ceases to exert the potency and valency it formerly had: when God as the condition of perfection of every substance is revealed only to be the monadic substance's desire to perfect itself. Perfection here always had a moral sense, as the *Monadology* makes clear, so that this tying together always has a moral underpinning. Leibniz speaks of the harmony between monads as "this City of God, this truly universal monarchy, [which] is a moral world in the natural world."[17] Intersubjectivity arises always as a moral and ethical problem, through what Heidegger calls "empathy" and others have called "compassion" or even "solidarity."[18]

The I-Thou relationship, re-presented as the basic postulate of all ethics, is in fact always in consequence of an act of will. Every I-Thou relationship will now be entered into through a choice, a decision, that determines both the "I" and the "Thou" in their interrelatedness, and takes the two subjects as absolute, irreducible terms. Appetition, or desire (as desire for, or toward, the other) is interpreted as the potential will for domination or totalization, where other bodies are instrumentalized to my (subjectival) desiring. Ethical intersubjectivity reverses this totalization, so that simply by my coming across it, the otherness of the other lays upon me a sovereign ethical imperative. In fact this imperative is no different from what it reverses, for instead of my instumentalization of the other to myself in a totalization of the other, I instrumentalize myself to the existence of another, or rather I reveal that both I and the other are simultaneously instrumentalized to appetition, or will, as such.

Every intersubjectival encounter, no matter how it appears or under what demands of sovereignty, is still a claim to sovereignty and so an instrumentalization of a self, mine or some other's. The intrusion of God into these intersubjectival events simply guarantees the absolutization of the ethical imperative, and unfolds as both absent and something to be willed and so attained all over again, God as the transcendental horizon to which all ethical intersubjectivity tends and aspires.

Moreover the desired reappearance of God in intersubjectivity is no longer a self-evidence, but is attained by a second invocation, a second act of will. God is the one alone who might break the *enfilade*. God, no longer invoked through being (as reason), must now be invoked through the good as the one who *should* appear, who must appear, or whose non-appearance has a moral valency, exacts a kind of judgment. Every attempt to reinstall God in this way, *especially* through intersubjectivity in the "exterior" encounters with other subjects, will therefore appear not just as an act of will, but as the exercise of the will to power, even if, as in ethical intersubjectivity, that will to power is depotentiated for the sake of the "other." Intersubjectivity understood as an ethics in this way is nothing other than the inclusion and so instrumentalization of the "other" for the sake of a devaluation (and such a devaluation is still only valuation as such, taking on a specific mode of its appearing as negation) of my-self. The otherness of the other is put to use for a reconfiguration of myself. I triumph through self-disempowerment, and so appear as the unreproachable, ethical subject, in virtue of what appears to be an invocation of God, and is still nothing other than a citation of myself.

Martin Heidegger criticizes intersubjectivity, particularly as it arises in Buber (although without naming him), through an elaboration of what he calls *Miteinandersein*, or being-with-one-another. He notes that "the problem of being-with-one-another is not just a question of the relation of subject to subject, but primarily a problem that belongs to the essential determination of a subject as such."[19] As Heidegger is able to demonstrate, however, this monadic understanding of substance is entirely in consequence of the "inside" and "outside" established through the Cartesian axiom. In consequence, every attempt to establish the structure of intersubjectivity will depend on the inside and outside of the Cartesian structure of the subject. Heidegger's critique of intersubjectivity is intended to show how Descartes' construction of "inner" and "outer," where "world" is always taken as "outside" to the interiority of the self, is in fact a construction.[20] He says: "Self and world belong together in the single being, *Dasein*. Self and world are not two beings, like subject and object, or like I and thou, but self and world are the basic determination of *Dasein* itself in the unity of the structure of being-in-the-world."[21] In the same place Heidegger notes the confusion of the definition of intersubjectivity with transcendence, stressing that "frequently the term is used to designate God" but in fact transcendence is what it means to be in the world, to reach out (transscend) to know anything at all.[22] The sphere of what is knowable is not the immanent, enclosed world, but the sphere of the transcendent, the transcendable. Heidegger stresses throughout his critique of intersubjectivity that the overdetermination of subjectivity results in a postulation of the subject's solipsism. He shows how there is no "outer" or "outside," because to be human is already to be constituted as "outside with," ready for encounter with others because being available to others is what it means to be human at all.[23] Human existence presupposes relatedness, even before any particular self comes to itself as particular and individual.

How did "the Transcendent" come to be a name for God in the first place? In the ancient, pre-Enlightenment understanding of the world, the cosmos is finite, and determined according to place rather than space. Space, as infinite space, has no correlate in the cosmos for either Plato or Aristotle. Highest, as that most reached out towards, is therefore the outermost limit of the heavens, a finite place, a limit, τὸ ἔσχατον. The outermost limit of the heavens, however, the apex of the cosmos, is the seat of the divine. Divinity here is understood as what makes the placements of place possible, the idea from which all other ideas flow. God, in other words, has a specific, locatable place in the cosmos, the place of the outermost reach, the limit of transcendence. When place, as τόπος, is no longer tenable, and when space is understood through an entirely geometrical arithmetic as the infinite and infinitely extensible, however, the Transcendent remains as a name for God, but is only reachable by an imaginary act, an abstraction from world, through a controlled, calculable act of reason. This act has no place, but must be performed as an act of the imagination, an act of will.

Discovering the other as other to the self is the basis of intersubjectivity, but is in fact a falsehood, arising exactly from the worldlessness that Heidegger traces. This "alterity" of the other is intended to protect the mysteriousness and unknownness of the other to myself, in the face of my self-transparency to myself.

I am, however, never really transparent to myself, for I have a future. The future is always unknown to me, and so hides me from myself (as forgetting does with respect to the past). The otherness of the other, moreover, is also never wholly *un*known to me, but just in my coming across you, you come into the place of my being, the event of my self-transcending. I am never subservient to the mystery that you are, but rather, together we are open to the future that commonly and separately neither of us yet has. Your mysteriousness lies ahead of me, as something to be discerned (which I could either instrumentalize or love), and yet, because you too have a future, I never overcome you totally, unless I take your future from you, as by an act of murder. My openness to my own future is at the same time my openness to the future that we share, that is at once the same and undivided. The self never knows what is not-itself, which is why even the self's coming to know God would have to be the divinization of the self. What is genuinely other to the self – "not-I" – is entirely hidden and concealed from the self, and remains entirely unknown to it, until I do indeed come upon it, as a mystery and something to be discerned, whose meaning cannot be exhausted because it has a future.

What are the consequences for prayer of this critique of intersubjectivity? A primary consequence of modern subjectival thinking is that, as I explained at the beginning, prayer is understood psychologically and intersubjectively, so that through an act of will (often described as an interiorization) I *elect* to step into, enact, produce the acts of shared prayer, in the prayer of the assembly or *ecclesia*. Recently a Christian composer was invited to speak about what he was doing when he composed contemporary religious music. He spoke of the way in which his faith informed his composition, and castigated the Catholic church for its abandonment of the use of Gregorian Chant, a chant, he claimed, which profoundly informed his music. One of the compositions he spoke of was to be performed for the first time in one of London's foremost concert venues, the Albert Hall. This prompted the question from the audience, "why the Albert Hall and not Westminster Cathedral?" I am making no criticism of him here, but the point is that for him, even composition concerned with faith was a self-articulation whose primary purpose was what we might call "auditory spectation." The tradition, chant, informs his work and is referenced by it, but as a genre, even if a genre of the sacred. The past tradition, the precursor and precondition for what he now does, exists now *for* him: it is his resource. He is himself constituting an access to an interior experience of faith which we, subsequent to his creativity, are invited to share. We "step in" to the place he opens up for us in performance, by purchasing a ticket to the Albert Hall. This is the music of *his* faith, not the music of faith as such. We may marvel, scoff, enjoy, or pass it by, but it is ours only subsequent to him. It is, in that sense, thoroughly postmodern.

What would it mean for prayer to take seriously Heidegger's demonstration that human being is always "outside" itself, that interiority is a fiction? In prayer we have no *private* access to God (which means that in prayer I do not address God through some non-worldly means, interior only to myself and discrete, but through words and language, even the language of silence). I offer one small example from the history of prayer to illustrate what I mean. In this example the language of prayer, rendered as singing, breaks the structures of mirroring and representation that constitute the human person subjectively, so that what is produced to be heard and understood is *not* the product of the human will, but the resonance of the human through invocation of the divine. The musicologist Marcel Pérès has examined in detail the Cistercian musical reforms of the thirteenth-century, and from his researches concludes: "The theoretical preoccupations of the Cistercians were not vain speculations; the intention of the reformers was directed at the incarnation of the Word through the agency of the most basic laws of the resonance of the human voice."[24]

Armed, however, with an understanding of human being and its relation to God, governed not by a modern conception of the spatiotemporal universe, but the ancient cosmology in a musical system still owing more to Pythagoras than to anyone else, and certainly not owing anything at all to the mechanization of music through the Baroque (the mathematical resolution of "equal temperament"), the Cistercians constituted by the harmonious collaboration of architecture, word, and practice, an icon of the heavens which was simultaneously an address, aimed at the wider church, in a reform that was also a figuration of the mystery of salvation.

What are the principles that underlay the chant for them? In the first place, the singing of the chant is constitutive of world as such (not *a* world, an imaginary, but the cosmos *entire*). This is not a community which an agent subject enters into, but rather, through the work that it undertakes (the *opus Dei* of Benedict's rule, prayer itself, as singing) the participant is revealed to be already a member of the company of heaven. Singing here is analogous to the unity and the movement of the heavens – an understanding derived directly from the Pythagorean and ancient understanding of the work of music in the movement of the heavens, a work that lifts the person into the heavens themselves, and so to the outermost limit of the heavens, the seat of the divine.

This view is Christianized in the sense that the heavens are understood as not of themselves eternal, but originate from God. The recitation of the psalms, and the participation in the sacrifice of Christ, therefore, constitutes the form the participant takes within the heavens in his or her relation to the God who creates *ab initio*. This form is that of Christ. In the second place, however, the Cistercian reform aims to reestablish a natural harmony between the heavens and the earth. Pérès makes the point that the great Cistercian abbeys – Fontenay, Sénanque, Le Thoronet, Fontfroide, and so on – were constructed to possess particular acoustic properties which amplified the human voice in such a way as to add harmonies to it that would not otherwise be apparent to the ear. Pérès adds: "Without recourse to the artifices of polyphony, a single voice, or the chorus in unison are able to produce harmonies that are not the work of the human will, but the effect of the fundamental laws of the vibration of sound-bodies, physical harmony, the impulse of matter that, by means of the absolute logic of its laws, renders the pereniality and the magnificence of the thought of God to the human ear."[25]

This form of being-with-one-another realizes, but does not enact, our common being in God, through baptism, through shared formation and faith, but never by a cogitative act of reason or deduction. Prayer, in this sense, has no ontology of its own, but is an event arising out of the constitutive ontological structures of the human person. The constitutive structure is being-with-one-another. This being-with-one-another will never need to reconstitute being with God through acts of compassion, empathy, or solidarity, because it does not need to recreate something which already is there, given by God and discovered in faith. Yet this being with one another will be filled with compassion, empathy, and is *already* solidarized because these are the conditions that you and I will both be drawn to, in finding ourselves already together with a God of love. We will not choose or will to be compassionate, but will be drawn (or even driven, as the Spirit so inflames us) to share with others the compassion we have received.

Being, as singing-with-others, can never be intersubjectival, for my singing is never directed towards the *thou*, towards you. Our singing directs us towards song as such, which by no will of ours lifts us to the heavens. And yet the Pythagorean cosmos is gone. If I take Augustine's maxim, "who sings, prays twice," who now sings? And is my yearning to sing the praises of God and so yearning, finding myself alone all over again, unsung, none other than the default of the absence of God in postmodernity?

Notes

1 Matthew 6. 6. "But when you pray, go into your room and shut the door and pray to your Father who is in secret; and your Father who sees in secret will reward you." (σὺ δὲ ὅταν προσεύχῃ, εἴσελθε εἰς τὸ ταμεῖόν σου καὶ κλείσας τὴν θύραν σου πρόσευξαι τῷ πατρί σου τῷ ἐν τῷ κρυπτῷ· καὶ ὁ πατήρ σου ὁ βλέπων ἐν τῷ κρυπτῷ ἀποδώσει σοι.)

2 René Descartes, *Meditationes de prima philosophia: Meditations on First Philosophy*, trans. George Heffernan (Notre Dame, IN: Notre Dame University Press, 1990), *Meditatio* III, p. 128. "Nam proculdubio illæ quæ substantias mihi exhibent, majus aliquid sunt, atque, ut ita loquar, plus realitatis objectivæ in se continent, quàm illæ tantùm modos, sive accidentia, repræsentant; & rursus illa per quam summum aliquem Deum, æternum, infinitum, omniscium, omnipotentem, rerumque omnium, quæ præter ipsum sunt, creatorem intelligo, plus profecto realitatis objectivæ in se habet, quàm illæ per quas finitæ substantiae exhibentur."

3 Ibid, p. 136. "Dei nomine intelligo substantiam quandam infinitam, independentem, summe intelligentem, summe potentem, & a quâ tum ego ipse, tum aliud omne, si quid aliud extat, quodcumque extat, est creatum."

4   G. W. von Leibniz, *La Monadologie*, in *G. G. Leibnitii Opera Philosophica*, ed. J. E. Erdmann, Berlin, 1840 (containing for the first time the original French text of 1714). Translated as *Monadology* in *Philosophical Writings* by Mary Morrison and G. H. R. Parkinson (London: Everyman, 1995 [1934]).
5   Leibniz, *La Monadologie*, §1. "La Monade, dont nous parlerons ici, n'est autre chose qu'une substance simple . . . sans parties."
6   Ibid, §38. "Et c'est ainsi que la dernière raison des choses doit être dans une substance nécessaire dans laquelle le détail des changements ne soit qu'éminemment, comme dans la source: et c'est ce que nous appelons Dieu."
7   Aquinas, *Summa Theologiae*, I Ia. 2, A. 3.
8   Leibniz, *La Monadologie*, §79. "Les âmes agissent selon les lois des causes finales par appétitions, fins et moyens. Les corps agissent selon les lois des causes efficientes ou des mouvements. Et les deux règnes, celui des causes efficientes et celui des causes finales, sont harmoniques entre eux.
9   Ibid, §15. "L'action du principe interne qui fait le changement ou le passage d'une perception à une autre peut être appelé appétition."
10 Martin Heidegger, *Einleitung in die Philosophie* in *Gesamtausgabe*, vol. 27 (Frankfurt: Klostermann, 1996), p. 144. "Jede Monade spiegelt je das Ganze des Seienden, aber jede von verschiedenem Augenpunkt her und verschieden nach Graden der Wachheit . . . von diesen gibt es eine Stufenleiter bis zur Zentralmonade Gott, Gott im Sinne der christliche Theologie gedacht."
11 See in particular Aquinas's discussion of the relation of the unity of things in the simplicity of God are reflected in their differentiation as in a mirror in *Quæstiones Disputatae: de Veritatae*, Qu. 8, Art. 4, Resp., and Art. 10. See also *de Veritate*, Qu. 3, and *Summa Theologiae*, I Ia. Qu. 14, esp. Art. 1, Resp.: "Similiter etiam in cognitivis aliquis qui est elevatioris intellectus, ex paucis principiis penes se retentis habet in promptu procedere ad varias conclusiones, ad quas pervenire non possunt qui sunt hebetioris ingenii, nisi per varias inductiones, et per principia particulariter coaptata conclusionibus." The same understanding of the hierarchy of intelligences is found in Aquinas's consideration of ideas and knowledge.
12 David R. Lachterman, *The Ethics of Geometry* (London: Routledge, 1989), p. ix.
13 Ibid.
14 Leibniz, *La Monadologie*, §7. "Les monades n'ont point de fenêtres."
15 Judith Butler, *The Psychic Life of Power: Theories in Subjection* (Stanford, CA: Stanford University Press, 1997), esp. ch. 3.
16 Martin Heidegger, *Identität und Differenz* in *Gesamtausgabe*, vol. 11 (Pfullingen: Neske, 1990 [1957]), p. 51. Translated by Joan Stambaugh as *Identity and Difference* (New York: Harper Torchbooks, 1969). "Inwieweit gelingt eine Erklärung? Insoweit wir beachten: Die Sache des Denkens ist das Seiende als solches, d.h. das Sein. Dieses zeigt sich in der Wesensart des Grundes. Demgemäß wird die Sache des Denkens, das Sein als der Grund, nur dann gründlich gedacht, wenn der Grund als der erste Grund, πρώτη ἀρχή, vorgestellt wird. Die ursprüngliche Sache des Denkens stellt sich als die Ur-Sache dar, als die causa prima, die dem begründenden Rückgang auf die ultima ratio, die letzte Rechenschaft, entspricht. Das Sein des Seienden wird im Sinne des Grundes gründlich nur als causa sui vorgestellt. Damit ist der metaphysische Begriff von Gott genannt. Die Metaphysik muß auf den Gott hinaus denken, weil die Sache des Denkens das Sein ist, dieses aber in vielfachen Weisen als Grund: als λόγος, als ὑποκείμενον, als Substanz, als Subjekt west." ["To what extent is an explanation successful? To the extent that we take heed of the fol-

lowing: the matter of thinking is beings as such, that is, Being. Being shows itself in the nature of the ground. Accordingly, the matter of thinking, Being as the ground, is thought out fully only when the ground is represented as the first ground, πρώτη ἀρχή. The original matter of thinking presents itself as the first cause, the *causa prima* that corresponds to the reason-giving path to the *ultima ratio*, the final accounting. The Being of beings is represented fundamentally, in the sense of the ground, only as *causa sui*. This is the metaphysical concept of God. Metaphysics must think in the direction of the deity because the matter of thinking is Being; but Being is in being as ground in diverse ways: as λόγος, as ὑποκείμενον, as substance, as subject."]

17 Leibniz, *La Monadologie*, §86. "Cette Cité de Dieu, cette Monarchie véritablement universelle est un Monde Moral, dans le Monde Naturel."
18 *Einleitung in die Philosophie*, p. 141. "'Einfühlung'"; cf., for instance, Martha Nussbaum, "Compassion: The Basic Social Emotion," in *Social Philosophy and Policy*, vol. 13, no. 1 (winter 1996).
19 Heidegger, *Einleitung in die Philosophie*, p. 142. "Das Problem des Miteinanderseins ist nicht erst eine Frage der Beziehung von Subjekt zu Subjekt, sondern vordem ein Problem, das zur Wesensbestimmung eines Subjekts als solchem gehört."
20 For Heidegger's critique of Descartes' establishment of interiority through mathematics, and the appeal to geometry as μάθησις, see *Die Frage nach dem Ding*, in *Gesamtausgabe*, vol. 41 (Tübingen: Niemeyer, 1962), pp. 52–82. Translated by Barton Deutsch as *What is a Thing?* (Washington, DC: Gateway, 1979).
21 Martin Heidegger, *Die Grundprobleme der Phänomenologie*, in *Gesamtausgabe*, vol. 24 (Frankfurt: Klostermann, 1996), p. 142. Translated by Albert Hofstadter as *The Basic Problems of Phenomenology* (Bloomington, IN: Indiana University Press, 1988). "Selbst und Welt sind nicht zwei Seiende, wie Subjekt und Objekt, auch nicht wie Ich und Du, sondern Selbst und Welt sind in der Einheit der Struktur des In-Welt-Seins die Grundbestimmung des Daseins selbst."
22 Heidegger, *Die Grundprobleme der Phänomenologie*, pp. 424ff. "Oft bezeichnet man mit dem Transzendenten Gott."
23 Heidegger, *Einleitung in die Philosophie*, p. 138.
24 Marcel Pérès, *Chant Cistercien du XIII*^{e} (Paris: Fondation, 1992). "Les préoccupations théoriques des cisterciens n'étaient pas de vaines spéculations: les réformateurs avaient pour dessein l'incarnation du Verbe par l'intermédiaire de lois de résonance les plus fondamentales de la voix humaine." Cf. Michel Huglo and Marcel Pérès, *Aspects de la Musique Liturgique au Moyen Age* (Paris: Éditions Créaphis, 1991).
25 Ibid., "Ainsi, sans avoirs recours à l'artifice de la polyphonie, voix seule ou chœr à l'unisson peuvent faire entendre des harmonies qui ne sont pas l'œuvre de la volonté humaine mais l'effet des lois fondamentales de vibration des corps sonores, harmonie physique, élan de la matière qui par l'absolue logique de ses lois rend accessible à l'entendement humain la pérennité et la magnificence de la pensée de Dieu."

CHAPTER 27
The Christian Message and the Dissolution of Metaphysics

Gianni Vattimo

For many of us in the English-speaking world Gianni Vattimo is known for his studies of Nietzsche and Heidegger. The essays collected in *The End of Modernity: Nihilism and Hermeneutics in Postmodern Culture* (Oxford, 1988) introduced him to the English public as a philosopher investigating the "closure of modernity and its consequences for the arts and sciences" (ibid, p. vii). Vattimo's was a philosophical approach to postmodernity, and although some of us drew upon his work in order to situate contemporary theological projects, he himself was not, at that time, known to be concerned with religious issues. What drew him into religious and theological debates was the question of interpretation. In a series of books, most recently *Beyond Interpretation: The Meaning of Hermeneutics for Philosophy* (Oxford, 1997), Vattimo has developed what he terms a hermeneutical ontology, where hermeneutics is related to the processes of becoming. It is the unavoidability and the endlessness of the hermeneutical task which, for Vattimo, challenges substantial notions of Being; if modernity can be characterized as in thrall to the metaphysics of Being, hermeneutics performs the dissolution of such a metaphysics. His hermeneutical approach differs from the romantic notion of interpretation providing access to the ultimately meaningful. Hermeneutics becomes a way of living in a world that is always a fiction. One can relate this work to Don Cupitt's, though the critique of metaphysics is shared with most postmodern theologians.

Vattimo was introduced to hermeneutics by his teacher Luigi Pareyson who, fascinated by existentialism, introduced Heidegger's work into post-World War II Italian philosophy. In 1968, following researches into the hermeneutics of Heidegger and Gadamer, Vattimo published a book still only available in Italian, *Schleiermacher, filosofo dell'interpretazione*. His treatment is not of Schleiermacher as a theologian, and by Vattimo's own account it was only during the 1980s that he began to see parallels between his thinking on the dissolution of Being and the emptying of the Word in Christianity's account of kenosis. Increasingly, his thinking was dominated by the "death of God," as for instance in a book translated as *The Adventure of Difference: Philosophy After Nietzsche and Heidegger* (Oxford, 1993). The ghost of Nietzsche, of course, haunts Turin, where Nietzsche first collapsed into a madness that silenced him and where Vattimo was born and now teaches. It was only with the English-language translation and publication of *Religion* (Oxford, 1996), a book he edited with Jacques Derrida, that Vattimo explicitly began to engage with religious questions. His essay in that collection points the way towards his more recent work. He treats there what has been understood as the Enlightenment's overcoming of religion (and the subsequent account of secularization) in the light of the current revival of religious thinking. Derrida, struck by the same phenomenon, suggested religion as the topic for discussion at a conference on the island of Capri in March 1994. Vattimo writes: "In religion, something that we had thought irrevocably forgotten is made present again, a dormant trace is reawakened, a wound reopened, the repressed returns and what we took to be an *Uberwindung* (overcoming, realization and setting aside) is no more than a *Verwindung*, a long convalescence that has once again to come to terms with the indelible trace of its sickness" (ibid, p. 79). The language of this essay still views religion, after Freud, as a pathology, and yet this religious trace has remained compelling for Vattimo. The English-language translation of his book *Belief* (Oxford, 1999) discusses in depth the question of the incarnation of God in language and kenosis as a movement of self-exhausting charity. These are themes evident in the following essay: "nihilism as the death of Jesus evoked by the gospel" or "why Christianity should be considered the starting point of the modern dissolution of metaphysics." This nihilism does not repeat Nietzsche's (or Heidegger's), for it is a nihilism of love, not a reactive nihilism – a charity dissolving truth. This brings his work close to that of John D. Caputo.

It could be stated, as a very general view, that what has happened in the two thousand years which separate us from that mysterious event to which our calendars refer (our calendars? Yes and no) is the progressive consumption, or dissolution, of the validity of the famous maxim "amicus Plato sed magis amica veritas" (attributed by ancient biographers to Aristotle). We can recall, for example, that an expression of this dissolution can also be found in an author such as Dostoyevsky. When he evokes the choice between Christ and truth (*The Devils*, part 2, ch. 7) Satov attributes it to Stavrogin. However, in a letter Dostoyevsky utters this on his own behalf. But it is not only in the name of love for Christ that this sentence is refuted or overturned. In fact, Dostoyevsky constitutes a paradoxical case since, generally speaking, starting from Jesus's words "ego sum via, veritas et vita," Christian thought has rather been inclined to identify Christ with the truth – understood in the classical sense of truth as corresponding to a state of things – and has therefore denied the possibility of any alternation between these two terms. It is perhaps here that the meaning of the exceptional position of Dostoyevsky in Christian thought or *for* Christian thought is to be found (I am thinking of the studies made by my teacher, Luigi Pareyson). Apart from Dostoyevsky, the classical feature of Christianity has been to identify truth as an exact and objective description of "reality" with the truth that is Christ. If truth has the power to liberate us it is because it is only by knowing what reality is that we can liberate ourselves (but from what? Surely not from truth/reality itself, however unpleasant and oppressive it may be . . .). Redemption ("Redimisti nos Domine, Deus veritatis," as a prayer of the *completorium* of the Roman breviary states) would therefore consist of "seeing" Being itself for what it is: "amor dei intellectualis," to use Spinoza's words. The traditional idea that eternal life consists of a (face-to-face) contemplation of God has in fact been interpreted in the Spinozian sense, which ends with identifying beatitude with a perfect knowledge of geometry. Could it be for this purpose that the second person of the Holy Trinity became incarnate and was sacrificed on the cross?

Starting from these reflections, it seems obvious, rather, that it is Dostoyevsky, with his paradox of the choice of Christ even against truth, who is the Christian thinker who is the most faithful to the meaning of the gospel. However, even more than in Dostoyevsky, and certainly more paradoxically, this faithfulness to the gospel is to be found in the work of Nietzsche, in his announcement of the death of God. Not only does this announcement, in its literal sense, simply repeat the evangelical history of the crucifixion, but most of all it means that since God who is dead, killed by his faithful, is justly, and only, the moral God – the supreme guarantor of this order of the (geometric) world who made the dying Socrates say that a righteous man has nothing to fear, either in this life or in life after death – it is primarily in Nietzsche himself that the most radical expression of Dostoyevsky's paradox is to be found.

Nietzsche does not understand this paradox to be a moral alternative with which every individual would be confronted during his path towards salvation. Rather, he sees it, and it is in this sense that I propose to interpret it here, as the very meaning of the history of Europe, of the West, and of "Christian" modernity. The death of the "moral" God marks the end of the possibility of preferring truth to friendship, because this death means that there is no "objective" or ontological truth, etc., which can claim to be anything other than simply the expression of a friendship, or of a wish for power, or of a subjective relationship. Even those who believe "magis amica veritas" do it in the name of love of another or of themselves, of the tradition which is expressed in them, or for the "human, too human" motives which Nietzsche so meticulously analyzed in the wake of the French moralists. Friendship, Will, or even, to use Pascal's words, "reasons of the heart."

If European nihilism (as stated in the famous article which bears this title and which was written in Lenzer Heide during the summer of 1887) is the end of belief in an objective order of the world, and thus justifies a fidelity to truth beyond any particular friendship or hostility, then what Nietzsche refused to see (namely did not wish to see or could not see, because of his own hostilities as a son of a pastor raised in the shadow of the church as recorded in one of his autobiographical articles) is the fact that this nihilism is not only the Nietzschean meaning of the death of God but is also the meaning of the death of Jesus as stated in the gospel.

In other words, it is what Heidegger calls the end of metaphysics. We know that, for Heidegger, the end of metaphysics is rightly accomplished in Nietzsche's nihilism and in the phenomenon of history and destiny which Neitzsche's doctrine acknowledges, describes, and proclaims. From the Nietzschean–Heideggerian point of view with which I am dealing here, nihilism is the loss of belief in an objective truth in favor of a viewpoint which understands it as an effect of power – in the many meanings of this expression: scientific experimentation which realizes the *principium reddendae rationis* – the foundation of which is based on the active will of the subjects constructing the experiment and of those who, in the context of a paradigm which even if it is not arbitrary is certainly historical, accept it as being valid; an ideology deemed to be true by those who belong to a certain class; a lie invented by monks to justify power and social discipline.

In what sense can this consummation of objective truth in the expression of different friendships – and therefore for "reasons of the heart" – be considered as an effect of the death of Christ, or as a development of this mysterious event which constitutes the basis of our modern calculation of time?

The author who is most likely to help us answer this question, or the one who in my opinion should be referred to, is Wilhelm Dilthey, who certainly took over Hegel's legacy but updated it in order to make Hegel's philosophy of history less rigid and systematic. In the second volume of his great unfinished work, *Einleitung in die Geisteswissenschaften*, Dilthey traces the history of European metaphysics, which is divided into two stages: the metaphysical stage of the ancients and that of modern man, the latter being destined to end with the dissolution of metaphysics which was completed by the criticism of Kant and by its developments until Dilthey's historicism.

What distinguishes the metaphysics of the ancients from that of modern man is the turning point which is manifested with the advent of Christianity, and which shifts the center of philosophical interest from the natural world to human spirituality. For Dilthey, Platonism is the emblem of the metaphysics of the ancients even if it is not strictly speaking naturalism. Its value as an emblem consists of the idea that Being (as Heidegger would later state, his vision of the history of metaphysics being deeply influenced by Dilthey's reconstruction) was conceived by Plato as visible form – idea, *eidos*; and consequently as an external "fact," placed before the eyes of the spirit as an objective form. Christianity, on the contrary, shifts the attention of thought towards spirituality, and in so doing places Will rather than intellect in the foreground. As is shown by the first few pages of the second volume of the *Einleitung*:

> to the Greek mind, knowing meant reproducing an objective Being in the intellect. Then (or with Christianity), the center of all the interests of the new communities

(Christians) became actual experience. But this simply means an awareness of what is occurring in the person, namely self-awareness. With their enormous advantage, the experiences of Will and heart devour any other object of knowledge. If the faith of these new communities had, even then, at once developed a science which completely corresponded to that faith, this science would have had to consist of a foundation based on spiritual experience.[1]

Christianity, to summarize it briefly but accurately, is the condition which prepares for the dissolution of metaphysics and its substitution by what is termed Gnosticism by Dilthey and Kant. Emphasis on the subject, the foundation of knowledge on a spiritual awareness of oneself, these are the principles which inspired Descartes and Kant and which have come to dominate modern philosophy. The latter for a long time remained a metaphysics which was dominated by an objectivist view of spirituality itself, because the principle of subjectivity introduced by Christianity did not immediately succeed in becoming influential. "During the Middle Ages, the connection, from the standpoint of the foundation of knowledge, between Christianity and knowledge based upon spiritual experience did not succeed in producing a corresponding basis for science. This omission can be attributed to the superiority of a classical culture in which Christianity only started to become influential in a slow and progressive manner."[2]

The conflict between the "new vintage" of Christian spirituality and the "superiority" of the "visual" or aesthetic objectivism of the Greeks is well represented by the thinking of St Augustine. In his thinking, the spiritual certainty of the relationship of the soul with God is combined with a theory of *veritates aeternae* derived from Platonism and Neoplatonism: "the soul grasps the truth by itself and not through the body or the sensory organs. We are thus right back in the middle of Plato's metaphysics, which we thought we had left behind."[3] "In St Augustine's 'spiritual experience' there are elements which transcend this Plato-like connection between the human intellect, the world and the God of *veritates aeternae* ... namely a component which transcends the thinking of classical antiquity."[4] What occurs in the thinking of St Augustine (it should also be noted that what is dealt with here is not simply the traditional opposition between Platonism and Aristotelianism in Christian thinking, but is rather a conflict between what remains of Greek thinking, especially Platonist thinking, and the "Kantian" newness represented by Christianity) can also be found, in different stages of development, in the history of Christianity as a whole, from the Middle Ages to modernity. Until Kant, who finally deduced the anti-metaphysical consequences of the inaugural movement represented by the Christian message, there was conflict between the new possibility offered to thought by Christianity and the resistance of metaphysics. The reasons for this resistance are numerous and complex: in his personal history, Dilthey now and then points out these reasons with regard to St Augustine, which are indicated by the influence of Neoplatonism. In a more general manner, for St Augustine as for all church Fathers and medieval thinkers, this resistance can be explained by the social and political responsibility which the church had to assume after the fall of the Roman empire, inasmuch as it had to shoulder the burden both of the vestiges of ancient social institutions and of the culture of which they were an expression. Most of all, however, both because of this responsibility as a "stand-in," to use a contemporary phrase, and because of its hierarchical organization, the church developed as a rigid structure, which was (inevitably) based on objectivist metaphysics and also on the claimed scientific knowledge of the natural world (as the case of Galileo clearly attests).

However, this view of the history of European thought as the history of a struggle between the principle of dissolution of metaphysics – spirituality, Will, the certainty of thought – which was introduced by Christianity, and the visual–naturalistic (aesthetic) objectivism of Greek culture, profoundly characterizes Heidegger's view of survival and of the dissolution of metaphysics. I emphasize the fact that, more explicitly in Heidegger but also in Dilthey, there is absolutely no question of a struggle between the "natural" (or paradoxically, "objective") truth of Christian subjectivism and a metaphysics which would ultimately reveal itself as a falsification of this authentic truth. The Christian assertion is actually a historical event and is not the revelation, through Christ, of an eternal truth. Rather, it is a struggle between two historical possibilities, or, it could be said, between two "friendships." This is also expressed, in different terms, in Husserl's *Krisis*: the crisis of European science does not consist of a betrayal of a claimed "natural" essence of science which modern science has forgotten and abandoned; it is (only) a lack of fidelity to the ideal of an "absolute" and totally founded science (although there may be a contradiction in Husserl himself here), an ideal which originated at a particular moment in history and which we can no longer live without (but why? Only the ontology of Heidegger's *Ereignis* can justify this).

Let us return to our theme. It seems essential to me to reconsider Dilthey in order to understand why Christianity should be considered the starting point of the modern dissolution of metaphysics. It is sufficient to acknowledge – and this is the sense of Heidegger's existentialism in *Sein und Zeit* – that Kantism is still a sort of Augustinism, namely it is a claim that spiritual certainty can be traced back to a non-historical, "natural" structure, which in this sense is an objective structure (the transcendental of Kant, which had already been criticized by Dilthey in these terms), in order to see that the most radical inheritors of the anti-metaphysical principle introduced into the world by Christ, are Nietzsche in his Death of God and Heidegger in his doctrine of *Ereignis*. A detail which I should like to emphasize is that there is something profoundly Christian in Dilthey's conclusion relating to history and the dissolution of metaphysics. For example, Dilthey writes that even though metaphysics has become impossible as a science, "the metaphysical element of our lives as a personal experience, or, in other words, as a religious and moral truth, still remains. The experiences of the Will of a person remain, but fall short of a universal demonstration which would be convincing and binding again for any other intellect."[5]

> However, where a human being breaks, by his Will, the connection between perception and liking stimulus and pleasure, in which connection he no longer likes himself, this is the metaphysical trait which, in the history of metaphysics which has been explained by us, has not ceased to be reflected in countless images. In fact, metaphysics is a historically delimited phenomenon, but the metaphysical conscience of a person is eternal.[6]

It would be difficult, but not impossible, to interpret this passage as a critical pointer which identifies the survival of metaphysical objectivism with Schopenhauer's denial of Will. Rather, this is an ambiguity. On the one hand we could suspect that the denial of self and of Will is an extreme way of preferring the object to the subject (this is indeed how Adorno, in a chapter of his *Negative Dialektik*, reproaches Heidegger's ontology). On the other hand, the tone of this passage rather makes us think that Dilthey sees this "eternal metaphysics," which is manifested as surpassing the will to live, as something positive, as a metaphysical residue, in the high and unsurpassable sense which this implies even for our post-Kantian modernity, a spirit of denial of the Will which also inspired a notion such as Heidegger's notion of *Gelassenheit*. Moreover, the ambiguity which I have just emphasized is more or less the same as the one we can find in Heidegger's vision of the end of metaphysics as a triumph of modern subjectivism and voluntarism: the ultimate stage of oblivion, but also the first *Aufblitzen* of the *Ereignis*, the first flash of the event of Being, as is stated in a famous passage of *Identity and Difference*.[7]

Finally, why *amicus Plato*, why friendship instead of truth? Here we possibly encounter the ultimate manifestation of the struggle between the resistance of the "objectivist residue" of Greek metaphysics and the force of Christian newness. In very brief terms, the nihilism of Nietzsche and the ontologism of Heidegger in the sense criticized by Levinas are still evidence of the same combination of Christianity and Platonic–Greek objectivism which was observed by Dilthey in St Augustine. (In passing, we could ask ourselves if these two thinkers, in different ways, are only expressing the presence, which is similar in each of them, of personal and psychological elements: Nietzsche, the son of a pastor, who rebelled against the authority of his father, his sister, etc.; Heidegger who distanced himself from the Catholic church at the very start of his academic career.) This was itself combined with intentions which are largely political or which relate to power (I am thinking of the last writings of Nietzsche, of his letters to kings and statesmen, and of Heidegger's Nazi adventures). Thus, Nietzsche and Heidegger themselves, to different degrees and for reasons which are broadly analogous to those of St Augustine, remained imprisoned by Greek objectivism and fundamentally refused to develop all the implications of the anti-metaphysical Christian revolution.

These implications cannot be fully developed without recourse to charity. To express this again in a very schematic way: it is only friendship which is explicitly acknowledged as a decisive factor of truth which prevents us thinking of the end of metaphysics as bringing to a head what we could call, with Nietzsche, reactive (and even reactionary) nihilism.

I will confine myself to an outline which seems to me to be at least an indicative one but which is in need of further clarification. It is impossible for me not to see, in the central role assumed by the other (the Other? Here we encounter the problem of the theological objectivism of Levinas himself), in theories as diverse as the thinking of Levinas and Habermas's philosophy of communication, or in the use of the term "charity" by Davidson, a confirmation of my own hypothesis on the central role of charity.

Why, then, should we not prefer Levinas, Habermas, and Davidson rather than the questionable authority of controversial thinkers such as Nietzsche and Heidegger? This could be answered, but this time in a simplified manner, by stating that it is only Nietzsche and Heidegger, with their reconstruction of history (because this is also in Nietzsche: I am thinking here of the chapter on "As the real world came to an end by becoming a fable" in *Twilight of the Idols*) and of the dissolution of metaphysics, who offer a rigorous philosophical foundation to theories which are more open to charity, such as those of Habermas and Levinas. To state this more explicitly, friendship can only become the principle, the factor of truth, if thought has abandoned any claim to an objective, universal, and apodictic foundation. Without a genuine opening to Being as an event, the other of Levinas always risks being seen as deposed by the Other (with a capital O) – which this time is a truth which "justifies" friendship for Plato only by eliminating the other as a historic individual. A similar discourse seems also to be valid for Habermas, for whom non-opaque communication which functions as a normative horizon is not based on respect for the other as such, but rather on an intent to reduce the other and myself to an idea of "transparent" rationality. This idea, even if it does not call to mind the rationalist metaphysics of Kant, or rather exactly because it claims to do so, is only in the final instance a colonization of the world of life by strategic rationality, which dominates science and technology.

The Christian preaching of charity is not only, or is not by any means, an ethical, or rather an edifying consequence of the revelation of "objective" truth regarding our very nature as children of God. Rather, it is an appeal which arises from the historical fact of the Incarnation (which is historical not only in the sense that it is a "real" fact but in the sense that in its *Wirkungsgeschichte* it constitutes our existence) and which speaks to us of a nihilistic purpose of Being, a teleology of the enfeeblement of any "ontic" rigidity in favor of an ontological being, namely of *Verbum*, *Logos*, words which are interchanged in the *Gespraech*, which we are inasmuch as we are historical beings.

Truth as charity and Being as *Ereignis*, or as an event, are two aspects which are closely associated with each other. The central role of the Other in many contemporary philosophical theories acquires the whole of its significance if we put it in the context of the dissolution of metaphysics, and it is only this condition which avoids the risk of what is purely and simply an edifying moralism, or of what is purely a "pragmatic" moralism. ("Anyway, it is still better to live in a world of friends.") With all the inaccuracies which a conclusion such as this (even a provisional one) allows to exist, it seems to me that it is from this point that reflection has to commence on what remains not only to be remembered but also to be done, two thousand years after the event of Christianity.

Translated by A. J. Wickens

Notes

This essay is taken from a paper given at the Sorbonne in December 1999, in the course of the congress "deux mille ans après quoi."

1 Wilhelm Dilthey, *Introduzione alle scienze dello spirito*, trans. De Toni (Florence: La Nuova Italia, 1974), pp. 324–5.
2 Ibid, p. 325.
3 Ibid, p. 338.
4 Ibid, p. 339.
5 Ibid, pp. 492–3.
6 Ibid, p. 494.
7 Martin Heidegger, *Identitat und Differenz* (Pfullingen: Neske, 1957).

PART VII
Derrideans

28	The Poetics of the Impossible and the Kingdom of God	469
29	Anti-Discrimination	482
30	Is There a Postmodern Gospel?	490
31	Indian Territory: Postmodernism Under the Sign of the Body	505

CHAPTER 28
The Poetics of the Impossible and the Kingdom of God

John D. Caputo

Schooled in Aquinas and Augustine from a continuing Catholic education (he holds a Chair at Villanova University, a Catholic institution), Jack Caputo's work has followed in the footsteps of Aquinas and concerned itself with the overcoming of the metaphysical project. There is a clear line of development and continuity between Caputo's first books, *The Mystical Element in Heidegger's Thought* (Athens, OH, 1978) and *Heidegger and Aquinas: An Essay in Overcoming Metaphysics* (New York, 1982), and the following essay, in which he examines the way "the kingdom confounds philosophers who are accustomed to arrange things according to the 'principles' of being, reason, order, possibility, presence, sense, and meaning." Caputo was first taught to read the world this way by Heidegger, particularly in Heidegger's lectures on Nietzsche and *Identity and Difference*. It seems to me that Caputo takes from Heidegger, not only a critique of the metaphysics of presence (and the ontotheology inextricably bound to such a metaphysics), but also an understanding of the destiny of thought. For it is not simply that Heidegger's examination of *Ereignis* critiques the possibility of things being fully present to themselves (the very basis for modernity's positivisms and empiricisms), but Heidegger demonstrates that any thing and any question concerning that thing, comes out of a certain epoch, a trajectory of what can be thought. After Nietzsche and the "death of God" a specific project gives itself to be thought, and that project is the overcoming of metaphysics. For Caputo, unlike Thomas Altizer and Don Cupitt (chapters 25 and 29, this volume) or Mark C. Taylor, this overcoming is not the dissolution of the theological in terms of various atheologies and mystical nihilisms. The overcoming of metaphysics is not the final nail in the coffin for a dead God. Rather, the overcoming of metaphysics opens again the God-question and, as is evident from his essay, the scriptural question concerning the coming of the kingdom. It is perhaps then no surprise to find Caputo turning from Heidegger (who always was ambivalent about his theological position) to certain forms of post-Heideggerian thinking which explicitly treat the theological. The work of Emmanuel Levinas and Jacques Derrida has profoundly influenced him. His relationship (both intellectual and personal) with Derrida has been a long one. In print it began with his book *Radical Hermeneutics: Repetition, Deconstruction and the Hermeneutical Project* (Bloomington, IN, 1987) and flowered into a passionate and poetic tribute to Derrida in *The Prayers and Tears of Jacques Derrida: Religion without Religion* (Bloomington, IN, 1997). Derrida speaks to Caputo not only about how to take Heidegger's observations further (with respect to a way of closely reading specific texts, the instability of interpretation, and the nature of undecidability). Derrida's words also recall Caputo to Kierkegaard's in the same way as Heidegger's words had recalled Eckhart's and Aquinas's. In his book *Against Ethics: Contributions to a Poetics of Obligation with Constant Reference to Deconstruction* (Bloomington, IN, 1993) Caputo drew out these associations between deconstruction and what Kierkegaard in *Fear and Trembling* called "the suspension of the ethical." He did this prior to the publication in English of Derrida's own commentary on *Fear and Trembling*, *The Gift of Death* (French text 1992). It is Kierkegaard who will write about the work of faith with respect to the absurd, and the expectation of the impossible. It is Derrida who will revisit these lines of thinking in developing his own "religion without religion" or "messianism without the Messiah." Thinking out a certain destiny of thought-opening by Nietzsche, announced by Heidegger, developed by Levinas and Derrida, reminiscent of Kierkegaard and figured within the Catholic tradition through theologians as different as Peter Damian and Thomas Aquinas, Caputo writes (with commitment, intensity, and rhetorical flair) of a Christianity refigured for postmodernity.

A Poetics of the Impossible

The "kingdom of God" abides by a certain logic, but it is a divine logic. From the point of view of the "world," which is its antagonist, what goes on in the kingdom looks mad and even impossible. Still, it can be said in defense of the kingdom, it is not simply impossible, but rather, let us say, *the* impossible. We might even speak of the "logic" of *the* impossible, on the perfectly logical assumption that with God all things are possible (Luke 1.37), including the maddest and most impossible. But beyond any possible logic, even a logic of the impossible, I prefer to speak of a "poetics" of the impossible. By a poetics I mean a constellation of strategies, arguments, tropes, paradigms, and metaphors, a style and a tone, as well as a grammar and a vocabulary, all of which, collectively, like a great army on the move, is aimed at making a point. We might say that a poetics is a logic with a heart, not a simple or bare bones logic but a logic with *pathos*, with a passion and desire, with an imagination and a flare, a mad logic, perhaps a patho-logic, but one that is healing and salvific. A poetics of *the* impossible describes the movements of a desire beyond desire, a desire beyond reason and what is reasonably possible, a desire to know what we cannot know, or to love what we dare not love, like a beggar in love with a princess, whose desire is not extinguished but fired *by* the impossibility of his plight. For our hearts are burning with a desire to go where we cannot go, praying and weeping for what eye has not seen nor ear heard, hoping against hope (Rom. 4.18). To desire what is merely possible, to curb our passion so that it remains confined by the parameters of a carefully calculated probability – what would that amount to if not a lover without passion, who is, according to Johannes Climacus, a "mediocre fellow"?[1]

This poetics has cultivated an ear for parable and paradox and a taste not for measure or moderation but for excess and going beyond, for the hyperbolic, for the odd system of accounting – the "aneconomy" – in the kingdom. The way things are counted in the kingdom confounds the calculations of the "world." If your brother offends you seven times a day, you should forgive him, and that still holds even if he offends you seven times seventy, which seems excessive. If one sheep among a hundred is lost and then found, there is more rejoicing over that one than over the ninety-nine, which is an unaccountably odd way to count, since there is more profit in the ninety-nine and the one is not worth the risk to the ninety-nine, as any cost accountant, who knows how to calculate risks, can assure us. In the kingdom there is an odd predilection for reversals: the last shall be first, sinners are preferred to the righteous, the stranger is the neighbor, the insiders are out. That makes for the astonishing hospitality portrayed in the story of the wedding banquet in which the guests are casual passers-by who are dragged in off the street while the invited guests snub the host. That seems like an excessively mad party, which would stretch the imagination even of a Lewis Carroll. In general, in the kingdom, the general rule is the rule of the unruly, the possibility of the impossible.

The poetics of the impossible does not spring from a taste for heady rhetoric or from impish authors with no head for logic. On the contrary, it is a discourse with a deadly serious concern, a *prophetic* concern to *contradict* the "world," to confound its calculations, and to *interdict* its hardness of heart, its cold-blooded logic, and heartless economics. When St Paul says that God chose the foolish and weak things of the world to *shame* the wise and strong, and that God chose the nothings and nobodies (*ta me onta*) of the world to *reduce to nothing* the things that boast of being and presence (*ta onta*), he was confronting the world head on, trying to shock and startle and antagonize the world with the way things happen in the kingdom (1 Cor. 1.27–9). For the kingdom comes to contest the economy of the world, to loosen the grip of the world's merciless rationality. The world keeps rigorous books. Nothing is for free and nobody gets off scot free. Everything is for sale, everything has a price, and nothing is sacred. The world will stop at nothing to get even, to even a score, or to come out ahead; the world is pomp and power and ruthless reckoning. In the world, offenders are made to pay for their offense and every investor expects a return; every equation is balanced and every bill is paid, in one way or another, with blood or money.

The poetics of the kingdom is prophetic – a diction of contradiction and interdiction – that "calls for" (*prophetein*) the rule of God, calls for things to happen in God's way, not the world's. The discourse of the kingdom gets in the world's face, which is a costly business, for the world keeps strict accounts and knows how to make its critics pay. If anyone comes into the world and puts it to the world, the world will receive them not, which usually means it will cost them dearly, maybe everything, which is not a good investment. It is this prophetic passion, which contradicts the world, that explains why the discourse of the kingdom takes such a contrarian form, why it is so unyielding, so full of poetic perversity. The poetics of the kingdom moves about in the distance between logic and passion, truth and justice, concepts and desire, strategizing and praying, astute points and mad stories, for it can never be merely the one or the other, can never occupy a spot that is simply exterior to one or the other. The whole idea is to speak out in the name of justice, in the name of God, and to call for the coming of the kingdom, to pray and weep for the coming of justice. For the kingdom comes to interrupt the business as usual of the world, to put the world in question, to bring the world up short. To proclaim the coming of the kingdom of God is to deny that the world is all in all, to resist enclosure by the horizon of the world, to refuse the totalizing grip of the world, and to insist that the merciless calculations that obtain in the world are not the last word. For the horizon of the world is set by the calculable, the sensible, the possible, the reasonable, the sound investment. In the world, we are made to pay for everything. The world is nobody's fool.

God's Own Good Time

The kingdom of God is not a place but a time, the time when God rules rather than the world. The rule of God contests the powers and principalities of the world, what Luke calls the *exousias* (Luke 12.11), which is a suggestive expression meaning the "powers that be," the powers that have prestige and presence and all the weightiness of being (*ousia*). The reign of God challenges the rule of the men of means, the men of substance, and the pomp of this world, by exposing them to the power and sovereignty of God, for there is no *ousia* and no *exousia* except from God (Rom. 13.1).[2] The rule of God resists the way things are done in the world, and rejects the order of rank, the *arche*, that is installed in the world. The kingdom is neither another world beyond this world, nor another time outside time, but rather the time of God's rule in the world, another way to be in time and to be in the world. It is the rule of a certain time, God's own good time, as opposed to the time-keeping that goes on in the world, for in the kingdom time is God's, not ours.

When we pray, we pray for the kingdom to come, asking that life in time become a time when God rules, that time be kept by God, as opposed to the way that time is kept in the world. Time is one of the keys to the kingdom, a sign or a clue that we are moving freely and easily with the rhythms of the kingdom, rather than being sucked into the vortex of the ways of the world. In the kingdom time is like God's pulse, God's echo, God's orchestration, whereas in the world time is money. In the kingdom time is the music God plays in our ears, whose fortes and pianissimos must be sorted out from all the background noise coming from the world. If no one has seen God and lived, we just might be able to hear God playing sweetly in time, and dance to God's own good time.

The world's time has been faithfully recorded by the philosophers, where time is said to keep a steady beat, to maintain the steady tick-tock of "now" succeeding "now" in a succession so regular that Husserl called it a "form" and was even able to draw a diagram of it.[3] The razor-thin source point of the now-phase is thickened by the now that has just lapsed and the now just about to come. Now-phases flow smoothly from the future into the present, enjoying their fleeting moment in the sun of the present, only to flow off just as smoothly into the past where they assume their inalterable place. Everything is tightly organized and regularized around the rule of retention and protention, memory and expectation, past-present and future-present, which is the basis of all the prudent long-range planning and careful record-keeping that goes on in the world. The time of the world is the sort of time that you can count, the time that you can count on, the sort that economics depends upon. It is regular and reliable enough for us to calculate equivalences and fair exchanges and to do a close cost analysis.

But time in the kingdom is decidedly different. The steady beat of *ousia*'s presence in the world fades before a more "ephemeral" openness to and dependence upon God's daily provision. Behold the lilies of the field, the day-lilies: they are not worrying about anything, for "today" is God's day, today is in God's hands, and God will provide. Give us this day our daily (*epiousios*) bread, the bread we need for today, for the cares of today are enough to worry about, and we should not even worry about them. "Ousiology" gives way to "epiousiology" (*epiousios*), which means the rule of God over the "quotidian" (*quotidie*) day-to-day time of the fleeting day-lily. The steady reliability of substance and of people of substance, the *ousia* and *exousia* of this world, gives way to a more fragile, lily-like, insubstantial, transient *un*-self-sufficiency. The "world" stands there on its own, in all its pomp and worldly adornment, boasting of its *Selbstständigkeit*, self-standing, self-sufficiency; it is as if the world thinks itself able to put up a kind of ousiological resistance to God or to declare its independence of God. But the towering lordship of the world is laid low by the lilies of the field, who neither sow nor reap, while God keeps watch over their every need. In the kingdom time yields to God's sway, becoming entirely transparent to God, alive to God, responsive to God, who watches over each day, each moment, from moment to moment, sustaining each moment. For God has counted every moment, just as he has counted every tear and every hair on our head (Luke 12.7; Matt. 10.30).

When God rules, when time is a tune played by God, the results are as a rule generally unruly. The expectations and assumptions, the patterns and regularities, the rules and regulations that are built up in economic time are ruptured.

The steady beat of the time of presence, which measures the regular rhythms of *ousia*, gives way to epiousiological initiative, innovation, and surprise. The regularities of kinetics succumb to the marvelous metamorphoses of "metanoetics" – from *metanoia*, to be of a new mind and heart – where things are given over to transformation and transfiguration. What is, is what is *given* – what have you that you have not been given? Even so, what is ever so given that it cannot be forgiven, so thoroughly done that cannot be undone or pardoned? Even as, in the kingdom, the unforgiving past can be forgiven, so the future is held open in messianic expectation for the coming of the unforeseeable.

With God All Things Are Possible

In the eleventh century Peter Damian argued that God's power was so great and extended so far that, were it good to do so, God could actually alter the past and make it to be that what had happened in the past did *not* happen. Damian did not make this point as part of a machismo effort to prove that our God is mightier than your God but as an argument about forgiveness. God's power to forgive sin was such that God could, were it good to do so, make it to be that the sinner did not sin, that the sinner was not only forgiven but rendered innocent.[4] The good is so much better and more powerful than being, so much beyond being, that the good takes the stuff right out of being and *ousia* and can even trump the difference between being and non-being. Things, being, *ousia*, presence, sense, and non-sense, indeed even the seemingly almighty principle of non-contradiction itself, all fade fast before the *exousia* of God, the power and benignity of God, who alone is almighty, who alone is good. These much honored philosophical principles, these "princes and principalities" of the philosophers, are no match for God's power and goodness. As a result, in the kingdom, when God rules, things take on an astonishing alterability, unpredictability, revisability, and contingency, the likes of which are not dreamt of by the philosophers.

I must confess my doubts about whether Damian can make the argument about the alterability of the past stick. For over and above the puzzling question of the sheer coherence of this suggestion, it seems to me that were God to annul the past offense, God would thereby also annul forgiveness, inasmuch as there would then be nothing to forgive. Forgiveness requires that the past offense be forgiven not annulled, that it be left standing even as it is *somehow* lifted, lest it become blind fate and inalterable destiny. But if I have my doubts about its logic, I am very much attached to the poetics of Damian's sometimes very technical argument. For Damian has dared to push the poetics of *the* impossible that is astir in forgiveness about as far as one can go. Like Angelus Silesius, he dares to go where you cannot go. Damian is one of the great theoreticians of *the* impossible and this because he has a keen sense for the difference between the world's time and the time in which God rules. Like Kierkegaard and like Levinas later on, he is a philosopher with a biblical ear, with an ear tuned to the divine rhythms, all of whom have noticed the idiosyncratic character of forgiven time.[5] Like them, he actually has two good ears, thanks be to God, one for the poetics of God's rule and the other for a good argument, two anti-Tertullian ears, one for Athens and another for Jerusalem. Two ears are better than one and they make it easier to write with both hands; monoauralism will only get you half way.

Damian thinks of time metanoetically, regarding each moment as a *new creation* in which the past lapses in order to let life begin anew, which means to make all things new, which is a basic idea in the kingdom. That idea also makes its way into Descartes, whom we are accustomed to think of as the father of rationalism, but to whom Levinas has lent a very biblical ear. This evangelic or metanoetic time is exemplarily realized in "forgiven time," in the time of forgiving, which requires a second chance, a turned-back clock, a "gift" of time and of a new birth, in which all things are made new, which is what it means to be "saved." In a very similar spirit, although the letter of their texts are very different, very early on in his career, Levinas spoke of repairing the irreparable:

> Time, which is a condition of our existence, is above all a condition that is irreparable. The *fait accompli* . . . forever evades man's control, but weighs heavily on his destiny. . . . Remorse – that painful expression of a radical powerlessness to redeem the irreparable – heralds the repentance that generates the pardon that redeems. . . . Time loses its very irreversibility.[6]

To have the time of a grievous mistake *back* – is that not our desire beyond desire, our hope against hope? If that were not possible, if the impossible were not possible, if we could not repair the irreparable, "how then can we live?" as the great prophet of turning around (*Teshuvah*) asks (Ezek. 33.10).

Damian believed that God's power to make all things new means that time no less than space can offer no real resistance to God, that the *ousia* of this world is no match for the *exousia* of God, even as the philosophers who offer resistance to theology are fuel for the flames (Damian was a little rough around the edges when it came to dissenters). Damian affirmed the central biblical motifs of *creation* and *recreation*, of making all things to begin with and then of making all things new, that is, making them again, in a divine repetition, for every yes yearns for repetition. There cannot be one yes, for every yes insists on saying yes again. God made the world, yes, and then he saw that it was good, yes, and so God kept on making it, yes, yes, and even after God rested from creating, the workweek of the created world went on which required his constant attention. The Greeks, by contrast, had a very different and worldly experience of time. For Damian, time has a radical contingency and revisability, which even extended to the contingency of the past, which was hollowed out for Damian by the goodness and omnipotence of God, who just might be of a mind and a heart to alter it. For the Greeks, on the other hand, the very idea of the divine meant the rule of the unchanging and immortal, which is what they meant by the divine. The Greeks divided everything up into unchanging being and changing being, immortals up above and mortals down below, and they bent their knee above all to the things that could not be otherwise, which were alone truly "divine," and about which there was alone true *episteme*.

For the Greeks to love things divine was to prize the necessary, immobile, and universal over the contingent, changing, and singular, which is exactly the opposite of the way things happen in the "kingdom of God." Like all men of good sense, the Greeks, who kept an eye out for how things happen in general and for the most part, would have preferred the ninety-nine to the one, the general rule to the unruly oddity, which should be cast away. Hence, the ideal way to think about God for the Greeks was to imagine God traveling in a circle while thinking endlessly and only of himself, quite heedless of and impassive about us bleeding mortals down below. Whereas in the kingdom God has counted every tear and every hair on our head and God grieves and suffers with us through our every crisis. The Greeks constantly recommended that changing things strive after and seek to be as unchanging as their humble circumstances permit, instead of acknowledging that the infinite elasticity and contingency of things is a sign of the gods. The Greeks were scandalized by the idea that being would come from non-being, that knowledge could come from ignorance, that any business at all could be transacted between non-being and being, two parties that must be rigorously prevented from making contact with each other. They wanted to subordinate the changing things that just happen to a thing (*symbebekos*) to what that thing steadily and permanently is (*ousia*). Necessity ruled in all things, which is what they would have meant by the "kingdom" of what they called "*theos*," had anyone coined such an expression among them. Which nobody did.

That is why forgiveness, which requires much humility, holds a pride of place in the kingdom of God, and that is why the poetics of Damian's project is so interesting and un-Greek. Forgiveness is an impossible attempt to do something impossible, to repair the irreparable, to make the sinner *new*, to say to the sinner, "it never happened!" Even and especially if it *did*. Forgiveness is a sign of our love of *the impossible*. For the impossible is just what we love. Love will not put up with the idea that the impossible is off limits, or rather, the impossible is the only thing that can fire love to the limit. Otherwise the lover would be a mediocre fellow who has carefully counted the coins in his pocket, carefully calculated what can and cannot be, who is never surprised or overtaken by the advent of the astonishing. The impossible is what sets our hearts afire, what we are driven *by*. Love begins *by* the impossible. Forgiveness is a blow struck by the Good against being and necessity, a *reductio ad nihilum*, which reduces the being of an offense to a certain non-being, which continues and extends the work of creation by leading the offender from non-being into being, into *metanoia*. The dead rise from their graves, the lame are made straight, a virgin gives birth, bodies pass through hard surfaces or are sustained on water, seas are parted, walls are brought down by trumpets. Wonders never cease. It is, all in all, a very unruly and anarchic world, but still, it is a very edifying and holy chaos, a sacred anarchy, a hier-an-archy that ought to make the established hierarchy nervous. In the kingdom things do not seem to be made of the stiff stuff of Greek *ousia* but to have a wondrous pliability and plasticity that would have left the Greeks themselves wondering, even though the Greeks were supposed to be famous for their wonder.

Raising Holy Hell

On the whole, the kingdom confounds the philosophers, who are accustomed to arrange things according to the "principles" of being, reason, order, possibility, presence, sense, and meaning, an intimidating parade of luminaries enjoying pride of place in philosophy, the men of means and of substance (Col. 1.16), the princes and principalities of philosophy, who sit at the head of philosophy's table. To that is opposed a kingdom which is foolishness, a joke, a kingdom *ironice*, where the last are the first, the weak are strong, the out are in, the crooked are straight, the nobodies and nothings are preferred, and the blind and the lame take the lead. A veritable anarchic kingdom, a kingdom whose *arche* is whatever is *an-arche*, without princely and principial authority. The kingdom marches to its own drummer, has its own beat, its own laws of space and bodily permeability, the key to which (the key to the kingdom) shows up in its own very non-standard time and its own sense of what is possible and impossible. That is why, exceeding any Greek sense of wonder, the texts of the kingdom read – if we may adapt a suggestion coming from Gilles Deleuze – like a veritable *Alice in Wonderland*, packed with stories of the most astonishing transformations and transfigurations, of paradoxes and aporias, of wedding feasts as mad as any hatter's party, of eventualities that confound the time of the philosophers, who do not have nearly as good a time.

If the truth be told – and this is my hypothesis, for which I fully expect to be made to pay – what comes about when the kingdom comes looks and sounds like what contemporary French philosophers call an "event" (*événement*). We could say of the kingdom what Deleuze says of *Alice*: to understand it requires "a category of very special things: events, pure events."[7] The coming of the kingdom is an out-coming, from *evenire* (Lat.), the coming-out or bursting out of something we did not see coming, something unforeseen, singular, irregular. Alternatively, the event is also what Derrida calls *l'invention de l'autre*, the in-coming (*invenire*) of something "wholly other," the breaking into our familiar world of something completely amazing, which shatters our horizon of expectations. In the military, when someone shouts "incoming" the sensible thing to do is head for cover lest we be blown to kingdom come. This outburst or out-coming shatters our horizons of expectation. Otherwise, nothing is happening, nothing much, nothing new; creation is grinding to a stop, and the yes is losing the strength to repeat itself, to come again. The "event" is something that does not seem possible, that for which no mundane horizon of possibility or foreseeability is able to prepare us. To wait for the event is to expect to be surprised and overtaken, to prepare for something for which you cannot be prepared, which is like knowing in advance that the kingdom will come like a thief in the night.

I am, in short, in imitation of the one who dined with sinners, allowing the kingdom to sit down to table with deconstruction and other disreputable French types. I am, to the great scandal of deconstructors and the "Christian Right" alike, contending that the way the kingdom contests the mundane powers that pretend to be and to have presence goes hand in hand with the notorious critique of the "metaphysics of presence" (*ousia*) in deconstruction. I am aligning the opposition of the "kingdom" to the "world" in the scriptures with the opposition of the "gift," which is *the* impossible, to "economy" in deconstruction. I am aligning the coming of the kingdom with the in-coming of the *tout autre* or the out-coming of the event in deconstruction. I am arguing that in the kingdom and in deconstruction we have to do with two different versions of the poetics of the impossible. I am not trying to reduce the one to the other, by any means, because they are importantly different, but to open up the lines of communication between them and to show the "good news" that they bear to each other.

In a poetics of the impossible things are highly deconstructible, but being "deconstructible" is not as bad as it sounds. In fact, my contention is that it is good news and arises in the wake of *the* good news. For something is deconstructible only if it has been constructed to begin with, which is why deconstruction comes along in the wake of a theology of creation, and why its critique of the metaphysics of presence springs from a frame of mind that keeps an eye out for the idols of presence. Deconstructibility is the condition of the "event." Otherwise things would be nailed down too tightly, and *ousia* would cling too tightly to *ousia*. That was what inflamed the desire of Parmenides, whose idea of a good time was an airtight perfectly spherical solid, which is, if you let yourself think about it, an exceedingly odd ideal to hold close to your heart. For anything new or surprising to eventuate, for anything strange or amazing to happen, which is what we long for and desire, pray and weep, things must be deconstructible. So far from being the enemy of faith and religion, far from being the last nail in the coffin prepared for the death of God, the deconstructibility of things is one of the hallmarks of the kingdom of God, one of the first things to come about when the kingdom comes, one of the first things to happen when God rules, one of the things we are praying for when we pray for the kingdom to come, when we pray and weep, *viens, oui, oui*. Deconstructibility is the principal thing we need for things to open up and be pliable to the rule of God, when time is God's rather than the timeless now of a rock-solid well-rounded sphere, which was the first form *ousia* assumed when it came into the world.

It is astonishing to me that anyone who reads the scriptures faithfully and who is in love with the idea of the kingdom of God, would also fall in love with "ousiology" or with Neoplatonic hyperousiology, with essentialism or hyperessentialism, or with Greco-Roman "natural law" theories with which ousiology often keeps company. True, nature has its laws, but God, who is the author of nature, is the law of these laws, the *exousia* that trumps all worldly *ousia*, which is why in the scriptural stories God will from time to time beg leave to set those laws on their head. That interruptibility, that deconstructibility, in the name of justice is what we *mean* by the kingdom. If, in the world, God's glory is shown in the regular course that nature follows, which is an idea that even philosophers can follow, then the rule of God is made still more manifest in the kingdom stories by the interruptions and contraventions of nature's regular course.

In the kingdom things happen a lot more like the way things fall out in deconstruction, whose least bad definition, Derrida says, is an "experience of *the* impossible,"[8] than they do in classical metaphysical theology, which, as Johannes de Silentio quips, "sits all rouged and powdered in the window and . . . offers its charms to philosophy,"[9] to philosophy's love of necessity, order, presence, essence, regularity, and stability. I do not know how to cushion this blow, either for the learned despisers of religion or for the learned despisers of deconstruction, for whom this good news signals an exceedingly bad turn of events: deconstruction, on my view, is *structured like a religion*, and makes use of religious structures. For Derrida can say, no less than St Augustine, *inquietum est cor nostrum*, our hearts are restless and driven by desire, a desire beyond desire, a desire for *the* impossible. For by *the* impossible Derrida does not mean just any wild or crazy eventuality, however bizarre, mean, or violent. The event begins *by* the impossible, is moved and driven by a desire for the *gift* beyond economy, for the *justice* beyond the law, for the *hospitality* beyond proprietorship, for *forgiveness* beyond getting even, for the coming of the *tout autre* beyond the coming of the same, for what Levinas, picking up on an ancient tradition, called the excess of the *good* beyond being, which is a lovely idea that lovers of the kingdom can use, if you drop the Neoplatonic metaphysics, which has next to nothing to do with the kingdom and would have left Jesus of Nazareth dumbfounded. The event is driven by a desire for the Messiah to come, a Messiah who will contradict the smug complacency and the pomp of the present, a Messiah who will put it to the world and to the way things are done in the time of the world. So if, on the one hand, the kingdom is the sphere where God rules, and if, on the other hand, deconstruction means the rule of the gift, of the good, of justice, of hospitality, and forgiveness, then it seems to me that the two of them, deconstruction and the kingdom of God, should get along famously, even if they have their differences, and even if their respective staff and campaign workers do not trust each other.

I am not proposing to put the New Testament on the same footing as *Alice in Wonderland*, even though I think the lovers of the kingdom have something to learn from Deleuze's love of Lewis Carroll in the *Logic of Sense*. I am only doing my duty, to keep time holy, and space, and to protect them both from idolatry, by saying that they are God's, that in the kingdom space and time are the scene of God's rule. But if, and we have this on the highest authority (*exousia*), the kingdom of God is within us, then what I am saying bears upon the transformability of our lives, having to do with the most powerful and transfiguring figures of self-transformation, in which we and all things are made new. The idea behind the poetics of the impossible, is *metanoetic* and transformative, prophetic and salvific, creative and recreative, to repair the irreparable, transforming the face of the earth, always beginning *by* the impossible, by a breathtaking transformation *ex nihilo*, which, according to the Greeks, is impossible. I stick to my hypothesis with devilish persistency, with unrelenting itchiness, and without the least compunction, trying to make life difficult both for the learned despisers of religion and the learned despisers of deconstruction, who are, alas, a learned legion. This is risky business and unlikely to win a large following. For the self-appointed Defenders of the Good have always been scandalized by the way the kingdom consorts with sinners (or deconstructors), which they denounce as a devilish lot, even as the Deconstructors of the Transcendental Signified have always worked themselves up into an unholy heat about religion, which they regularly denounce as the slave revolt in morals or as pitiable people longing for their mommy.

The kingdom ought to be as hospitable as possible, in the spirit of that impossible story about a very strange wedding feast, a veritable hatter's party, where the distinction between who is in and who is out in the kingdom starts to look a little mad. I am very interested in the question of the borders of the kingdom, of its inside and outside, and its politics, a question that also spills over into other important questions about the borders that divide the "religions of the Book," or the borders between orthodoxy and heterodoxy, between the community and the excommunicated, between theism and atheism, theology and atheology, and in general between religion and what has been called in a devilishly delicious phrase "religion without religion." Are there rigorous walls around the kingdom? Do they have border patrols there? Do they have a problem with illegal immigrants? Who is in and who is out? Is anyone there who rightly passes for an atheist? The guidance we get from the story is that the insiders are out, and the outsiders are in. That, I readily agree, is perfectly mad – it makes perfect sense or non-sense, is in perfect compliance with the poetics of the impossible, with the sort of goings on you come to expect when the kingdom comes.

For, according to my hypothesis, the rule of God is a bit unruly, and the kingdom has the look of a holy or sacred anarchy where, truth to tell, it seems like all hell has broken loose.

Holy hell, that is.

Notes

1 Søren Kierkegaard, *Kierkegaard's Works*, vol. 7, *Philosophical Fragments*, ed. and trans. H. Hong and E. Hong (Princeton, NJ: Princeton University Press, 1985), p. 37.
2 Although, *pace* Paul, who is being an excessively good Roman citizen in this text, it seems to me to follow from this point that the ruling government is precisely *not* to be confused with something invested with divine power.
3 Edmund Husserl, *On the Phenomenology of the Consciousness of Internal Time (1893–1917)*, trans. John Barnett Brough (Dordrecht: Kluwer Academic Publishers, 1991), pp. 237–8.

4 See Damian's "*De divina omnipotentia*" in *Die Briefe des Petrus Damiani*, ed. Kurt Reindel (Munich: Monumenta Germaniae Historica, 1983–93), vol. 3, Brief 119, pp. 341–84. For the English translation see Peter Damian, *Letters*, 4 vols, trans. Owen J. Blum, *The Fathers of the Church* (Washington, DC: Catholic University of America Press, 1989–98), vol. 4, Letter 119, pp. 344–86. For an excellent commentary in English see Irven M. Resnick, *Divine Power and Possibility in St Peter Damian's De Divina Omnipotentia* (Leiden and New York: Brill, 1992).

5 Johannes Climacus also noted the paradoxical character of forgiven time, its "retroactive power to annul the past," as a thought that faith spends a lifetime trying to realize, while the Hegelians claim to go further. See *Philosophical Fragments*, p. 77; and Søren Kierkegaard, *Kierkegaard's Works*, vol. 12, 1, *Concluding Unscientific Postscript to "Philosophical Fragments*," ed. and trans. H. Hong and E. Hong (Princeton, NJ: Princeton University Press, 1992), p. 224.

6 Emmanuel Levinas, "Reflections on Hitlerism," trans. Séan Hand, *Critical Inquiry*, 17 (Autumn, 1990), p. 65.

7 Gilles Deleuze, *The Logic of Sense*, trans. Mark Lester with Charles Stivale, ed. Constantin V. Boundas (New York: Columbia University Press, 1990), p. 1.

8 For a more carefully elaborated and documented implementation of the claim that deconstruction lends itself to a religious interpretation, see my *The Prayers and Tears of Jacques Derrida: Religion without Religion* (Bloomington: Indiana University Press, 1997).

9 Søren Kierkegaard, *Kierkegaard's Works*, vol. 6, *"Fear and Trembling" and "Repetition,"* ed. and trans. H. Hong and E. Hong (Princeton, NJ: Princeton University Press, 1983), p. 32.

CHAPTER 29
Anti-Discrimination

Don Cupitt

It is impossible to do justice to the scope of Don Cupitt's work, which began in the late 1960s with a commitment to Kantian epistemology, and continues today with a series of books offering everyday guides to religious thematics, articulating what he terms "democratic philosophy." Nevertheless over the course of his many books and articles a distinctive logic can be discerned. Cupitt's Kantian roots accepted a constructivism which, by the mid-1970s, had developed into a sophisticated philosophical non-realism. This development came through rejecting Kant's universal categories of the understanding and arguing instead for categories that were always culturally and historically relative. At this point Cupitt retained an intense focus upon the liberal subject, but if with Kant the transcendent God remained a regulative principle whose existence was, possibly, only authenticated through ethical action, then the move in the direction of cultural relativism opened the door to atheism. This was a move being made on the Continent by Gilles Deleuze and later by Jean-François Lyotard.

Don Cupitt is certainly no coward soul, and he followed the trajectory of his thinking to *Taking Leave of God* (London, 1980), in which he wrote: "over the years I have tried to combine belief in God with spiritual freedom by pressing the themes of 'negative theology' and divine transcendence even harder. Eventually I was saying that God does not determine and cannot be thought of as determining the spiritual life from outside, for God is altogether unspecifiable. God has to become objectively thinner and thinner in order to allow subjective religiousness to expand. It is only one step further to the objectively atheous position here propounded." Two further elements in his thinking begin to emerge in the 1980s. The first is a "linguistic turn" that receives its full articulation in *The Long-Legged Fly* (London, 1987) and *What is a Story?* (London, 1991). With this Cupitt's theology of culture is deepened and linked to a theology of desire: we continually make the worlds we inhabit through the language that we employ. Our language incarnates our desires. We tell stories, we weave texts. The second element is the nihilism which can be implicit in certain forms of negative theology (Buddhism and, according to Cupitt – influenced no doubt by his reading of Heidegger – the negativity of Eckhart). Cupitt now pushes the unknowability of God towards a radical disinterestedness which defines what is. In this he shares something with the work of John D. Caputo, and in fact produced his own account of the kingdom of God in *Kingdom Come in Everyday Speech* (London, 2000). As Cupitt expresses it in *The Last Philosophy* (London, 1995): "In the movement of words we come to feel and understand that moving energies, formed into words, are what everything's made of." All is relative, fleeting, and immanent; true happiness is being able to go with the flux. He has called this religiousness "ecstatic immanence," "humanist non-realism," and "the mysticism of secondariness," and the style of his thinking that began with *Creation Out of Nothing* (London, 1990) he called "expressionist."

The essay contributed to this volume reveals once more the way Cupitt tackles the questions, the issues, and the texts that are prominent today. His is a commitment to the continuing relevance of demythologizing theological language, so that all might appreciate the centrality of religious belief unshackled from ecclesiology.

In traditional cultures the world is very commonly thought of as having been created by a series of acts of discrimination or discernment. The two words have a common root in the Latin verb *cernere*, to separate, with special reference to the sifting or sieving by which the wheat is separated from the chaff, and good stuff from rubbish generally. Discrimination or discernment evidently involves evaluation, because it does not simply divide the flux of experience into two equal and similar zones: on the contrary, it seems to *structure* the world, so that two markedly different things or principles or regions appear. One of them is prior, founding, normative, and lucid, and the other is its secondary, darker, and less stable counterpart or "Other." They thus make an asymmetrical, complementary pair: familiar examples from mythology include light and darkness, which are usually associated with a whole series of other and closely related pairs: waking and sleeping, consciousness and unconsciousness, Day and Night, Sun and Moon. In the universally familiar Genesis narrative we then hear of Heaven and Earth, Land and Sea, Animals and Plants, and Man and Woman.

Mention of the male–female distinction invites the question: "Is it true that the way people in the past – and we ourselves in our infancy – have perceived and internalized the sexual difference has come subsequently to act as a model or template for our entire construction of the world?" There is some confirmation of this hypothesis in the theogonies of polytheism, where the cosmological pairs are not established by a chain of distinct utterances of the creative Word of one God, but are themselves pairs of divinities, each of which is begotten by its predecessor, and begets its successor. In which case, it is indeed the sexual difference that gives birth to everything else.

We should be wary, however, of the conclusion drawn by some, to the effect that all traditional symbolic thinking, and the whole traditional construction of the world, is applied sexism. There are too many very awkward exceptions, such as the fact that in ancient Egypt the sky is female, Nut, and the earth male, Geb. To most people that will surely seem horribly wrong-way-round. It is all wrong that in Egyptian art Geb, on his back, should be straining upwards so awkwardly as he tries to penetrate the sky. And isn't it also horribly *wrong* that in German, which surely ought to be reliably patriarchal, the Sun is female? And there are many other such seeming inconsistencies: for example, in our own culture a tradition of portraying Woman as more fickle than Man coexists happily with another tradition that portrays Woman as more virtuous and faithful than Man. We seem quite happy to invoke whichever stereotype suits us at any one moment.

Perhaps then we should change the hypothesis, and consider instead the possibility that people everywhere tend to think and to structure their worlds in terms of asymmetrical binary oppositions, a pattern that then gets applied to the human man–woman difference just as it gets applied to everything else. The reason is probably (in a *very* broad sense) ethical. Everywhere language is used to advise and admonish, telling people which way round to see everything, which way to go, and what to prefer. Choose this and leave that: there is always a Way of Life and a Way of Death, a right and a wrong, a kernel and a husk, a winner and a loser. Language is cruel: the runner-up, the one that comes second, is the loser, the one whom God "hates." "Is not Esau Jacob's brother? Yet I have loved Jacob but I have hated Esau," says God.[1] But that's the way it has to be. So in traditional society thinking is in terms of asymmetrical binary contrasts, which then generate a worldview that embodies and confirms traditional values.

Now we have two possibilities. We may regard the sexual relationship as the original unequal, asymmetrical binary opposition which – endlessly permutated and recycled – becomes the basic building-block of all culture and worldview. Or, alternatively, we may say that, if the world was originally just a featureless flux, then the mere drawing of a great line across it would not by itself create anything. The drawing of the line must introduce some difference of priority, of power, and of value between right and left; between what's on one side of the line and what's on the other side. *Thus a cosmos cannot be created at all except by establishing unequal, asymmetrical binary contrasts.*[2] For there to be a world, there must be discrimination, and that means discrimination in the hard sense: there is always a loser, always something that comes second. Without that ordering and preference, there doesn't get to be a world at all. In sum: to structure Chaos, inequalities must be imposed. Without inequality, no reality.[3]

On the first of these theories sexism seems to be the chief culprit, and it would seem that if we could create a non-sexist human psychology then we might be able to build a non-sexist Cosmos. But, on the second view, inequality, asymmetry, and difference (or "*différance*") are inescapable features of any ordered world – as indeed they are of language itself. For is not meaning itself always produced by prioritizing Something and differentiating it from its Other, that stands just behind it? And are not all words accompanied by their shadowy antonyms, metonyms, correlates, counterparts, so that we always think of back and forth, up and down, right and left, give and take, in and out, before and after, and life and death? Perhaps the bilateral symmetry of our own bodies – and their slight *a*symmetry, too – is what first sets us thinking this way.

We should further notice that if binary thinking is a pervasive feature of myths and cosmologies, it has played an even greater part in subsequent philosophical and religious thought. Plato is steeped in it, and does not he himself declare that "matter and form are the mother and father of being"? Because Plato himself is so highly binary, the entire Western philosophical tradition has remained so until modern times. We still use his binary vocabulary of time and eternity, form and matter, being and becoming, appearance and reality, and so on. Similarly, in the religious tradition, thought has always been shaped by very sharp contrasts between the sacred and the profane, the holy and the common, the clean and the unclean, the divine and the human, Holy God and sinful man, Grace and Nature, salvation and damnation, and Heaven and Hell. In many faith-traditions the ritual marking of the distinctions just *is* the practice of religion.

The way this works out in religious thought is neatly illustrated by the Elizabethan Reformed (or Calvinist) writer, William Perkins (1558–1602). In *A Golden Chaine, or the Description of Theology* (1690) Perkins draws the whole Plan of Salvation in a big diagram that shows all cosmic history as a dance of the binaries.[4] The Grand Narrative begins with the eternal decree of election in God's right hand, and the eternal decree of reprobation in God's left hand. It ends with the sealing of Heaven and Hell. In between the beginning and the end of the story everything is black or white, being rigidly controlled by the power of God and by the clarity with which the opposing principles are contrasted and played off against each other. God is, you might say, the Great Discriminator, who makes sure that in the end everything is exposed as being – and as having been all along – either snow white or jet black. As was decreed in the beginning, everything ends up either at God's right hand, or on his left.

The purpose of this discussion so far has been to recall the extent to which, in the Western tradition, we have seen reality as produced by acts of distinction, discrimination, discernment. Great lines were drawn across the primal Chaos, each line bringing into being a complementary unequal pair like light and darkness. By such acts of division and discrimination the world of linguistic meaning was produced, values and disvalues were produced, the Cosmos was ordered, and History was set in motion.

It is evident, then, that the main Western philosophical tradition since Plato, and the main theological tradition at least since the Jewish apocalyptic writings, have been both firmly committed to realism and to discrimination. So we have been committed to a highly unequal world-picture, with numerous inbuilt ethical/ontological scales. Notice that the cause of realism and the cause of discrimination – including God's negative discrimination, his just rejection of that which ends up at his left hand – the two causes, I say, are one and the same, for it is discrimination that alone produces reality. The Creator and the Judge are one and the same.

Now I begin to understand why, in the much-discussed writings of John Milbank, "theology" and "nihilism" are set up as being *themselves* a pair of binary opposites.[5] For him as much as for a Muslim, the great choice is the choice between theological realism and secular nihilism. Milbank recognizes that since about the time of Schelling and Hegel Western thought has been gradually turning away from Plato and has been attempting to transcend, or undo, or "deconstruct" the great binary oppositions that he imposed upon it. In effect – Milbank is saying – Western philosophy and secular culture have been driving very successfully towards nihilism. But, in Milbank's own scheme of thought, nihilism is regarded as a very bad thing. Only theology (and an eclectic sort of catholicized neo-Calvinism at that) can deliver us from it. To speak more plainly, only God can conquer the Nihil at which Western thought has arrived. *Fiat lux*, says God: "Let there be light." So God will reinstate the old discriminations, and bring back the good old days.

There are however some very serious objections to the way Milbank describes our present religious and cultural situation. In effect, Milbank identifies the cause of theology with the cause of a highly differentiated sacred cosmology, produced by multiple acts of discrimination. For him and his allies, Christianity was most itself at the peak of the Middle Ages. But we do not live in a world of that type any longer. Our world is now the world as pictured by natural science, and we are energetically fighting our moral battles *against* the various surviving forms of negative discrimination left over from the religious past. Our ethical humanitarianism is magnificently nihilistic: one gives succour to the other simply on the basis of our barest co-humanity and quite *regardless* of race, color, creed, gender, sexual orientation, doctrinal soundness, and moral desert.[6] Thoroughgoing anti-discrimination – i.e., *nihilism* – is "political correctness," and is what makes our brand of religious humanism so novel and so beautiful. We very consciously do *not* discriminate: that is, we do not even *wish* to classify people and fix their position on various value-scales, before we agree to minister to them. On the contrary, we remember that in our tradition religion at its best has always yearned to see the end of religion: that is, "in those days," in the kingdom of God on earth, in the heavenly world, in the longed-for perfect world at the end of the world, the great binary distinctions are undone. There is no longer any chasm between God and man, between the sacred and the profane, between the clean and the unclean, between saints and ordinary citizens, between masters and servants, nor between light and darkness, and the manifest and the hidden, for in the Kingdom of Heaven there are no shadows or concealment, and everything is open and explicit.

The point here is very familiar in the Bible. The prophets and Jesus criticized the sacrificial system and the whole elaborate apparatus of mediated religion. It does not save. It offers, not religious happiness, but only "belief," which is worthless by comparison. Mediated religion locks the ordinary believer into lifelong dependency: he is like a kidney patient who is chained to his dialysis machine and will never be free of it; he *must* get his regular transfusions of forgiveness and Grace from the ecclesiastical salvation-machine. So the prophets and Jesus, like other religious prophets and innovators, want to see the end of the ritual universe and the salvation-machine. They look for a new world in which the great distinctions between the divine and the human, the sacred and the profane, the clean and the unclean, and between different degrees of sacred rank have disappeared, so that religion becomes immediate and beliefless: they look for a world without violence and oppression, globalized, post-ethnic, supercommunicative and humanitarian, a world of reciprocally transparent and equal persons, a "kingdom of ends" in Kant's phrase, and a world in which the divine is no longer objectified but has become scattered and dispersed into people's "hearts." They look forward to the sort of world we are now trying to build. Thus the sacred universe, *minus* all the discriminations that built it up, equals the kingdom of God. Ecclesiastical theology, deconstructed, equals kingdom theology.

We now see two radically different theological interpretations of our present cultural and religious situation opening up before us. For the neo-orthodox, Jesus came to earth "to found the church" and to validate the claims of the higher clergy. The developed church and its theology represents a true continuation of his project, and "Christianity" is most itself at the peak of its historical development in the sacred civilization of the high Middle Ages. The secularization of culture that has been accelerating since the Enlightenment represents a rebellion against God, and therefore a movement into nihilism, that was completed by the twentieth century. Postmodernity, acknowledging the failure of secular man's attempt to go it alone, represents the chance to reinstate the old Latin Christian culture. Secular reason is bankrupt, and it is time to return to Augustine.

The radical Christian interpretation of our present situation is entirely different. In our view, Jesus did *not* come to earth "to found the church." He was a prophet of the kingdom of God, in the hope of which he lived and died. But the kingdom was delayed, and after his death the church came into being as a stopgap. It was a disciplinary organization that recruited people and trained them so that they would be ready and waiting for the kingdom-world. But generations went by, and still the kingdom did not come. The church gradually changed character: instead of preparing people for the coming of the kingdom on earth, it now prepared people for divine Judgment and life in the heavenly world after death.[7] It was ruled by the higher clergy, who controlled the sacraments, and it began to think of itself as "indefectible." It was no longer a merely transitional stage in the religious history of humankind: it was permanent. Ecclesiastical discipline and mediated religion would be the human fate *forever*: it is very noticeable that in ecclesiastical theology religious alienation is sealed-in. In the doctrine of Christ, and in mystical theology, the God–man disjunction is very strictly maintained. In order to keep undiminished the need for religious mediation, and so for the church, ecclesiastical theology defers our final salvation and our religious happiness forever. It is always "belief" and never enjoyment; always jam tomorrow and never jam today.

Radical theology cannot endure such severe pessimism. It is committed to deconstructing ecclesiastical theology into kingdom theology, and above all to deconstructing the God–man distinction. It seeks liberation through mysticism,[8] and then through Protestantism. Then it is impelled to attempt to leave the ecclesiastical era behind altogether, and to create the kingdom-world on earth. This attempt has taken many forms: congregationalism, Quakerism, "America," anarchism, socialism, communism, liberal democracy, humanitarian ethics.

Hence our painful and paradoxical present-day condition, as radical theology interprets it. Since the seventeenth century the old church has forgotten its own merely transitional character, and has lost touch with its own radical tradition of kingdom-theology. Instead, the church has made an absolute of itself, of its own merely mediated kind of religion and its own doctrine-system. The church has declared itself indefectible and inerrant. So it no longer saves, because it no longer knows of anything higher and better than itself. (It is not the True Church any more, because it says it *is*.) Meanwhile the surrounding secular culture of the West has been steadily developing, by the progressive deconstruction and democratization of the old medieval heritage. Led especially by "America," itself the New World, we still battle against discrimination of every kind: our humanitarian ethics, our feminism, our anti-racism, our political correctness, and our environmentalism show us still striving to build the kingdom of God on earth. The paradoxical result of all this is that today the best secular morality outside the church represents a much more developed form of Christianity than is available from within the church. In matters such as the treatment of homosexuals, the church today needs to learn *its own religion* from what it calls "the world."

So, for the radical Christian, postmodern culture, with its ubiquitous, scattered religiosity and its opposition to discrimination, is a secular realization of the traditional kingdom of God. I don't go quite as far as Mark C. Taylor, who sees in the city of Las Vegas the kingdom of God on earth,[9] but I do see in our postmodern humanitarian ethics the best realization of the Christian ideal yet seen on earth.

Notes

1 Malachi 1.2–3.
2 On the relation of the early Derrida to the Genesis creation-myth, see Eve Tavor Bannett, *Structuralism and the Logic of Dissent: Barthes, Derrida, Foucault, Lacan* (London and New York: Macmillan, 1989), ch. 4.
3 See my *Kingdom Come in Everyday Speech* (London: SCM Press, 2000), appendix 2, "Inequalities."
4 Reproduced in John R. Hinnells (ed.), *A Handbook of Living Religions* (Penguin Books, 1985), pp. 76ff.
5 John Milbank, *Theology and Social Theory: Beyond Secular Reason* (Oxford: Blackwell Publishers, 1990), etc.

6 On humanitarianism, see for example my *Kingdom Come*, ch. 7; and my "Humanitarian Ethics" in the forthcoming Hebblethwaite *Festschrift*, ed. Julius Lipner. For the connection between humanitarianism and nihilism, the best starting point is still Albert Camus's novel *La Peste* (1947), ET *The Plague* (1948).
7 On the deferral of the kingdom and its consequences, see the fine late essay by Albert Schweitzer, "The Conception of the Kingdom of God in the Transformation of Eschatology . . .", reprinted in various places, including E. N. Mozley's *The Theology of Albert Schweitzer* (1950), and Walter Kaufmann (ed.), *Religion from Tolstoy to Camus* (New York: Harper Torchbooks, 1964).
8 See my *Mysticism After Modernity* (Oxford: Blackwell Publishers, 1998), which is about the implications of the fact that the church only promises salvation, and does not actually deliver it.
9 Mark C. Taylor, *About Religion: Economies of Faith in Virtual Culture* (Chicago: Chicago University Press, 1999), ch. 7, "The Virtual Kingdom"; and *The Réal: Las Vegas NV* (CD-ROM, issued in the US with the book, 1999).

CHAPTER 30
Is There a Postmodern Gospel?

Walter Lowe

Walter Lowe's work represents a contemporary trajectory of the Yale School of postliberal theology. Having worked under Hans Frei and George Lindbeck, Lowe carries some of their concerns into a negotiation with postmodern thinking. His work is characterized by its philosophical and theological intensity, and by its attention to cultural context. Stimulated by Paul Ricoeur's observation that Bultmann short-circuited the examination of the representation of the Word in words, and trained in the hermeneutics of both Gadamer and Ricoeur, Walter Lowe's work begins from the Christian perspective attuned to the philosophical legacy of modernity and the critique it is currently undergoing. To this extent his writing is Protestant – placing scripture into a negotiation with the historical movements of Enlightenment thinking and Romanticism, and rehearsing the ideas of the theologians (particularly Schleiermacher, Kierkegaard, and Barth) working within these contexts. One sees these same elements in Frei's work: the scriptural, the historical, the philosophical, and the theological. The Yale School developed a Barthian theology quite distinct, in English, from the Barth of Tom Torrance and, more recently, Bruce McCormack. What is distinctive about Walter Lowe's work is the way a commitment to the ongoing destiny of thought has led him to take up the challenges and critiques of poststructural discourse.

Having completed and published his doctoral work on Freud (read through Ricoeur's developing anthropology), he published his first book, *Evil and the Unconscious* (Atlanta, 1983), which treated psychoanalysis as an archeology of caughtness and loss, tapping the "dangerous memory" of human suffering. Against those who dismiss Freud as a reductionist, Lowe argued that Freud had released modernity from the notion that there can be a univocal language. Lowe's third book, *Theology and Difference: The Wound of Reason* (Bloomington, IN, 1993), opened a conversation between Kant, Hegel, Kierkegaard, Barth, and Derrida. Just as Lowe was one of the first theologians to recognize the importance of Ricoeur's work, he was also one of the first to see in Derrida's analysis of *différance* an important tool for the continuing reworking of the Christian legacy. If Ricoeur attempted to think through Bultmann's problematic without the short-circuit, then Derrida's examination of the nature of representation, and his explicit appeal to theological discourse to illustrate and further this examination, opened a new and fruitful approach to Christian hermeneutics. Unlike other *rapprochements* between Derrida and religion (represented in this volume by Caputo and Raschke in particular), Lowe always maintains a distinction between Derrida's ideas and those of Christian theology. Derrida is useful both negatively, to facilitate an internal vigilance within Christian discourse by those who employ and enlarge it, and positively, to point up deconstructive parallels as the theological disrupts the secular, the immanent orders of the self-grounded. Derrida's own critique of modernity through his analysis of the deferral and slippage of meaning in discourses of reason, deepens the Yale School critique of liberal theology. Postliberal theology thus takes a new and more philosophically nuanced direction. Lindbeck made passing reference to certain Wittgensteinian philosophemes (as employed by Clifford Geerzt), but avoided a more meticulous engagement. Busy writing and researching for his fourth book, the following essay illustrates how Lowe's work is continuing this theological negotiation between the legacy of modernity and the present cultural context through Derrida's construal of deconstruction.

Postmodernity has arrived, or almost arrived. It is arriving even now. It has arrived for those who have eyes to see and ears to hear.

Postmodernism announces an event, the emergence of postmodernity. That announcement, itself an event or act, has a certain form and tone. It participates in a certain literary genre, which is that of a gospel. *Behold, the New has come, the Old is passing away.* It is well known that the English word "gospel" derives from the Latin *evangelium*, "good news." We commonly use the phrase "good news" of any favorable event. But even the most ardent capitalist would hesitate to attach the word "gospel" to a rise in the Nasdaq index. On the other hand, there are many who announce a "new world order" in gospel tones.

So a gospel is good news, but radical. The claim to radicality, however, entails a problem. For if something is truly new, if it upsets existing standards and patterns, by what criterion is it known to be good? Conversely, if it fits given standards of discernment, is it new? Schematically put, the latter has been the particular problem of Christianity; the former, of postmodernism. In modernity, the particularity which binds Christianity to the Christ event has tended to evanesce, leaving a pale notion of Christianity as "being good," about which there is absolutely nothing new.[1] Derrida, in treating "messianism," will speak of that which is to come as perhaps "the monstrous." What remains of the good?

In the hands of some, postmodernism reiterates a too-familiar gesture of Western culture, namely the muttered assertion that whether or not what is happening in the culture is good, its expansion is inevitable. Here as elsewhere, assertions of inevitability are the kiss of death for discussions of the good. Yet Christianity too has trafficked in inevitability, in the form of apocalyptic. That intensest form of the new against the old is close at hand any time one speaks earnestly of revolution. Is that a good thing?

The present essay represents a wager that by shuttling between the Christian gospel and "gospel" as a genre one may expose some problems common to Christianity and postmodernity, and examine how the problems have been treated in the two instances. The title question "Is there a postmodern gospel?" may thus be twofold. Is postmodernism, which has the form of a gospel, good news? And can there be a Christian gospel in the context of postmodernity?

The essay does ask to be read as a work in progress. Though it sometimes aspires to be such, it is not a single seamless argument.

General over Particular

Kierkegaard's question of whether one could become a Christian in Christendom is well founded. Constantine's establishment of the Christian religion made it difficult any longer to receive Christianity as news. Kierkegaard's whole effort was to make it strange, so that it might again be heard as gospel. During the medieval period there were of course strong social–cultural reasons why the question was seldom raised whether the given of Christianity was a good. One way modernity defined itself was by introducing the question.

A major reason for the modern interrogation was what is commonly called "the scandal of particularity," the fact that Christianity is so profoundly tied to particular alleged historical events. The grounds for skepticism are distilled in Lessing's dictum that "accidental truths of history can never become the proof of necessary truths of reason."[2] Now Lessing's words breathe the spirit of his time. It was an age newly committed to the project of extracting the universal laws of nature from the particularities in which they happen to be observed. For the empirical sciences, a "necessary" truth is one which can be replicated in a variety of circumstances. It is a general truth, in contrast to the event *per se*, the particularity of which is unrepeatable. The Enlightenment critique of Christianity thus operates within a schema of general versus particular, where, for all the claims to objectivity, the concept of the general tends to be normative.

This predilection was reinforced by the Enlightenment's concurrent advocacy of democratic structures, which was in part a response to the wars of religion, where particularity conspired with intolerance. Sanity demanded an orientation toward that which is held in common, the general good, and the rule of the many, not the few. To know the amplitude of the Enlightenment concept of reason one must appreciate how the concept permitted discourse to circulate among several senses of "the general" – scientific truth is democratic, confirmable by anyone; democracy works because in principle all have rational capacities; and education empowers the many to enter more fully upon the truth of science/reason. Given this modern synergy of the general, a Christian "God story" which does not regard its historical specificity as incidental will inevitably bear the onus of "the scandal of particularity." Now a cultural complex so cathected deserves a name. Let us hyphenate "the general-good" to indicate a cultural context where a presumption in favor of the general is frequently overextended, determining the culture's very notion of what can and cannot be true (cf. Foucault).

So the schema becomes the general-good versus the particular. Now if one perversely wished to intensify the antinomy even further, no more would be required than to mention apocalyptic. J.-B. Metz, who has called for a Christianity "with an apocalyptic sting," writes: "The shortest definition of religion: interruption."[3] Rational inquiry after the general-good requires (to anticipate the next section) a certain consistency of "tone." As in a court of law, it requires consistency in its procedures and self-consistency in its result. The effect of apocalyptic in such a setting is rather like that of a fog horn in a string quartet. Its tone overrides all dialogue; it is seldom well disposed toward the generality of humankind; and the end of the world of which it speaks is scarcely conducive to replication. We can thus say that modernity operates, *in extremis*, within a schema of general-good versus apocalyptic. Modernity's answer to the question of whether Christianity's introduction of apocalyptic was a good thing is resoundingly negative.

Enlightenment adhesion to the general-good has three consequences for religion. (1) There is a determination to purify language. Any affirmation of apocalyptic, even the least, must be forsworn if one would seek admission to the modern discussion. Any one who has affirmed belief in God in a skeptical intellectual setting has probably felt moved to add, "but I'm not one of those people who think that the world is about to end." (2) Advocates try to fashion an apologetic case on behalf of religion within the parameters of the general-good. Inevitably this means disengaging some value from the particularities of its original religious setting. But commonly the result is that, at best, modernity "recognizes" the proffered good – while by the same gesture it completes the process of disengagement. That is to say, modernity implicitly affirms that the good (e.g., the golden rule) is, after all, something that had really been known all along.[4] Thus (3) revelation is reduced to being a reminder; it is understood as a "republication."[5] At a fundamental level modernity requires *a priori* that it not be disturbed. It excludes any suggestion that revelation might deliver something that would really be news. Which is to say that modernity excludes the Christian gospel insofar as it is indeed a gospel.

Looking back over the three consequences, we may ask whether there might not be a link between the first and the third, between the exclusion of apocalyptic and the evisceration of gospel. Liberal theology sought, on the one hand, to disavow the apocalyptic and, on the other hand, to reaffirm the Christian gospel. But that is to assume that a firm line may be drawn between the two.

May not the limitations of liberal theology stand as evidence that such a line cannot in fact be drawn? Might it be that in order to understand the Christian gospel one must come to terms with apocalyptic?

From Particular to Singular

It is a common wisdom among those sympathetic toward religion that it is no longer necessary to confront the questions posed by modernity. This, it is said, is the good news of postmodernism for religion. Postmodernism has shown that the Enlightenment worldview is but one perspective among others, thus opening the way for various religious worldviews as being equally legitimate perspectives in their own right.

This is the short way for handling modernity. For Christian theology it is, I believe, inadequate. One evidence is the fact that Christian claims on behalf of one particular particularity, viz. Jesus of Nazareth, continue to be a scandal in postmodernity. Jacques Derrida has affirmed a certain messianic hope, but he like most of his supporters remains resistant to the claims of any particular messianism.[6] And so be it: deconstruction is vigilance. But with regard to the vigilance, a certain clarity is required. (1) As regards the legitimate democratic *concerns* of the general-good, vigilance against the dominance of any messianism is necessary and appropriate. But (2) insofar as it goes beyond that to invoke a hierarchy of general over particular, or general over singularity – thereby excluding *a priori* the possibility that the good might be decisively instantiated in a specific singularity – the vigilance oversteps its bounds and becomes itself a policing of discourse. Finally, once the second point has been affirmed, one must return to the spirit of the first point and say (3) that the character of Christianity is such as to require of *everyone* – of those within the community as surely as of those without – the exercise of utmost vigilance; a vigilance of which deconstruction has now become an indispensable part.

Vigilance is required because the Christian gospel is a "messianism" in the specific sense that it does not subscribe to unqualified perspectivalism. Liberal theology found ways to soft-pedal or deny this but Schleiermacher, for one, was candid in according Christianity a certain primacy. Such claims might seem to spell the end of dialogue. The Christian gospel's disinclination to regard itself as but one perspective among many poses problems which might seem to foreclose the discussion. But the problems are not exclusive to Christianity, and that reopens the possibility of discussion. One way of making this point is of course retortion. Do those advocating perspectivalism regard perspectivalism itself as being but one perspective among others? A more concrete approach is to note that while postmodernism is clearly allied with some form of perspectivalism, it is also generally determined to take seriously the questions raised by the Holocaust. But the questions dissolve the moment one lets slip the actual historical event, in all its facticity.[7]

We need to reflect further. Let us begin with the classic Enlightenment thinker, Immanuel Kant, whom Derrida treats in an essay entitled "On an Apocalyptic Tone Recently Adopted in Philosophy."[8] Derrida's title plays upon that of a 1796 essay by Kant which Derrida translates as "On an Overlordly Tone Recently Adopted in Philosophy."[9] In this essay Kant champions the general-good. Philosophy, whose task it is to distinguish truth from superstition, proceeds by a process of discussion and debate which is both rational and democratic. But some believe themselves no longer accountable to such procedures; they refuse to present their claims before the bar of reason. These persons Kant calls "mystagogues."[10] Contrary to Enlightenment principles, they lay claim to a special revelation.

What is important for our purposes is the fact that Kant's chief criticism of the "mystagogues" does not turn upon the "general/particular" distinction but upon another, namely that between a truth claim based upon some unreflective *immediacy* and one which has tested or *mediated* by rational, reflective examination. "They are partisans of intellectual intuition" (p. 70). Obviously the latter distinction is related to the former, but it may have the advantage of being less "metaphysical." The terms "general" and "particular" are commonly inscribed within a hierarchical worldview in which particularity, associated with materiality, gravitates downward; and generality, associated with rationality and spirit, triumphantly ascends.[11] In contrast, the critique of (alleged) immediacy continues right into contemporary discussions, where it is often framed as the issue of "presence."

Derrida enters the discussion via a term which Kant uses somewhat informally, that of "tone." Kant argues that to be true to its calling, philosophy needs to maintain a steady tone, just as a court of law must treat both sides in a serious and evenhanded way. Philosophy, in tone and procedure, needs to stay "on track"; it must follow "due process." In contrast, mystagogic immediacy claims exemption from having to defend itself in public debate. It does not stay "on track" because it claims to have already arrived. It claims to possess the truth directly. Kant holds that such a claim would have the effect of derailing philosophy; it would prevent philosophy – and human reason more generally – from fulfilling its purpose and reaching its proper goal. (Hence the necessity of recasting the claims of religion "within the limits of reason alone.") Let us call this line of reflection the first moment of Derrida's reading of Kant. The first moment is in its own right pertinent to our own investigation. For Kant, the Christian gospel as commonly presented would of course be an instance of mystagogy. But now the face-off between gospel and reason is portrayed not in terms of particularity versus the general-good, but in terms of (purported) immediacy versus mediation. This is an advance in that it makes possible a critique of that modernity which identifies itself with the general. A general concept such as "progress" or "the New World Order" can function as a "presence," i.e., as a reality which is taken to be immediately self-justifying, fully as much as any particular can. Some of the onus is thus lifted from particularity.

Kant has ruled appeals to immediacy to be out of order in the court of reason. In a second moment of his reading, Derrida inquires whether Kant himself can abide by this rule. It is well and good to require that thinking be consistent, that it stay on track in order to attain its proper goal. But the one who makes this requirement implicitly affirms that she or he does have some knowledge of what that goal is. Is *that* knowledge gained stepwise, indirectly, by discursive reasoning? If it were, how would one know that *that* process was moving in the right direction? Derrida's point here is close to Heidegger's disorienting discovery that Truth itself is not "true." The point is important but no less so is the fact that it is Derrida who makes it. For early deconstruction seems to have been, quite consistently, a critique of immediacy or "presence"; whereas here Derrida indicates that some sort of immediacy, or something rather like immediacy, is at some point essential. This reasoning may throw some light on the philosophic grounds for Derrida's more recent interest in religion. Certainly it renders porous the barrier Kant sought to erect between philosopher and "mystagogue." It further disturbs the Enlightenment's hegemony of the general-good.

Commenting on Derrida's discussion of Kierkegaard's "knight of faith," John D. Caputo contends,

> Deconstruction wants to universalize this exception, to say that we are always already caught up in exceptionality, caught up in a singular secret that we cannot communicate to others. The religious exception, the singularity of the religious situation in which ethical generality is suspended, is always upon us.[12]

Deconstruction represents a radical reappreciation of particularity; or better, since the "particular/general" binary has ceased to be determinative for us, an appreciation of *singularity*. It is sometimes forgotten that however much deconstruction is a disassembling, it is no less surely a careful process of "agglutination," a tracing of the chains of supplementation, which simultaneously occasion and distend the singularity, the quasi-uniqueness, of a specific text. At the same time, deconstruction stands guard against any policing or narrowing of public discourse in the name of one singularity or another. This is perhaps the calling, the necessary "eternal vigilance" of deconstruction, or of philosophy as deconstruction understood it. Paying tribute to the Enlightenment, Derrida asserts:

> We cannot and must not forego what compels recognition as the enigmatic desire for vigilance, for the lucid vigil [*veille*], for clarification, for critique and truth, but for a truth that at the same time keeps within itself enough apocalyptic desire, this time as desire for clarity and revelation, to demystify, or if you prefer, to deconstruct the apocalyptic discourse itself and with it everything that speculates on vision, the imminence of the end, theophany, the parousia, the Last Judgment, and so on. (p. 82)

Again, vigilance is required of all, those within communities of belief and those without. "And what I say to you I say to all: Watch" (Mark 13.37). To Caputo, vigilance suggests that one does best to speak of singularity in general, as it were.

Like the deconstruction he describes, he "wants to universalize." Well and good. But as far as I can see, nothing that has been said thus far prohibits the alternative. Nothing dictates that truth, elusive as it is, *cannot possibly* be revealed in, and linked to, a specific singularity; a specific event.[13]

To paraphrase a bit of folk wisdom, God must love singularity, to have created so much of it. And what God has created, we are called to protect. But *to create singularity* – that is something extraordinary, something utterly beyond the cookie-cutter process of forming particulars from a general pattern. The ability to create singularity bespeaks a unique relationship of unfettered transcendence and utter intimacy. "For thou didst form my inward parts, thou didst knit me together in my mother's womb" (Ps. 139.13). A god so loving and so free as to do that could also do something more. Such a god could also become incarnate, if so disposed, in a specific singularity.[14]

Postmodern Good

From the foregoing it follows, on the one hand, that some sort of presentation of the logic of the Christian gospel may be possible in a postmodern context. The next section will indicate one direction such a presentation might go. At the same time it also follows that if such a gospel is to be received as (conceivably) good, it must be mindful of deconstruction's distinctive vigilance. What criterion would this imply? Is it even possible to fashion a criterion of the good in the context of postmodernity? To respond, let us recall Derrida's reading of Kant. To introduce a figure of our own, Kant accuses the "mystagogues" of short-circuiting philosophy. But his opponents could well reply that an electrical current does not flow unless the circuit is already in some fashion complete. In making such a point, Derrida moves in some sense beyond Kant – but he does so by using an argument that is classic Hegel. Put sweepingly, Hegel is true to the Enlightenment in insisting (against Schelling's mystagogic "night in which all cows are black") that determinacy is essential and that one must proceed discursively, step by step. But he is Romantic in that he holds that a "spirit" which is more than discursive reason is at work, conveying the sense of direction and end for which Kant cannot account. The pressure created by that twofold insistence is what makes the *Phenomenology* work.

Much of this purpose or direction is conveyed, of course, by Hegel's complex notion of *Aufhebung*, a "lifting up" to another level of reflection where conflict is to some extent resolved. In Hegel there is little to question the achievement of such a surmounting functions as an implicit norm. Not surprisingly, postmodernism rejects major aspects of this norm. In Hegel the "lifting up" is a step toward ultimate unity which postmodernism judges totalitarian, however much the friends of Hegel may insist upon its rich and dynamic character.[15] Against unification postmodernism pits its themes of otherness and difference. But sheer difference is not enough; one must acknowledge the enigmatic operations of a certain elusive "call" without which critique itself would be impossible. After all, it is one thing to forswear a predetermined goal, but quite another to have no *sense* of direction at all. This is an important aspect of Derrida's move from Saussurian difference to *différance*; and from apocalyptic to an "apocalyptic *sans* apocalyptic" within which a certain "call" yet remains.

That "call" cannot be predetermined or contained. Derrida will say at points that it may presage "the monstrous." Is postmodernism so understood good news? If so, by what sort of criterion?[16] On my reading, there is still quite enough of the *Aufhebung* in deconstruction to provide an initial answer. For one finds in the practice of deconstruction a constant effort to get beyond the situation which Hegel epitomized in the face-off of master and slave, i.e., an effort to get beyond the often violent stalemate of *oppositionalism* or *mirroring*. Catherine Keller deploys such a norm with subtlety and verve in her book *Apocalypse Now and Then*, which seeks to move beyond both apocalyptic and anti-apocalyptic.

> So I do not abandon apocalypse. I have argued that our history cannot delete it without committing it. At the same time, I have undeniably been hoping that its oppositions might generate a "third" space, open but not empty, in which the presuppositions of endism may be positively overcome – "sublated," at once preserved and transcended.[17]

In Derrida's essay on Kant the "apocalyptic *sans* apocalyptic" comes from attending to a certain tension (cf. "tone") between discursivity and immediacy. But it does not simply negate the elements. It rather holds them "in suspension." More generally, deconstruction may be said to proceed by taking a particular text, perhaps a single phrase or word, and holding it "in suspension" so that its many resonances may be heard. One might well say that suspension is essential if singularity is to be honored. Such a procedure often proves fruitful where other ways prove sterile. It is a good. And whether or not it achieves it, suspension points toward a norm, perhaps an impossibility – what one might brashly call "the good *Aufhebung*."[18]

One reason postmodernism presents itself as good news is that it understands itself as a liberation from imprisoning dichotomies. With that in mind, we may now ask whether a Christian gospel beyond the no-news gospel of Christendom, a Christianity which affirms its singularity and with that, a certain irreducible messianism, can be indeed good news.

Christian Gospel

Remarkably, Karl Barth, archenemy of the mixing of theology with philosophy, made vigorous use of a certain concept of *Aufhebung* in his commentary on Romans. The term is consistently paired with *Begrundung* in a phrase –

translated "dissolved and established" – which recurs so frequently as to become a fundamental trope.[19] The sense of "dissolved and established" is reinforced when Barth affirms that with the Christ event the power of this world "is pronounced to be something and – nothing, nothing and – something."[20] Taken in context the passages are unmistakably apocalyptic. Barth suggests that some notion of *Aufhebung* provides a way of delineating the impact, effect, and significance of Christian apocalyptic. Whether it is to be judged a "good *Aufhebung*" is the question we now address.

I propose to do so by turning from Romans to Galatians and from Barth to a contemporary commentator. Let us begin our exploration with the premise that it is unfruitful to seek, as liberal theology has often sought, to erect a fire-wall between the Christian gospel and Christian apocalyptic. For better and for worse, gospel and apocalyptic bleed into one another – in Christianity and in the culture at large. Let us also note that while deconstruction may be judged indispensable to the vigilance which Christian theology must exercise *vis-à-vis* its own apocalyptic, it does not follow that deconstruction should define beforehand the nature of that apocalyptic. If we wish to be attuned to otherness, we should not conclude too quickly that Derrida's "apocalyptic *sans* apocalyptic" is, or ought to be, "the same" as Christian apocalyptic. In the emphasis given to this concern, my approach diverges, I believe, from that of Caputo, Keller, and others.

"There is neither Jew or Greek, there is neither slave or free, there is neither male and female . . ." (Gal. 3.28, RSV). This is good news, this is liberation; no passage in all of Paul is more readily embraced by champions of the general-good. Even more in keeping with the spirit of modernity is the translation preferred by the New RSV: "There is *no longer* Jew or Greek, there is *no longer* slave or free, there is *no longer* male and female . . ." This is the rhetoric of gospel: in the time of darkness, some were slaves and some were free; but that is no longer so, a new day has arrived! The modern gospel. But Paul then adds, "for you are all one in Christ Jesus." Is this incidental? Can it be dropped in view of the larger democratic truth? Or have we to do with a singularity?

In 1997 there appeared in the Anchor Bible series a remarkable commentary on Galatians which places apocalyptic front and center.[21] The author, J. Louis Martyn, notes that already in his greeting Paul refers to "the present evil age" (1.4), a distinctly apocalyptic expression. In traditional apocalyptic, however, the contrast term would be "the coming age." For Paul, on Martyn's reading, the contrast term is rather "*the new creation.*"[22] The centrality of this concept, or event, is apparent as Paul writes, "For neither is circumcision anything nor is uncircumcision anything. What is something is the new creation" (6.15). The parallel with "neither Jew or Greek . . ." is striking. It is as if all the antinomies were "suspended" within "the new creation."

Let us examine Martyn's reading more closely. There are four occurrences within Galatians of words of the stem "apokalyp-". Two refer to the event on the road to Damascus (1.12, 15–16), one pertains to a revelation which directed Paul to go to Jerusalem (2.2). The fourth is 3.23, which the NRSV translates,

"Now before faith came, we were imprisoned and guarded under the law, until faith would be revealed." But Martyn notes that

> Paul speaks of "the apocalypse of faith," using that expression interchangeably with "the coming of faith" (3.25) and with the coming of Christ (3.24). Paul thus explicates the verb *apokalyptô* with the verbs *erchomai*, "to come [on the scene]," and *exapostellô*, "to send [into the scene]" (4.4, 6).[23]

The latter verbs have resonances which are distinctly apocalyptic. The usual translation of *apokalyptô* as "to reveal," "to unveil," is thus misleading in that they suggest the unveiling of something that was previously hidden, as though it had been eternally standing behind a curtain; whereas:

> The genesis of Paul's apocalyptic – as we see it in Galatians – lies in the apostle's certainty that God has *invaded* the present evil age by sending Christ and his Spirit into it. There was a "before," the time when we were confined, imprisoned; and there is an "after," the time of our deliverance. And the difference between the two is caused not by an unveiling, but rather by the coming of Christ and his Spirit.[24]

We may recall what a contribution it was to twentieth-century theology when Jürgen Moltmann insisted that eschatology was not just a single doctrine, but a lens through which all doctrine should be reconceived. Moltmann made of eschatology an adverb and a generation of theologians began to "think eschatologically." It may be that something no less radical is afoot when, on the strength of this passage and other clues such as Paul's references to "the present evil age" and a "new creation," Martyn argues that throughout the epistle, from beginning to end, Paul thinks and speaks "apocalyptically."[25]

If Paul's gospel turns not on a concealed truth, now revealed, but on a quite specific event, viz. the crucifixion and resurrection, that would speak to its singularity. But if Paul's gospel is indeed apocalyptic, how is it good news? To the leaders in Jerusalem Paul with his claim of having himself received a decisive revelation could well have seemed a mystagogue, or more colloquially a loose cannon. Is Paul to be counted among those whose tone conveys "I have the truth"? Does he profess to know, or control, who is and is not to be saved? Is he deaf to the legitimate concerns of those who, whether ancient or modern, have care for the common good? Crucial to Martyn's account is a distinction made by scholars of Jewish apocalyptic between two "tracks" within the complex heritage Paul would have known. In what may be called "*cosmological apocalyptic*,"

> evil, anti-God powers have managed to commence their own rule over the world, leading human beings into idolatry and thus into slavery, producing a wrong situation that was not intended by God and that will not be tolerated by him [sic]. For in his own time God will inaugurate a victorious and liberating apocalyptic war against these evil powers, delivering his elect from their grasp and thus making right that which has gone wrong because of the powers' malignant machinations.[26]

In contrast, "*forensic apocalyptic*" turns upon human beings, who have rejected God, thereby earning God's wrath and occasioning the evils of this world. "Given this self-caused plight, God has graciously provided the cursing and blessing Law as the remedy, thus placing before human beings the Two Ways, the Way of death *and* the Way of life."[27] At the last judgment individuals will be rewarded or condemned in accordance with the way that each has chosen.

One need hardly say it has been commonly assumed that whatever else there may be in Paul, there is some form of what is here called forensic apocalyptic. It is Martyn's contention, however, that the key to Paul's theology in Galatians and beyond is to be sought in his adhesion to a specifically *cosmological* apocalyptic. To drive the point home, Martyn further argues that the rhetoric of the Two Ways, with its antinomies of pure and impure, saved and unsaved, is the stock in trade of "the Teachers" – the very persons whom Paul fervently believes are leading the Galatian Christians astray. As a worldview, forensic apocalyptic represents the very thing that Paul opposes. To press the matter into a formula, one might almost say that in Galatians Paul has his own version of "apocalyptic *sans* apocalyptic," namely cosmological apocalyptic *sans* forensic apocalyptic.[28]

Strange as it is, Martyn's reading of Paul, and by implication of Christianity, does have one significant precedent in modern theology. This is Gustaf Aulén's *Christus Victor: An Historical Study of the Three Main Types of the Idea of Atonement*.[29] The parallel is indeed striking; the "classic" view of soteriology which Aulén champions closely resembles cosmological apocalyptic and the "objective" theory which Aulén critiques recalls the conventional forensic view which Paul himself attacks. Now Aulén observes that a major reason the "classic" vision of God's triumphant warfare against the powers of darkness fell into disfavor, after having had a formative influence throughout the first millennium of Christian theology, was what its critics considered to be its "mythological" character. Paul, for his part, is no less "mythological" in speaking of the "powers" which have held creation in thrall. Now Martyn is quite explicit that the device by which the powers hold humankind captive has been the perpetuation of certain binary oppositions such as pure versus impure, sacred versus profane. These are the structures by means of which the evil powers have imprisoned humankind. And it is from the dominance of such structures that we have been freed, according to Paul, "in Christ." Thus it is not just a changed social pattern but a radically transformed cosmic order that Paul proclaims when he says that in Christ "there is no longer Jew or Greek, there is no longer slave or free, there is no longer male and female . . ."

This brings us to "another way" that Christian theology might proceed. It might proceed from the assumption that the Christian gospel is in some sense irreducibly apocalyptic; that, following Paul, the apocalyptic turns upon one particular event, namely the crucifixion and resurrection of Jesus; and that, Enlightenment preconceptions notwithstanding, this apocalyptic event is to be interpreted in a manner which is "cosmological." To indicate why this direction might be of interest despite its difficulty, we may observe that forensic apocalyptic, for its part, is a virtual paradigm of what Derrida has called a "closed economy." In order to assure that each human action will count toward reward or retribution, there can be no "leakage" or loss, each act must have its commensurate effect.

It follows that Paul may have adopted the language of cosmological apocalyptic precisely because it offered an *alternative* to the antinomical mindset of the forensic. We would then have to read in the awareness that Paul is not simply presenting another apocalyptic, but is rather using apocalyptic in what is truly "another way." It would be a way where (cosmological) apocalyptic deconstructs (forensic) apocalyptic from within. It would be a way that proclaims the return of the good Creator and the restoration – which is neither negation nor absolutization – of the manifold differences, such as that of female and male, within the good creation. It would be a way that proclaims (to use language that is admittedly not Pauline) "the good *Aufhebung*."[30]

And as for Paul, so too perhaps for Christianity. A Christian gospel which dissolves such social dichotomies as master and slave might be received as prospectively good news for anyone, modern or postmodern, who shares the legitimate concerns of the general-good. Of course, those committed to the modern (Enlightenment) principle of constant tone will judge unacceptable any disturbance of natural processes and the presumed continuity of history. But those mindful that any tone is already a disturbance have the wherewithal to imagine the possibility that one might receive this Christian apocalyptic as being simultaneously profoundly other – thus new – and liberating – thus good.

Notes

1 For a trenchant examination of this issue, see Bruce Marshall, *Christology in Conflict: The Identity of a Saviour in Rahner and Barth* (Oxford: Blackwell Publishers, 1987). Behind Marshall lies the work of Hans Frei, particularly *The Eclipse of Biblical Narrative* (New Haven, CT: Yale University Press, 1974).
2 Gotthold Lessing, "On the Proof of the Spirit and of Power," in *Lessing's Theological Writings*, ed. Henry Chadwick (Stanford, CA: Stanford University Press, 1972), p. 53.
3 Johann Baptist Metz, *Faith in History and Society: Toward a Practical Fundamental Theology* (New York: Seabury Press, 1980), pp. 73, 171.
4 See Kierkegaard's contrast between God as teacher and God as savior in Søren Kierkegaard, *Philosophical Fragments* (Princeton, NJ: Princeton University Press, 1985), pp. 23–36. The text bears the pseudonym Johannes Climacus.
5 In the seventeenth and eighteenth centuries there were many who "were content to argue that such supernatural revelation as had been given . . . could be nothing more than what they called a 'republication,' for the benefit of weaker minds, of truths which a sufficiently sustained and honest exercise of reason could know independently." John Baillie, *The Idea of Revelation in Recent Thought* (New York: Columbia University Press, 1956), p. 6.

6 For a helpful interpretive reading of Derrida's writings on religion, see John D. Caputo, *The Prayers and Tears of Jacques Derrida: Religion without Religion* (Bloomington: Indiana University Press, 1997).
7 The work of Jean Baudrillard seems particularly problematic in this regard.
8 Jacques Derrida, "On an Apocalyptic Tone Recently Adopted in Philosophy," *Semeia 23: Derrida and Biblical Studies* (1982), p. 63.
9 "Von einem neuerdings erhobenen Ton in der Philosophie," in Kant, *Schriften von 1790–1796 von Immanuel Kant*, ed. A. Buchenau, E. Cassirer, and B. Kellermann, vol. 6 of *Immanuel Kants Werke*, ed. Ernst Cassirer (Berlin: Verlegt bei Bruno Cassirer, 1923), pp. 475–96.
10 Derrida, "On an Apocalyptic Tone," p. 68. My exposition of Kant's essay follows that of Derrida. In this section, references to Derrida's essay will generally be given in parentheses.
11 I examine the metaphorics of infinity and ascent in "Can Transcendence be Finite?" in *Questioning God*, ed. John D. Caputo (Bloomington: Indiana University Press, 2001).
12 Caputo, *Prayers and Tears*, p. 208.
13 Cf. Derrida, "On an Apocalyptic Tone": "Truth itself is the end, the destination and that truth unveils itself is the advent of the end. Truth is the end and the instance of the Last Judgment. The structure of truth here would be apocalyptic. And that is why there would not be any truth of the apocalypse that is not the truth of truth" (p. 84).
14 If God were *not* truly transcendent, if God were in some sense a part of the world, then the incarnation attested by the Christian tradition would be impossible. For, as Robert Sokolowski observes, "the union of any two natures in the world is bound to be, in some way, unnatural, because of the otherness that lets one thing be itself only by not being the other. But the Christian God is not a part of the world and is not a 'kind' of being at all. Therefore the incarnation is not meaningless or impossible or destructive." See Robert Sokolowski, *The God of Faith and Reason: Foundations of Christian Theology* (Notre Dame, IN: University of Notre Dame Press, 1982), p. 36. Note that Sokolowski does not claim that the incarnation is either necessary or rationally demonstrable. Either of those contentions would contradict the incarnation as gift (pp. 39–40).
15 See the nuanced discussion in Joseph C. Flay, *Hegel's Quest for Certainty* (Albany: State University of New York Press, 1984), pp. 249–67. Flay notes Hegel's crucial "presupposition of a single referent for totality and intelligibility" (p. 260).
16 For a fuller treatment of this disputed topic, see Richard Kearney's essay "Desire of God" in *God, the Gift and Postmodernism*, ed. John D. Caputo and Michael J. Scanlon (Bloomington: Indiana University Press, 1999), pp. 112–30, 136–45, and the responses of Jacques Derrida and John D. Caputo (pp. 130–6).
17 Catherine Keller, *Apocalypse Now and Then: A Feminist Guide to the End of the World* (Boston: Beacon Press, 1996), p. 276. Keller is fully aware of the Hegelian connotations.
18 Kevin Thompson's illuminating study "Hegelian Dialectic and the Quasi-Transcendental in *Glas*" concludes: "The 'profound affinity' between deconstruction and speculative philosophy may finally prove inescapable and their relation irresoluble." The essay appears in *Hegel After Derrida*, ed. Stuart Barnett (London: Routledge, 1998), pp. 239–59; the quotation is from p. 259.

19 Karl Barth, *The Epistle to the Romans* (Oxford: Oxford University Press, 1933); within the first chapter the phrase is found on pp. 30, 36, 38, 46, and 51. For a fuller study of this aspect of Barth's thought, see Lowe, *Theology and Difference: The Wound of Reason* (Bloomington: Indiana University Press, 1993), pp. 33–47.
20 Barth, *Epistle to the Romans*, p. 36.
21 J. Louis Martyn, *Galatians: A New Translation with Introduction and Commentary* (New York: Doubleday, 1997).
22 6.15; Martyn, *Galatians*, p. 98. With this passage and those that follow, I adopt Martyn's translation (see pp. 3–10).
23 Ibid, p. 99.
24 Ibid; emphasis Martyn's.
25 See Lowe, "Prospects for a Postmodern Christian Theology," in *Modern Theology*, 15: 1 (January 1999), pp. 17–24.
26 Martyn, *Galatians*, p. 97, n. 51. Martyn's understanding of the two apocalyptic traditions draws upon the work of M. C. de Boer; see de Boer, "Paul and Jewish Apocalyptic Eschatology" in *Apocalyptic and the New Testament: Essays in Honor of J. Louis Martyn*, ed. Joel Marcus and Marion L. Soards (Sheffield: JSOT Press, 1989), pp. 169–90; and de Boer, "Paul and Apocalyptic Eschatology" in *The Encyclopedia of Apocalypticism*, vol. 1, ed. John J. Collins (New York: Continuum, 1998), pp. 345–83. Martyn and de Boer speak of "cosmological apocalyptic eschatology."
27 Martyn, *Galatians*, p. 98, continuation of n. 51.
28 More exactly, perhaps, a forensic apocalyptic which has become "nothing – and something, something – and nothing" within a determinative cosmological apocalyptic.
29 New York: Macmillan, 1951.
30 For a fuller treatment of the specifically Christological character of Paul's apocalyptic gospel, see Lowe, "Christ and Salvation" in *The Cambridge Companion to Postmodern Theology*, ed. Kevin Vanhoozer, (Cambridge: Cambridge University Press, forthcoming).

CHAPTER 31

Indian Territory: Postmodernism Under the Sign of the Body

Carl Raschke

In 1982 a group of American theologians, trained in philosophy (particularly the death-of-God thinking of Hegel and Nietzsche and the linguistic turn taken by Wittgenstein and Heidegger), encountered the work of Jacques Derrida and saw the potential of deconstruction for theological discourse. A book emerged, *Deconstruction and Theology*, featuring essays by Thomas J. J. Altizer, Mark C. Taylor, Robert Scharlemann, Charles Winquist, Max Meyer, and Carl Raschke. In the same year Mark C. Taylor published his full-length study *Deconstructing Theology*, followed in 1986 by his edited collection *Deconstruction in Context*.

Derrida (with Paul de Man) took the American literary world by storm from the mid-1970s when English translations of his work began to appear, and the influence of his thinking for those schooled in hermeneutics, for those waiting for the next move that might be made following Gadamer, began to be felt. Raschke was one of the first to register the importance of Derrida's work. In the summer of 1977 he was busy reading the later Heidegger and thinking through the relationship between the semantic emphasis of hermeneutics and the semiotic emphasis of pragmatists like Peirce. In his book *The Alchemy of the Word: Language and the End of Theology* (Missoula, MT, 1979) the chapter in which Derrida appears involves a discussion of transcendence that examines Wittgenstein, Peirce, and Ricoeur before finally arriving at Derrida. Derrida's critiques of logocentrism and presence, his account of *différance*, according to Raschke, provide the *apparatus criticus* "for making the appropriate gestures towards conceiving language as transcendence, which is at once an epochal break with the metaphysics of certainty." And yet, at this point, Derrida promptly disappears from Raschke's argument; instead, the later writings of Heidegger are discussed along with Martin Buber's dialogicalism. It is as if the importance of deconstruction is not fully grasped by Raschke until the early 1980s.

> Derrida and Heidegger have been central to Raschke's project of rethinking the nature and operation of theological discourse at the end of theology as an ecclesial discipline – theological discourse after the death of God. In *Theological Thinking: An In-Quiry* (Atlanta, GA, 1988) he draws on Derrida and Heidegger in an attempt to rehabilitate theological discourse as thinking that is heterological, that meditates upon the impossible other. There is no mention of Buber. In this rehabilitation the move is made away from the hermeneutical emphasis upon textuality towards deconstruction's concern with writing; *scripture* as Derrida plays on the term.
>
> By the mid-1980s another voice comes to complement Derrida's: Lacan's. A new thematics also arises, in which Lacan's thinking acts as the *apparatus criticus* for elucidating the body and desire. This turn in Raschke's work is signaled by an essay which appeared in a volume he edited with Edith Wyschogrod and David Crownfield: *Lacan and Theological Discourse* (Albany, NY, 1989). A later draft of the same essay appeared in Raschke's book *Fire and Roses: Postmodernity and the Thought of the Body* (Albany, NY, 1996), in which deconstruction is interleaved with an analysis of eros, and the heterological project now negotiates the Freudian rather than the Heideggerian appraisal of *Unheimlichkeit*. "The uncanny" registers a not-being-at-home, the magical presence of a mobile desire. In the following essay, it is the outlaw which now figures Raschke's preoccupation with the uncanny.

> *"The real . . . originates from the determination of a place."*
> Michel de Certeau, *The Writing of History*

> *"Can signs be trusted?"*
> Mark C. Taylor, *Hiding*

> *"Besides the written laws there are many usages in force which are not written. Their peculiar ceremonies and customs are not written."*
> Ethan Allen Hitchcock, *A Traveller in Indian Territory*

Increasingly, the question of postmodernism as a theological movement has been cast in terms of ontology or, more precisely, of *onto-theology*. What might be characterized as Derrida's own "Deleuzian" interpretation of Heidegger[1] has framed the chassis for virtually all of the controversy that has run the gamut from Mark Taylor's efforts to write an "a/theology," or theology of absence, to John Caputo's attempt to appropriate deconstruction as a kind of piety of difference.[2] In many respects the debate has remained, despite its rhetorical pyrotechnics and literary riffs, a scholastic debate. The sensibility of the postmodernists circles like some strange and distant planetoid around the central and unresolved issue first raised by Hegel in his *Science of Logic*: how can predicative determination be a critical function in the act of negation? To what degree is the logico-syntactical relationship between sameness and difference a matter of "substance," as the Aristotelian tradition would have it, or a revelation of emptiness, as Buddhist philosophy might argue just as cogently?

The irrepressible anxiety among theological traditionalists over the "nihilistic" ramifications of postmodernist thinking indicates in large measure what Nietzsche himself prophesied about the philosophy of the twentieth century, and those centuries beyond. Nietzsche himself foretold that there would appear a curious "alterity" in Western philosophy, a kind of "uncanniness" (*Unheimlichkeit*), a prescience concerning the *nihil* implicit in the very notion of *ens*. This discovery was first made by Spinoza. And it became the operative insight of the Hegelian dialectic – *omnia determinatio est negatio*. It is also the signature of "postmodern" thinking. To signify is to nullify. To construct is to deconstruct. To reveal is to conceal. To take a stance is to hide.

This inherent ontological dyadism – what might be characterized as the great postmodernist aporia, which rests upon an only partially perceived fracturing within modern philosophy – can also be viewed in an ethico-political light as well. The drive of postmodern is engendered not so much in the ontotheological problem of identity and trace, which Heidegger and Derrida have framed as the very architecture for contemporary thought, as from the distinctly "de-ontological" issue of moral and metaphysical pluralism. In other words, the much maligned "relativism" and "nihilism" of postmodernist thinking actually derives from a weak reading of the polysemy of modern democratic thought. Postmodernism need not be construed as some dusky revolt against the transcendent order of things. It is most aptly understood as an intrinsically "liberal" preoccupation with maintaining a balance of power among a multitude of constituencies. It concerns what Michael Hardt has termed the "political refusal of teleology," corresponding to a "philosophical refusal of ontology."[3] This refusal is intrinsic to the history of critical philosophy in the West, which commences with Kant's deployment of his "transcendental" method to overthrow the suzerainty of classical ontotheology in the name of a "religion within the limits of reason alone," a "rational faith" founded on the freedom of the moral will, in short a *de-ontology*.

Furthermore, American pragmatism, particularly the radical empiricism of William James, crafted its own philosophical idiolect for an attack on classical ontology. The "discovery" of Derrida in the 1970s by Richard Rorty is no fluke of contemporary intellectual history. The movement known as "deconstruction" gave a more current, if not precise, voice to philosophical themes of the American pragmatist school. But American philosophical pragmatism is not to be associated straightaway with postmodernism as an intellectual and historical phenomenon. While there has been a subtle, and almost ingenious, effort on the part of political and theological neo-liberals since the mid-1980s to rebaptize themselves as "postmodernists," the results have been confusing. French poststructuralism, closely aligned in its early days with Marxism, may have been hybridized with the core "libertarian" strands of American thought to generate what we broadly recognize as the "postmodernist" style of conversation.

However, something more trenchant has been going on all the while. Recently a full-dress challenge to postmodern theology has been launched by a group of British-trained religious thinkers who espouse a perspective they call "radical orthodoxy." The perspective of radical orthodoxy is sweeping, eclectic, and in many ways neo-scholastic. But the most persistent feature of the argument of radical orthodoxy is that postmodernism merely completes the "idolatry," as John Milbank puts it, of modernism. Modernism, in turn, is founded on the great defection of ontology in the late Middle Ages under the impact of Duns Scotus toward "ontotheology," where "one can first understand Being in an unambiguous, sheerly 'existential' sense ... without reference to God, who is later claimed 'to be' in the same univocal manner." Scotus hence, according to Milbank, brings about "the late medieval commencement of the decline of metaphysics, in the opening to an autonomous, secular sphere of knowledge."[4]

Like Derrida before them, the exponents of radical orthodoxy make a forward sortie in the advance of post-metaphysical thought by carefully misreading Heidegger. Milbank, for instance, seeks in his own way to deploy Heidegger's critique of ontotheology to revive the Thomistic idea of revelation as illumination of the intellect and to argue that the former's notion of "fundamental ontology" actually applies to Christian theology in its premodern forms. "If Christian theology prior to Scotus avoided ontotheology (metaphysics), then this was because it was able to elucidate the hidden manifestness of God in terms of the hidden manifestness of Being in beings."[5] The difficulty, however, with radical orthodoxy's attack on postmodernism is that it overplays the Heideggerian move and ignores the other streams and influence that have created theological postmodernism. Our argument, therefore, is that theological postmodernism has less to do with the "history of Being in the West" – although the Heideggerian hermeneutic has certainly established the framework for a critical theory of representation and language that undergirds much of the postmodernist idiom – than it does with its development as a post-Enlightenment narrative of ontological freedom. In this respect postmodernism, in contrast with radical orthodoxy which claims to be the rightful heir to it, can be perceived as a distinctively American narrative. It runs up against not only "radical orthodoxy," but American liberal orthodoxy as well, as the historical bearer of what we may term the "deeper semiotics" of American cultural experience.

The underlying syntactics of this experience may be called *radical modernism*, which may in fact be what "postmodernism" is all about. Radical modernism suggests that postmodernism can be regarded neither as a movement in itself nor as a kind of "end game" to the modernist project, as radical orthodoxy contends. Radical modernism weighs in with the insight that the question of the "originary" cannot be settled simply in terms of the Kantian/Heideggerian critique of the language of metaphysics. Indeed, the current campaign of radical orthodoxy against what amounts to a caricature of a neo-Nietzschean theology of immanence presumes that there is some kind of strange dividing line between postmodernism and "truth." What both radical orthodox thinkers and their opponents miss entirely, however, is Kant's own response to the "problem" of metaphysics – the assertion of radical freedom, and *pari passu* the possibility of "radical evil."

As Kant wrote in the second preface to the *Critique of Pure Reason*, his eminent aim was to "annul *knowledge* in order to make room for *faith*."[6] And Kantian faith is the authentic modernist faith – faith in the divinely endowed freedom by which moral and social action is possible in the first place. No matter the appeal of the Nietzschean critique of metaphysics and morality, the modern celebration of individual *libertas* underwrites the postmodernist project. As Aryeh Botwinick argues, "in order for postmodernism to be an adequate metaphilosophical theory, it must presuppose the existence of modernism. Otherwise, postmodernism emerges as a tautology possessing zero explanatory power."[7] Postmodernism emerges as a postscript to the text of the Enlightenment, as a radicalization, and hence an overdetermination, of the discourse of freedom. In postmodernism the discourse of freedom deconstructs the metanarrative of reason.

The discourse of freedom, of course, is more far-reaching than the paleoutilitarian doctrines of knowledge and motivation, such as we find in Lockean theory, that anchor historically so-called "liberal" political thought. From an ontological standpoint, the discourse of freedom emanates from the Cartesian stance of subjectivity – the necessity of an ego positing itself in order to put itself in question. As Heidegger understood, the modern experience of the liberty of the *ego cogito* redirects the momentum of ontotheology away from the *ens qua ens* in the direction of the *ens qua voluntas*. The "theological" position of modernism, fully articulated for the first time in Kant's *Critique of Practical Reason*, thus hinges on the insuperability of will. The transition in late Scholasticism away from the notion of God as supreme essence to an identification of the *Deus absconditus* with absolute will constitutes the real "red shift" in Neoplatonic and Augustinian thought, revealing the roots of the modernist mentality. Indeed, this movement in the late fourteenth and fifteenth centuries, associated with such figures as William of Ockham, Jean Buridan, Gregory of Rimini, and Gabriel Biel, was known as the *via moderna*. The attack on ontotheology came from a philosophical nominalism and a "voluntarist" doctrine of God, which like postmodernism seven hundred years later, asserted the freedom of the signifier over the priority of essence.

In its religious form the so-called *devotio moderna* laid the groundwork for Protestant pietism and ultimately the Kantian critical philosophy.[8] This shift is far more important in the genesis of modernism than the identification of God with Being *qua* Being by Scotus, as radical orthodoxy argues. It is Ockham, not Scotus, who can be called the first "modernist." Any critique of postmodernism as a kind of dissymetrical reading of modern philosophy must recognize that it is nothing less than the "sacred," particularly of the freedom of the will, that is at stake. The alleged nihilism of postmodernism is but a way of reading tendentiously the discourse of freedom, which emerges *tout ensemble* in the sixteenth and seventeenth centuries as the theological "double sentence," most recognizable in Luther's writings as the transcendence of God and the spiritual liberty of the Christian. Pietistic voluntarism is what makes the epistemological and political rules of modernism thinkable in the first place.

In contrast, however, postmodernism is about something much more than the freedom of the subject as the *a priori* condition, as it was in Kant, for conceiving

God. The modern meditation on the self was always a venture, as both Hegel and Heidegger understood, into the experience of truth. It was an experience that could no longer be chartered in the Augustinian language of sacramental participation and the gradations of nature and supernature. The venture of postmodernism must be understood, as John Caputo reminds us, as a wager of "radical hermeneutics," as an inventory of "transactions [that] have roots which extend far below the surface, into the depths of textuality, of the unconscious, of history, and of who knows what else, and that we have only limited hope of disentangling them."[9] The issue, for Caputo, is whether freedom in the postmodern sense transgresses the borders established by the nineteenth-century truce between Hegelian rationality and Augustinian illuminationism. The "transactivity" of postmodern experience overrides both the voluntarism of the modern and the metaphysical authoritarianism of classical Christianity. Caputo asks: have we postmodernists inscribed a new law of the sign, or are we "outlaws."

"The police of truth . . . are after us and it is high time to make the case that we are responsible citizens, not outlaws. Still the very idea of outlaw is not intrinsically bad, not bad by its essence. . . . Historically, some of the very best people have been judged and even punished as outlaws by the law."[10] The question of the postmodernist as "outlaw" is critical, because it is superimposed on the issue of how we configure, philosophically and theologically, what we understand as "rationality." In medieval times the law of subjectivity was the province of the theological outlaw, the heretic. The heretic was contrasted with the "orthodox." He, or she, was "outside the truth." The law of the sign was bound up with the system of dogmatic theology, compiled from ancient authority and proof text, the so-called *via antiqua*. The problem of postmodernity has less to do with either the boundaries, or the possibilities, of reason in the Kantian sense than with negotiation of what we mean by the expression "heterological." Although since Batailles first coined the term we have come to denominate the science of "heterology," yet we still do not know its terrain. The band that demarcates the terrain of the outlaw – the hetero-writer – from the "rule of law" is often a problematic type of sequestering – a slum, a mountain range, a river, a cave.

The outlaw "hides out." The outlaw's "hideout" is beyond the "reach" of the law, but it is close to the law. It is exterior to the jurisdiction of grammar; yet it is interior to the ascendant discourse. The outlaw moves routinely, and undetected, within the "territory" from which he or she is a fugitive. Whereas the nomad has no "home," no territory to signify as place, the outlaw knows his, or her, "site." The terrain is familiar. The postmodernist is like the *habiru* of ancient Egypt, an outlaw that "displaces" the *topos* of imperial signification to the desert. Yet the desert is always a place from which to stage raids on the empire, to wander in and wander out, to settle and rule, then return. As Caputo argues, he or she must always be wary of the police, though most successful outlaws maintain a necessary, supplementary relationship to "law and order." There would be no respectable vice without the mafia, and vice versa. The relationship between the two "regimes" is one of *co-territoriality*.

As an example, during most of the nineteenth century America's most famous outlaws – the James Brothers, Billy the Kid, John Wesley Harding – all hid out in the region between the Arkansas and the Red Rivers, the area that is now part of the state of Oklahoma and was known as "Indian Territory." Indian Territory was the place to which the aboriginal inhabitants of America, the "native Americans," were "removed" during the 1830s either by guile or by brutal force. Thus Indian Territory became the "place" for all Native Americans – a place set aside for the displaced, a place that to this day defines America, yet is incomprehensible to most Americans, even many who consider themselves "Native American." Indian Territory was a highly strategic place during the Civil War. It was a place to be fought over, a strategic locus for the control of other terrains. It was, and is, like the postmodern itself, the territory of outlaws.

The ancillary relationship between Indian Territory and other familiar sign-terrains is incised in Josef Simon's "philosophy of the sign." Simon's philosophical semiotics has not yet exercised the leverage it commands in this country. But it is becoming increasingly important for comprehending what Lyotard calls the "postmodern condition." Simon says, "*all* signs as such are freedom signs." The reason is that "freedom is exercised in the understanding of signs."[11] The sign, according to Simon, is guarded in the self-presence of the body as the synthesis or "chiasm" (Merleau-Ponty) of phenomenal immediacy and noumenal freedom. The strange combination of self-certainty and the experience of infinite alterity, which Levinas uncovers in the Cartesian circle of self-reflection, derives from such a phenomenological correlation of the sign as intention. The "primary sign of freedom," Simon remarks, "is the body."[12] For the body, contrary to the Husserlian argument, radically situates the sign as subjective agency. If Descartes could have thought away the body, he could have thought away the self, although the infamous "Cartesian dualism" masks this peculiar facticity within perception.

Semiotics, unlike phenomenology, cannot forge an *epochē*; it requires a "thesis," because it requires the freedom of sign-production and interpretation made available by the body. Semiotics is essentially "somatological," as I have argued elsewhere.[13] The "body" of the sign hides out from the act of reflection. It is not a self-presence, but an appurtenance for the experience of presence.[14] Such a distinction, of course, is evident in Heidegger's analysis of the relationship between *zuhanden* and *vorhanden*, between "equipment" as the condition for signifying praxis and the formal templates of meaning that constitute the representational character of language.

But the hiding of the sign to itself is what not only depicts the rhythm of representation, but puts ontotheology at issue.[15] The nihilistic reading of postmodernism hinges fatefully upon a refusal to acknowledge that signification by its very nature proceeds from an ontology of freedom that leaves every form of substantialism, even a "Christian" substantialism, under the guise of sacramentalism, impossible. The Calvinist rejection of Christ's "real presence" in the eucharist, for instance, was more than a quibble over any permissible degree of theological realism. It signified the genesis of the modernist, and by the same token postmodernist, understanding that the experience of redemption is impossible without the liberty of conscience. The Protestant doctrine that the elements of the "body" and the "blood" in the Lord's Supper are substances was an intuitive and pre-theological statement about the genesis of the sign itself. The sign is not only somatological; it depends on the moment of signification, the revelation of freedom. Negation is the "immediately syntactic sign."[16] Metaphysics is a forgetfullness of the origin of the sign. It is syntax that signifies. Syntax is the "flesh" of language. Signification is its redemption.

But this moment of redemption must proceed from another "context" of signifying relations that manifests the representational order of discourse, the Derridean double inscription. In its moment of "subjecticity" (Heidegger), which founds the modern position in both philosophy and theology, the sign shows its Janus face. The sign signifies both the exteriority of a natural or "empirical" structure of correlative associations, and the interiority of "self-consciousness," according to which the "thetic" composition of ontology itself can be discerned. This bifurcation of the sign, of course, is the phenomenological fulcrum upon which the notion of "deconstruction" itself rotates. Deconstruction is not so much a postmodern innovation as it is a rhetoric for unfurling the double coding that dominates all modernist texts, which in themselves are distinguished by the syntactical parallelism of author and *oeuvre*, subject and knowledge, freedom and experience.

The much catalogued intellectual sins of the deconstructionists can be viewed as nothing more than a writing of the aporias of modernism itself. But the philosophical desire to move beyond these aporias, which distinguishes postmodern thought from deconstruction *per se*, requires a rereading of the entire theory of the sign. As Hassan Melehy shows, the "Cartesian circle," in which the signs "I" and "God" are reciprocally inscribed, is the founding aporia of modern discourse.

> In the *cogito* Descartes discovers the possibility of the complete disruption of signification; he "fixes" the *cogito* – reinscribes it – through recourse to a system of axioms that is part and parcel of the Western institution of the sign. God, in Descartes, becomes the name of the institution, in which the philosophy of the subject is inscribed. And since he has the ability to institute those relations with such completeness, God also has the power to disrupt it with equal thoroughness ... the "false" is error, determined in strict accord with the specifically modern notion of truth as the institution of the sign, in which the sign becomes a transparency, guaranteed in God. Error is a wandering, a wandering of signifiers away from their instituted signifieds. Again, the *cogito* is a finite being, and because of its finitude it is not in the full presence of this institution whose limits are marked in the signature of God – but its finitude is also its freedom, through which it will come to know God and the world and institute itself as knowing subject.[17]

Hassan's semiotic interpretation of Descartes points up the way in which much of so-called "postmodern theology," such as that of Mark Taylor, can be called a "reverse Cartesianism." It is a modern subjectivist metaphysics that has been turned upside down rather than surpassed because of the death of God. The Cartesian mirror epigraphy of God, self, and knowledge becomes "the disappearance of the self, the end of history, and the closure of the book."[18] Because of the negative valency of the sign, its "wandering" makes plain what underlies the institution discourse of the divine, in short, its "theology" or, as Taylor calls it, an "a/theology."

Modernism is the "law" that has been revealed for what it is, the law that has been deracinated. But modernism at the same time amounts to a grandiose construction, a cathedral erected upon the double coding of all levels of signification. The emptiness beneath the foundations, the *nihil* that stalks the spaces between the double folio, cannot be construed as some perversity of the ontological project. The double coding itself arises from the reflexivity that is introduced into metaphysics, and by implication Western theology, through the Cartesian *skepsis*. Any "radical" appeal to the pre-Cartesian innocence of theological experience is a form of bad faith.

The postmodern project, like the American experience itself, is administered by the sign of freedom. But it is a *tensive* freedom. The tension emerges not from the Cartesian double coding of representation, but from the segregation of the law of representation as the institutionalization of sign-functions and the territory of the outlaw. The outlaw is recognized by a refusal of teleology, by a commitment to the freedom that figures forth from the signifying capacity of the body, from the certitude not of the *cogito*, but from the opacity of desire. Postmodern thought fills out a discourse founded on Simon's "primary sign," the freedom of the *soma*. But the postmodern *soma* differs radically and essentially from the sacramental "body." The sacramental body is a *substantia duplex*, a peculiar type of *res materialis* that lacks the self-intelligibility of the *soma per se*. As with the elevated host in the Latin mass, it is a spectacle rather than a primary signifier. It remains inside the terrain of representation with its common law and codices. It embodies the purposive movement of desire toward the infinite in the Augustinian way. It involves *telos* rather than *semiosis*. The sign of freedom is subordinated to the kinetics of grace, the rescript of divine will. The negative is wanting.

It is indeed Hegel's "power of the negative" that positions postmodern thinking as somatological thinking. But this negativity is not the abstract negativity of nihilism, or any so-called "negative theologies." It is the negativity that highlights the borderlands between two differing laws of signification, between two different territories, between the "civil" and the "native." Civil law is configured from the rules of representation. But the idea of the "native," which is at the same time the realm of the "outlaw," belongs to a different kind of territority – "Indian Territory." Indian Territory is the topography of freedom, because it is "outside" the law. But it also remains on native soil. It is the fullness of presence that inhabits the body as *primum signum*. Yet this fullness remains differentiated, disseminated. In its *diaspora* the transcendent, the infinite, comes to be enfleshed.

American thought is the *diaspora* of Western thought, which tells why postmodernism is uniquely American. But there is also the "native" stratum of thinking in America. And it is in this setting that postmodernism "institutes" the sign of freedom as a relationship to the soil. To the territory that cannot be enclosed or bounded by the law. By the "postmodern condition" we do not mean so much the de-institutionalization of the sign as its *trans-gression*, its "crossing over" the boundary where the territories themselves diverge, to where the double coding of the system of representation can now be read as the relationship between the self-presence of the *soma* and the sign that transcends itself toward the infinite. It is here that we recover the true meaning of the word "freedom." But it is now the freedom that comes from the capacity of the body to posit beyond itself in the splendor of the chiasm, to penetrate many veils, to de-institute what has been institutionalized, to overthrow the empire of representation.

We acquire a sense of this overture in reading Derrida's essay on "Faith and Knowledge." For Derrida, the terrain of primary signification must be understood in a peculiar sense, as a "testimonial sacredness," of which Heidegger speaks "under the name of *Zusage* ('accord, acquiescing, trust, or confidence')" as "that which is most irreducible, indeed most originary in thought."[19] Derrida construes ontotheology as an "encrypting of faith." Faith betokens the "place" from which the ontotheological imagination, which we may call "religion," egresses. "The place is unique; it is without name."[20] It is the One that can only be "deconstructed" as the infinity of gods, spirits, and place names, as revered texts and their distinguished commentaries, as the production of theological innovations and critical glosses. The One is always "One + n," which "incalculably engenders all these supplements."[21] It is the One that demands, unlike ontic monuments, sacrifice and prayer. It is not the Absolute to be comprehended in the spiral of reflection, but which does not allow itself to be misappropriated, that deciphers the manifold grammars of "world theologies" with the violence of penance, atonement, and immolation. It is found in the "space and time of a spectralizing messianicity beyond all messianism."[22] Religion is the terrain. Faith is its locus.

But as a house is not a home, a terrain is not a territory. Of what territory do we have in mind then? We speak of a territory that is not written as any kind of sovereignty, but allows the regime itself to be accessed, disrupted, and called to the bar for its false teleology of suprapersonal transcendence. We speak of the territory that is native, yet is not some romantic and pseudo-essentialist, but is telluric and connotes what de Certeau calls the "space of the other." The native is not a text captured in alternation of representative signatures, but a voice, the voice that "can create an *aparté*, opening a breach in the text and restoring a contact of body to body."[23]

To indemnify the postmodern in this way is not to transgress reason. It is to swap territories, territories that adjoin and adhere, but cannot be annexed, territories that replicate each other in a signifying oscillation that discloses the relationship between language and liberty, between religion and faith, between teleology and freedom.

We no longer have to say, as Taylor says, that we "are in a time between times and a place between which is no place."[24] We are in the place from which we are free to raid and return.

We are in Indian Territory.

Notes

1. The indebtedness of the early Derrida to Giles Deleuze is a topic that has been largely overlooked in retrospective studies of poststructuralism and contemporary French philosophy. One can make the case that Derrida simply picks up within the context of Husserlian phenomenology the Deleuzian insight, drawn from Bergson, that "difference marks the real dyamic of being – it is the movement that grounds being." Michael Hardt, *Gilles Deleuze: An Apprenticeship in Philosophy* (Minneapolis: University of Minnesota Press, 1993), p. 2. For the philosophy of "difference" see also Gilles Deleuze, *Bergsonism*, trans. Hugh Tomlinson and Barbara Habberjam (New York: Zone Books, 1988); Gilles Deleuze, *Difference and Repetition*, trans. Paul Patton (New York: Columbia University Press, 1994).
2. The phrase "piety of difference" is mine. For Caputo's major work in this area, see John D. Caputo, *The Prayers and Tears of Jacques Derrida: Religion without Religion* (Bloomington: Indiana University Press, 1997).
3. Hardt, *Gilles Deleuze*, p. 120.
4. John Milbank, *The Word Made Strange: Theology, Language, Culture* (Oxford: Blackwell Publishers, 1997), p. 44. For a collection of essays by representatives of radical orthodoxy, see John Milbank, Catherine Pickstock, and Graham Ward, *Radical Orthodoxy: A New Theology* (London: Routledge, 1999).
5. Milbank, *The Word Made Strange*, p. 41.
6. Immanuel Kant, *Critique of Pure Reason*, trans. Werner S. Pluhar (Indianapolis, IN: Hackett Publishing, 1996), p. 31.
7. Aryeh Botwinick, *Postmodernism and Democratic Theory* (Philadelphia: Temple University Press, 1993), p. 17.
8. For a discussion of the *via moderna*, see the classic by Heiko A. Oberman, *The Harvest of Mediaeval Theology: Gabriel Biel and Late Mediaeval Nominalism* (Cambridge, MA: Harvard University Press, 1963). See also E. A. Moody, "Ockham, Buridan and Nicholast of Autrecourt," *Franciscan Studies*, 7 (June 1947), pp. 113–46.
9. John D. Caputo, "On Being Inside/Outside Truth," in James L. Marsh, John D. Caputo, and Merold Westphal (eds.), *Modernity and Its Discontents* (New York: Fordham University Press, 1992), p. 54.
10. Ibid, p. 45.
11. Josef Simon, *Philosophy of the Sign*, trans. George Hefferman (New York: State University of New York Press, 1995), p. 191.
12. Ibid.
13. See Carl Raschke, *Fire and Roses: Postmodernity and the Thought of the Body* (Albany: State University of New York Press, 1996).

14 This is largely Terry Eagleton's argument. "What is special about the human body . . . is just its capacity to transform itself in the process of transforming the material bodies around it. It is in this sense that it is anterior to those bodies, a kind of "surplus" over and above them rather than an object to be reckoned up alongside them. But if the body is a self-transformative practice, then it is not identical with itself in the manner of corpses or carpets, and this is a claim that soul language was also trying to make. It is just that such language locates this non-self-identity in the body's having an invisible extra which is the real me." *The Illusions of Postmodernism* (Cambridge, MA: Blackwell Publishers, 1996), p. 72.

15 This observation is expressed in slightly different words by Mark C. Taylor. "To experience immediacy would be to enjoy a presence uninterrupted by absence in a presence undisturbed by memory of the past or anticipation of the future. Such a moment would be totally present here and now. Representation negates this moment of immediacy, or, more accurately, disclosed that it has always already been negated by showing that presence is never totally present and the present is never simply presence. As a structure of substitution, representation involves an irrepressible interplay of presence and absence." *The Picture in Question: Mark Tansey and the Ends of Representation* (Chicago: University of Chicago Press, 1999), p. 24. The rhythm of representation, on the other hand, does not necessarily sustain the kind of interpretation both Derrida and Taylor give to it. It is based on the *differend* inherent in the poststructuralist understanding of the sign. As Umberto Eco notes in his treatise on semiotics, "the sign-function exists by a dialectic of presence and absence, as a mutual exchange between two heterogeneities." *Semiotics and the Philosophy of Language* (Bloomington: Indiana University Press, 1984), p. 23.

16 Simon, *Philosophy of the Sign*, p. 96.

17 Hassan Melehy, *Writing Cogito: Montaigne, Descartes, and the Institution of the Modern Subject* (Albany: State University of New York Press), p. 137.

18 Mark C. Taylor, *Erring: A Postmodern Theology* (Chicago: University of Chicago Press, 1984), p. 8.

19 Jacques Derrida, "Faith and Knowledge," in Jacques Derrida and Gianni Vattimo, *Religion* (Stanford, CA: Stanford University Press, 1998), p. 60.

20 Ibid, p. 66.

21 Ibid.

22 Ibid, p. 51.

23 Michel de Certeau, *The Writing of History*, trans. Tom Conley (New York: Columbia University Press, 1988), p. 235.

24 Taylor, *Erring*, p. 7.

Index

A-reasonings, 338–40, 342–3
Abraham, 27, 63–4, 195, 344
Absolute, 351, 352, 354–5
absolutism, 415–19, 436–8
Adorno, Theodor, 464
Adventure of the Kings in the Snow, The (Bruegel), 33
aesthetics, 112
Alfred, Lord Tennyson, 71–2, 73, 74
"The Altar" (Herbert), 56, 59–60
Anasthasis, St., 381, 383
Andersson, Bibi, 40
angels, 27, 43, 45, 46, 198, 283
Anselm, St., 355, 403
anthropology, 74–5
Antonioni, Michelangelo, 114
Anzaldua, Gloria, 240, 270
apocalyptic, 152, 431, 432–3, 441–2, 485, 492, 493, 498, 499–500; cosmological, 500, 501–2; forensic, 501
Apostle, The (film), 6
Aquinas, St. Thomas, 135, 148, 156, 404, 448, 449
Arendt, Hannah, xix, 233, 236–7, 287
Aristotle, 78, 109, 111–12, 125, 135, 136, 140, 164, 170, 213, 375, 401, 452, 459
Armstrong, Louis, 88
Arnold, Matthew, xii

art, 423, 424; ambiguity in, 17–18; ambition in, 16, 17, 18, 20; displayed in church, 7–14; displayed in museums, 14–21; work of, 21, 396
art history, 6–7; dogma concerning, 7; and painting of *Judith*, 14–21; reluctance to study female nude, 8; and study of Caravaggio, 7–14
as-if, 372
atheism, 358, 379, 397, 436, 437
Auden, W. H., 32, 33
Aufhebung, 498–9, 502
Augustine, St., 197, 201, 213, 216–17, 218, 289, 295, 404, 418, 423, 433, 462, 464, 479, 487
Aulén, Gustaf, 501
Austin, J. W., 13, 50

Bacon, Francis, 288
Bakhtin, Mikhail, 274, 278
Balthassar, Hans Urs von, 65–6, 201
Barnett, Angie, 37
Barth, Karl, xvi, 27, 210, 215, 414, 420, 432, 498–9
Barthes, Roland, xxi, 26, 194
Basil of Caesarea, 218, 404
Batailles, Georges, 510
"Batter-my-Heart" (Donne), 59
Baudrillard, Jean, xvii, xxiii
beauty, 289–92

"Beauty Way," 99
Beckett, Samuel, 146, 442
Being, 65, 395–6, 409, 429, 434, 436, 438, 442, 460, 461, 464, 508, 509
being-in-the-world, 418, 452
being-with-one-another, 452, 455
Benedict, St., 139
Benhabib, Seyla, 296
Benjamin, Walter, 233, 383
Bentham, Jeremy, xxiii, 112
Bergman, Ingmar, 40
Bernard, St., 404
Bhabha, Homi, 270
Biel, Gabriel, 509
"Bitter-sweet" (Herbert), 56–7
Blake, William, 46, 285, 288, 430, 440, 442
Blanchot, 120
Blond, Philip, 147–8, 156
Blood Feast (film), 47
body, the, 448, 511–12, 513
Boehm, Rudolf, 353
Boehme, Jacob, 430
Bol, Ferdinand, 20
Bolan, Marc, 36
Book of Common Prayer, The, 61
Borowitz, Eugene, 327–8, 347
Botwinick, Aryeh, 509
Boulez, Pierre, 87
Bourdieu, Pierre, 275, 276
Bowie, David, 36–7, 46
Boyle, Nicholas, xiii, xxiii, 145, 146–7, 149, 153–4, 157, 159, 160
Boyle, Robert, 284
Bruegel, Pieter, 31, 32, 33–4, 44
Buber, Martin, 336, 448
Buchan, John, 126
Buckley, David, 36
Buddha, 422
Buddhism, 415, 422, 423, 431, 506; two levels of truth in, 417–18
Bultmann, Rudolf Karl, 441
Buñuel, Luis, 25
Buridian, Jean, 509
Burke, Edmund, 290
Burrell, David, 156
Butler, Judith, 296, 450

Cain, curse of, 50, 54
Cammell, David, 47
capitalism, 150, 157
Caputo, John D., 496, 499, 506, 510
Caravaggio (film), 10–11
Caravaggio, Michelangelo Merisi da, 18; according to Jarman, 10–11; claustrophobic space in, 11–12; illusion/realism in, 10–11; performativity of, 13–14; reasons for seeing paintings by, 9; relationist activism in, 11; sensual/religious tensions in, 7–9; site/conditions of viewing, 9–10; standard research on, 7; visual erotics in, 12–14
Carlyle, Thomas, xii, xxv
Carpenter, John, 45
Carroll, Lewis, 471, 477, 479
Castels, Robert, 84
Catholicism *see* Roman Catholics
Cavarero, Adriana, xxi, 287
Cavell, Stanley, 396
Celan, 377
Census at Bethlehem, The (Bruegel), 33
Certeau, Michel de, xiii, xv, xxii, 196
charity, 464–5
Cherubinic Wanderer, The (Silesius), 214–15
Chopp, Rebecca, 297
Christ, 148; as Bread (Monstrance), 55, 387, 393; crucifixion of, 187, 198, 199, 223, 386, 430; death of, 62, 127; different identities of, 268; divinity of, 417; as epiphany in the mundane, 34; as familiar and strange, 42; as fetish of presence, 380; filmic allusions to, 30–1, 33, 34–5, 42; as final Adam, 382; and gift of the Spirit, 212; God in, 219; last words from the cross, 63; messianic transfiguration, 378–81, 382, 383; passion narrative, 34–5; resurrection of, 385–8, 392–3; sacrifice of, 55; suffering of, 198–201; trial/punishment of, 188; union without confusion, 380, 390–1
Christianity: and ascetism, 207; attitude to punishment, 178, 186–9; as challenge to postmodernism, 147–8, 151–5; conflict with aesthetic objectivism, 462–3; divided, 431–2; economy of charity, 204–5; and

giving, 127–8; internal/external tensions, 109; Jewish beliefs in, 326; and moral enquiry, 140; and moral luck, 108, 109–11, 116–17; and myth of the fall, 118–19, 120–1; pain/pleasure in, 197–203; premises, 5; relationship to Plato, 164; as running into reverse, 116; and sacrifice/death, 124, 125, 126, 128; secularization of, 111, 116–17; spiritual, 212; subversive core, 205; and suffering, 204–6; and surpassing of understanding, 205, 208
Cistercians, 454
citizens, 81, 328
city: described, 165–8; as fundamental, 165–6; identified with the Cave, 170–1, 285, 288; spatial/temporal aspects, 166; tripartition of, 167–72
City of God, 433, 451
Cixous, Hélène, 196, 207
Clark, Elizabeth A., 252, 256
Clemente, Francesco, 350, 362
Climacus, Johannes, 471
Clockwork Orange (film), 30
Coca-Cola advert, 133
Coleridge, Samuel Taylor, 77
Collins, Patricia Hill, 87, 93–5, 296
Color Me Blood Red (film), 47
Colson, Charles W., 179
Commedia (Dante), 433
communication, 465
communion, 54–62
community, 302, 329, 417; Christian, 267, 269, 272, 273, 278
comprehension *see* incomprehension
Connolly, William, xviii, 275
consciousness, 351, 352–3, 354–5, 359, 364, 372, 437, 439
Constantine the Great, 492
conversation, 59; circulation in, 61–2; cry and answer, 62–4; as gift, 65; signification of, 65–7; speech/silence in, 51, 57, 62; transformation of, 51
Conversion of Saint Paul, The (Caravaggio), 9–14
Corman, Roger, 47
Cornell, Drucilla, 296
creation narrative, 51, 204, 212, 382
creativity, 91–2, 94

crime *see* prison; punishment
critique, 94; necessity/danger of, 80–6; and social engagement, 99
Critique of Practical Reason (Kant), 509
Critique of Pure Reason (Kant), 508–9
Cronenberg, David, xx
Crouch, Stanley, 88
Crucifixion of Saint Peter, The (Caravaggio), 9–14
culture, 289; dominant/marginal meeting point, 86–93; interdisciplinary study, 5; postmodernism as style of, 156; and science, 75; and theology, 5–6, 17, 21; transformation of, xi–xiii; understanding of, 4
cyborg, 242
Cyprian, St., 268

Daedalus, 31, 33, 44
Daly, Mary, 142
Damian, Peter, 474–6
Dante Alighieri, 148–9, 433–4
Darwin, Charles, 70
Das, Veena, 272
Davidson, Donald, 465
Dawkins, Richard, xxii
De Lubec, Henri, 56
death, 55, 117, 223, 286, 288, 291, 420; acknowledgment of, 329, 330–1; of Christ, 62; cultural portrayals of, 284–5; of the deity, 430; as ethical, 122, 124–5, 127; of God, 73, 284, 435, 439, 449, 460–1; as loss, 117; of man, 71–2, 74, 76, 284; pragmatic rules for reading, 337–8, 339–42; as sacrifice, 123, 125, 127; of self, 113, 126
Debord, Guy, xv, xxiii
deconstruction, 312, 313, 436, 479, 480, 494, 496, 509, 512
Deleuze, Gilles, xvii, 194, 477, 479
Dellum, Ronald, 87, 95–8
democracy, 83, 328, 492
"Deniall" (Herbert), 57
Derrida, Jacques, xiv, xvi, xx, xxiii, 55, 108, 165, 203, 315, 477, 479; on alterity, 371; "apocalyptic *sans* apocalyptic," 498; on "closed economy," 502; critique of ontotheology, 49; on deconstruction,

Derrida, Jacques *cont.*
227, 287, 296, 312; on *différance*, 65, 497–8; "discovery" of, 507; on economy of sign, 195; on the Enlightenment, 496; on faith, 514; on gift and sacrifice, 116, 120, 122, 123, 124, 195–6; and giving of oneself to another, 116; and heretical Christianity, 111; interpretation of Heidegger, 506; and *jouissance*, 195–6; on Kant, 495–6, 497, 498; on "knight of faith," 496; on locus of Christian essence, 127; on messianism, 382, 491, 494; on naming and negative theology, 352, 355, 356–7, 358; on response, 66; on speech–act theory, 50; spiritual aspects of, 213–15; on the sublime, 290

Descartes, René, xvi, xix, 336; and dualism, 511; on errors/inadequacy of philosophy, 330; on essence of thinking, 409, 411; failings of, 337; on God, 446–7, 448, 449; and the Infinite, 361, 401, 403, 404; on inner/outer world, 452; as late medieval thinker, 156; on rationality, 78; on self-knowledge, 215; and *skepsis*, 513; and substance, 353; on tradition, 331

desire, 194, 204, 207, 216, 285, 292, 352; Platonic, 171–2; sexual, 217

Destruction: Chorban, first destruction, 332, 344; Chorban, second destruction, 332–3, 334, 345; Galut, 333, 345–6; Mitzrayim, 332, 344; modernity, 333–4, 346–8; rabbinic pragmatism/logic of redemption, 334–43; Shoa, 333, 346–8

Detienne, Marcel, 125
Deuteronomy, 58
différance, 65, 195, 356, 484, 498
Dilthey, Wilhelm, 415, 461, 462, 463, 464
Dionysius the Areopagite, 405
discrimination, 483, 484, 485–6
divine, 475–6
Divine Comedy (Dante), 148–9
Donne, John, 39, 46, 59, 285
Dostoyevsky, Fyodor, 459–60

Douglas, Ann, 90
dualisms, xviii–xix, 507; as language of opposites, 483–8; mind–body, 193–4, 448; in Plato, 163–5
Duns Scotus, John, 147, 148, 149, 401, 402, 508, 509
Duvall, Robert, 6

Eagleton, Terry, xxiii, 151, 155–6, 157, 313
Eckhart, Johannes, 430, 439
education, 159
Edwards, James, 157
El Paso, 266–7
Ellington, Duke, 88, 90
Emerson, Ralph Waldo, 449
Encyclopedic enquiry, 135
Engels, Friedrich, 183
Enlightenment, 73, 135–9, 202, 235, 237, 241, 327, 335, 415, 417, 492, 493, 494–5, 496, 509
environment, 210–11
epistemology, 74; feminist standpoint, 241–2, 243–4
Ereignis, 463–4
error, 83–4, 94, 338, 417, 512
ethics, Christian, 188–9; eudaemonist, 111–12; as everyday hope for life in common, 117; as gift-exchange/openness to divine grace, 122–8; and giving of self, 115–16; global/regional, 134–5, 140; of goodness/fortune, 109–10; as mythical, 117–18; as other-regarding, 110–14; post-Enlightenment, 112–14; of promises, 236–8; and security, 110; and self-possession/self-government, 111
eucharist, 55, 127–8, 395–8, 512
evil, 419
existentialism, 463

faith, 508–9; decline in, 69–70; effect of science on, 70, 71–2
fall, the, 216–17, 430
fallibility, 80, 82, 84, 86, 97
fate, 157
Faubion, James, 84
feminism, 250, 269, 488; discarding of

religion, 284; and oppression of modernity, 284
feminist theory/theology, 296–7; and bounded openness, 302, 307; and community, 301–2; companionable wisdoms, 297, 298, 302; and doctrine of sin, 301, 307; and essentialism, 300; and gender relations, 300; justification/sanctification, 299, 306; and management of normative claims, 298–9; and nature of self, 299; shared insights, 303–4; shared narrative, 297–8
Ferry, Brian, 36
fetishism, xx–xxii, 157, 194, 372, 375, 380
Fichte, Johann Gottlieb, 430
Fish, Stanley E., 155, 315
Ford, David, 337
forgiveness, 236–7, 239, 244, 272, 476
Forms, 124, 125
Foucault, Michel, xiv, 74, 91–2, 98, 145, 146, 194; on Boulez, 87; on criticism, 80–2; on government, 158; on punishment, 183, 184–5, 283; on reason, 283, 415; on sado-masochism, 205; on sexuality, 283
framing, concept of, 14–15, 22; exhibition experiment, 15–18; as link between work/world, 15; thematic, 17–18
Francis, St., 432
Frankfurt School, xvi, xvii
freedom, 137–8, 237, 291, 292, 295–6, 419, 508, 509, 511, 513–15
Frei, Hans, 341
Freud, Sigmund, xvi, xx, 195, 207, 285, 286, 287, 288
Fried, Michael, 22
friendship, 460, 461, 464
Fukuyama, Francis, xxii
Fulkerson, Mary, 297

Gabbard, Krin, 88
Gadamer, Hans, 384
Galileo Galilei, 64–5, 401, 449, 463
Gates, Skip, 266
Gathering the Ashes of Phocion (Poussin), 239–40

Gauguin, E. H. P., 115–16
gay movement, 159
gender, 267, 269, 278, 283–4, 286, 288, 291; roles, 252, 253–4, 256–62
Genealogical enquiry, 135–6
Genesis, 118, 197, 483; creation narrative, 51; violence of language in, 50
Gentileschi, Artemisia, 18
ghettos, 266
Gibbs, Robert, 340
gift, 110, 418, 479; austerity of, 111; Christ as, 387; Christian, 127–8; in conversation, 62; economic, 120–1; fragility of, 115; mutual, 119–20, 123; receiving, 116, 124; recognition of, 123–4; as reduced, 123–4; as sacrificial/unilateral, 122–8; self-giving, 112
Gill, John, 37
Gillespie, Michael, 156
Girard, René, 183, 184
"glitter rock," 36
global ethic: and common areas of agreement, 140–1; conflicts/clashes, 141–2; economic/political basis, 135; found within religious traditions, 134–5; importance of religion, 134, 135; and liberal Enlightenment, 136–9; suspicions concerning, 143
globalism, 149–51, 158–9, 266
Gnosticism, 429–32, 442
God, 110, 124; banishment of, 282; bartering with, 63–4; as charitable, 53; as creator/redeemer, 219, 325, 330–1; death of, 73, 435, 439, 449, 460–1; and desire, 56; and dialogue, 66–7; and earth, 221–3; as Earth Spirit, 211, 213–15, 224, 225; existence of, 283; face of, 42, 47, 337, 361; hope in, 69, 76; incarnation of, 326; knowledge of, 155, 161; and love, 58, 59–61; love of singularity, 497; as mask of self, 450; naming of, 58, 66, 215, 355–8, 359, 443, 448, 452; as omnipotent, 147, 156; as other, 122; phenomenology of, 352–5; power of, 474–7; praising, 55–7, 59; (re)appearance in intersubjectivity,

God *cont.*
    448–52; of scarce blessings, 51–2; and
    self, 361–2; self-saving of, 430, 439;
    substance of, 445–8; as Transcendent,
    452–3, 503; trinitarian enfleshment of,
    219–20; as underfoot, 215–18;
    univocity of, 148; worship of, 152
Godhead, 429–31, 433, 435, 437, 438,
    439–40, 441
godlessness, xix–xx
Goethe, Johann Wolfgang von, 430, 442
Golding, Arthur, 31
good, 109, 116–17, 123, 126, 196, 476,
    480, 491; general, 493, 494–5; is good
    in itself, 355; Platonic, 165, 169–70,
    171–2; postmodern, 497–8
Good Samaritan United Methodist
    Church: conflict in, 272–3; finding
    identity in, 274–7; and problem of
    identity, 267–70; worship at, 270–2
Gorgias (Plato), 182
gospel, 491–2; Christian, 498–502; from
    particular to singular, 494–7; general
    good over particular, 492–3; as
    instance of mystagogy, 495
government, 158
grain, 53–4
grammatology, 312, 317
Great Church, 432–4
green pneumatology, 212–15, 221
Gregory of Nyssa, 201–2, 203, 208,
    252–62, 405, 407, 423
Gregory of Rimini, 509

Habermas, Jürgen, xv, 328, 465
habitus, 275–7
Hajdu, David, 88, 91
Halivni, David Weiss, 347
Halperin, David, 252, 256, 257
Ham, curse of, 50
Handelman, Susan, 312, 313, 314,
    315–17
happiness: as comparative, 112; inner
    possession of, 110; as nowhere in time,
    112; as punctual, 111–12; as secure,
    108–9, 110; self-fulfilling, 115–16; as
    tranquil, 109; as virtual, 111
Haraway, Donna, 241–2
Hardt, Michael, 507

Hardy, Daniel, 341
Harnack, Adolf von, 414
Hart, Kevin, 65
Hartshorne, Charles, 383
Harvey, David, xiv, xxi, xxii, 149–50, 157
Hasidism, 329
Hassan, Ihab, 210
Hauerwas, Stanley, 137, 153, 341
Hayes, Richard, 337
heavenly visitations: biblical, 25, 27; and
    the Christ figure, 30–5, 42; and
    crossing of sexual boundaries, 35–9;
    fictional, 25–6, 27, 30–4, 35; filmic,
    25–6, 27–30, 31, 33, 34–6, 37–42;
    modern, 25; sleeping with, 39–42; as
    welcomed then destroyed, 29–30, 34
Hegel, G. W. F., xxii, 116, 383, 420;
    Absolute Idealism of, 436, 440;
    critique of Kant, 112; Engels's
    comment on, 183; on God, 201, 213,
    432, 434; influence on Dilthey, 461;
    influence on Heidegger, 438, 441; on
    the negative, 196, 506, 513; notion of
    Aufhebung, 498–9, 502; and
    sacramental presence, 395; on self,
    509–10
Heidegger, Martin, xx, xxiv, 49, 375;
    critique of God, 437–42, 448, 450–2;
    critique of intersubjectivity, 454; denial
    of the past, 157; on the end of
    metaphysics, 461; influence of Greek
    objectivism on, 464; influence of Hegel
    on, 438, 441; and nihilism, 414;
    notion of Being, 65, 395–6, 409, 429,
    434, 436, 438, 442, 460, 461, 464,
    508, 509; notion of *Ereignis*, 463–4;
    notion of *Gelassenheit*, 464; obsession
    with Silesius, 356; "only a god can save
    us now," 282; on the self, 510; on
    zuhanden/vorhanden relationship, 511
Hell, 435, 439, 440
Hengel, Martin, 125
Henry of Ghent, 147
Heraclitus, 166
Herbert, George, 55, 56–8, 59–62, 120
hermeneutics, 415
Hesse, Mary, 75
heterology, 510
Hinduism, 141, 142, 143

INDEX

history, 5, 149, 157, 160, 420, 429, 437, 438, 439, 461, 463, 465, 510
Hobbes, Thomas, xviii, 74
Holderlin, Johann Christian Friedrich, 430
Holy Spirit *see* Spirit
Homily on the Transfiguration (St. John Damascene), 378–9
homosexuality, 36–7, 46
hooks, bell, 236, 242–4, 243
hope, 69, 76–7, 117–21, 123, 146, 305–6
Horton, John, 139
humanism, 82, 92
Hume, David, xvii, 282, 415
Husserl, Edmund: on the body, 511; on conscience/reality, 408; on nothingness, 435, 442; phenomenology, 350, 351, 352–5, 359; on time, 473; as transcendental idealist, 436, 437–40
hybrids, 270, 272, 274–5, 277, 278, 279

"I," 436–7, 438
I–Thou relationship, 451
Iamblichus, 163
Icarus, 31, 33
Idealism, 436, 436–7, 438
Ideas (Husserl), 351, 352–5, 364
identity, 110, 122, 164; finding, 274–7; *idem*-identity, 237; *ipse*-identity, 237; Jewish, 328; and multiple oppression, 269; personal, 237; problem of, 267–70; sexual, 159; and spatiality/mobility, 269–70; uncertainty of, 28
"In Memoriam" (Tennyson), 71–2
incomprehension: and auto-objectivation of man, 410–12; knowledge of, 403–6; man as incomprehensible to himself, 407–10; sensation of, 404–5, 410
Infinite, comprehension of, 403–6; in reason, 400–3
inner/outer, 447–9, 452
Inside/Outside (Clemente), 350–1, 362
intentions, 119; knowledge of, 115–16
intersubjectivity, 447, 450–2
Iqbal, Muhammed, 341

Irenaeus, bishop of Lyons, 268, 278
Irigaray, Luce, xvi, xxiii, 74, 242, 250–1, 256, 296
Isasi-Diaz, Ada Maria, 297
Iser, Wolfgang, 23
Islam, 139–40

Jael Showing the Body of Sisera to Barak (Speckaert), 15, 18–19
Jaggar, Alison, 74
James, St., 380
James, William, 507
Jameson, Frederic, xiii–xiv, xxiii, 149, 414
Jantzen, Grace, xxi, 242
Jarman, Derek, 10–11, 12
jazz, 86, 98; ceremonies of gratitude in, 90–1; and happiness, 92–3; healing properties of, 88; individual/larger community interaction, 89–90; power of, 87; risk in, 90; sorrow/joy in, 89; success as ephemeral/real, 91; white interpretations of, 88
Jeremy (gay magazine), 36
Joachim of Fiore, 210
Johannes de Silentio, 479
John the Baptist, 198
John Chrysostom, 408
John Damascene, St., 378–9, 380, 383
John of Patmos, 152
John Paul II, xxii, 152
John, St., 384, 387
Johnsonn, Elizabeth, 305
jouissance, 194, 195–6
Joyce, James, 442
Judaism, 139; condition of today, 327–31; emancipation of, 327–8; and identity, 328; liberal modernist, 328–30; Orthodox, 329, 330; and the redeemer, 330–1; and religious renewal, 334–5; spiritual dissipation of, 327
Judith Shows Holophernes' Head to the People of Bethulia (Sweelinck): ambiguities of framing, 18; ambition/portraiture in, 16, 17, 18, 20; comparisons with other depictions, 18–19; exhibition/presentation of, 15–21; as masterpiece, 16; thematic framing, 17–18

Jüngel, 337
Justice Fellowship, 188–9
justice/injustice, 80–1, 85, 86, 91, 93, 95, 98, 240, 244, 472, 479; distributive, 167–8; meanings of, 166–7; and problem of rule, 168–70; visible, 164

kabbalah, 326, 329, 342, 346–7
Kadushin, Max, 347
Kafka, Franz, 442
Kant, Immanuel, xiii, xvii, 111, 237, 330, 377, 463; and beauty, 290; Derrida on, 495–6, 497, 498; Dilthey's criticism of, 461; failure of Critical project, 330; on faith, 508–9; as harbinger of Romanticism, 156; and indifference, 110; and the infinite, 361; on "kingdom of ends," 487; and moral law, 215; on our thinking essence, 409; on punishment, 181–2; and rationalism, 238, 405, 465; on tension between Christianity/metaphysics, 462
Kazantzakis, Nikos, 385
Keenan, Thomas, xviii
Keller, Catherine, 498, 499
Kepler, Johann, 401
Kepnes, Steven, 340, 341
Kierkegaard, Søren, 126, 195, 419, 430, 474, 492, 496
King Lear (Shakespeare), 116, 117–18
King, Martin Luther, 96
kingdom of God: all things are possible in, 474–7; coming as an "event," 477–8; on earth, 488; Jesus as prophet in, 487; poetics of the impossible, 470–2; and raising Holy Hell, 477–80; as time not place, 472–4
Knight, Kevin, 137–8
knowledge, 495–6, 513; authentic, 403–4; crisis of, 74; of the incomprehensible, 403–6; and language, 75
Kristeva, Julia, xxiii, 20, 239, 371
Kubrick, Stanley, 30, 36
Küng, Hans, 132–5, 137–40

Lacan, Jacques, xx, xxi, 73, 194, 195, 204, 207, 286

Lachterman, David R., 449
Laclau, Ernesto, xviii, xx, xxi
language, 418, 419–20, 439, 440, 442, 511, 512; as conversation, 50–1; cruelty of, 484; instrumental, 49–50, 53; mystery of, 61; of opposites, 483–8; philosophy of, 75; rhythm of, 51; speech-act theory, 50; as tool, 50, 53
language-games, 73
Latour, Bruno, xvi
L'Avventura (film), 114, 120
Laws (Plato), 172–3
Le Colonel Chabert (film), 114, 120
Le Guin, Ursula, 41
Left Hand of Darkness, The (Le Guin), 41
Legenhausen, Muhammad, 139
Leibniz, Gottfried Wilhelm, 447–50
Lessing, Gotthold Ephraim, 492
Levene, Nancy, 340
Levinas, Emmanuel, xxiii, 112, 126, 464, 474; and centrality of God, 448; on consciousness, 358–9, 364; on the face of God, 336; and "free" gift, 120; on the good, 479; on the Infinite, 361–2; on infinite alterity, 511; and Messianic Time, 382; the other of, 465; and the *persona*, 372, 374; and recognition, 396; and revelation, 338; on sacrifice, 108, 122, 196; on self/Other, 359–60; and thoughts concerning Christ, 384
Lewis, Herschell Gordon, 47
Leyden, Lucas van, 20
liberalism, 509
Life of Macrina (Gregory of Nyssa), 258–9, 260–2
Lightfoot, J. B., 200
Lindbeck, George, 341
Lindbeck, Kris, 341
Little Hans, 287
liturgy, 446
Locke, John, 118, 282, 284, 342
logic, 335, 470
love, 207, 236, 338, 476
Lubac, Henri de, 56
Luke, St., 60, 378, 472
Luther, Martin, 418, 430, 509
Lyotard, Jean-François, xiii, xiv, xvii, 70, 73, 147, 194, 290

McClintock, Barbara, 76
McFague, Sallie, 225
MacIntyre, Alasdair, 135–7, 139–42, 155
Mackinnon, Donald, 118
Magid, Shaul, 340
Maharsha, 320
Maimonides, Moses, 360–1
Male–female distinction, 483–4
Malebranche, Nicolas, 409
Maleuvre, Didier, 16
Mallarmé, Stéphane, 442
Man Who Fell to Earth, The (book/film), 25–6; divine/human relationship in, 39–42; identity in, 28–30; opening scene, 25–6; religious aspects of, 30–5; sexuality in, 35–9, 41; "watcher" in, 34, 45
Mander, Karel Van, xxiii, 16
Marcel, Gabriel, 374
Marion, Jean-Luc, 49, 55, 65, 112, 120, 122, 123, 124, 337
Mark, St., 152, 381
marriage, 120, 121
Martin, Joan, 297
Martyn, J. Louis, 499–501
martyrs, 125
Martz, Louis, 55
Marx, Karl, xiii, xix–xx, xxi, 137, 157, 372, 432
Marxism, xviii, 507
Mary Magdalene, 35, 45, 385, 386
Mary of Nazareth, 35
Masque of the Red Death, The (film), 47
Massacre of the Innocents, The (Bruegel), 33–4
Matthew, St., 60, 186
Maxwell, James Clerk, xvi
Mayersberg, Paul, 28
Melehy, Hassan, 512–13
Melody Maker, 36
Melville, Herman, 379
memory, 336, 344; of the body, 276, 277; creation of just, 240; described, 232–3; ethics of, 234, 236, 242; forgiveness, 236–8; as form of knowledge, 233; of past losses, 331–4; and postmodern theology, 234–6; as representing the past, 238; storytelling as, 233; yearning, 239–40
Mendus, Susan, 139
Mennonites, 152–3
Merleau-Ponty, Maurice, 374, 393, 511
messianic, time, 377, 382–4, 391–2; transfiguration, 378–81
messianism, 491, 494, 514
Metaphysical Elements of Justice (Kant), 181
metaphysics, 49, 137, 215, 226, 355, 395–6, 409, 429, 434, 450, 461–2, 463–5, 465, 495, 508, 512, 513
Methodius of Olympus, 252
Metz, J.-B., 69, 493
midrash, 312–13, 338–9; compared to a "hammer on the rock," 313, 315, 316, 317–21
Millbank, John, 139, 156, 188, 486, 508
Miller, James, 100
Milton, John, 434–5
Moby Dick (Melville), 379
modernism, 147, 156, 508, 513
modernity, xviii–xix, 281–2, 283–4, 291, 414, 434, 449, 491; anxiety of, 72; apocalyptic aspect, 493; Jewish, 326, 333–4, 346–8
Moltmann, Jürgen, 200–2, 222, 500
Momigliano, Arnaldo, 252
Monads, 447–8, 450
money, 149, 157
Montaigne, Michel Eyquem de, 147, 404
moral luck, 108, 122, 125; Christian, 109–11, 116–17; Greek conception, 108–9; and pursuit of self-fulfilling happiness/regard for other, 115–16; secularization of, 111–14; and self-sacrifice, 115–16; in Shakespeare, 114–15, 117–21; Stoic, 109
morality, 81; thick/thin, 134–5, 137, 138–9, 140–2
Moses, 53, 62, 66, 336, 337, 357, 360, 379, 380, 381
Mouffe, Chantal, xx
mourning, 236, 239–40, 329, 330; dancing after, 331, 332, 337, 344–8; and memory of past losses, 331–4; as never ending, 334
Mowinckel, Sigmund, 56

Mozart, Wolfgang Amadeus, 396, 423
Mukta, Parita, 236
Murdoch, Iris, 74
"Musée des Beaux Arts" (Auden), 32, 33–4
music, 453, 454–5
mystical theology, 64, 65, 66
Mystical Theology (Pseudo-Dionysius), 54–5, 58
myth, 19–20, 164, 420, 422, 484; ethical, 117–18

Napoleon Bonaparte, 65
narrative, 95; of God, 49; grand, 152, 154, 485; of idolatry, 53; legitimating, 73; little, 154; multiple allusions in, 26–7; of neglect/rejection, 52; performativity of, 51; of promise-keeping, 239; reception of, 51–4; science in conflict with, 73; theological, 279; third-person standpoint, 243; under strain, 26; visual representation, 10, 22
nation-states, 149, 150–1, 158–9, 328, 372
Nazism, 438, 440, 442
necrophilia, 285, 287–8, 290–1, 292
needs, 166
negation of negation, 195
negative theology, 350–1, 352, 355, 356–8, 513
neighborliness, 267, 277
Neoplatonism, 163, 164
New Age narrative, 372, 384–5, 392
Newton, Isaac, xvi
Nicene Creed, 211, 267
Nicolas of Cusa, 401
Nietzsche, Friedrich Wilhelm, xvii, 135, 136; and alterity in philosophy, 507; atheism of, 437; and fate, 157; and God as No-saying, 430; nihilism of, 73, 419, 429, 432, 435, 442, 449, 460–1, 463, 464, 465; on sin, 282; and Zarathustra, 355–6, 441
nihilism, 49, 69–70, 73, 116, 136, 156, 419, 429, 432, 435, 438, 442, 460–1, 464–5, 486, 507, 509
nothingness, 435, 442–3
Nussbaum, Martha, 109, 125, 159

Ochs, Peter, 340, 341
Ockham, William of, 509
On the Soul and the Resurrection (Gregory of Nyssa): desire/anger in, 254–5; gender roles in, 252, 253–4, 256; links with Plato, 252–3, 255–7
ontology, 118, 396, 508
ontotheology, 49, 434, 507, 508, 509, 514
Origen, 216
Other, 266, 270, 277, 351, 352, 359–60, 452, 465, 483, 485; alterity of, 453; appropriation of *persona*, 373–4; dying for, 122; figure/*persona* of, 371–2; presence of, 122–3
other-regarding ethics: as altruistic/self-sacrificial, 110–11, 113, 115; and happiness, 112; life/death dichotomy, 114–15; and loss of duty/loss of self, 113, 115; and mourning, 113–14; and self-fulfilling happiness, 115–16
outlaws, 510–11
outsiders, 276
Ovid, 31–2

pain–pleasure: Christian, 197–203; confrontation, 203–6; contemporary, 194–7
Pannenberg, Wolfhart, 213
Pareyson, Luigi, 460
Parfitt, Derek, 112
Parmenides, 166
Pascal, Blaise, 408, 419, 460
Patocka, Jan, 108, 116, 122
Paul, St., 39, 193, 198–201, 217, 381–2, 383, 384, 409, 419, 441–2, 471, 499–502
Pauline legacy, 381–2
Pauw, Amy Platinga, 297
Peirce, Charles, 334, 335, 338, 341, 342
Pérès, Marcel, 454
Performance (film), 47
performativity, 13–14, 18, 23; as act of faith, 62; of language, 62; of narrative, 51
perichoresis, 219, 228
Perkins, William, 485

persona: beyond fusion, 374–6; as chiasm, 376–7; as *eschaton*, 372–4; of Other, 371–2
Persona (film), 40
Pessoa, Fernando, 112
Peter, St., 378, 380
Petrosini, Silvano, 364
Phaedrus (Plato), 165, 172, 252, 253
Phallus, 374
phenomenology, 350, 351, 352–5, 376
Philo Judaeus, 436
philosophy, 434, 437–8, 495, 496; anxieties of, 72; gaps in, 241–2; loss of, 170–2; turning period in, 85–6
phronesis, 169–70, 173
Pickstock, Catherine, xxi, 156
Plato, 124, 125, 182, 216, 252, 255–6, 257, 258, 259, 285, 288, 375, 377, 401, 452, 462, 465; on the city, 165–8; dualistic understanding of, 163–5; and loss of philosophy, 170–2; and problem of "rule," 168–70; reception of, 163; and the soul, 165; and true tragedy, 172–3
Plotinus, 163, 423, 430
poetics of the impossible, 470–2, 478, 479–80
poetry, 283; and incarnation, 58–9; representation of women in, 285; sacramental, 54–62; and the soul, 57–8; verse/converse, 56, 57
polemics, 81–2, 100–1
politics: and joy of connections, 97–8; lament/self-critical affirmation, 98–9; openness in, 95; providing alternatives, 96–7; and unanticipated consequences, 97
Pollack, Griselda, 22
Portman, John, xxiii
portraiture, 16, 20
positivism, 73, 372
postmodern theology: interdisciplinary aspects, 6; visual, 6–7
postmodernism, xiii–xv, xxii–xxv, 73, 116, 135–6, 140, 266–7, 372, 414, 491, 494, 513; and Christian difference, 151–5; and the global market, 149–51; historical debates concerning, 145–9; as metaphilosophical theory, 509; as outworking of mistakes in Christian theology, 147–8; as pessimism of obsolescent class, 145, 151; playful use of, 145, 155; as style of culture, 156; as theological movement, 506–8
postmodernity, xiv, xxii–xxv, 133, 281, 487, 491
Poussin, Nicholas, 239
power, 83, 84–5, 91, 94, 99, 447
pragmatism, 334–43, 507
praise, 271, 397; of the divine, 164, 173; of God, 55–7, 59
prayer, 472, 514; interiority of, 445, 453; ontology of, 445; as worded, 445
presence, 396–8, 496
Priest, Josiah, 50
Prigogione, Ilya, 73, 75
prison: Christian practice in, 188–9; conditions in, 179–80; and creation of crime, 185; as punishment, 181–4; racial aspect, 179; and reduction in crime rates, 180–1; as "soft" system, 180; statistics, 189–90; statistics concerning, 178–9; substance-abuse treatment in, 190; and unemployment, 179
Prison Fellowship, 188–9
Procession to Calvary, The (Bruegel), 34
Proclus, 163
promises, 236–8, 239, 244, 381
Psalms, 55, 56
Pseudo-Dionysius, 54, 56, 58, 59, 65, 381
pseudo-religion, 421
psychiatry, 81, 84, 85
psychoanalysis, 286, 313
public/private sphere, 164–5
punishment: Christian view of, 186–9; as deterrent, 181–2; flaws in, 184; and forgiveness, 188; realities of, 183; recommendations for, 185; as retribution, 182, 185, 187–8; and scapegoat mechanism, 183–4; types of, 180
Pynchon, Thomas, xxiii
Pythagoras, 125

rabbinic Judaism *see* midrash
rabbinic pragmatism, 334–43
Rabinow, Paul, 81
racism, 50, 266
Rad, Gerhard von, 56
Radner, Ephraim, 160
Rahner, Karl, 76
rationality, 400–3, 415, 493, 509, 510; comprehensible, 403–6
reading of text, 314–22
redemption, 325, 326, 331, 336–43, 430, 460, 512
Redondi, Pietro, 65
Reed, Carol, 35
Reformation, 55, 289, 435
Reid, Thomas, 338
religion: affinities between, 423; binary opposites in, 485–8; as cause of strife, 134; common global ethic, 132, 133; conflict/clashes between, 141–2; criticism of other, 142; de-absolutizing, 415–19; and dialogue, 142; and gender, 142, 143; of literature, 158; moving outside of, 142; Platonic, 164; political power of, 134; role of imagination in, 423; ultimacy of, 421–2, 423–4; understanding of, 283; and world peace, 134
Republic (Plato), 164, 165–7, 171–3
resurrection, 120–2, 123, 420, 439
revelation, pluralistic, 419–24
Richardson, Kurt, 341
Ricoeur, Paul, 76, 232, 234, 237–8, 352, 353, 372
Rieder, Jonathan, 91
Rime of the Ancient Mariner, The, 77
risk, 87, 90, 118
Roeg, Nicolas, 25–31, 32, 34, 35, 37, 42
Roland, Jacques, 364
Roman Catholics, 138, 141, 143, 422; moral authority of, 154, 160; universality of, 153–4
Rorty, Richard, 134, 150–1, 158, 159, 507
Rose, Gillian, 236, 239–40
Rosenzweig, 336, 337, 341
Roth, Catherine, 252
Rothschild Canticles, 219
Ruether, Rosemary, 142

Rushdie, Salman, 270
Ruskin, John, 71
Russell, Letty, 297

sacramental presence, 395–8
sacrifice, 55, 108, 110–11, 122–3, 195, 460, 514; Christian, 126–8; economic, 124; and gift, 116; as gift, 116, 120, 122, 123, 124; morality of, 124–5; as necessary/unavoidable, 196; of passions, 125; secular, 122, 125–7; will to, 122–4
sado-masochism, 100, 203, 204, 205, 207
Sanchez, Carol Lee, 99
Sartre, Jean-Paul, 373, 377
Saussure, Ferdinand de, 342, 498
scapegoats, 183–4
Scarry, Elaine, 290
Schelling, Friedrich Wilhelm Joseph von, 336, 430, 442, 497
Schlabach, Gerald, 153, 160
Schlegel, August and Karl, 147
Schleiermacher, Friedrich Ernst Daniel, 414, 494
Scholasticism, 509
Schopenhauer, Artur, xvii, 116, 464
Schussler-Fiorenza, Elizabeth, 142
science: complicit with epistemological crisis, 74; in conflict with narrative, 73; and faith in beauty, 71; link with culture, 75; objectivity of, 75; and the punctual self, 75; reductionism of, 72–3; and religion, 70, 71–2
secularism, 283–4, 285, 286, 288–9, 487; implosion of, xvi–xx
self, 78, 417, 513; disclosure of, 446; disengaged/punctual, 74–5; and God, 362; knowledge of, 166; Other as higher than, 359–60; as responsible for Other, 361; spiritual awareness of, 462; subjective, 446–7; technologies of, 91–2
self-sacrifice, 110–11, 115, 117, 126
semiotics, 342, 508, 511, 512–13
Serres, Michel, xxi
sexuality, 18–19, 151, 269, 272–3, 315
Shakespeare, William, 117
Shlomo ibn Aderet, Rabben, 319

Shmuel Ederles, Rabbenu, 316, 317–18
Shoa, 326, 329, 333, 346–8
Sidgewick, Henry, 111
sign, 510, 511, 512–13
silence, 62–7, 454; beyond, 54–5; mystical, 64; papal, 64–5; political, 64; as waiting, 62
Silesius, Angelus, 214, 356, 357, 474
Simon, Josef, 511
Simon Peter, 387
sin, 419, 476; original, 117–19, 432
Smith, Warren, 253
Society for Scriptual Reasoning, 340–1
Society for Textual Reasoning, 326, 340–2
Socrates, 124, 164, 166, 169, 170, 171, 182, 255–6, 257, 258
soul, 289, 448, 462; battle between good/evil, 172; centrality of, 164–5; enfleshed, 193, 194; as just, 169–70; subordination to divine reason, 172–3
sovereignty, 158
2001: A Space Odyssey (film), 36
Spaemann, Robert, 111, 112, 117
Spinoza, Baruch, 409, 435, 436, 437, 438, 460, 507
Spirit, 268, 340, 342, 419; biocentric identity of, 218–20; as enfleshment of God, 211; as forgotten member of the Trinity, 211–12; green pneumatology approach to, 212–15; and matter, 216–18; postmodern, 210; recovery of, 224; renewed longing for, 210–11; use of different pronouns for, 226; wounded, 220–4
Starman (film), 45
Steiner, Mark, 320
Stengers, Isabelle, 73, 75
Stern, David, 313–15
stoicism, 109, 111
Strayhorn, Billy, 88–9, 90, 91
Suarez, Francisco, 396, 402
subject: conceptions of, 449–50; disengagment of, 74–5; inner/outer, 447–9; unity of, 450
subjectivity, 462, 510, 513
sublime, 290
substance, 353
suffering, 193, 195–6, 223, 337, 346; Christian, 198–203; of humanity, 331; nature of, 203; of Other, 362; primordial, 197
Sweelinck, Gerrit Pieterszoon, exhibition of painting by, 15–21
Symposium (Plato), 252, 255–8, 259–60, 375

Talmud, 338–9
Tam, Rabbenu, 317–18
Tanner, Kathryn, 297
Taylor, Charles, 74, 78
Taylor, Mark C., 488, 506, 513, 515
Temple, The (Herbert), 55, 56–8, 59–62
Teresa of Avila, 423
Terry, Clark, 91
Tertullian, 46
Tevis, William, 25, 30, 35, 37
Text Reasoners, 326, 341–3
Theologico-Poetical Fragment (Benjamin), 383
theology, 172, 424; and culture, 5–6, 17, 21; modernist, 8; and placing of sensuous/erotic within, 7–14, 15; potential placed away from, 14–21; radical interpretations of present-day condition, 487–8; skepticism in, 156
Third Man, The (film), 35
Thomism, 135, 136–7, 140, 141
Timaeus (Plato), 173
time, 472–4, 475, 478
Tisha B'av, 331, 332
Toole, David, 145–6
Torah, 325, 326, 337, 340, 342, 346
Touraine, Alain, xvi–xvii, xviii
transcendence, 351–2, 354–5, 364, 436–7, 438, 439, 452–3, 503; erotics of, 352, 355–8; ethics, 352, 358–62; infinition of, 1–2
transfiguration, 430, 432, 477; messianic, 378–83; New Age controversy, 384–5; Pascal testimonies, 385–9; Pauline legacy, 383–4; of the *persona*, 370, 371–7
transformation, 243, 477
trinitarianism, 211–12, 219–20, 228, 326, 375, 422, 460
Troeltsch, 415
"True Hymn, A" (Herbert), 57–8

truth, 359, 417–18, 435, 459–60, 461, 463, 464–5, 465, 492, 503, 508, 510
Tyrrell, George, 415

Ullmann, Liv, 40
unity, 267, 268, 272, 278
universalism, 375
utopian visions, 93; elite, 83; free-market, 82; green, 83; religious, 83; technological, 83

values, 72–3, 98
Van Gogh, Vincent, xviii
Vatican, 64–5
vision, 86
visionary pragmatism, 93–5, 98
Voltaire, François Marie Arouet de, 415

Wachowski brothers, xx
Waiting for Godot (Beckett), 146
Wallerstein, Immanuel, xxii
Walzer, Michael, 134
Warhol, Andy, 371
Watts, Michael, 36
Weber, Max, 70, 157

Weil, Simone, 290
Weinberg, Steven, 82
White, Dan, 268, 270–2
Whitehead, Alfred North, 433, 438
Will, 460, 461, 463–4
Williams, Bernard, 111, 115
Williams, Mary Lou, 88
Williams, Rowan, 253
Winter's Tale, The (Shakespeare), 118–21
Wittgenstein, Ludwig, 74, 409
Wolfenden Committee, 37
Wolfson, Elliot, 341, 346
women's history, 250–3
writerly texts, 26
Wyschogrod, Michael, 326, 328

yearning, 239–40, 241–2, 244, 486
Yoder, John Howard, 146, 152, 160
Young, Iris, 296
Young, Robert J. C., 270

Zank, Michael, 340
Žižek, Slavoj, xviii, 194, 195, 204, 384, 385, 392–3, 414
Zoloth, Laurie, 340